The American Western in
Canadian Literature

THE WEST SERIES
SERIES EDITOR: George Colpitts

ISSN 1922-6519 (Print) ISSN 1925-587X (Online)

This series focuses on creative nonfiction that explores our sense of place in the West – how we define ourselves as Westerners and what impact we have on the world around us. Essays, biographies, memoirs, and insights into Western Canadian life and experience are highlighted.

No. 1 *Looking Back: Canadian Women's Prairie Memoirs and Intersections of Culture, History, and Identity*
S. Leigh Matthews

No. 2 *Catch the Gleam: Mount Royal, From College to University, 1910–2009*
Donald N. Baker

No. 3 *Always an Adventure: An Autobiography*
Hugh A. Dempsey

No. 4 *Promoters, Planters, and Pioneers: The Course and Context of Belgian Settlement in Western Canada*
Cornelius J. Jaenen

No. 5 *Happyland: A History of the "Dirty Thirties" in Saskatchewan, 1914–1937*
Curtis R. McManus

No. 6 *My Name Is Lola*
Lola Rozsa, as told to and written by Susie Sparks

No. 7 *The Cowboy Legend: Owen Wister's Virginian and the Canadian-American Frontier*
John Jennings

No. 8 *Sharon Pollock: First Woman of Canadian Theatre*
Edited by Donna Coates

No. 9 *Finding Directions West: Readings That Locate and Dislocate Western Canada's Past*
Edited by George Colpitts and Heather Devine

No. 10 *Writing Alberta: Building on a Literary Identity*
Edited by George Melnyk and Donna Coates

No. 11 *Ranching Women in Southern Alberta*
Rachel Herbert

No. 12 *Rocking P Ranch and the Second Cattle Frontier in Western Canada*
Clay Chattaway and Warren Elofson

No. 13 *The American Western in Canadian Literature*
Joel Deshaye

THE AMERICAN WESTERN IN CANADIAN LITERATURE

JOEL DESHAYE

The West Series
ISSN 1922-6519 (Print) ISSN 1925-587X (Online)

© 2022 Joel Deshaye

University of Calgary Press
2500 University Drive NW
Calgary, Alberta
Canada T2N 1N4
press.ucalgary.ca

All rights reserved.

This book is available in an Open Access digital format published under a CC-BY-NCND 4.0 Creative Commons license. The publisher should be contacted for any commercial use which falls outside the terms of that license.

LIBRARY AND ARCHIVES CANADA CATALOGUING IN PUBLICATION

Title: The American Western in Canadian literature / Joel Deshaye.
Names: Deshaye, Joel, 1977- author.
Series: West series (Calgary, Alta.) ; 13.
Description: Series statement: The West series ; 13 | Includes bibliographical references and index.
Identifiers: Canadiana (print) 2022013927X | Canadiana (ebook) 20220139431 | ISBN 9781773852676 (softcover) | ISBN 9781773852683 (open access PDF) | ISBN 9781773852690 (PDF) | ISBN 9781773852706 (EPUB)
Subjects: LCSH: Western stories, Canadian. | LCSH: Canadian literature—American influences. | LCSH: Canadian fiction—Canada, Western—History and criticism. | LCSH: Canadian literature—Canada, Western—History and criticism. | LCSH: Canada, Western—In literature.
Classification: LCC PS8191.W4 D47 2022 | DDC C813/.087409—dc23

The University of Calgary Press acknowledges the support of the Government of Alberta through the Alberta Media Fund for our publications. We acknowledge the financial support of the Government of Canada. We acknowledge the financial support of the Canada Council for the Arts for our publishing program.

This book has been published with the help of a grant from the Federation for the Humanities and Social Sciences, through the Awards to Scholarly Publications Program, using funds provided by the Social Sciences and Humanities Research Council of Canada.

Printed and bound in Canada by Marquis
This book is printed on 57lb Enviro Smooth paper

Copyediting by Ryan Perks
Cover image: Colourbox 14882132
Cover design, page design, and typesetting by Melina Cusano

Contents

	Acknowledgements	VII
★	Introduction *Signposts and Scales*	1
1	Scaling and Spacing the Genre *Transnationalism, Nationalism, and Regionalism*	43
2	Tom King's John Wayne *Indigenous Perspectives on the Western*	111
3	The Northwestern Cross *Christianity and Transnationalism in Early Canadian Westerns*	155
4	From Law to Outlaw *The Second World War, Westerns, and the '40s Pulps*	205
5	CanLit's Postmodern Westerns *Ghosts and the Cowgirl Riding Off into the Sunrise*	245
6	Degeneration through Violence *Contemporary Historical Westerns and Post-human Horsemen*	297
★	Conclusion *Mining the Western in the Twenty-First Century*	347
	Works Reproduced in Part	378
	Works Consulted	379
	Index	403

ACKNOWLEDGEMENTS

This book is dedicated to the memory of Herb Wyile, who committed his generous expertise and kind advice to this book when I was still dreaming it up. If he had not been the first to encourage it, I would not have written it. Early support from Brian Trehearne and D. M. R. Bentley also gave me confidence in the project. My heartfelt thanks!

Part of chapter 2, "Tom King's John Wayne," was first published in 2016 in a slightly different form in the journal *Canadian Literature* (no. 225), whose editors and peer reviewers offered insightful comments that contributed to its improvement.

Most of the later chapters were earlier presented in different form at the following conferences:

- "Distant Reading and the Range in the Genre of the Canadian Western." Canadian Society for Digital Humanities Conference, University of British Columbia, 3 June 2019.

- "Ghostmodernism and the Post-Western: Ondaatje, Eastwood, and Jiles." Popular Culture Association/American Culture Association Conference, Washington, DC, 19 April 2019.

- "Genre, Parody, and Postmodernism in Luke Price's Smokey Carmain Westerns." Association of Canadian College and University Teachers of English Conference, University of Regina, 29 May 2018.

- "The Genre of the Quebec Western and Postmodern Regionalism in George Bowering's *Caprice*." Association for Canadian and Quebec Literatures Conference, University of Regina, 26 May 2018.

- "Ironies of the Western and the Public Domain in Jordan Abel's *Un/inhabited* and *Injun*." Association of Canadian College and University Teachers of English Conference/ Congress of the Humanities and Social Sciences, Ryerson University, 28 May 2017.
- "Transnational Nostalgia and 'Cowboys & Riels' in Frank Davey's *The Louis Riel Organ & Piano Company*." TransCanadas Conference, University of Toronto, 27 May 2017.
- "Mining the Western: Coal, Gold, and Masculinity in Gil Adamson's *Outlander*, Patrick deWitt's *The Sisters Brothers*, and Dayle Furlong's *Saltwater Cowboys*." Popular Culture Association/American Culture Association Conference, San Diego, 17 April 2017.
- "The Western Genre and Adventures for Boys in H. A. Cody's *Rod of the Lone Patrol*." Association of Canadian College and University Teachers of English Conference, University of Calgary, 29 May 2016.
- "Transnational Outlaw-Lawman: Ralph Connor and His Border Crossings." Trans 2016 Conference of the University of Toronto Comparative Literature program, 5 March 2016.
- "The West Turns North: The Western in Canadian Literature and Culture." Northeast Modern Languages Association Conference, Ryerson University, 30 April–3 May 2015.
- "Tom King's John Wayne: The American Western in Canadian Literature." Popular Culture Association/American Culture Association Annual Conference, New Orleans, 1–4 April 2015.

The project in general was supported by an Insight Development Grant from the Social Sciences and Humanities Research Council of Canada from 2017 to 2019, extended for revisions and spinoff projects into 2022. Kelley Bromley-Brits's suggestions in helping me to shape the grant application were razor-sharp and highly productive.

In Saskatoon, Delvin Kanewiyakiho sparked my interest in contemporary Indigenous (specifically Cree) culture by explaining to me, shortly after the beginning of the millennium, that the West was still (and still is) in a state of "acute colonialism," a realization that I had not yet admitted and acknowledged. Some of my oldest friends, Ted View, Clayton Boyer, and Dustin Kasun, expanded this horizon of knowledge in conversations about our families and their experiences.

In Montreal, Allan Hepburn at McGill suggested that I teach a course on the Western, partly because I was from the West. In one of the classes I taught there, Lana McCrea, Nicholas Cameron, and Zev Steinlauf were especially engaged and helped me to see the relevance of the Western to contemporary students and other interpreters of pop culture. Seeing the Coen brothers' remake of *True Grit* (2010) with Benjamin S. W. Barootes led to many enlightening conversations about Westerns and medieval genres such as the epic and the romance (and on one occasion Disney's *DuckTales*). And Ned Schantz's insightful probes about genre, and his ideas about national monuments and landscapes in the West, were compelling as we visited the Westerns exhibit at the Museum of Fine Arts.

In St. John's, my research assistants have been invaluable. Amy Donovan conducted early bibliographical research on specific authors and advised me on geography-related topics. Collin Campbell came on board and became the digital designer of the multi-book index of generic conventions—the dataset parallel to this book—and his editorial comments throughout the process have led me to many warranted revisions of the manuscript. Elizabeth Hicks and Mandy Rowsell were enthusiastic and questioning readers of Westerns, post-Westerns, and even non-Westerns. Sam Lehman dug deeper to improve my existing bibliographies on saloons and horses. Yining Zhou and Chris Newell assisted me swiftly and cheerfully with distant reading and editorial work in the penultimate stages of the project. Melanie Hurley and Morgen Mills pursued final questions and refinements with diligence and acuity. And Ericka Making from my graduate seminar told me the likely origin of the title of Dayle Furlong's 2015 novel *Saltwater Cowboys*, while Andreae Callanan crystallized our class's discussions into a brilliant essay on Jordan Abel and the simulation of language loss.

My film class at Memorial helped me to develop my ideas about *Pale Rider* in many amazingly inductive discussions; I wish to give special thanks to Hailey Ryan, Cassandra Miller, and Connor Fitzpatrick. My Westerns class included Adrian Bell, who introduced me, fortuitously, to the German Western *Sons of Great Bear* when I was thinking about the transnationality of the Western.

My esteemed colleagues John Geck, Lisa Moore, Chris Lockett, and Andrew Loman read or heard me talk about parts of the book and gave me fresh leads on obscure materials, new and old—and friendly, expert writing advice. Plus all the needed reassurances. Other helpful suggestions came from Danine Farquharson, Helene Staveley, Brad Clissold, Rob Ormsby, Arn Keeling, Mark C. J. Stoddart, Kurt Korneski, and Matt Rise.

Through my father, Lloyd Deshaye, and the playwright Mansel Robinson, I contacted Robert Gagné from the National Arts Centre, who generously arranged for me to see the script of *Gabriel Dumont's Wild West Show* when I could not travel farther west to see the show itself. Through my mother, Mary Deshaye (née Albers) and her brothers and sister-in-law in Alberta, I became better acquainted with ranching culture and points of view in the West.

In the United States, Helen Lewis has been unstintingly welcoming as organizer of the Westerns meetings at the various Popular Culture Association and American Culture Association joint conferences held around the country. Christopher Conway invited me to contribute to a book on globalization and the Western in comics, which led me to the work of the Métis painter and scholar David Garneau, and then to a book on the global literary Western (in my case, a chapter on Canadian Westerns by Alix Hawley and Natalee Caple), all of which resonated with me as I finalized this book.

Helen Hajnoczky from University of Calgary Press expressed interest in this project, and that was also a powerful motivator for me to finish it.

My mentor Robert Lecker provided keen feedback when I needed it most.

And Jordanna and Lucy—thank you for everything.

Introduction
Signposts and Scales

The Western genre is about dry land, the dusty expanses of the American Southwest or the grassy plains of North America—and yet when the poet Don McKay alluded to the Lone Ranger in his 2010 Pratt Lecture in St. John's, he was nearly within sight of the Atlantic Ocean. In the same year, the popular television program *Republic of Doyle* went on the air, the first episode about two Albertan cowboys causing trouble in Newfoundland. The hero Doyle—like the Lone Ranger in taking the law into his own hands—paddles both of the interloping Albertans with the lid of a toilet tank, telling them to "saddle up." He then threatens to electrocute one of them with a gun-like hair dryer in a bathtub full of water, the man in a tub being a motif of the Western (Gaines and Herzog 180).[1] In his parting words he exhorts them to "ride off into the sunset together." Meanwhile, on Water Street, not far from some of the typical filming locations for *Republic of Doyle*, the Rocket café displays old coffee tins newly decorated with an imaginary brand called NFLD MOON and featuring the image of a silhouetted cowboy with the sunset behind him. Next door, the awning above an out-of-business restaurant advertises the Stetson lounge upstairs. A few blocks north is an abandoned store, the First Western Boutique (re-located elsewhere), with an awning depicting cacti, the sunset over the cordillera, and another cowboy in silhouette. Some signs of the Western in easternmost St. John's imply a ghost town, when in fact the city sometimes

---

[1] See also Aritha van Herk's 2004 historical work in "Washtub Westerns."

booms with oil—not from Alberta, but from under the sea.[2] Terrestrial oil and gas companies have been known to use Western imagery to suggest that the roughneck is the new cowboy, even if his landscape is ecologically damaged rather than pastoral (Hitt); offshore oil companies have done something similar with frontier narratives (Polack and Farquharson 252-3). So, too, with the Newfoundland fishery, as seen in the documentary TV series *Cold Water Cowboys* (2014-17), about the long aftermath of over-fishing and the 1993 cod moratorium. Partly in the context of a cultural refusal to see land and water holistically, as an ecosystem, McKay speaks out against the "either/or" reductionism that arguably underlies the desperate commitment here to oil or cod. Still, his passing reference to the Lone Ranger invokes several binaries. The Lone Ranger is typically seen as a "hero" despite (or because of) his position of privilege over his Native American "sidekick," Tonto; he is lone, but in a duo; a Texas Ranger, but also an outlaw, a wearer of a white hat and black mask. Similarly rife with dichotomies and paradoxes, the Western itself has nevertheless gained new complexities and dimensions, moving farther and farther from the American West, into the East, over water, and around the world.[3]

The Western is not only an American genre now. This claim might once have elicited objections (and maybe it still would in some corners); now it might elicit nostalgia for a time when the United States appeared to be both the origin and the only true custodian of the genre—when the Western was the work of American literature and film par excellence (Bazin 141, 145, 148). A primary contention of this book is that it is Canadian too, as demonstrated by the many Canadian books that inform this study, even if a lot of them depart from the formula enough that "Canadian literature"

---

2   The vagaries of resource economies in relation to the Canadian Western are also evident in Dayle Furlong's *Saltwater Cowboys* (2015), which I consider in the book's conclusion; it is a post-Western (in Neil Campbell's conception of it) about Newfoundland miners who move to northern Alberta. Resettlement in Newfoundland has also created ghost towns around the bays. For some suggestive reflections on ghost towns and nostalgia, see Carlton Smith's *Coyote Kills John Wayne* (2000, 7-8).

3   As Sherrill E. Grace does in *Canada and the Idea of North* (2001), I capitalize the term "the North" "as a small reminder *passim* of [the North's] fundamentally *created* status" (15); I capitalize "the West" partly for this reason, and sometimes to distinguish it from the cardinal directions, which is why the genre of the Western gets a capital *W* while film noir gets no capital *F* or *N*.

was a better phrase in my title than "the Canadian Western."⁴ Katherine Ann Roberts pinpoints the genre as "*imported but not foreign*" (14, original emphasis—a remark to which I will later return). Although Owen Wister's paradigmatic Western novel *The Virginian* (1902) was American and based on a historical figure, this same Virginian, Everett Johnson, had already moved to Canada by the time of the novel's publication (Jennings 200–1). Alberta's famous Black cowboy, John Ware, had also already moved from the United States to Canada and met Johnson there (Jennings 201), and much later he inspired the Canadian novelist Bill Gallaher's *High Rider* (2015). But American precedence for Canadian derivation is not quite a satisfactory explanation for the development of the genre in either country; in fact, its development is multifarious and often simultaneous across nations and geographies (and, in fact, within them), and these real and imagined spaces have far more nuance than implied in the singularity of the name "the Western." Although genre studies are beset with the problems of being able to seek "infinite" precedents and to define genres "retrospective[ly]" (Altman, *Film/Genre* 30, 36) and with "retrospective coherence" (Mitchell, *Late* 5), you might say that the first major literary Western in Canada was written by a Far Easterner, Michael Ondaatje, whose *The Collected Works of Billy the Kid* (1970) contains a photograph of Ondaatje as a boy in Ceylon costumed as a gunslinger.⁵ It is an ironically nostalgic image, now, when we think of how geographically close Ondaatje was to being a "real Indian"—an Indian from India rather than the mistakenly named "Indian" of the continent colonized as North America.⁶

---

4   A parallel contention appears in Christopher Conway's *Heroes of the Borderlands* (2019), a book that "corrects the dismissal of Mexican Westerns as derivative and unworthy of deeper reflection. What matters about Mexican Westerns is not that they are exotic or weird but that they are deeply connected to both Mexican and US cultural history" (23). Canadian Westerns are "connected" too, if not as "deeply." The Canada-US border is less fraught, historically, than the Mexico-US border, but Canadian Westerns are a point of interest for any Mexican, American, or Indigenous reader or scholar of the frontier narratives of North America.
5   Admittedly, my use of the term "literary" here amounts to a value judgment, one that coincides with the related designation of "major," both of which judge once popular but now forgotten Westerns such as those of Ralph Connor or H. A. Cody as less literary and, by association, less major. Literary (or high) and popular (or low) cultures have much in common, but readers looking for entertainment in the Western in 1970 probably did not start with Ondaatje's book about Billy the Kid or even bpNichol's ribald riff on the same figure.
6   Even for real Indians, and Indian writers elsewhere in the world, "[t]his word 'Indian' is getting to be a pretty scattered concept" (Rushdie, "Imaginary" 17), for the simple reason that

Introduction   3

These remarks might seem facetious, but geography, authenticity, and nostalgia are precisely the issues with Eastern, Northern, and otherwise foreign appropriations of and coincidences with the American Western. Nostalgia refers to *nostos* (Greek for "return home") and *algos* ("pain")—the pain of being separated from a home inevitably idealized by the heart that grows fonder. Citing Fredric Jameson's 1989 notion of "nostalgia for the present" and an example of Filipino popular music that reproduces American classics, Arjun Appadurai states that "[t]his is one of the central ironies of the politics of global cultural flows, especially in the arena of entertainment and leisure. It plays havoc with the hegemony of Eurochronology. . . . Here, we have nostalgia without memory" (30). With a similar example, Svetlana Boym describes the temporal paradox of a tourist listening to local music: "It is this living presence [i.e., of folk song], outside the vagaries of modern history, that becomes the object of nostalgic longing" (12). This nostalgia is not very different from that of Brewster Higley, the man who in 1872 probably wrote the poem that soon became the famous song "Home on the Range" (Catherine Cooper 154), which has been called "the national anthem of the cowboy" (165). He asks in the lyrics, "give me a home / where the buffalo roam / where the deer and the antelope play." He most likely would not have seen the ever symbolic buffalo at "home" in Kansas around the time he wrote the lyrics (157), the buffalo having been almost exterminated in that decade, the 1870s, but he might have remembered them from before.[7] Curiously, when my partner and I bought a house in St. John's some years ago, she was digging holes for perennials and found two buried pistols—each a tin toy gun, its rusty barrel packed with dirt and inscribed beneath the cylinder with "Young Buffalo Bill." They had belonged to the twin boys who had grown up in the house a generation earlier. Unlike Higley with his buffalo, the boys probably had no memory of Buffalo Bill; they probably knew him instead as a generic cowboy, and I imagine that the nostalgia of their role-playing with his name was the nostalgia of their father remembering *his* youth, as if once upon a time *he* had been a Buffalo Bill in

---

India is comprised of a huge population with enormous diversity magnified by global connections.

7   A brief but haunting description of the buffalo slaughter appears in Cormac McCarthy's 1985 novel *Blood Meridian* (316–17).

another country—and, indeed, he would probably have been old enough to remember Newfoundland before it joined Confederation in 1949. For many Newfoundlanders, for Ondaatje in Ceylon (now Sri Lanka), and for Americans as leaders in twentieth- and even twenty-first-century globalization, "the past is usually another country" (Appadurai 31).[8] This nostalgia can now seem old-fashioned, which is one reason why Appadurai believes that some cultures "have entered a postnostalgic phase" (31). But because it is almost always premature to argue that something cultural has reached an absolute end, regardless of the trend of imagining postness, I would rather stand on Appadurai's firmer ground: "The crucial point . . . is that the United States is no longer the puppeteer of a world system of images but is only one node of a complex transnational construction of imaginary landscapes" (31), such as a fondly "remembered" West full of Buffalo Bills.

It is another contention of this book that the Westerns studied herein describe "imaginary landscapes" that are themselves "complex" and "transnational," and that map onto Appadurai's explanation of modernity and globalization through what he calls "scalar dynamic[s]" (32). For Appadurai, globalization must be understood as a movement through social and geographic strata—for example, in the now commonly heard invocation to "think locally, act globally," or in the inversion of "top-down" and "grassroots-up," strata that are also dispersed through time at a historical moment when both temporal and spatial dimensions can be instantly (if only partly) collapsed through media.[9] I will remark upon the "mapping" metaphor shortly, which has been a tendency in cultural theory since the spatial turn led by thinkers such as Walter Benjamin, Gaston Bachelard, Michel Foucault, Henri Lefebvre, Michel de Certeau, and Edward Soja. But the related ideas of "scaling" and "rescaling" a liter-

---

8   The line can be traced back at least as far as L. P. Hartley's *The Go-Between* (1953), as Salman Rushdie points out. Writing partly about his life away from Bombay/Mumbai, Rushdie remarks that "my present . . . is foreign, and . . . the past is home" ("Imaginary" 9). In the more general context of the West, Eli Mandel claims that "regional literature is . . . a literature of the past" (206), but all of Canada can be described as regional. In "Journey through the Past," Neil Young sings, "Now I'm going back to Canada / On a journey through the past." Later in this introduction and especially in chapter 1, regionalism is another concern.

9   I also want to acknowledge Susan Stewart's *On Longing: Narratives of the Miniature, the Gigantic, the Souvenir, the Collection* (1993) for its theorizing of scalar relationships between space and time—for example, in the experience of time while playing with a doll's house. More explicitly critical than Arjun Appadurai and Svetlana Boym, Stewart calls nostalgia a "social disease" (ix).

ature have gained and regained prominence in Canada in the past decade or so thanks to Kit Dobson's *Transnational Canadas* (2009) and a 2019 issue of *Canadian Literature*, guest-edited by Eva Darias-Beautell.[10] These and related studies show how the transnational movements of Canadian writers and texts can expand markets and spheres of influence but also further complicate national identities. My book does the same, while suggesting that in the case of the Canadian Western the markets and influences have been limited, partly because of the strength of the American Western here in Canada, in the United States, and elsewhere in the world. So, as a guide, the first chapter of this book will duly proceed in a scalar fashion—globe, country, region—to help show how the Western was a synecdoche for not only the United States but also Canada and now at least parts of the world (or the whole world, according to Jon Favreau's 2011 film *Cowboys & Aliens*). We get a hint of the synecdoche in Higley's "national anthem of the cowboy," in which a single member of society stands in for the country. Sometimes that member stands in for other countries too. I recall pictures of most American presidents and Canadian prime ministers (and at least one Mexican president) of recent decades in cowboy hats or buckskin jackets (with canoe, if you are Pierre Elliott Trudeau); these symbols also make a show of lessening class distinctions so that the wealthy governing elite can be seen to pay at least a token of respect to "the rest of us," imagined here as honest, hard-working, and grass-rooted if not grass-fed. And in playing this game of national identification, the makers of the Western have also turned the cardinal directions around, spinning a compass so that getting lost on a frontier can still happen—even after the vaunted closing of the American frontier—if the new frontier can be Canada, Mexico, or outer space.[11]

---

10   These studies owe a debt to the conferences organized and the books assembled by Smaro Kamboureli, whose TransCanadas conferences and her leadership therein produced, among other outcomes, her and Roy Miki's co-edited collection *Trans.Can.Lit* (2007). These studies are also related, beyond the Canadian context (though the first of its editors is at the University of Calgary), to Michael Tavel Clarke and David Wittenberg's *Scale in Literature and Culture* (2017), which I consider briefly in chapter 1.

11   After Edward McCourt's *The Canadian West in Fiction* (1949), Wilfrid Eggleston's *The Frontier and Canadian Letters* (1957) seems to be the earliest book-length study to entertain ideas of the frontier in Canada, and it was published in the same year as the Soviet launch of Sputnik 1 and thus the beginning of the space age. Instead of a conceptual reflection on its contemporary moment or the ethical ramifications of frontierism, Eggleston's book is mainly a cultural-material

Strictly, one can assert a border, a property line, by saying that the Western is American. In claiming that it is Canadian too, in the face of occasional objections to this claim, I do not mean to perpetuate literature's nationalistic complicity in supposedly justifying the colonization of Indigenous lands, as explained in Margery Fee's *Literary Land Claims* (2015), which begins with the premise that "a national literature constitutes a land claim" (1). The existence of the Canadian Western should not elicit the claim that American soil is somehow Canadian; more to the point, it should not affirm that Indigenous lands taken by the British Empire should forever be held by Canada. I would hope quite the opposite, in fact: that anyone convinced that there is a Canadian Western would reopen the question of settled land and consider, as Fee does, how "the formation of a Canadian literature [has] been complicit in the colonial process of occupying and claiming land" (4). In this context of questioning nationalism, and in looking transnationally at American and Canadian literatures (and cinemas), I am adopting a perspective that remains meaningful partly because the study of literature and culture remains bordered by nations, even as nations—especially Indigenous nations in North America—cross borders and make different claims to land and nationhood. The interplay of multiple nations within one nation-state suggests that nationality will always be contested and debated before being resolved (if it ever is). Roberts's *West/Border/Road: Nation and Genre in Contemporary Canadian Narrative* (2018) is presently the only other book on the Western in Canada, and she offers a crucial nuance: "the oppositional aspects of Canadian national culture . . . must, in my view, constantly negotiate its relationship with cultural forms that are *imported but not foreign*, that is to say, that come from elsewhere, yet are read, consumed, digested, and interpreted as only partially 'other' " (14, original emphasis).[12] Kathy-Ann Tan's

---

history. Although it conceives of the West in the then familiar pioneering terms of the garden and the hearth, its preoccupation is social Darwinist: the survival of an environment that can be adapted through colonization until a market for literature and "great" authors could appear to define that environment nationalistically. Partly because of this approach, it does not serve as a source or study of genre fiction, though it does briefly consider the situation of Ralph Connor (e.g., 144)—but as a Prairie writer alongside Frederick Philip Grove and Sinclair Ross, not a writer of Westerns (or Northerns or Northwesterns).

12 Johannes Fehrle's dissertation is another book-length study. Both Fehrle's and Roberts's studies focus on postmodern and contemporary Canadian Westerns with greater emphasis on American literature than readers will find here.

Reconfiguring Citizenship and National Identity in the North American Literary Imagination (2015) is another recent example of a book-length study of the literatures of both nation-states; her thesis is "that prevailing notions of citizenship and national identity are, in periods of emergence and crisis, reimagined along transnational and post-national lines of social, political, cultural, sexual belonging" (11). Tan's work is aligned partly with "the recent 'turn' to hemispheric methodologies of analysis and inquiry" (252) articulated by writers such as Colin Woodard, Joel Garreau, and Dante Chinni and James Gimpel. She sees, too, "the limitations of nation-based models of liberal and civic republican citizenship" (253).[13] These limitations will not become less pronounced in the future. In spite of what isolationists say, the world is not becoming any smaller. Our sense of it only grows bigger as we come to recognize that problems such as climate crisis and environmental racism are global in scope. They require proportionate solutions. But partly because of the often manufactured sense of danger on our doorstep, we frequently feel the political influence of wanting to make claims on a national scale.

So, even among settler-colonists in the United States there is debate over where the Western belongs. Displaying both entrepreneurial and folk-cultural ideals, various interests from around the United States claimed copyright to the song "Home on the Range"; many people in the 1930s and '40s said they had written it, or that their fathers had written the song, which they had sung to their kids, thereby fostering a "sense of ownership" over aspects of the fundamentally acquisitive frontier myth (Catherine Cooper 148–9). This "sense" is also a sense of home, and it was imagined all over the place, in both real and symbolic Wests.[14] Douglas Brode, for example, argues that the John Wayne movie *The Alamo* (Wayne, 1960) failed commercially not only because John F. Kennedy pre-empted its Republicanism with his Democratic "New Frontier" message, but also because it reminded audiences that America had failed to beat Russia to the new frontier of outer space (176). The crossover genre of the space

---

13   See also Spivak's *Death of a Discipline* (2003) for her term "planetarity" as an alternative to "globalization."
14   For related scholarship on the variable symbolic values of home in the regional fiction of the West, see Deborah Keahey's chapter on "Relative Geographies" in her book *Making It Home: Place in Canadian Prairie Literature* (1998).

Western proposes a new colonial vision for humanity, one sometimes defined by non-American interests—as with Sean Connery's *Outland* (Hyams, 1981), which was one of the sources of the title for Gil Adamson's *The Outlander* (2007)—but more often defined by the American television and movie industries, as with Joss Whedon's *Firefly* series (2002–3) and *Cowboys & Aliens* (Favreau, 2011). In that vision, the frontier is always in motion, whether in orbit or space travel. "Home" is not only this new frontier. It is also the result of a race *to* the new frontier—a frontier defined by *agōn*, or contest, in which the prize might always be a little out of reach.

The *agōn* here is also between two political extremes—a world order associated with the regulatory Left, and the individual associated with the libertarian Right—in spite of macroeconomic and personal complications that defy the simplification of a left-right/liberal-conservative spectrum. I will not attempt to define these shifting terms rigorously, because a basic definition of the word "conservative," such as "favouring free enterprise, private ownership, and socially conservative ideas," as per the *Oxford English Dictionary*, reveals significant overlap with "liberal," which describes those "favouring individual liberty, free trade, and moderate political and social reform." Both positions privilege freedom but neglect the "freedom to" and "freedom from" nuances of Isaiah Berlin's "Two Concepts of Liberty" (1958/1969). The *OED*'s definitions differ mainly in the "social" dimensions that partly relate to Berlin's concepts, and in my experience people who identify as conservative often assume that the people they call "liberal" are socialist and overly sensitive (i.e., "bleeding hearts"), while people who identify as liberal often assume that the people they call "conservative" are libertarian and too comfortable with violence as a solution to problems. These assumptions about others underlie the simplified spectrum, but something like the Nolan chart might be required to illustrate a multi-dimensionality, even in Westerns, because many Westerns or their writers can occupy both positions, if they are only described by way of a binary.[15] For one example, skip ahead to Luke Price's

---

15 In a master's thesis that proposes an alternative "culture cube," David Bruce Hollis MacKenzie surveys models of the political spectrum that add another axis or dimension—for example, Brendon Swedlow and Mikel L. Wickoff, James Devine, David Nolan (the "Nolan chart" being probably the most familiar of these examples), and D. O. Miles (the Miles model being a sphere).

Dynamic Western storyline in chapter 4.[16] Even in this case—formulaic pulp fiction from the 1940s—we can discern preferences for local business over big business, white people over brown people, empowered women over acquisitive men, and individualized or community-based law over a broader justice system. I can imagine that, today at least, a self-styled liberal and a self-styled conservative would debate each other's attributions of an ideology to Price's stories.

I mentioned Kennedy to invoke the political contexts of the Western in mid-century—contexts that still help to explain the surprising popularity of the Western in Canada since the 1990s. The short explanation for that popularity is that Thomas King's *Green Grass, Running Water* (1993) and Guy Vanderhaeghe's *The Englishman's Boy* (1996) appeared in the mid-1990s, but the longer explanation involves events outside of literature. A potted history of the shared political contexts of the genre would show that American and Canadian Westerns in the first three decades of the twentieth century were almost uniformly conservative, albeit sometimes in the "compassionate conservative" mould of a Zane Grey or a Ralph Connor.[17] I look to Steve Neale to sketch out the increasing liberalism of the Western resulting from the Great Depression and subsequent American milestones of the New Deal and the anti-fascist campaigns of the 1930s ("Vanishing" 15). By the end of that decade, the ideological jockeying was made visible in a series of A-list American Westerns—*Dodge City* (Curtiz, 1939), *Stagecoach* (Ford, 1939), *Jesse James* (King, 1939), and *Destry Rides Again* (Marshall, 1939). In Canada in those years, domestic film production of fictional narratives was marginal, and not many Westerns were being published; they were not among "the most popular types of escape literature" (Pacey 660). The latest on Desmond Pacey's list was A. M. Chisholm's *Red Bill* (1929); Chisholm had established what we now think of as conservative themes of patriarchy, industry, and resulting progress in *The Land of Strong Men* (1919).[18] Later wartime comics and pulps (the

---

16 Admittedly, there is a chance that the probably pseudonymous "Luke Price" is a collective of authors, but ideological complexity, even incoherence, is simply a feature of pop culture and its genres—a result of trying to appeal to people broadly.

17 See Patrick McGee for commentary on the typical conservatism of the classic Westerns (xiv).

18 Pacey's list of Canadian Westerns includes Luke Allan's *Blue Pete: Half Breed* (1921), which is part of the dataset informing this study; Harwood Steele's *Spirit of Iron* (1923) and *The*

latter being the subject of chapter 4) did not yet register a significant response to early manifestations of conservatism here. Then came, in the United States, "the advent of the Cold War, the initial post-war activities of HUAC [the House Un-American Activities Committee], and the consequent attack on liberal values," which led in turn to "the cycle [of liberal, pro-Indian Westerns] that emerged in 1949" (Neale, "Vanishing" 15). Even if the Second World War and its Cold War aftermath created boomtime socio-economic aspirations and chauvinism that the Western served very well (Corkin, "Cowboys" 66–7), they also cannot be underestimated as reasons why the Western soon became more politically diverse, reflecting a diversifying society, its different visions of moral responsibility in national and international arenas, and a troubling introspection about global power and imperialism. As liberal Westerns in the United States were published and screened in the 1960s and '70s, thereby questioning—from within—one of America's most conservative cultural trends, the Canadian writers Margaret Atwood, Michael Ondaatje, and bpNichol (and very few others that I know of until the 1980s) saw an opportunity to join the critique while bolstering their own new product, CanLit. They were outliers driven in part by youthful insouciance: in 1970 bpNichol was subjecting an American anti-hero to a short-dick joke in *The True Eventual Story of Billy the Kid*. And being "anti" to "anti" is complicated, like the word "antidisestablishmentarianism."

The complexity has much to do with how Canada's underdog status disguises its own imperial, or at least colonial, history, one that mid-century liberalism in Canada—badly flawed in the first Trudeau government's notorious White Paper (1969) but mitigated, imperfectly, in the official multiculturalism of the 1980s—helped to gloss over.[19] In Canada, from the end of the 1930s to the beginning of the twenty-first century, there were only two prime ministers from the Conservative Party who held power for any length of time (John Diefenbaker and Brian Mulroney), and from the mid-1960s to the early 1980s the spirit of the times was especially liberal and Liberal. Coupled with the nationalist symbolism of 1967 in Canada

---

Ninth Circle (1928); and Chisholm's *Prospectin' Fools* (1927), in addition to the aforementioned *The Land of Strong Men* and *Red Bill*. Each of these writers wrote several genre fictions in short order.
  19 In a different context, a helpful overview of the White Paper's effects is available from Kevin FitzMaurice (2011).

(its centennial), for a while it was retrograde to appeal too much to the United States. Bruce C. Daniels explains:

> In the twentieth century, as everywhere in the western world, . . . conservatives and liberals reversed their historic nineteenth century positions on basic values. By the 1960s, being a conservative in Canada meant essentially that one embraced a free-market entrepreneurial system: this inclined the Conservative Party to look more favorably at the United States . . . [and] an unregulated economy . . . [and] the free flow of goods across the border. Add to this . . . the conservative fear of international communism and their support of American foreign policy, plus the political necessity of opposing the Liberals, and one finds the Conservative Party of the mid-1960s portraying the Liberal government as the saboteur of good relations with Canada's closest friend and ally. (96–7)

For the up-and-coming Canadian writers of the 1960s, that "sabotage" was probably fine with them. They had internalized or were internalizing the modernist and especially the postmodernist imperatives of remaking or breaking the system, including politics (as seen in chapter 5). But there was still not much motivation for Canadian writers to produce many Westerns, probably because in that somewhat liberalizing moment there was distaste for the genre's earlier tendencies toward conservatism; a stronger motivation was required.

As the ground shifted in the United States and Canada with the election of leaders such as Ronald Reagan—the "cowboy president" who had acted in several Westerns from the 1930s to the 1950s—and then Brian Mulroney, a new conservatism or neoconservatism emerged that tipped its cowboy hat to the American Western.[20] Again within the limitations of a potted history, the late twentieth-century liberalism of Canadian

---

20 Reagan gained the moniker "cowboy president" because of his prior appearances in films such as *Santa Fe Trail* (Curtiz, 1940), *The Last Outpost* (Foster, 1951), and *Law and Order* (Juran, 1953), and he was a guest star on the television series *Wagon Train* (1957–62).

prime ministers Jean Chrétien and Paul Martin seemed to approach conservatism via neoliberalism—an economically driven politics promoted by Reaganomics and the supposedly inevitable capitalism espoused by Margaret Thatcher.[21] As with the liberal-conservative spectrum, neoliberalism and neoconservatism conjoin in valuing the economy above almost everything else, but the latter justifies its economics with social views derived partly from religion (Wendy Brown 691–2; Worden, "Neo-Liberalism" 223). Thus far, the ultimate manifestation of neoconservatism in Canadian federal leadership has been Stephen Harper, Conservative prime minister from 2006 to 2015 and a Westerner (or mid-Westerner).[22] During the Harper years, a related rhetoric intensified as military historians and conservative politicians worked toward "rebranding" Canada (a rancher's metaphor) as both a Western and a "warrior nation" (McKay and Swift 9). The cover of Ian McKay and Jamie Swift's *Warrior Nation* (2012) displays an intriguing photograph by Jeff McIntosh. It features General Walter Natynczyk, the chief of the Defence Staff in Canada, posing astride a torpedo or missile, as did Major "King" Kong (Slim Pickens) in Stanley Kubrick's *Dr. Strangelove* (1964), cowboy hat waving in the air as General David Petraeus, of the United States Army, looks on laughing. Is that a parody of a satire, or just missing the point to endear Canada to the American military with another image of the "cherished anti-intellectual cowboy" (Pitts 14)? The federal government's 2009 *Discover Canada* promotional publication includes a photograph of former Governor General John Buchan, a Briton who had been involved in the Second Boer War (1899–1902), in a feathered headdress that marks him as an "Indian," suggesting both that he had "gone Indian" by adventuring in the far reaches of the empire—and that he had dispossessed " 'real' Indians." Not long before *Discover Canada*, Canadian soldiers in Afghanistan had been overheard

---

21   As liberals and Liberals in the context of what was called the "compassionate conservatism" of the American president George W. Bush, perhaps the term for Jean Chrétien and Paul Martin is "compassionate neo-liberalism," which implies that these ideologies are more similar than they appear. The coinage is not mine but apparently Jason Hackworth's in a 2010 issue of *Studies in Political Economy*.

22   Perhaps "mid-Westerner" would be more accurate, given that in Canada as in the United States the often conservative West is bordered by the often more liberal West Coast, but for now the suggestion that the national East-West dynamic changed is enough. Harper, incidentally, was often called "neoliberal" in the discourse of federal politics, even if "neoconservative" was a slightly more accurate term for him.

describing the battleground as "Indian country" (McKay and Swift 234). Significantly, Buchan had been in South Africa at the same time as Robert Baden-Powell, who founded the Boy Scouts. Buchan wrote a series of adventure novels aligned in their imperialist spirit with the early Canadian Westerns of Ralph Connor and H. A. Cody, the latter of whom wrote *Rod of the Lone Patrol* (1916) to promote the Boy Scouts and an image of the Western hero that depended on appropriation and adaptation of the "Indian scout" into an imperial role (as seen in chapter 3). My book, then, is partly a response to a Canadian culture that has circled back to the 1900s and 1910s in some aspects of its militarizing conservatism. Fred Stenson, for example, moves the frontier from Alberta to the Second Boer War in his cavalry Western *The Great Karoo* (2008). There in Stenson's imagined South Africa, the "big and fenceless prairie" of the "wide open" (107) Karoo becomes the setting for his transplanted "dime-novel heroes" (67) and his war game of "cowboys and Indians" (326). These military and political contexts, of a diversifying left-leaning globalization and attenuating right-wing countercurrents, are a major reason why Canadian writers have turned their words to the West and the Western again.

As per my earlier remarks, I do not mean to imply that Canadian writers of Westerns are necessarily conservative or liberal; any one of them could probably be identified (by others, at least) as both, depending on the contexts and the full range of the Nolan chart. And I hope that readers of this book will be of various political persuasions. What I mean to do, however, is to call attention to some of the more extreme political currents in the Western world, and their identity politics, as informed by the Western genre. Shortly before Harper and his Conservatives were elected in 2006, William H. Katerberg accurately described the moment just before conservatism in Canada—and its West—started drawing everyone's attention again; however, he underestimated the power that was building in the West under leaders such as Harper and Stockwell Day. Following Benedict Anderson's keywords for the definition of nation, Katerberg explains that

> images of the frontier and mythic narratives of the West continue to represent something larger than a specific region, and still define key aspects of the "imagined" American nation. The same does not seem to be true in Canada,

> where Western identities have become "limited" ones. Indeed, it is not clear that even Northern identities unify Canadians as they once did, however loosely and inconsistently. In part, this situation may be so because regional identities have weakened national visions even within English Canada. It may also reflect the effort of many Canadians (and their governments) to distance themselves from the negative aspects of classic myths of Northernness (e.g., racism and imperialism) by appealing to multicultural definitions of Canadian citizenship. Despite similar dynamics south of the border, classic Western frontier myths continue to play a powerful role in American popular culture and politics. (555–6)

Since the publication of Katerberg's essay, of course, not only did Harper come and go in Canada, but Donald Trump came and went (at least temporarily) at the end of his presidency (2016–21) in the United States.[23] And the messages of these national leaders are unusually complex, if indeed "regional identities have weakened national visions." I should say outright that I do not think that Trump and Harper are exactly comparable; one's style was much more reasonable and competent than the other's. Nevertheless, Harper was elected partly because of Western alienation and nostalgia for the good old days before transfer payments and other national (read: Central Canadian) projects. Trump's 2016 electoral campaign succeeded partly because of regional appeals in the midwestern

---

23   Notably, when Trump was on the campaign trail in 2016 in Winterset, Iowa, at the John Wayne Birthplace Museum, he accepted Wayne's daughter's endorsement and said, "I was such a fan of John Wayne, and the one meeting I had with him was just an amazing meeting. John Wayne represented strength, he represented power, he represented what the people are looking [for] today, because we have exactly the opposite from John Wayne right now in this country. But I think . . . having a John Wayne and John Wayne family endorsement means a lot" ("Trump Receives"). Behind Trump, against the museum's backdrop of Monument Valley, was a wax figure of Wayne. Later, echoing Trump's admiration of "strength" and "power," the Cowboys for Trump organization publicized its support for his policies of "securing our border, protecting our second Amendment, and protecting the lives of the unborn" ("Cowboys for Trump"). Partly because the Western has these sorts of political connotations, Westerns rise and fall in popularity in the United States. In Canada, the appearance of clusters of new Westerns is far less frequent, and they come to attention less obviously because of the lesser power and money in Canadian marketing and politics.

Rust Belt, and partly because of his so oft-repeated calls for a wall between Mexico and the United States. The wall in particular has called attention and focused the international media on the Southwest, where what Trump repeatedly called an "invasion" of migrants is altering the American imagination of the frontier. Although I have seen Trump photographed in front of a wax figure of John Wayne and a Monument Valley backdrop, his vision of the frontier is both Western and anti-Western: it idealizes a border, but a closed one rather than an open frontier, contrary to earlier international views of the border—for example, when "[b]oth [Zane Grey's *Lone Star Ranger* and Ralph Connor's *Corporal Cameron*] celebrate what the authors see as the democratizing influence of the frontier, an influence important to the North American experience" (Tranquilla 73). Trump's wall stokes fears and hatreds of un-American, non-anglophone, brown-skinned Others—but Central and South Americans more than Native Americans. The "America first" agenda—and to a lesser extent the West-oriented neoconservatism or neoliberalism under Harper—is in effect *a strategy of folding the world back into a region*, of remaking a small world in which a nation can be proportionally great.

And so, because the Western is closely associated with quintessential Americana (not Canadiana), it sometimes rallies its defenders when foreign Westernness is under consideration. Frayling explains that "[i]t was generally considered [by English and American film critics] that *any* Westerns which were not made in Hollywood, using American desert locations and based on American literature or history, had by definition to be rootless parodies" (118). Some Americans have even assumed that American myths remain at home and that other nationalities can identify them but cannot identify *with* them, as when the leading scholar Lee Clark Mitchell muses,

> whatever history is invoked to explain why the American myth of the West did not extend much above the 49th parallel or below the 42nd and the Rio Grande—whether broad imperialist aspirations, or the quality of prairie soil, or even more immediate resonances of the cattle trade—these are rarely touted as the explanation for what makes the overall Western myth so powerful that for countless people it

would define Americans as American. The image that is always invoked is the land itself, and the implications of that image in the construction of the myth of the American West are what concern me here. For it is the very capacity of the American western landscape to become metaphorized that contrasts with the Mexican South's and Canadian North's apparent resistance to this process, and thereby helps to explain the role of myth in making the West American. ("Whose West" 498–9)

Although in the same piece Mitchell subsequently states that "it is precisely the imperializing aspect of the Western American myth that lends it a quality overwhelming the more nuanced, historically-informed, attentive view of the West that both Mexican and Canadian writers have provided" ("Whose West" 506), he names not one Mexican or Canadian creative writer or scholar (notably, in the *American Review of Canadian Studies*), and he sometimes relies on the same exceptionalist assumption that he briefly attributes to Frederick Jackson Turner and his ideas about the frontier.[24] I doubt that the Mexican landscape resists metaphor (partly because to think it does would be to attribute a lack of imagination to Mexicans and others), but the Canadian North certainly does not. Any invocation of "the true North strong and free" is a personification of the North, and personification is a type of metaphor. In H. A. Cody's *The Frontiersman* (1910), which I interpret in chapter 3, "the North was gripping her hard" (316); "Chains had been forged which were binding her to the land" (316). In Cody's *The Long Patrol* (1912), the North is metaphorically a "complete blank" (6) on a policeman's map, signifying its lawlessness but also its semblance of openness to colonization. Jack Warwick believes that the North in French and English Canadian literature signifies a "rebel spir-

---

24 Although Neil Campbell's *Post-Westerns* (2013) has helped to expand our understanding of Westerns transmedially and transnationally (Fehrle 4), Stephen Teo notices a blind spot in Campbell's work: "It contains homilies of the post-West as a veritable movement towards a configuration that is non-American but it remains strictly obsessed with the U.S.-centricity of the form albeit as a more critical overview of American history beyond the classical framework of the frontier" (2). On the topic of American exceptionalism, Robert Warrior argues that "transnationality has become an alternative to the exceptionalism that has been a preoccupation in these related fields [such as American literary studies] for generations" (123).

it" and "the feeling of the artist as non-conformist" (qtd. in Wood 19). Similarly, Aritha van Herk thinks of it as a metaphor of escape and remoteness (qtd. in Grace 199). William Westfell claims that the North as a metaphor "proclaim[s] national values at the expense of regional ones" (qtd. in Grace 67). Sherrill E. Grace herself explains that the North is so meaningful—through metaphor, metonymy, synecdoche—that it sustains "nordicity," an existential regionalism that expands personal experience into national consciousness; Northern texts imply that their region "is a part of/a synecdoche for Canada: from metaphor to metonymy" (264). And one of my main arguments in my writing on the idea of West and the Northwestern is that the North is metaphorically the West, partly because Canadian writers saw in American culture of the West an already familiar and expedient rationale for their own inklings about vast "unexplored" lands; Katerberg explains that "in Canada the North has played a mythic role like that of the West in the US, as a frontier producing a 'new world' people," and "[i]n the culture of Canadian nationhood, then, the West is 'Northwest,' West of the Old World and North of the US" (553). Upon reflection, I, too, am a defender—not of Canada to its inhabitants, nor even of Canada to the world (however much we are one of the least worst countries), but of the idea that Canada has a West and a Western, and shares these or a version of them with the United States and much of the world.

So I admit to feeling rankled when someone assumes that there are no Canadian Westerns, or ignores Canadian Westerns (and their implications for Indigenous points of view), or asserts that they are mere "parody," when parody is in fact quite serious (as chapters 4 and 5 suggest). Although he is indeed serious about the Canadian Western, Robert Thacker asserts that "[c]haracter and caricature—that is the difference between American and Canadian western heroes" ("Mountie" 166). In fact, however, non-American Westerns are often homage, or a way of reminding Americans of shared values that some feel to be exclusively or exceptionally American. Even if, according to Thacker, the Mountie is presented "for juveniles and tourists" (166), at least "tourists" from the United States would see a version of their sheriff.[25] Indeed, Thacker later implies that we

---

25 The inverse is also true. In 2014, police officers in Quebec dressed as sheriffs, complete with star badges and cowboy hats and boots, to protest pension reforms ("Old-West"). In other

need more international or transnational dialogue: "extended thoroughgoing examinations of historically or structurally relevant US parallels just have not happened: Canadian Literature is *here*, American Literature is *there*" ("Reading North" 409–10).[26] Although the existing scholarship on the American Western is so vast that this book cannot survey it without excluding the Canadian Western and displacing Canadian voices, I offer here a partial response to Thacker's concern about isolationist and exceptionalist readings. When Mitchell claims that "something about the myth requires American citizens to imagine it as intrinsically American" ("Whose West" 498), that "something" is not as much in the myth as in the Americans *and others* who identify with it. For homage, one might start with Ondaatje's Billy the Kid, or Fred Stenson's Karoo cowboys, or Patrick deWitt's *The Sisters Brothers* (2011); these authors treat their characters fondly, and their plots too. Franco Moretti has remarked that transnational literature often features a triad: "foreign *plot*; local *characters*; and then, local *narrative voice*" (qtd. in Nir 228, original emphasis), the last of which may criticize the foreignness but also adapt itself to it, and then incorporate it. Frayling, cataloguing national variants of the Western, notices how so many of them are stereotyped as touristy and therefore inauthentic (and I would add Othered and perhaps even domesticated and feminized) by being nicknamed according to food (118) (something to incorporate, to bring into the body): the "Spaghetti" Western, the Curry, the Borscht, and the Meat Pie.[27] There have been many parodies of the Western here and abroad *and* in the United States; my favourite cinematic Canadian example is the movie *Gunless* (Phillips, 2010), which derives in part from the television series *Due South* (1994–9), both of which star Paul Gross and Callum Keith Rennie. Gross, in both roles, is a fish out of water who adapts and endears himself in a foreign country by showing qualities that

---

words, police officers in Canada sometimes imagine themselves as American.

26 Thacker's own work, and the work of Dick Harrison, might count among exceptions to the lack of transnational studies.

27 The Meat Pie Western needs clarification as Australian, because some Canadians would locate it in Quebec—the home of the meat pie known as tourtière and the Festival Western de Saint-Tite, the large rodeo and Western music festival. See Aritha van Herk's *Stampede and the Westness of West* (2016) for a great many reflections on food and the Western at the Calgary Stampede. For more on Australia and Samoa, look to Sarina Pearson's "Cowboy Contradictions: Westerns in the Postcolonial Pacific" (2013).

others in his environment can appreciate as familiar and real. His performances are a foreign/national rapprochement.

Foreign examples simply cannot be dismissed as inauthentic, especially when the genre's iconography comes from the essentially touristy and performative travelling Wild West shows popularized in the mid-1880s by Buffalo Bill Cody and others.[28] The iconic American Western has never been "authentic" in the sense of natural and not performative, so van Herk suggests that "authenticity" can only "measure . . . its own imitation" (*Stampede* 58).[29] The power of American Westerns derives to some extent from the generic but also ideological repetition that enables such stories to seem natural and right (Slotkin, *Gunfighter* 5–6). The presumed authenticity of the Western is a major aspect of the myth of the West that Richard Slotkin indirectly exposes by examining the "myth-production" (*Gunfighter* 10) by the mass media in his trilogy concluding with *Gunfighter Nation* (1992).[30] An American fan's appreciation for the Western is an appreciation partly for a myth, partly for a nostalgic and homey feeling that had to be created in the United States as much as it had to be created in Canada—and not only for fans but also for the pioneers who had to be attracted to the West. In chapter 1, drawing on the scholarship of Herb Wyile and others, I suggest that—then and now—movements between regions depend sometimes on persuasion or interpellation (in the Althusserian sense of hailing ideological allies). The pioneers were not necessarily duped, because the colonial enterprise in general profited enormously; what I mean is that their own transformations from "foreign" to "national" were being produced, as in a performance, as they moved across oceans and lands.

---

28   The phrase "Wild West" was popularized by Cody and his vaudevillian performances, certainly, but also by Henry David Thoreau and his more philosophical entertainments: "The West of which I speak is but another name for the Wild" (qtd. in Marovitz 97). In other words, for Thoreau it is associated with wilderness. Today, however, "wild" often connotes libertarianism, an anything-goes ethos, which is usually associated with conservatism (but not necessarily, as per the Nolan chart).

29   Rushdie, in an essay that happens to mention van Herk and his memory of her description of "the great emptinesses of Canada" ("Commonwealth" 62), calls authenticity "the respectable child of old-fashioned exoticism" (67).

30   Slotkin also recently proposed, rather directly, that the "cumulative genre effect" is life imitating art (Slotkin and Desmarais 147).

As I will also illustrate in chapter 1, through a quick survey, the Western Hemisphere has produced and continues to produce many Western-like texts in addition to Westerns, alongside related cultural production from places such as Europe, Asia, and Australia. The Western travels far, farther than the (North American) West is wide. One might argue that the chauvinistic failure of imagination when someone asserts that the Western is only American is also a hypocritical denial of the idealized borderlessness of the West. Reflecting on the idealization of the West, the aptly named Elliott West puts his namesake in the context of utopia, which means "no place" (qtd. in Catherine Cooper 153). A rootlessness, a drifting, is part of it. Perhaps the most significant contribution of a reading of the Western in Canadian literature is to recognize the Western and the West as synecdoche—as a part of the whole, of the continent if not the Western world, a world that has not been isolated from the East (an equally complex "place") for centuries. It is not a symbol of a fenced-in or fenced-off grassland of pure Americana. If anything, the westward expansion and moving target or moveable frontier of American history attests not to isolationism but exploration—to the drive to see (and sometimes problematically conquer) new places, even when such places are or were wildernesses or tribal lands that deserve to be defended, renegotiated, and reclaimed.

The new places reimagined and re-placed by the books in my study are not merely replicas of entirely familiar Western backdrops and main streets, and so they are not always immediately recognizable as Westerns, or they are called literary Westerns or literary fiction. Christopher Conway, while he proposes that the Western is "the most important and instantly recognizable US cultural export" (13), acknowledges that it is "versatile and adaptable enough to be used by Europeans and Latin Americans [and Canadians, I would add] to explore national identity or challenge US myths" (13). (I would also add "archetypes" to "myths" here, to invoke Northrop Frye's influence on the parallel discourse in Canadian literature and its criticism.) Being "adaptable" is a tenet of genre theory. Such theory, and the received wisdom of comparative literature, suggest that any genre is not only "generic" but also "genetic" (a metaphor that the comparatist Claudio Guillén often uses), coming as it does from a lineage of precursors that cannot always be immediately recognized. The face of a great-grandfather is not always familiar in that of the great-granddaughter; there is always the ambiguity of what Ludwig Wittgenstein called "family resemblance" (qtd. in Mitchell, *Late* 3).[31] Neil Campbell and the currently expanding University of Nebraska Press series on "post-Westerns," which includes books by Campbell, Mitchell, and others, have repeatedly shown how easily contemporary urban texts can be understood as Westerns that have outlived and transplanted themselves.[32] The prefix "post" has of course been debated ad nauseam in theories of postmodernism and post-colonialism, among others; I like Thomas King's oft-repeated insight that we are not "past" colonialism.[33] In his 2018 book *Late Westerns*, Mitchell offers the explanation that new genres emerge through a "backward glance" (5) at older genres whose histories evince our changing assumptions about which examples are classic (4);[34] thus, if we can recognize them only retrospectively, "the Western has been effectively 'post-' all along" (5). Indeed, the Western in its historical trappings comes after the epic (and its quasi-history), the parent of many a genre, and Mitchell cites the examples of Owen Wister and Zane Grey, both of whom were recognized initially as writers of romances, which are also related to epics.[35] Mitchell's theme in *Late Westerns* of the "persistence" of the genre is not surprising if we think of the Western as one child of the epic. In fact, I would suggest that, unlike the genetic metaphor of people's lineages, genres almost never come to

---

31 Notably, Rick Altman criticizes the "family resemblance" analogy (*Film/Genre* 64–8), partly because it assumes that something like a DNA test could be used to identify, accurately, members of the same genetic line—whereas genre as a family is more like a result of births, yes, but also adoptions, marriages and divorces, deaths, faked deaths, and false identifications (as I imagine it after Altman). For a more recent consideration of the pros and cons of this metaphor, see John Rieder (194–6). With less evolutionary terminology, Robert C. Post defines genre simply as a set of "common aesthetic attributes" (370). Relatedly, John Frow defines genre in terms of conventions and constraints (10). I return to Post and Frow later in this book.

32 I have written elsewhere about Clint Eastwood's transition from Westerns to post-Western or Westernesque cop movies, demonstrating the theory of post-Westerns from a different perspective. See my 2017 article, " 'Do I Feel Lucky?': Moral Luck, Bluffing, and the Ethics of Eastwood's Outlaw-Lawman in *Coogan's Bluff* and the Dirty Harry Films."

33 Kit Dobson explains: "Theorists of transnational economics and cultures have repeatedly argued that the contemporary moment can no longer be seen as one of decolonization or postcolonialism, but rather as one of brutal recolonization or neo-imperialism" (75).

34 Susan Sontag, in her 1965 essay "On Style," makes a similar observation about the related concept of style: "our perception of the style of a given work of art is always charged with an awareness of the work's historicity, its place in a chronology" (23).

35 Generally, while epics have historical and geographic residue spread thin across their fictionalizations, romances are less grounded, more "nowhere and anywhere," as a medievalist friend of mine explained. Westerns, as I understand them, are both epic and romantic.

the end of the line. They go through phases of change intermittently and thereby persist or, as Robert Scholes puts it, "reincarnat[e]" ("On Realism" 271). But Mitchell also asserts that Westerns are "always recognizable" (*Late* 2), which implies a litmus test: Could we ever miss or misrecognize a Western? (Does everyone see the cowboy in Clint Eastwood's Dirty Harry movies?) If we missed it, what did we call it instead? And what happens when someone disputes the recognition?

I agree with a lot of Mitchell's statements, but here I beg again to discuss. The *sine qua non* of the Western, what it cannot live without, is arguably a more archetypal than realistic story in which an outsider figured as a cowboy fights for a social order (not necessarily law) somewhere along a frontier.[36] But it depends. Mitchell's own circumspection about how to define a classic testifies to the difficulties that we face as interpreters of genre. The Western is perhaps the most recognizable of American genres, but this recognizability depends partly on the audience. And the audience's recognition has major consequences: "an interpreter's preliminary generic conception of a text is constitutive of everything that he subsequently understands" (E.D. Hirsch qtd. in Scholes, "Towards" 103). At an American conference I attended, an American scholar once asserted to the audience that if it's not American, it's not a Western—but even in the American context, some audiences might watch Eastwood perform in Italian Westerns and not realize that they are not American films. Most audiences would be familiar enough with the genre to pick out a Western from the wide variety of Western sub-genres that Slotkin identifies in his trilogy of studies. Slotkin organizes them by figures such as the town-tamer, the cattle driver, the rancher, the railroader, the outlaw, the cavalry, and the "Indian" (*Gunfighter* 352).[37] But what about films that

---

36 I have already footnoted definitions of genre that are based more on aesthetics than contents, but defining the Western would probably be impossible without reference to conventions—for example, cowboys and frontiers—as "content" of the genre. It might be impossible anyway, to everyone's satisfaction. I return to questions of aesthetics in relation to genre and mode in chapter 1.

37 See also the typology in which Frank Gruber includes the "empire story," the "outlaw story," and the "Marshal story" (qtd. in Yates 7), which for Canadians means "Mountie story." In both Gruber's and Slotkin's typologies, except for in the "empire story," most of examples are set later than the fur-trading and pioneering Westerns. Unlike the "cavalry Western," too, with its earlier Indian Wars settings, the empire, town-tamer, outlaw, and "pro-Indian" Westerns tend to happen during or after the American Civil War of the 1860s, when conflicts between isolated

audiences identify as Westerns even if they do not contain cowboy hats or American locales? Scholes, in a different context, argues that genres are a "spectrum [that] cannot be turned into a set of pigeonholes, but must be seen as a system of shades" ("Towards" 106). A friend of mine, an ocean scientist, reflected on the recognizability of Westerns and post-Westerns with a key question: "So, James Cameron's [2009] movie *Avatar*—is that sci-fi or Western?"[38] The question raises the issue of endless similarity between genres, an issue grappled with in the field of comparative literature. In effect, according to Jie Lu, over-generalization in comparative literature is a problem accentuated by "the cultural turn and pan-cultural study" (2) of related discourses and other cultural products. According to Scholes, however, a genre undergoes "modifications . . . [that are] most noticeable when it crosses temporal or cultural barriers" ("On Realism" 271). In other words, a genre's essences and variations can become clearer through comparison.

My study's transnationalism is not quite "pan-cultural," but it certainly moves in that direction; however, it also minimizes some of the problems because of the obvious cultural and geographic closeness of the United States and Canada. What can't the *Canadian* Western live without? Here the answer is a little clearer: the American Western. As soon as we add a nationality, a (trans)nationally comparative relationship appears necessary, even if the Western was always already part of folk traditions in other countries, as I will explain in the following chapter. Although we might guess today that the Canadian Western must be oppositional or anti-imperial, it was actually fairly consistent with the historical development of the American Western, only with a later start; and today's revisionist Westerns and post-Westerns are often parodies or critiques, whether they are to the north of the border, as in the already mentioned Canadian film *Gunless*, with its lovingly critical portrait of a hapless, gunless gunslinger, or to the south of the border, as in the American film *The Ballad of Buster Scruggs* (Coen and Coen, 2018), with the sudden death of its smarmy titular

---

pre-modern individuals (especially postwar drifters and outlaws) and a newly settled society (including representatives of the law) were at their height. These categories generally map onto Canadian Westerns. For other, less immediately recognizable typologies, see Will Wright's *Sixguns and Society: A Structural Study of the Western* (1975).

38   In fact, M. Elise Marubbio argues that, yes, *Avatar* is a "revisionist Western" (167).

duellist.³⁹ The problem is that the number of Canadian Westerns is small compared to the very big number of American Westerns,⁴⁰ with various consequences. (Why small, incidentally? One answer is that, because the most recognizable genre of Canadian literature is societal, social, or conventional realism, Canadian writers are ushered away from unrealistic genres such as the Western—even though many of its most prominent writers seek to comment on the Western with a Western or post-Western of their own, sometimes thereby gaining or maintaining said prominence.)⁴¹ One consequence is that the plethora of American Westerns makes room for greater diversity, so contemporary pro-American Westerns are served alongside less patriotic fare. The perceived need to differentiate from American Westerns means that contemporary Canadian Westerns tend to be at least subtly critical of American culture, while also reinscribing most of the definitive elements of the American Western. Furthermore, possibly because of the difficulty in marketing such a Western, very few people in Canada or the United States are familiar with Canadian Westerns, but many Canadians know American Westerns.

As a result, when necessary, I have chosen Canadian books that acknowledge the Western most obviously, as with Dayle Furlong's *Saltwater Cowboys* (2015), over equally post-Western but less explicitly Western texts such as Nadia Bozak's *El Niño* (2014). The nuance here is that post-Westerns can be located on a spectrum of Westernness, from more subtle, like the American television series *Breaking Bad* (2008–13), to more obvious, as in an American (but pointed toward Canada) hybrid or crossover film such as *Logan* (Mangold, 2017). At one pole of the spectrum, the Westernness is no longer a question—take, for example, the television series *Deadwood* (2004–6) and *Deadwood: The Movie* (Minahan, 2019).

---

39   A pair more contemporary with each other at the historical emergence of oppositional, anti-imperial, parodic, and critical Westerns would be the Canadian bpNichol's *The True Eventual Story of Billy the Kid* (1970) and the American *Blazing Saddles* (Brooks, 1974).
40   The numbers of Mexican Westerns are big too: "in the 1950s when the Mexican film industry was in decline after its so-called Golden Age . . . at least 20 percent of Mexican-made films were Westerns" (Conway 3).
41   The interest in the Western genre shown by "prominent" or "major" Canadian writers might be a reflection of the American context: "It is remarkable how many major American authors wrote at least one revisionist Western attempting to target the formula from within in the second half of the 20th century, yet such works are seldom the source of extended critical study" (Fehrle 6).

In a Canadian example such as Furlong's *Saltwater Cowboys*, the Western might not occur to readers as a cypher of her novel without its title (which she borrows from the 1981 folk-country album by Simani, who used it to critique the influence of Alberta on Newfoundland identity), whereas Bozak's novel and its Canadianness are still less obvious, resonating as a Western primarily when readers are familiar with American borderland narratives and post-Westerns such as Cormac McCarthy's border trilogy or his novels *Blood Meridian* (1985) and *No Country for Old Men* (2005).[42] Bozak's novel could certainly be studied in depth in this book, as could several others that are mentioned only in passing, and I hope that this book will call further attention to them.

While I excluded several recent novels, I have included early Canadian "outliers" such as Ralph Connor's *Corporal Cameron* (1912) and H. A. Cody's *Rod of the Lone Patrol* (1916) despite their being less familiar today as Westerns, mainly because they predate John Wayne and Clint Eastwood and the still-iconic mid-century Westerns that crystallized some versions of the outlaw-lawman while occluding others.[43] The latter examples corroborate Mitchell's emphasis on the "backwards glance." Indeed, looking backwards in Canada became a trend around the same time that New Historicism was developing toward Stephen Greenblatt's coinage of the term in the 1980s. In that decade, it was partly the legitimation of genre fiction in Margaret Atwood's *The Handmaid's Tale* (1985), a speculative fiction, that laid the groundwork for the Westerns by George Bowering and Paulette Jiles that soon followed. Then more generally there was the boom during the late 1980s and early 1990s in acclaimed genre fiction in other media (Howell 35–6). And finally, there was a series of Westerns in the early 1990s that all responded in their own way to changing views of American history (in tandem with the changing political contexts that I have already outlined), including *Dances with Wolves* (Costner, 1990), *Unforgiven* (Eastwood, 1992), *The Last of the Mohicans* (Mann, 1992), and *Geronimo: An American Legend* (Hill, 1993). These films set the stage for

---

42 The border trilogy is *All the Pretty Horses* (1992), *The Crossing* (1994), and *Cities of the Plain* (1998).

43 I have written elsewhere that "the Western outlaw and the renegade policeman . . . are symmetrical and easily reversible figures—two sides of a coin that might be thought of as the outlaw-lawman" ("Do I Feel Lucky?" 20).

the Western to ride out in Canada in the mid-1990s with Thomas King and Guy Vanderhaeghe. By the 1990s, with New Historicism gaining popularity in the academy, Vanderhaeghe was turning toward the trilogy of historical Westerns that he would begin with *The Englishman's Boy*—the book that, with King's less historical and more mythic *Green Grass, Running Water*, turned serious attention to the Western in Canada.[44] There was a resulting surge in Canadian Westerns and post-Westerns, such as Brad Smith's *All Hat* (2001) and *The Return of Kid Cooper* (2018), Garry Gottfriedson's *Whiskey Bullets* (2006), Gil Adamson's *The Outlander* (2007) and its sequel *Ridgerunner* (2020), Patrick deWitt's *The Sisters Brothers* (2011), Sean Johnston's *Listen All You Bullets* (2013), Natalee Caple's *In Calamity's Wake* (2013), Nadia Bozak's *El Niño* (2014), Dayle Furlong's *Saltwater Cowboys* (2015), Alix Hawley's *All True Not a Lie In It* (2015) and its sequel *My Name Is a Knife* (2018), Clifford Jackman's *The Winter Family* (2015), Bill Gallaher's *High Rider* (2015), Jordan Abel's *Un/inhabited* (2015) and *Injun* (2016), Emily Ursuliak's *Throwing the Diamond Hitch* (2017), Tyler Enfield's *Like Rum-Drunk Angels* (2020), and most recently Gary Barwin's *Nothing the Same, Everything Haunted: The Ballad of Motl the Cowboy* (2021) and Bob Armstrong's *Prodigies* (2021), plus a small set of Canadian films, television series, and at least one play.[45] These authors are a big group for a small span of time in the small Canadian market for Westerns and post-Westerns. Unfortunately, the chapter-by-chapter historical arc of this book, after chapter 2, might superficially diminish the relatively high degree of activity since the turn of the millennium, but the trade-off is a better historical scope, which is helpful in a study that is one of the first. If my selection may be described as idiosyncratic, it is partly a result of the challenges of ex-centric genre studies over time, and, relatedly, because

---

44   Lee Clark Mitchell affirms this timeline in the American context too, stating that the Western on film "had been put out to pasture, [but] it reemerged in the 1990s with a vengeance" ("Who" 260).

45   This list does not include self-published Westerns, for example, by Arthur C. Eastly, nor Western romances in the Harlequin tradition, like those by C. J. Carmichael, nor Christian Westerns, like Janette Oke's. Although later chapters think through crossover genres, I must also manage the scope of this book. In chapter 3, I include Westerns in the earlier mode of Muscular Christianity because, at that time, Christian ideals were more central than they are now to the social and cultural vision that was shaping Canadian literature.

no canon of Canadian Westerns exists in the relative absence of dedicated fans and critics of the genre here.[46]

My selection is skewed for another reason implied in the title, *The American Western in Canadian Literature*. Although this book refers to a few classics of American literature, it usually compares Canadian literature to American film, a case of apples and oranges with several ramifications. This book is not quite a study in comparative literature and culture, mainly because it is almost entirely English, but partly because its relatively few American sources are mostly films, and its much more numerous Canadian sources are mostly books. My specialization in Canadian literary sources means that I am not one of the pure comparatists that Claudio Guillén idealizes in *The Challenge of Comparative Literature* (1993) who "refuse . . . specialization in one nation or one nationality" because it is not "practical" (6). Actually, it is eminently "practical" to minimize the huge corpus of American Westerns and to seek a comparatively manageable body of work elsewhere, though there are risks. Guillén explains that "a culture consists of different levels, and often what is brought along by a stronger economic and military power may be the most elementary or utilitarian level of its culture, serving only to spread over the host country a visible but superficial glaze of predominance, without any intellectual substance" (243–4). Hollywood has this effect around the world, but it also creates its own "intellectual substance" as filmmakers think through America's foreign relations and influences. And Canadians have to think through these all the time. Even my friends and colleagues who are Canadianists and literary scholars in Canada probably have more lifetime exposure to American film and television than their Canadian equivalents. Most members of the public, including most creative writers here, are probably in the same situation. American film and television influence all manner of Canadian art. They are practically inescapable.[47] So, demanding the study to compare only literature to literature would

---

46   This adjective, "ex-centric," appears occasionally in Canadian literary studies, such as Dobson's, and it can playfully confirm Appadurai's explanation of globalization extending through space *and* time: something once central, such as the Western, becomes ex-centric, even as it extends beyond its American centres to other locations, whether margins or otherwise.

47   Richard Slotkin and Mary-Dailey Desmarais wrote the same thing of Westerns themselves in his American context; they were "inescapable" and "everywhere" (Slotkin and Desmarais 147). They add: "From 1946 to 1960, Westerns were the most popular and widely

not respect the real channels of influence and inspiration-seeking across media and national borders. One reward of acknowledging these channels is that the literature serves as if it were film criticism, or at least intertextually self-aware creative writing. The literature therefore becomes what we sometimes now call the "knowledge base," a doubling of nouns that needlessly implies that "knowledge" on its own is insufficient (even "debased"—some additional metaphorical power being required). One risk is that I am also comparing *well-known* films, such as Clint Eastwood's *Pale Rider* (1985), to *lesser*-known books, such as Paulette Jiles's *The Jesse James Poems* (1988), potentially re-inscribing the canonization of a select few texts and their national contexts. However, it matters that well-known American Westerns are truly but a handful of the works considered in this study. They loom large, but mainly as shadows or ghosts, as I will explain in chapter 5. Undoubtedly, because of the smaller number of American Westerns included here, readers will notice many connections to other American Westerns—both in film and literature—that I have neglected. In genre studies, connections can never be exhausted, and half the fun is adding nodes to connections noted by others.

Another risk is in the expectations surrounding the mismatch between high-cultural and low-cultural products (to invoke a Bourdieuian difference in fields of cultural production).[48] In a study of the Western, we might expect B movies, pulp fiction, and comics to be more prominent. The fact is that there was, historically, very little of the Canadian Western in these media, in contrast to the Mexican Western that Christopher Conway examines in *Heroes of the Borderlands* (2019). I have written elsewhere of the Canadian Western in comics, which mirrors the history of the Canadian Western in pulp fiction that I assemble around Luke Price's probably pseudonymous contributions to *Dynamic Western* magazine in chapter 4. I have not yet read about or found any "slicks" among the pulps in the Canadian Western–related archival studies and materials (slicks being glossy magazines that were a step up from the pulps in quality). The

---

produced film genre" (147). Further details on this popularity are available through Slotkin's various publications.

48   I am thinking, of course, of Pierre Bourdieu's *The Field of Cultural Production* (1993 in English), which builds on his previous book, *Distinction* (1984 in English), to theorize literature's various roles in the power dynamics of culture-defining economies.

American counterparts of these media were not to my knowledge imported into Canada to anywhere near the same degree as A-list Hollywood films, partly because they were banned for most of the 1940s, as I explain in chapter 4. Most of the Canadian literature in this book is arguably a high-cultural product—literary fiction and poetry—which I first began to consider through Ondaatje's reflections on the materials that make legends in *The Collected Works of Billy the Kid*, published in 1970 by the now very chic Anansi Press. The exceptions are Ondaatje's friend bpNichol's simultaneous publication of *The True Eventual Story of Billy the Kid* in a slyly pornographic pamphlet; others are in the early years of the twentieth century, when almost all Canadian production was a fly-by-night operation; and especially when Canadian pulp fiction and comics came to the fore in the 1940s. Nevertheless, despite the high-cultural scarcity of Canadian Westerns compared to American or Mexican Westerns, not all the books and films included here are what I would describe as great literature or film. Many of them are dated; some of them are not especially well-made; some of them appear to have paid homage to pulp fiction and B movies without fully embracing the slapdash, careless love of genre evident in pulpy, B-list styles.

Given the already prominent occurrences of my opinions and anecdotes above, I think it essential to rationalize their presence a little more. In this introduction, with its emphasis on nostalgia and our felt experience of nationalized space, it would feel irresponsible not to situate myself according to the principles of post-colonial theory that Gayatri Chakravorty Spivak made familiar to me. Spivak engages with deconstruction throughout *A Critique of Postcolonial Reason* (1999) to acknowledge and assess our own critical limits and blind spots. She unpacks the West as "the Northwestern European tradition (codename 'West')" (6). Thinking of the West*ern* as such helps us to see that it is not merely a light entertainment for teenage boys; it is also the aforementioned synecdoche for the West, a microcosm of the Western world with serious implications for literature and culture more generally. Given the coded strength of this tradition, Spivak argues that to attempt to reverse, invert, or upset colonial power will be ineffective. Rather, our studies "require a persistent attempt to displace the reversal [and] to show the complicity between" (37) the powers at home in our countries and the powers that impress from our neighbours and elsewhere abroad.⁴⁹ The Derridean aporia that Spivak accentuates is highly applicable to the problems of being (and caused by acting as) a white, cisgender man, and a settler-colonist by birth, one who has inherited privileges that came and still come at a cost to others. This land is "home on Native land," as the twist on the Canadian national anthem goes—but our singing of even this one ironic line can be interpreted as a celebration of dispossession. In referring *un*ironically to Canada Day and "this home on my native land," Susana Deranger, of the Athabasca Chipewyan First Nation, also mentions "the birth of a nation that stole my land" (40), an allusion to D. W. Griffith's white-supremacist epic, *Birth of a Nation* (1915). Deranger furthermore provides a set of reasons why we should think of colonization in Canada as an act of genocide—which I, too, have written about, on the occasion of the report from the National Inquiry into Missing and Murdered Indigenous Women and Girls in 2019.⁵⁰ In these contexts, and in spite of its complicities, this book is subversively anti-colonial in spirit, especially in chapter 2, where I attempt to orient us toward Thomas King's, Jordan Abel's, and Zacharias Kunuk's Indigenous perspectives on the Western (among others), while also following a settler-colonial tradition of "unsettling" Canadian literature that goes back at least as far as Gary Geddes's *The Unsettling of the West* (1986) and continuing with important studies by Dee Horne, Laura Moss, Alison Calder, Owen Percy, and their counterparts elsewhere in Canada and the United States.⁵¹ My occasional critiques of the American Western and its scholarship do not mean that I uncritically promote the Canadian Western or Canadian studies, nor do I consider myself a nationalist, except when under pressure from other, stronger powers.⁵²

---

49   Here I am eliding Spivak's use of her coinage, "the native informant" (4, 6), which she borrows from ethnography. The risk for me and anyone from the West in attempting to be self-conscious about our Westernness is "the cover story ... of a fully self-present voice-consciousness" embodied as "the self-marginalizing [not in my case] or self-consolidating [perhaps] migrant or postcolonial [more likely] masquerading as a 'native informant' " (6). My purpose here is simply to admit, again, certain limits of my critique.
50   See my blog post, "The Word 'Genocide' in Canada," *Publicly Interested*, 18 June 2019, http://www.publiclyinterested.ca/blog/the-word-genocide-in-canada.
51   For more contributors to the tradition, see also the essays collected in Cynthia Sugars and Gerry Turcotte's *Unsettled Remains: Canadian Literature and the Postcolonial Gothic* (2009).
52   I do believe that national democratic government is the only organizational alternative to the much less accountable transnational corporation, whose hierarchies and efficiencies are

One such power is empire, which can make other nations appear minuscule in contrast—but imperialism as it helped to define Canada is also patriarchal. This book as a whole does not concentrate on patriarchy or its effect on women in Canadian Westerns or Westerns more generally,[53] but substantial portions of it are devoted to critical examinations of gender in the Western. This theme emerges with the proposal that the problematic masculinity of "Muscular Christianity" (in chapter 3) is a gendering sometimes meant to prepare boys for war, and it echoes later in the parodies of the cowboy that begin with Luke Price's Smokey Carmain (in chapter 4) and develop into bpNichol's Billy the Kid (in chapter 5). More contemporary concerns are prominent in the feminist reimagining and reframing of the figure of the cowboy, especially through the cowgirl in George Bowering's 1987 novel *Caprice* and the cowboy's (or outlaw's) mother in Jiles's *The Jesse James Poems*, which appeared the next year (also in chapter 5). Masculinity and violence come under scrutiny again, alongside the possibility of genderless post-human existence, in my readings of historical Westerns by Guy Vanderhaeghe and to a lesser extent Fred Stenson (in chapter 6). Finally, the book's conclusion involves feminist and post-humanist theorizing of gendered landscapes and industrial violence against them in books such as Gil Adamson's 2007 novel *The Outlander*. With the exceptions of Margaret Atwood's poem "Backdrop Addresses Cowboy" (1968) and of Price's serialized short stories, which are herein assembled as a novelistic arc, I have focused almost entirely on books, with the unfortunate result of not including the several Western-related short stories by Aritha van Herk that Katherine Ann Roberts considers in *West/Border/Road*, though I do quote from her *Stampede and the Westness of West* (2016) on occasion. Although the enthusiasm for rodeo in van Herk's *Stampede* is an endorsement of values such as competition that might

---

powerful, and whose transnationality frustrates national law. For more on this topic, see Frank Davey's *Post-National Arguments* (1993) and Kit Dobson's *Transnational Canadas* (2009), the latter of which explains "how Canadian texts have debated the national as a means of resisting transnational capitalism" (71).

53   The perennially relevant statement on gender by Judith Butler is entirely consonant with the Western: "That gender reality is created through sustained social performances means that the very notions of an essential sex and a true or abiding masculinity or femininity are also constituted as part of the strategy that conceals gender's performative character" (141). A statement by Katherine Ann Roberts makes the link to Butler: "Westerns involve dress-up; it is impossible to completely renounce the aesthetic power of costuming" (128).

seem conservative, her project of "explor[ing] . . . the difficulties women writers face in writing themselves into the West" (Roberts 85) might seem liberal (another example of the inadequacy of the left-right binary), and Jiles, Adamson, Dayle Furlong, Nadia Bozak, Natalee Caple, and Alix Hawley have responded with books that figure into this one. Following van Herk's critiques of Clint Eastwood, and echoing Spivak's call for "persistent attempt[s]" to question and resist imperial-patriarchal powers, Roberts acknowledges "the impossibility of pronouncing the death of the western (since he [Eastwood] is very much alive), only the possibility of subjecting it to an ongoing critique" (129). I have already footnoted my own research on Eastwood, who appears again, spectrally, in chapter 5. This book's "ongoing critique" partly examines the extension of supposedly heroic figures such as Eastwood and his characters through popular culture and into conceptions of history, where patriarchal attitudes become dangerous precepts that affect how we treat other individuals, other nations, and the land.

Relatedly, trying to reflect on my own "postcolonial reason(s)" in this book, I need to comment on my modes of thinking and writing, which I would describe as leaning toward induction and inquiry from training in deduction and theory.[54] Although the deduction and theory are mainly here and in the first chapter, more theory unfolds inductively, as needed by inquiry, in the chapters that read the Westerns. There will probably be some surprises. Most readers want clear expectations and a certain efficiency, and I do not want to hamper them without cause, but our academic habits of "signposting," "flagging," and "foregrounding" throughout our texts are obvious metaphors of settler colonialism and extractive industries such as those for oil and gas: naming spaces, planting flags, and parcelling them dimensionally with fences and roads. So are the metaphors of "surveying" and then "staking a claim" to an "area of inquiry," and of "mapping" a theory onto an unfamiliar situation or a puzzle; so, too, is the comparatively inductive metaphor of "intellectual exploration."[55] In her readings of Canadian literature in *Mapping with Words* (2018), Sarah

---

54   Robert Scholes describes deduction and induction as two different, but "complementary," approaches to genre ("Towards" 104).
55   With a focus on allegory instead of metaphor, Fredric Jameson explains "cognitive mapping" as the way in which an individual thinks through a world that capitalism has served to

Wylie Krotz identifies "cartographic aesthetics and strategies . . . in the discursive claiming of settler space" (167). Although Krotz also shows how some settlers produced "counter-maps" (153) that acknowledged Indigenous lands and people, among other complexities, the mapping metaphors are in my experience one of the commonest ways in which scholars talk to each other about their writing, along with related scalar metaphors such as "weighing an argument." In the scholarly discourse on genre, we sometimes hear people talk of how a genre signposts itself to be marked or identified as that genre.[56] More relevantly, these signposting-related metaphors also refer to the modernizing activities that the Western nostalgically rejects but also tacitly and pragmatically accepts as inevitable. As I reflected on this sense of inevitability, I was reminded of how my training and my colleagues romanticized a bygone era of contemplation and "slow professors" while pushing many of us toward intellectual shorthand for systemic processes of imperialism and capitalism. Susan Stewart, in *On Longing* (1993), has suggested that a collection of essays or chapters, such as this one, pulls together threads of narrative and becomes "the place where [such narratives are] transformed into space, into property" (xii). How different was I from the frackers seeking new oil reserves? Yes, quite different, except that I sometimes drive a car that still runs on gasoline. How different was I from settlers, then and now, who could find new opportunities on lands made available by the destruction of the population (e.g., the Beothuk in Newfoundland) or the establishment of "Indian reserves"? Less different, still complicit. I am from the West, once felt "settled" on the grasslands and wetlands of the Prairies, but the petro-cultural narrative of the West's modernization—driven by precisely the same metaphors—is no longer responsible when cultural imperialism can flow through oil pipelines, and we are engineering and capitalizing on an environmental disaster of global proportions.

Partly for this reason, and because almost all of the chapters in this book were road-tested at conferences across Canada and the United States, the tone of this book is usually more personal, public-facing, risk-taking,

---

us as a figure and a product but that we might not experience directly ("Cognitive" 349–50). See Oded Nir for how this "mapping" signifies in other work by Jameson and by other spatial theorists.

56   See, for example, Tessa Dwyer's chapter on the *Mad Max* movies in *Locating the Voice in Film* (2016), p. 142.

and energetic than that of my previous book, *The Metaphor of Celebrity* (2013). That project happened to become my transition from literary and celebrity studies through film studies to genre studies. Celebrity as a system depends on the disposability of most stars alongside the recycling of a select few into sacred objects of resilience and renewal. It is wasteful but produces illusions of durability through the classics and the canons. Celebrity obviously cannot be ignored if we want to understand the dominant cultures of the West, and it is also important to the once-dominant Western, as the genre shifted cultural registers from pulps and B movies to Wister's *The Virginian* and A-list stars such as John Wayne, Jimmy Stewart, and Clint Eastwood (and, in Canada, eventually Paul Gross). Intentionally or not, these and other stars regenerated unsustainable eighteenth- and nineteenth-century American ideas of panoramic natural resources, personal and cultural independence, and moral clarity in a century of (un)natural depletion, growing international interdependence, and ethical dilemmas. Although the Western affirms a conservatism toward nature that derives from sources such as American transcendentalism and ranch-oriented land management, it also suggests that this conservatism is obsolete, and that the new conservatism seeks not to conserve nature so much as the right to exploit nature's products, whether raw, refined, or synthesized. I mean gold, oil, and gunpowder. As I wrote this book and imagined my future studies, I realized that my research and teaching needed to confront social and environmental problems more directly if I wanted to help solve these problems, and I wanted more keenly to show how reading and writing literature and film are processes that can help too. Hence the change of tone. In *The Metaphor of Celebrity*, I had tried to strip my own language of metaphor because I had theorized that some writers ultimately lose control to metaphor—an inevitability for almost all of us, actually, but still I did not want to be one of those writers.

This concern is esoteric to most people, but how we think and talk about our environments and sources of energy is not. They are now far more ethically significant than ever. Reading for *The Metaphor of Celebrity* introduced me to George Lakoff and Mark Johnson's indispensable *Metaphors We Live By* (1980), which evokes the Jungian archetypes that William Indick considers in *The Psychology of the Western* (2008)—archetypes being akin to the deeply rooted, profoundly ideological conceptual metaphors that underpin our thinking and acting. Immediately after Lakoff and Johnson's book, in 1981 Fredric Jameson rebranded "ideology" as the "the political unconscious" with his book of that title.[57] Perhaps not coincidentally, some of the conceptual metaphors that Lakoff and Johnson identify are also orientational: *happy is up; sad is down* and *conscious is up; unconscious is down* (16). Their related metaphors of centres and margins might be superficially more explanatory when it comes to the Western's expansionist drive, especially given the prevalence of these metaphors in Canadian literature and criticism, but the affect of *happy is up* seems better. It offers implicit relief from ethical dilemmas: *heaven is up; hell is down*—it's that simple.[58] On the one hand, in the context of the Western the vertical orientation of *heaven is up; hell is down* is a pillar of the anti-intellectualism of this anti-modern(ist) genre, compelling us not to over-think whatever is unconscious or that derives from the unconscious.[59] (The genre's supposed "moral clarity" means that we don't have to think about it.) On the other, the Western is deeply informed by the Freudian model of the psyche, revelling in power struggles and identity formation, and especially the id's greed and lust, its spasmodic satisfaction of desire, and its snap judgments. Nowhere has this been better illustrated than in the film adaptation of Upton Sinclair's *Oil* (1926–7), Paul Thomas Anderson's *There Will Be Blood* (2007), in Daniel Day-Lewis's famous "I drink your milkshake" scene. Derisively bragging about his success in

---

57   Slotkin agrees: metaphors can be "masked by the traditional form of narrative [e.g., a genre such as the epic], its conformity to habits of thought, generic conventions, and literary expectations so deeply engrained that we are unconscious of them" (*Fatal Environment* 22).

58   It's also about the same in Canada as in the United States, though I have not devoted much time or space in this book to national differentiations of the Western in the context of the ethical turns in criticism in the past fifty years, with some exceptions from other comparatists a little later on. I do, however, devote part of chapter 6 to a critical reversal of Slotkin's regeneration-through-violence theory that is probably similar to some American Westerns that were also becoming critical of the genre—for example, Robert Altman's wintry and hardly regenerative 1971 film *McCabe and Mrs. Miller*, which would be countered by major regenerative and revivalist texts such as McCarthy's 1985 novel *Blood Meridian* and Eastwood's 1992 film *Unforgiven*. Lee Clark Mitchell appears to disagree about *Unforgiven*, in which "violence represents nothing more than itself . . . [and] it fails to restore social order" ("Who" 260), in spite of the hero's restoration of the "social order" of capitalism at the site of the brothel. And in the epilogue, according to Patrick McGee's cultural-materialist interpretation of the film, Eastwood's character "discovers that he is not just a man, but a businessman" (197).

59   A notable Western film whose title invokes but also depolarizes this orientational binary is *Hell or High Water* (Mackenzie, 2016).

getting a neighbour's oil, Day-Lewis's character says that it was easy to "drain it . . . just like that," and he strikes upon a milkshake metaphor to explain how he got the oil: "My straw reaches acr*aaah*sss . . . and starts to drink your milkshake. I . . . drink . . . your . . . milkshake! *Sluuurp!* I drink it up!" Although I have not crystallized the Western's "metaphors we live by" into an aphorism quite so memorable, such an aphorism would need to account for the orientational dynamics of *crossing* the West but *digging down* for the resources of power and desire, chiefly oil and gold.

This need is another reason that this book is scalar in some places, though I regret the signposting. After this introduction, it starts big (a lot of the planet) then goes small (the nation) and smaller (the region) before expanding outward again through the historical arc of Canadian Westerns. Conceptually, I adhere to Michel de Certeau's maxim in *The Practice of Everyday Life* (1980) that "[s]pace is a practised place" (117). This introduction and the first chapter focus on "space" as a set of constructions of ideology tethered to land, such as nationalism and regionalism, and the later chapters focus on "time" as a line of chronological development. Chapters 3 to 6 are linear because this book amounts to a brief history of the Western in Canadian literature, from its turn-of-the-century beginnings (ca. 1898) to its post-millennial present (the early 2020s)—about a hundred and twenty-five years. Although the American Western is older, it is not older because it had a more original national vision, though you could argue that it did; it is older because of the continuity between earlier literature such as the accounts of Daniel Boone (most recently fictionalized in Canada by Alix Hawley in her 2015 novel *All True Not a Lie in It* and its 2018 sequel, *My Name Is a Knife*) and James Fenimore Cooper's *The Last of the Mohicans* (1826), which Thomas King re-framed as Western in 1993 in *Green Grass, Running Water*. American society in the later nineteenth century needed a genre whose fictionalized violence was rationalizing an earlier and more sustained colonial violence, which itself was rationalized as a temporary and ultimately more benign civilizing feat than the ancient history of supposed savagery. Meanwhile, and more banal as a claim, the Canadian publishing industry did not exist in its legally protected form until the late nineteenth century (a situation illustrated by Ralph Connor's experience with the piracy of his first book, one of the first Canadian

Westerns, *Black Rock* [1898]), so it could not "have" an earlier Western.[60] And almost all the Westerns in this book are set around that time, with major national initiatives and power fluctuations in the background: the two transcontinental railroads, the American Civil War, the North-West Resistance, the North-West Mounted Police, and the American purchase of Alaska from Russia.

Although American acquisition and imperialism are frequently a straw man in Canadian literature and criticism, this book begins by finding many ways in which Canadian movement through the West is imperialistic, from its railways to its missionaries. After the reflections on scalar global, national, and regional relationships pertaining to the West and the Western in chapter 1, and building on my previous book, *The Metaphor of Celebrity*, chapter 2 presents "Tom King's John Wayne"—in other words, some of the views that Indigenous writers have made public on the effects of celebrity and Hollywood's cultural and economic imperialism abroad. I focus on the fictionalized death of the historical movie star John Wayne in King's *Green Grass, Running Water*, a (Canadian) response to the American Western and the West (in Spivak's conception) in general. In a magic-realist scene, the mythic ancestors of the Blackfoot rewrite a John Wayne movie so that the "Indians" defeat the whites and kill the celebrity. Wayne was not a historical cavalryman, like George Custer, or a historical outlaw who became infamous, like Billy the Kid, and so King's "Indians" are symbolically attacking popular culture because it can be more harmful than history. King directs his critique not toward what has been called " 'history-history' [but] the history made up by movies" (Slotkin and Desmarais 148). Drawing attention to the imperialism of popular culture, King's novel recasts earlier Canadian Westerns in which the fictionalized historical figure is killed, such as Paulette Jiles's *The Jesse James Poems* (1988), bpNichol's *The True Eventual Story of Billy the Kid* (1970), and Michael Ondaatje's *The Collected Works of Billy the Kid* (1970), as a collective fantasy of the death of American celebrity—and as a rebuttal to the arguments implied in the Western. I also highlight the significance of other Indigenous perspectives. Writers such as Thomas King and Jordan Abel have produced major works in this vein, and the

---

60 See the various references to the work of Eli MacLaren in chapter 3.

filmmakers Zacharias Kunuk and Natar Ungalaaq answered John Ford's *The Searchers* (1956) sixty years later with *Maliglutit* (2016). The primary insight that I derive from these Indigenous perspectives is that the effect of popular culture can be as pernicious as that of colonial history, and that Indigenous writers and filmmakers—rather than "vanishing" according to the very doctrines (e.g., Manifest Destiny) underlying the reservation systems—have made concerted and creative efforts to subvert or at least resist the Western and its ideological manifestations in national policies in North America.

When going west brought settlers and then the railroad to the West Coast, the idea of the West had to turn, and this turn was conceptualized in the early variant of the Western that I will consider in chapter 3, "The Northwestern Cross." One "crossing" of this chapter is that of the East-West and North–South axes, a geographical turning of the cardinal directions that helps to explain the American interest in the North as a new frontier. (The implied senses of direction and spatial relationship also raise questions about the terms "transnational," "international," and "global" in this chapter, especially in the biographical and historical contexts of the authors.) The sub-genre called the Northern or Northwestern was often set in the Yukon or Alaska—the Northwest. It originated with American authors and was popularized in American novels such as John Mackie's *Sinners Twain* (1895) and Jack London's *Son of the Wolf* (1902) and, from a year later, *Call of the Wild*, but it had Canadian proponents such as H. A. Cody and Ralph Connor. Cody and Connor were Christian ministers, and the physically imposing and morally assertive heroes in Cody's *The Frontiersman* (1910) and Connor's *Corporal Cameron of the North West Mounted Police* (1912) exemplify what Candida Rifkind, Daniel Coleman, and others have referred to as "Muscular Christianity." This style of Christianity is part of Western ideology in general—an indefensible rationale for thinking of Indigenous "heathens" as savages to be "civilized" through religious colonization and the accompanying imposition of Western-world patriarchy, government, and economy. Connor's and Cody's fictional minister-lawmen are genuine and not especially hateful, but they have serious failings that became anti-heroic in subsequent generations of writers. But at a time of generic instability and imminent cohesion, even if their principles were otherwise socially conservative, they experimented almost liberally with crossover genres to appeal to readers of different ages.

In chapter 4, we see the (mostly) morally upright heroes of Cody and Connor set in partial contrast with the anti-heroes of the Westerns of the 1940s pulp fiction industry in Canada. The "industry's" very temporary growth and limited range cast some doubt on the term, but the wartime laws of the 1940s limiting American imports had the effect of creating a market in Canada, even if writers of the Western tended to imitate American models with their national markers and settings. In fact, the increasing strength or saturation of Westerns in the American market from the late 1930s through to the early 1950s is one reason why the scope of this chapter is limited to only one author's series of short stories rather than a set of books. It appears that so many American Westerns were circulating during this period that Canadian Westerns could not emerge here, or at least have not stood the test of time. And so it also appears that the Canadian Western skipped ahead from turn-of-the-century models to postmodernism, just as Robert Kroetsch proposed that Canadian literature in general had done (qtd. in Nischik 303). In both American and Canadian contexts, we usually think of anti-heroes as figures that emerged alongside postmodernism in the rebellious 1960s, but Luke Price's short stories in Toronto's *Dynamic Western* magazine in the 1940s suggest that the Western had significantly earlier, and significantly self-conscious, experiments of this type. Price's main character, Smokey Carmain, is fundamentally stereotypical, but the wordplay around his name and his allusions to gun smoke create a self-consciousness that is almost metafictional, anticipating postmodern developments—from as early as the 1940s—in literature and politics in Canada and abroad. This revised timeline of conventional wisdom calls for further study of the Western's anti-intellectual challenge to its contemporary high modernism, whether inter- or postwar.

In chapter 5, "CanLit's Postmodern Westerns," we see that not until the post-1960s flourish of postmodernism was the heteronormative masculinity of the Western hero often called into question (with exceptions from the United States such as the arguably queer Shane in George Stevens's 1953 film of that name), and we reflect on various deaths and hauntings as literalizations of what would come to be known as "post-Western" commentaries on American cultural influences. Partly because of the emerging postmodernist trends, and partly for nationalistic reasons associated with the perception of foreign threats and undefended cultural borders, the Western in Canadian literature after the 1967 centennial is usually a critical response to American power—as are many American Westerns from this era. Through texts such as Michael Ondaatje's *The Collected Works of Billy the Kid* (1970), Frank Davey's *The Louis Riel Organ and Piano Co.* (1985), George Bowering's *Caprice* (1987), and Paulette Jiles's *The Jesse James Poems* (1988), I further develop many of the aforementioned themes while engaging with current models of the post-Western alongside Sylvia Söderlind's 2010 coinage of "ghostmodernism," a concept that helps to literalize some of the "cowboys and Indians" who metaphorically haunt postmodern and contemporary literature and, again, lend credence to Neil Campbell's concept of the post-Western as a contemporary text haunted by the Western.[61] In brief, the genre begins to be more obvious about the death and obsolescence of the cowboy (as such), even if the genre had been implying it for years.

Chapter 6, "Degeneration through Violence," speaks especially to the work of the American cultural historian Richard Slotkin, who argues in his 1992 book *Gunfighter Nation* that the Western promotes a myth: that American society was established and must be perpetuated through violence (10)—an echo of his *Regeneration through Violence* (1973). In response to Slotkin, this chapter proposes that the Western in Canadian literature tends to counter the American Western with its own myth: that *degeneration* is the result of violence, and that society should be peaceable. Developing this argument, I focus on the first two (and most conventional) of Guy Vanderhaeghe's unofficial trilogy of Westerns, *The Englishman's Boy* (1996), *The Last Crossing* (2002), and *A Good Man* (2011). Putting *The Englishman's Boy* in the context of postmodernism and other historical moments to which it refers, I look at some of its scenes of what might be called degenerate violence, which reappears symbolically in the syphilitic and brutal aspiring hero in *The Last Crossing* and in other Canadian

---

61   Although I see the contemporary as an adjacent to postmodernism, or as the envelope that postmodernism pushes, they seem to be treated as equivalents in Josh Toth's *The Passing of Postmodernism: A Spectroanalysis of the Contemporary* (2010).

Westerns. I also focus especially on horses in this chapter—the Western being also known as "horse opera," in a coinage widely attributed to the early film star William S. Hart. The close, familial, even intimate feelings and relationships between horses and humans raise questions about whether our rapprochement with non-humans is degenerative or regenerative. The contrastive motif of degeneration and regeneration also calls up the concept of the post-human, which develops into the ecocritical concerns of the end of the book.

So, finally, in the conclusion, I look to millennial and post-millennial Canadian Westerns, such as Robert Kroetsch's *The Man from the Creeks* (1998), Gil Adamson's *The Outlander* (2007), Patrick deWitt's *The Sisters Brothers* (2011), and Dayle Furlong's *Saltwater Cowboys* (2015). Mainly, I examine their representations of extractive industries, as when I interpret barrels of whisky as symbolic barrels of oil in *The Man from the Creeks*, or when I read the ore-related accidents in *The Outlander* and *The Sisters Brothers* as natural defences against patriarchal-industrial extractions. Although the writers in this conclusion might not agree with me entirely, I view these Westerns as deeply concerned about mining, if not other big businesses, because of its externalities, such as the damage done to human bodies and to nature, especially wilderness. Partly as a result, I join in the call for a rapid energy transition based ideally on a changing world view of human progress, or at least pragmatically on the recognition of the unwise insistence on still fuelling industrial and social development primarily with oil and gas—the black gold of the nineteenth and twentieth centuries that seems more and more regressive now.

1

Scaling and Spacing the Genre
Transnationalism, Nationalism, and Regionalism

In their introduction to *Scale in Literature and Culture* (2017), Michael Tavel Clarke and David Wittenberg begin with a dialogue from Galileo Galilei's *Two New Sciences* (1638). In that book, an allegorical character who represents intelligence—but not expertise—misunderstands "that when one increases the size of an object in one dimension (for instance, length), the cross-sectional area of that object is enlarged by the square of the same increase, and its volume (along with its mass) increases by the cube" (Clarke and Wittenberg 2). This is why some miniatures could never be greatly enlarged in their original proportions without collapsing under their own weight. Clarke and Wittenberg use *Two New Sciences* and Immanuel Kant's notion of the sublime object, among other ideas, to contextualize various theories of globalization and the environment; they point to Timothy Morton's theory of the "hyperobject," which they describe as "a phenomenon so large that it cannot in principle be perceived by humans, but nonetheless must be conceptualized" (7). As their introduction proceeds, Clarke and Wittenberg suggest that the growth and globalization of literary studies happened "without substantial controversy" (11), with the possible exception of "the controversy over Franco Moretti's *Distant Reading* [2013]" (17), a book that posited the end of close reading. Moretti observed that literature has been expanding as time passes, so a historical scope eventually becomes impossible for even an obsessive and rapid reader to manage (at least without recourse to limiting constructs such as taste). When a reader then wants to increase the scope of research beyond traditional national boundaries, the problem is magnified, both temporally and spatially. Literature itself does not collapse when it becomes *global* or *literatures*, but categorization and reading processes might, and these might *feel* like collapse; however, genre studies and quantitative methods such as distant reading can offset the limits of other methodologies.[1]

Although there is a distant-reading dataset behind *The American Western in Canadian Literature*, which I intend to publish separately, this book on its own does not offer a satisfactory solution to the problem of scale that Moretti explained and that Clarke and Wittenberg further contextualized. As I rationalized in the introduction, limits such as language and nationality are practical in literary studies. But they can also be compensated for in theory. This chapter is meant to theorize—or, perhaps more accurately, contextualize—the genre of the Western by scaling it down from the globe, through the nation, to the region, while also spacing out different regions in relationship with each other.

Ironically, to justify this study of a national literature, some perspective on transnationalism—on an area of bigger scope—is required. Canadian literature simply cannot be isolated from other national literatures and from other national cultures more generally, and the Western is an ideal example, because the genre is more strongly associated with the United States and Mexico (and even Italy, thanks to Sergio Leone and several others) than Canada. While not what I referred to in the introduction, following Arjun Appadurai, as a "puppeteer," the United States remains fascinating in a world of devolving superpower, partly because people everywhere in the ostensibly free world, and in aspiring nations, are drawn to the idea of West—imbued with "nostalgia without memory"—that dates from the pre-superpower, even pre-modern, era of America. In those days, the superpower was not a country but an individual—the "superhero" of the late nineteenth-century Western who became the Superman and the

---

1   To tease out these implications—of expansion and collapse—in more detail would be quite a thought experiment, but Clarke and Wittenberg include in their collection an essay by Oded Nir that acknowledges various reasons to prevent "world literature" from becoming too theoretical (237–40). For Nir, following Fredric Jameson, "the system [of world literature is] ultimately unrepresentable" (241; see Jameson, "Cognitive" 356), though Nir does assemble a typology that could help. See also Salman Rushdie's optimistic thoughts on "a new shape of the [English] language in . . . a world literature" ("Commonwealth" 70).

Batman of the 1930s (Wachhorst 15). Much of the thought and feeling cast back to those days is also contextualized by what living people outside the United States *do* remember, such as late-imperial American aggression during the wars in Vietnam and Iraq, which accounts for not only some of the anti-Americanism but also a relieved anxiety of influence in non-American Westerns; we do not have to see the Western as all good, and we do not have to imitate it exactly or feel the pressure of mimicry. Such pressure assumes that the Western is defined as a powerful, only-American frontier story, but I have already found reason to suggest, as I did in the introduction, why that is not the case. In contextualizing the American Western in Alberta, Aritha van Herk succinctly expresses the paradox by claiming that "[w]e yearn to recapture what we have never seen but dreamed" (*Stampede* 82) while admitting that "[n]ostalgia isn't what it's cracked up to be, creaking with extinction and / forgetfulness" (91). She summarizes that, when you love something, "you cherish its faults as much as its strengths" (91). Van Herk seems to "cherish" the Calgary Stampede in particular and the West in general, but, in the nostalgic discourses of the Western and the West, there is also an undeniable fondness for the United States—for example, in van Herk's poem about the Stampede's American founder—one that might be described as "restorative nostalgia" (Boym 402) in line with Richard Slotkin's regenerative theme (to which I return in chapter 6). Briefly, what I mean to suggest is that nostalgia is sometimes *more* than "what it's cracked up to be," because it scales up; it almost always stretches toward something geographically distant, an Odyssean homeland.

The Western in the East and Old World

Whether *of* or *in* the East, the homages are especially curious, many of them appearing during a time of cultural revolution in the English-speaking world, some of them part of a cultural feedback loop. One of the classic American Westerns took inspiration from Japan not long after Japan came to matter more to Americans during the Second World War; *The Magnificent Seven* (Sturges, 1960) was a remake of Akira Kurosawa's *Seven Samurai* (1954), from the genre of samurai cinema, *chanbara*, a type of *jidaigeki* or period drama. In *Eastern Westerns* (2018), Stephen Teo cautions against interpreting *Seven Samurai* as a Western because it inspired a Western (4, 5), though in chapter 9 of his book he does call *The Magnificent Seven* "the prototype" of specifically Eastern Westerns, suggesting that prototypes were being transnationally exchanged.[2] The final episode of the first season of *Westworld* (2016) shows samurai rehearsing for an American *jidaigeki* too. Sergio Leone's and Clint Eastwood's first Italian Western, *A Fistful of Dollars* (1964), was inspired by Kurosawa's *Yojimbo* (1961) (Smart 19), amplifying resonances between Japan, Italy, and America—hence Quentin Tarantino's mash-up of cowboys and samurai in the *Kill Bill* movies (2003, 2004); Tarantino later appeared in Takashi Miike's *Sukiyaki Western Django* (2007), a title that refers partly to the Italian Western cult favourite *Django* (Corbucci, 1966).[3]

These are cases of interplay and not only influence, cases that show how intertextual and interchangeable our "mental models" (Guillén 244) of narrative can be—at the risk of letting similarity slip into assumptions of sameness or identification with an American model. In China, which also has a tradition of regional realism pertaining to its own West, there are also mythic kung fu engagements with American Westerns, such as *Once upon a Time in China and America* (Lau and Hung, 1996), and studies are emerging in the wake of Teo's *Eastern Westerns* that show strong resemblances between Westerns and *wuxia*, or Chinese martial arts genres. Relatedly, in fact, Ian Teh's ecocritical photo essay entitled "China's New Deserts" (2019) happens to include an image from Madoi County in China that could well be the set of a Western, with its deserted small-town main street, its wide dusty sidewalk, its shops with false fronts, and even a man in jeans and a fedora ambling toward the camera from the middle ground. Elsewhere in the relative East, there is the Indo Western, such as the movie *Adima Changala* (Raj, 1981), which was based on an Italian Western called *The Five Man Army* (Taylor and Zingarelli, 1969). The Spaghetti Western in Italy and the Red Western and its Eastern/*Ostern* variant (Hillhouse 221) from Germany, Yugoslavia, and the Soviet Union gained attention internationally starting around 1966, partly because of the long-standing popularity of Karl May's turn-of-the-century German Western novels,

---

2   Teo is rigorous about terminology related to categories of Asian film throughout his introduction to *Eastern Westerns*.

3   Tarantino later riffed on the title in his own *Django Unchained* (2012).

partly because of their themes related to American freedoms in the context of divided and repressive regimes, and partly because of DEFA's *The Sons of Great Bear* (*Die Söhne der grossen Bärin*, Mach, 1966).[4] In this film, the character Adams (Horst Jonischkan) tells the captured Dakota warrior Tokei-ihto (Gojko Mitić), "When you're free, flee to Canada." The implication is that Canada was a better "model nation" than the United States for Indigenous people, but the model *genre* was still American.

Writing not specifically about Westerns but about American popular culture such as the movie and merchandise of *Jurassic Park* (Spielberg, 1993), Svetlana Boym in 2001 offered a related explanation—one that seemed almost quaint during the isolationist Trump administration:

> American popular culture has become a common coin for the new globalization. Cultural differences are often masked behind visual similarities. While the availability of American entertainment in Eastern Europe and Asia was greeted at first as a sign of new openness, its expansion and ubiquity became more problematic over time, especially when Western popular culture gradually became synonymous with democratization and supplanted other experiments with democracy. (39)

Because of its ostensible openness to settlement, America's landscape (which was often actually Italy's or Spain's, in Spaghetti Westerns, or Canada's in others) became a metonym for freedom, that glittering generality. For a fistful of years after the mid-1960s, the Europeans released more than six hundred Westerns, especially in Italy, where Westerns accounted for a third of all new films in 1967 (K. Grant 12), including many Italian movies of the *Zapata* variant set during the Mexican Revolution of 1910 (Gaberscek 45). According to Christopher Frayling, such films "forced [North American] critics to articulate a basic assumption which

---

4   Slightly preceding Karl May, but in Russia, was the late nineteenth-century Irish-American novelist Thomas Mayne Reid, whose novels were translated into Russian and whose idea of "the American West was used to create a territory that we term conceptually the Russian 'West.' ... The fact that Reid's novels escaped censorship in both communist and pre-revolutionary Russia reflects the 'emptiness' of his American West" (Naughton and Naughton 143–4).

has seldom been made so explicit before—that 'the Western' really belonged to a folk culture rather than an entrepreneurial culture; a folk culture which may have contained some Biblical, medieval and European motifs, but which, in the end, was essentially American in character" (118). In this formulation, the Western was partly borrowed and not altogether innovated—and, regardless of the plausibility here, we critics in the West finally admitted that we thought the world was always or eventually going to be American.

We should question this "assumption" before it is essentialized: the Western was not entirely a new and self-made ("entrepreneurial") American product, and, however true it was ("essentially") to America, it was also quite worldly. The Spanish director Joaquín Luis Romero Marchent was annoyed with the allegation that Europeans did not understand Westerns, and he and others noted that American filmmakers hardly deserved accolades for their accurate retellings of "Old World legends" (K. Grant 32) or Indigenous myths. The "world Western" was produced by people who thought about elsewhere and how it connected to home, and by people who came from abroad and brought their ideas. So it is about longing for another country, a country of the past (a prime example of nostalgia), and making it new. The implication is in some ways a revelation about the ambivalent capitalism and the nostalgic anti-modernism of so many Westerns around the globalized world, including those from Canada and the United States: they are as much a tradition as an innovation and commodification.[5] Leone sums this up like so: "Several great Western directors come from Europe: Ford is Irish; Zinnemann, Austrian; Lang, German; Wyler and Tourneur, French. . . . It is the Far West reinterpreted by Frankenstein and Disneyland" (qtd. in Frayling 118). In fact, one may claim, as Christine Bold does, that "[a] network of patrician easterners created the western as we now most commonly know it" (*Frontier* xvii), and that these "easterners" (not those mentioned by Leone) cultivated "a club mentality" among unofficial members who "sought to exclude . . . women, African Americans, 'new' immigrants [such as those

---

5   Examples of Canadian anti-modernism include the nostalgia for the Mountie (Dawson 143). Sharon Wall, in *The Nurture of Nature* (2009), also points to the work of T. J. Jackson Lears in the United States and Donald C. Wright in Canada.

mentioned by Leone, I would think], and Indigenous peoples" (xviii, xix).[6] Bold is referring to figures such as Owen Wister, Frederic Remington, and Theodore Roosevelt.[7] Their vision of the West—to spell out Leone's mixed metaphors—was hacked up and stitched back together by foreigners (hence "Frankenstein"), then made slick (hence "Disneyland").

And as with Frankenstein and Disneyland, the subtext is modernity and its dynamics; the Western becomes a vestige of cultural imperialism disguised by cosmopolitan immigrants to appear (counterintuitively) modern—*not* in its settings but by association with the New World and the newness of its frontier, or by nostalgia, which always implies our position in a relatively modern or contemporary time. Nostalgia colours the frontier through rose-tinted lenses that distort hindsight and obscure the frontier's ethical blind spots. Nostalgia renders it psychological and often immediate, or, as John G. Cawelti explains, not merely "geographical" but also "social and historical." For Cawelti, the frontier is a moving target, a symbol that speaks for many different particularities: "the Western is a story which takes place on or near a frontier and consequently the Western is generally set at a particular moment in the past" (*Six-Gun Mystique Sequel*, 20). Nostalgia enables a temporally paradoxical symbolism: the frontier is a symbol of promise and, therefore, the future, even while it is a symbol of a past when first contact was still possible.

Both the mythic and historical narratives of American culture and modernization from the nineteenth to early twenty-first centuries have also affected the rest of the West—the close neighbours of the United States, especially Mexico and Canada. In the field of Canadian literature, Northrop Frye explains the national imagination as a garrison mentality—the garrison being a metaphor or myth of a remote society "surrounded with a physical or psychological 'frontier,' separated from [its own communities] and from their American and British cultural sources" ("Conclusion" 205). In Chicano literature, "the Anglo American westering experience and all that it precipitated did make a decisive mark" (de Dwyer 212); along with

---

6   For a detailed expansion of classic and revisionist Westerns to include African-American and Indigenous works, see Shane Joseph Willis Frankiewicz's dissertation, *Revisionism and the Subversive Cowboy in the Classic Western* (2017).
7   For the historical details of this "frontier club," see not only Bold but also Patrick McGee (22–5, 41–2) and his sources.

the transition from hero to anti-hero in the American Western and in American youth culture in the 1950s and '60s, in Chicano literature "[t]he virtuous epic heroes of the frontier *corridos* [or border ballads] have been replaced to a great extent by the antiheroes of modern, urban barrios" (208). In American Westerns that represent Mexicans, "Mexicans have been symbolically trapped in a fairly rigid bandido complex" (Conway 33), but Mexican Westerns include the *vaquero* (the cowboy) and the *charro* (the horseman), the latter a costumed performer, sometimes a local wanderer, a bandit, or a revolutionary (Betz 511), but usually aristocratic rather than working class (Conway 38). As a not-quite cowboy but nonetheless a related symbol, the *charro* "came to represent the traditional and Catholic values in defiance of the leftist, modernizing tendencies emanating from the cities" (Mora 47)—an anti-modern figure who would be at home in the Western as I understand it. Still farther into the South but still in the Western Hemisphere, in Argentina and Uruguay is the *gaucho*, another horseman who appeared in fiction between the 1840s and the 1920s, not in Westerns exactly but in Western-esque plots about law and order, civilization and savagery, and town and country ("Gaucho"). These plots derived in part from well-known tales about the outlaw Martín Fierro and the bandit Juan Moreira (Acree ix). Partly because of their populist inclinations and popular results, these texts are often read as representations of a country's founding myths.

Transnationalism and Indigeneity

One such founding myth, however, partly belies the transnational diversity of the previous examples. That myth is suggested by the titles of James Fenimore Cooper's *The Last of the Mohicans* (1826) and Zane Grey's *The Vanishing American* (1925), later entitled *The Vanishing Indian* (1939). In Canada, "the Vanishing Canadian" was the focus of Paul Kane's mid-nineteenth-century paintings, inspired by his American contemporary George Catlin (Francis 16–18). Kane's memoir, *Wanderings of an Artist among the Indians of North America* (1859), "laments the inevitable disappearance of the Indian, and though the rest of the book does not deal with this subject in any detail, most reviewers took it as their theme" (Francis 23). In the spirit of the times, "Cooper's 'last Mohican' was for many a symbol of all Indians" (38). The symbolic totalization here is crucial.[8] In the at worst racist and at best romantic symbolism of the "Indian," the "Indian" is a nostalgic figure: a symbol of nature and of a wild youth who died young—a sort of James Dean whose maturity would always be before him, an influence acceptable to responsible adults as long as he is dead. Dead, he cannot interfere with how others symbolize and generalize him. "The misnomer 'Indian,' ironically so, now binds many native peoples, several thousand tribes spread all over the Western Hemisphere . . . first glossed wrongly by Columbus as one mythical subgroup" (Lincoln 8). By locating such diverse peoples in an imagined "India," the very diversity of their cultures and their movements was reduced. Wolfgang Hochbruck notes that "Europeans are probably a more homogenous lot" (266).

However sympathetic Westerns such as *Dances with Wolves* (Costner, 1990) can be, they have rarely been optimistic toward Indigenous peoples. Even in *Buck and the Preacher* (Poitier, 1972), a Hollywood Western that answered the classics by focusing positively on Black cowboys and their Indigenous allies, the "Indian" chief says through his translator that "tomorrow we will be like ghosts."[9] And *Dances with Wolves* helped to revive the genre of the Western in the 1990s but without returning the Vanishing "Indian" from the retreat of the Sioux into a snowy forest. In the United States, what Kenneth Lincoln calls the *Native American Renaissance* (1983) in literature began with N. Scott Momaday's *House Made of Dawn* (1968), but no Indigenous writer in Canada had similar success until Thomas King's anti-Western *Green Grass, Running Water* (1993) (which I consider in the next chapter) was widely Canadianized in Canadian literature courses, in spite of the view that King "cannot be a Canadian Native writer because the Cherokees [to whom King's paternal relatives belong] are not 'native' to Canada" (Andrews and Walton 605). Born in the United States

---

8 It extends even further. Shortly after the American Civil War, a theory of "black extinction" (Interlandi) emerged—a grave misunderstanding of the reasons why African-Americans, with freedom finally theirs, were struggling with epidemics. The reasons were what they tend to be: malnutrition and unsanitary conditions related to poverty, not a racial incompatibility with modernity.

9 Coincidentally, Buck's nemesis Deshay (no final *e*) has a variation of my rather rare anglicized name, "Deshaye." Deshay is a white man from the American South who has travelled northward after the Civil War with a posse to coerce African-Americans to return to work (or wage slavery) in the South. Instead of appearing in the climax, Deshay is killed by Buck midway through the film.

but living and writing primarily in Canada, King has travelled and moved from country to country, a paragon of transnationalism, "bound" to the Canadian nation writ large, who has raised doubts about nationalism and its derivatives as appropriate concepts for understanding his work. In *The Inconvenient Indian* (2012), King explains why he felt compelled to write about Canada and the United States as two sides of a border: "I would have found it impossible to talk about the one without talking about the other. For most Aboriginal people, that line doesn't exist. It's a figment of someone else's imagination" (xvi; see also *Truth about Stories* 102).[10] If the continuity of lands here may be paralleled with Indigenous theories, I would add that King has proposed terms such as "interfusional" and "associational" to describe Indigenous writing ("Godzilla" 12). What settlers saw as a vanishing was partly an assumption about their total neutralization of earlier (but also cohabiting) inhabitants, their own Manifest Destiny as landowners, and their superior Darwinian fitness—an assumption probably worsened by their misunderstanding of some Native American and First Nations migratory patterns as nomadic. If "Indians" did not settle, then they were transnational and homeless, transient, *aboriginal* in the sense of "without origins" and thus rootless as a tumble weed: always out of place in, and ultimately gone from, the nation-states that settlers were helping to build in North America.[11]

Such a misunderstanding is one reason why transnationalism, when used alongside "globalization" and "neoliberalism," is not ideal as a concept that might locate the "Indian" of "cowboys and Indians" in the Western. In fact, it can also suffer as a result of slippage from "misunderstanding" to "misinformation." As critics such as Richard Slotkin, Alan Trachtenberg, and Christine Bold have explained, the American government and media had a practice of perniciously homogenizing the identities of immigrants

---

10   For more on Indigenous views of borders, see the introduction to Carlton Smith's *Coyote Kills John Wayne* (2000, 3–5).

11   Boym notes: "By the early twentieth century modern experience became identified by George Lukacs as 'transcendental homelessness' " (22), but King in *The Inconvenient Indian* and Francis in *The Imaginary Indian* argue that the symbol of the "Indian" is not modern but hopelessly primitive and, by the internal logic of the symbol, destined to vanish and never be a force in the modern world. I thank Len Findlay for observing this very problem of being supposedly "without origins" in an honours seminar many years ago—an observation I have never forgotten, and an early touchstone in my education on these matters.

and Indigenous peoples, "repeatedly substitut[ing] the one for the other as a way of demonizing both throughout the second half of the nineteenth century" (Bold, *Frontier* 170). Generally, the assimilationist policies directed at immigrants and Indigenous peoples in both the United States and Canada worked on assumptions of their transience and lack of origins (or the erasure thereof), and this distorted sense of transnationalism has been used as justification for removals and relocations or other forced transportations, especially of Indigenous peoples.

A different transnationalism is required. Robert Warrior argues that transnational theory "has had little impact in Native literary studies" (121) and that "[a] major reason for the lack of engagement with transnationality by Native American scholars is the widespread rejection of postcolonial studies" (122), a rejection that King articulates in his often-quoted essay "Godzilla vs. Post-Colonial" (1990): "the term [post-colonial] itself assumes that the starting point for that discussion [about not only oppression but also progress] is the advent of Europeans in North America," and the term remains "a hostage to nationalism" (11, 12). Warrior in turn asserts that "Native Americans remain colonised peoples rather than people facing post-independence realities and challenges" (122). He is also concerned that transnational theories that focus on globalization are not sufficiently critical of the homogenizing tendencies of both globalization and nationalism (126), and so

> Indigenous scholars have contributed to discussions of transnationality specifically by refusing to get with the program, failing to adopt its premises, and continuing to focus on the concerns that have fueled the agenda of their world. In effect our nationalism is born out of native transnationalism, the flow and exchange of ideas and politics across our respective nations' borders. (125)

The differentiation of not only "nationalism" but also "transnationalism" from "native transnationalism" is Warrior's tactic for preventing the assimilation of Indigenous scholarship into post-colonial studies. He also seems to suggest, however, that Indigenous peoples on Turtle Island have an unexpected opportunity in an era of globalization because "the effects of capitalism, which were once contained and constrained by the sovereignty of nations [specifically nation-states], now supersede and trump the power of states. Put in another way, states as opposed to different groupings increasingly are incapable of effectively addressing the needs of people within their borders. Indigenous peoples are among those different groupings" (119). Until the American government under Donald Trump began to look increasingly inward, one could have said that, in an era of neoliberal globalization, "going Indian" is going local, seeking local sovereignties and self-determinations.[12] In *Green Grass, Running Water*, King's "Indians" fight John Wayne to reclaim their land in parallel with an attempt to stop a massive hydroelectric project that serves national political ends and, often, transnational or multinational corporate ends. In *Un/inhabited* (2015) and *Injun* (2016), both composed of hundreds of excerpts from American Westerns that are now in the public domain, the Nisga'a poet Jordan Abel takes back representations of the Wild West that were once owned by colonial writers and publishing companies, and thereby "prompts a reconsideration of the land 'found' by pioneers" (Stefanucci iv). The "native transnationalism" in these examples is microeconomic. Textual lands change hands for decentralization and, more idealistically, decolonization. The result of "native transnationalism" is both an unsettling of the place of the West in the Euro-American mindset (to follow the trend of the unsettling double entendre) and a reclamation. It once more invites the question of where the Western belongs, or to whom.

National Genres, Myths, and Histories

Having begun big, with the world, we now move into the country.[13]

---

12   In the related context of comparative and global Indigenous literary studies in English, Chadwick Allen emphasizes how a huge diversity of so-called "Indigenous" literatures may be considered "together (yet) *distinct*" (xiii). He also thinks that "*trans-* seems the best choice" (xv) among additive and comparative terms: "The point is not to displace the necessary, invigorating study of specific traditions and contexts but rather to complement these by augmenting and expanding broader, globally Indigenous fields of inquiry. . . . Similar to terms like *trans*lation, *trans*national, and *trans*form, *trans*-Indigenous may be able to bear the complex, contingent asymmetry and the potential risks of unequal encounters borne by the preposition *across*" (xiv).

13   The previous section was not truly about "the world," given that it omitted big places such as Africa, but it was about transnationality as one step up from nationality.

Transnational and national theories and genre theories all have correlations. Although nationalists want to be strict about national borders, transnationalists show the ways in which aspects of culture such as myth move across borders—and the borders themselves can change. Although some genre theorists want to be strict about the borders of genre, others show how these borders are almost always overlapping. In *Film/Genre* (1999), Rick Altman uses the same analogy: "Just as our knowledge of the changing borders of France underlies any current use of the term 'France,' so categories like *poetry, drama* and *comedy* coexist with *the musical*" (69); furthermore, "the notion of genre parallels that of nation" (86), partly because genres are sometimes thought to have organizational structures akin to that of nation-state > province > city > neighbourhood. Curiously, we might now be in an era where the nation is branded in ways similar to the branding of genres—for example, in the latter case when brightly coloured optimistic superheroes are the brand of Marvel comics in contrast with their dark counterparts in DC. In a coincidental metaphor or cultural echo of Appadurai's explanation of modernity and globalization through "scalar dynamic[s]" (32), Margaret Cohen states that "[i]n the case of the modern novel, genre is an essential scale for producing a thick history of the novel's diverse aesthetics" (55). Cohen puts genre alongside poetics and style; indeed, taken together these are ways in which writers practise their art and work to use conventions idiosyncratically. Altman, too, explains that "the constitution of *film* cycles and genres is a never-ceasing process, closely tied to the capitalist need for product differentiation" (*Film/Genre* 64). Broadly speaking, one might say that cultural production of transnational genres is process-oriented not only to differentiate but also to disseminate genres for profit, and that "product differentiation" (e.g., Hollywood's setting of hundreds of Westerns in Canada) can have the unexpected result of *minimizing national-cultural differentiation* when, for example, consumers internalize the transnational genre as their own—which is arguably the case for Canadian consumption of the American Western, *and* the American consumption of the Canadian Western. For the bigger cultural producer, this internalization is an advantage, because it emboldens cultural producers at home and minimizes cultural resistance abroad. And the minimized national-cultural differentiation is also a creator of nostalgia—for the country as it once was—that encourages further marketing of the brand.

"The country," by which I mean "nation" but which I want to use for a moment to connote both the nation-state and the landscapes around its centres, has bearing on the Western because of a shared nationalism or patriotism that is supported in part by myth.[14] According to Leo Braudy, the dynamic is that "[g]enre films essentially ask the audience, 'Do you still want to believe this?' Popularity is the audience answering, 'Yes' " (qtd. in Altman 16). This question and its answer, of course, are never stated so simply or explicitly in films or books themselves, but from them we can infer a connection between genre and myth, if myth is a story that people want to believe and affirm. In the context of the Mountie in the Canadian Western, Keith Walden suggests that the production of a myth might begin with what we think to be "a self-evident reality," but that the "reality" is only "what [we] wanted to see" (11). Myth and genre therefore seem to be related concepts, indispensable to the Western. For Rick Altman in *Film/Genre*,

> [l]ikening genre to myth provides clear gains for genre theorists. This strategy provides an organizing principle for genre study, transmuting what might have been a hollow commercial formula into a culturally functioning category. . . . In return for these benefits, however, genre critics have been forced to forego serious historical considerations in favour of the transhistorical model offered by myth. (20)

It would be easy to misunderstand "transhistorical" as "ahistorical," but in the view that Altman explains here the myth applies universally throughout history. It is not absent from history or without bearing on history. I prefer F. W. Galan's view that "genre is a historically conditioned concept,

---

14   Partly because of the familiarity of the metaphor of centres and margins in Canadian culture and literature, nationalism (of the centre) cannot be separated from regionalism (of the margins). Frank Davey writes that "we would not be here discussing Canadian regionalism were there not also a nation-state called Canada" ("Toward" 3). Although national genres and myths are the main topic of this section, regionalism cannot be entirely relegated to subsequent sections. Colin Hill would seem to agree: "realist portraits of particular locales were a feature of the larger, national movement in Canadian literature" (102).

not a universally valid one" (qtd. in Beebee 270), and so my study compromises between transhistorical and historical models. There are various reasons for the compromise, but the most significant—the one from which the rest extrapolate—is that mythmaking and the appreciation of myth are *ideological* in the Lacanian and Althusserian sense of ideology as a mystifying system of hidden and serial assumptions, desires, values, and differentials of power (Beebee 15; Kellner 10)—what Fredric Jameson means, I think, when he refers to "the political unconscious." In the 1981 book of that name, Jameson explained that "[g]enres are essentially literary institutions, or social contracts between a writer and a specific public, whose function is to specify the proper use of a particular cultural artifact" (106). The reference to a "social contract" is about expectations: the reader's and the writer's and what they are supposed to do for each other. Using Janice Radway's terminology related to romance and Will Wright's historical positioning of the Western (itself a romance), Thomas O. Beebee in *The Ideology of Genre* (1994) explains that Westerns are "compensatory literature" (4). They compensate for men's felt lack of individual agency—in an era of "postindustrial capitalism that has de-emphasized the individual" (6)—with the proposition that "[a] man acting alone can solve a collective problem" (6). This explanation is historically situated in economics but is also mythic, partly because of its connotations of the hero, a romantic archetype one step removed from the heaven and hell of gods and demons into the world of human experience (Frye, *Anatomy* 139–40). During the 2016 Democratic National Convention, President Barack Obama said that one person—namely, the Republican nominee, Donald Trump—cannot solve all of America's problems, contrary to Trump's assertions ("Barack"); Obama was identifying a myth at work in Trump's campaign and the popular support for his candidacy. He could have called Trump a cowboy to situate the latter's self-styled heroism. (I have already footnoted the Cowboys for Trump organization.) In effect, the Western historicizes a myth, a myth closely associated with the hero in transhistorical romances and epics. Beebee's and Obama's ideological insights can help us to understand historical attitudes, causes and effects, and (through Beebee and Altman) the phases of genres.

This book is, in fact, a study of the phases of the Western in over a century of Canadian literature, beginning at the turn of the twentieth century and extending to the present. Consider, for example, how the early Canadian Westerns, such as Ralph Connor's *Black Rock* in 1898 or H. A. Cody's *The Frontiersman* in 1910, might be (mis)recognized as other genres—or unrecognized entirely—unless they are understood in their historical context and seen as precursors. They can be described as sentimental romances, or melodramas, or adventures. Any early example of a genre is easy to associate with similar precursors and contemporaries, contrary to Aristotle's attempt to isolate them, which has ironically had "the effect of narrowing genre theory ever since" (Altman, *Film/Genre* 2). To the contrary, Frye argues that the ur-categories of romance, tragedy, comedy, and satire are "pregeneric elements of literature" (and arguably also film) that can be described as "*mythoi* or generic plots" (*Anatomy* 162). For his part, Frye thus allows for a widening of genre theory. Altman, meanwhile, counters Aristotle by showing that in the late nineteenth century the Western began as Wild West films, Western chase films, Western comedies, Western scenics, Western melodramas, Western romances, Western adventures, and Western epics (*Film/Genre* 36, 52)—the adjective "Western" describing other genres before being christened as its own. As I wondered with less context nearer to the beginning of this book, are Eastwood's Dirty Harry movies Westerns, considering that he used *Coogan's Bluff* (Siegel, 1968) as an obviously self-conscious transition from his penultimate Westerns to his early cop movies? Not quite, but they cannot be fully understood unless their titular rogue cop is compared to the outlaw-lawman of the Western or other heroes. Significantly, the early Canadian Westerns were not "Canadian Westerns" that became a genre called simply "the Canadian." Nor were they labelled with food, as Italian Westerns were—Spaghetti Westerns—or as others that I mentioned in the introduction, possibly because the contiguity of the Canadian and American landscapes enabled directional terms to work perfectly well. They were simply called "Northerns" or "Northwesterns," as Pierre Berton points out in *Hollywood's Canada* (1975) and elsewhere, so that region rather than nation was in the foreground, just as it is with the Western, regardless of its American associations. (Alan Ladd, famous for playing the eponymous hero in the 1953 film *Shane*, also played a Mountie in Raoul Walsh's 1954 film *Saskatchewan*.) Certainly most people, even many scholars, do not know about or recognize the existence of the Canadian Western as I write this book. Altman asks why "some structures fail to achieve generic recognition" (*Film/Genre* 50) while others are canonized. One answer is that the ideology of nationalism enforces borders, and a genre with strong associations with a nation may be policed by its nationalism so that the borders of the genre become more difficult to cross. Another is that the American Western assimilated the Northwestern into a phase of its development as a renewed and repositioned vision of the frontier, providing variation on a theme—Canada as spinoff—during the increasing popularity of the Western into the 1950s, when overexposure eventually demanded recourse to the new cycle that is now strongly associated with Sergio Leone and Clint Eastwood. In fact, as the genre moved from nearer (Canada and Mexico) to farther countries, Leone's and Eastwood's roles in transnationalizing the Western were a widening of the Western's scope that was already happening in the very early twentieth century with the Northwesterns, as I will show in chapter 3. It also seemed to be happening in the United States in novels such as Pauline Hopkins's *Winona: A Tale of Negro Life in the South and Southwest* (1902–3) (Frankiewicz 168–9, 174–7), which happens to begin with a line about the Canadian border and the intersection of Black, Indigenous, and white people there.[15]

Presented with the historical arc of the Canadian Western, Canadian as well as American readers will be more likely to accept that Canadian literature is a home of the genre—even if genres themselves are not exclusive homes for texts, and if texts never really feel that sense of "belonging" (Derrida 65) in a single genre. The Canadian Westerns that are most explicit about their lack of belonging only in the genre of the Western are, predictably, the postmodern Canadian Westerns—such as Ondaatje's *The Collected Works of Billy the Kid*, George Bowering's *Caprice* (1987), Paulette Jiles's *Jesse James Poems* (1988), and (though he has distanced himself from the colonial implications of the term "postmodern" just as he has with "post-colonial") Thomas King's *Green Grass, Running Water*. These can also be read as examples of what Linda Hutcheon calls (in various essays and books) "historiographic metafiction," itself a genre,

---

15   Mourning Dove's (Hum-Ishu-Ma's) *Cogewea* (1927) might also be included here as a prototype of expanding the Western, but its Westernness is highly debatable and problematic, perhaps more so than with Hopkins's *Winona*.

one that raises self-conscious questions about the writing of history and about myth. In suggesting that historiographic metafiction is a genre but that it is not the exclusive name for some of these books that should also be called Westerns, and in surveying quite widely to find analogues and mutual influences of the Western, I am obviously not suggesting that all analogues are classic Westerns or that any genre has "clear, stable identities and borders" (Altman, *Film/Genre* 16). Rather, I like Beebee's focus on "generic instability" (256–67) and the analogues that Beebee finds in use by other scholars, notwithstanding the inaccuracies of the genealogical analogy that Altman debunks (*Film/Genre* 64–8): genre is like a family resemblance; genre is like a colour spectrum; genre is like a Venn diagram, as Beebee himself demonstrates (252, 256–7, 259–60); and so on. These analogies are of continuity. So, I mean to help readers see the genre's border crossings and crossovers with other genres, such as the literary and historical Western developed by Guy Vanderhaeghe, and such as adventure stories for boys and girls along the lines of Cody's *Rod of the Lone Patrol* (1916) and *Jess of the Rebel Trail* (1921). And I want us to recognize the temporal continuity between Cody and Vanderhaeghe, separated though they are by seventy-odd years, even if the continuity is debatable. According to Beebee, it is precisely the text whose genre is debatable that will "expos[e] its ideology" (19) when we attempt to classify it. He explains that ideology, as invisible as a dream but all the more effective,

> simultaneously holds a society together by allowing it to communicate with itself in shorthand and pushes society apart by conflicting with people's realities. It is only in the deformations and contradictions of writing and thinking that we can recognize ideology; genre is one of those observable deformations, a pattern ... that reveals the force of ideology. (18)

The "generic instability" proposed by the "Canadianness" of the Western has the potential to lead to more ideological insightfulness than would a study of the stabilized American Westerns, by which I mean the classics that are the least revisionist and the least revised. In fact, for the same reason, many critics are drawn to complex American Westerns such as

Unforgiven (Eastwood, 1992) because they at least temporarily seem to offer generic alternatives, such as the anti- or post-Western premise of what later becomes the unapologetically pro-Western conclusion of *Unforgiven*. And as we read Westerns through time, a Jamesonian historical method enables us to see how the genre bends according to how commodified it is, whether in the middlebrow phase of Connor's and Cody's 1900s and 1910s, the lowbrow pulp fiction of the 1940s, or the mainly highbrow literary Westerns from the 1970s to the present. According to Ortega y Gassett, "each epoch favors a certain genre" (qtd. and trans. in Beebee 272), as almost any study of popular culture would confirm—were it studying a time before satellite radio and the Internet's on-demand broadcasting, at least.

On the topic of media, this book assumes that genres are mobile not only across the borders of nations but also across the borders of media. The early Canadian Westerns are situated at a phase when comparative exemplars such as Owen Wister's 1902 novel *The Virginian* had already appeared, prior to the imitation of these exemplars and their temporary stabilization into the genre of the Western in film later that decade (Altman, *Film/Genre* 35). One of Altman's perplexing arguments is that the temporary stabilization of the genre in late nineteenth-century fiction was very different from the temporary stabilization of the genre in early twentieth-century film, where it had to be "recreated" (*Film/Genre* 35)— an argument that poses a problem for this book, which is mostly about literature but draws on theories of genre in various media, as Beebee does in *The Ideology of Genre*. Different media, according to Altman, produce different genres even when "the outward trappings" are very similar and they have a "shared name" (*Film/Genre* 36, 35); thus, pre-1910 films that used iconography from Buffalo Bill's Wild West Show were not Westerns, because the "Show" was not a film. If this claim is true, what happens when we read Ondaatje's *The Collected Works of Billy the Kid*? Although Ondaatje integrates a dime-novel cover and narrative into the book, along with other print media such as the newspaper, scholars such as Dennis Cooley and Linda Hutcheon have demonstrated that the cinematic point of view and treatment of sound associate the book with films. Presumably, these associated films are Westerns, given the photograph of Ondaatje as a boy dressed in a cowboy costume that resembles what's worn on film more than what's described in literature. The generic sources of the first major literary Western in Canada were not only other print media but also the moving pictures. The same is true of so many earlier books.

Why would Altman draw the line at intermedial origins of genres when he connects them intramedially? (What would Altman do with adaptations of novels into movies, or with the effects of fan fiction on producers and directors?[16]) Since the first decade of the twentieth century, novelists have been watching movies, and filmmakers have always been reading novels and other books. Although I agree with the McLuhanism that adaptation into a new medium can fundamentally change the message, this change does not necessarily exclude the new text from the genre(s) of its precursors. Genres are not entirely message-dependent, otherwise a revisionist Western would be impossible, but some genres are obviously better suited to some messages than others. The translation and variation of a genre across media are simply more expressions of the instability of any genre. When Altman asks where genres are located, he finds them not only in texts but also in the intentions, uses, and expectations of the writers, producers, institutions, and readers surrounding those texts. Genre is not a closed system. I also agree with another McLuhanism, which is that new media contain old media, so—like nesting dolls—they can be recursively opened up. Altman's own openness suggests that his closing of the borders between media is a convenience to ensure a manageable scope to his research. Moretti's distant reading is another management of scope.

I have already (in the introduction) rationalized the scope of my book, so here I leave you with a thought experiment. What if we replaced "genre" with "nation" in the previous paragraph?

Nations are not entirely message-dependent, otherwise change would be impossible, but some nations are obviously better suited to some messages than others. The translation and variation of a nation across media are simply more expressions of the instability of any nation. Nations are located not only in texts but also in the intentions, uses, and expectations

---

16 Possible inconsistencies in *Film/Genre*, such as Altman's classification of *The Great Train Robbery* (Porter, 1903) as a blend of travel and crime genres (35) but his later acceptance of it as a Western (48), may be attributable to his remarkable ability to alternate and compare his critical methods, as in chapter 3, where he interprets genre from the point of view first of the critic and then of the producer.

of the writers, producers, institutions, and readers surrounding those texts. Nation is not a closed system.

Frontier Theses and Myths

Given the close relationship between the United States and Canada, and their centrality as producers of the Western in English, what are their comparable myths, and how should they be situated historically? William H. Katerberg argues that Canadians did have historians, as the United States had Frederick Jackson Turner, who created a "frontier thesis" that informed Canadian mythopoeia: "Together, the 'staples thesis' of Harold A. Innis and the 'metropolitan-hinterland' paradigm of J. M. S. Careless [based in part on Innis's centre-margin dichotomy] provide the basis for a Canadian frontier thesis" (548).[17] Basically, Innis recognized Canada as a resource economy that sent staples or basic goods such as pulp and wheat back to Britain and, without other economies of its own, would remain a frontier. Careless developed the idea to suggest that centres are needed to spread civilization outward. Katerberg further explains that "the frontier West in American culture typically is a land all its own, with its own logic and dynamic, where people go to escape the burdens of the civilized world. But in the Canadian imagination, frontiers usually are tied to the larger world, as peripheries shaped and controlled by distant cities and capitols" (545). This view agrees with that of Brian Dippie, who raises the possibility that there is "one West, two myths" (509); he uses Daniel Francis's terms to differentiate "the Mild West north of the border, and the Wild West south of it" (510). Dippie also acknowledges that historians have often demanded that the sensational histories of the Indian Wars and Custer's Last Stand be considered alongside the usually peaceful social history of the American West; however, in terms of myths rather than history, Francis's Mild/Wild distinction seems to stand. It also supports the Frygian theory of the garrison mentality in which a Canadian society bands together in a centre for protection against an extreme wilderness at the margins, rather than going it alone the more American way.

---

17   A preceding and often parallel study is that of D. M. R. Bentley, "The Mower and the Boneless Acrobat: Notes on the Stances of Baseland and Hinterland in Canadian Poetry." *Studies in Canadian Literature*, vol. 8, no. 1, 1983, pp. 5-48.

Katerberg's view also indirectly affirms that of Dick Harrison, one of the significant regionalists whose work during Canada's nationalistic 1970s was meaningfully comparative, and I want to focus on Harrison partly because he was not a historian but a literary scholar whose breadth of reading in *Unnamed Country* (1977) is a major contribution to genre studies. Harrison looked mainly at Prairie fiction but also reflected on some examples of the "formula Western" ("Across" 52; *Unnamed* 157) in the United States and Canada. He claims that the myths made in Canada were just not quite the same myths as in the United States:

> The Canadian West was not, of course, a frontier in the sense that the American West was, and this was not merely because order usually preceded settlement. It had much to do with what the West represented to the country as a whole. The prairies were not thought of as the leading edge of a continuously expanding nation but as a colony developed separately which had to be tied in to confederation with a railroad and two armies. Canada itself was not an Atlantic seaboard nation seeking cultural independence from Europe but a landlocked nation struggling to maintain its British character. Canadians were not looking to an advancing frontier to provide their identity or mature their national character, and western writers could not think of themselves as at the centre of forces which were shaping their nation's ideals. The fact that the Canadian fictional prairie is not a frontier in the usual sense and does not yield to the application of Turner's thesis remains the most salient and the most consistent distinction between the literary fictions of the two Wests as it was between popular fictions. ("Across" 51; for echoes, see also *Unnamed* 74)

Although Harrison's diction here does suggest that he is thinking not of history but of literature (i.e., "represented," "thought of," "fictional prairie," "literary fictions"), he also explains several historical facts, possibly overemphasizing history because of an assumption that Canada had not only *different* myths but simply not enough of them. In " 'Across the Medicine

Line': Problems in Comparing Canadian and American Western Fiction" (1977), Harrison concludes that Canada's "under-mythicized West" and America's "over-mythicized West" (55) conceptualize subtly divergent national identities. Katerberg's view of the independence of the American Western aligns with Harrison's perspective on the interdependency of Canadian and British identities, and this binary of independent and inter/dependent nationalities is a theme in the scholarship that echoes throughout this book too.

The North complicates this binary, however. In " 'Across the Medicine Line,' " Harrison compares Wister's *The Virginian* (1902) to Connor's *Corporal Cameron* ten years later (1912) but does not reflect on the widespread popularity of other examples of the Northwestern and how, in hundreds of stories, novels, and movies set in Canada, it could have "under-mythicized" the region—a mistake that we have already seen with Mitchell's comparative views. Still, in *Unnamed Country* he counts at least "150 volumes of fiction in which Mounties play a prominent part" (157). *Corporal Cameron* (as Harrison's gold standard) is one such example of Mountie fiction, but its geographical range in the latter half (after Cameron's movement from Scotland through Canada) is mainly Northern or Northwestern. The novel is set partly around southwestern Alberta while invoking the midlands of Saskatchewan and the North-West Resistance of 1885 when, in Canada, the West was synonymous with the Northwest. The North-West Resistance concluded at Batoche, Saskatchewan, which is about as far to the north as North Battleford—still a long way south of the midpoint of the province that demarcates the beginning of Northern Saskatchewan at La Ronge. Furthermore, today we still talk of "Northern Ontario" when referring to locations as far south and west as Lake of the Woods, barely north of the 49th parallel, or even Sudbury, which is around the 46th. The relativity of these terms helps me and others to suggest that Canada has a North that is conceptually parallel to the West (Grace 12). We simply cannot underemphasize nordicity when we accept that Mountie fiction and other Northwesterns create "the nearest approach we have to a popular art form of the Canadian West analogous to the American Western" (Harrison, *Unnamed* 156)—with the exception, I would add, of "Canadian" books set in the United States that feature fictionalized American historical figures such as Billy the Kid, Jesse James, and Calamity Jane. Significantly, in the many movies that Berton reflects upon in *Hollywood's Canada*, the geography is always Northern and almost always historically inaccurate, and the compulsion to reproduce a fantasy (not merely a falsehood) is a defining trait of mythmaking (Walden 8–11). Harrison does not neglect the North, but he underemphasizes its relevance to the Western.

The only other dispute I have with Harrison's perceptive explanation is that the Canadian West *does* seem to have been a continuous expansion, an "advancing frontier," an "edge." Surely Connor's *Black Rock* and Cody's *The Frontiersman* attest to expanding settlements in their representations of the hard labour, isolation, and associated intemperance of early industrial towns in the Northwest, and *Corporal Cameron* attests to the North-West Mounted Police's role in protecting that expansion. Surely the gaining of the North-West Territories and the spanning of the continent from east to west also played a part in defining a national consciousness, even if "Canadians were not looking" for one. If for Britain it was only another colony, people in Canada must surely have understood that it was special because of its vast size, as with Australia, and that the also considerable size of the United States and its potentially related independence would create similar possibilities for Canada. (The United States' population was much bigger too, and so Canada's sense of possibility might have been disproportionate in terms of that metric.) Harrison elsewhere admits that by 1870 "romantic traditions" (*Unnamed* 5) in the depiction of the American West, and possibly already the Canadian West, were influencing perceptions of the actual West, and this, too, is a point that deserves more emphasis. The Canadian West was sometimes following American "romantic traditions" of the West rather than its own history.

The fact of Canada's longer existence as a British colony informs Harrison's related statements about an alternative to the frontier myth. Remember Harrison's view that, in Canada, "order usually preceded settlement." He also claims that the alternative to the frontier myth is an Edenic garden myth based on an idea of order:[18]

---

18   See also Leo Marx's *The Machine in the Garden* (1964) for a theory of the pastoral American landscape marked by technology, and Annette Kolodny's *The Lay of the Land* (1984) for a vision of the landscape as a feminine entity cultivated into "a maternal 'garden' " (5). In Canada, see Shelley Boyd's *Garden Plots: Canadian Women Writers and Their Literary Gardens* (2013).

> The West to be found in English Canadian fiction is rarely a "frontier." If a "frontier" is taken to be that meeting point of advancing civilization and untamed nature, *where civilized order confronts unordered wilderness*, then there is no reason to expect one, since the frontier era was virtually over by the time the literature began. . . . When most of the early novelists began to come west with the bulk of settlement from Ontario, Great Britain, and the American Middle West, they came into incredibly rigorous pioneer conditions, but not to the edge of a trackless wilderness. (*Unnamed* 73, emphasis added)

Although Harrison might have read Connor's description of the Northwest as "God's own open country" (*Corporal* 187) and inferred that, with God in it, it has the orderliness not only of an English garden but also of Eden, it is nevertheless "open" (not walled as in Andrew Marvell's English garden). In Cody's *The Frontiersman* (one of Harrison's few meaningful omissions but one that demands to be considered partly because of its title) there are only two tracks: one behind the heroic Keith Steadman, whose trek into "the great white silence" (9) of the snowy North leaves a trail for a dog thought to be a wolf to follow (10); the second "an Indian trail which wound its devious way through the wilderness" (311) that is also described as "a roadless wilderness" (30). These examples from the genre suggest that, in fact, Canadian literature has its own "trackless wilderness." But then there is that idea of order, as Harrison continues:

> One could say that the conception of order in Wister's West is inductive—order is generated from the immediate particulars of experience—while that of Connor's West is deductive—order descends logically from higher precepts to which the individual has no access. . . . This willingness to see the encompassing *order as in some way sacred* is a strong element in the Garden Myth of the early fiction. (*Unnamed* 79, emphasis added)

These are indeed appropriate inferences based on the comparison of Wister's style of hero (à la outlaw) and Connor's (à la Mountie). For Connor, these "higher precepts" were British authority and Christian ethics brought together through imperialism. In the "Northwestern Cross" chapter, my reading of Connor and Cody—both of whom were ministers and missionaries— shows that Christianity and related aspects of the theory of Manifest Destiny are a part of the idea of West. Katerberg explains that, "[t]o be sure, Anglo-Canadian dreams of the Dominion as an equal partner with Britain differed from American notions of manifest destiny, but they did so in the details more than in scope" (547); "both re-envisioned the region as marvelously endowed by the Creator" (546) with a "unique vitality" (547). Doug Owram in *Promise of Eden: The Canadian Expansionist Movement and the Idea of the West, 1856–1900* (1980) links the parts of Manifest Destiny in his title: Eden, expansion, West. The syllogistic logic of Owram's title makes it almost commonsensical.

If you recall from the introduction of this book that the political contexts of leftward and rightward swings are relevant to the Canadian Western, my conclusion here is that Canada and the United States both had conservative dimensions in their different frontier theses and Manifest Destinies. There was not yet a leftward swing, but there was a different baseline for shared conservatism. In Canada, the frontier destiny was both less and more conservative than in the United States: less conservative because it was imagined as less violent and less chaotic; more conservative because writers of the Canadian Western did not yet want to break with the authority of Christianity and the British Empire. American writers wanted to build the next big thing, and for it to be new. In this era, Canadian writers wanted that thing to be suitable to the old.

The Individual in Myth

Eventually we scale down to the individual, the atom of the nuclear family, but the mythic resonance of the individual is so strong that it arcs between region and nation. The so-called myth of the West depends largely on the individual in both countries, and this individual is strongly associated with the nation and the land. One of the most memorable visual examples (also American) is when the namesake of the movie *Shane* (Stevens, 1953) rides out of the background of plains and mountains in the opening sequence, sighted along a toy gun and associated through his rawhide jacket with the dun colours of both the deer and the prairie. When Canadian regionalist scholarship came of age in the 1960s and '70s, it argued that the land and the landscape were defining features of the individual in the West. Henry Kreisel's "The Prairie: A State of Mind" (1968), Laurie Ricou's *Vertical Man / Horizontal World: Man and Landscape in Canadian Prairie Fiction* (1973), and Harrison's *Unnamed Country* all have this focus, to different degrees. Harrison states that he wanted to correct Edward McCourt's neglect of Prairie uniqueness in *The Canadian West in Fiction* (1949) and Ricou's lack of concentration on "the influence of culture on man's reaction to the landscape" (*Unnamed* xiii). According to Alison Calder and Robert Wardhaugh, however, the studies that predate *Unnamed Country*, and that study too, "constructed a category of 'Canadian prairie writing' in which landscape dominates culture and geography effaces history" (8). According to Calder, Wardhaugh, and other critics, the corrective was in the writing of Robert Kroetsch and an associated set of authors who were trying to show how mythic the landscape was—how created by the imagination, how historiographic, and yet how independently influential. Not until Robert Thacker's *The Great Prairie Fact and Literary Imagination* (1989) did regionalism become transnationally mythic as an exploration of the psychological frontier in both Canada and the United States.

Although the notion of the land as one's own mind is compelling, partly because it would entail the formation of self and the revelation of self-knowledge, the individual's association with the land may never be assumed to be friendly. The Western needs to be acknowledged as Western fiction that depends on violence, usually individual acts of violence that are trigger-happily protective or retributive, but sometimes the more general cultural violence involved in the engagement with First Nations, Native Americans, Mexicans, and—crucially—the land itself, or "Indians" as metonyms of the land. Following Harrison, and Frye's concept of the garrison mentality, Ronald Tranquilla explains that "the myth of the Western developed part of [the garrison mentality]. Here, the hero is in combat with nature—'knowing it, measuring it, controlling it, and, if need be, fighting it'" (74). The series of gerunds Tranquilla quotes here is from Connor's *Corporal Cameron*, a novel in which the Mountie usually reserves "fighting" for the last resort and whose knowledge is power: to know is to control. Knowing nature, we can "measure" out our own defences against it. Tranquilla notices that Harrison describes the symbol of the house as a defence against the environment (74), and this observation I think deserves emphasis; preoccupied with the garrison mentality, a defensive concept (the shield), we might forget that the Western almost always prominently involves aggression and violence: "combat," usually involving firearms (the sword). The garrison mentality is thus anti-Western, a mentality that might have been created by the myth of the West or, perhaps more accurately, to counter that myth. Explanations of the Western would be incomplete if they did not consider the emphatic, morally charged human violence that drives and resolves almost all stories in the Western and its spinoffs. In my chapter on "Degeneration through Violence," I offer an interpretation of Canadian Westerns that seem to suggest, contrary to Slotkin's theory of American regeneration through violence, that violence irreparably damages the individual. For fictional violence to be cathartic and vicarious in its effects depends in part on a viewer's identification with an ideology of individualism that has heroic potential: me against the world, or more accurately, me against society.

Harrison suggests that in the United States there is "a fascination with individualism which makes the hero unable to submit to the social contract even when he has helped to draft it," whereas in Canada "the isolation of characters . . . results from a life of self-abnegation" ("Across" 52). Here he, too, echoes Frye, whose concept of the garrison mentality suggests that Canadians faced with the frontier tended to become less individualistic and more socially responsible. Frye explains: "A garrison is a closely knit and beleaguered society, and its moral and social values are unquestionable. In a perilous enterprise one does not discuss causes or motives: one is either a fighter or a deserter. . . . The real terror comes when the individual feels himself becoming an individual, pulling away from the group" ("Conclusion" 226). In other words, you fight alongside your comrades or you leave them and face the wilderness alone, whether to triumph over it or to run back to some other home. I wonder about this idea; it is questionable as an explanation of ideology that is specifically Canadian. Some prominent Canadian writers of the Western were and are highly individualistic in temperament and interests, such as Connor and Ondaatje, and though Connor with his loyalties and wartime experience may never really be described as a "deserter," Ondaatje is a radical individualist in his fascination for characters with strong social connections who become anti-social, such as Billy the Kid, Pat Garrett, and Buddy Bolden (the latter from the 1976 novel *Coming Through Slaughter*). With similar reservations, D. M. R. Bentley argues that the garrison mentality is useless as a concept, partly because American literature is no less concerned with the threat of the wilderness than Canadian literature is:

> Frye attributes the emergence of the "garrison mentality" in "the Canadian imagination" to the existence of "[s]mall and isolated communities surrounded by a physical or psychological 'frontier,' [and] separated from one another and from their American and British cultural sources." . . . Since the concept of "frontier" is at least as suggestive of American as of Canadian culture, it is not at all surprising to find a parallel (and possible source) of the "garrison mentality" in Oscar Handlin's *Race and Nationality in American Life* (1957), where early European migrants to what became the United States are envisaged as "living in clearings" in the "dark forest, the secret home of unknown beings," and attempting in a "circumscribed area . . . [to] keep out the wilderness that ever threatened to break them." Whatever its origins, sources, and evidential basis, the "garrison mentality" is at best an idiosyncratic, limited, and reductive notion that has little explanatory power. (6–7)

Unless, of course, it applies not only to Canada but also to other countries that have a frontier or had one during their formative phases. Frye himself acknowledges this possibility when he writes, in the same text, that "many Canadian cultural phenomena are not peculiarly Canadian at all, but are typical of their wider North American and Western contexts" (214). For younger countries, the formative phases might still be a recent memory that continues to influence their sense of national identity, as may be the case in both Canada and the United States. On the theme of youth, Harrison argues that the search for self is a basic drive of Western fiction in Canada—and this search, too, must in some way be individualistic.

But no one except a hermit or a survivalist is equipped to live as a true self-reliant and self-sufficient being, and so a pure individualism is mostly a myth. Frye argues that "the Canadian literary mind, beginning as it did so late in the cultural history of the West, was established on a basis, not of myth, but of history" ("Conclusion" 231). I do not quite agree, but we can look to the history and present of our laws and institutions, which do in fact reveal Canada to be substantively less individualistic—less capitalist, more socialist—than the United States. But the Western usually places less emphasis on interdependence than on self-reliance, and themes of interdependence in the Canadian Western are more noticeable in the literary Westerns after the 1960s, which are as close to "anti-Westerns" as there are in Canada.[19]

In sum, the Western as a national genre is transnational and even interdependent, insofar as some American Westerns look to the North as a new frontier. The Western yokes together in North America the United States and Canada (and almost certainly Mexico, though that is beyond the scope of this study). The overlap is extraordinarily significant, and figures such as the Mountie that are supposed to differentiate national temperaments are not as consistently special as we tend to assume. Even nordicity is relative, partly because all of these figures and tropes are made to suit our fictions. Scholars such as Thacker and Harrison are better-read than I am, but I am skeptical of the notion that Canada's West or North is somehow truer and less mythic than that of the United States, or vice versa. Myths are essential to the genre of the Western, as they are to literature in general, and these myths seep out of fiction into our political water supplies. It is our expectations of genre, including national genre, that allow us as readers to find more differences than similarities, so that most Canadians and Americans (I would bet) want to think that they are really very different from each other. Genre theory and its focus on adaptability and overlap produce its own kind of readers who read things transnationally. Meanwhile, theories of ideology expose national difference (in terms of the nation-state) in North America as a symptom of trying to force categories upon national identities and tendencies. I know that there

---

19   The historical placement of this shift is corroborated by Ronald Sutherland in *The New Hero* (1977) (7–8, 10, 16).

is a difference, but not in most Westerns, partly because—as its name implies—it is a regional genre that can stand in for a national one.

Regionalism and the Canadian West

Although the beginning of this book might seem to have opened up an anything-goes frontier for the Western to justify a study of the Canadian Western, I have commented in the preceding pages on the genre's historical scope and limits related to national myths. However, according to Ronald Sutherland in *The New Hero* (1977), "[i]n Canada, what myths did develop ... were generally regional ... [in] the absence of all-embracing positive myths ... of 'Canadianism' " (5).[20] In Canada, "[p]revious to [the latter 1840s] there had been very little attention paid to the West" (Owram 36), but soon thereafter a concern over American expansionism inspired further attempts—now with the railway in mind—of "an overland route to Asia" (32) that would economically support British imperialism and protect Canada from the United States. The railway would not be completed until 1885, but the intervening years did much to inspire national dreams and the associated myth of the West. (The North-Western Territory was transferred to Canada in 1870, when it became officially known as the North-West Territories.) Although Canadians now pay more attention to the Canadian West, regionalism is still essential to this book because book-length studies of the Canadian West*ern* are few and far between (e.g., those of Katherine Ann Roberts and Johannes Fehrle), and a critical framework that was closer to home than American frameworks was necessary even to my equivocating nationalism.

In terms of my own borders, I draw as boundaries my own experience of writing in the early twenty-first century (and in the Atlantic East) about a West associated with late nineteenth-century visions of the Prairies, from Manitoba to the Rockies, where "the far West" of Alberta becomes "the near East" of British Columbia (McCourt, qtd. in Harrison, *Unnamed* xv) or "the West beyond the West" (Katerberg 554). On the other axis, my boundaries begin south of the Far North: from the Yukon down to the Medicine Line (the 49th parallel) and into the northwestern United

---

20   Sutherland's "positive myths" of America are " 'Manifest Destiny' and 'Garden of the World' [and] 'American Dream' " (5).

States, sometimes as far as the Southwest (the likely setting of the Luke Price Westerns in my chapter on the '40s pulps) because of its favoured position as a setting in so many American Westerns. Occasionally I draw on Westerns or Western-like texts from Eastern Canada, such as Cody's 1916 novel *Rod of the Lone Patrol*, as evidence that the West was, especially early on, seen by " 'Eastern' eyes" (Harrison, *Unnamed* 1; see also Bold, *Frontier* xviii, and Bowering, *Caprice* 34). Generally, the Westerns in this book are set in Western Canada or the Western United States, and sometimes both. Sometimes, the West is represented generically enough that readers must watch for telling details to distinguish state from state, province from province, or state from province.

Any region, however, is not strictly delimited. Aritha van Herk refers to an "unlimited and undefinable space, the westness of west" (*Stampede* 97) that is "a real place" only in "story" (92). Relatedly, using keywords of "imagination" and "community" from Benedict Anderson, Herb Wyile explains that, "[i]n more recent theorizing about the concept [of region] in various disciplines from geography to political science to literary criticism, region is increasingly being viewed not as a geographical/cultural/political given but as a construct, a kind of imagined and at times strategic sense of cohesion and community, projected usually from without but also from within . . . as an assumed or imposed homogeneity and/or unity" (*Anne* 8). I return to this view of region soon, in the section entitled "The West Turns North." Of course, the North and West have to be considered too—for example, as the compound North-West. Sherrill E. Grace estimates that "at first glance it seems that, perhaps since [the] Meech Lake [Accord] (1987), there has been a rush of voices struggling to create and enter a debate about Canada and the North. However, a closer look reveals that Canadians have been attempting to define themselves and Canada by invoking the North or their nordicity for a very long time" (31). Indeed, when political summits and Olympics make their way to Canada, the staging of nordicity is obvious, it, too, projecting Wyile's "cohesion and community"—regions staged for national gains.

Whereas in thinking through region Henri Lefebvre focuses on sites of production, and Edward Soja focuses on the uneven production, concentration, and redistribution of resources, Wyile brings together their economic definitions of regions, arguing that regional literature is now characterized by the frustration that the (Eastern) region's compact with the nation is no longer a *fair deal*. The reason is that the deal depends on trapping the East in the same tourist trap that was supposed to capture the imaginations and dollars of seasonal visitors: the idea of the East as "an unspoiled, authentic, pre-modern culture" and "quaint pastoral retreat" (22). Almost the same can be said of ranchland in the West, where the theme of Western alienation comes from a frustration with the unfair deal of national energy programs and transfer payments that redistribute Alberta's wealth. One difference is that Alberta, for at least fifty years— Gordon Pitts claiming in 2010 that "[t]his westward push of power has been the story of Canada over the past one hundred years" (10)—has been a consistent leader in the Canadian economy in spite of the nation, unlike Newfoundland or the Maritimes. The East can be seen as "reduced to selling back to the rest of the country a very stylized and romanticized version of the underdevelopment in which those more powerful regions have played a large part" (Wyile, *Anne* 23). Janice Kulyk Keefer suggests in *Under Eastern Eyes* (1985) that a Canadian version of Turner's frontier thesis is at work when we assume that the East is the place of tradition and the West of adventurous experimentation (qtd. in Wyile, *Anne* 23), and yet to me the movement to the West and "the idea of West"—to echo Glenn Gould's radio documentary entitled "Idea of North" (1967)—are at least as conservative, partly because they depend on (or else comment liberally upon) theories of ever-expanding property and capital, and the myth of an Eden that can still be, temporarily, exploited. In this book on Westerns, the region like the frontier is a moving target, ideational as well as real, lost in time and found not only in its place but in many of the places where its ideas have travelled.

Regions of the Past

In some ways, Alison Calder has the same concern about the West as Herb Wyile has about the East, insofar as both regions have had to remain timelessly and idealistically rural or become generically urban, to gain from readers who buy books for a spectrum of reasons such as nostalgia, on the one hand, and as a confirmation of their globalized sensibilities on the other. In *History, Literature, and the Writing of the Canadian Prairies* (2005), one of Calder and Robert Wardhaugh's most significant questions about the West is more temporal than spatial: "When is the prairie?" (3) The question echoes, of course, one that is familiar to Canadianists but just as enigmatic, Frye's "Where is here?" ("Conclusion" 220). Frye's question was already an adaptation of "Who am I?" By removing the first-person pronoun, Frye points away from the individual toward the "where," the place that is also the "here," which becomes a self-effacing but nation-defining landscape consistent with his theory of the garrison mentality. There are remarks upon the limitations of this theory elsewhere in this chapter, but it also questionable here in terms of regionalism; Donald G. Stephens claims that "[the West] is a land of optimism, of hope, for everyone knows that the cycle will go on, and that some year, sometime, it will be the best year yet. The 'garrison mentality' so obvious in the writing of Eastern Canada . . . is not prominent in that of Western Canada" (2). For Stephens, the West is a place of looking forward to the future ("the best year yet"), even if the writing of the West is so often nostalgic (the best future being the past). Calder and Wardhaugh's alternative to Frye is in the same tradition but privileges the temporal dimension to redress the balance between spatial and temporal terms—especially because the balance often tips toward the past in our imagination of regions, and might need to be tipped to the present.

Why would Canadians want to indulge in Westerns when these Westerns encourage people to think that, in the West, everyone is stuck in the past? Nostalgia, of course, and its rose-coloured glasses, but the answer requires more than that. Sue Sorensen writes that "[t]o get the wheels of your snazzy new SUV stuck in the ruts of the old dirt track of *rural versus urban* is to demonstrate that you haven't been reading your Kroetsch" (18, emphasis added) or, as she also suggests, your Vanderhaeghe. Sorensen reports that Guy Vanderhaeghe complained that cities are ignored in Prairie fiction (15), and yet she observes that "Vanderhaeghe's most recent novels, *The Englishman's Boy* and *The Last Crossing* [and then *A Good Man*] are, for the most part, forays back into prairie history and into the countryside" (16). Why? I have already answered the question by suggesting that Westerns respond to a contemporary but anti-modernist shift back to the conservatism of the turn of the century to the 1920s (see also Brégent-Heald, "James" 692), when cities were not yet where most Canadians lived; however, there is a related, more specific, answer.

To set up this answer, I want to digress for a moment into Calder's essay, "Why Shoot the Gopher?" Therein, Calder identifies the gopher as "a prairie icon" that, when viewed positively, has "an underdog quality ... that fits well into ideas of western alienation" (254). This positive view disguises an ambivalence. Calder also quotes Kroetsch's *Seed Catalogue* (1986) and its answer to the question of how to grow a Prairie town: "Stand up straight" but then "[v]anish suddenly: the / gopher was the model" (qtd. in Calder, "Why" 243). Perhaps the gopher offers insight into the "rural versus urban" rut, especially when we think of town versus city in the context of Appadurai's "scalar dynamics" of globalization.[21] Kroetsch's association of the iconic gopher with the town, a small version of the city, raises the question of whether the gopher is a small version of a related and even more iconic animal—such as the buffalo. Indeed, why shoot the buffalo? In the 1870s, when settlers and complicit Native Americans and First Nations almost entirely destroyed the buffalo (Jennings 61), the extermination was for the same reason as with the gopher, which was "an obstacle [to settlement and agriculture] that must be eradicated or controlled" (Calder, "Why" 245). Calder also links the gopher to its historical "use-value" as a source of food and a narrative figure for some First Nations (245), a "use-value" that the buffalo had too—yet presumably in far greater concentration of biomass—and she concludes in part that "[i]mplicit in this representation is the belief that the prairies belong to the farmer; it is the gophers, not the settlers, who are invaders" (247). Like the gopher and like the buffalo, the town has to "vanish" as the "Indians" have to "vanish" to make way for the next phase of civilization—the next *big* thing—which is the city and capital-C Country, Canada. During a shift to the right in politics, then, the Western is a nationalistic reminder of progress or, more accurately, the renewal of a myth of progress. Instead of cowboys on horses, we have cowboys in sport-utility vehicles: progress. Same hat, different ride. Same hat, different time.[22]

---

21   Mark Jackson, following Dipesh Chakrabarty and others, has continued the thinking about micro/macro and universal/particular dynamics in *Coloniality, Ontology, and the Question of the Posthuman* (2018).

22   After the Dirty Harry movies, one of the most obvious representations of this mixture of progress and anti-modernism in the American context is *Justified* (2010–15), the Graham Yost television adaptation of an Elmore Leonard story.

Time and the periodizations of the Canadian Western cannot be neglected, partly because of the "postnostalgic phase" that Appadurai theorizes. While an American who is nostalgic for America might recover it in the present in the Philippines, thereby alleviating nostalgia (to the extent that it survives defamiliarization), a Canadian nostalgic for a bygone West can don a Stetson and go to the Calgary Stampede, seemingly recovering a shared North American history of the West and laying claim to Western iconography that is sometimes thought to be only American (i.e., of the United States) or fawningly American.[23] In fact, the term "stampeder" referred to prospectors rushing to the West *and North* for gold, as Kroetsch claims in *The Man from the Creeks* (1998), and the precursor to the Stampede was "a reasonably sedate agricultural fair with limited cowboy elements" until an American, Guy Weadick, founded the modern Stampede in 1912, "a borderless affair, with American contestants and bucking horses . . . , a contingent of vaqueros brought all expenses paid from Mexico, an encampment of 2,000 costumed Indians from the Blackfoot, Blood, Stoney and Sarcee reserves, a reunion of . . . the 1874 Mounted Police attired in period uniform, and a replica of Fort Whoop-up" (Dippie 514)—all pan-American. In *Stampede and the Westness of West* (2016), van Herk implies that something essential, the "ness" of "Westness," can be rediscovered at the Stampede—the "unlimited and undefinable space" already quoted—and this Westness does not appear to map onto only one nation-state. Sociologically, however, the Stampede's nostalgia does map onto colonial nation-building anachronisms, as when twentieth-century Stampede ads depict bare-chested Indigenous men who align with Victorian codes of savagery rather than Victorian codes of modesty and civility (Joudrey 27). And Calgary today is a city of big trucks and long, wide highways, so the Stampede also evokes the transition into "the post-equine era in North America (1910–1930)" (Nance 12). Surrounded by car culture and the businesses that fuel it, the Stampede has historically used horses for "nostalgia entertainment purposes" (13). Susan Nance suggests that "the collective fiction" of the Stampede "came

---

23 The cowboy hat, as one possible souvenir of the Stampede, "contracts the world in order to expand the personal" (S. Stewart xii). It reminds you of where you have been, somewhere in the distance, and reifies your memory in an object of nostalgia.

to symbolize the city's modern business brand, perhaps because [competitive rodeo] performed a ... moment symbolizing infinite possibility" (13). Again, the region expands: it is "unlimited" and "infinite," partly because the timeline points both forward and backwards, and partly because the Stampede annually renews the past-future dynamic.[24]

For Calder, however, the past-future dynamic manifests itself in the West as a limit, not the lack of one, and the problem is that of living vicariously in the past through the regionalism of the West. Writing specifically about the Prairies and not precisely the West of the Western, though I want to call attention to the connections, Calder argues that

> here [on the prairie], place = rural = past, and the present is a kind of unrooted urban space that is radically disconnected from this past. The construction of this urban prairie present as post-prairie [in the titles of two earlier anthologies] is plausible only if we allow the prairie to be defined within these terms: as incompatible with either modernity or postmodernity, as irretrievably located in a vanished and obsolete rural landscape. Why we would accept these limitations is puzzling. But if the history of the agricultural prairie is the history of colonialism, does it then follow that, in the post-prairie, colonialism is over, and we are now all starting fresh, on a field that is as level as, well, the now-vanished prairie? ("Importance" 173)

The answer, she implies, is "no." Colonialism is not over, which is why the prairie is still here and now. Rushing into "postness" in various fields is so often theoretical or wishful, and wishful thinking is one of the operations that enable us to enjoy the Stampede or any Western (some of these cultural texts being enjoyable even for some Native Americans and First

---

24 Ironically, however, the Stampede might help to expand the region symbolically, but the Stampede itself has supposedly shrunken according to one (proportional, not absolute) metric: "there has been a steep relative decline [in attendance] compared to population growth. Between 1976 and 2009, Stampede attendance grew by just 17 percent. During the same period Calgary's population grew 127 percent and Alberta's population grew by 90 percent" (Peter Fricker of the Vancouver Humane Society qtd. in Killingsworth 9).

Nations, as scholar JoEllen Shively and novelist Thomas King, through his character Lionel in *Green Grass, Running Water*, have suggested; see the chapter on "Tom King's John Wayne" for more). In those moments, there is the conservative impulse to be "incompatible with either modernity or postmodernity," and thereby to remain on stable, settled ground, surrounded by horses and acceptably isolated from the modernizing and progressive East.

At the same time, however, Stampeders do refuse "these limitations." They drive to the rodeo in shiny twenty-first-century trucks, live more often in suburbia than on ranches, and have in recent memory elected in Calgary a Muslim mayor of South Asian and African descent (Nasheed Nenshi, three times) instead of a white man from a European background. A problem of condescending chauvinism emerges if the Stampede, like other expressions of multiculturalism, is seen as only a ritual re-enactment of a culture that is "over" or elsewhere, such as Montana or Wyoming.

For Wyile in *Anne of Tim Hortons: Globalization and the Reshaping of Atlantic-Canadian Literature* (2011), this is a problem for Atlantic Canada in much the same way that I pose it for the West: "tourist promotion of the region . . . has had a pronounced impact on how the region is seen from outside and, indeed, how it sees itself" (4). For the Stampede to be understood as an authentic expression of a culture of the West that is alive and well, it must be accepted as a performance of a way of life or set of values that remains meaningfully a part of people's everyday lives. For me, the prime example of a real life playing a part in the spectacle of the Western's iconography is Gabriel Dumont, the Métis ally of Louis Riel who, after participating in the North-West Resistance of 1885, fled as an outlaw to the United States and joined Buffalo Bill Cody's Wild West Show, "enjoy[ing] minor celebrity" as a "rebel leader and wanted man" (Gaudry). Already by 1885, with the railway-enacted closures of the frontiers in the United States (1869) and Canada (1885), the West had become a myth, a thing of the past that had to be remembered in Westerns. An acceptably earlier beginning for the Western as such is in the *Leatherstocking Tales* (1823–41) of James Fenimore Cooper, including *The Last of the Mohicans* (1827), which are all set in the eighteenth or early nineteenth centuries. I tend to prefer that the Western begins a little later, when—especially in the

Western regions of the United States and Canada—the West had become a show for others and for itself.

Regionalism, Realism, and Genre

When I refer to "people's everyday lives" and a "past-present dynamic" in regionalism, these phrases are also coded references to realism, which developed in literature when the Western was emerging or re-emerging in the late nineteenth century, alongside modern and modernist literatures. (The cultural coincidence of modernism and the Western deserves further study.) Then, in the final quarter of the twentieth century, realism contributed to redefining the Western as "revisionist" or "historical," terms that partly meant "more realistic" and sometimes "less mythic." The topic of realism is too complex for a thorough consideration here, but it puts (other) genres into perspective; it helps us to position the (often mythic) Western relative to (often realistic) Prairie fiction.

Realism is also one of the most obvious ideological and aesthetic engagements with both nationalism and regionalism, regionalism being the suffusion of "local colour" that imparts believability on a text.[25] According to Colin Hill, modern (more or less twentieth-century) realism in Canada was at times quite regional, as demonstrated by his choice of writers who are strongly identified with the West but also skeptical of its promises, such as Sinclair Ross. Regionalism can thus be "incompatible with an idealistic nationalism" (Hill 34).[26] And yet, in spite of exceptions such as wartime propaganda, nationalism "usually privileges [realist forms]" (51; see also 129). For Robert Lecker, nationalism is "displaced into" (5) or "morphs into" (10) realism; "literature has always been seen as a vehicle through which authors bore witness to the country [i.e., the nation]. In this context, mimetic literature was a kind of testimony; it provided

---

25   Situating local colour as a late nineteenth-century development in realism that was later perfected, in the early twentieth century, as regionalism, Jonathan David Shelly Schroeder states that "regionalism . . . redefined local-color fiction as its failed precursor" (552–3). Regionalism can also be defined as "cultural rather than geographic . . . not geography itself but a strategically resistant mapping of geography" (Davey, "Toward" 4). For Frank Davey, regionalism is often defined against nationalism.

26   Hill gives another reason: realism was sometimes also "incompatible" with nationalism because realism was meant to represent psychology and the mind, an inner world that was not necessarily shaped by or preoccupied with the nation (21).

evidence that the country was real" (304). This "testimony" or "test" was and is all the more relevant to a nation-state often assumed to be "really" or "basically" American or, in the past, British. Realism probably helped to put "Canada" on the map in Canada before the regions were there (even literally as "Canada West"), at least initially, because Canada had a greater need for nationalism; it hadn't attempted to break away from its European heritage with a revolution as the United States had. In the United States, which had a stronger national identity at the end of the nineteenth century, realism and even regionalism could serve a more local purpose, helping to put up-and-coming states such as California on the map of places that had to be dealt with and not merely imagined as distant sites of no political consequence (Mexal 189). In literature and film, realism arguably also promoted a modern (if not modernist) idea of order—of things as they are—and this idea neatly rationalized national-industrial social hierarchies (Corkin, *Realism* 54).[27] Today, however, these hierarchies are points of contention that regions raise to their nations, and the debates often seem painfully informed by the differences between the idealism of nation and the pragmatism of region.

Again, it is a question of scale related to genre: how big ideas are too general or generic and superimpose imperfectly onto smaller constituents. Harrison, Thacker, and others quoted earlier in this chapter seem to think of the Western as a sub-genre of regional literature—i.e., Prairie fiction and usually Prairie realism—while more and more I invert the paradigm, thinking of so much literature as a sub-genre or at least reflection of the Western, especially if the Western is an exemplar of today's epic (superseded recently by the superhero genre). The Western's relationship to epic helps to distinguish it from the literature of the West by calling attention to its heroic, larger-than-life qualities, which imply that the Western is not realism (or at least not usually in a realistic mode), unlike so much Prairie fiction.[28] Admittedly, this distinction can be construed as a straw

---

27 While I am offering these comparative glosses, I might add that regionalism in the United States was arguably integrated in the melting pot on a national level; in Canada, it was more geographically discrete (Roger Gibbins qtd. in Davey, "Toward" 1).

28 Beyond Harrison and Thacker and in an almost strictly American context, Sanford Marovitz explains prevailing preferences to realism in the literature of the West as a moral imperative galvanized against the violence of the Western. Marovitz quotes Jay Gurian's *Western American Writing* (1975): "The real cowboy ... does not require fiction to announce him; history

man if you believe that realism is defined as an accurate view of reality—one of the views that Robert C. Post calls "naive" (368). There are simply too many dimensions of reality to reflect adequately even in realism. And, for Post and the philosophical tradition leading to John Dewey (and the post-structuralism coincident with Post's essay), reality itself is an idea. But Prairie fiction and the Western are not equidistant from that idea. Prairie fiction often distinguishes itself from the Western by insisting on being unpretentious or simply not flashy in its representation of ordinary lives and times, while the Western tends to be more noticeably stylish in its representation of exceptional heroes and the definitiveness of their decisions and actions. Westerns, especially revisionist Westerns, are sometimes presumed to be realistic because of their vague historicity and regional grounding—usually identifiable American states in the late nineteenth-century West—but epics are vaguely historical and sometimes regional too. And even especially mythic Westerns can be presumed to be realistic because they tend to be not only historical (in being set at a mine site that once existed, or after the American Civil War, or in a Western town recently linked to telegraphs and rail lines) but also gritty.[29] In the context of the "true grit" of the Western,[30] Patrick McGee argues that we "need to be careful about imagining that 'realism' of any sort ever truly transcends the conventions of the Western" (202), conventions being too powerful, and the Western being less interested in the accuracy of realism than in the supreme determination and resilience of its heroes (qualities that might be inverted in revisionist Westerns but that continue to exist, in the subtext, as standards of comparison).

Realism itself, however, is either a genre or a mode, depending on whom or what you are reading.[31] There is critical confusion because these

---

can do that" (99). He also quotes Jack Brenner, whose view of the realism in the literature of the West was intentionally narrow, because the West was mythologized and stereotyped "almost before it was settled" (103), leaving little room for realism.

29   These references to grit in the context of realism may evoke the concept of "dirty realism," which was theorized as the next phase after postmodernism as early as 1983 in an issue of *Granta* introduced by Bill Buford (Toth 3).

30   I am alluding of course to Charles Portis's novel *True Grit* (1968), adapted to film with the same title in 1969 by Henry Hathaway, and in 2010 by the Coen brothers, Joel and Ethan. Patrick McGee himself is not alluding to any of these texts.

31   See for example Sanford E. Marovitz's "Myth and Realism in Recent Criticism of the American Literary West" (1981) (109).

"terms are used in so many different ways" (Scholes, "Towards" 105). I will not attempt to differentiate them as laboriously as do Northrop Frye, Robert Scholes, and others. I think of genre as a set of conventions in the content of a book or film, conventions such as the Stetson hats worn by so many cowboys, and this genre can be stylized through different modes or ways of communicating the genre—modes that can become so readily recognizable as to become genres of their own. Seemingly in the inverse, Alastair Fowler simplifies it as "genre tends to mode" (qtd. in Whetter 36), because he thinks of modes as less strict than genre, as Linda Williams does (42), and genres tend to open up over time. Following Williams, Jaimey Fisher explains that "a particular historical moment might favor a generic mode over discrete genres and ... the contingencies of a particular moment might turn a genre into mode to create hybrid works that met different cultural needs" (93). These are reasonable views, but I want to avoid a chicken-or-egg argument. The consensus seems to be that, regardless of which comes first, modes operate as adjectival qualifications, something less than definitive, whereas genres are more like nouns, which are more definitive; furthermore, there is interplay between them.[32] Realism is actually modal too.[33] It is, like a style writ large, an identifiable manner of expression that eventually becomes recognizable as its own thing, or—more in agreement with the previous few quotations—it is used to lend legitimacy to genres when they have started to become stereotype factories or parodies of themselves. The legitimacy is not the stuff of reality (if reality exists) but the construction of an illusion that can develop into its own category of art, such as genre, which is driven more by convention than

---

[32] Later in this book (in chapter 3), I will consider Rick Altman's and Paul Monticone's related work on what can be called "hybrid" or "crossover" genres such as the noir Western or the space Western. These examples combine genres, so that film noir "colours" a Western, becoming a philosophically and even visually darker Western—or we may call it a hybrid.

[33] Beyond this further simplification, Linda Williams argues that "[m]elodrama [not realism] is the fundamental mode of popular American moving pictures. It is not a specific genre like the western or horror film" (42). She continues: "We should not be fooled, then, by the superficial realism of popular American movies, by the use of real city streets for chases, or by the introduction of more complex psychological motivations for victims and villains. If emotional and moral registers are sounded, if a work invites us to feel sympathy for the virtues of beset victims, if the narrative trajectory is ultimately more concerned with a retrieval and staging of innocence than with the psychological causes of motives and action, then the operative mode is melodrama" (42).

by reality or originality. (You can see that chicken-egg circularity here.) In fact, the location of realism within the conventions of genre is hinted at in terms such as "conventional realism" (Scholes, "On Realism" 269). Most mainstream contemporary literature is conventional realism, and our biases in favour of it entail the demeaning of "genre fiction," whether Western, science fiction, fantasy, Harlequin romance, hard-boiled, et cetera. Genre fiction loses credibility mainly because the formulas of genre fiction are more obvious than in most realisms and certainly in everyday life. If I go to the bar, I can be reasonably sure that I will not witness a fistfight or shootout. The Western's stereotypes of masculinity, femininity, whiteness, and Indigeneity do not convincingly reflect the people I know, even if we feel pressure from modelled roles. However conformist we might be, we are not quite conventions in a genre.[34] Realist fiction that minimizes the appearance of convention is most of the literature of the West, but not the Western. And Western films can be superficially realistic but are probably melodramatic (Williams 42); they dramatize and stylize their conventions, wearing them like hearts on their sleeves.

John Frow explains that genre "is a set of conventional and highly organised constraints [which he defines in turn as 'shapes' and 'guides'] on the production and interpretation of meaning" (10). His notion of a "constraint" is helpful because it reminds us that conventions are chosen from alternatives that are not usually allowed or, if they are, then only as quirky exceptions. The first and foremost convention of the Western is the cowboy, not an astrophysicist or a ballerina—but the cowboy could

---

34 In spite of my recourse to potential events in any of our own lives here—and to my admittedly inconsistent belief in my discernment of reality and my own related self-determination—another way of seeing the question of realism and the Western is to consider how its myths have begun to inform not only history but also reality. Richard Slotkin and Mary-Dailey Desmarais in *Once upon a Time ... The Western* (2017) argue that the politics of films such as Fred Zinnemann's *High Noon* (1952) later became real-world politics: "those who have (or can claim) the knowledge to recognize and the power to conquer evil have an absolute obligation to act against it regardless of the law or the will of the people. Democracy is weak and must rely on the strong, cold man of power who holds us in contempt even as he saves us" (150). They go so far as to claim that the plot of "*High Noon* is [the] foundational myth" of "the present Global War on Terror" (150). Such conclusions might seem outrageous, but they are precisely those that seem to corroborate postmodern theories of media and society such as Jean Baudrillard's *Simulacra and Simulation* (1983 in English); Baudrillard's theory of the precession of simulacra is that illusions create reality: art before life. Hence, Buffalo Bill Cody "began to think of himself as the heroic figure of the Dime Novels [written about him by Ned Buntline], and he acted accordingly" (Marovitz 103).

be a related stock character such as the sheriff or Mountie, or even the outlaw. There are at least this many alternatives or variants—or mutants. In his book on distant reading, Franco Moretti thinks of distant reading in terms of genre and one of the ironically dead metaphors of genre: evolutionary theory. Genre theorists such as Altman and Steve Neale write of how genres "evolve" or "mutate." Moretti also focuses on Darwinian "rivals" (66) and "the market" (68), conceiving of them as powers that no professor could ever influence until it was irrelevant anyway, and for these and other reasons I am not a fan of Moretti. I simply recognize similarities in some of our methodologies. In his research on nineteenth-century detective fiction, Moretti samples the fiction and goes looking for a "well-defined formal trait" (63) that might change over time or over other boundaries such as the edges of sub-genres. He chooses the clue, which is a trait or in other words a convention of detective fiction. In later work, Moretti expands his methodology beyond a single trait or convention to what he calls quantitative formalism and multivariate analysis (64), which does seem necessary for genre studies because, in a genre, there is never only one thing that is definitional.

Instead, we need to identify a set of conventions that suffice to differentiate and identify the genre in some combination most of the time. In terms of Western-specific methods, my approach is similar to that of Christopher Conway in *Heroes of the Borderlands* (2019): "to trace a network of visual cues, formulas, and archetypes that are sometimes self-referential citations tied to a genre formula and other times meaningfully linked to social, political, and national themes" (23). Not every convention needs to be in every Western. The "Indians" often have vanishingly small roles, if any, and can help to define a Western by their very absence (Tompkins 8). Women, too, are fictionalized as rare birds in Westerns or they are marginal and stereotyped (as are most men). Sometimes, the characters are beyond or before the reach of trains. The range is far more common a setting than the saloon. Only guns and cowboys seem ubiquitous—"It is doubtful that a movie without revolvers could be considered a Western" (Conway 29)—and usually horses. But if most of the conventions are present, and especially if they interact with each other, we probably have a Western, or a so-called post-Western, which usually means a contemporary Western, or a sub-genre or crossover.

Students or fans of the Western will already realize that this set applies to a relatively late iteration of the Western, later in the nineteenth century when trains and whisk(e)y trading, for examples, were realities in the West. This later iteration is right for my purposes because Canada came later to the genre, and, as a relative outsider with a more recent history of Westerns, Canada has Westerns that tend to imagine and revise the post–Civil War Westerns popularized since the 1950s by John Ford and John Wayne, and then Sergio Leone and Clint Eastwood, among others. Despite the gritty trappings of the classics of the 1950s and '60s—such as styles of acting, costumes, locations, and cinematographies that could be realistic at times—these Westerns and their iconic, unbendable heroes were unapologetically mythic. As I argue in chapter 6, in Canada we have historical Westerns that push back against myth, often realistically, but they tend to debase one myth and raise another. Ultimately, we have better options than to work much with realism as a heuristic for the Western, except as a framing device for the Western and Prairie fiction, in spite of realism's mainstream position and its dominant role in defining modern and contemporary literatures.

And in spite of its value to regionalism, realism—because of the influence of myth—has been a problem for literary representations of the West. According to Owram in *Promise of Eden*, already by 1870 a "new and extremely enthusiastic image of the West was in danger of becoming as unrealistic as the more cynical view of the first half of the century" (5). The balance has been difficult to achieve or has perhaps never been achieved or maintained—and, as centres and margins tilt against each other, other regions are implicated. Owram explains that the "image" of the Canadian West prior to 1870 was an inaccurate view of the *North*west that was overly influenced by northern exploration and fur trading routes so that it seemed "much harsher and more northerly" (12), even "semi-arctic" (13). Later texts such as those of Connor approached the North, via the West, to make it a little more familiar and less intimidating—not an Eden but a place that could be cultivated or excavated by hard work and a work ethic that was implicitly a manifestation of Muscular Christianity. The *new* "image," this emerging myth of progress on a slightly more hospitable frontier, is one reason why some of the texts under consideration in this book can be described not only as Northwesterns but also as early Canadian Westerns. Even if the North lost relative ground again as Westerns dwindled in mid-century Canada—eventually and emphatically reoriented by *Maliglutit* (Kunuk and Ungalaaq, 2016)—the North has been crucial for perceptions of the West in Canada.

The West Turns North

On 28 December 1967, as Canada's centennial year was about to elapse, Glenn Gould aired the program "Idea of North" on CBC Radio's *Ideas*. The first of his "Solitude Trilogy," "Idea of North" was commissioned by *Ideas* (Lucht 11) and was followed by two more programs about isolated communities, one about outports in Newfoundland and one about rural Manitoba. The first, however, gained additional prominence when it was adapted for television in 1970 by Judith Pearlman. This CBC-PBS international co-production[35] visually translates Gould's Canadian odyssey in some of the terms that would be very familiar to American viewers, with imagery associated with Westerns and the West: a 1962 poster for a gold rush festival at Dawson City, some footage of wagons lined up for a "land rush," and oil wells and telegraphs that remind us of the economic rationale for western expansion. For a film based on a Canadian centennial-nationalist documentary, the American connections were many—such as the focus on the train as the means to the ends of the continent.

Pearlman, however, was not appropriating Gould's documentary through these images. In fact, one of the narrators describes the North as a "frontier" that must be understood as such "in much more than a physical sense" or latitudinal sense. "North of 60" is also idealized as "the land of the possible," which is similar to the view of the West—not only in the United States but in general—as a place wide open geographically, economically, and culturally. One of the only references to the Inuit in the film is a short clip of Inuit children watching themselves on television followed soon afterward by an equivocatingly critical remark about the "white master race." The children seeing themselves on television—undoubtedly a great novelty at the time—also calls attention to the fact that Indigenous people were a televised spectacle who were in reality unknown

---

35 This detail of the CBC-PBS collaboration is according to the former Glenn Gould Foundation website, which is no longer accessible.

to most viewers in the predominantly white South, an ignorance that was a historical factor in rationalizing the displacement, dispossession, and assimilation of Indigenous peoples during colonial expansion to the West by wagon and rail. Margery Fee in *Literary Land Claims* (2015) is less equivocating: "The railway itself became a symbol of the (white settler) nation while the Chinese and Irish men who laid the rails were excluded" (11), as were the First Nations and Métis who would remain for much longer an obstacle in the eyes of settlers in the West (as would some of them, plus the Inuit, in the North). In identifying the North as a frontier or margin similar to the West, Pearlman was recognizing a Canadian-American kinship, a shared ideology based on the assumption of limitless wealth deriving from resources open to the white man, whose cunning exploits and interloping travels would be interpreted as heroic. Canada's renewed nationalism depended in part, as Gould and Pearlman suggested in 1967 and 1970, on the imagining of a new land of opportunity.

And so, not much less than a century after the last spike in the railway purported to unify Canada, the two versions of "Idea of North" suggested that the national cultures of Canada and the United States might realign the axes of their ideology, West to North. In the opening scenes of the filmed version, we see Toronto's Union Station and the first destination of the film: Winnipeg, from which the Muskeg Express would carry the filmic eye northward along the rails to Churchill. As I explain in the next chapter, on Indigenous views of the Western, Zacharias Kunuk and Natar Ungalaaq's 2016 film *Maliglutit* realigns John Ford's iconic American epic *The Searchers* (1956). The ideological differences between *The Searchers* and *Maliglutit* are obvious—Chris Knight's review in the *National Post* calls the latter a Northern—while Kunuk himself is as damning of colonialism in Canada as *Maliglutit* is of colonialism in the United States. In a different context, Sherrill E. Grace writes, "That this North so closely resembles the American [W]est is perhaps obvious only in hindsight" (12). The implication is clear. To go north, you must go west. The West turns North.

Turned Around, and Lost Around Lines

I do not conclude that the West *transforms* into the North; I mean it *turns* that way, or, more accurately, that cultural perspectives turn and the landscape seems to turn relative to the eye of the beholder. Although this chapter has had a fairly straight, telescoping line from world to nation to region, now I want to allow it to wind its way to the conclusion. The next sections are admittedly theoretical, even playful, but they do snap back in the end to a relevant question about region and climate that is undoubtedly (though not exclusively) Canadian. Here the chapter rides off a little madly. It explores (that mapping metaphor again) some of the implications of regions that suddenly become unmoored, or slip seismically, or disguise themselves and seem other than they "are."

How can the West "turn" without a discombobulating disorientation? I do not imagine a compass spinning so that the disorientation is that of placelessness or circularity; I mean the loss of balance from a change in movement along a line or a vector, and this loss can feel at least momentarily like lostness. If the so-called progress of Western civilization was ever imagined as a directly western route to the New World (and perhaps ultimately to Asia), remember the quest for the Northwest Passage—really an Arctic route, northwest then southwest. The Franklin expedition in the mid-nineteenth century went looking but ended in disaster, a tragic failure of navigation through shifting ice. They were "lost" for more than a century—until found, on 27 September 2014, when a long search sponsored in part by Stephen Harper's Conservative government discovered the sunken wreck of the HMS *Erebus* and gave the Conservatives a symbolic victory ("Lost"), both in their assertion of Arctic sovereignty and their colonial pride in nineteenth- and twentieth-century exploration. The Conservatives are not the only party with a stake in such symbolism; it was the Liberal minister (later prime minister) Lester B. Pearson who said that " 'Go North' has replaced 'Go West' as the call to adventure" (qtd. in Grace 9); he was echoing the American writer and resource economy enthusiast Courtney Ryley Cooper, who, already in 1926, had published *Go North, Young Man*, himself echoing "that famous advice of Horace Greeley: 'Go West, Young Man' " (vii). What is the West in Canada before its turn North? Donald G. Stephens explains that, for writers such as Ralph Connor, the Prairies of Manitoba, Saskatchewan, and Alberta were "the end of the frontier rather than the place to go through before reaching the mountains and the West Coast" (3). In the imagination of the West, the West begins on the plains of Manitoba and reaches the Badlands just east of the Rockies. In this Canadian literature, it does not appear to cross them.[36]

Rather, it turns, looking especially for seemingly available flatlands to develop (with so little such land west of the Rockies). Similar to Cooper as a rhetorician but eventually more pessimistic, Farley Mowat claims that foreign traders, not Canadians (and he could almost have been thinking of Cooper himself), "undertook the first 'development' of the North—exploiting its animal and mineral resources, the while maintaining and elaborating on the northern mythology in order to discourage competition and perhaps also to conceal what they were doing from the myopic view of the people of southern Canada" (10). This was 1976; Mowat argued that sovereignty needed to be asserted but without causing "its physical ruination" and "the ultimate dissolution of the native Northerners" (11); he feared "multi-national corporations who owe allegiance to no nation" (12) and governments committed to being smaller to interfere less with the economy preferred by such corporations. Until 2015, Harper's quest for Arctic sovereignty reiterated that the North was the new West,[37] and his tenure was only one span in a recent history of associating North and West. The fictionalized Harper in Michael Healey's play *Proud* (2015) calls the North "big" and "completely empty," which was one of the same assumptions that drove western expansion. Although Susan Kollin argues that it is "premature to speak of a New West" (251) in the context of the American West and the Western, she and I concur that our North American society has not progressed much beyond our historical approach to the Old West, which persists today seemingly anywhere we go.

---

36   In fact, the only two Westerns that come to mind that do cross the mountains and reach the West Coast are American: Annie Dillard's post-Western novel *The Living* (1992) and Jim Jarmusch's revisionist Western film *Dead Man* (1995).

37   Shelagh D. Grant suggests that the quest for Arctic sovereignty was delayed by the quest for Western sovereignty: "Preoccupied with settling the West, it was not until the turn of the century that Canadian officials learned that prior British claims to the Arctic Islands were considered inchoate (or incomplete) according to international law of that time and would require additional administrative measures and eventual settlement to ensure the country's inherited title was respected" (60).

The Rail Line and Train

Being "lost," like the ships *Terror* and *Erebus*, is a theme of Canadian literature that is often and perhaps strangely associated with the train—one of the great symbols of modernity and of the winning of the West. In this section on "The Rail Line and Train," I want to work through some ideas about the West's turn to the North by thinking about representations of trains in Canadian Westerns alongside subversive imagery of the West from authors engaged with the Western.[38] The subversions "twist" and turn not only rail lines but also our conceptions of the West's directionality. In *Mapping with Words* (2018), Sarah Wylie Krotz states that "[e]arly Canadian literature [e.g., of the eighteenth century] is marked by settler preoccupations with orientation and emplacement, with mobility and accommodation, with not getting lost" (152). Although these "settler preoccupations" and the resulting "geographical awakening[s]" (Krotz 159) are not always so strong in Canadian Westerns, with their fictionalized, mythopoeic landscapes that in fact encourage readers to "get lost in the story," they can often be dramatized. The stories themselves are also, perhaps ironically, dramas of disorientation. Krotz explains:

> That one map-maker's stories can chafe against others confirms their tenuous hold on the land. The world moves in and out of focus, the literary cartographer's lines merely spatial stories marked with others that fray the edges of the myths of emptiness, *terra nullius*, and wilderness wastes upon which colonial expansion relied. (167)

In Canadian Westerns, as with other Westerns, characters are often lost or risking lostness in blizzards, deserts, and forests. A skill or tool is needed to find the way. They need what Krotz calls, in a different context, "dreams for the future" (166). In Vanderhaeghe's *The Englishman's Boy* (1996), the train is precisely this symbol: "The knowledge that the new century was going to be a century governed by images, that the spirit of the age would express itself in an endless train of images, one following upon the other

---

38 See also chapter 3 for a couple of paragraphs on trains in Connor's *Corporal Cameron*.

with the speed of the steam locomotive that was the darling of the last century and symbolized all its aspirations" (106).[39] Trains helped to define cinema: Vanderhaeghe might have had in mind *The Great Train Robbery* (Porter, 1903), often considered the first fictional narrative film, where the window in the railway-ticket office could almost be a movie screen whose "train of images" is literally a train. But Westerns are anti-modern narratives that look back nostalgically to the days before trains and their enabling of big business and big government. In *The Great Train Robbery*, the locomotive is surprisingly vulnerable to outlaws; in *High Noon* (Zinnemann, 1952), the train and the clock are twin symbols that herald not civilization but the return of the outlaws. In *The Good, the Bad, and the Ugly* (Leone, 1966), an approaching train has a dead man tied above the cowcatcher as a warning, and on the back is a cannon; but then Tuco (Eli Wallach) finds himself chained to his dead captor, and he escapes the corpse by laying the chain of his manacle onto the track so that the train breaks it—the train enabling his freedom but only along the straight and narrow line that he otherwise avoids. In *Dead Man* (Jarmusch, 1995), the long trip by train to the West is an incremental voyage into the past, with each stop introducing passengers with an older fashion of clothing. In the comparatively obscure and seemingly post-apocalyptic Canadian Western *Six Reasons Why* (Campagna and Campagna, 2008), the railroad is about to be extended over the Badlands to a mysterious utopia, but the arrival of the train and its business interests—having depleted the resources of the known civilization—could result in a disruption of the utopia. Although each of these films deserves consideration for representations of the train that are more complex than I have time or space to explain here, the train always has a cost: you get something, but you lose something.

Cooper declares that in the North "the inexperienced can easily become lost within a quarter of a mile of a railroad" (8)—and the train too is imagined as something lose-able. Michel Foucault imagines that the train is "the place of . . . nowhere" (25) because it can escape "geographical markers" (25), or at least enable someone to disappear rapidly into

---

39   As with the sense of time expressed here, the train is also a passing symbol, if I may play with words; Michel Foucault explains that "a train is an extraordinary bundle of relations because it is something through which one goes, it is also something by means of which one can go from one point to another, and then it is also something that goes by" (23–4).

the distance.[40] The theme of lostness appears in Don McKay's *Deactivated West 100* (2005)—not a Western but a poetics of the colonial imagination in the West—when the narrator in a chapter entitled "Five Ways to Lose Your Way" describes himself as "the seeker, more than that, the questor, the ardent archaeologist of missing logging locomotives" (85). Unlike a ship such as Franklin's, however, the train is not supposed to be able to drift and lose its heading. It is on tracks. But in an earlier section of *Deactivated West 100*, "Waiting for Shay," the poet watches as a Shay locomotive "slides by on the tide" (80), an engine shipped to the West Coast for logging as "another brand of predator" (79) in the forest. Fascinating, then, that in the forest McKay's speaker discovers an abandoned "carcass of the myth of progress" (85) and declares himself "Parsifal of locomotives lost" (86), as if he had found the Holy Grail: an unerring machine that had erred.[41] In the contexts of "West" as both a direction and location, and of the questing that was needed to find it, McKay seems to suggest that going off the rails is quite possible.[42] Directions that seem fixed—arguably even the cardinal ones—can be turned.

The train is so compelling as a symbol of conquering the West that Thomas King seems, like McKay, to have felt a grim pleasure in taking it apart. In King's novel *Truth & Bright Water* (1999)—again, not a Western, but relevant in the context of King's *Green Grass, Running Water* in the next chapter—the conceptual artist, painter, and sculptor Monroe Swimmer designs an installation of buffalo made of iron—the material

---

40   Even in Wayne Johnston's novel about the history of modern Newfoundland, *The Colony of Unrequited Dreams* (1998), being lost, or "unfound," is related to the train. Its narrator, the historical figure Joseph Smallwood, leaves Newfoundland for New York via the railway, upon which he remarks, "This is not an island . . . but a landlocked country in the middle of an otherwise empty continent, a country hemmed in and cored by wilderness, and it is through this core that we are passing now, the unfoundland that will make us great someday" (141). After returning to Newfoundland, the fictionalized Smallwood ironically finds himself lost on the tracks when a blizzard numbs his senses, including his sense of distance—implying that only a force of nature can redraw an unerring line.

41   A similar image later appears in Brian Bartlett's *Ringing Here & There* (2014): "The old National Dream, leading to the Last Spike, has detoured into another dream: Rails to Trails, coast to coast" (114). On the bike trail, a heterotopian overlay upon abandoned railroad, Bartlett's speaker hears "a cyclist's jingling bell" that reminds him of a train's "blast," and the memory of "the past" seems to be "searching for the lost train & the elusive rails" (114). Alliteration connects to end-rhyme to associate, through poetic and remembered sound, different historical technologies of transportation.

42   In Lee Henderson's *The Man Game* (2008), "[t]he forest lost track of itself" (314).

of the "iron road" or railroad. Monroe and the allusively named teenage narrator Tecumseh fix the buffalo in place upon the plains "with a long spike, the kind they use for laying track" (140), and Tecumseh says that his grandfather had worked on the railroad. The narrator, however, makes no indication of knowing its significance to his heritage or to buffalo (141) until later, when he wonders if the few live buffalo in his area "can remember the good old days when they had the place to themselves, before they had to worry about Indians running them off cliffs or Europeans shooting at them from the comfort of railroad cars" (249) (the latter a scene in *Dead Man*). During the decade or so of carnage in the 1870s, settlers decimated buffalo populations to deprive Indigenous peoples of a major resource and to make way for the rails. Iconic photography from the era depicts buffalo bones piled high alongside the rails near train stations ("Buffalo"), where collectors, some of them Indigenous (Barnett 6), would be paid for bones by the ton. The sheer volume was mortifying when I first saw the pictures. The bones, a formerly renewable resource from 25 to 30 million buffalo reduced to as low as 100 (M. S. Taylor 3163), provided material for fertilizer and sugar refineries (Barnett 3). In Canada especially, the skins were destined for the fur trade, "Canada's premier industry" (Jennings 61). The colonial expansion from the East and the industrialization of the West depended in part on the active ruination of sustainable, traditional economies and lifeforms—trains over buffalo.[43] King therefore alludes to the famed "last spike" in the railroad when the narrator describes the end of his first day of work with the artist:

> We make three trips back to the church, and it's early evening before we've hammered in the last spike. Monroe sits on the tailgate of the truck and looks back the way we've come. You can't see the church, and you can't see the bridge, and you can't see Truth or Bright Water. "Look at that," says Monroe. "Just like the old days." (143)

---

43   The association between the railroad and the destruction of the buffalo was illustrated vividly in Jim Jarmusch's *Dead Man* (1995) when the Johnny Depp character watches his fellow passengers open the windows and fire at buffalo from the train—a sequence that also implies, through the changing fashion of passengers at different stops, that going West is also going back in time.

He later says, "I didn't lose the church. . . . I just lost track of it" (230). Painting the church so that it disappears by optical illusion, recovering the buffalo symbolically from the repurposed colonial site of the church, and finding a site without a vantage point of the bridge, Monroe attempts to reverse time and rewrite history. Although his buffalo are made of iron, as were trains and railroads, he tells his helper, "Watch them in case they try to run away again" (142). Monroe is sardonically joking about losing the iron buffalo; he imagines that they have the same mobility as live buffalo—or as the "locomotives lost" in *Deactivated West 100*. Monroe wants the train to disappear, and he wants to replace it with an artwork that ironically fixes in place a species that roamed with a freedom unknown to trains.

McKay and King share a fantasy involving the erasure of cardinal directions through a lostness that would "deactivate" the colonial drive, a change that would, coincidentally, prevent the North from being treated as the West. The title of *Deactivated West 100* refers to "the road deactivated—bridges torn out, culverts removed, delivered over to neglect" (114). For McKay here, "neglect" is a positive term, because it entails a natural renewal in the absence of destructive humans. He projects his thoughts out of the forest and into a city and a future beyond human extinction when the deactivation would include "boulevards and cul-de-sacs" (115). Although various federal governments (and political parties) wanted the North opened not only to passage but also to sovereignty through economic development/disruption/destruction of natural environments, McKay and other theorists of geography—whom he names, following Harry H. Hess, "geopoets" (42–3)—might prefer it to remain as is. He might in fact prefer the government to "get lost" and thereby learn a lesson about respecting nature instead of promoting the canard (partly disproven by Germany and other countries) that ecology and economy are mutually exclusive, that we must choose one over the other. At the very end of *Deactivated West 100*, the poet mistakes a bear for a stump and narrowly avoids drawing her attention in the presence of her cubs, and he realizes through his mistake that the bear and the mountain are practically interdependent: "that place where lava cooled so fast it kept its muscle tone and passed directly into mammal, quickening, sitting up to sniff the breeze, and ambling off among the alders" (117). McKay, expert in metaphor (his 2013 Pratt Lecture being on that topic precisely), imagines connections rather than exclusions, oneness instead of binaries—but he also recognizes that not only roads but also the idea of West must be dramatically changed. To approach the North as we did the West will be another environmental and cultural mistake unless the reorientation of our geographical axes includes our ideologies and ourselves.

Notably, one alternative might be to approach the North as we did the West but in an Indigenous way. In 2005, the Iron Ore Company of Canada, based in Quebec, sold its railroad to three Indigenous groups: the Innu nations of Uashat Mak Mani-Utenam and Matimekush-Lac John, and the Naskapi nation of Kawawachikamach (Ellingson 54). The train—Tshiuetin, meaning "the wind of the North" in Innu—goes from southern Quebec into the North, which is otherwise inaccessible (by automobile). Although talk of digging a mine and lengthening the railroad (Ellingson 55) would scar the land, at least the financial benefit to the railroad and its nearby communities would be mostly to Indigenous peoples.

McKay implies that the Western is a driving force that might push us to lose our way in our geography, and that the metaphoric "turn" (114) of the road toward deactivation depends somehow on the Western. He alludes to the genre in a passage that is oddly difficult coming from an aficionado of grammar and style. The Western in *Deactivated West 100* is mentioned in a sentence fragment that seems either to contain the incorrect pronoun—"who" instead of "that"—or to create an image that would never be seen in a Western:

> And a short way beyond, the crest where Loss Creek's valley falls suddenly away with that lurch made familiar
>   by Westerns, always accompanied by the theme, now swollen from the inside by French horns, who [sic] have appeared from nowhere. (McKay 114)

He might mean "French horns" as synecdoche for "French horn players," but of course we would rarely if ever *see* French horn players in a Western—a harmonica player (like Charles Bronson in Sergio Leone's 1968 film *Once Upon a Time in the West*) being more likely. Maybe, however, this is McKay's purpose. Hiking through the forest, his speaker is disoriented by "that lurch" of the Western and the appearance "from nowhere" of a foreign (i.e., European) interloper associated with the colonization of the West. The Western is not naturally a part of the West; instead, it is an often clumsy product of the idea of West created by Europeans and their migrating descendants, who have "swollen" the population of North America. McKay's unusual grammatical awkwardness here could be a syntactically apt expression of the now ideologically "familiar" but formerly new and disorienting conception of the West. The turn in the road, then, must be away from the Western—a cultural version of the seismic realignment imagined in the title of McKay's *Strike/Slip* (2006)—if we are to regain balance by deactivating the West and its related, problematic ideas.

The train's unerring sense of direction is too often conflated with historical progress, partly because, built into its industrial history, it had its own wild side, which it eventually tamed in some respects. Carlos A. Schwantes and James P. Ronda state in *The West the Railroads Made* (2008) that because of the train "the Wild West would vanish, and in its place might come a region more urban and eastern . . . than a West of fur trappers, cowboys, and Indians" (11). In *Time Lord* (2000), Clark Blaise's book on Samuel Fleming's role in standardizing time through the railroad industry, Blaise states: "The frequently drawn analogy of nineteenth-century railroads to the contemporary world of computer entrepreneurs and dot-com cowboys is not misapplied" (99). As Schwantes and Ronda do, Blaise evokes the Western with his reference to cowboys, icons of the genre who rode through the unfenced wilderness on actual horses, not the Iron Horses that would later demarcate lands, "fencing" them with rails. In the early days of the industry—I mean before 1883 and observance of "railroad standard time" (Blaise 103)—travelling by rail was complicated by a wilderness of competing temporal standards that differed by city and corporation. At one point, there were seventy standards in effect (101), and the various interactions between them were chaotic and bewildering.[44]

---

44 Blaise provides an example: "[I]f you were a Philadelphia businessman in the 1870s with an appointment to keep in Buffalo, transferring in Pittsburg (as it was then spelled), you would of course have to know the departure time in Philadelphia local time (just as you would today)—*unless* the train had originated in Washington or New York, in which case it might depart according to the local time of those stations, a few minutes earlier or later than your local

Railroad standard time in 1883 and then universal time in 1884 greatly simplified travel and communications.

There was a related psychological effect, or at least the promise of such an effect. According to Svetlana Boym, "[i]n the nineteenth century, many believed that railroads would take care of displacement and that the speed of transportation would accommodate trips to and from home" (346); the train was imagined to be fast enough that a traveller or settler would always be within reach of home, and so no one would need to feel nostalgia. The promise of the train was a promise of enabling the past to keep up with the present. It was synchronicity. For the Western, however, the train was a symbol of time that was often a threat—as in *High Noon*, when it brings the bad guys to town, or in *Dead Man*, when, in a nightmare of gunfire and burning coal, it transports people through time not to the future but to a more dangerous past. In *Back to the Future III* (Zemeckis, 1990), however, the train is a more literal time machine, the only alternative to the DeLorean sports car that could enable the heroes to sort out the various timelines.

The generally straight line of a railroad, too, came to be associated with order. With order, civilization supposedly came to the West. But even Fleming was doubtful: "Fleming, looking southward in the early 1870s from his surveying encampment on the prairies, wondered to his friend George Grant if a more humane way of development than the American model of wholesale slaughter of all inconvenient human and animal life could not be found (though he was not overly optimistic)" (Blaise 127). Indeed, around 1865 the American general Winfield S. Hancock had said explicitly that when "the great railroad brings civilization . . . , the wild Indian and the buffalo will have passed away" (qtd. in Schwantes and Ronda 26). It seems to me that uniting the country by rail was less bloody in Canada than it had been earlier in the United States. The Blackfoot led by Crowchild were mainly peaceful in spite of encroaching railroad developments, whereas there was more violence south of the border; north of the border there was in effect a mounted police escort for the railroad in the final phases of its development. But "bloody" or not, genocide or at

---

Philadelphia time. It was your responsibility to know the difference. Thereafter, you entered a twilight zone of competing times" (70).

least cultural genocide was at work, with the train's effect on buffalo an analogue of the colonial effect on Indigenous peoples.[45]

The train has a history of unbridled competition and territorial desire. The competition was not only between railroad execs but also nations, and it did not end as the train and its economic and cultural engineers "won" the West. When the end of the American transcontinental railroad (finished 1869) was in sight, the US secretary of state, William Seward, was, not coincidentally, looking to the North as the next frontier: "Seward, a leading advocate of 'Manifest Destiny,' held the notion that the United States was not merely a continental power but destined by its dynamism and the full exercise of its republican virtues to *be* the continent, as his 1867 purchase of Alaska from Russia would soon bear out" (Blaise 51). Manifest Destiny was the exceptionalist doctrine that Americans had a duty and a right to conquer the West. With relevance to this doctrine, Blaise reflects on what happened after it was symbolically effectuated by completing the railroad: "We are fond of saying that the railroad 'tamed the West,' that it civilized the world, but there is a rakish counternarrative. Railroads emboldened us. The distant whistle fed our dreams, our hunger, made us, by prevailing standards, wanton" (138). Canada and the North became an object of desire. Whether the Overland Route or the Orient Express, the train was a technology of imperialism—and, for a Canada beginning to imagine a transcontinental railway in the 1840s, the protector of British imperialism against American interests (Owram 28, 32–4). For people committed to the idea of West and the allure of the frontier, settlement was no satisfaction. Another frontier was needed—another "savage" but "empty" land that could bear the repeating of narratives of civilization and modernization. Another old land was needed to make new.

And so Cooper describes the railroad's advance into the North with remorseless nostalgia in the final words of *Go North, Young Man!*: "It was the pioneer track layer of the Hudson Bay line, laying steel as though there were no storm to hamper. A strangely animated thing, this track layer, a combination of trams and lifts and cranes and adjustable hoists" (269), a

---

45 In more neutral terms, W. H. New criticizes the notion that Canadian settlement by rail was somehow "placid" (83). The railroad effectively introduced and defined police work as the policing of Indigenous peoples, an issue with which we still contend.

"monster that was devouring a frontier" (270), a "giant, spidery, voracious thing" that meant "a march of civilization and a funeral of another frontier" (271). Although Cooper's metaphors occasionally admit to the destructiveness of the industrial technologies that invade the North—e.g., "an army of big business" (23)—his book is boosterish and Westmongering, suggesting always that new geographies to exploit remain when the West and even Northwest are exhausted: "the excitement of new money is as fervent today in Canada as it was even back in those days when the name of Cobalt became synonymous with silver, and the sour-doughs of the Klondike, their first flush gone, turned from the Western North to the Eastern North in hopes of new riches" (7).

These reorientations of power and money are also coincident with Confederation. In 1867, the United States gained Alaska, and Canada gained a union of three colonies—going only so far west, however, as Ontario (then known as Canada West). The last spike in the Canadian railroad would not be nailed until 1885 (R. Daniels 63), drawing a line both material and symbolic that helped to fortify the Canada-US border and block the American incursions into the North-West Territories that we see in some of Vanderhaeghe's books (discussed in chapter 6). The West's turn North has arguably continued along with refinements to Canadian territory, the focus being more recently the Far North, with Nunavut gaining its own ground in 1999. Based in Ottawa but partying, so to speak, in Calgary, the Harper government engaged in a search for the wrecks of the Franklin expedition partly to claim sovereignty over the unoccupied (again, empty) North Pole in 2014 (Weber). This claim extended a geo-cultural shift that has been happening in North America since the middle of the nineteenth century, at least in terms of the Canadian Western.

So, one of the ideas of West is that of the range, the open country, the place that the railroad can only border. And as I have tried to show here so far, the place is geographically West but has turned North. Is there a feature of northern geography that helps to explain or justify this idea of openness, of blankness, of *terra nullius*?

The Blank Space of No Man's Land

I thought it was the snow. It is a symbol of nordicity and a related mistaken assumption sometimes made in white cultures, which is—as Daniel Coleman explains—that Canada's "rugged northern climate and untapped natural resources posed a challenge that would thicken the blood and callus the hands of any delicate British young man" (137). But in retrospect, the civility that this "challenge" was supposed to help create was highly, rampantly destructive. There is a sepia-toned monochromatic 1874 photograph reproduced in Pierre Berton's *The Last Spike* (1971) that seems to capture a field of tall grass pocked with snow but which, upon closer inspection, reveals not snow but sun-bleached buffalo bones covering the prairie from foreground to middle distance (12). Each bone is so white that the overexposure seems almost the result of a scratch on the negative letting all the light through. Each bone is in that sense a pock, not a mound but a hole, an absence (of buffalo, of Indigenous peoples) that is even brighter and emptier than the sky.

The whitest sky, however, can be filled with cloud and snow, the snow differing from cloud and rain as a solid that partially extends the solidity of earth *upward*. Snow is associated with the North (and of course a South far deeper than the American Deep South), but in addition to nordicity it also means altitude, which is why snow may appear unproblematically in American Westerns set in the mountains of the Southwest (e.g., *The Searchers*). Whether you are going north on a map or climbing against gravity, nordicity and altitude are similarly *up*. I once proposed to a Canadian literature class at McGill University that, for the United States, the North was the new frontier (as I have been explaining here), and one of my American students countered that his passport said that outer space—the epitome of upness—was now the frontier. Perhaps they are both this new frontier that upness is. Both are Olympian, as in Mount Olympus and the Olympics; the Olympian adjectives are faster, stronger, *higher*. Upness in the North and in the snow is Olympian because this real place is the conceptual space of bold quests (being that "[s]pace is a practised place," as I already quoted from Michel de Certeau), such as racing against the Russians for outer space and the moon, or seeking the Northwest Passage along the polar ice.

Although snow (like almost any signifier in the Western) is often slippery and drifting[46] and associated with the North, it re-inscribes the frontier myth of the West through its evocations of desire and ambition, uncharted territory and open country, and a narrative freedom and originality that problematically counter the *ab-originality* of the West. Simultaneously, snow couples the hospitality of this "free" space with a manifest hostility of the wilderness—a Derridian "hostipitality," a paradox of the warm welcome and the powerfully cold shoulder. Students often ask me what makes Canadian literature different from other literature, a question that assumes there are national differences. Often there are, but Frank Davey is compelling when he argues, in *Surviving the Paraphrase* (1976 as essay, 1983 as book), that the same themes can be found in many places around the world. (I will return to Davey more than once, especially in chapter 5.) Broad swaths of geography can help to explain shared themes. Regional approaches isolate the North, the prairie, the island, and other geographies that can be found in more than one place but are not the same as all other places.

Snow is not so common in the Western, or so perpetual even in the Northwest, that it should be considered a feature of landscape rather than weather. Tim Ingold writes that "[t]he question comes down to this: is the sky a part of the landscape or is it not?" (127). Ingold points out that medieval farming was "done close-up, in an immediate, muscular and visceral engagement with wood, grass and soil—the very opposite of the distanced, contemplative and panoramic optic that the word 'landscape' conjures up in many minds today" (126). He later writes of going with his class to the seaside on a stormy day to demonstrate a counterpoint to "landscape phenomenology" (129): as much as we might feel connected to the weather, we can do little to change it immediately and certainly (global warming being a long process whose necessary correction might never be fully realized), unlike the land, which can be terraformed. A snowstorm or snowfall is a phenomenon of weather that, like a dust storm, comes uncontrollably out of the sky and is thereafter only temporarily a feature of the landscape that can be manipulated—swept away, shovelled up, tracked through.

---

46   Here I am conflating, with slipperiness and the drift, post-structuralist ideas from Jacques Derrida and D. H. Miller.

Similarly, one night in Connor's *Black Rock* (1898), one of the early Canadian Westerns, snow is not part of the landscape but an effect on it: "the dazzling snow lay like a garment over all the open spaces in soft waving folds, and crowned every stump with a quaintly shaped night-cap" (140), and above the "garment" the sky is "like the roof of a great cathedral" (140). The welcoming landscape here is the perceived result of Connor's religious colonialism, where the welcome is partly because of the assumption of "open spaces" whose blankness is highlighted by the snow. That the landscape is consumable is evident in the narrator's appreciative gaze: "I stood silent, drinking in at every sense the night with its wealth of loveliness" (140)—the allusion to "drinking" also an ironic comment on the total prohibition sought in the Northwest by Connor (here both the author and narrator) and Craig, the missionary.

It is also not only part of the weather's effect on landscape but also on the mindscape. The exterior becomes interior in H. A. Cody's *The Frontiersman* (1910) when snow prompts the hero's self-discovery, even religious epiphany:

> It was early dawn as the two plodded their way through the deep snow. The furious storm of the night had ceased, and a hush reigned over the land, as if in honour of the birth of the Great Prince of Peace. All around lay the virgin snow, unsullied as yet by its contact with earth, and untrodden save by the two night watchers. "How like my life," thought Keith. "Last night, the storm howling and raging; this morning the stillness of God. Ah, I see it clearly."
>
> "Hey? what d'ye see?" asked the prospector, suddenly stopping and looking at his companion.
>
> Keith laughed. "Nothing outwardly," he replied. "I must have been dreaming and forgot myself." (97–8)

Although Keith associates the snow with his life, the prospector has a different idea. The prospector tells Keith that he sees on the snow "a new trail bein' blazed out fer ye by the hand of the Almighty," and that "it'll make all the difference in the warld when the shinin' light of a true woman lightens yer path" (98). The prospector associates the snow with "the Almighty" and "a true woman," and this woman obviously relates to the "virgin" quality that Keith perceives when he looks at the white landscape. The men's anthropomorphisms imply their belief in the innocence and goodness of Keith's ministry, his colonialism. The glaring and sublime reflection on snow prompts self-reflection. For Cody, as an early imaginer of the West through the lens of the Western, the snow has a religious significance akin to Manifest Destiny.

In the moments of emerging out of shelter into the snow, it can seem like the blankness of an unmarked page or an unpainted canvas. Ingold asks, "is the sky . . . the epitome of emptiness?" (127) No, he implies as an answer, but the myth of the West encourages us to imagine a transfer of sky to earth when snow falls: the sky's emptiness comes down to earth, reducing variations in hue and tone, smoothing surfaces so that the heterogeneity of landscape appears temporarily more homogenous and, in a Baudrillardian precession of simulacra long preceding the hyperreal, reminds us of the page or canvas that can convey the picture of anything we imagine. Ingold rightly cautions us that "there is something oxymoronic about compounds [such as "lightscape" or "soundscape"] that couple the currents of sensory awareness with a regime, implicit in the modernist equation of *scape* with the *scopic*, which reduces such currents to vectors of projection in the conversion of objects into images" (134).[47] In other words, he cautions us against seeing the landscape as an image—or, in the case of the unpainted canvas, as an image-to-be. The equation of image with landscape is precisely the error that Thomas King criticizes when Monroe Swimmer, in *Truth & Bright Water*, vandalizes classic landscape paintings by painting the First Nations back into them. The irony is that the colonial impression of emptiness is so easily disturbed in the snow by tracks, but, just as easily, blowing snow can erase the signs of animal life and human occupation.

Because I am interested in visual images here, I want to remark on how, in various American Westerns on film, snow is a symbol of danger, mystery, blankness, and barrenness—and even of a lack of mothers

---

[47] In Ingold's writing about *scape* and *scope*, there are echoes of Arjun Appadurai's metaphors of the scape—for example, mediascape and ideoscape, which he uses in *Modernity at Large* (1996) to conceptualize movements between cultures.

who can produce surviving children. In the 1956 film *The Searchers*, snow signals a change of seasons as Ethan (John Wayne) follows the trail of his kidnapped niece, seemingly with no hope of finding her and thereby renewing the fecundity of spring for his family. In *McCabe & Mrs. Miller* (Altman, 1971), John McCabe (Warren Beatty) finds that his experience of the American Northwest results in his dying unheroically in a snowbank after being shot in the back. In *Buck and the Preacher* (Poitier, 1972), there is no snow, but there is the threat of what will happen if the Black families travelling northward cannot recover the money that was stolen from them before winter. In *Jeremiah Johnson* (Pollack, 1972), the snow in the Rocky Mountains is metonymically associated with the mountain man rechristened Bear Claw (Will Geer), an old white man with a preference for wearing white or light-coloured furs. He tells his protégé Jeremiah Johnson (Robert Redford) that a woman's breast is the hardest rock in the world and that he prefers to live alone, as Johnson does. Johnson's forced marriage to a Flathead woman named Swan (Delle Bolton) ends in her death at the hands of vengeful Crow men, suggesting that, in the eyes of the filmmakers and their "Indians," the whiteness of a swan is only beautiful until it is coloured by miscegenation; in parallel, Bear Claw's racialization as "Indian" through his animal name is allowable because as a hermit and bachelor (his maleness notwithstanding) he is no threat to racial purity. In *Pale Rider* (Eastwood, 1985), the preacher (Clint Eastwood)—also like a hermit or bachelor—is similarly associated through metonym with the snowy mountain that is often his personal backdrop, and its whiteness implies his ghostliness. *Dances with Wolves* (Costner, 1990) suggests as much when the Sioux led by Kicking Bird (Graham Greene) vanish into the snowy forest at the end of the film, the snow implying (falsely) the winter of their culture. At the beginning of *The Hateful Eight* (Tarantino, 2015), a horse-drawn carriage drives through the snow past a crucifix, and the semblance of the reversed direction of the carriage in a cut between scenes breaks the 180-degree rule and implies that the purity of Jesus Christ is about to be stained red in one of Quentin Tarantino's signature bloodbaths. In *The Revenant* (Iñárritu, 2015), the snow forces Hugh Glass (Leonardo DiCaprio) to shelter himself, naked, in the dead body of his still-warm horse—his re-emergence being a symbolic rebirth that calls attention to the lack of real and living mothers in the story.[48] (I consider the born-from-a-horse scene with several other examples in chapter 6.) In these American films, snow is associated with death, perhaps the death of a style of masculinity—such as the strong, silent type—associated with a supposedly vanishing Indigeneity.

But I have seen far less snow in the Canadian Westerns that I have watched. I don't recall it in the film adaptation of *All Hat* (Farlinger, 2007), or the television adaptation of *The Englishman's Boy* (Smith, 2008) (though the novel it was based on does have snow), *Six Reasons Why* (Campagna and Campagna, 2008), or *Gunless* (Phillips, 2010). Even in *Gunless*, which is so self-consciously and parodically Canadian, the Montana Kid rides up from Montana kicking up dust. The landscapes are the southern Alberta Badlands and grasslands in summer, and in *Gunless* it is dry enough that Jane's (Sienna Guillory) preoccupation is finishing the pump to activate her well and draw water. Whereas, on film, the American Western has a diversity of Western landscapes that include altitudes and northern locales that rationalize the use of snow, the Canadian Western has landscapes that tend to be in the American West or South or could stand in for them. Its proof of concept is in the fact that so many American Westerns have scenes filmed in Canada, such as *Saskatchewan* (Walsh, 1954), *Little Big Man* (Penn, 1970), *Unforgiven* (Eastwood, 1992), *Last of the Dogmen* (Murphy, 1995), *Open Range* (Costner, 2003), *Brokeback Mountain* (Lee, 2005), and *The Assassination of Jesse James by the Coward Robert Ford* (Dominik, 2007).[49] Admittedly, contrasting a small sample size of Canadian films without snow is not statistically significant, but it is almost as if the makers of Canadian Westerns on film want to distance themselves from weather or landscapes that might appear too Canadian

---

48   The only mothers in *The Revenant* are a bear and some Native American women, especially the Pawnee woman (unnamed in the film) who was in love with Glass and gave birth to their son. She, however, is killed by colonists. When Glass surprises the bear and her cubs, he barely survives the ensuing attack, but in the struggle he kills the mother, leaving the cubs to flee the trappers without parental guidance. Presumably David McGimpsey would quip that this is about normal in Canada: "Life in Canada is just bear attack / after bear attack. It always happens" (29). Indeed, there are bear attacks in Canadian Westerns such as H. A. Cody's *Rod of the Lone Patrol* and Guy Vanderhaeghe's *The Last Crossing* (2002)—the point here being that the bear can simply sleep through winter, and that the bear and snow are parallel threats that the settler is not perfectly equipped to survive without help.

49   See, too, the British-Canadian co-production *Welcome to Blood City* (Sasdy, 1977).

(and might alienate those American viewers who do not know the history of Northerns featuring Canada made in the United States). Or they want to cordon off the North to protect it from the West's turn to the North as a generic Americanization; or Prairie fiction with its greater realism has enough snow already.[50] Of course, some of the early Canadian Westerns in literature that were more self-consciously exploring the Northwest have snow, as in various examples from Connor and Cody. And Zacharias Kunuk and Natar Ungalaaq's recent *Maliglutit* is set on a very wintry Baffin Island, but the snow has far less Canadian-American relevance than the Inuit reality of snowpack and sea ice at many or most times of all seasons (thus far, in the brief history of anthropogenic climate change and crisis).

We have seen that both American and Canadian writers have turned the idea of West northward so that Canada becomes the new frontier. Snow and climate are not defining factors, though it is possible that in the American Western it suggests a greater desire to imagine and turn toward new frontiers than we see in Canada. From the perspective of the Western, in Canada and in the United States, there is no feature of northern geography that justifies the notion of *terra nullius*; it is a construction of myths and texts. Still, the Western is oriented toward it: American Westerns look west and north; Canadian Westerns look west and south, except when they are more obviously Northerns. Although the straight line of the train is sometimes seen as a (time)line of progress—a civilizing development that brought law and geographic containment to savages and the wilderness—it is also a symbol of modernity whose "roads" and "ways" imposed a built structure on natural geography and whose "last spike" concluded the virtual extermination of the buffalo and of related Indigenous traditions and economies. While Blaise articulates a history of ideas in which the train demands time to be understood as relative rather than constant, King and McKay imply that the West needs to be "deactivated" by breaking the line of the train and the strong sense of direction that underlies western expansion. Such expansion is not only "western" but also "Western," in the sense of a direction aligned inseparably with the idea of West that Westerns illustrate and epitomize. And yet in the

---

50 I thank Morgen Mills for these latter two speculations about why Canadian Westerns on film have so little snow.

Western the train is also a source of apprehension, because modernity and the relativity of time and space involve easy compressions that come with speed, and the ease with which one technology can be superseded by another and abandoned in the wilderness. But, whether snowy or not, this *terra nullius* is the blank space, a nothing, that can be moved to anywhere colonists imagine, part of the transnational imagination.

2

Tom King's John Wayne
Indigenous Perspectives on the Western

Explaining the decline of Prairie regionalism, Alison Calder states that "[o]ne problem that has not been talked about, but that eclipses all others, is that there is no way that Aboriginal people can be accommodated in this agri-centric definition of prairie literature" ("Importance" 171). One solution is to "centre" ourselves with help from Indigenous perspectives, as this chapter does (instead of situating it later, in the chronological chapters, in spite of its generally recent texts). Another is to consider the Western, as this chapter obviously does too, because Indigenous people cannot be ignored in a study of the Western in which "cowboys and Indians" are definitive iconography. Stereotypes of the "Indian" are widely critiqued in Indigenous literature and in scholarship such as Leslie Monkman's *A Native Heritage* (1981), Daniel Francis's *The Imaginary Indian* (1992), and Armando José Prats's *Invisible Natives* (2002). The one by Prats is the most pointed at the Western and its representations. Rather less well-known, however, are Indigenous perspectives on the genre of the Western—perspectives conveyed in popular culture that predated Hollywood's studio system but were later marginalized (Bold, "Did Indians" 137–8). This is indeed a concern, partly because Indigenous writers understandably seem to avoid writing the Western per se. And yet several creative writers north of the Medicine Line have written *around* the Western, most notably Thomas King in *Green Grass, Running Water* (1993), Garry Gottfriedson in *Whiskey Bullets: Cowboy and Indian Heritage Poems* (2006), Jordan Abel in *Un/Inhabited* (2015) and *Injun* (2016), and Zacharias Kunuk and Natar Ungalaaq in *Maliglutit* (2016, written in Inuktitut with Norman

111

Cohn). King's novel is arguably the inspirational Canadian Western, or post-Western, that started the contemporary boom in Canadian Westerns (followed by Guy Vanderhaeghe's more Western-focused 1996 novel *The Englishman's Boy*). Its publication in the early 1990s and its representation of John Wayne coincided with a time when John Wayne often either came out on top in polls asking Americans about their favourite stars, or else lost to Clint Eastwood (Wills 11). Hence, the title of this chapter.

There is also one text mostly by non-Indigenous writers in this chapter: the director Mani Soleymanlou's *Gabriel Dumont's Wild West Show* (2017/2021, written by a collective of French, English, and Métis playwrights—Dalpé et al.). I was advised by the playwrights that the play *in toto* should not be presumed to be Indigenous given that most of the writers are non-Indigenous, and that the Cree and Michif in the play are minimal compared to the English and French. I am non-Indigenous too and have no authority in defining Indigenous identities or deciding the issues. Nevertheless, I want *Gabriel Dumont's Wild West Show* in this chapter as a brief example. In responding to the American Western, it proposes a comparatively real, historical, Indigenous figure to counterbalance "cowboys" such as John Wayne and of course Buffalo Bill Cody, whose power to affect Indigenous peoples and non-Indigenous views of them is derived from popular culture.[1]

Sherman Alexie's and Louise Erdrich's perspectives on Wayne merit attention too, but as arguably American examples, I will reflect on them mainly in passing, as I do with (other) American texts later in this book. Daniel Heath Justice explains:

> Critical currents in the United States have had an important influence on discussions of Indigenous literatures in Canada, but they have not constituted those discussions; there are substantive historical, social, and political differences between Aboriginal peoples in Canada and American Indians in the United States, and these are as influential on the

---

1 See chapter 5, "CanLit's Postmodern Westerns," for a related example that invokes Gabriel Dumont by way of his more famous ally and leader, Louis Riel, in Frank Davey's *The Louis Riel Organ and Piano Co.* (1985).

literatures and scholarly studies of those literatures as are the inevitable exchanges. One necessary caveat regarding such exchanges, however: as is the case with many things, Native lit scholars in Canada tend to be far more inclusive of and familiar with the literature and criticism coming out of the States than is evidenced by many of our counterparts in the United States, to the great detriment of the latter. (337)

So, although this chapter (re)casts the long shadow of John Wayne, its counterpoints are primarily Canadian, insofar as "Canadian" is an accepted term for people who live or have lived for long periods on the land now officially called "Canada." The examples of Indigenous peoples on Turtle Island, or North America, are instructive: they show that sharply defined borders are historically contingent and not often, or not for long, capable of demarcating cultural movements and influences. Further, in that "Indigenous literature reaches out to settler communities to advance social justice, to heal the wounds of oppression, and to reconcile our communities" (Jo-Ann Episkenew, qtd. in Justice 337), the "Indigenous literature" of this chapter is what King defines as "interfusional"—that is, literature that blends genres of oral tradition and colonial writing ("Godzilla" 14). They are not "associational" (14) examples that centre on Indigenous communities and cultures outside of the context of colonization. They are starkly responsive to the colonial culture on display in the Western, yet also interested in stepping into popular culture to popularize Indigenous concerns.

Indeed, Christine Bold shows that Indigenous writers and performers have been aware of this popular culture and engaged in it since the earliest dime novels and the related Wild West shows of the late nineteenth century ("Did Indians" 138, 151–2). Although they rarely had control over their own representations in this culture, there were exceptions, such as the Indigenous director James Young Deer and his influential silent films, including *White Fawn's Devotion* (1910).[2] In fact, Joanna Hearne demon-

---

2   Young Deer's tribal identity is not entirely clear; usually he is considered to be Ho-Chunk (a.k.a., Winnebago) (e.g., Hearne 5, 45), but he was not registered as such (Sweet), leading to some speculation.

strates three phases of more than a century of Indigenous involvement in Westerns in *Native Recognition: Indigenous Cinema and the Western* (2012).³ It is not a case of Indigenous people who have been represented by others in what Renée Hulan calls "the absence of dialogue, that is, when some have no voice" (203), but neither is it a case of mainstream non-Indigenous writers and filmmakers co-operating as equals with Indigenous counterparts to produce Westerns that represent Indigenous peoples harmlessly or fairly. I do not consider myself to be co-operating with Indigenous counterparts (except insofar as one of my research assistants has identified as Indigenous, specifically Mi'kmaq), but I am trying to relay and amplify Indigenous voices—"amplifying" rather minimally because most or all of the Indigenous writers in this chapter have greater public profiles than I do. Partly because of their own steadily rising status in Canadian arts and letters, Indigenous creators have not been silent in the face of the Western and its key figures.

John Wayne and the Reel of the Western

One such figure is the American movie star John Wayne. When Wayne died in 1979 after a long career, the American poet Louis Phillips commented on the star's historical significance in "Considering the Death of John Wayne,"⁴ a poem that predates by fourteen years Thomas King's even more daring "consideration" in his novel *Green Grass, Running Water*:

> Mouth-sore with bad breath,
> A runny-eyed roan, sway-backed,
> What kind of a horse is death? (265)

In 1974, *CBS News* reported that the "conservative Wayne" had visited the comparatively liberal Harvard University upon invitation from the

---

3 According to Hearne, the phases are Indigenous involvement in (1) early silent films; (2) mid-century documentaries; and (3) late-century and millennial feature films (as per the tripartite structure of her book). For more Indigenous perspectives on the Western in cinema, see "studies by . . . Jacqueline Kilpatrick (Choctaw and Cherokee), Beverly Singer (Tewa and Diné), and Angela Aleiss" (Hearne 7).

4 With "Considering the Death of John Wayne," Phillips is possibly alluding to an e. e. cummings poem, "Buffalo Bill's" (1923), where Bill is a "blue-eyed boy" who rides "a watersmoothsilver / stallion" toward the waiting "Mister Death."

provocative *Harvard Lampoon*, arriving on an "armoured personnel carrier" (*CBS*) offered to him by supporters in the reserves. Phillips remembers the scene in his poem: "He went to Harvard in a tank / Which is one way to get there" (265). If you remember Wayne's voice, you can hear it in the second of these lines. Phillips is partly ventriloquizing, which helps to show how any persona is like a dummy that someone else can manipulate, as King does with Wayne in *Green Grass, Running Water*. Although the "tank" can also be manipulated or driven as a symbol of modernity after the First World War, Philips gives John Wayne a nineteenth-century form of transportation as a metaphor of death in his poem. He describes Wayne's death from cancer as a ride on a "runny-eyed roan, sway-backed" and "bob-tailed," "a terrible old nag" (Phillips 265). The metaphor of death as transportation is actually a conceit that spurs the poem from the beginning, with the reference to the "tank" as "one way to get there." In Phillips's poem, the metonymic transition from tank to horse ironically reverses the evolution of horse to "Iron Horse" or train, a tank-like vehicle in its power over landscape. The transition humanizes Wayne, but it also suggests that he is historically backward, even degenerate, in spite of his perennial celebrity. The poem and its historical contexts introduce many of the ideas that preoccupy me in this chapter, such as the politics of celebrity and the fascination with dead celebrities.[5] King, too, is preoccupied with these ideas, and in *Green Grass, Running Water* and other texts he articulates his stake in a popular culture that has a pernicious influence on opinions of the First Nations and Native Americans beyond and within those groups. As King suggests, the problem is that figures such as Wayne spin off from popular culture into history, or at least into popular conceptions of history, and give the false impression that modern Indigenous

---

5   In John Wayne's final film, *The Shootist* (Siegel, 1976), Mrs. Rogers suggests that Wayne's character J. B. Books should see a priest before he dies, but he retorts, "I'm tired of people pawing over my death for this reason or that or for any reason. A man's death is about the most private thing in his life. It doesn't belong to Dobkins or Reverend Saunders or Thibodeau or you, it's mine." In addition to the coincidental parallels between Wayne and Books here, there is also the film's commentary on celebrity. Young Gillom Rogers (Ron Howard), starstruck, says to Books, "You're the most famous person to ever come into this town. And when I was a boy I heard all about your shootout at the Acme saloon." Not long afterward, when Books's presence in the town is common knowledge, the reporter (Richard Lenz) visits and says, "You must appreciate, sir, that you are the most celebrated shootist extant."

culture is an oxymoron; it was *supposed* to have died in the nineteenth century.[6]

As King does in his novel, and as Phillips does with his contrast of the horse and tank, Louise Erdrich uses Wayne as a pretext for commenting on figures of the Western and their positions in modernity. Her poem "Dear John Wayne" (1984/2003) is set in a drive-in theatre where Indigenous viewers are sitting on the hood of a car watching a Western, starring Wayne, and "the drive-in picture is packed" (21). Phillips used a horse and tank in relation to modernity, but here Erdrich sets up the same relationship with a car, a "Pontiac," a name that refers not only to the twentieth-century brand but also to the eighteenth-century Odawa chief who fought against the British around Fort Detroit. The appropriation of the historical figure's name for a car is also his dehumanization (or "degeneration" to the symbolic equivalent of a horse, a trope that I consider in chapter 6). Similarly, the poem's title alludes to the tradition not of love letters but breakup letters, suggesting that her presumably Indigenous speaker wants to cut ties with Wayne, whose star power helped to popularize cinematic representations of Indigenous peoples that are often dehumanizing or abusive. Although he, too, is dehumanized when "[h]e smiles, a horizon of teeth" (Erdrich 22), the implication is that his onscreen charisma is powerfully colonial (expanding toward the frontier of the "horizon") and consumerist (associated with "teeth" and eating). And whereas the viewers leave the drive-in "speechless and small / as people are when the movie is done" (22), Wayne has a "voice" that is "still playing" (22), sustained and amplified by the technologies of film.

These technologies in Erdrich's "Dear John Wayne" are juxtaposed with military technologies associated, perhaps unexpectedly, with "the Indians." Seemingly describing the action onscreen, the speaker says,

> Always the lookout spots the Indians first,
> spread north to south, barring progress.

---

6   Following King, Carlton Smith offers a gloss, that Frederick Jackson Turner's famous speech about the frontier (and his book on the topic) "inaugurated a kind of cultural monologue, a long history in which pop culture became the refractory point for oppressive colonialist allegories" (3) that either neglected or maligned non-white peoples and thereby set them against Turner's Americanness.

> The Sioux or some other Plains bunch
> in spectacular columns, ICBM missiles,
> feathers bristling in the meaningful sunset. (21)

In a series of figurative associations produced by the act of looking at the screen, the viewers are metonymically associated with, first, "the hordes of mosquitoes" (21) that are pestering them; and, second, the onscreen image of "the Indians" appearing metaphorically as "spectacular columns, ICBM missiles" (21). Of course, no Western starring Wayne was ever set at a historical moment when ICBMs (intercontinental ballistic missiles) existed. The "Indians" in their "spectacular columns" seem to remind the speaker of images of ICBMs, thereby implying that the Indigenous people are a growing threat of modern warfare. Ironically, however, the viewers' lack of agency as they leave the drive-in suggests that they are indeed powerless, in keeping with their being stereotyped as a pre-modern or primitive threat.

These binaries of powerful and powerless are valid but also called into question in "Dear John Wayne," because Erdrich invokes various kinds of screens and thereby implies that the whole scene of the drive-in is hyperreal: a Baudrillardian illusion. In one of the poem's deft shifts of point of view, "the lookout" in the movie might be looking *not* at "Indians" elsewhere in the diegesis but *out of the screen* at the Indigenous audience, whose positions on the hoods of cars would also frame them with the windshield, which is sometimes also called a wind*screen*. Furthermore, Erdrich plays on the military technique of a "smoke screen" (21) by invoking "the slow-burning spirals" (21) of mosquito deterrents that the viewers use (in vain) to make their viewing experience more comfortable. In effect, there is a (wind) screen whose reflections of a (silver) screen are filtered through a (smoke) screen, and the viewers are stuck in the middle. Their powerlessness could be a result of their liminality, their in-betweenness, a state of being that is intensified by their highly mediated environment. In that mediascape (to borrow a term from Arjun Appadurai), Indigenous people are as modern as anyone, but modern technologies such as mosquito deterrents are ineffective against threats of a natural environment that is generically associated with Indigenous peoples and their traditions. Are these nineteenth- or late twentieth-century "Indians"? According to

Carlton Smith in *Coyote Kills John Wayne* (2000), Erdrich's acknowledgement of temporally complex identities means that "[h]istory too is ... destabilized, moving in and out of the present, leaving 'tracks' that will keep altering the present" (111). I agree; I only shift the emphasis. In "Dear John Wayne," the movie that they watch both narrates and visualizes their loss of power, but they have little recourse to the advantages of their own historiography, partly because their histories have been popularly misunderstood as histories of loss, defeat, and disappearance.

Popular culture as a threat bigger than history—that is one concern of this chapter, and it is one possible motivation for King's wading into the literary end of popular culture: to question it from within, as Erdrich does by implying that her position is fully screened-in. When King wrote *Green Grass, Running Water*, he had not yet made all of those strides, but he was imagining them. Although the next part of this chapter is about the popular culture of the Western in *Green Grass, Running Water*, it is also about the publicity of John Wayne compared to that of "Tom King," and the former fantasized by the latter. Although I have corresponded once or twice with King, I am not familiar with him personally; I call Thomas King "Tom" here and in the title as a reminder of the public persona he developed in the late 1990s on CBC Radio's *Dead Dog Café Comedy Hour* and during his candidacy for a seat in Parliament in 2008—where in both cases he is "Tom." In *Green Grass, Running Water*, King is teaching us lessons about popular culture and the publicity of "Indians" that he would develop not only on radio but also through his photographic series of "Native artists in Lone Ranger masks" (qtd. in Christie 76) and in the short film *I'm Not the Indian You Had in Mind* (King, 2007). ("Indian" is one of King's preferred terms, and it reminds me of how this essentially geographic error forms identities and shapes the idea of West; its continued use—not so much by King as by uncritical others—reminds me that newcomers still have a long way to go in arriving at a correct understanding of the First Peoples.) Following, for example, Gerald Vizenor's short film *Harold of Orange* (Weise, 1984), and anticipating later examples such as *Reel Injun* (2010), King pioneers what Stuart Christie calls "Indigenous Convergent Media" to insert Indigenous peoples into the reel of popular culture and *then* a new history.

The reel of the Western specifically is the object of attraction and scrutiny in *Green Grass, Running Water*, the first but not the only of King's book-length genre fictions. In brief, this novel interweaves a cycle of creation stories from Indigenous and Christian sources, classic literary symbols such as the whale from Herman Melville's *Moby-Dick* (1851), contemporary plots such as the collapse of a hydroelectric dam, and the fantastic sequence in which the "Indians" insert themselves into a John Wayne movie and rewrite the ending so that he dies and they win. Of all King's work, this novel is the one most completely devoted to deconstructing genre and popular culture.[7] *Green Grass, Running Water* is a postmodern and post-Western twist on the earlier sub-genres of the Western that Richard Slotkin identifies as "pro-Indian" and "alternative" (*Gunfighter* 366–8, 628–33) and of what has been called the revisionist and literary Western (Evans 407). *Green Grass, Running Water* begins by critiquing the Western from the non-diegetic *outside*, from the vantage of a frame story in which most of the characters watch the same televised Western featuring John Wayne, but then inserts newly mythologized "Indians" into the movie to change the genre from the diegetic *inside*.

The Western is a historically engaged and nostalgic genre, but the implicit comparison of the present to the Old West or Wild West is not often made obvious through framing narratives such as those in *Broken Arrow* (Daves, 1950), *The Man Who Shot Liberty Valance* (Ford, 1962), *Back to the Future III* (Zemeckis, 1990), and *The Hateful Eight* (Tarantino, 2015). These films are exceptions, as is Guy Vanderhaeghe's novel *The Englishman's Boy* (1996). The Western tends to bring us close to the action. The framing narrative in *Green Grass, Running Water*, however, creates a distancing effect that also helps King's own readers to avoid the nostalgia so crucial to Westerns. Coincidentally, another book by a Native American writer

---

7   King has also published five detective novels (2002, 2006, 2018, 2019, 2020) that also critique popular culture (e.g., detective films and reality TV), and some of the later ones begin to play with fiction/reality and diegetic/non-diegetic binaries. He once said that he "wanted to separate [his] serious work from [his] detective fiction" (qtd. in Breitbach, 84)—presumably "serious work" like *Green Grass, Running Water*. Julia Breitbach, however, claims that the serious versus generic distinction is "artificial" (88), partly because King "wittily rewrites not just genre formula, but—even more so than in his take on the hard-boiled mode—debunks stereotypes of Nativeness on the go" (89). To me, *Green Grass, Running Water* is serious because King implies that the genre would be better if it were significantly changed (e.g., had different outcomes), and I don't get the same impression from his detective fiction.

published in 1993 similarly avoids nostalgia; in Sherman Alexie's *The Lone Ranger and Tonto Fistfight in Heaven*, one of the "Indian" characters dreams of being "a gunfighter with braids and a ribbon shirt. He wouldn't speak English, just whisper Spokane as he gunned down Wild Bill Hickok, Bat Masterson, even Billy the Kid. . . . [W]hite and Indian people would sing ballads about him" (232).[8] As Smith implies in the title of his book, *Coyote Kills John Wayne*, the nostalgia for an alternative history suggests that King's fantasy about the death of American celebrity is not simply a "Canadian" affair; it is a concern other Indigenous writers have about the pop culture of the Western. Conventionalized through repetition of narrative and trope, the genre encourages us to appreciate rather than critique nostalgia. When generic conventions are repeated but not challenged, they enable fictional representations to support real-life ideology—a slippage from illusion to reality. Such a slippage is like the biographical fallacy of assuming that the character is like the actor. *Green Grass, Running Water* treats John Wayne distantly, as the Other, refusing to personalize or historicize the man behind the persona. To do so might be to create sympathy in readers and to individualize a key problem of the Western genre: the idolization of gunfighters and the related nostalgia for their passing. Correspondingly, in *I'm Not the Indian You Had in Mind*, King considers "this Indian you idolize" to be the detrimentally kitschy idol of a cigar-store "Indian," an equally problematic figure because of nostalgia for the Vanishing "Indian" instead of support for contemporary Indigenous cultures. The nostalgia encourages overly selective memories and distorted histories. In *Screening the Past: Memory and Nostalgia in Cinema* (2005), Pam Cook argues that "the distinction between nostalgia, memory and history has become blurred" (3), and that "nostalgia is generally associated with fantasy" (3). Cook prefers to see history, memory, and nostalgia as a "continuum" (3) on which memory partly validates nostalgia so that it is not dismissed as inauthentic or fantastic. King would probably agree with her in that respect. Indeed, one reason why he disavows nostalgia might be to reduce its effect on notions of history. Another is the likelihood that

---

8   See also the memorable scene concerning John Wayne's teeth—possibly a deliberate echo of Erdrich's mention of the "horizon" of Wayne's smile—in the book's film adaptation, *Smoke Signals* (Eyre, 1998) (also noted in LaRocque 150).

nostalgia in the Western tends to be imperialistic (Abel 87), and that the West now needs to be won "from the shady forces of illusion and fantasy" (Evans 408). Although David H. Evans argues that such "forces" are to some extent straw men in other revisionist Westerns (408), I find few replications of the problems of the Western in *Green Grass, Running Water*. By refusing to treat John Wayne nostalgically through history or pseudo-history, but rather through a genuinely *alternative* fantasy (I mean as a subversive construction), King minimizes the effect of generic star power on his readers, though some of his Western-watching characters (most importantly Lionel) are under that influence.

When King fantasizes about the death of John Wayne, he is thinking less of the man born Marion Morrison and more of his persona—and, in fact, as much a *type* as a *trope* that appears often in narratives of stardom. To want to see a celebrity knocked off his high horse is a cliché of popular culture that partly explains these rise-and-fall narratives. Consider the relatively recent *Birdman* (Iñárritu, 2014), the exemplary *Sunset Boulevard* (Wilder, 1950), and of course some of the nine films in which the John Wayne character dies, perhaps most importantly *The Shootist* (Siegel, 1976), the last of his career. In the latter two examples, the star is synecdoche for an era, and the narrative comments on history. At other times, the star is allegorical, standing in for a morally charged historical figure, as happens in *Citizen Kane* (Welles, 1941). The deep and abiding problem mentioned earlier is that history and popular culture are not separate, nor are the person and persona as neatly divisible as even the stars themselves might hope: *The Shootist* refers semi-autobiographically to the imminent death of the actual man. When celebrities perform deaths while their own deaths are imminent, Thomas H. Kane calls it "automortography" (410), a form of self-promotion that enables stars to set some of the terms of memorialization. It's what some people do when they know that their compulsively followed dramas as celebrities—as public personas—give them the status of historical figures too.

John Wayne had that status, and it is almost certainly one of the main reasons why King chose to kill him fictionally at the hands of the "Indians" in a movie—a magic-realist reversal of the usual fate when cowboys meet "Indians" in Westerns. King could have chosen to re-enact the scene of George Armstrong Custer's death at the Battle of the Little Bighorn, as in the movie *Little Big Man* (Penn, 1970), but he chose Wayne. The only historicity he acknowledges in Wayne is that of the public persona; he alludes to how John Wayne movies might have been marketed to kids (214), and he alludes to real John Wayne movies such as *Stagecoach, Hondo,* and *The Searchers* (Ford, 1939; Farrow, 1953; Ford, 1956). In his work on King, Brian Johnson is wary of "collaps[ing] history into geography" (30), as Marshall McLuhan allegedly does, and in parallel I am wary of collapsing history into popular culture. For the character Professor Alberta Frank in *Green Grass, Running Water,* "[t]eaching Western history was trial enough without having to watch what the movie makers had made out of it" (214). Partly because of the movie within the novel, Johnson calls for more critical attention to the mass media in *Green Grass, Running Water,* which "is most explicitly engaged in questioning the effects of Western technology and electric media on Native subjectivity and culture" (28). In 2012, King wrote in his non-fictional book *The Inconvenient Indian* that "film, in all its forms, has been the only place where most North Americans have seen Indians" (xv). That he chose Wayne suggests that non-Native popular culture is the real enemy of Native American, First Nations, and Métis cultures, partly because it influences how we understand history and even becomes mistaken for history.

John Wayne has power as a historical figure in and out of his movies, and he is arguably even more historically important than Custer and many other leaders, simply because of star power (which is not to say that many leaders do not have their own star power). His historical airs are partly contrived, of course; the film scholar Edward Buscombe shows that Wayne's typical costumes are realistic and help him to project a sense of historical authenticity (9, 78). Slotkin calls him the "supreme example" (*Gunfighter* 243) of an "icon of authenticity" (242), one who was given a congressional medal "honoring him as the embodiment of American military heroism—although he had never served a day in uniform" (243). In one film, the collaboratively directed 1962 epic *How the West Was Won,* he even plays a major historical figure, to my surprise not a Confederate but the Union Army general William Tecumseh Sherman, whose middle name "Tecumseh" ironically refers to the famous Shawnee chief who fought against American soldiers and temporarily allied with the British in the War of 1812. But outside the diegesis, Wayne is historically significant too. Russell Meeuf states that "Wayne's international drawing power and the transnational appeal of his body in action helped circulate Hollywood globally in the 1950s" (6). Meeuf also writes that "[a]s movie audiences around the world experienced the often-disturbing social and economic changes of capitalism becoming increasingly global, as well as pressure to conform to a particular form of Western modernity, Wayne was the world's most popular movie star, offering an appealing image of modern manhood managing those social changes" (4). Meeuf convincingly demonstrates the range of Wayne's global appeal, finding examples from Germany, Australia, Afghanistan, Peru, and even Japan and the Soviet bloc (5). He also quotes assertions about the Western's popularity in France, Italy, and Northern Rhodesia (now Zimbabwe) (70). Nowhere is Canada mentioned, but Canada's proximity to the United States and the centrality of American pop culture on Canadian screens suggest that John Wayne would be at least as well-known here as in other countries. By promoting Hollywood as synecdoche for the United States when American superpower was growing, and as Hollywood's and perhaps the world's most popular star of his generation, John Wayne became a special target of critique.

He is highly political, obviously, and King has reason, given his political differences from Wayne, to be critical of him. Wayne was a Republican "supporter of Joe McCarthy, Richard Nixon, and the Vietnam War" (Newman 158) and "came to symbolize hard-line conservative politics of the 1960s and 1970s" (Meeuf 2), thereby polarizing his reception, according to Meeuf, as either "a necessary but benevolent patriarchal and national authority, or . . . a racist, sexist totalitarian who represented all of U.S. culture's oppressive past" (2). Wayne's persona could be as hard and even "indomitable" (Wills 17) as the tank that Phillips relates to him in the poem that opens this essay. Nearer to the liberal end of the spectrum, Thomas King ran as "Tom King" in 2007 as a parliamentary candidate for the New Democratic Party of Canada, which was once a socialist party and is now left-leaning but centrist. How serious he was as a politician remains a question for me, partly because he seems to imply a used-car salesmanship joke in the video in which he sells himself as a candidate ("NDP"), and partly because *The Inconvenient Indian* is extraordinarily cynical compared to the false "monumental optimism" (King,

"Interview") of King's novels, nowhere more so than in its commentary on federal politics. Regardless, he is in many ways opposite to Wayne on the political spectrum, and he presumably sees Wayne as a cowboy in something other than a white hat.

The differing views of Wayne, however, are not as racialized as one might expect in the context of King, a writer of Cherokee, Greek, and Swiss-German descent whose primary interest as a writer is the racial politics related to his Indigenous heritage. Greg Bechtel argues that most critics are "reductive" (205) in their interpretations of *Green Grass, Running Water* and perpetuate a " 'Whites' versus 'Indians' " (206) mentality that does not perfectly reflect a novel in which, for example, some of the enemies of "Indians" are people who could identify as "Indian." And the novel aligns with JoEllen Shively's small study of Indigenous and white viewers' responses to *The Searchers*, which revealed that many Indigenous viewers really like John Wayne movies, especially Wayne's "toughness" (731) in them; they don't interpret it as "totalitarian."[9] King's character Eli Stands Alone in *Green Grass, Running Water* also thinks that "he liked Westerns. It was like . . . eating potato chips. They weren't good for you, but no one said they were" (163). Eli's opinion is not impossible to find among Indigenous people in the real world either (LaRocque 138; Miller 281; "Zacharias Kunuk Reimagines") In contrast with the study done on the reservation, however, Shively's study with Indigenous college students revealed that her viewers did not like John Wayne and associated his character with interview-based comments they perceived as racist (732). Wayne's notorious *Playboy* interview and his racism were criticized again recently by Mi'kmaw filmmaker Jeff Barnaby in a series of tweets (@tripgore) in 2018 and especially around 20 February 2019. King, university-educated like Barnaby and a professor for most of his career, has more in common with the Indigenous college students—but his residence in Canada is not a preference that means the "U.S. culture's oppressive past" is the main concern of his politics. King refers to the "political push-pull" ("Interview")

---

9   I thank Morgen Mills for pointing out that Indigenous and non-American viewers could appreciate Wayne's "toughness" as resilience (a hard-earned and admirable trait, perhaps especially for oppressed people), without necessarily agreeing with the goals that the toughness might serve. Notably, too, many viewers might enjoy Wayne's acting without liking his off-screen comments.

of his national identities; not only his identities but also his politics are transnational, and he is as critical of Canada as he is of the United States in *The Inconvenient Indian*, pointing to the complex histories of mutual antagonism between Indigenous peoples and colonial governments in addition to the oppressive influence of the newcomers.

Mixing "Cowboys and Indians"

I want to digress briefly into a related, important example in the work of the poet Garry Gottfriedson, who has a similarly complex and ultimately ambivalent critique of the Western in his 2006 book *Whiskey Bullets: Cowboy and Indian Heritage Poems*. Gottfriedson, who has Okanagan (Sqilxw), Shuswap (Secwepemc), and Cree (Nêhiyaw) ancestry (Schneider and Gottfriedson 138), has been a Shuswap language teacher and rancher. His ranching background is key to his partial identification with the figure of the cowboy.[10] However, he also recognizes the cowboy as a figure with a colonial view of the West and of its original inhabitants. His shifting persona says at one point,

> I ponder roping
> a painted Indian on canvas
> . . . .
> I am the cowboy artist
> who gazes at Indian art (54)

Here Gottfriedson associates a cowboy "gaze" with cultural appropriation and the dehumanization of "roping / a painted Indian" as if he were a cow, horse, or buffalo. Later in *Whiskey Bullets*, however, he offers a reconciling view: "cowboys and Indians / are the same" (66); "their love is geometry: / elements at right angles & triangles" (83). But this middle view is also offset by an Indigenous, decolonial view:

---

[10] See also Morgan Baillargeon and Leslie Tepper's *Legends of Our Times: Native Cowboy Life* (1998) (qtd. in LaRocque 150), which helps to explain Indigenous views of the cowboy in relation to ranching, rodeo, and horses, among other things.

> the Indian smiles with crowned teeth,
> *You have to go, Babe.*
> so the cowboy packs
> his rig ... (36)

"Pack[ing] his rig" to leave is a strict interpretation of decolonization, but decolonization is probably not quite what Gottfriedson had in mind here. Rather, the three perspectives that I discern in *Whiskey Bullets* are, like King's, directed at a specific colonial mentality that transmits through popular culture. In "Cowboy Up," Gottfriedson's persona claims to be "resistant / to Hollywood and reality tv" (*Whiskey* 60). In the words of reviewer Connie Brim: "[R]eplacing the lone, silent, white cowboy are Aboriginal cowboys who crack the whip, observe council politics, lecture on alternative histories, participate in rodeos, speak of love, and write poetry" ("Review"). The "alternative histories" and alternative political frameworks of "council politics" jump out at me here. Gottfriedson seems to see the cowboy as a colonial figure while recognizing that many Indigenous people seek decolonization or are engaged in anti-colonial resistance, in tandem with their seeking reconciliation, possibly "the best of all worlds" ("Acknowledgements," *Whiskey*).

While Gottfriedson's persona and King's character Eli are circumspect about the Western's appeal, Eli's nephew Lionel Red Dog in *Green Grass, Running Water* is enthusiastic about John Wayne. One of the main characters in *Green Grass, Running Water*, Lionel is a TV salesman whose aunt Norma tells him, "I would sometimes think you were white" (7). Among scholars, Brian Johnson states that Lionel is "complicit in his own oppression" (39); Dee Horne calls him a "mimic" ("To Know"). Lionel identifies with Wayne as fans often do with movie stars. Contrary to his cousin Charlie Looking Bear's view of Wayne as a reprehensible killer, Lionel—at the even younger age of six—"knew what he wanted to be. John Wayne. Not the actor, but the character. Not the man, but the hero.... The John Wayne who saved stagecoaches and wagon trains from Indian attacks" (241). Lionel's father suggests that he "keep his options open": "We got a lot of famous men and women, too. Warriors, chiefs, councillors, diplomats, spiritual leaders, healers" (241). But Lionel is set on John Wayne, partly because he has been convinced by advertising aimed at children; King writes that "[o]ne of the cereal companies offered a free John Wayne ring for three boxtops and fifty cents handling charge" (214). Later in life, however, Lionel gets a fringed leather jacket from four strangers (to him) on his birthday that makes him "look a little like John Wayne" (303)—though Wayne's comparatively realistic costuming means that "John Wayne" here signifies any generic cowboy. Lionel himself thinks he looks less like his uncle Portland Looking Bear and "more like John Wayne" (318). At one point, Lionel makes the healthy decision to walk to work instead of driving: "it would be a good way to start the day, a good way to start his new life.... That's what John Wayne would do" (243).

Here, King seems to recognize a positive aspect of fandom, but the movie itself to which he alludes necessarily returns an interpretation to ambivalence. In the 1953 movie *Hondo*, "a good way" is a catchphrase of the main character, Hondo, played by Wayne. Hondo embodies traditionally American and libertarian values such as self-reliance, that keyword of Ralph Waldo Emerson and ideal of most Westerns, but Hondo's ethics are suspect, and his admiration of self-reliant beings occasions explanation only in circumstances involving the dog Sam and the Apache. When Angie (Geraldine Page) wants to feed his dog, Sam, he refuses because he is proud of the dog's self-reliance; when she offers Hondo the food for Sam, he says, "No ma'am. I don't feed him either. Sam's independent. I want him to stay that way. It's a good way." Midway through the film, the Apache kill Sam, but we never see Hondo show grief. Much later, as the pursuing Apache are repelled and the pursued whites comment on the imminent arrival of major reinforcements for the cavalry, Hondo's old friend Buffalo Baker (Ward Bond) says, "That'll be the end of the Apache." "Yeah," says Hondo, typically stoic. "The end of a way of life. Too bad—it's a good way." Hondo seems to have character here; Robert Pippin speculates that Wayne is so effective at portraying "great integrity" (243) that most viewers ignore his persona's racism. The repetition of Hondo's catchphrase means he *is* comparing "the Apache" and the dog. This comparison might not be so negative given his stated respect for both, but—epitomizing so many North American and Western attitudes—he is nostalgic, not remorseful.

Probably only King, in his humorist guise, would try to find something funny in this scene, if in fact he was thinking of it while writing *Green Grass, Running Water*. In his novel, King introduces the Dead

Dog Café (108), which he later parlayed into CBC Radio's *Dead Dog Café Comedy Hour*, which ran to eighty-five episodes between 1997 and 2000. Michael Enright describes the series as "irreverent, political and sometimes breathtakingly politically incorrect. And funny" ("Dead"). Arnold E. Davidson, Priscilla L. Walton, and Jennifer Andrews describe it in *Border Crossings* (2003) as "a show that deliberately highlights the ludicrousness of clinging to reductive racial stereotypes that don't allow for alternatives" (112). On the show, King plays himself, Tom, alongside characters Jasper Friendly Bear (Floyd Favel) and Gracie Heavyhand (Edna Rain), the latter of whom manages the café-cum-broadcasting studio. One of the show's running jokes is that Louis Riel would appear as a special guest (e.g., as "a famous Indian" in the first episode); however, its infamous joke is that the café serves puppy stew. In the second episode, Tom worries about Gracie's plans to "butcher a puppy on a radio show," and she relativizes about eating one kind of meat and not another. The joke cannot or should not be separated from the show's commentary on the Western; Gracie also relativizes about sentencing in the criminal justice system in the "Trust Tonto" segment of the show, which Jasper introduces by playing some cavalry music that might be heard in a Western. Jasper claims that the Lone Ranger cannot be trusted because he is a white man in a mask, a man who rides around the West to make the world "safe for democracy and multinational corporations." Speaking for Tonto, Gracie then remarks on a problem common throughout North America: that "Natives get tougher sentences for the same crimes as whites" and outnumber whites in prison. In this context, Jasper asserts again that Louis Riel is alive, indirectly raising the question of the fairness of Riel's death sentence in 1885 following the North-West Resistance. King alludes to dead dogs to criticize the low value placed by the dominant culture on the lives of Indians—and, in fact, their dehumanization. No people have ever been as harmless as puppies, but King's purpose is to accentuate relative harms, as he does by comparing figures and arguing in *The Inconvenient Indian* that white settlers "were considerably more successful at massacre" (5) than Indigenous peoples were.

King's Mass-Mediated Celebrity

The controversies and hijinks of *The Dead Dog Café Comedy Hour* helped King to establish a degree of celebrity in the mass media, and this celebrity is theoretically a type of power to be used against the ghost of John Wayne—or, more accurately, the longevity of Wayne's persona and views. *The Dead Dog Café* had an "average weekly audience of nearly one hundred thousand CBC listeners" (Flaherty 313). As Davidson, Walton, and Andrews argue, King's popularity is partly the result of his challenges to the American-Canadian border (11, 13), and to the accessibility of his work beyond "the book-buying public" (97). The fictional killing of John Wayne is one such challenge. A related challenge to borders is broadcasting. King writes in *The Truth about Stories* (2003) that "instead of waiting for you [non-Indigenous people] to come to us, as we have in the past, written literature has allowed us to come to you" (114). Radio and other mass media extend this rapprochement. Although "[t]he elevation to celebrity status for King's Native characters [such as Portland in *Green Grass, Running Water*] requires the submission to commodity status" (Rodness), and although King himself has had to resist being stereotyped as Cherokee, American, or Canadian in interviews, the mass media are for King an opportunity *to play with* stereotypes and thereby influence culture. Brian Johnson explains that "*The Dead Dog Café* not only affords King the opportunity to parody and contest stereotypical representations of Natives for a mass popular audience, it also enables him to do so orally, and thus to revitalize and reinvent oral traditions in a non-traditional medium" (44). King uses the mass media to be simultaneously creative, resistant, comic, and promotional of his messages and himself.

Davidson, Walton, and Andrews add that "King himself is a newsworthy figure, who does not simply write books, but also is a frequent presence on radio programs, an occasional actor, and a sometimes critic" (76–7). His connection to the "mass public audience" and his status as a public intellectual (e.g., in his Massey Lectures in 2003, which became *The Truth about Stories*) mean that he has a status that can resist celebrity on his own terms—not as an entertainer among those who "ceased being a people and somehow became performers in an Aboriginal minstrel show for White North America" (*Truth about Stories* 68). He writes in *The*

Inconvenient Indian about the "public face" (153) of the American Indian Movement, recognizing the disproportionate effect of publicity on the public's understanding of which movements are influential. In the context of his own activism, King jokes that "Hollywood might even make a movie about us. I wonder who they'd get to play me" (144). Although he is the underdog in a metaphoric battle against John Wayne, he has star power to fight star power—fire with fire—at least in Canada.[11]

As celebrities tend to do, King sometimes engages in grandstanding, but ironically. Rather than insinuate himself into the circles of people who are much more widely recognized, he plays with an invocation of religious significance to suggest his ambition, as other Canadian literary celebrities have done (Deshaye, *Metaphor* 10, 28, 61). He invokes for example the religious figure of Coyote and associates himself with the trickster spirit. Coyote is "good and bad, creator and disrupter" (Davidson, Walton, and Andrews 80), a force of chaos and shaper of narratives. King himself is not only a writer but also a photographer, and one of his series of portraits of Indigenous writers is a self-portrait with a taxidermied coyote. In the photograph, the coyote is stretching up as if to howl or bark, and its tongue ripples between its open jaws. King is leaning in and looking surprised, positioned so that the coyote's tongue is at his earlobe, as if the canine were whispering to him or licking his ear. According to Davidson, Walton, and Andrews, "[t]he photograph plays tricks with the eye by aligning King with the coyote in his own visual form of trickster discourse" (100). King's ludic propensity has a satirical bite when he compares the Christian God to Coyote in a scene from *Green Grass, Running Water*. Faye Hammill summarizes it like so: "One of Coyote's dreams is about a dog, but the dream gets loose, reverses its name, and proclaims itself

---

[11] His views remain relevant when Conrad Black, arguably another public intellectual and certainly a figure of celebrity in the national media that he helped to expand, still feels justified in writing that pre-contact "Indian society was not in itself worthy of integral conservation, nor was its dilution a suitable subject for great lamentations" (9). Neither Black nor King are sentimental or overly idealistic about pre-contact "Indians," but King decries Black's sort of smug and condescending dismissiveness of "Indians," a dismissiveness that remains problematic for First Nations even in the era of the Idle No More movement, the Truth and Reconciliation Commission, and the National Inquiry into Missing and Murdered Indigenous Women and Girls. Black's *Rise to Greatness* (2014) is unapologetically a history of great white men—one whose impressive scope is diminished by its focus on winners in war and politics, and whose integrity is deeply suspect because of its omissions, erasures, and rationalizing of cultural genocide.

GOD; subsequently, GOD's attempt to rename and reclassify everything in Canada according to a Christian worldview is counteracted by a group of shape-shifting Indigenous deities" (1). On the one hand, King's comedy equalizes Christian and Indigenous traditions while noting the spiritual significance of non-human animals for Indians. On the other, if King had *Hondo* in mind, then he is being wickedly funny in killing off Wayne alongside God.

King doesn't apologize, either, when he kills John Wayne. For someone who campaigned for an erstwhile socialist party in Canada, his implied author is remarkably conservative in his embrace of retributive justice at the moment when magic realism meets realism in this novel—quite different from in the realist sections, where his Indigenous characters refuse to engage in violence. Let me set the stage, which is "Buffalo" Bill Bursum's audio-video store, where Lionel's cousin Charlie has come to talk about jobs and money; Bursum is playing the John Wayne movie on his wall of TVs, the TVs set up to look like a map of the country. Throughout the novel the only program on TV is this very Western (177, 220), a fictional movie called *The Mysterious Warrior*, which Bursum thinks of as "[t]he best Western of them all. John Wayne, Richard Widmark, Maureen O'Hara. All the biggies" (188).[12] The realist and magic-realist sections of the novel finally combine when the aforementioned "group of shape-shifting Indigenous deities" enter into *The Mysterious Warrior* and act out an alternate ending. These deities name themselves after characters in "imperial master-narratives" (Davidson, Walton, and Andrews 88) that have race as a major theme: Hawkeye, Ishmael, Robinson Crusoe, and the Lone Ranger—all characters "paired with indigenous, colonized sidekicks" (Wyile, "Trust Tonto" 115). Incidentally, Hawkeye and the Lone Ranger affirm Bill's opinion by saying, rather too innocently, it's also their "favorite" (302) movie. King bases his movie on a fictional novel mentioned in his own novel in which a "stagecoach was attacked by Indians led by the most notorious Indian in the territory, the Mysterious Warrior" (162), a warrior who kidnaps a young woman from the stagecoach. The plot echoes such

---

12   Johannes Fehrle notices that, in Kurt Vonnegut's *Slaughterhouse Five* (1969), the kidnapped protagonist is in a cage designed as a typical American apartment, in which "[t]here was a picture of one cowboy killing another pasted to the television tube" (Vonnegut qtd. in Fehrle 9)—a possible source for King's scenes in which the only thing on TV is the same old Western.

John Wayne films as *Stagecoach* and *The Searchers*. Whereas the battle scenes of these real movies are grim indeed, in *The Mysterious Warrior* "Hawkeye, Ishmael, Robinson Crusoe, and the Lone Ranger [are] smiling and laughing and waving their lances as the rest of the Indians flashed across the river to where the soldiers lay cowering behind some logs" (221). King's vengeance against the American soldiers is joyful here, not in the slightest remorseful—and why should it be, given that the historical reality of oppression is so much worse than the fantasy of surviving it without trauma?

The death scene's joyfulness dissipates quickly, however. Initially embarrassed to see his father, fictional B-list movie star Portland Looking Bear, onscreen and about to lose to John Wayne, Charlie starts to identify with him as it becomes apparent that the four deities have "fixed" (317) the movie. They do so by erasing the cavalry that came to the rescue of Wayne and his party: "There at full charge, hundreds of soldiers in bright blue uniforms with gold buttons and sashes and stripes, blue-eyed and rosy-cheeked, came over the last rise. And disappeared. Just like that" (321).[13] Outnumbered and missing most shots, John Wayne and Richard Widmark lose the fight. King describes it as follows:

> John Wayne looked down and stared stupidly at the arrow in his thigh, shaking his head in amazement and disbelief as two bullets ripped through his chest and out the back of his jacket. Richard Widmark collapsed facedown in the sand, his hands clutching at an arrow buried in his throat.
> "Jesus!" said Bursum, and stabbed the remote....
> Charlie had his hands out of his pockets, his fists clenched, keeping time to the singing [of the four deities]. His lips were pulled back from his teeth, and his eyes flashed as he watched his father flow through the soldiers like a flood.
> "Get 'em, Dad," he hissed.

---

13   A parallel appears in King's later novel *Truth & Bright Water* (1999) when the artist Monroe Swimmer explains that he dealt with the erasure of Indians from the landscape by painting them back into classic images.

"Yahoo!" shouts Coyote.

And then the movie ended and the credits rolled to black and all the screens ran to static. (322)

Charlie's intense reaction is cathartic, a vicarious release of his frustrations with the popular culture of the Western that costumed his father in "a large rubber nose" (217) to suit a stereotype, and that directed him to perform his own defeat in Western after Western. As Herb Wyile observes, King turns some whites into literalized "cartoon characters" ("Trust Tonto" 112) as a revenge against Indigenous stereotyping. And the fantasy is not only that the "Indians" had beaten back and humiliated the cowboys and the colonists. It's also that they had finally been represented as succeeding—no "tragedy or doom" (Cox 220).[14] Charlie is a successful lawyer but realizes that he, like his father, had to sell out for success. Although Lionel registers vague apprehension when his idol dies (322), he later renews his affiliations with his Blackfoot family by going to a Sun Dance. The alternate ending of *The Mysterious Warrior* seems to inspire Lionel to be more involved in tradition, and yet there can be no full recovery of pre-colonial, pre-modern Indigenous ways. Shively argues that "[w]hat makes Westerns meaningful to Indians [and probably anyone from the West] is the fantasy of being free and independent like the cowboy and the familiarity of the landscape or setting" (729), whereas anglophone settlers enjoy Westerns as "primitive myths" (729) that affirm that colonization was good.[15] King disputes the historical validity of the "myths" and *partly* aligns with Indigenous viewers who want their "fantasy."

King argues insistently that a major problem in the majority's view of First Nations and Native Americans is that the "Indian" remains a "primitive" figure—not a modern and complex figure but a singular reductive

---

14   The inversion is in contrast with the problem in non-Indigenous literature that "dead Indians, even whole extinct tribes, work as well as or better than 'live,' contemporary Indians" (Fee, "Romantic" 16).

15   The identification of "Indians" with cowboys continues today beyond literature. A recent article in *The Walrus* includes Birthe Piontek's large photograph of Tsilhqot'in chief Roger William wearing a cowboy hat and fringed buckskin jacket against a backdrop of mountains in British Columbia, the caption reading "Cowboy and Indian" (Kopecky 31). Later in the piece, Arno Kopecky writes: "Modern Tsilhqot'in, to put it crudely, are both cowboys and Indians. They depend on moose and salmon as much as on the cattle they ranch. William, a rodeo champ in his youth, wears a black Stetson and never leaves home without a drum" (33).

figure "trapped in a state of stasis" (*Inconvenient* 78). The alternate ending of *The Mysterious Warrior* represents King's entry into the world of film and of mass media, which he wants to complicate and Indigenize; "King ... remains cautiously optimistic that, like the book, electric mass media can ... accurately reflect divergent cultural perspectives" (Johnson 43). Active in such mass media as the Internet, the hundreds of Indigenous nations in Canada and the United States can add perspective to the problematic view by sidestepping the cultural gatekeepers of Hollywood movies.[16]

Canadians Reading American Westerns

Andrews and Walton explain that "[t]he counter-narratives or alternative visions within King's texts also perform a political purpose," which is "cultural resistance to the dominance of nation" (609); elsewhere, they call these narratives "alterna(rra)tives" (Davidson, Walton, and Andrews 87).[17] Despite King's justified resistance to this "dominance," and "the larger issue of the uneasy place of Native writers in 'Canadian' culture" (Wyile, "Trust Tonto" 122), I want to conclude this section by thinking about how the death of John Wayne in *Green Grass, Running Water* encourages Canadians to read American Westerns. Admittedly, these national categories are impositions on King; he writes in his book *The Truth about Stories* that "the border doesn't mean that much to the majority of Native people in either country. It is, after all, a figment of someone else's imagination" (102). It is also likely that he knew he was writing his novel at a time when "many Americans [had recently] been surprised and hurt by reports in the media of or by personally experiencing anti-Americanism on the part of Canadians" (B. Daniels, 87). Whether or not Americans and Canadians generally interpret King as Canadian, university teachers

---

16   The big, colourful guide to the Montreal Museum of Fine Arts and Denver Art Museum joint exhibit *Once upon a Time ... The Western*, by Mary-Dailey Desmarais and Thomas Brent Smith (2017), includes three illustrations in coloured pencil by an unknown Cheyenne artist, ca. 1875–6. They depict Indigenous people in battle. In two cases, an Indigenous man on horseback is attacking a man on foot, identifiable at least in the first case (fig. 80 in the guide) as a cowboy, with hat and holstered pistol. The illustrations are on ledger paper whose ledger lines give the impression of comic-book panels. Although they are not a mass-mediated alternative to the history written in the Western, they are suggestive of it; they are also at least another example of Indigenous visions of their own power.

17   For similar wordplay but with more emphasis on "Native," see Drew Hayden Taylor's play *alterNatives* (1999).

in Canada have Canadianized *Green Grass, Running Water* such that it is the second-most popular text by an Indigenous writer in English literature courses in Canada (Fagan and McKegney 36). As both "Tom" and "Thomas King," now a star to some degree in Canadian literary circles if not in politics, King realizes that his large readership now draws on the majority—mostly non-Indigenous people, most of whom identify as Canadian or American. He could not have been ignorant of the political risk of his novel, and in fact he might also have foreseen that its "Canadian" objection to American influence would prompt self-reflective readers to consider the parallel of Indigenous objections to Canadian influence.

Margaret Atwood had already done so in *Survival* (1972) when she wrote that "white Canadian identification with the Indian-as-victim may conceal a syllogism something like this: 'We are to the Americans as the Indians are to us' " (100). Although Atwood is not writing in the context of the Western, her identification with the "Indian-as-victim" is a major problem of the Western. John Wayne's Hondo, "part Indian," represents a fantasy of guiltless colonial Indigenization. That the cowboy in the Western thinks he can Indigenize himself without also victimizing himself (or caring much about others) is an assimilation-without-consequences idea. If Atwood's suggestion applies to the Canadian Western, then one implication is that the cowboy here is *doubly* identified with the "Indian"—but is perhaps not much more sympathetic. Atwood does not describe the cowboy as such in her poem "Backdrop Addresses Cowboy" (1968), which I address in the chapter on postmodern Westerns, probably because she was thinking of the Western as exclusively an American genre, and her nationalism was hiding (even from herself) the Canadian complicity that, in *Literary Land Claims* (2015), Margery Fee discovers in Atwood and her precursor Northrop Frye's nationalist tracts (6–7).

To many Canadians, the dominant nation is the United States, and they are concerned about the economic pressure of "free trade" and the supply side of the cultural globalization that I have already mentioned. "[T]he spirit of manifest destiny became even more chilling to a small nation" (B. Daniels 90) as Canadians from the nineteenth century to the present witnessed the United States use force on other small nations abroad and on American soil. Some Canadians resent the "American indifference" (91) to Canada when Canada cannot afford to be indifferent to its southern neighbour. According to the self-described "American-Canadian" historian Bruce C. Daniels, "Canadians have developed an increasing tendency to overstate problems and defects in American society" (86, 92), a questionable behaviour (one of which I am sometimes guilty) given that many Americans (including my friends and colleagues) are at work on those problems and defects; one might argue that King, born in California and holding a PhD from the University of Utah (Davidson, Walton, and Andrews 5), is one such "American" critic—one to whom I look for guidance when trying to understand my own position as non-Indigenous and Canadian, and the extent of my own openness to the ideology of the Western.

Rereading the Canadian Westerns published after the Canadian centennial in 1967 but before *Green Grass, Running Water* in 1993, I note that an American historical figure—the main character—is always killed. (I am only including books that signal the genre in obvious ways.) There are only three that end with a dead American historical figure that I know of in this time frame (the true resurgence of the Western coming after King): Michael Ondaatje's *The Collected Works of Billy the Kid* (1970), bpNichol's *The True Eventual Story of Billy the Kid* (1970), and Paulette Jiles's *The Jesse James Poems* (1988). There is at least one further example in Canadian Westerns on film, William A. Graham's *Harry Tracy, Desperado* (1982). Although these are small numbers and would be dwarfed by the number of American Westerns that focus on the death of an American historical figure, in the comparatively small field of Canadian literary production it is notable. The scene of the "Indians" killing John Wayne in *Green Grass, Running Water* also makes me wonder if the Western in Canada can teach us something about the interest in dead celebrities in the work of Canadian poets such as Ondaatje, Gwendolyn MacEwen, and Irving Layton (Deshaye, *Metaphor*, chs. 7 and 10). For Layton and Ondaatje, the examples are almost always American; many of their texts were published in the 1970s, when nationalistic feeling was strong in Canada, which partly accounts for the paranoia about American cultural imperialism or colonialism. So, these Canadian books that focus so much on Jesse James,

Billy the Kid, and John Wayne seem to be part of a general commentary, not only a generic precedent.[18]

Because these figures are not purely fictional, these books are often read as metahistorical; however, King's novel encourages us to read them as critiques of popular culture instead of history. My view here is that King's vision of John Wayne re-frames Canadian Westerns about Billy the Kid and Jesse James *as a collective fantasy of the death of American celebrity*—or at least an attempted subversion of American pop-cultural influence. The killing of John Wayne in *Green Grass, Running Water* is hardly the restorative justice of the stereotypical leftist Canadian way; it is retributive—but *creative, fantastic,* not *real*. King recognizes John Wayne and the American Western as pop-cultural factors in a representational stigma that perpetuates historical losses. Partly through King, the American Western in Canadian literature is rewritten to adjust popular culture's negative effect on history, ultimately to encourage "Indians" not to leave it to the cowboys.

John Wayne vs. Gabriel Dumont (and Louis Riel)

What figure stands up to Wayne now, given that King works against the myth of the violent hero through the passive resistance of his character Eli, who refuses to leave his home in the path of environmentally destructive development? Is there an "Indian" hero who fits into this myth and the bigger myth of the West—that of the open range, open to cowboys who need only be stoic in defiance of the wilderness and its occasional manifestation in the "Indian"? The Métis painter and scholar David Garneau, in a 2015 issue of *Geist*, published an illustrative painting entitled *Cross (Ad)dressing* that depicts two men.[19] Slightly closer to the viewer but facing away is a chief in headdress, over whose shoulder we see a cowboy in his cowboy hat. The cowboy and "Indian" share a thought bubble that asks their unspoken mutual question: "Métis?" The implication is that the fig-

---

18   For additional recent examples that consider the real or symbolic deaths of American historical figures who are also celebrities, see Natalee Caple's *In Calamity's Wake* (2013) and Alix Hawley's *All True Not a Lie in It* (2015).

19   *Geist* entitled the painting *Cross Addressing*, but Garneau in an email to me on 30 July 2019 stated that it is *Cross (Ad)dressing*. Garneau, a Métis professor and painter at the University of Regina, has since the late 1990s painted many canvases in response to the Western.

ure who bridges the gap between the cowboy and the "Indian" is the Métis, the same occupant of the Red River mentioned in the Lomax-McCurry version of the classic tune "Home on the Range":

> The red man was pressed from this part of the West
> He's likely no more to return,
> To the banks of Red River where seldom if ever
> Their flickering campfires burn. (qtd. in Catherine Cooper 171)

Gabriel Dumont is such a figure: the Métis leader, warrior, and ally of Louis Riel who called up Riel from exile in Montana and who then himself fled into the United States after Riel's hanging; the "Hero of the Half-breed Rebellion" (Barnholden 24) recruited by Buffalo Bill during his time in the United States; the historical figure recently reoriented to the front of the stage by the director Mani Soleymanlou in the multi-authored *Gabriel Dumont's Wild West Show* of 2017/2021 (Dalpé et al.). Dumont—whom Garneau has painted alongside Riel in his *How the West Was . . .* (1998–2008) series—was a rebel but tactically respected the law when it was in his interest: he was alleged to have travelled with Buffalo Bill to tour in Europe, but he claimed to have refused to go because he did not yet have his amnesty (Dumont 56). Despite his exploits and the revival of interest in him after *Gabriel Dumont's Wild West Show*, he remains under-recognized outside of Saskatchewan and Manitoba.[20] *Gabriel Dumont's Wild West Show*, however, comments on the Western more directly than anything about Riel that I have found. In fact, the stage directions in *Gabriel Dumont's Wild West Show* suggest that Dumont's first words in the play should be spoken "à la Eastwood" (11), another alternative to Wayne.

---

20 Instead of Dumont, the figure who has captured the popular and national imagination sufficiently to stand up to John Wayne is more likely Riel, the Métis politician whose roles in the Red River Rebellion and the establishment of the province of Manitoba, his exile in the United States, and his eventual hanging qualify him as an outlaw too. Better yet, he, too, is clearly an outlaw-lawman, the iconic figure who straddles the border or rides both horses. Northrop Frye writes, "Canada has not had, strictly speaking, an Indian war: there has been much less of the 'another redskin bit the dust' feeling in our historical imagination, and only Riel remains to haunt the later period of it" ("Conclusion" 224). As I footnoted earlier in this chapter, sections on Riel (fictionalized by Frank Davey) are in chapter 5.

Taking a cue from *Green Grass, Running Water*, *Gabriel Dumont's Wild West Show* interrogates the effect of popular culture on history. It does not absolve itself from this problem; the play is also self-conscious about its own salesmanship and inauthenticity, displaying a poster that reads "1-888-NARRATION CANADIENNE" (9) shortly before one of its characters amusingly assures us: "Hover and Séguin Epic Narratives and Storytelling is recognized by the department of Canadian Heritage and the Canadian Food Inspection Agency" (9). Such self-reflection is important, because in a multi-authored, multicultural play about Métis heroes it is possible to indulge in the idealization of what Chelsea Vowel calls "the myth of Métissage," or mixedness/hybridity, which is related to what she describes as "the myth of authenticity" (43, 165).[21] In Canada, it is a particularly dangerous myth if it encourages Canadians to absolve themselves of responsibility for colonization because multiculturalism supposedly solved that problem (43). But *Gabriel Dumont's Wild West Show* helps remind us that problems of colonization are still with us, as in the striking image of residential schools that appears near the end of the play (and which I consider in more detail below). And so the play also recaps the history of surveying the West, the Métis resistance to this surveying and the resulting dispossessions, the *Manitoba Act* (1870), Riel's relationship with Dumont (in act 1, parts 2 and 3), and the Battles of Duck Lake and Batoche—and the tragic consequences—with all the main historical figures cast as characters (in acts 2 and 3). It also highlights several women's voices—for example, that of Madeleine Dumont—to counteract the masculinity of written history.

In fact, near the end, Buffalo Bill himself finally appears on stage to comment on popular culture and history—and he is played, if I am reading the typescript correctly, by the same woman cast as Madeleine

---

21   One of the earliest Canadian Westerns to deal with hybridity at length is the Blue Pete series by Luke Allan (pen name of William Lacey Amy), e.g., *Blue Pete: Half Breed* (1921). In terms of the myth of authenticity, Collin Campbell explains: "Constable Mahon [the novel's protagonist] goes on to remark that Blue Pete is dressed less like a practical and authentic cowboy and more like a caricature from a *Buffalo Bill* theatrical performance, but Blue Pete's superior wilderness skills simply add to the enigma here. He is both the least and most authentic cowboy of them all" (3). The novel's ambivalence toward hybridity is never quite resolved.

Dumont, Dominique Pétin (who also performs as John A. Macdonald).[22] When the Métis performer Montana Madeleine (Krystle Pederson) rides in, "a veteran star of the Wild West Show, attired in a long traditional-style dress, beaded leggings and double holster" (23), the character named Hover (Jean Marc Dalpé, one of the writers) says dismissively in French, "[c]'est juste du théâtre" (23)—but Montana Madeleine and Madeleine Dumont object to "these white men [who] won't listen to her story" (24). Later, when Montana Madeleine is imploring others to "wake up to . . . the systemic racism built into the founding Canadian," she is interrupted by "the Historian" (Dalpé again) who tells her to "[c]ease and desist" (82) the "historical revisionism . . . [of] socio-politico-artistico, tree-hugging, guitar-strumming, agit-prop Lefties" (84)—suggesting that pop culture can at least attempt to speak truth to powers such as history and its often nationalist and martial biases.

According to the play, however, the risk is that embedding history within pop culture is sleeping with the enemy. Buffalo Bill, captioned on a screen at the back of the stage as "Buffalo Bill Cody, Producer" (91), tells Dumont,

> I am offering you a lead role in my Wild West Show. I got braves, I got squaws, I got stage-coach robberies 'n buffalo wrasslers. I got Annie Oakley and I even got the Great Sitting Bull on the bill, all kinds of hullaballoo for our high-falutin' friends on the Eastern Seaboard. What I need is you: a bona fide prairie revolutionary. (91)

Buffalo Bill wants Dumont because he is "bona fide" or authentic, but his true incentive, according to the writers, is less commonly associated with authenticity. He continues: "Canada's a small caliber outfit, Mr. Dumont, just a derringer in some wallflower's purse. In America we got that big iron on our hip. Fame, Mr. Dumont, is what I'm talking about and you won't find fame in Canada" (92). He says "fame" but more precisely means the notoriety of an outlaw, and when Dumont is pardoned, Buffalo Bill

---

22   I was unable to travel to see the play, but Robert Gagné at the National Arts Centre helpfully gave me a final or near-final script.

says, "that's bad for business" (97). Although Dumont retorts that he is a businessman too, their styles are completely different. J. Kelly Nestruck states that "[i]n a letter Martin and Dalpé stumbled upon in their research, the playwrights discovered that Dumont even dreamed of creating his own Wild West show that would tell the story of his people more directly" ("Welcome"). That he did not create "his own Wild West show" might tell us about his style, and about how different the playwrights here are from him too. The historical Dumont may well have wondered whether it was right to stage these shows, and this question is probably one reason why the playwrights were so self-conscious and almost metacritical in this play. The concern is that the prototypical business of Hollywood makes money from "bad" guys.

The fictionalized Buffalo Bill's marketing strategies also appear to be racist and nationalist. Elsewhere in the play, the historical figure Bishop Vital Grandin is reimagined as the ring master—the stage becoming a circus—and calls the Métis "the savage, the feral, the uncivilized" (37). They disobey him rather than act out the part he expects and demands. For the writers, "the Show" as appropriated from Buffalo Bill is a hegemonic device of colonization. And when the circus later transforms into "a hockey arena" featuring "René Lecavalier and Don Cherry, two Canadian sport casting [sic] legends" (44), national history is again recontextualized by popular culture, and the Métis resistance against the nascent nation-state is described as "a very special match" (45). Similarly, in act 3, part 1, Dumont and Riel are portrayed in a quiz show that serves as a sort of leadership debate between them (71–4), highlighting their different methods of achieving the same goals.

With innuendo that suggests the bad guy of big business is in real-life politics today, act 2, part 2 begins at the Battle of Duck Lake, but this deadly skirmish is recontextualized by the RCMP Musical Ride (48) and is broadcast by a fear-stoking "Foxy Fox News" (51)—one of Donald Trump's mouthpieces. It is another satire of historical infotainment. Then "John 'Locomotive' Macdonald" is announced in a boxing match "like WWF [World Wrestling Federation]" (53) against "Gabriel 'The Métis' Dumont" (53). When Macdonald hears of Riel's death sentence, he says, "game over" (95), as if Riel is only playing. Immediately thereafter, however—to remind us of how real the "game" was—the scene changes into a residential school (in my own community of Battleford, near where I grew up) and shows Indigenous children's clothes turning white as they are forcibly assimilated into a colonial culture. Although the play seems at times to be articulating an especially French-Canadian perspective on an anglophone prime minister and his forces while simultaneously asserting a stronger French-Canadian alliance with Indigenous peoples, the image of the whitening clothes significantly expands the scope of the critique— while also implying that something more resilient remains underneath the whiteness.

In sum, however much *Gabriel Dumont's Wild West Show* implicates itself as a "play" in the pop-cultural transmission of the Dumont-Riel history, it is more concerned with farther-reaching media such as television and its real and symbolic sports. These media are contextualized as stereotypically and parodically Canadian extensions of an older American performance, Buffalo Bill's Wild West Show. (Pushing this idea further, it is almost as if the media themselves were a spinoff of the Western—and, indeed, how many people bought televisions in the 1940s and '50s to watch Westerns? Or hockey with its "shootouts"?) Ultimately, by ironizing Canadian storytelling and Canadian nationalism, *Gabriel Dumont's Wild West Show* questions the system of white privilege that was unquestionably the dominant bias of Canadian literature until long after the country's centennial year. Although the writers of the play are mainly non-Indigenous, they call attention to various Indigenous identities, not only men's, as heroes of history and not only of a genre.[23]

Cultural Appropriation and Jordan Abel's *Injun*

The risks of cultural appropriation in almost all of the texts considered thus far now lead me to be a little more self-reflective too, especially as an academic who quotes and in that way appropriates the voices of others. A more clearly problematic version of this potential problem manifested as I was writing this section when a white painter who works in Norval Morrisseau's Woodland style reignited the cyclical scandal of the cultural appropriation of Indigenous art in Canada (Szklarski). Shortly before that,

---

23   An even greater emphasis on the women surrounding Riel and Dumont is in Maia Caron's novel, *Song of Batoche* (2017).

it was Joseph Boyden's debunking as Indigenous spokesperson (Barrera), hot on the heels of mascots and the so-called hipsters in headdresses.[24] To cite recent examples is not enough, of course, and Indigenous writers sometimes respond with exasperation when they encounter still more in a history of cultural appropriation; it's *"ad nauseum,"* wrote Drew Hayden Taylor (11)—and he wrote that in 1995. He wrote again, in the *Globe and Mail*, as the cycle continued a few years ago ("It May be Harmless").

The recent appropriations seem all the more current and crucial in light of Jordan Abel's *Un/inhabited*, which came out in 2015, and *Injun*, in 2016. *Un/inhabited* and *Injun* are highly conceptual "found poems," meaning that they are pastiches or collages of words by other writers that he has artfully reorganized. Significantly, the words he searched for and "found" are from around a hundred novels in the genre of the Western, a genre famous for its iconographic landscapes and its convention of the cowboy and "Indian." In Abel's case, the cultural appropriation is his re-appropriation of white men's words from a genre that has a myth of the open country and, in some of its sub-genres, is more specifically about defeating Indigenous peoples and taking their land. Taylor recalls a typical question and his answer: "Question one: What do you feel about cultural appropriation? My answer: About the same as I feel about land appropriation" (11). As a result of the interdependence of land and Indigenous cultures, I worry that quoting someone's words, which are a crucial means of cultural expression, is like taking someone's land. But I also recognize Abel's books as published and public, only not in the public domain.[25] Critically acclaimed writers such as Abel and King would be overwhelmed with requests if they had to be asked for permission to quote their published texts.

---

24   For some literary-historical context about the potential for such appropriations, from a critical but non-Indigenous perspective, see Wolfgang Hochbruck's essay on Indigenous literatures as a twentieth-century industry and cultural phenomenon (272–4).

25   I do not object to Abel's use of white men's words for oppositional purposes, partly because I am not comfortable identifying myself as a white man, though I also cannot disavow the imperial histories of my French and German ancestors. I would prefer to think of myself as an ally, but Indigenous literature and studies are not my main focus, so I have not earned that "label ... [by] continually work[ing] at [it]" (Keene), as Adrienne Keene of the *Native Appropriations* blog advises. I also have not been invited into an Indigenous community by an Indigenous person in recent years, so I am definitely an outsider—but also definitely trying not to speak up for the Western (except to establish an understanding of its history in Canada), which is a genre with too many problems to enjoy or even accept uncritically.

Germane to my reading of Abel here—and of my reading of Frank Davey's *The Louis Riel Organ and Piano Co.* in chapter 5—is Davey's debate with Terry Goldie over the problems and potentials of being a non-Indigenous reader and critic of Indigenous writings. Goldie had written various essays "in which [he] refused to continue as a white critic commenting on Native Canadian literature" (Goldie 119). His reasons, in brief, were to stop writing "just one more white version of Native culture," to stop functioning as a "cultural gatekeeper," to stop presuming to be the intended audience of Indigenous writing, and to stop implying that white people are natural to this land and that Indigenous peoples are the others or aliens (qtd. in Davey, "On Not" 8–9). Then, following Gayatri Chakravorty Spivak, Davey argued that white readers can earn a right to be critics if they interrogate themselves and their historical positions as a practice of their criticism. Davey believed that for white teachers to stop commenting on Indigenous writing would mean for them to stop teaching with it, and that the effect of such a silencing would simply re-marginalize Indigenous writers. Writing in 2008, Davey did not think that there were enough Indigenous teachers in universities to prevent such re-marginalizing. (This is unquestionably true of my university today.) Goldie wrote back to Davey that he "would be more open to non-indigenous criticism in a world defined by indigenous critics" (126), but, as Goldie implies, that "world" does not exist in most universities or literary circles. I agree with Davey and intend to continue teaching with Indigenous writings as long as they are published and are made available ethically to the public, but whenever possible I want to find Indigenous criticism and commentary that can "defin[e]" this world. Much of it is online. Coincidentally, the Anishinaabe comedian Ryan McMahon describes the exciting "creative space" of the Internet as "the new Wild West. The Internet and this medium [are] the new Wild West for us, except... there's no—John Wayne is dead, if you will" ("New"). So, my research on the Western involves trying to find Indigenous views of the genre that put the "Indian" before the cowboy, as McMahon does with the title of his podcasting network, Indian & Cowboy.

Abel's *Un/inhabited* and *Injun* are special cases, because they are largely re-appropriations of the words of white writers, and so white readers who quote these books are perhaps less complicit in cultural appropriation. As with King's *Green Grass, Running Water*, which appropriates plots and actors such as John Wayne from classic Westerns, I feel slightly more confident in approaching these books. However, despite (or because of) his PhD, Abel does seem wary of scholars or academics. His book *Un/inhabited* has an unusual feature, an additional essay that is described on the back cover as "the first piece of scholarship on Abel's work." Its author, Kathleen Ritter, is herself described not as a scholar but as "an independent curator" (she is an artist who has worked for the Vancouver Art Gallery). Ritter calls *Un/inhabited* "a welcome provocation to reinvent these narratives [of the Western] alongside [Abel]" (xviii). Ritter was probably invited to contribute to the book and thereby ensure that the "first piece of scholarship on Abel's work" is by an ally who can avoid some of the tendencies of academics. In an interview for the *Lemon Hound* blog, Abel expresses concern about academics: "I definitely found that the 'Indian' as described by [the anthropologist Marius] Barbeau was objectified in the same way as the totem poles that Barbeau removed from their places of origin. In Barbeau's case, this objectification was not subtle but a visible extension of his academic training as an anthropologist. Barbeau was comfortable using the same anthropological process to study and catalog totem poles and to study and catalog First Nations peoples" ("In Conversation"). For white readers of Indigenous poetry, we risk appropriation when our ways of reading, ways that include marking the text and quoting the text, transform and conform the meaning of the text to a colonial idea of Indigenous poetry.

That's why Abel's *Injun* is so fascinating to me: because it re-appropriates the Western's colonial idea of the "injun" or "Indian" and, in the process, comments on the similarly colonial idea of intellectual property.[26] In brief, intellectual property is colonial partly because traditional

---

26 His practice of dealing with property, especially intellectual property, is one of my interests, and just for a moment I want to comment on this word "interest" and its relation to intellectual property. "Interest" obviously has financial connotations related to having money, which is the symbolic equivalent of properties such as land or gold. In the intellectual context, an "interest" is something that attracts your attention from all the other trivial or generic things that you could contemplate (Ngai 950). This is one of Sianne Ngai's observations: that the concept of *interesting* is also "modern, emerging in tandem with or against the development of markets, the rise of civil society, economic competition, and an increasingly specialized division of labor" (952). Because of these connotations, I try (at least in my writing) to prefer the terms "fascinating" and "curious," though "curious" does refer to commodities such as curios.

Indigenous knowledge is often of the land, and so taking the land and restricting its resources to exploit them has effects on the continued availability of that knowledge (Khan 37), and partly because it imposes the concept of individual ownership on nations that did not have the same concepts of individualism (Tan 63). Intellectual property remains a central concept for the university and the discourse of citation that gives credit for ideas and expressions. Universities in Canada are usually publicly funded because they are thought to be a public or a common good, something that is a benefit to everyone and everyone's progress: the ripple effect of education. As a public good, it should not be an opportunity for privatization, though this ideal is not what it once was. The public domain is supposed to be free of personal or private property but can be *government*-owned, which from an Indigenous perspective is likely to be ironic: it's public but colonial, thus not in the interests of Indigeneity within the public of the nation-state. Hutcheon's conception of irony as a critical "edge" in the title and contents of one of her books is all the more relevant at the truly spatial edges of the West, where "the public" and "the public domain" have not always been hospitable to marginalized or "edgy" people.

This connection between the public domain and the colonial mentality is one explanation for Abel's choice of intellectual property. He is taking it from old classic Westerns written by Americans such as Owen Wister, Zane Grey, and the ridiculously pen-named Max Brand—some of the people most responsible for popularizing stereotypes of "Indians" and for promoting the ideologies of the Western. These are the dead white men of pop-cultural literature, but both Ritter and Julie Mannell in *Vallum* magazine refer to these writers as canonical (Ritter xix; Mannel, "Featured"), as if they were Shakespeare or Dickens or Melville, say, in *Moby-Dick*. I take their point, because (as I wrote earlier in this book) the genre of the Western is a synecdoche for the literature of the Western world, a lesson I learned from King in *Green Grass, Running Water*, where John Wayne and *Moby-Dick*'s Captain Ahab are symbolically side by side. In contrast with the stereotypes of thieving "Indians" in imperialistic narratives and the Western genre, Abel's practice respects copyright laws and intellectual property. He is not stealing anyone's real or symbolic land, because even the symbolic land is in the public domain. Ritter explains that, with *Un/inhabited*, "[t]he resulting book is thus composed of entirely found text.

Nothing is 'written' in the conventional sense of the word" (xi). Nothing is "taken" in the conventional sense either.

As a tactic of cultural appropriation, the lesson of Abel's found poetry seems to be that appropriation should not include restricted symbols. (It should also produce something unrecognizable as the other's work. Abel's data mining has the wide scope of genre, not the narrow scope of individual style or achievement.) Restricted symbols include culturally specific things such as war medals or eagle feathers (Vowel 81-7), but also creations such as privately told stories, including family secrets or certain First Nations myths. Abel's chosen Westerns are in the public domain, unrestricted. They are different from contemporary works of art, such as Morrisseau's Woodland style. Although a rare interlocutor might conceivably argue that the Western should be restricted because Manifest Destiny was a more or less sacred precept for the white man, Western culture writ large has developed copyright law that allows appropriation according to the principles of fair use—that is, only partial, relatively focused, and non-commercial or scholarly use. Ironically, perhaps, Abel obeys the law; it's the restricted or sacred symbol. He seems to be saying that if you want to appropriate First Nations symbols, then you should do it on the terms of those First Nations, just as I have done it on the terms of Canadian and international law.

By limiting his selection to the public domain, he avoids the intellectual property of others and implies an alternative to the colonial assumption that the West was free land, or open country, uninhabited by the First Nations and Native Americans. Echoing Taylor's link between culture and land, Ritter explains that Abel "appropriates and transforms the genre [of the Western] to produce something unique: a meditation on the relationship between text and land. The question *Un/inhabited* poses is a political one: Can a reader inhabit a text the way one inhabits land? This question is at the core of Abel's process of appropriation, extraction and reterritorialization" (xi). Although I don't think "a meditation on the relationship between text and land is unique," nor is erasure poetry unique, I agree that "Abel's use of appropriation as a methodology is classic: he takes a source text and, without changing any of the words, subjects it to a number of processes that ultimately recontextualize and politicize it in a way that the original authors could never have imagined" (xvi). In that sense, it's unique, and I agree with the explanation and the emphasis on the question of how reading—reading the Western especially—is a claim on land. Ritter again explains that "it is a reclaiming and reversal of the genre, as a comment on the fraught relationship between this narrative history, identity and indigenous rights to the land" (xvii).

Abel also, however, seems to foreground his "own" voice in a lyric sequence about "play[ing] injun in gods country" (3) that ultimately breaks down, "progressively," as extra spaces and gaps appear in the text, symbolizing how Western ideas of ownership and progress have been detrimental to Indigenous voices. Abel writes found poems but also erasure poetry. In both *Un/inhabited* and *Injun*, the act of reading a progressively more blanked out or erased text simulates the incapacitation or destruction of the reader's language. It simulates illiteracy. It parallels the destruction of Indigenous languages by processes of colonization such as residential schooling; Abel identifies himself in an interview with rob mclennan as "an intergenerational survivor of the Canadian residential school system" ("Seven"). When Abel copies a line from a Western that contains one of his keywords, such as "injun," he blanks out the keyword so that the reader has to fill it in to make sense of the line. Calling attention to erasure is one of the strategies of *Un/inhabited*. Ritter explains that "absences are as important as text" (xv) in *Un/inhabited*, as they are in *Injun*. As the reader says the word, mentally or aloud, the reader is also implicated in the damaging erasure and the insulting re-inscription of the word.

Abel's *Un/inhabited* and *Injun* offer non-Indigenous readers a powerful experience of simulated colonialism, including the overwhelming generic repetition of racist, disempowering representations of people and places. This experience can remind non-Indigenous readers that we are the outsiders, as in books such as James Welch's 1986 novel *Fools Crow* (Chester 93). It also reminds them that the West denies Indigenous conceptions of "Indian Territory" and its related sovereignty, contrary to the alternative "West" in books such as John Milton Oskison's *Black Jack Davy* (Kirby Brown 79-80). Although some Indigenous scholars of Westerns describe ambivalent Indigenous responses to the genre, as in King's *Green Grass, Running Water*, Abel's books are almost entirely negative in their assessment, because the "found" text disperses and excludes Indigenous voices. There's a somewhat positive twist: the "found poem" conceit. It enables a productive irony (however depressing it might also be) of the "Indian" finding his voice or at least *a* voice in all the words of "cowboys."

The Searchers and *Maliglutit*

Having considered some significant examples of rethinking the Western through Indigeneity, with significant representation from Indigenous writers such as Abel, King, Gottfriedson, and the collaborators on *Gabriel Dumont's Wild West Show*, I want to approach the following chapter and its realignment of the West toward the North by transitionally considering Zacharias Kunuk and Natar Ungalaaq's 2016 film *Maliglutit*, the second-ever feature film in Inuktitut (the first being their *Atanarjuat: The Fast Runner*, from 2001). The film's Inuktitut title, which is translated as "followers" in the subtitles, refers to John Ford's 1956 film *The Searchers*. Both films involve a kidnapping and a quest to retrieve the kidnapped person or people, but they differ greatly in location and racial commentary. *Maliglutit* is set in the Far North and comprised entirely of Inuit characters; *The Searchers* is set mainly in the American Southwest and features white, mixed, and Indigenous characters. *The Searchers* gave John Wayne one of his most unforgettable roles, as a former soldier driven both to racist desecration of a Comanche body and to unspeakable rage at the thought of miscegenation between his niece and a Comanche chief. Its ending is iconic, an almost still-life picture of a seemingly injured Wayne turning away, blocked off by the backlit doorframe of a home where he can never belong. This symbolism of the hero who cannot settle and must move on, even as he enables others to settle, is a Western convention that depends on a dichotomy of wide open space and settlement. "I grew up on the land," Kunuk said in 2017 of the area around Igloolik; "when I was a child I thought we were the only people on Earth" (qtd. in "Zacharias Kunuk Reimagines"). Kunuk and Ungalaaq move *The Searchers* into the North, where wide open spaces remain partly protected by the harshness of the landscape itself. Cian Cruise explains that, "[d]espite being set in the north, *Maliglutit* is a western through and through. It's got a harsh landscape where folk eke out an existence, a homestead vibe with each isolated igloo days apart on the tundra and a social space where individuals must enforce their own law" ("*Maliglutit*"). (It also needs a figure of the cowboy—more on this below.) Kunuk and Ungalaaq's Indigenous intervention into the Western is to use the North as a stand-in for the West, an intervention that other writers and directors have already suggested but without such a direct relationship to a single classic American Western such as *The Searchers*. In creating the direct relationship, they can go beyond geography and symbolism into differences of narrative, implying that geographic and symbolic analogues do not determine the narrative.

Kunuk did not start out with questions but was subjected to the sway of the Western. At some residential schools, where Indigenous children were forcibly re-educated in English, children were shown Westerns, and, as one survivor of these schools has said, they often "re-enacted some of the more dramatic scenes of the movie and of course we played cowboys and Indians. Everyone wanted to be a cowboy; nobody wanted to be an Indian" (Miller 281). Echoing many other Indigenous people who have been fans of Wayne, Kunuk remembers being sent to school in Igloolik, where there was "a little community hall where they would show 16 millimetre movies. A lot of it was cowboys and Indians and John Wayne. . . . John Wayne was our hero" (qtd. in "Zacharias Kunuk Reimagines"). Later, Kunuk realized that the influence of the Western had been insidious, along with less subtle influences from Wayne's culture: "Four thousand years of oral tradition silenced by fifty years of priests, schools, and cable TV" (qtd. in Cruise). For this reason, Kunuk's two major films pay anthropological attention to the recovery of historical and cultural details. Kate Taylor describes it as "an almost documentary examination of pre-modern life in the Arctic" ("Maliglutit"). It ranges from types of clothing, food preparation, and travel, to invocations of oral tradition and religion, including, I presume, the spirit of the loon that Kuanana (Benjamin Kanuk) receives as a helper from his dying father, an elder. The loon's call sets Kuanana on the trail toward his kidnapped family, and it is simultaneously the narrative's call to its mythic past and to its parallel in the here and now.

When *Maliglutit* was being made, the Canadian government and various Indigenous organizations were beginning the consultations that eventually led to the National Inquiry into Missing and Murdered Indigenous Women and Girls (MMIWG), but reviews of the films have not yet emphasized how this context invites us to interpret the narrative. Most provocatively, the coincidence or the intention of the timing speaks back to the Vanishing "Indian" motif of Westerns, implying that in

Canada today a trope of genocide persists: "Vanishing" becomes "Missing and Murdered." With recent revelations of hundreds of unmarked graves near former residential schools in Western Canada (Eneas), the Vanishing "Indian" motif becomes even more relevant and real. (Some might argue that the trope cannot be genocidal if the violence is somehow limited by its gendered and unsystematic methods—however *systemic* it is—but the implication is compelling, especially under the broader rubric of cultural genocide.) Whereas *The Searchers* involves the kidnapping of a white girl by Comanche people, *Maliglutit* involves the kidnapping of an Inuit woman and her daughter by a banished Inuit gang. "Gone is the racial conflict at the core of Ford's film" (Cruise); instead, in *Maliglutit* the antagonism is all within a community. This variation in plots speaks to the MMIWG inquiry, which tends to focus on systemic problems introduced to Indigenous communities by colonists and the enforcers among them. Among its priorities, the MMIWG inquiry often airs the concern that the police are not equally diligent and determined when they are searching for Indigenous women compared to white women. *Maliglutit* offers a very Western solution: in the absence of law (at least, the absence of colonial police), seek justice on your own. Thus, Kuanana and his eldest son become "searchers" (or "followers") when Kuanana's wife and daughter are kidnapped in an assault on his family that leaves his youngest son and his two elders dead. With closer family ties than the uncle and niece in the precursor by Ford, *Maliglutit* emphasizes an intergenerational diversity that is not unlike the addition of "G" to the "W" in "MMIWG." Similarly for the males, Kuanana and his son are at risk because they are outnumbered by the gang, and they are aided (despite the women's efforts to escape) only by the gift of help from the loon. The spirit of the loon implies—as a commentary on the MMIWG inquiry—that Indigenous self-reliance and familial co-operation are not all that is required: so is a belief in the stories that draw power from myth and land.

The power of the loon, however, is spiritual or mental (i.e., as direction, as determination) compared to the physical power that Kuanana brings with him: his gun. Set around 1913, *Maliglutit* includes various signs of contact with explorers, and the gun is the most prominent. In his essay on the film, Cruise asserts that in *Maliglutit* "retribution is . . . a travesty. It is a failure" ("*Maliglutit*"). Much like the gun, this is a loaded statement.

On one hand, it is a success, not "a failure," when Kuanana and his family kill the kidnappers. On the other, it is indeed a failure if a colonial and Western symbol, the gun, must be used in the achievement of justice, and if justice must be death. Interpreted in this latter way, *Maliglutit* is deeply ironic: a "pro-Indian" Western that concludes with the social Darwinism of surviving by "virtue" of having the better weapon, not (necessarily) a better idea of justice or community.

The representation of the gun in *Maliglutit*, however, is nothing like the venerating gaze upon the phallic six-shooter that we see in so many Westerns. Although Kuanana's gun is the only one in the story and gains importance through this fact, it is a simple rifle with a worn stock, and until now he had used it primarily for hunting caribou. Contrary to the fantastically infinite supply of bullets in most action movies, in *Maliglutit* there are only three bullets. When Kuanana goes hunting on the advice of the elder who spoke with one of the spirits, Apisaaq, for guidance, his first shot is heard by Kupak from a distance, alerting him to the likelihood that the igloo would be relatively undefended—no armed man. The gun here is a liability, but Kuanana does get a caribou. The second shot, like the first, is not shown onscreen. Kuanana is chasing the gang and presumably fires at the gang member who was ordered to slow down for reconnaissance (killing him, I think). The distant sound sets off the women's escape attempt. In both cases, the gunshot is a signal that prompts action. Near the end, through terrain near Igloolik that is vaguely like Monument Valley—flat barrens with (short) flat-topped rocky outcroppings—Kuanana sneaks up and clobbers one of the three remaining bad guys with his gun stock. With his third and final shot, he kills the man who was straddling his beaten-down son and about to knife him. He then finds Kupak (Joey Sarpinak), the bear-spirited leader of the banished men. Kupak guesses correctly that Kuanana is out of bullets, and Kuanana's attempted intimidation with the gun therefore doesn't achieve the desired effect. Larger, stronger, and a murderer, Kupak beats Kuanana with his cudgel. Then Kuanana's wife Ailla comes out of nowhere and spears Kupak when he is on Kuana, about to bludgeon him to death. In the context of MMIWG, the woman's action encourages women to fight back. Ailla becomes as much the cowboy as her husband is. In the context of the genre, her mastery of her own phallic symbol when her husband's is failing is a partial revision of the Western's strong association between men and guns.

It is a symbolic mastery, and it helps to return the shooting, for its viewers, to the realm of the unseen that Kuanana had to disturb to save his son. Keeping the first two shots out of sight minimizes the violence; it is not gratuitous, unlike in most Westerns. The third shot centres our attention on the gun as a tool to shift the dynamics of power and to defeat our enemies, but Ailla's effectiveness with a more traditional weapon implies that the filmmakers would prefer that guns remain distant—close enough to hear, but too far to be a danger to the people. In this respect, and probably only this respect, the gun is like Kalluliik, the spirit of the loon: invisible in its actions and therefore mythically powerful. For *Maliglutit*, there is a balance between the gun and Kalluliik. Both are necessary to find and defeat the enemy, but Kalluliik is not violent. Like Apisaaq, Kalluliik is a source of knowledge, not a destroyer.

Pushing gun violence off-screen is an example that I would use to support Jaymes Durante's conclusion that, as a potential "anti-colonialist rebuke," the film is "surprisingly composed and non-confrontational" ("*Maliglutit*"). But this semblance is not only a result of the film's long shots, which sometimes hardly stray from establishing shots; it is also a result of the remoteness of colonial activity. Durante observes: "That it's set in 1913—nine years before *Nanook [of the North]* and 45 after Ford's Civil War-set *The Searchers*—isn't at all evident, barring the ongoing presence of a set of binoculars [actually, a telescope] and the late appearance of a rifle. The film has a peculiar, culturally specific relationship with time, influenced no doubt by the far north's extreme location and its eternal days and nights" ("*Maliglutit*").

While Durante points the film up, if up is north, and if the North is a new West (as I argue in the next chapter), Travis Hopson orients it differently: "If you thought *The Revenant* looked cold, *Searchers* [*Maliglutit*] is closer to an icy Hell" ("Filmfest"). Certainly the notion of a bi-directional, vertical Christian frame for the story has some merit, because the directors are so obviously alluding to the Ford and Wayne collaboration—but Hopson also echoes a colonial discourse in his conclusion: "*Searchers* may prove too culturally specific for some audiences, but for those looking to experience a rarely-explored civilization through the frame of a Western classic, this is a film to seek out" ("Filmfest"). Searching, for viewers, becomes a problematic exploration, but at least it's of the art of cinema.

The third chapter will consider exploration and settlement in greater detail, mainly in relation to the "Muscular Christian" that Candida Rifkind and Daniel Coleman have investigated in early Canadian Westerns and their Mounties, but in this chapter we have considered the related figures of John Wayne and Gabriel Dumont. For Soleymanlou and the writers of *Gabriel Dumont's Wild West Show*, Dumont is the historical figure who can resist the cultural persuasion of a star of the Western such as Wayne. Dumont's recontextualization alongside the Western appears to be mainly a non-Indigenous act of imagination, and it may evince a feeling of identification that problematically extends from a more justifiable recognition of similarities between the Métis resisting Canada, on the one hand, and Canada resisting the United States and its popular culture, on the other. But Kunuk, Gottfriedson, Abel, and even King are less preoccupied with fighting fire with fire and look instead to more novel methods of resisting. For Kunuk and collaborators on *Maliglutit*, the entire narrative of colonial versus Indigenous violence is rewritten as an intracultural drama in which race is not an issue except in the subtext of its response to Ford's *The Searchers*. For King in *Green Grass, Running Water*, despite his sympathy for fans of John Wayne, the alternative is less a Canadian star or hero than the mythic figures of Coyote and the spirits of what he calls the Old Indians. For Abel in *Injun*, the alternative is the non-Indigenous reader whose experience of simulated assimilation and dispossession leads to a new awareness, but at the same time his method of distant reading effectively depersonalizes the reader's experience (another simulation, in fact) and inhibits many of the identifications with the characters of the Western. For Gottfriedson in *Whiskey Bullets*, characters of the Western such as the cowboy and the "Indian" are similarly appealing but also deeply problematic as stereotypes and role models, and so the alternative is Horsechild (a figure I will try to explain in chapter 5): a return to the land and to other animals whose spirits, like Kalluliik in *Maliglutit*, animate a relationship with the world that is more balanced and more just. These Indigenous texts (and one non-Indigenous) all contend with the Western and attempt to offer guidance in thinking through the personal and systemic problems exacerbated by the genre.

3

The Northwestern Cross
Christianity and Transnationalism in Early Canadian Westerns

In North America, the modern axis of colonialism—now mostly in its cultural-economic rather than settler phase—is vertical, or north–south, as the United States becomes arguably more and more successful as an arbiter of artistic culture and governmental affairs, at least in Canada if not also Mexico, and as a transnational corporate occupant of the entire continent and much of the world. Canada, too, has been recently vertically colonial, encouraging renewed military surveillance, economic exploration, and settlement in the North. From the very late fifteenth century to the late nineteenth, however, the primary axis of colonialism here was horizontal, east–west. The east–west railroad was completed relatively peacefully because the North-West Mounted Police were there in the later 1870s and 1880s to protect its development and because Indigenous peoples were therefore already exhausted after years of fighting. The Mountie is a crucial figure in the settling of the West—a figure equivalent to what I have elsewhere called the outlaw-lawman: often a vigilante but sometimes a sheriff akin to the modern "rogue cop" that Clint Eastwood popularized through the Dirty Harry films beginning in the 1970s.[1] This chapter will show that the Mountie and symbolic lawmen in Canadian Westerns were, at times, surprisingly different from the upstanding and dutiful ideal. And as this sort of lawman—a figment of the imagination as

---

1   See the bibliography for my already noted essay on the outlaw-lawman in Eastwood's transitional and rogue-cop films.

155

opposed to a historical figure—he brought the law not only to the West; Robert Thacker explains that "[o]nce the prairies were settled, of course, the Mounted Police moved into the north as the next frontier" ("Mountie" 165). Novelists such as Ralph Connor and H. A. Cody often imagined that the law the Mountie carried from west to north was fundamentally Christian, a moral code suitable to what their American contemporary James Oliver Curwood called "God's country" (qtd. in Brégent-Heald, "James" 692). If we may imagine two maps of the same land and water, the later version superimposed over the earlier, the horizontal and vertical axes would form a cross.[2]

The image of the cross, on the one hand, has no necessary symbolism: it is simply a geographical coincidence that this chapter uses to stitch geography to genre and religion. On the other, the cross as a symbol of Christianity was and is a motivating factor in the colonial settlement of the West and North, one that cannot be ignored in the early Canadian Westerns, just as crossing over between genres was a technique that enabled Connor and perhaps especially Cody to transmit their religious messages. Building on the genre-nation connections from chapter 1, this chapter suggests that crossover genres—the Northern or Northwestern and the Western, but also adventures for boys and the Western—were strategically transitional, serving the nation-state and its nascent military-industrial complex by training young readers into adults who would be morally receptive to imperial actions such as westward expansion, settlement, and war.[3]

When the railroad reached the already settled West Coast in 1885, horizontal colonialism was symbolically complete, and so the symbolic expansion had to change direction; the industrial capitalism of the railway, its associated national project, and Christianity all worked on principles of expansion and growth (Wood 204). Creating the appeal of this

---

2   I do not mind the echo in this vertical-horizontal cross of Laurie Ricou's *Vertical Man / Horizontal World* (1973). I briefly mentioned some of Ricou's work in the first chapter of this book in one of the sections on regionalism.

3   I leave "the nation-state" deliberately vague here, but some might argue that Canada does not have a military-industrial complex, at least not one anywhere near the magnitude of the one in the United States. As I will show, however, Connor and Cody offered both real and fictional support to the United States and the internationally shared war effort, so if nothing else it refers to the United States.

"next frontier" in the United States and the Canadian East has been called "destination branding" (Brégent-Heald, "James" 692). The new direction was evident in the immediate emergence of a variant of the Western—e.g., John Mackie's *Sinners Twain* (1895) and Jack London's *Son of the Wolf* (1902) and *Call of the Wild* (1903)—called the Northern or Northwestern, whose earliest Canadian proponents, Ralph Connor and H. A. Cody, happened to be Christian ministers.[4]

Although I try to avoid re-inscribing a hierarchy by thinking of the Northern or Northwestern more as a variant and less as a sub-genre, Richard G. Baker correctly identifies the power dynamics when he writes that, "in replacing the Western's amorphous and generic frontier with Canadian territory, the Northern implicitly redefines Canada as the American frontier. In this sense, the sub-genre itself positions Canada as a subordinate element inside an American self-narrative" (109). If the generic lineage of Western and Northwestern is implausible even in the slightest, notice that almost all the characters in Cody's *The Long Patrol: A Tale of the Mounted Police* (1912) get classic Western names, like Buckskin Dan, Siwash Bill, Shifty Nick, and Old Meg—everyone a sobriquet. And the vernacular is pure Western. In Connor's *Black Rock* (1898), one of the men exclaims about the minister, "Ain't he a clinker! I'll be gee-whizzly-goldusted if he ain't a malleable-iron-double-back-action self-adjusting corn-cracker" (149). He might as well be riffing on a banjo. And in *The Long Patrol*, "If we kin, we must reach Hishu afore Windy Pete gits thar" (135), says Buckskin Dan. The elision of the cussing—for example, "them d— Yellow-legs" (54)—is one of the usual tactics of purifying the genre in the novels by Cody and Connor. Although they could be liberals in blending genres, they were usually religious conservatives in their messaging.

Connor is known today among diligent readers of Canadian literature and its history, but Cody is not, nor was he as popular in his and Connor's day—but they worked together with later writers to establish the genre that provides the best literary evidence of the West's turn to the North

---

4   Others included the American James B. Hendryx's 1918 novel *Connie Morgan with the Mounted*; the Scottish-American Laurie York Erskine's series that began in 1922 with *Renfrew of the Royal Mounted*; the American James Oliver Curwood's 1926 novel about Mounties, *The Flaming Forest*; the British-Canadian Roderick Haig-Brown and his somewhat later 1954 novel *Mounted Police Patrol*.

that I theorized while thinking through the idea of North in the introduction and first chapter. In this chapter, I will eventually consider some of the subtleties of genre, such as crossover, in which they worked; but first I will show how various representations of the Northwest—focusing on its iconic Mountie and other symbols of law and order—concentrated on a brand of heroism that conveyed colonial attitudes about the West and North and the First Nations and Inuit who had preceded them in living there. Cody's *The Long Patrol* and Connor's *Corporal Cameron of the North West Mounted Police* (1912), with their physically imposing and morally assertive heroes—"Christians in action" (Gordon 15)—exemplify the "Muscular Christianity" (Rifkind 134; Coleman 128-9) associated with the new Boy Scout movement (est. 1910) that Cody promoted in his Westernesque *Rod of the Lone Patrol* (1916) and that Laurie York Erskine perpetuated in his later series of Mountie novels and their spinoffs. Candida Rifkind, in an essay on Erskine's Renfrew of the Mounted novels, quotes a *New York Times* reviewer of Erskine's *The River Trail* (1923):

> Most of the novels that are concerned with the life and people of the wilder regions in the west and northwest of Canada represent the flow of population as being wholly between the east and the west of the Dominion. . . . But Mr. Erskine indicates a considerable movement north and south, not only across the boundary line but far south in the United States. (qtd. in Rifkind 131)

In fact, this "considerable movement" has a parallel in literature that was made prominent through earlier examples such as Connor and Cody. Through them, the imagined line from east to west gained a new dimension, a north–south line, which promised that the wilderness (however inhabited and understood it already was by Indigenous peoples) would remain open to adventure and prospecting—and open to taming.

The Nation in the Northern and Northwestern

In beginning this chapter with an emphasis on a transition from the West (and South) to the North, I also hope to explain some of the transnational dynamics of both the American and Canadian Westerns. Canada produced or was the setting for hundreds of the variant known as the Northern or Northwestern, whether in magazines, novels, or films, from the 1910s to the 1940s. In truth, most of the films were American visions of Canada, usually the Northwest (and so Northwesterns are not necessarily Canadian, and Canadian Westerns do not necessarily include all Northwesterns, though I do call Northwesterns "Canadian Westerns" when they are written by Canadians or published in Canada). American authors of comic books and pulp fiction looked northward to Canada for heroes and tales, such as *Zane Grey's King of the Royal Mounted* comic (1935–54). Although critics who were writing as early as 1911 were complaining of the historical inaccuracies in the Western (Altman, *Film/Genre* 38), Pierre Berton in *Hollywood's Canada* (1975) echoed the grievance, partly because impressions of Canada could be distorted by those inaccuracies. He noted that, between 1907 and 1975, "American film companies . . . produced 575 motion pictures in which the plot has been set entirely or mainly in Canada" (16). When Berton examines the titles of these films (in an early example of distant reading), he discovers that "Canada was never Hollywood's favourite word" (19). Instead, of the several hundred films, 79 include in their titles the words "North, Northwest, Northern, or Northwoods," and fifty use the words "Wild, Wilderness, or Trail" (19). Although Berton argues that "everybody knew . . . that the setting was north of the border" (19), the occlusion of "Canada" might also suggest that, paratextually, American producers wanted to minimize the Canadianness of the films to appeal to the American desire for a general nordicity that could include the northern states or, more likely, be "the next stage of the frontier" (Walden 170). Novels by Americans that served a similar purpose include London's *Call of the Wild*; they renewed the sense of the open frontier that Americans sought after that part of the American West was settled and mythologized in the wake of the Civil War, the transcontinental railroad, and Buffalo Bill Cody's Wild West Show. These novels and films probably should not be described as a "Canadian influence" on American culture, because Americans were usually in charge of the productions. In many cases, Americans such as James Oliver Curwood—"history's most prolific screen contributor" (Berton, *Hollywood* 26)—wrote both the films and the stories on which they were based. Remarkably, however, Curwood was for a decade employed by the government of Canada as a travel writer in the Canadian West and North (Berton, *Hollywood* 27; Brégent-Heald, "James" 694–7); therefore, much of what he produced can be described as a Canadian influence, whether or not he wrote what the Canadians intended.

Assigning a single nationality to a text, writer, figure, or genre can be difficult, even when the Western seems to be so geographically specific. In *Visions of Order* (1982), Keith Walden names several writers of Northwesterns who had one or two nationalities and lived and/or wrote in other countries: Joseph Holliday, James B. Hendryx, Louis Charles Douthwaite, William Lacey Amy (a.k.a. Luke Allan), and Laurie York Erskine. Similarly, William H. Katerberg observes that Robert Service was an "Englishman-become-Canadian" (543) whose memorable poem "The Shooting of Dan McGrew" (1907) later became the American president Ronald Reagan's favourite, a "classic 'American' story" set in Canada's North that belies Canada's relatively moderate gun culture but "suggests the influence of American myth on how Canadians imagine their own frontiers" (544); it also suggests that "Western myths do indeed cross borders, and in more than one direction" (557).[5] Walden asks, "What national perspective did they [from the list above] write from? In many cases it is impossible to tell, although it may be significant that the figure of the Mounted Policeman appealed to authors with migrant backgrounds" (152). The promise of a new frontier was probably a more significant factor, and on this new frontier a modern cowboy was needed. What nationality was the Mountie? British? Canadian? Walden explains that the Mountie was, crucially, a figure of *order* whose appeal declined in Britain when the British dream of order through empire began to decline too, and a figure who was temporarily appealing to Americans because he was, in effect, a cowboy-detective: a hero familiar from a different and more urban genre who could sustain "the old individualist ethic" (169) of the cowboy while

---

5   Beyond the scope of this chapter, Luke Price, my prime example of uncertain nationality from the 1940s era of pulp fiction (in chapter 4), might have been an American writing under a pseudonym and publishing in Canada. From the contemporary set interpreted in other chapters of this book, Michael Ondaatje, Paulette Jiles, Thomas King, and Patrick deWitt are further examples. Their border crossings attest to an ever-increasing personal and cultural mobility associated with globalization, and globalization—despite all its estrangements—can minimize national differences even as it increases national subtleties.

managing with ease the modern, efficient, technocratic, orderly world.[6] Although Berton argues that Hollywood's version of Canada in general is primitive (*Hollywood* 75), and Dawson argues that "Mountie literature was an expression of Canadian antimodernism" (43), from an American perspective the Mountie himself was relatively modern: an emissary of Eastern cities, the first protector of the railroads and telegraph lines of modernity. He was a compromise. During the Mountie's cinematic heyday in the first half of the twentieth century, he therefore offered hope, through his appropriation into the American imagination, that the United States could forestall the future implied in Frederick Jackson Turner's 1893 warning about the closure of the American frontier and the total modernization and decline of American society (Walden 168–9). In that respect, the Mountie was an American figure who reassured viewers that an urban-rural/modern-traditional balance would be possible in the future. In fact, for five much later years (1995–2000), the Disney Company even gained ownership of the licensing rights to the Royal Canadian Mounted Police. Incredible, eh?

The Mountie's Americanization was not only the result of American anxieties, prognoses, and writings. In some cases, novels by Canadian writers served as source material, however loosely, for the films in Berton's catalogue. Connor's *The Sky Pilot* (1899) was adapted into what was described in the media as "an exceedingly good western," which meant partly that it had a lot of "thrilling punches" (qtd. in Berton, *Hollywood* 20). Connor's novels do stage several fight scenes, but they are often not so gratuitous as they are signs of the Muscular Christianity of his heroes—such as in the titular Mountie in his 1912 novel *Corporal Cameron*. "But in Hollywood's Canada, Mounties drew their guns on the slightest provocation" (Berton, *Hollywood* 122). In fact, such gunplay appears in a novel by a Canadian as early as 1912, before the trend of the Americanization of the Mountie; in Cody's *The Long Patrol*, the Mountie shoots first—and at *the back* of a retreating enemy (129–30)—a wild departure from the ideals of the never-shoot-first North-West Mounted Police. Quite possibly,

---

6 See also Ronald Sutherland's *The New Hero* (1977), which succinctly traces this "old individualist ethic" through different strains of Puritan thought in the United States and Canada, and which finds the origin of the later anti-heroism in the figure of "the loser" who is "crushed by a regimented system" (4), whether a government, an economy, or a family.

The Long Patrol is a Canadian Americanization in this detail: a writer in Canada dramatizing a Canadian figure through a lens trained on (or by) quick-shooting American cowboys and sheriffs. Much later, from the 1970s through to the 1990s (when in the latter part of the decade Disney owned the "brand"), this American influence turned from sensationalism to revisionism, helping to clean up the Mountie's image and "sanitiz[e] narratives of the North American West" (Gittings, "Imagining Canada"). Ultimately, producers of American culture, not exclusively of the American Western, used Canada as it wished and influenced Canadian writers, while Canada had a small influence on the United States thanks to Canadian writers—but a much larger influence thanks to their geography, which was close and continuous with the relative South.

Cody and Connor

Cody was an Easterner—like some writers who popularized tales of the frontier, such as Owen Wister, who was from Philadelphia,[7] and Theodore Roosevelt, who was from New York City—and, like these men, Cody gained insight into the West by travelling there. He lived and worked in Whitehorse as an Anglican minister from 1904 to New Year's Eve 1909. He returned to New Brunswick and eventually published twenty-four novels in a career that was closely contemporary with Connor's. Rodger J. Moran states that Connor's and Cody's books "were amongst the first to be mass-produced in North America due to their accessible prose, Christian themes and appeal to a broad audience" ("Hiram"). Although the reviews of Cody's novels were mixed, they were generally positive initially (Jones 192; Scott 144). Cody's first novel, *The Frontiersman* (1910), was in an edition of ten thousand copies (Jones 180) and "placed Cody's name with some of the most popular writers of his day" (179)—a popularity in the thousands rather than Connor's millions at that time (MacLaren 508), but an accomplishment. It was due partly to the fact that there were many promotional Christian newspapers and magazines when Cody began writing in the first decade of the twentieth century (Jones 118), and partly because

---

7   Wister was from Philadelphia, but his model in *The Virginian* (1902)—the twentieth-century origin of the cowboy—appears to have been Everett Johnson, a Virginian who later became an Albertan, as John Jennings argues throughout his 2015 book *The Cowboy Legend*.

he intentionally followed the success of writers such as Connor, Gilbert Parker, and London (Scott 142; Jones 112, 122, 177), with the latter's *Call of the Wild* in 1903 and *White Fang* in 1906 also set in the Northwest. In 1906, Cody entitled one of his poems "The Call of the Deep" (Jones 117); later he entitled another "The Call of the Parson" (Jones 144), titles that seem to allude to *Call of the Wild* and to a poem from 1907 by Service that borrows London's title verbatim. Service was a friend of Cody (Jones 104), and he and London served Cody as a mix of precedents and contemporaries.

Moran also states that "[w]hile HA Cody is not considered a pioneer of Canadian literature, his novels deftly capture the interests and spirit of the age in which he lived and wrote" ("Hiram"). Cody is certainly not yet "considered" as such, but he was more or less contemporary with Connor. Eli MacLaren describes Connor as a "pioneer" (507) for having been so successful as a Canadian writing about Canadians when the country was still under imperial copyright, as it would be until 1924. Connor preceded Cody in writing works set in the Northwest, as with *Black Rock* in 1898 and *The Doctor of Crow's Nest* (1906), but Cody was on his heels and was an equal "pioneer" of the Northwestern, insofar as the genre needs a Mountie. With *The Long Patrol* in 1912, Cody expanded his earlier interest in the Northwest to include what Thacker calls "the embodiment of the human force necessary to create Canada out of a vast wilderness" ("Canada's" 302)—a pioneering police force. Although Connor was "undoubtedly the most influential Canadian writer of Mountie narratives" (Dawson 42), his novel *Corporal Cameron of the North West Mounted Police* was published in 1912, the same year as Cody's *The Long Patrol*, and two years after Cody's *Frontiersman*. Cody was no latecomer. Along with Connor, London, and Service (who wrote about Mounties in a ballad published in 1911 called "Clancy of the Mounted"), Cody and his early success with the Mountie was contemporary with Curwood's *Philip Steele of the Royal Northwest Mounted Police* (1911) and the later *The Flaming Forest* of 1923, and Erskine's series of Renfrew of the Mounted novels, which were published between 1922 and 1941 and which spun off into American film, radio, and television (Rifkind 136–7). He was a pioneer, but, as I have suggested, the Northwestern was an expression of a zeitgeist that inspired many.[8]

Connor needs less introduction, but he still might be "the most popular Canadian novelist that most Canadians have never heard about" (Dummitt 68)—and "a name which is virtually lost in the mists of time" (Watt 7). "Ralph Connor" was born Charles W. Gordon in 1860 in Canada West, now Ontario. He studied at the University of Toronto and at Edinburgh, became a Presbyterian minister in 1890, and in that decade worked for almost four years as a missionary in Banff, Alberta, before settling into a job in Winnipeg, which was then still "a frontier town notorious for its tavern brawls" (Wilson 14, 16). In 1897, he began writing fiction to raise money for the church. After the runaway success of *Black Rock* in 1898 and a series of quickly written and quickly published novels, he was producing something resembling pulp fiction except for its Christianity and hardback format. In other words, it was not seedy or as cheap as the stuff published in magazines, but it had some of the qualities that result from haste or urgency. His early novels are accurately described by Terrence Craig as "fast-paced, sentimental melodramas, with stereotyped characters dramatizing the conflict between good and evil in frontier settings presided over by exemplary churchmen" ("Ralph Connor"). (In this respect, he was like Cody.) Connor "always believed that the church should be militant in social issues and he never shied away from any consequent political involvement" (Wilson 22). Then Connor served in France during the First World War. He was "a padre in the field" (Webb 42) and had the rank of major, a dual role that gave him credibility when he travelled to the United States to drum up support for the war. Later he wrote the frankly propagandistic novels *The Major* in 1917 and *The Sky Pilot in No Man's Land* in 1919, which Peter Webb includes among other "ideologically complacent, aesthetically dated, and perhaps morally troubling" (46) war fictions. Connor died in 1937, and his reputation persisted until the 1960s (MacGillivray 8).

Critics tend to agree that his best books were his first—*Black Rock* (1898), *The Sky Pilot* (1899), *The Man from Glengarry* (1901), and *Glengarry*

---

8   See also Desmond Pacey's lists of Northwesterns and Canadian Westerns (660) (the latter of which I relayed in the introduction).

School Days (1902)—the first two of which were set in the West. People now have a divided view of where to place Connor. W. L. Morton calls him "a clerical Jack London" (qtd. in Gordon 13), and Connor's own son, J. King Gordon, writes of his father that "[h]e never ceased to be a Westerner" (13); "[f]or half a century his work was built into [the West's] history" (15). Although Connor lived in Manitoba and Alberta, Donald G. Stephens claims that he had the approach of "the visitor, the person from another background, schooled in the traditions of the nineteenth century and spurred on by his great faith in God" (3). (In this respect, too, he was like Cody.) Roy Daniells describes Connor as a man whose true landscape was the Ontario in which he was born and raised, and which featured in some of his novels (17, 18); he claims, too, however, that "Connor's own emphasis is on western expansion as absorptive of all energies, a cure for all enmities" (25). As I wrote previously about regions functioning as nations, the West was therefore a feature of his "utopianism" and his participation in a "tradition of national ebullience" (MacGillivray 8).

His nationalism was strong enough that he not only earnestly repeated propaganda in some scenes of his war novels *The Major* and *The Sky Pilot in No Man's Land* (Webb 32, 40); he also brought his message to politicians in person. Connor was to some extent influential (at least with the potential of having had influence) in the United States, having been invited to the White House in 1905 by the American president Theodore Roosevelt—himself a defining figure in the ideology of the West—and sent on a speaking tour of the country in 1917 by Canadian prime minister Robert Borden to encourage American involvement in the First World War (MacLaren 508). "His international fame as a novelist . . . stood him in good stead" (Wilson 35) as he sought contributions to ending the war swiftly and decisively, to the extent that "his success did something to hasten American entry into the war" (36).

Mountie Fiction and the Northwestern as Genre

Rifkind states that, as a perhaps surprising result of the work of authors such as Connor and Cody, "northern and western Canada . . . occupied a central place in American and British popular culture of the early twentieth century" (137). Some of the hundreds of American films set in Canada before the mid-twentieth century starred major Hollywood players such as Errol Flynn and Alan Ladd (Hutchison xiii). "Between 1890 and 1940, authors produced well over one hundred and fifty Mountie novels" (Dawson 35) that were published in Toronto but also New York and London. This production was part of what Dominique Brégent-Heald calls "the Dominion's experimental media strategy" ("James," 693), specifically in the government's hiring of Curwood to write of the North. Dawson explains that "[w]hile the popularity of Mountie movies peaked in the 1930s, the classic Mountie myth was by no means exhausted" (49). In 1925, the pulp magazine *North-West Stories* emerged and was so popular that *Complete Northwest Novel Magazine* and *Real Northwest* responded as competition in the 1930s (Hutchison xii). Illustrated Mounties followed trends from the 1930s and appeared with their pistols drawn on the covers of magazines such as the French-Canadian *Policier* and others during the Canadian pulp fiction boom of the 1940s (Driscoll, "Tales from the Vault!"). Genre specialists such as Ryerson Johnson and William Byron Mowery made names writing Mountie fiction (Hutchison xvii). The American movies eventually stole the show, playing the lead role in crystallizing the genre for audiences in the United States and probably also in Canada. MacLaren recounts that Americans effectively stole Connor's first novel, 1898's *Black Rock*, by taking advantage of its lack of copyright protection in the United States, thereby bringing the North into the South. On the one hand, you might say that the American culture appropriated the Canadian, or on the other that the Canadian culture promoted the Northwest to take advantage of American interest.

One might even argue that the heyday of the iconic Western of the 1940s and '50s would not have been quite so heady if it were not for the earlier success of the Northwestern—a case of the spinoff promoting the original, or the sub-genre helping the genre to rise to its zenith. For Rifkind, "Mountie fiction" (127) is a sub-genre of the Northwestern, itself a sub-genre (a term I will call into question below), and I think this is true, but the generic lineage circles back to the top, as Rifkind acknowledges by calling Northwesterns "adventure stories of a frozen northern territory in which Mounties replace the heroic sheriffs of American Westerns" (124). Rifkind continues: "Northwesterns typically draw on similar values to Westerns when it comes to the conquest of indigenous territories and the civilizing mission of white settlers and soldiers in North America" (127).

Ronald Tranquilla sees differences in how the two genres "seem to embody divergent perceptions of national identity in the two countries, especially egalitarian and democratic vs. elitist and oligarchic values; the primacy of self-indulgence vs. the necessity of self-restraint; and individualism vs. collective behavior" (75), but some of the examples below are exceptions to Tranquilla's rule and help to explain why the Northwestern would be so appealing to Americans. Thacker argues that "Americans were longing for another frontier and so adopted and adapted the Canadian mountie— first in fiction, then in film—as a way of obtaining one" ("Mountie," 165). More than any factor in the Western's popularity in the 1940s and '50s was probably the widespread adoption of television in the latter decade— but genres tend to need occasional variants to remain popular, and there were many years between Wister's *The Virginian* (1902) and the 1940s. The Northwestern is an example of the West turning North for new but related material.

The relatedness is close indeed, as a comparison of representations of the West and North reveals. One film critic commented on a Mountie movie by writing that "Saskatchewan might as well have been in Texas" (qtd. in Hutchison xiv). In Wister's *The Virginian*, one of the classics of the American Western, the West is an "unfeatured wilderness" (7). In Cody's *The Long Patrol*, the North is "the vast wilderness" (33). In Connor's *Corporal Cameron*, echoed later by Curwood (in an echo chamber of ideological statements then and now), it is "God's own open country" (187). Implicitly or explicitly, here the North and West are open to colonization, open to being shaped by the dreams of the colonizers. Both regions are therefore understood, from the very beginning, as constructions or as places where the idea of West or North could be performed. Signalling the fact of his persona and its potential inauthenticity, Wister's Virginian is introduced as "a false alarm" (5, 6) (some of his first actions being those of a prankster), and the town of Medicine Bow has many houses that "wore a false front to seem as if they were two stories high" (13). Connor's Cameron has "his vision of himself as a wealthy rancher, ranging over square miles of his estate upon a 'bucking broncho,' [sic] garbed in the picturesque cowboy dress" (138). For Cody in *The Long Patrol*, "the vast wilderness was the stage, with rushing rivers, foaming rapids, wind-swept lakes, sweeping plains and towering mountains, the setting, and dare-devil white men and roving Indians the chief actors" (195). On this "stage," the players play for rewards that are not only spiritual. Near the end of *The Virginian*, Molly's great-aunt says, "New Hampshire was full of fine young men in those days. But nowadays most of them have gone away to seek their fortunes in the West. Do they find them, I wonder?" (501). The Virginian replies, "Yes, ma'am. All the good ones do" (501). In *Corporal Cameron*, a character tells of the "big ranches further West" and says, "The railways are just building and people are beginning to go in. But ranching needs capital, too. It must be a great life! They practically live in the saddle. It's a glorious country!" (102).[9] Another then surmises that "a young man has better opportunities of making his fortune, so to speak, in the far West rather than in, say, Ontario" (102). Here, their language is of capitalism: capital, opportunity, fortune—all of which coincide with the putative openness of the frontier, North or West. It could also be described not only as "tourism promotion" but also "immigration propaganda" (Brégent-Heald, "James" 695).[10]

Why else would such a shift to the North be necessary? Recall that the Western and its icons of cowboy and "Indian" were established when the North American frontiers were already basically closed—Buffalo Bill's Wild West Show of the mid-1880s coinciding with the extension of the Canadian Pacific Railway to the West Coast in 1885, the American precedent having reached the West by 1869 (Blaise 40). Although the CPR's success led to what might be called a "boisterous era of western expansion" (Watt 8) when "all eyes were on the West" (13), a time that lasted until after the First World War, the earlier expansion in the United States was slowing. Richard Slotkin, paraphrasing Turner, explains that "an epoch... had ended in 1890 with the disappearance of the vast reserve of undeveloped land that had constituted the frontier" (*Gunfighter* 29). Slotkin brings together the major concerns of this turning point in American history:

> Many of the elements of the "Frontier Thesis" put forward by Turner and Roosevelt already belonged to the complex of

---

9 Actually living life in the saddle would most likely produce more saddle sores than exhortations of "a great life."

10 To my amusement, Curwood traded promotional articles for land in both cities of the West in which I have lived, Saskatoon and North Battleford (Brégent-Heald, "James" 697). He thus appeared to have bought his own shtick.

> traditional ideas that had accumulated around the idea of the "Frontier" since colonial times, including the concept of pioneering as a defining national mission, a "Manifest Destiny," and the vision of the westward settlements as a refuge from tyranny and corruption, a safety valve for metropolitan discontents, a land of golden opportunity for enterprising individualists, and an inexhaustible reservoir of natural wealth on which a future of limitless prosperity could be based. (*Gunfighter* 30)

Although the frontier was in reality still open to new developments in farming, logging, drilling for oil, and gold mining, its closure in the American imagination was a crisis (Slotkin, *Gunfighter* 30–1). Slotkin does not seem to consider it, but the remaining open frontier in the American and Canadian imaginations was in the Northwest, whether Alaska or the Yukon or the Canadian Badlands, and so the Northwestern helped to keep alive the myths of the West, including the imperialistic myth of continual territorial expansion and settlement—in other words, Manifest Destiny, the still problematic doctrine of justifiable colonization (and, less euphemistically, dispossession and destruction).

In Canada, the "destiny" of such an expansion relied partly on the Mountie, who is a key figure in Northwesterns as a variant of the Western. Referring to Connor's works but with relevance to Cody, Robert A. Kelly claims, "[w]hereas the American sense of Manifest Destiny is that the United States is destined to cover the continent from Atlantic to Pacific with the benefits of democracy and capitalism, [Connor's] sense of Manifest Destiny is connected with the place of Western Canada in the whole British Empire" (10–11). Much the same can be said about Cody and the Mountie fiction of *The Long Patrol*, and indeed Dick Harrison and Thacker identify the Mountie as "a metaphor of Canada's imperial ties" (Thacker, "Canada's" 299)—the main difference with American Westerns being simply the question of which empire.

The Outlaw-Lawman and Manifest Destiny

The Mountie is a figure whose code is upheld by "moral rather than physical force" (Hutchison xiv). Dawson explains that, "[f]rom the 1890s until the 1950s, books and films—as well as TV programs and comic books—depicted Canada's federal police force as a daring group of individuals who brought British justice and fair play to the less civilized peoples of the world: Native peoples, Eastern European immigrants, and French-Canadians" (53). One might add Americans, given that Americans tend to be represented by Cody and Connor in stereotypical ways too. As Connor implied when he told Roosevelt that Mounties made their arrests without drawing their guns (as I retell more fully later in this chapter), the Mountie code involved never shooting first, always respecting women, and dealing fairly with Indigenous peoples. Such restraint was supposed to be contrasted with the code of the American sheriff and federal marshal, who behaved a lot like the Lone Ranger, breaking the rules as if they were vigilantes, because the law was such a minor presence in the far-flung settlements and towns of the West that it was hardly in effect, and Indigenous protocols were not known or respected. Christine Bold explains in *The Frontier Club* (2013) that, in fact, the American laws themselves, from the late nineteenth century to at least the 1920s, were already encouraging different types of violence against Indigenous peoples and immigrants (169–70). In Canada, the laws have often been just as bad, but the idea persists that Canadian law and its representatives have been significantly more progressive.

Berton, however, offers a contradictory account from popular culture: "Movie Mounties always shot first and asked questions later" (qtd. in Dawson 49), and Dawson suggests that this "tendency . . . indicates Hollywood's incorporation of the Mounties into the myth of the wild American West" (49). Not everyone agrees entirely; George Bowering, in his novel *Caprice* (1987), reflects on earlier representations of Mounties in a dialogue between two outlaws, one American and one French Canadian (the latter speaking rather unexpectedly for his imagined community of Canadians[11]):

> "Well, when they get them wanted posters up everywhere, then we'll be famous, leastways in these parts, I mean in the

---

11   I am alluding, of course, to Benedict Anderson's *Imagined Communities: Reflections on the Origin and Spread of Nationalism* (1983).

beginning. And once we get famous folks will start to think of us as heroes. I mean like Jesse James and all. Especially the kids, eh? Kids really look up to famous outlaws."

"Not up here in this goddamned country," said Spencer. "Up here they think the goddamned Mounties are heroes. Cops!"

"No, no. You don't understand the way we are up here. I mean all that Mountie stuff. That's just the government version. That's just what some grown-ups and government people are trying to get across. I never heard of a kid yet that really thought the Mounties was heroes. No, everybody up here follows what's going on down there, 'cause that's where the books and songs comes from." (220–1)

Here, the morality of the outlaw or the Mountie is a perception determined by fame or infamy, and the perception is mainly determined by "where the books and songs comes from." Indeed, the many cover images from pulp magazines collected in Don Hutchison's *Scarlet Riders* (1998) glorify violence, almost always representing Mounties as intimidating, gun-firing heroes. "In many stories the Mountie did not follow the letter of the law but used his common sense and compassion to do the 'right' thing" (Dawson 34). Going back as far as Cody and Connor in 1912, the lawman is a Christian lawman, but there are some strange deviations from expected codes of conduct that show the strong resemblance of the figures of the lawman and outlaw even in these early Canadian Westerns.

Supporting Berton's view of these deviations, my favourite example is in Cody's *The Long Patrol* when the Mountie shoots first. A plot summary is probably in order. Set in "the North" (61), specifically "Northern Yukon Territory" (1–2) west of the Rockies (5), this is the story of Constable Norman Grey of the North-West Mounted Police and his final mission: to venture into unmapped territory to save a kidnapped child, Donnie, from the unfortunately named Siwash Bill and his gang, who are ransoming him for twenty thousand dollars (75). Among the novel's many credulity-straining coincidences, the mission is the pretext for Grey's reunion with his lost girlfriend Madeline, who was presumed dead six years earlier on a sunken steamer. She survived and has been living in the North when

Grey happens to find her, along with the boy. Ultimately, when Grey returns triumphant, having found not only the boy but also Madeline, they learn that her father's huge estate was destined for her, and they are immediately happily engaged.

Now, more to the point, Cody's *The Long Patrol* includes the premise that "there was the strict command instilled into every new recruit not to shoot first" (36). However, when Grey sees someone sneaking toward his camp in the middle of the night, along with "a sudden gleam from polished steel" (129), he does shoot first—and at someone's back.[12] "Quickly Grey brought the rifle to his shoulder and sent a leaden missive after the retreating form" (130). He interpreted the steel as "a gleaming knife" (130), not even as a gun that might require a proportionate response. Later, sneaking up on the "Indians" who kidnapped Donnie (after Donnie had been rescued from Siwash Bill), Grey

> longed to pick off those two dusky braves. Two quick reports and the deed would be done. . . . But another voice soon silenced this blood-thirsty desire. "Cowards," it whispered, "would you shoot them down without giving them a chance? You call yourself a man. You a member of a famous Force." (196)

When the "dusky braves" do force Grey and Dan to turn and fight, Grey is the one to want to snipe at the Indigenous men and kill them, but Dan says, "Don't do it, pardner. . . . Ye don't know them Big Lakes. We mustn't shoot unless they come at us fust" (204–5). There is obviously a moral dilemma here, a tension between a desire and a code. According to Christopher Dummitt in a line that applies as well to Cody, "[b]eing a hero in a Connor novel meant overcoming not only external foes but also the demons within" (74). Cody's Grey is a lawman who is almost an outlaw.

The outlaw-lawman is a classic symmetrical figure present in Westerns throughout the genre's evolution. In one of the first classic Westerns on

---

12   Patrick McGee explains that, in the historical context of Wister's *The Virginian*, "most of the victims of the WSGA [Wyoming Stock Growers Association] were shot in the back" (23). Wister himself was sympathetic to the WSGA (McGee 23).

film, *Stagecoach* (Ford, 1939), John Wayne plays the Ringo Kid, an escaped prisoner who takes the law into his own hands by seeking revenge for the murder of his brother and father at the hands of the Plummer brothers. King Mabry in Louis L'Amour's *Heller with a Gun* (1955) is a known killer who functions as a policeman by protecting life and property, while killing many a bad guy along his wandering way. Michael Ondaatje's Billy the Kid from 1970 is symmetrical with the sheriff, Pat Garrett (Deshaye, *Metaphor* 140, 146–7). Clint Eastwood's classic outlaw in *The Good, the Bad, and the Ugly* (Leone, 1966) is so aligned with his primary foe, Angel Eyes (Lee Van Cleef), that they are even partners for a time, as he is with the chaotic Tuco (Eli Wallach). One "ugly" or unpleasant to realize fact is that the good and the bad are so easily inverted. Eastwood's outlaw-lawman transforms in *Coogan's Bluff* (1968) into the rogue cop in the Dirty Harry movies of the 1970s (Deshaye, "Do I Feel Lucky?" 20). Images of symmetry and twinning help to define the morality and immorality of the bloodthirsty brothers in Gil Adamson's *The Outlander* (2007) and Patrick deWitt's *The Sisters Brothers* (2012). The outlaw-lawman—the "cowboy" in "cowboys and Indians"—might be called the bedrock of the Western if he were not such a shifting figure, one whose symmetry means moral ambiguity, an adherence to an unstated code.

Even before he shoots at the back of a retreating man, Constable Grey in *The Long Patrol* is introduced as a classic outlaw-lawman, one whose effortless intimidation and clothing are less like classic images of the early Mountie, in his red tunic and pillbox hat ("Uniforms"), and more like the stereotypical cowboy:

> the man ... straightened himself up to his full height of six feet with a sudden jerk, while his dark piercing eyes flashed questioningly from beneath the broad brim of his Stetson hat. A deep silence now pervaded the room; the poker chips ceased their rattle; the rustling of the newspapers stopped; the man behind the bar stayed his hand in the act of pouring a glass of ginger beer, and even pipes were allowed to go out. (1)

Cody writes soon thereafter: "A belt filled with cartridges encircled his waist, and his revolver sheathed in its leathern holster hung at his hip" (2). Grey later wears a buckskin jacket made by Buckskin Dan (138, 139–40). Grey is immediately established as "the man for [a difficult job]" (2), which is to save the boy kidnapped for ransom (4). Grey accepts the job despite his being only two weeks from leaving the force (7–8) after five years as a policeman (12), exhibiting some of the recklessness of the outlaw-lawman. In fact, it might be said that the symmetry of the outlaw-lawman is an enabler of Manifest Destiny, of the colonist who purports to adhere to an ethics but whose moral compromises include the (now) obvious blind spot toward Indigenous rights and precedence.

Explaining Grey's orders, the major shows Grey a spot on the map: "Everything else was a complete blank, no name of town or village appearing. Here the Major made a small circle, and wrote over it the one word 'Hishu' " (6)—a place "up Hishu Creek" (7) known only to the Indigenous people of the area. When the gang of kidnappers speculates, mystified, about the unlikely appearance of Grey to save the boy "in the nick of time" (53) (a theme of the novel) at the rapids, Shifty Nick exclaims, "How did he happen to be there! How does he happen to be here? How does he happen to be everywhere? Don't you know he's one of them d— Yellow-legs [i.e., a Mountie]? . . . Don't ye know that them Mounted Devils are everywhere?" (54). The dramatic irony is that the Mounties were not "Devils" but guardian angels presiding over even the "complete blank" of unmapped and supposedly unclaimed territory. They claimed the land not only for country but also king. When Cody published the novel in 1910, the word "Royal" had been added six years before (1904) to the name "North-West Mounted Police," signifying the monarchy and by extension the British Empire (Butts) and through it the Canadian desire to assimilate the "Indians" and their lands and be distinct from other nations.

The Canadian analogue of Manifest Destiny was partly a defensive expansion to prevent a revolutionary country from gaining ground. It was, too, a defensive expansion against the Métis and Cree who were involved in the North-West Resistance of 1885 in what is now Saskatchewan. Several forts already existed in the West, and so the railway as symbol is to me more relevant as a defence against American Manifest Destiny as expressed by the purchase of Alaska from Russia in 1867 (the year of Canadian Confederation, thus a year in which the United States and Canada were evidently jockeying for position). By now it should also be obvious that, as I consider different threats to Canadian nationalism, I am more sympathetic to First Nations and Native American influence than to American influence (though I have had far more exposure to the latter). Although treaties with the First Nations were well under way by the 1870s, their consent to the treaties was not freely given (King, *Inconvenient* 87); one of the major problems with Manifest Destiny in both countries was that, as ideology and policy, it was not a platform for dealing fairly with the legitimate presence of Indigenous peoples in the supposedly open, empty North and West. According to Thomas King, the impression of emptiness was produced partly by "removals and relocations [which], as federal policies in both countries, allowed Whites to steal Aboriginal land and push Native people about the countryside" (*Inconvenient* 97), out of sight and partially out of mind.

The dealings were predisposed to unfairness partly by the biases of missionaries who went to the North and West, the same people—like Cody and Connor—who later told stories about the region that circulated widely in the relative East and encouraged an East-West rapprochement. I am wary of what Coleman has called the "scholarly dismissals" (129) of Muscular Christianity, as if not a single dimension of Christianity could ever be called "progressive"; I accept Christopher Dummitt's argument that a contemporary analysis of Connor's Northwesterns (and I would add Cody's) might problematically "reduce a complex moral vision of the good to only one component [e.g., colonization], leaving the larger whole from which it emerged [i.e., the social gospel] unrecognizable" (79). I also admire many of the traits of Connor's (and Cody's) heroes, including "the democratic and egalitarian sensibility" (Dummitt 82) that they and their authors seem to have. I cannot, however, be other than critical of the genre's position in that "whole," partly because genre tends to be remarkably coherent and repetitive, and therefore ideologically powerful and potentially systemic. Dawson writes that, through authors such as Connor, "the Mounted Policeman . . . emerged as the personification of Christian social harmony and conservative gender, class, and ethnic ideals. He was a symbol of divinely ordained hierarchies, against which ethnic minorities, subordinate classes, and feminists could struggle but never prevail" (42–3).

The imagined destinies and religious missions in these novels are troubling; they are associated with an imperialism that magnifies their problems and extends their reach. Connor was a missionary while at Banff, as was Cody during his years in the Yukon. Jamie S. Scott shows that, in *The Frontiersman*, Cody's missionary in the Northwest is an "imperial hero" (142) akin to the Mountie. In *The Long Patrol*, Cody implies that the "vast unknown wilderness" (101)—and the Indigenous peoples therein—could be encompassed and drawn in by Christian love. Cody's fictional adventures also usually have a Christian romantic subplot. In *The Long Patrol*, Grey's loved one is presumed dead after her ship sinks during a voyage across the Atlantic. In a book published in October 1912 (Jones 193), this was probably a reference to the sinking of the *Titanic* in the previous April that has implications for the novel's significance in relation to globalization. Although *The Long Patrol* is in retrospect not very progressive, Madeline's survival of the *Titanic*-like shipwreck is a sign of hope that globalization, modernity, and civilization (all implicitly Christian) would not be set back by one symbolic loss. From the beginning, in fact, Grey is not convinced that she is dead. When he contemplates his very early retirement from the force, he thinks that he "could go home, but what was home without her? . . . How beautiful she was then in all her virgin purity! That was six years ago—and where was she now? Six years, and not a trace of her since!" (8). "He would find her, oh, yes. The world was large, he knew, but love would make it small" (12). In one of the incredible plot points of *The Long Patrol*, Grey finds her in the same unmapped territory in which he finds the kidnapped boy. She has gone to work in a log cabin known for sheltering at least one "fallen woman" (216, 249), so her "virgin purity" is at risk, partly because Siwash Bill intends to get her by whatever ominous "ways" (276) are necessary. Bill is a "white man" (217) but is married to Nadu, a Big Lake "Indian" (79), the miscegenation being one reason for his derogatory nickname. The missionary in the novel, Charles Nordis, remarks somewhat pointedly that his wife buried in the "Indian cemetery" (217) was not an "Indian." Although he is racialized as different from the Indigenous people, his name, Nordis, suggests that he is at home in the North—home because Christianity as a force of globalization will "make [the world] small" and safe for "virgin" and Christian "purity." The change of scale from large to small here is classic globalization.

According to some theorists, globalization is characterized by the "scalar dynamic[s]" (Appadurai 32) that I partly explained in the first parts of this book. In *Modernity at Large: Cultural Dimensions of Globalization* (1996), Arjun Appadurai coins the term "scape," a widely applicable suffix that I understand as a scalar landscape metaphor that helps us see human activities in terms of globalization—the plastic that I throw away that blows out of a landfill into the ocean and expands a gyre on the other side of the world, for example; or the money I contribute to a micro-lending program in my own city that indirectly benefits micro-lending abroad; or indeed the European idea of the colonized "Indian" that preceded North American colonization and later became a misconception of the North American "Indian" that circulated around the world and displaced Indigenous self-identifications. Appadurai states that "[t]he suffix *-scape* allows us to point to the fluid, irregular shapes of these landscapes" (46) of ethnicity, finance, technology, media, and ideology. For Cody and Connor and so many others, going West in Canada was a version of going West across the Atlantic from the United Kingdom and Europe. Before the railroad, travelling across the country would likely be more time-consuming and arduous than riding the waves; afterward, reaching the nascent towns and cities of the West was relatively easy. The future policeman's voyage in *Corporal Cameron* from Scotland to the Canadian West was so uneventful that it warranted not a single scene, except a minor drama with a train (described below). Journeys beyond the towns and cities into nature are the dangers. The thrill is going back to a place-time when world travel was not yet, not *quite*, so easy.

Transnational Crossing in the Canadian Western

If the invocation of globalization—a word that came to vogue in the 1990s—seems inappropriately anachronistic to the Western and its late nineteenth- and early twentieth-century origins in Canada, we might look to Nataša Ďurovičová's distinctions between *transnational, international,* and *global* in her work on world cinema. *Global* implies a totality, and that is too big a claim for the sub-genre of the Northwestern, which has even greater geographical specificity than the Western. *International* connotes diplomatic negotiations around mutual benefits related to the sovereignty of nation-states and governmentally organized trade across borders. It also implies "parity" between countries, according to Ďurovičová (x), and obviously parity does not always apply to the cultural exchanges of the United States and Canada today, though it still applied to the diplomatic era of the 1950s and '60s, when Canadian diplomacy expanded the St. Lawrence Seaway and Canadian peacekeeping was popular. In comparison, *transnational* suggests "unevenness and mobility" (x)—a flow, and both Ďurovičová and Appadurai think of this flow in terms of differential scale and cultural-geographic "scale jumping" (Ďurovičová x)—from local to global, or just "below-global" in the case of Ďurovičová (x). Partly because of such scale jumping, the categories of *transnational* and *international* are not mutually exclusive, but I would argue that *transnational* is the most appropriate description of the Western. We can put the Western on a scale of local to just below global: first, we can see the regional sub-genre of the Northwestern as a synecdoche for the Western and the Western as a synecdoche for America and the Western world, as King does in his novel *Green Grass, Running Water* (1993); second, we can consider the Western's typical settings—fur trading routes, open countries scouted for ranchland, boom towns associated with nearby ranches, mines, and oil fields—and the related subtext of capitalist growth in the West; third, we can inquire into the cultural production of the Western across borders and as an asset to both capitalism and national ideologies.

Across borders—this is one of the two most significant movements in the West (the other being the exploration of seemingly borderless lands), and it is the movement of transnationalism. Transnationalism is an aspect of globalization, and although globalization first gained momentum with imperial expansion in the late fifteenth century when the world was just beginning to seem borderless or at least technologically opened to global movements (Appadurai 28), this same borderlessness is a crucial feature of the Western. It is an aspect of the myth of the frontier and of the so-called open country or range. Borderlessness enables plots in Westerns that involve hunting, tracking, cattle driving, smuggling, and other activities in which resources are mobile and national boundaries are either not yet defined or under pressure from colonization, as we see in historical Westerns such as Guy Vanderhaeghe's *The Englishman's Boy* (1996) and

Fred Stenson's *The Trade* (2000); in the former, a gang of American wolfers chases Assiniboine horse thieves back into Canada, and in the latter, Canadian and American fur traders compete for resources while negotiating with First Nations and Native Americans for access to lands that are being steadily colonized. Appadurai's insights are surprisingly appropriate to the Western when we consider the scalar dynamics of globalization and the interactions between economies and nation-states when capitalism crosses borders and cannot be policed nationally. *Transnationalism* connotes the multinational corporate agency of a globalization that destabilizes the very concept of the border.

The best early example of this transnationalism in the Canadian Western and its contexts of production is Ralph Connor. When we include the facts that his popularity in the United States developed partly through the piracy of *Black Rock* and that the publishing industry was involved in his political activities, his border crossings become transnational. The pirating was enabled when the book's British publisher failed to secure American copyright by printing it in the United States and depositing two copies with the Library of Congress (MacLaren 516). Its resulting popularity in the late 1890s created a market for Connor's later editions and books and led to an invitation to the White House from President Roosevelt in 1905. Later, as I explained in more detail above, at the behest of Prime Minister Borden in 1917, Connor met President Wilson and went on a speaking tour of the United States to urge Americans to help in the First World War. Connor's access to American leaders demonstrates some of the potential influence that he had in international politics. His border crossings also probably contributed to an American fascination with Canada's North and Northwest, including a fascination with the figure of the Mountie—the North-West Mounted Policeman—and related lawmen and outlaws. In the Unites States, Connor's publisher, George Doran, organized a speaking tour, which Connor called a "campaign" (*Postscript* 296), that brought him to university clubs, political rallies, and other events where "some of American's most influential citizens" (Wilson 35) were present. Doran's role here is significant. Doran was born in Canada but had become an American citizen (Connor, *Postscript* 281). Connor described his own work as "internationalism" (*Postscript* 296), which is a term associated with intergovernmental activities, but his diplomatic role depended on his Canadian-American publisher's impressive network of elite businessmen and their institutions. Hence the transnationalism.

In Connor's imagination, his own novels seem as transnationally significant to his encounter with Roosevelt as Doran's involvement was. Connor's meeting with Roosevelt was arranged and chaperoned by Doran; Connor writes that they "were invited through Doran's good offices to meet him at the White House" (*Postscript* 156). According to Connor, Roosevelt approached him as a fan might, asserting an identification and a proximity: "Ah! I know you well, Mr. Connor. I know your country, lived across the line from you for two years. I know your books. I could pass an examination in *Black Rock* and *The Sky Pilot*" (qtd. in Connor, *Postscript* 157). Connor's emphasis on Roosevelt's claims to "know" him and Canada is a sign of Connor's approval of American-Canadian identifications and shared values. These commonalities are spatial, oriented around "the line" of the border. His transcript also suggests a potential slippage when Roosevelt reportedly says he "could pass an examination," which is like "passing over" from one side of the border to the other, a transfer that has the metaphoric potential of transforming Connor's books into transnational documents: passports.

The implicit presence of laws and regulations in the symbolic passports and "examination[s]" becomes explicit as Connor and Roosevelt proceed with their discussion. As Connor remembers it, despite their alignments they had different views of the West—more specifically, a contrast of assumptions and experiences of the Canadian West:

> [H]e knew something about my work in the new wild West country. He became serious and gravely earnest as he spoke of "that big raw West country with its vast possibilities and its perils."
>
> "It's a great country, but it is wild, the 'wild West' all right with its lawlessness and—"
>
> "Lawlessness? Why, Mr. President, the law runs in the western country that I know just as it does in Toronto. I never saw a man offer resistance to one of our Mounties. And what's more I never saw a Mountie pull a gun to enforce the law." [As I consider below, Connor does imagine a

Mountie in *Black Rock* taking away a gun, a gun owned by an American, but not by pulling a gun of his own.]
    He was genuinely interested.
    "Never pull a gun in making an arrest? You amaze me! And you have seen men arrested?"
    "Yes," I said, "and gun men, too, from across the line. They do come across, you know, Mr. President."
    "Oh, don't apologize. I know them. Splendid chaps, but—wild, wild! (*Postscript* 158)

Why would Connor "apologize"? Presumably, Roosevelt detected an apologetic tone when Connor otherwise accusingly noted the brazen border crossings of "gun men" into Canada from the United States. Connor implies that Roosevelt was appreciative, even proud; although Roosevelt contrasted "great" and then "splendid" with "wild," he takes no offence (not according to Connor, who would benefit from a public impression of their friendship) at the insinuation that Americans are breaking Canadian law, or are threatening the Canadian West, by coming armed into Canada.

In a meeting years later with another American president, Woodrow Wilson, Connor is much more pointed in criticizing Americans, but he could also be seen as mildly hypocritical. The contexts of the presidential rendezvous were entirely different: the visit with Roosevelt appears to have been essentially a social call, whereas the meeting with Wilson was arranged by Borden for diplomatic purposes. The potential hypocrisy is that Connor, above, may have been criticizing Americans for crossing borders with their guns, whereas below he is criticizing Americans for *not* crossing borders with their guns—his point being to exhort Wilson to join the First World War by shipping American soldiers to France and elsewhere. The appearance of hypocrisy disappears when we recognize that Connor wished, in both situations, for Canadian allies to help each other rather than harass each other. Although by Connor's own description he was haranguing Wilson because the United States appeared to be delaying its entry into the war to minimize costs while profiteering—Connor going so far as to claim that Canadians "hate and despise" (*Postscript* 282) Americans—their meeting ultimately resolved diplomatically. Wilson listened patiently, even actively, and convinced his guest that he intended to join the war when it had become bad enough for the American people "to unite" (qtd. in Connor, *Postscript* 285) in full support rather than joining ineffectively or symbolically. Although the major biographies of Roosevelt and Wilson make no mention of Connor, Connor's biographer Keith Wilson asserts that "his success [with President Wilson and the speaking tour organized by Doran] did something to hasten American entry into the war" (36). Regardless of the degree of Connor's influence, he clearly served a diplomatic and international role.

Earlier I suggested that transnationalism and internationalism are not mutually exclusive, and indeed Connor's border crossings were either a combination of both or were in quick oscillation, phasing from internationalism (with his studies, jobs, and military service) to the transnationalism that enables *further* internationalism. The key example is the piracy of *Black Rock* and its consequences. Connor had serialized parts of *Black Rock*, and these instalments qualified the novel for British imperial copyright in advance of publication as a collection, so his publisher was confident enough to do an initial print run of five thousand copies. Five thousand was "incredibly large for the Canadian market," but the books sold out, which is when Doran "agreed to bring out an American edition" (Wilson 28). It sold in the hundreds of thousands. Here I quote MacLaren's aptly cultural-materialist explanation of what happened next:

> As [Connor's] publishers well knew, an anomaly lay at the foundation of his career: [his] first novel forfeited copyright in the United States. . . . *Black Rock* entered the American public domain the moment it was first printed in Toronto, because no simultaneous American edition had been arranged. Because of this error, American firms were free to reprint the novel without authorization, and they soon realized this opportunity, as the number of surviving editions indicates. . . . [Connor] became a famous Canadian author because his first novel was "pirated" in the United States. (510)

Because of the "error" that MacLaren mentions, a "profusion" (510) of pirated editions appeared, thereby undercutting editions that were legal in

Canada and Britain (526–7). The lack of alignment between international laws allowed businesses to profit from Connor without paying him, but this piracy had an unexpected promotional effect. MacLaren's study also demonstrates how the prices of Connor's later novels were influenced by transnational economics (528); the availability and cheapness of American editions in Canada helped Connor to gain and maintain a readership here (530). His Canadian reputation as a respectable writer with American connections, and the preceding border crossings of his novels, led to his diplomatic role. Like an ambassador, he belonged at least temporarily in both places.

Americans Reading Canadian Westerns

Partly because of this context of *Black Rock*'s reception in the United States, some American readers saw this Canadian novel as their own. This appropriation was not an isolated incident of contemporary reception; Susan Wood's essay on "Ralph Connor and the Tamed West" appeared in a collection entitled *The Westering Experience in American Literature* in 1977. According to MacLaren, one reviewer of *Black Rock* dismissed the stereotyped French-Canadian and Scottish-Canadian characters and ignored the "vilification of the gun-toting American, 'Idaho Jack,' " and "saw the novel as a frontier romance with a racial message consonant with the American ideology of manifest destiny" (521).[13] I agree with the latter quotation from the review, and presumably many patriotic Americans and nationalist Canadians would too, because of the nationally parallel "ideology of manifest destiny," which the novel endorses through positive representations of the westering missionaries, policemen, and trains. This "manifest destiny" also appears in problematic representations of the landscape as open to colonization because, in *Black Rock*, there are no First Nations. Although the novel does not have the "Indians" to go with the cowboys, nor the heroic violence of an ultimate fatal gunfight that is so strongly associated with the American Western, it does have a few crucial

---

13   Another reason might be that American readers thought that Canada needs more cowboys: "The presence of the iconic cowboy in the Canadian wilds implies a lack of homegrown, Canadian agency and implicitly asserts the need for a violent, masculine, and explicitly *American* response to Canadian territory and its inhabitants" (Baker 109, original emphasis). Idaho Jack *almost* meets this "need."

fistfights in saloons, won mainly by a character named Graeme who works for the mining industry and, later, the railroad. He and his idol, the minister Craig, are stand-ins for the mostly absent sheriff or Mountie, and they win their battles through a rather funny combination of brawling, property damage, and temperance union meetings. The complex of symbolic lawmen in *Black Rock* was evidently acceptable, possibly identifiable, to American readers looking for an affirmation of their ideology—assuming that the ideology would also override more personal responses to the stereotypes of Canadian ethnicities and the "vilification" of the American character.

These characters do offer further insight into Connor's imagination of related, but not identical, Canadian and American cultures. MacLaren implies in passing that the "minor" (521) characters in *Black Rock* are unexpectedly meaningful to national identifications, and I would like to develop this idea with a brief close reading. But first, another plot summary will help. At Black Rock, a mining/company town (265) in the Selkirk Mountains of British Columbia (132, 322), there is a drinking problem. The minister Mr. Craig encourages prohibition to save the souls of the miners from Slavin, the barkeep and owner at the saloon. Craig gets help from his friend Graeme, who basically punches his way through the bad guys (62–3, 182–6) all in the name of Jesus Christ. Together, they (I mean Craig and Graeme) defeat the evils of whisky and gambling and convert Slavin to Christianity. Mrs. Mavor, in love with Craig and loved by all the men, leaves to look after her dead husband's mother, and Craig leaves to live in the East and Britain. Eventually, Mrs. Mavor's mother-in-law dies and she (Mrs. Mavor) is able to move again, so she returns to the West; Craig goes back too, and they marry in the mountains; Graeme also returns. The novel ends with their keeping the peace during the development of the West.

Alongside Slavin, Idaho Jack is a crucial enemy, and he is symmetrical with the North-West Mounted Policeman, Stonewall Jackson, who appears in only one scene. The symmetry is obvious in that they both have "Jack" in their names. (Connor also shares his own name—technically, his pseudonym—with the narrator in the novel, a "Connor" who is an illustrator for the railway; the multiple proxies create the possibility that Craig, too, may be proxy to the Mountie, as I have already suggested, or even to Christ, given the wordplay with names: Slavin/Slaving/Satan, etc.) By extension, Canada and the United States are also symmetrical, and therefore both similar and opposite. In contrast with Idaho Jack, Jackson the Mountie illustrates Connor's idealistic and arguably self-consciously Canadian perspective on the law and gun control, and this Mountie encourages Canadian readers to see *Black Rock* as a Canadian rather than American novel.

The scene in which the Mountie confronts Idaho Jack is notable for its brevity, for how rapidly and neatly Connor tries to nationalize the novel as both un-American and conciliatory toward Americans. Idaho Jack is a "professional gambler" (158), so he is a metonym of the American "smuggled whiskey" (180) that is the social detriment of the mining town and that, historically, was one reason that the North-West Mounted Police were deployed to the West in 1873 (Katerberg 545–6).[14] Connor writes that "Idaho was never enamoured of the social ways of Black Rock. He was shocked and disgusted when he discovered that a 'gun' was decreed by British law to be an unnecessary adornment of a card-table" (158–9). Here we see Idaho Jack's gambling in a saloon enabled by smuggled whisky, and the smuggling is another contravention of Canadian law. In the 1890s, of course, the law was still "British," and even today the name of the Royal Canadian Mounted Police invokes the monarchy. British or Canadian—the point then was that it was not American or First Nations. From Idaho, Idaho Jack would have relatively easy access to the sparsely policed Albertan foothills and the interior of British Columbia. Connor writes that the Mountie is "her Majesty's sole representative in the Black Rock district. Jackson, . . . after watching the game for a few moments, gently tapped the pistol and asked what he used this for" (159). Idaho's threatening response leads Jackson to say, "sweetly" but "with a look from his steel-grey eyes, 'I'll just take charge of this,' picking up the revolver; 'it might go off.' Idaho's rage, great as it was, was quite swallowed up in his amazed disgust at the state of society that would permit such an outrage upon personal liberty. He was quite unable to play any more that evening"

---

14   For more on the multifariously symbolic use of alcohol in Canadian Westerns, see the conclusion of this book, where I offer a reading of Robert Kroetsch's *The Man from the Creeks* (1998), which, like *Black Rock*, is also about mining.

(159–60). How quaint that evoking "amazed disgust" is enough to maintain law and order. Of course, there is some subtle intimidation too; Idaho Jack refuses to push the Mountie any further, and "in Stonewall's presence Idaho was a most correct citizen" (160). Referring to him as a "citizen" is ironic because he is American; he gains Canadianness through the "correct" way to be prudent with money, and the language of being "*quite* swallowed up" and "a *most* correct citizen" suggests that the Canadianness is, so to speak, quite British. In Connor's imagination, Britain and Canada are less violent than the United States, and one's nationality is determined in part by whether one does business peacefully or violently. But here the American is shown to suppress his feelings and make a sensible decision not to fight the law. Whether an American reader then or now would like these attributions remains a question.

Corporal Fitness, Corporal Rank, Inc.

In *Unnamed Country*, Harrison has a similar comparison between the heroes of Wister's *The Virginian* and Connor's notable later Western *Corporal Cameron*, which, like *Black Rock*, involves a Mountie who stops a gunman in a gambling den. Harrison chooses *Corporal Cameron* because in it "Connor presents what may be the central archetype of the Mountie" (*Unnamed* 77), an archetype that pairs well with archetypes in *The Virginian*, chosen "because it seems to contain everything—rustling, lynching, a gun duel at sundown, complete with a weeping bride. In action and world view it epitomizes the elements of frontier fiction from Cooper through the 'Dime Novels' to Zane Grey and the movie western" (*Unnamed* 76).[15] The comparison is "epitome" to "archetype." Harrison describes the main difference: "The Virginian draws the gun with which he will enforce the right, while in Connor's scene ["scenes," I might add] it is the man with the gun who backs down" (*Unnamed* 78). Harrison's explanation is that difference is in "the source of the justice" (78), which is embodied in the Virginian but channelled in the Mountie: "One could say that the conception of order in Wister's West is inductive—order is

---

15   See Christine Bold's *The Frontier Club* (2013) for how Wister "whitewashed the vigilantism" (9) of one of the Frontier Clubs, the Wyoming Stock Growers Association, as an already standard technique of late nineteenth-century capitalist rebranding.

generated from the immediate particulars of experience—while that of Connor's West is deductive—order descends logically from higher precepts to which the individual has no access" (79), including British authority located eastward, not only in Ottawa but also across the ocean. Harrison's simplification works very well, but Connor also ensures that other "precepts," if not justice, are "embodied" in Cameron. His strength is a virtue. His body gains a symbolically industrial power even if he does not fully understand it.

Although *Corporal Cameron* is likely the earliest Canadian Western with which readers of this book might be familiar, it probably still needs a quick summary. It focuses on Allan Cameron, in Scotland, who causes trouble for himself by drinking too much booze, falling out of shape, and losing an important rugby match. Soon falsely accused of forgery (39), he plans to run from ignominy and establish a new life in Canada, starting in Montreal. Finding himself unsuited to offices, he goes west to London, Ontario (158), where he saves a drunken farmer by fighting some hoodlums. As a result, he goes to work for the farmer, a Mr. Haley. Cameron befriends Haley's teenage son Tim and learns turnip-hoeing and other skills from him, but thereby starts a jealous conflict with the hired man Perkins, who loves Haley's daughter Mandy. Mandy is described as almost thoroughly undesirable but stirs both love and contempt in Cameron, who eventually leaves the farm—in good physical condition again—to prevent the worsening of trouble between himself and Perkins (265). He joins a surveying crew on the Macleod Trail but is soon ambiguously kidnapped, or saved, in a blizzard by the morally chaotic Raven and his sidekick Little Thunder, a former chief of the Bloods. They part ways when Cameron himself saves a North-West Mounted Policeman (371), thereby gaining the officer's trust and his own entry into the force, in which role he eventually helps to prevent an "Indian war" by arresting "Indians" and the railway builders who were on strike during the Resistance of 1885. (Connor's own brother actually tried to do this, as Dummitt recounts.) Injured while arresting a man during a riot at a saloon, Cameron is nursed back to health by Mandy, who is now Nurse Haley and has come to the West (412); she has been transformed through her training (427). Cameron's real heart has improved throughout the novel; now his symbolic heart is transformed too. After a rejected proposal of marriage prior to the injury (442), he proposes again from his sickbed and is accepted, virtually simultaneously with his promotion to corporal. The moral of the story appears to be that personal ambitions are satisfied by the nation when individuals do something for their country.

There are two scenes in *Corporal Cameron* that I wish to consider, the first of which involves his movement—even before he joins the NWMP—by train across the country. The train is a symbol of nation-building, because it brings settlers farther and farther into the West, but for Cameron it also provides a model of strength, personal strength modelled on that of industry. (Here again we see the relationship between transnationalism and internationalism.) Waiting for the Camerons to arrive by train at a waypoint in the United Kingdom before they leave for Canada (126), a young admirer of Cameron rushes to the oncoming vehicle: "There before their horrified eyes was young Rob, hanging on to the window, out of which his friend Cameron was leaning, and racing madly with the swiftly moving train, in momentary danger of being dragged under its wheels. . . . But as he fell, a strong hand grabbed him, and dragged him to safety through the window" (129).[16] By saving Rob from the train, by taking him into and "through" it, Cameron asserts the Western ideal of natural human strength over industrial strength (which is itself an extension of other animal strength, specifically the horse that becomes the Iron Horse). But Cameron is associated with the train too, and his westward move from Scotland to Canada imitates the westward expansion of railroad technology from Europe and across the continent of North America. When he arrives in Canada and goes to work on a farm, the roles are reversed: Cameron admires the boy Tim, who is self-reliant and industrious and whose strengths have similar associations. When Tim races the troublemaking Perkins in a hoeing competition, Connor compares the boy to a train: " 'Good boy, Tim!" called out Cameron, as Tim bore down upon them, still in the lead and going like a small steam engine" (194). One

---

16   In 1916, in a slightly later novel, Cody's *Rod of the Lone Patrol*, young people are warned about trains through the story of Alec Royal, who dies with "[m]any people" (50) in a derailment. But *Rod* has a younger implied reader than does *Cameron*, and its author wants to keep the boys closer to home, so the train in *Rod* has none of the romantic associations of Captain Josh's safer boat (notably not a seafaring ship). Nevertheless, both novels have some of the Western's antimodernism.

might say that Tim has already symbolically gone "through" the train, as if he were born of it, and has become its "small" version. Trains here are associated with evolution and industry through competition, and time through racing. The lesson Cameron learns is to use his strength for a *purpose*, not merely spontaneously. Going west disciplines him so that he is like a train, even as the Western idealizes the pre-modern times in which strength was only natural.

The purpose now is more agrarian than when Cameron first arrived in Montreal. He is at first disillusioned with the surrounding "business" and "smokestacks" (140), thinking that "everything seems closed up except to the capitalist, and yet from what I heard at home situations were open on every hand in this country" (140). Then he finds a job in the office of a railroad company whose general manager is "Wm. Fleming, Esquire" (141)—an obvious reference to Sandford Fleming, whose influence on time appears, in a reductive form, in the following dialogue:

> "Oh!" said Cameron, carelessly. "Eight? Yes, I thought it was eight! Ah! I see! I believe I am five minutes late! But I suppose I shall catch up before the day is over!"
>
> "Mr. Cameron," replied Mr. Bates earnestly, "if you should work for twenty years for the Metropolitan Transportation & Cartage Company, never will you catch up those five minutes; every minute of your office hours is pledged to the company, and every minute has its own proper work. . . . In case you should inadvertently be late again, you need not take the trouble to go to your desk; just come here. Your cheque will be immediately made out. Saves time, you know—your time and mine—and time, you perceive, in this office represents money." (149)

Cameron becomes a (temporary) slave to time at his office job in the bureaucratic city, and he goes west partly to find a land still free of such strictures and of industry's lockstep of time and money. But as Tim's race with Perkins demonstrates, the farm was driven by time too. Cameron must internalize time, incorporate it, absorb the skills of corporate management, integrate them into the physical strength that he has basically gained from the same sources: the train and nation.

Those sources add up so that we can see Cameron as an embodiment of national movement or transnationalism. The Metropolitan Transportation & Cartage Company prepared Cameron for his later work as a police officer serving distinctly nationalist purposes, and the company is part of the symbolic power of the train that drives Cameron and yokes his self-reliance, ironically, to the nation. The company's transnationalism and its nation's internationalism are obviously linked, and they are also linked in Connor's life and times. Whereas the Internet since the 1990s has created new types of piracy and globalization, an older type enabled Connor's American publisher's success and their mutual internationalism as agents of diplomacy. And his novels, in producing identifications and political positions for readers inside and outside of Canada, use the Western as a literally border-crossing genre that illustrates these transnational themes of imperial empowerment.

Evidently, the imperial and Christian ideological thrust of early twentieth-century globalization was involved in the spinning off of the Northwestern from the Western. The spinoff created a transnational relationship between an imperial America and a nascent Canada with imperial allegiances. In this relationship, Canada influenced the United States—or the United States went looking for symbols of the North that were adaptable to the Western and could maintain interest in one of the classic American genres and the myth of the West. In their novels, Cody and Connor encourage us to notice the Christian elements of Manifest Destiny that were also implicitly globalizing and changing the ideational scale of the vast wilderness of the Northwest.

Genres and Crossovers

Given these themes of Christianity alongside violence rationalized by Manifest Destiny, it might seem strange, at least in retrospect, that these representations of the Mountie and other lawmen, in spite of their potential bad influence, should be written for boys or to be read aloud to boys. Although Norris Yates in *Gender and Genre* (1995) considers several American Westerns written by women with marriage plots that imply a readership of girls,[17] in Canada—where there are far fewer examples and thus less diversity—the Western appears to be gendered for an expected readership of boys in at least the first half-century of its development as a genre, even if it also appears to seek out other audiences in different ways. In keeping with this chapter's symbolism of the cross, I will focus now on Cody's *Rod of the Lone Patrol* as a crossover text of the type that crosses a genre to appeal to both children and adults (increasing its potential market, because even adults without children might want to buy it and read it). Although there is some evidence that boys quickly grew out of Westerns in the early years of the genre (Altman, *Film/Genre* 38), Westerns have often been marketed to boys, as seen on covers of pulp fiction magazines depicting boys caught up with heroes in their adventures. They are also marketed (to use the words of the singer-songwriter Tom Cochrane) to "the boy inside the man." According to Wyn Wachhorst, "[t]he passing of the Old West . . . was like the coming of adulthood" (12), and so, contrary to other legends, the West(ern) is where to find the fountain of youth, to return to innocence—or at least moral clarity—as in the classic melodramas.[18] Perhaps unsurprisingly in a novel for boys, *Rod of the Lone Patrol* is about learning not only self-reliance but also familial loyalty and co-operation. It has that paradox in the title of "lone" and "patrol." With its theme of adoption, it also proposes different kinds of family: biological family, adoptive family, the symbolic family of the Boy Scouts troop, and maybe even the genetics of genre. Some of the heroes in this novel are separated from their families, which is a common theme in Westerns. Some of these heroes are also like Western outlaws in their willingness to take the law into their own hands, but there is a higher law: what Cody calls the "Scout Law" (*Rod* 134). This Scout Law in *Rod of the Lone Patrol* helps to

---

17 In fact, owing to its influence on Wister and his publication of *The Virginian* in 1902, Yates proposes that Mary Hallock Foote's 1883 novel *The Led-Horse Claim* "could be labeled the first formula Western" (11) by any writer anywhere. Other examples include Frances McElrath's *The Rustler: A Tale of Love and War in Wyoming* (1902) and Frances Parker's *Marjie of the Lower Ranch* (1903). Yates identifies Alfred Henry Lewis—author of *Wolfville* (1897)—as a rare "male author who during the early years of the formula Western paid more than token attention to women in his Western fiction" (14), though Zane Grey was "the first male writer of longer Western fiction to make a woman the protagonist" (15), in *Riders of the Purple Sage* (1912). In terms of obvious and unquestionable Westerns, Canada had to wait for George Bowering's *Caprice* (1987), though I am open to considering Cody's 1921 novel *Jess of the Rebel Trail*.

18 Here I am thinking of the work of Linda Williams on melodrama, mode, and genre.

teach boys a late-imperial war readiness, fiscal prudence, and what Cody calls a "spirit of true chivalry" (193) strongly associated with the anti-modern conservatism of the Western. To avoid too many more digressions into politics, I will focus on the late-imperial war readiness to position *Rod of the Lone Patrol* as a Western alongside another option, the war novel, and thereby to discuss this novel as a crossover text within a crossover genre.

Notably, *Rod of the Lone Patrol* is not set in the West; its setting is rural New Brunswick mostly around 1911, and Rod's mentor and Boy Scout leader is Captain Josh, a retired sea captain, not a cowboy. Suffice it to say that he is a so-called saltwater cowboy and that the conventions of the Western were appealing in Eastern Canada (as I suggested in the introduction), though not to the same degree as in the West. In fact, they were appealing around the world, and, in his survey of French Westerns, Mark Wolff finds that "young authors seeking to claim a position in the space that had been opened by [James Fenimore] Cooper not only imitated the American's tales of life on the frontier, but they also tried their hands at writing novels that described adventures on the high seas" ("Western Novels"). Rod's adventures are around smaller bodies of water but constantly evoke the sea as a frontier that he will explore when he's old enough.

The plot can be outlined as follows. On the day that would have been their dead son's twenty-fifth birthday (13), Parson Dan Royal and his wife Martha enjoy the news that Captain Josh has become friendlier to the missionaries and churchgoers in their New Brunswick community of Hillcrest. More important, a stranger abruptly pushes an orphaned baby named Rod into the parson's arms (15). With this second chance at parenthood begins the education of a boy who is encouraged by the parson and the captain into the Boy Scouts. Melodramatically, Cody interrelates the narratives of the separated mother and son through a series of increasingly unlikely coincidences, finally prompting incredulity when Rod turns out to be the biological grandson of the Royals. In an episodic form reminiscent of nineteenth-century novels such as R. M. Ballantyne's *The Young Fur-Traders* (1856) and more familiar examples such as Mark Twain's *The Adventures of Tom Sawyer* (1876) and *Huckleberry Finn* (1884), Cody creates a series of adventures as Rod the Boy Scout helps to catch robbers, shoots an angry bear, and braves a storm to save a neighbour. I don't think catching robbers is in the *Boy Scouts Handbook*, but saving people is straight out of the Bible, and all of the Boy Scouts troop's activities—including catching the robbers for the reward money—are charitably directed to raise funds to pay for an operation to save a girl with a degenerative spinal disorder. At the end of the story, the troop succeeds. Everyone is saved and everyone reunited, especially families.

Through *Rod of the Lone Patrol*, I want to consider a different kind of family—genre—in relation to what is sometimes referred to as the "crossover text." I do not define this term as in fan studies, where a crossover is a sub-genre of fan fiction in which characters from one author's universe are transported into another author's universe.[19] Crossover literature has other connotations too. Rachel Falconer explains:

> "[C]rossover" is still rather a slippery term that can be used to signify very different things. In postcolonial studies, for example, crossover is the critical term for texts that cross cultures or (like [Salman] Rushdie's *The Ground Beneath Her Feet*) represent such cultural shifts in the narrative. In gender studies, crossover is used to signify shifts in gender perspective (as in [Angela] Carter's *The Passion of New Eve*). In children's literature criticism, however, crossover is generally meant to refer to a crossing between age boundaries, the boundaries (for example, young child, nine to fourteen, young adult, adult) themselves being subject to constant redefinition. Even in this field, "crossover" can refer to different aspects of the narrative communication act: the relation between authors and texts, the internal attributes of texts, or the relation between texts and readers, for example. Surprisingly, more has been written about crosswriting and

---

19   A fan writes a crossover text to create and explore "a new world at the intersection of . . . one or more other universes" (Samutina 6). An example of a crossover in fan fiction would be if Clint Eastwood's character Blondie, from Sergio Leone's trilogy of Italian Westerns, were to cross the river and find himself in a showdown with Han Solo on a planet in the *Star Wars* universe. Blondie's universe and the *Star Wars* universe are already specific, with their own casts of characters, narratives, and settings. The specificity of individual characters seems essential in this type of crossover. In this conception, the generality of genre is less meaningful. Natalia Samutina argues that "[a] comparison of the genre of the new text in relation to the genre of the canon . . . is almost irrelevant" (13). Although the crossover is a genre itself (14), genre is not usually the focus of the crossover in fan fiction or fan studies.

dual address (with a focus on authors and narrators) than about texts or crossover reading. (3)

Indeed, because a genre's definition depends so much on a reader's expectations, we have to consider how trends in taste change over time. So I use the term partly historically, as when Misty Krueger uses the term "crossover" "to see synchrony in the canon, as opposed to abrupt breaks from one period to the next" ("Teaching Jane Austen"). Krueger's historical method applies to genres such as the Western, because genres establish conventions, and these conventions move through time to sub-genres and new genres in a process that Steve Neale describes as "cycles and trends" (*Genre* 141). Although Rick Altman cautions against a "synchronic approach" to genre because of its tendency to become "ahistorical" and to find "homogeneity" ("Semantic" 8) that does not exist in any genre, we recognize patterns of conventions among so many otherwise diverse examples that some generalization is inevitable; indeed, it's definitional to the word "genre."[20] Altman therefore proposes that we look for patterns and then interpret them both as conventions and as historical meanings, a method that he calls "semantic/syntactic" ("Semantic" 12). You might say that he wants the parents in the family to be respected, but he allows the children to grow into their own.

One of the proposed results is what Paul Monticone and others call the "hybrid," which is debatably synonymous with "crossover genre." (It also has the racial connotations mentioned in chapter 2.) Monticone's example is the noir Western. Another would be Joss Whedon's space Western *Firefly* (2002–3). In music, crossover genres include Western swing and alt-country. According to Altman, a crossover genre can be explained as a phase in the development of a new genre. Monticone paraphrases Altman: "For a new genre to form, the adjective must be 'substantified' as a noun—that is, 'western chase films' and 'western scenics' must give way to 'the western' " (341). Monticone then argues that "the adjectival term is not merely added on to a noun genre . . . but, as an adjective should, substantially modifies the noun genre" (344). The "noun genre" of *Rod of the Lone Patrol*

---

20   The Latin word *genus* and its derivative *generalis* are the sources of the English words "genre" and "general."

might be epic or romance or, more colloquially, heroic adventure story. Its "adjectival term[s]" are "for boys" and "Westernesque." I hesitate to say that this novel "substantially modifies" the epic (or romance), but these adjectives do set expectations about the adventures: they are like those in Westerns (e.g., they peak with moral clarity derived from action), and they are appropriate for boys. In terms of *hybridity*, the biological metaphor encourages us to stop thinking of adventure stories for boys and Westerns as children of the parent known as the epic. Hybridity occurs between different species, but I doubt that the genres of *Rod of the Lone Patrol* are different enough to be inter-species. Probably not, because they seem to be close relatives. So, when the degree of separation is high enough, "hybridity" seems to be the right word. When it is closer, the right words might be "crossover genre." Although I have been implying hierarchies by referring to genres and sub-genres, or superordinates and derivatives, or parents and children, the term "crossover genre" has an even less vertical orientation than "hybrid," more like a Venn diagram.

In the absurdly unrealistic conclusion to the novel, however, Cody reasserts the patriarchy and the hierarchy of the family "genre." Rod's mother, the famous American singer Anna Royanna, is revealed to have been legitimately married to Rod's father, Alex Royal, though Cody never explains why Alex never told the parson and his wife of his marriage before dying. Why she did not introduce herself as Alex's wife instead of abandoning Rod and vanishing into the night is also never explained, except insofar as she describes her sense of personal responsibility for becoming self-reliant and able to support Rod financially, which she does eventually through hard work as a singer. In accordance with melodrama's value of innocence, her self-reliance protects Rod from allegations of illegitimacy until it also enables her to join the traditional family. In this respect, *Rod of the Lone Patrol* hews to the genealogical line and allows no hybridity, crossing over, or other alternatives in the context of family.

The linear simplicity of *Rod of the Lone Patrol* is a sign both of the Western's moral simplicity and of the closeness of genres interacting in its story. The adjectives "Westernesque" and "for boys" come together partly because, according to Wachhorst, "[t]he sense of personal limits in an abstract society is assuaged by combining the hero's childlike moral purity and social isolation with the power of the adult, resolving complex problems in a single action" (16). Rifkind describes other early Canadian Westerns as "heavy-handed and didactic material . . . very much in keeping with the moral reform discourse of the era's Muscular Christianity, most obviously the Boy Scout movement founded in both Canada and the United States in 1910" (134). Applying Rifkind's observation to *Rod of the Lone Patrol* is easy because of the explicit Boy Scouts content in *Rod of the Lone Patrol* and the Muscular Christianity of Captain Josh as both an outlaw and "Scout Law" man. Another reason to associate *Rod* with Westerns is the similarity of the title *Rod of the Lone Patrol* to Cody's earlier Western entitled *The Long Patrol: A Tale of the Mounted Police*.

And there is one more factor: the cover of the book, which is ambiguous enough to imply a crossover related to genre and to age. The editor and young adult fiction writer Maureen Garvie notes, "it's hard to imagine a children's book that wouldn't have at least some adult appeal. Adults write them, after all" ("Not Just for Children"). A children's book that also appeals to adults may be marketed as a crossover. According to Falconer, "[p]ublishers have recently been directly involved in promoting this kind of crossover writing, for the obvious reason that a fanbase has already been established in one reading age group and may the more easily cross over into another" (4). I don't want to judge a book by its cover, but crossover texts in the marketing sense *are* judged in part by their covers when readers are shopping; Thomas O. Beebee interprets book covers to show "how . . . genres carefully differentiate themselves" according to "how they are to be used by their readers" (7). The cover of the 1916 edition evokes the myth of the West in all its seriousness, though it is a story for boys. The image is a silhouette of a rifle-wielding cowboy standing like a giant on the horizon, surrounded by the redness of the cloth cover and some gold highlights stratified above the horizon to illustrate the sunset. (The redness and styles of hat and pants also imply the Mountie.) Because the red pervades the sky and the foreground, and because the cowboy flatly appears to be on the horizon, scale is impossible to determine. It *could* be a boy with a gun, but it could be a man, or it could be a giant—at least a hero planted firmly on the land, defending his claim. Although Cormac McCarthy had probably never heard of the book before publishing *Blood Meridian: Or, the Evening Redness in the West* in 1985, the cover certainly depicts "the evening redness" and the cowboy's West, even though the story is set in

New Brunswick, in the relative East. And *Rod of the Lone Patrol* is as radically different from *Blood Meridian* as you could imagine—an innocent, wholesome, and hopeful story of a boy who will become a good man, rather than the degenerate, brutal, and deeply cynical story of a boy destroyed by evil in *Blood Meridian*. Tonally, they are diametrically opposed; no one would ever want to read *Blood Meridian* to a child or allow a child to read it. It could never have a crossover audience of children to adults or adults to children. Quite different, *Rod* has potential as a crossover text because of its generic crossings, its readership, and its marketing.

Nevertheless, I admit to the purists that I *am* using the term "crossover" to justify a deliberate misreading of *Rod of the Lone Patrol*, because despite its Western conventions it lacks the essential climactic violence of the Western genre. Krueger refers to "crossover" as a text that "simultaneously represents intersection and transition between time periods," but she also refers to "Miriam Wallace's phrase 'crossover audiences,' a term that [Wallace] uses to describe readers who examine texts across two literary periods rather than in separate ones" ("Teaching Jane Austen"). This usage is different from the crossover audience that buys children's literature and reads it themselves. So, for example, any recent Western in the mode of historical fiction, such as those by Guy Vanderhaeghe, has the potential to comment not only on the nineteenth-century West but also on the present. In reading Vanderhaeghe's novels as dual commentaries in my book, I am a "crossover audience" of the type that synchronizes or at least compares time periods; however, in reading *Rod of the Lone Patrol*, which was written around 1915 and is set in a short span of years around 1911 (153), I am relating it not to my life and times but to the historical contexts of the rise of the Boy Scouts and, somewhat differently, the ongoing First World War, which isn't mentioned in *Rod of the Lone Patrol*. Why not set the novel a few years later, during the war? Probably the answer involves the novel's intended "audience" or readership: boys, boys for whom war was too adult a concern.

For a genre to cross over between readerships by age, the scholar Jeffrey Canton argues that adults will read children's literature that has "compelling writing" and "strong appeal to adult nostalgia" (qtd. in Garvie, "Not Just for Children"). The Western is already a highly nostalgic genre, one that looks back upon an essentially mythic time and place when life was supposedly simpler, the morals clearer, and the Edenic potential of the West seemingly within the colonial grasp. *Rod of the Lone Patrol* uses childhood and a rural setting to evoke similar feelings, but, more than that, I can imagine an adult reading *Rod of the Lone Patrol* to a son during or after the war as a reminder of a not-too-distant past in which there was peace—a return to innocence. For the adult reader, many of the novel's scenes can be read as allegories, perhaps especially the climactic attempt to seek a doctor to save a young neighbour's life at the entreaty of his father. During the attempt, Rod is swept overboard by the storm and seems for the duration of a chapter to be a young sacrifice to a greater cause. Think First World War. Instead of a showdown between outlaw and lawman, there is a confrontation with nature that signifies the historical context of a confrontation with another seemingly elemental enemy, the Central Powers. This allegory might be appealing to some of the adult readers of *Rod of the Lone Patrol*.

To help with these questions of expectations and appeal, Maureen Garvie provides a typology of children's literature crossovers on which we can attempt to position *Rod of the Lone Patrol*:

a) the children's book written for children that appeals to any age (classics like *Anne of Green Gables*, new books like *When Smudge Came*);

b) the children's book that appeals mostly to adults (*Love You Forever, Tuck Everlasting, Tales from Gold Mountain*);

c) the children's book written for adults but taken over by clever children (*Watership Down, Lord of the Rings, Treasure Island*, the pre-Waldo puzzle books of Graeme Base);

d) the book written for young adults but challenging enough to pass as an adult book (*The Outsiders, The Chocolate War, Up to Low*);

e) the book written for adults, taken over by children for a while, but now out of favour (*Catcher in the Rye*, the heavily religious *Swiss Family Robinson*); and finally,

f) the book written for adults to look like a children's book, but which any real child wouldn't touch with a 10-foot pole (*Jonathan Livingston Seagull*). ("Not Just for Children")

Having never spoken to another adult or child who has read *Rod of the Lone Patrol*, I hesitate. I proceed by process of elimination. Would *Rod* appeal at any age? Not likely, because the Boy Scout context itself tended to become unpopular for children over the age of fifteen or sixteen, according to David MacLeod (11); most Boy Scouts enlisted at fourteen but quickly became bored and preferred sports. Would *Rod* appeal mostly to adults? Not likely, partly because, as Garvie suggests, young readers often prefer "formulaic stories with action a-plenty and a few basic, baser emotions like fear, greed, and envy" ("Not Just for Children")—a description apt for *Rod of the Lone Patrol*. Is it or its readers likely to be "clever" or "challenging"? No, because it's an almost excruciatingly simple book whose cleverness seems limited to *deus ex machina*. Was it "written for adults, taken over by children . . . , but now out of favour"? I do not know its history of reception, but I arrive at the end of the list thinking that Rod must be "the book written for adults to look like a children's book, but which any real child [at least today] wouldn't touch with a 10-foot pole." It's too didactic and wholesome for the "real child" whom I imagine, but a sufficiently idealistic parent might like it as a text to read to a child.

Why does all this theorizing about crossovers matter so much to the Western? In an essay on the Western and children's literature, Wolff explains that "[c]ritics of children's literature have wrestled with the unsettling truth that adults construct notions of the child for whom children's literature was and is produced" ("Western Novels"). In *Rod of the Lone Patrol*, the "unsettling truth" is that adults such as its author, Cody, and Robert Baden-Powell, the lieutenant general in the British Army who founded the Boy Scouts, saw boys as future soldiers. The Western was and is one of the many ways in which the popular culture of the Western world contributes, at least in theory, to war readiness: to prepare to solve problems with violence, beginning with the imagination of children and crossing over into an adulthood of action.

Captain Josh sees Rod and his troop in this way too. He is initially presented as an outlaw—a man outside the church who takes the law into his own hands whenever necessary, as when he arrests the robbers with a little help from Rod. Advising the boys on how to deal with confrontation, the captain warns his troop: "Some day ye'll come bang up aginst another troop, and how'll ye feel if ye git licked" (159). In the city with Rod to get a Boy Scouts uniform, Captain Josh learns of a competition among troops, and he decides to enter. Upon their return to Hillcrest, another character joins the captain in linking the Boy Scouts not only to competition but expressly to war; the girl Whyn immediately pines for more uniforms for the troop and says, "Soldiers never seem of much account until they get their uniforms on" (169). Later, when the troop decides to spend their money to save Whyn's life rather than win the contest with the other troops, Cody describes Captain Josh in military terms: "He felt at that moment like a general whose men had consented to make a mighty sacrifice for a great cause" (290). And when the lieutenant governor comes to Hillcrest to review the Lone Patrol and the other troops, "[i]t was a proud moment for Captain Josh, as he marched ahead of the procession. Drawn to his full height, and with his long beard sweeping his breast, he might have been taken for a great warrior of olden days leading his men into action" (313). In his present, however, "his men" are in fact boys, and here's where categorical breakdown is dangerous.[21]

---

21 According to David I. MacLeod, however, troop leaders were in reality worried less about wartime readiness than the dissolution of traditional families and the transformation of men's roles. MacLeod quotes Ernest Thompson Seton, a Briton appropriated by Canadians as Canadian, and the first chief Scout of the Boy Scouts of America: "farmboys had once been 'strong, self-reliant,' yet 'respectful to . . . superiors [and] obedient . . . to parents.' But the rise of industry and growth of spectator sports had turned boys into 'flat-chested cigarette smokers with shaky nerves and doubtful vitality' " (qtd. in MacLeod 5). The values expressed here imply an association between families (namely "parents") and armies (via "superiors"). Seton was and perhaps still is Canada's best-known naturalist writer, in the sense of *naturalism* as a type of realism. He was born in England in 1860 but was raised in Ontario, and he moved to the United States at the age of thirty-six, where he wrote *Wild Animals I Have Known* (1898) (appearing in the same year as Connor's pirated *Black Rock*), *Two Little Savages; Being the Adventures of Two Boys Who Lived as Indians and What They Learned* (1906), and a book on woodcraft that developed into the *Boy Scouts of America Official Manual* (1910). He, Baden-Powell, and Daniel Beard established the Boy

Crossing Over into Pulps

In this context of the various dangers I have just considered, and as we approach the next chapter, which is on the morally censured Western in Canadian pulp fiction of the 1940s, it is worth remarking on the pulpiness of some of Cody's and Connor's writing. I know less about Cody's method than I do of Connor's, but the results—flat characters, clunky plots, and other unrealistic elements—are similar enough that I assume their methods were at least occasionally similar. The flatness of Connor's heroes and villains was partly the result of how he wrote his twenty-five novels—and sold up to thirty million of them (Wilson 30). His long-time publisher and promoter, George Doran, explained the process this way:

> The beginning of each year we would make a contract for a manuscript to be delivered by July, for his readers wanted [i.e., Doran himself wanted, partly for the readers] a new book by Christmas. July would come and go with only a portion of the manuscript in hand. Finally it became a recognized procedure for me to get him to Chicago, and later to New York, and literally put him under lock and key until the manuscript was completed.... Sometimes... we would be printing up to page two hundred fifty-six while he was writing page two hundred and fifty-seven onward. (qtd. in Wilson 31)

Few writers could be expected to produce a book a year with fully developed characters in each one. Connor and Doran's "procedure" was much the same as that which delivers a steady supply of pulp fiction to the marketplace, except Doran produced hardcover books rather than cheaply made magazines (and, of course, Christian texts). Although both Cody and Connor aspired to chronicling a place and time and thereby rallying their audiences—as they did from the pulpit and lectern—to enact social change, their novels in retrospect suffer from a pulpy lack of complex

---

Scouts of America. Later disillusioned with the Scouts, "[h]e levelled charges of militarism and they, in turn, charged him with pacifism" (Redekop).

characterization. It is a criticism that I might levy as an adult that might not be a problem for children and teenagers.

Connor, in fact, predicted the demand for his work and his obliging output in his very first novel, *Black Rock*, in which the narrator has his name—his pseudonym, Connor—and a job not that different from his job as a writer. In *Black Rock*, Connor is a painter who has relinquished his romantic ideals for the regular income of illustrating, probably for magazines:

> There is no doubt in my mind that nature designed me for a great painter. A railway director interfered with that design of nature, as he has with many another of hers, and by the transmission of an order for mountain pieces by the dozen, together with a cheque so large that I feared there was some mistake, he determined me to be an illustrator and designer for railway and like publications. I do not like these people ordering "by the dozen." Why should they not consider an artist's finer feelings? Perhaps they cannot understand them; but they understand my pictures, and I understand their cheques, and there we are quits. (157)

Later, reflecting on his memories after leaving Black Rock, he echoes this passage: "I was filling in my Black Rock sketches for the railway people who would still persist in ordering them by the dozen" (263). The magazines or "like publications" promoting the railway are a commercial publication akin to a pulp magazine in that they have few literary or generally artistic pretensions, such as the pretension of being "a great painter." When Craig returns from Britain and reunites with Connor, he tells of meeting "a man who had written a great book" (310) and of the "sinful waste of God's good human stuff to see these fellows potter away their lives among theories living and dead, and end up by producing a book!" (310–11). Here Connor reveals his misgivings about literature and his preferences for instrumental, practical work; shortly after this scene, Mrs. Mavor writes to Connor to state, "I knew you would not be content with the making of pictures, which the world does not really need" (314). Connor the author presumably sustains the hope that a *useful* book—such as one that promotes abstinence from alcohol—is acceptable. He likewise has no compunctions about the commercialization of such books, however pulpy they are; in fact, his didactic novels simply reflect a Presbyterian work ethic surprisingly aligned with pulp cultural production though at cross purposes with pulp fiction's typical seediness.

So, in conclusion, Connor and Cody were dealing with cultural-material conditions, audience expectations based on historical circumstances and the ages of their potential readers, and moral concerns associated with their chosen genres. These were not simple to balance. Cody's *Rod of the Lone Patrol* can be read as a novel all about the growth of an adopted boy into his real family. His adopted status encourages him and the novel's readers to join symbolic families such as the army. The theme of family relates to genre, but genre might be better understood intertextually, as a network of crossings, rather than a genealogy or some other hierarchy. On the one hand, *Rod of the Lone Patrol* is an allegorical war novel for adults. On the other, it is a Western. On yet another, though it does not veer into fantasy, it is an adventure story for boys. (Genre always seems to juggle conventions.) It is therefore a crossover by age of audience and by genre. And Connor's *Corporal Cameron* appears to have a slightly older audience of boys growing into manhood, when moral lessons become more and more practical and pressing, especially in a wartime context of Boy Scouts becoming men. Connor's famous Mountie is different partly in the fact that Cameron is introduced as a heavy-drinking youth who does not grow up until he goes West. "The 'north'—or, more precisely, the Northwest—often played the vital role of 'masculinizing agent' " (Dawson 38) in Mountie fiction, including *Corporal Cameron* and later examples such as Curwood's *The Golden Snare* (1921). As Coleman and Rifkind have shown, this agency is particularly Christian. The "cross" produced by these novels is not only that of the crossover genre but also that of Christianity, which appears in such a different guise in the pulp fiction of Luke Price and his almost mythical outlaw-lawman, the entirely imitable Smokey Carmain, in the next chapter.

4

From Law to Outlaw
The Second World War, Westerns, and the '40s Pulps

Clint Eastwood once said that he was "one of the people who took the hero further away from the white hat" and that you could identify him "only because everybody else was crappier than he was" (qtd. in McNaron 152), but the villainous hero—whom I called the outlaw-lawman in the preceding chapter to emphasize the symmetry—long predates Eastwood's 1960s roles. To be fair, Eastwood probably had in mind "the white hat" of a film such as *High Noon* (Zinnemann, 1952), in which Gary Cooper plays one of the most upstanding lawmen imaginable, a man perfectly suited to the occasionally puritanical moralism of the 1950s (and his new Quaker wife). Even one decade earlier, however, the questionable hero can be found in the Westerns of the 1940s that preoccupy this chapter; he (usually he) can even be found in some of the Westerns of the 1910s of the preceding chapter, such as Ralph Connor's and H. A. Cody's, one of which—*The Long Patrol: A Tale of the Mounted Police* (1912)—involves a Mountie who shoots not only first but also at the back of a retreating interloper (130). Cast the lasso far enough into the past and the outlaw-lawman appears in the skin of the medieval Robin Hood, whose thievery was meant to right imbalances and restore justice. Even farther, he appears in Lucifer himself—a devil who was once an angel. The binary in these contexts is generally Christian, which is one reason why Thomas King in *Green Grass, Running Water* (1993) deconstructs the fallen angel and recontextualizes him as First Woman, who falls from the sky, lands in the ocean, and is

205

involved in bringing up the land and creating Turtle Island, more widely known as North America.

In chapter 2, the so-called Indian was duly complicated, not only by King but also by Jordan Abel in *Injun* (2016), Garry Gottfriedson in *Whiskey Bullets* (2006), *Maliglutit* (2016), Zacharias Kunuk and Natar Ungalaaq's epic rewriting of John Ford's *The Searchers* (1956), and—as an outsider to this Indigenous group—the multi-authored *Gabriel Dumont's Wild West Show* (2017/2021). Starting with First Nations perspectives and figures was to respect their primacy on Turtle Island and to set the remainder of this book in their context, rather than the inverse, as much as I can, given that the genre does so much to push them out. In the chapter before this one, for instance, I was critical of some of Cody's and Connor's examples of the Muscular Christian lawman, whose idea that they could do good in the West was based in part on a flawed premise of the vacancy of Indigenous lands.

Regardless of the political orientations, we have seen, in the work of the authors just mentioned, rather literary literature. Of all the subject matter in this book, the stories in this chapter are the most popular and the least literary, the least portentous, insofar as those adjectives are meaningful in a study of the Western. Western films such as *The Searchers* and *High Noon* are classic because they are major accomplishments of drama, character study, and cinematography, and are aesthetically parallel to the later literary Westerns of Cormac McCarthy in the United States or those of Guy Vanderhaeghe in Canada. The '40s pulps under consideration in this chapter are analogous, instead, to B movies, made in such numbers that the conventions were crystallized or, in a more appropriate metaphor, distilled into hooch. This chapter focuses on the 1940s and the Americanizing pulp fiction that made it clear that the lawman and outlaw are figures that are not only set side by side but also on top of one another—not only a duo, but also superimposed.

Insofar as Canada and the United States are a related duo, Canada obviously the sidekick, or the sleeper crushed under the elephant (as the saying goes here in Canada, anyway), the superimposition also flips in curious ways. In the Western, regionalism trumps nationalism and in fact *becomes* nationalism, with the West often expressing its resentment of the East and its traditions of nationalism, whether Washington, DC, or

Ottawa. I know from experience that people in Saskatchewan and North Dakota often feel more affinity for each other than for their imagined communities in distant capital cities. Reading Canadian Westerns, however, emphasizes a North-South tension instead of an East-West tension. For the record, I think of it as the tension between partners, not (necessarily) between competitors, though I have had second thoughts since the Trump administration's hard-line approach to renegotiating and renaming the North American Free Trade Agreement. And Canada has sometimes been strict about trade with the United States too, as it was when Westerns were involved.

I have two purposes now: first, to historicize the Canadian outlaw-lawman alongside wartime law, specifically the *War Exchange Conservation Act* that made it illegal to sell American Westerns in Canada, and the alleged cultural colonialism of American mass culture around the 1940s; and second, to read an American character of seemingly Canadian origin, the itinerant and intermittent sheriff Smokey Carmain, through his serialized appearances in the issues of *Dynamic Western*, available at Library and Archives Canada (LAC)—issues that I helped to rediscover, not yet catalogued, one fateful December. I am reading Westerns here, but, in the crossover spirit of the previous chapter, I am also a little of the detective, rummaging around and looking for clues about who wrote these pulps and what they were thinking.

Wartime Canadian Law and Western Transnationality

Clive Bloom, in *Cult Fiction* (1996), one of the few books to attempt a theory of pulp fiction, claims that "pulp is not to be defended, nor is it to be made more available for serious study at the academy—pulp never went to school and hates the academy. Academic respect kills pulp with kindness. Pulp does not wish to be part of the canon except to plunder and pastiche it" (133–4). How ironic, then, that in a sense I was "plunder[ing]" the archives, partly for academic purposes, partly to wonder about the Western's relationship to national canons, when I went looking for *Dynamic Western* and other pulps. I had had the impression from an out-of-date LAC website, Tales from the Vault!, that there was more to the archives than had been made available up to then, such as only one issue of *Dynamic Western*, and my repeated inquiries led to a more thorough search by one of the archivists, who found ten more issues and arranged their cataloguing. There is still not much: only, for instance, two partially represented years of *Dynamic Western* magazine (1941 and 1942), and parts of others such as *Bill Wayne's Western* magazine. Both of these magazines were part of Alec Valentine's publishing empire in Toronto in the 1940s (M. Smith 286), and a few hundred issues from his various genres of pulp magazines are now in Ottawa at LAC. (Slightly beyond the purlieu of the literary field, there are Canadian Western comics from the same era, many of them accounted for in the Grand Comics Database, such as Bell Features's *Triumph Comics* series prior to 1946, when they started reprinting American comics; LAC also has some of these. Having to limit the scope somehow, I have not included comics in this book, though I have written about them elsewhere.) When Valentine was publishing, there was no LAC, and "the three best collections of print Canadiana were [in the United States] at the Library of Congress, the New York Public Library, and Harvard University" (MacSkimming 24, 25). LAC got a building only in 1967. Its collection of pulp fiction is rare, small, and fragile—rare and small partly because these Westerns were published in Canada by publishers that did not last long, and partly because of their physical condition. The magazines are fading and yellowed, the paper brittle and torn, the stapled bindings (aptly called saddle-stitching) rusting. The March 1942 issue of *Dynamic Western* is missing too many pages to be read effectively and too damaged to be copied safely. None of these issues will sustain repeated hands-on viewings—the great historical peril of not making things to last.

And yet they tell a story that we should not forget, one germane to Canadian-American relations and the transnationality of the outlaw-lawman. As told, the story of the Canadianization of the outlaw-lawman is incomplete and thus open to question. If I were to speculate wildly, I would venture that the now-unknown writers in *Dynamic Western* magazine could have included Americans posing as Canadians and side-stepping Canadian law at a time when it was illegal to sell American Westerns in Canada. More likely, they were Canadians slavishly imitating an American genre, possibly not only for Canadians to enjoy. Some evidence suggests that Canadian publishers in the 1940s sold pulp fiction, probably including made-in-Canada Westerns, back to the United States (M. Smith 267). This evidence complicates the power dynamic and demands us to accept that the transnationality of the Western in the 1940s was not merely northward—a trail of exports out from the United States.

The Canadian law governing such trade was the *War Exchange Conservation Act*, and it was supposed to help indirectly with two moral obligations. The first was the war effort, as a result of keeping disposable income in Canada, where economic activity would add to state coffers. The concern was not unreasonable; Graham Broad estimates that, while disposable income increased by almost 50 per cent during the war, 90 per cent of that was spent on the movies, almost all of which would have been American (13, 169). The second obligation was perhaps the bigger concern for politicians in Canada: the protection of youth from the corruptive influences that circulated in the most cheaply available media—that is, magazines, effectively the Internet porn of the 1940s. According to the statute, the *War Exchange Conservation Act* banned American pulps that represented "detective, sex, western, alleged true or confession stories" (qtd. in Strange and Loo, "Hewers" 12). Although these identified threats were part of the language that echoed in future legislation such as the *Foreign Exchange Conservation Act* of 1947 and the Fulton bill of 1949 (explained further below), the *War Exchange Conservation Act* partly backfired. Note that "[i]n 1948 English-language publishers [in Canada] had issued a mere fourteen books of fiction and thirty-five works of poetry and drama" (MacSkimming 24), a sign that the industry in general needed investment, even without the wartime challenges. The act kept money in Canada, but, in Western terms, it "spurred the growth" (Strange and Loo, "Hewers" 11) of the Canadian pulp fiction industry, effectively nationalizing the worst that America had to offer, which was by today's standards very mild indeed. It proved Canada perfectly capable of writing and publishing its own smut, its own sordid tales of criminals and detectives, loose women (and men), and trigger-happy gunslingers—quite possibly the worst that *Canada* had to offer (as *art*, if we can accept that we did considerably worse in reality).

These sorts of characters come from genres that are different from each other but still related, often the same characters in different contexts. Keith Walden, Michael Dawson, and Carolyn Strange and Tina Loo agree that "the Mountie pulps" (Strange and Loo, "Hewers" 12) had heroes who were morally simpler or at least clearer than those typical of American

Westerns, though the preceding chapter also demonstrated some exceptions to this rule. These "Mountie pulps" might be considered "Northerns" but are some of the texts that I want us to think of as Canadian Westerns, to acknowledge their many shared conventions of the Western genre, such as their typically late nineteenth-century settings, anti-modernism, open country, "cowboys and Indians," violence often involving guns, and moral simplicity—the space- and time-sensitive chronotopes of Bakhtinian theory (Druick 300)—as I showed in the preceding chapter. Continuing into this chapter, Smokey Carmain is another, because his *Dynamic Western* vehicle is supposed to be Canadian but his settings are the American Southwest, and as sheriff he is not much like the upstanding Mountie in Canadian myths. The fact that this magazine was made in Canada demonstrates that some Canadians wanted American-style Westerns; Canadian publishers saw an opportunity to replace American product with "American" product.

The latter case is how Toronto's Alec Valentine started his business in the pulps (M. Smith 261): "Rather than designing his magazines in a manner that would emphasize their status as new publications produced in Canada, Valentine imitated his American counterparts at the visual and tactile level in order to benefit from their already established popularity" (268). Thus, stories in *Dynamic Western* usually happen in the American Southwest or occasionally the West, and, for most readers of *Dynamic Western*, its Canadian provenance would have been almost unnoticeable in the small print of the front matter. Bart Beaty states that American comic-book publishers had created Canadian editions that simply reprinted American comics in Canada (101)—early versions of the "branch plants" in Toronto that Al Purdy and other Canadian writers and figures called attention to and deplored in the 1970s—but this does not appear to be the case with *Dynamic Western*.[1] (See, instead, *10 Story Western*, which the narrator of Robert Kroetsch's 1966 novel *Words of My Roaring* mentions as some of his reading material.) Nevertheless, the complex and questionable national identity of *Dynamic Western* is yet another reason to

---

[1] Besides Beaty, some of the other especially notable scholars of Canadian comics of this era are John Bell and Ivan Kocmarek. For more on Purdy's nationalist views of the United States, see his book *The New Romans: Candid Canadian Opinions of the US* (1968).

sweep away some of the generic border between Northerns and Westerns and to think of them as versions of the same thing. Although Strange and Loo explain, for obvious reasons, that comics, crime magazines, and pulp fiction can be separate genres with different characteristics ("Hewers" 20), they also describe the "morally dark places, particularly the remote north and the far west," of the true-crime genre, and they link these genres explicitly: " 'Northerns' and westerns amplified detectives' capacity to restore order by depicting the added burden of their civilizing mission" (17, 28). I have already hinted that this Western-detective linkage was an element of characterization for Smokey Carmain in *Dynamic Western*, and the introduction to this book also demonstrated that, in much the same way as national borders can be permeable, genres of national significance can blend together too.

Crossing the border is one of the tactics of the outlaw. To escape the law, you sometimes have to get out of town, go past the county line, vamoose from your own country. With the '40s pulps, the "Americanization" of the Canadian market, or this "Canadianization" of the Western, was driven by outlaws in publishing. While we might be accustomed to thinking that the genre creates the market, as when ad agencies effectively tell us what to want, in this Canadian situation the outlaws in publishing might have been creating the genre: "The conventions which develop in these most formulaic Westerns . . . are more insistent and derive not from the influence of literary genre, but from the pressures of the market-place" (Bold, "Voice" 45). Even if these "outlaws" were not, in fact, Americans faking their names for *Dynamic Western* and *Bill Wayne's Western*, they had at the very least found their way around the prevailing moral codes— the de facto laws—that would be further codified in the 1950s: upstanding respect, honour, neighbourly watchfulness, conformity, the order of the picket fence. The potential for simply rebranding American content was a threat to both Canadian solidarity and Canadian individualism, in both cases a resistance to prevailing notions of a spreading American orthodoxy.

And so it is ironic that, in the pulps, the individualism of the author was one of the sacrifices to the market, because they were paid to churn out stories that conformed to identifiable genres and that thereby reified the genres through repetition (Bold, "Voice" 30). Christine Bold historicizes the example of one American publisher,

> Street and Smith, who entered the field in 1889 and stayed in it until after World War II, [and] streamlined their production to the smallest detail. In the [late nineteenth-century] dime novel days, they laid down specifications of character, scene and plot; they forced writers to re-write installments; and they shuttled them from one series to another in mid-story. By the time of the pulp magazines, which superseded dime novels around the end of the First World War, the conventions of commercial Western fiction were so entrenched that their production needed only perfunctory surveillance. ("Voice" 31)

Bold's research also shows that some prominent writers of dime novels and pulp fiction were remarkably self-reflexive in implying that there was a "marketplace function" (37) to their stories; she argues, however, that over time these authors lost their self-reflexivity—and ultimately their voice—to the genre (44–5).

I would add that another result of this "function" (in Foucauldian terms, an "author function," or in Barthesian terms, the death of the author) is in the names of some authors of the pulps, and indeed Bold alludes to "the anonymous publishing voice" ("Voice" 47) of pulp fiction. In a concession to their publishers and, I suspect, to Canadian law, the possibly American writers "in" Canada published in Toronto pseudonymously. Although Michelle Denise Smith claims that many of Valentine's magazines were produced in Toronto and that his busiest writers lived there (273), I have not, to date, found a Canadian biographical record of the most frequent contributor to *Dynamic Western* in LAC's eleven issues: Luke Price, creator of Smokey Carmain. (If the Bakhtinian method of interpreting genre is to locate its utterances culturally, materially, and historically, we are partly stymied here: we know the time and place of the utterance, but not who said it.) Several of the other writers sharing space in the magazine with Luke Price had unlikely names, such as Miles Canyon, Wiley Horton, and Terence Dawson. These, at least, suggest pseudonymity. Without ascribing or implying a national identity to pseudonymous writers, Strange and Loo state that pseudonyms were common across the pulpy genres ("Hewers" 30n); Thomas P. Kelly had at least thirty of them (M. Smith 283) and contributed to some of the Western magazines under the name of Zed Kelly (284). Furthermore, the use of pseudonyms partly enabled the transnationality of the Western, creating a new and untraceable set of "Canadian" writers whose very rootlessness enacts a trope of the colonial (or potentially diasporic) outlaw-lawman: escaping, wandering, movin' on.

Pseudonymity was also an escape from critics who could denigrate the quality of pulp fiction by recourse to standards such as grammar and spelling. (In *Dynamic Western*, the spellings are American, not British or Canadian.) *Dynamic Western* has many editorial errors, as do other pulps and comics of the day that I have read, but Smith finds an almost artfully egregious example in crime fiction: "In terms of textual content, the handful of manuscripts in the archive indicate that the stories were printed without many editorial changes. In getting these stories ready for printing, there was much room for error, and little time for corrections. In the text of a true crime story called 'Edmonton's Maniacal Killer and the Innocent Girl,' for example, a murder witness is identified in the story as 'Private A.J. Lajoie,' but the caption beneath his adjoining photograph reads 'Primate A.J. Lajoie' " (M. Smith 274). Bloom offers an explanation that helps us to understand the history:

> These "invisible" writers and their forgotten publishers produced an imaginative space at once banal and luxuriant, naïve and yet oddly complex. Somewhere between the written culture of the nineteenth century and the visual culture of the late twentieth, these writers act as an historical link which is also and at the same time an aesthetic link in its appeal to readers sophisticated in the media of film and television and perhaps only merely competent in the realm of the written. (24)

Any critic of literary taste must accept that, by the late 1940s, readers, including the critics, were highly influenced by televisual writing in film and even television (regular American broadcasting having started in 1939). Film on its own had already been affecting the language, structure, pacing, and points of view of modern writing. It is no wonder that a conservative segment of society would react against the pulps. Michael Warner argues that "good style often turns out to be not just grammatical or aesthetic but political" (129). Probably like all texts, the "political" dimension of *Dynamic Western* is made sometimes gleefully apparent, and sometimes complicated enough to demand a critic's expertise, a deft exploration of nooks and crannies, if not a critical hammer. But politicians took to the hammer.

Postwar Anti-Americanism and Canadian Sensitivity

After the end of the Second World War, the *War Exchange Conservation Act* was repealed, but new anti-Western—and residually anti-American—legislation replaced it. The sorts of complaints that Canadian nationalists such as Purdy registered against the United States in the latter half of the twentieth century had many justifications, not all of them realistic, such as the sense of having been robbed of "Canada's Century" when the Second World War demonstrated American superpower quite differently from Canada's primarily diplomatic influence on the world stage, following its contributions to the First World War at Vimy and other pivotal sites. Writ large, the complaints responded to cultural colonialism—the huge influence of American market-oriented cultures on Canadian cultures trying to preserve difference from America. Many of the regulations and state interventions emerging from the Massey Commission and its 1951 report, expanding to Canadian-content quotas in some of the mass media in the 1970s, can be traced to anxieties of the 1940s. In the public imagination at least, American influence had real-life consequences:

> It was November 13, 1948, and two young boys, age 11 and 13, stole a rifle. They set up camp by the side of a road in Dawson Creek, British Columbia, at Mile 0 of the Alaska Highway. With what could be described as a youthful disregard for consequences, they started trying to flag down cars and fired shots into the air; they later told police they were "playing highwayman." When a couple of cars failed to stop,

they fired directly into a vehicle in which James M. Watson, age 62, was a passenger. He was fatally wounded, and died three days later. . . . Among other facts, it was established that the two boys were avid comic-book fans, each reading dozens of crime comics a week. The correlation between crime and violence in the media and real-life crime and violence is still a matter of debate today, but at the time the debate was foreshortened and a connection was made between the boys' reading habits and their criminal activities. (Driscoll, "Corrupting")

In the aftermath of a media sensation in British Columbia, E. Davie Fulton, a Conservative member of Parliament, introduced a bill that passed and thereby outlawed crime comics and pulps. It was an incomplete gesture. In their article on "Maple Leaf Pulps" (2004), Carolyn Strange and Tina Loo claim that there was a "selective morality" at work: Canadians such as Fulton wanted stories that showed that "crime did not pay," but they accepted racist and sexist stereotypes ("Maple Leaf Pulps"). For Strange and Loo, it was a "tellingly Canadian" and "conservative morality" ("Maple Leaf Pulps"). In their earlier article, they joked that a conservative and anti-American Canadian government should have been willing to subsidize the magazines rather than ban them (Strange and Loo, "Hewers" 14). Although as of 1997 "fewer than a dozen charges have been brought to the courts" (Beaty 85), the Fulton bill (1949) remains in effect today in the Criminal Code, part v, section 163 (Driscoll, "Corrupting"), outlining "offences tending to corrupt morals," and including "crime comics" alongside child pornography. The legal definition of "crime comic" specifies magazines, other periodicals, or books that depict real or fictitious crimes and accordingly included Westerns, which routinely involve theft, kidnapping, assault, murder, and massacre. Beaty argues that "anti-comic book sentiment" (85) existed in the United States (91) but in Canada (and Britain) was partly anti-Americanism: "notions of Canadian literary production and consumption have historically been tied to a paternalistic conception of Canadian readers as children who require the moral guidance of the state in order to withstand the predatory suasion of American cultural industries" (85).² As the Dawson Creek manslaughter case suggests, Canadian sensitivity is associated with children's impressionable minds even by Canadians themselves (or probably mostly by Canadians themselves). The concern was with a set of genres—crime, true crime, Western—that already had American connotations and thus served to conjoin morals and one resistant idea of Canadianness: Canada as child of Britain who could eventually develop a high culture, a literature, that would be "counterhegemonic" (Beaty 102).

When the restrictions on trade were lifted at the end of the 1940s, coincidentally the pulp industry in Canada started to slump. The Fulton bill and competition from the reintroduced American pulp industry were only part of the reason, because the disappearance of the pulps was in fact "a continent-wide phenomenon, a product of changing products, changing tastes and changing markets" (Strange and Loo, "Hewers" 28). The new product that Strange and Loo emphasize was the paperback novel and its drugstore availability. The technology of paperback was necessary for literature of the "low culture" to compete with another new product: television. By this I mean that paperback was an innovation for the written word that generated excitement for it even as viewers were excited by the prospect of television in their living rooms or, as Irving Layton once said to Leonard Cohen, in their bedrooms (Deshaye, "Irving" 33). And without paperback, literature of the "high culture" would never have reached the masses through the many new publishers that emerged in the 1960s and '70s in response to federal funding for the arts, during a time of multiplying and expanding universities. Soon, this now more affordable literature was required reading in university courses. We now designate it "Canadian literature," but we also call it "CanLit" and, consciously or not, we acknowledge it as a brand and an inseparable element of popular culture here—in spite of the recent and reductive discourse of its "raging dumpster fire."[3]

---

    2   Incidentally, *true*-crime magazines were less worrisome than the supposedly more fictional crime magazines, because they were marketed to adults more than children, as Strange and Loo explain ("Hewers" 18).

    3   The phrase was popularized partly by Alicia Elliott in her article "CanLit Is a Raging Dumpster Fire" (2017).

In my previous book and other research, I have written about the inseparability of so-called high and low cultures in the development of Canadian literature, primarily through the examples of poets in mass-cultural media such as popular music, radio, and television, but also through examples of attractive public personas and manufactured controversy that could sell poetry across fields of cultural consumption. On the topic of controversy and the Western, television in particular is fascinating here at the historical junction of the 1940s and '50s. Shows such as *The Lone Ranger*, which debuted in 1949, could draw some readers away from their comics and the Western genre, but the show could also enable crossover marketing not only between genres but also between media. I have an image of a 1948 *Lone Ranger* cover (the November issue) on which the Lone Ranger bursts into a room full of criminals with a boy at his side, a boy stepping through the frame of a door that could be the frame of the television screen. As with Cody's *Rod of the Lone Patrol* (1916) and other books from the previous chapter, the image calls out to a public of boys—and to their parents looking for wholesome content for them. I imagine parents asking each other, "What can we allow the kids to do that isn't homework?" I can imagine the kids saying, "But Mom, the cowboy is a good guy!" In his book on pulp fiction, Bloom accordingly writes: "Speaking a secret language of desires unfulfilled, pulp is truly a type of embarrassing perversity negotiated between producers and consumer—a guarantee of order and yet anarchically sub-cultural" (150). One form of this "order" is the respectability promised by the Lone Ranger in his white hat. Elsewhere Bloom claims that "[p]ulp is the illicit dressed up as the respectable, but it is not disguised, nor does it hide its true nature from the consumer. Thus it becomes a type of coded play" (133). The boy's negotiation with parents over television and comics is a similar "coded play," a testing of limits and of parental patience leading to the inevitable judgment that a popular genre isn't "good."

As William Boddy explains it, "[w]ith the precipitous end of the [rigged] prime-time quiz show [in the latter half of the 1950s], Hollywood-produced episodic series, including a flood of TV Westerns . . . quickly filled the empty schedule slots" (125). But the Western on TV didn't last long either, partly because "[t]he war replaced the frontier as the subject everyone wanted to read about" (MacSkimming 29), and partly because of the same juvenile-delinquency concerns in the United States that had preoccupied Fulton and allied politicians in Canada. Boddy relates that the "director of the US Bureau of Prisons . . . reported that TV Westerns were some of the most popular programmes among incarcerated juvenile delinquents" (132), but he also explains that

> although some observers pointed to [Senator Thomas Dodd and his subcommittee's] TV violence hearings as a major factor in the near-disappearance of the TV Western, the effects of the congressional hearings were probably marginal in relation to wider shifts in prime-time programming. The adverse publicity from the Dodd hearings was certainly unwelcome to the industry, and there is some evidence to suggest that the networks adjusted their selection of summer reruns and the specific handling of dramatic violence. More importantly, the decline in the number of prime-time Westerns in the early 1960s reflected an earlier shift within the action-adventure genre from Westerns to contemporary crime series, and the fate of the Western was also linked to the more general shift to prime-time medical dramas, animated series, and, most significantly, situation comedies. (133)

I have written elsewhere about "an earlier shift within the action-adventure genre from Westerns to contemporary crime series" ("Do I Feel Lucky?"). Upon reflection, I think that one of the lessons about genre to learn from the shifts between comics, pulps, literature, television, and film is that any shift can be a bait and switch, a repackaging of offensive material that forces critics to rethink, regroup, and revise while someone else is making a dollar.

Ultimately, these cultural-material circumstances are another dimension to the legal history that worked against Westerns and other pulps in the 1940s and '50s, resulting partly in the rise and fall of genres. As one would "fall," it would in fact sometimes transform, crossing over into another genre in much the same way that an outlaw crosses borders. In the Canadian situation, the Western itself functioned as an outlaw, working perhaps against Canadian law but definitely against shared Canadian and American morals of the time, morals that increasingly demanded a conformity to national values while pulp writers negotiated their own creativity through the notoriously restrictive and repetitive conventions of pulp, a pinnacle (or abyss) of genre. The conventions were not and are not merely aesthetic, and nothing aesthetic is ever mere; they were political and motivated responses in law and in the involved cultures, high and low.

To get away from it all, *Dynamic Western*'s Smokey Carmain is always on the move, installing himself temporarily as the sheriff of a frontier town before gettin' while the gettin's good—that is, before the public realizes how much of a scoundrel he can be. And before he's bored with all the justice and order he grudgingly creates. He is, in a sense, the essence of genre: a character driven to compulsive repetitions that define the expectations for all his readers, who—just as he and they both settle into their roles—see him break all his good habits as soon as possible.

And now, ladies and gentlemen, Smokey Carmain, so bad he's good:

> "Smokey, huh? That's a heck of a moniqer [sic]. How do you come by it?"
> "Reckon it's 'cause I like the smell of it," he drawled.
> "The smell of what—smoke?"
> "Gun-smoke, I reckon." (Price, "Smokey Carmain" 56)

Back to the Future: Prototypical Postmodernism

"[T]here ain't nothing I like better than the smell of gunsmoke" (Price, "Gunsmoke" 103). These in fact are the first words to explain Smokey Carmain's moniker in the extant series penned by Luke Price for *Dynamic Western* in the early 1940s. Soon afterward, when Smokey is asked by Tessie Tailor how he got his name, he says, "Reckon it's 'cause I like the smell of it." She asks again, "The smell of what—smoke?" He concludes: "Gun-smoke" (105). He tells the same story of his name again—and a story it is, with character, suspense, plot, and climax all implied—in the next available issue of *Dynamic Western*, in "Smokey Carmain Shoots It Out!" The near-verbatim explanation demonstrates on the one hand the repetitive nature of episodic literature and of genre, and on the other the affinity for storytelling that even a laconic cowboy has, when it suits him. And the story grows taller with the telling: in "Valley of Vengeance," a man who knows Smokey's reputation describes him as "[t]he guy who has to breathe gunsmoke to keep livin' " (63); in "Smokey Defies an Army," he is "the smoke-eating sheriff" (27). The fantastic supernaturalism of this dragon of the American Southwest even becomes religiosity in "Six-Gun Thunder": "Men who had known him before he became sheriff had christened him 'Smokey' because of the aura of gun smoke that had surrounded him then" (56). He is "christened," not merely named; he has an "aura," a halo and a cowboy hat. What's in a name? Certainly, when it's so reflective, naming is quintessentially and indulgently self-reflexive, a hallmark of postmodernism.

One might argue, as John Frow does in *Genre* (2006), that any genre and any text has "metageneric" (8) and "metacommunicat[ive]" (17) potential. By extension, these "meta" qualities may be associated with postmodernism, but postmodernism is—to simplify—not merely a genre of content but more importantly a mode or a style (cf. Frow 64–5), one of performative excess (among other things). In Smokey's naming, there is also an outrageous affection for something other than the person so christened, and in Smokey's case more generally there is an obsessive compulsion to announce his violence. Like Judith Butler's maxim that gender seems natural only because we perform it so repeatedly, Smokey's name calls attention to the performance of violence that only seems essential to him. It does not merely verge on parody. As I will explain with help from Linda Hutcheon's maxims that postmodernism is defined by parody ("Politics" 180) and that parody is "repetition with difference" (*Theory* 101), Smokey Carmain is an outlaw-lawman whose naming and repetitions suggest that his genre is at a historical moment when a nascent postmodern mode is inclining it to parody. The repetitions are not merely modal (i.e., the way that Smokey laughs at himself). As seen above, the repetitions become part of the content of the genre, increasing their significance and furthering his characterization with each example.

This claim has several implications, including the consequence of having to historicize Canadian postmodernism differently by aligning it with a period, the 1940s, that is over a decade earlier than the start of Hutcheon's own timeline of postmodernism in *The Canadian Postmodern* (1988), which is bookended by Leonard Cohen's *Beautiful Losers* (1966) and various later works by Margaret Atwood, Robert Kroetsch, and others in the 1980s. Ultimately, I find that Smokey's modal inclinations must stop before postmodernism, at least if we understand postmodernism as "oppositional" and "contestatory" (Stacey xiii, xvii), as critics such as Frank Davey and Robert David Stacey do. The stories in *Dynamic Western* are, in form and most of their contents, simple imitations of American models and their (up until then) agreement on the natural superiority of American ideals. These authors do not oppose or contest—except, as I showed earlier in this chapter, they *were* deflecting their own authority by using pseudonyms, and they *were* dodging Canadian law and the increasingly puritanical social mores of the 1940s. Because of this international and cultural-material context, which is necessary to understand genre, I am compelled to examine just how far we can go with Smokey Carmain and the '40s pulps on a road to postmodernism, accomplishing at the very least a premature introduction to the next chapter.

Echoing Frow's comments on mode, Frank Davey asserts that postmodernism "is not a period, not an aesthetic, but an understanding of how meaning is constructed" ("Canadian" 10), and I agree—except that we can discern trends in such "understanding" that are historically specific, for example in the 1960s and '70s, when Davey and his peers were coming of age and coming to attention as postmodernist writers.[4] In a talk at the conference that generated Robert David Stacey's *Re: Reading the Postmodern* (2010), a talk produced by shuffling fragments, Davey provocatively wondered whether theories of postmodernism that are not in their form postmodern—Hutcheon's first and foremost—should be "qualified, or disqualified" ("Canadian" 9) as theories.[5] He also claimed that "Canadian understandings" were "harmed" especially by Fredric Jameson's "confusion" of postmodernism with postmodernity (Smokey Carmain being, indeed, more a result of postmodernity than postmodernism), and our alleged refusal (which I am refuting) to read "theory that is more than a

---

4   Another definition, one that agrees with Davey's, is that postmodernism is "a strategy of representation that foregrounds representational systems and their ability to make epistemological and ontological claims" (C. Smith 9).

5   Davey's method of presentation at the conference is reminiscent of the "frames" and "slippages" in the chapter called "The Critic as Innovator: A Paracritical Strip in X Frames" in Ihab Hassan's *The Postmodern Turn* (1987).

few years old" (Davey, "Canadian" 11, 12). In Hutcheon's contribution to *Re: Reading the Postmodern*, she tacitly agrees with Davey, observing that living in postmodernity, or being able to look at it retrospectively, will not necessarily produce an understanding of postmodernism ("Glories" 40). In spite of Davey's claims, however, he does situate postmodernism historically and spatially, especially in the Canadian West of the 1960s and '70s that he shared with Kroetsch and everyone who made the *Tish* magazine happen; various critics suggest in fact that Canadian postmodernism is Kroetschean and therefore "Western" to some extent (Stacey xiv), rather than even more cosmopolitan or global than modernism. Davey also mockingly predicts our future (now present) interest in delimiting postmodernism further ("Canadian" 15, 18, 30, 32). Although Hutcheon still argues that postmodernism evolves through parody ("Glories" 50), Davey tries to show, by rearranging his text, that it is multiple and discontinuous and not amenable to the uni-linearity of historical evolution, regardless of his own historicisms. In fact, by satirically mocking the periodizing dimension of historicism, and by quoting himself and contradicting himself in the partial disjunction between style and content, he, too, implies that historically situated parody cannot be ignored in the study of postmodernism.

I am interested in this debate, and in Hutcheon's and Davey's concerns about America's centrality, through Jameson, in the discourses of postmodernism. In *Postmodernism, or The Cultural Logic of Late Capitalism* (1991), Jameson offers a suggestion about how postmodernism may be historicized. He first considers the Nietzschean view of an ahistorical or non-historical world in which "period concepts finally correspond to no realities whatsoever" (282), but he ultimately dismisses this view. Jameson explains:

> Historicity is, in fact, neither a representation of the past nor a representation of the future . . . : it can first and foremost be defined as a perception of the present as history; that is, as a relationship to the present which somehow defamiliarizes it and allows us that distance from immediacy which is at length characterized as a historical perspective. (284)

Davey, Hutcheon, and Jameson all started writing about postmodernism at a time when their period could be described as postmodern, and so Jameson's concern over "a perception of the present as history" was then especially relevant and vexing. He continues: "what is at stake is essentially a process of reification whereby we draw back from our immersion in the here and now (not yet identified as a 'present') and grasp it as a kind of thing—not merely a 'present' but a present that can be dated and called the eighties or the fifties" (Jameson, *Postmodernism* 284). His primary example is Philip K. Dick's *Time Out of Joint* (1959), a science fiction that explicitly compares the 1950s to the imagined 1990s. It helps that *Time Out of Joint* projects the "present" into the future so that readers can imagine their present as "dated." The Western is not the same, because it tends to look backward from a not-yet reified, always modern or contemporary present, usually to the late nineteenth century. Imagine Price in the 1940s writing his stories set forty or fifty years earlier. First, he's writing about the past. Second, however, in most of his stories, Smokey Carmain tells the same story about how he got his name, and this seriality implies a perpetual present. Think of it as a time loop if you prefer. Or consider a more literal exception, the sci-fi Western film *Back to the Future III* (Zemeckis, 1990), in which the inventor Doc Brown travels from 1885, far beyond 1985, to a point in time when his time-travelling locomotive can be rebuilt to fly. The *Back to the Future* trilogy is fascinating partly because each sequel parodies at least one earlier film in the trilogy. And *Dynamic Western*'s stories featuring Smokey Carmain have a crucial similarity: in almost always repeating and embellishing his christening, they parody the first story about how he got his name, and they imply a series—a future—in which the legend will grow: smoke, fire, dragon, god. Based on the structural insistence on formalism in his essay in *Re: Reading the Postmodern*, Davey might well respond by saying that my examples here are, at best, postmodern ideas in conventional narratives—thus not postmodern in his way. But he also accepts the plurality of "postmodernisms," and I think that the dependence of parody on earlier texts, its seriality, is in itself a structural or formal feature that creates meaning and qualifies it as a postmodernism.

That it *might* be Canadian is delightful, because outside of Canada and apart from Canadianists, few onlookers would describe Canada as sly, postmodern, or sophisticated, except when trying on "American" clothes, being American in disguise, a dialogism that Mikhail Bakhtin would appreciate. More seriously, however, it suggests that *the Western*, almost always recognized first as an American genre, *can indeed teach us about historicism*, about a future-oriented society whose love of its history often seems to circle around to the future. Ronald Reagan, "the cowboy president," said, "Let's Make America Great Again!" Donald Trump said, "Make America Great Again!" Trump's slogan is not parody, unless we interpret it as unintentional parody. Hutcheon explains in one of her first works on the subject that "postmodernism is a fundamentally contradictory enterprise: its art forms (and its theory) use and abuse, install and then subvert convention in parodic ways, self-consciously pointing both to their own inherent paradoxes and provisionality and, of course, to their critical or ironic re-reading of the art of the past" ("Politics" 180). Trump has a "use" for Reagan but no sense of "abuse" of Reagan's Democratic origins or his career's "paradoxes": actor in many Westerns, first Democrat, then Republican. When Reagan says, "Let's," he is at least recognizing that an American narrative is not singular and altogether united, and that there might be more than one way to arrive somewhere (wherever it is) "again." For me, interpreting Trump, the destination is clear: Reagan. Although I have seen a photograph of Trump shaking hands with Reagan, and a photograph of Trump giving a speech in front of what appears to be a wax figure of John Wayne with a Monument Valley backdrop, Trump himself has reportedly denied that he had Reagan in mind, and if this is true (which is not likely) his slogan may be interpreted instead as an instance of the nostalgic ideology of the Western functioning as the political unconscious. Although Trump does not often seem self-conscious, he seems terrifically postmodern as a condition if not intention: subversive, destabilizing, relativistic, unpredictable, ahistorical. Perhaps this difference—condition not intention, which comes from Jean-François Lyotard's *The Postmodern Condition* (1979)—is at the heart of my inquiry into *Dynamic Western* and Smokey Carmain. From condition came intention (probably).[6] Thus, postmodern Canadian Westerns approach the

---

6   Admittedly, the inverse is possible. A conspiracy theorist might argue that late capitalists intended to create a postmodern condition that would reduce societies to lawless

American past very differently: *as do postmodern American Westerns*—for example, Michael Crichton's film *Westworld* (1973) and its television spin-offs (more postmodern ideas in conventional narratives—postmodernism as such). As the next chapter shows, various postmodern Canadian Westerns are at home on Hutcheon's timeline and are definitely engaged in "critical or ironic re-reading of the art of the past"—think Margaret Atwood's "Backdrop Addresses Cowboy" (1968), Michael Ondaatje's *The Collected Works of Billy the Kid* (1970), bpNichol's *The True Eventual Story of Billy the Kid* (1970), Frank Davey's *The Louis Riel Organ and Piano Co.*(1985), George Bowering's *Caprice* (1987), Paulette Jiles's *The Jesse James Poems* (1988), and (from chapter 2) Thomas King's *Green Grass, Running Water* (1993).[7] Like Crichton's *Westworld*, all of these Canadian Westerns represent the American past as a construct, a false front, a grand narrative, a metahistorical narrative. Every Canadian Western suggests that there is more than one way into American mythology. The pulp fiction in this chapter does too, though it handles textuality differently, without appealing to fragments, re-enactments, historical documents, or other textual backdrops, which are the main reasons why Luke Price's stories in *Dynamic Western* would not be individually identifiable as parodies or as postmodern texts. They need to be read cultural-materialistically and serially, maybe even sequentially, to be recognized as parodies.

The historical positioning of the Western in relation to Canadian postmodernism is especially fascinating, because nationalities have different and inconsistent temporal connotations, such as the notion that Canada as a nation is younger than the United States (arguably untrue) or Britain (obviously true), or, less officially, that the Canadian character is stodgily old fashioned and rather British or European compared to the American character, which is youthful (arguably true) and unfettered by Old World history (obviously untrue).[8] If postmodernism is not only a movement and a set of styles but also a *character*, which is reasonable to

---

enterprises governed only by "free markets."

7   In terms of "rereading" or at least "re-viewing," Nichol's title might be an allusion to *The True Story of Jesse James* (Ray, 1954).

8   Damien-Claude Bélanger explores these nuances more fully in his essay, "L'antiaméricanism et l'antimodernisme dans le discours de la droite intellectuelle du Canada, 1891–1945" (2008).

suggest of something so often described as "self-conscious" (as Hutcheon and Jameson both do), then it seems to me the sort of inventor who is a time traveller, maybe Doc Brown or the cinematic, rewound Billy the Kid of Ondaatje's book (as Dennis Cooley thinks of him), someone at home in different periods.

Postmodern Westerns of any nationality are curious because the Western itself is usually thought to be "anti-modern"—for example, resistant to changes related to the communications revolution after the invention of the telegraph by Samuel F. B. Morse in 1844. "Anti-modern" is not exactly the opposite of "postmodern." The opposite would be "pre-modern," if prefixes were definitive, but the opposite of "postmodern" might more accurately be "conventional," which is itself another way to understand genre. But postmodernism and genre are not opposed. More accurately, postmodernism's engagement with "the art of the past" is often with that art's generic conventions. Genre is conventional; it is always stuck in the past until a time traveller leaps out with it. The time traveller changes the context of the genre, and so the genre transforms. John G. Cawelti explains that there are four types of "generic transformation," and the first is parody (though he calls it burlesque), in which exaggeration and contrivance remind us of how far from reality the genre has strayed (*"Chinatown"* 504). In the case of the Western, thusly reminded of our distance from reality and a historical moment when the characters and plots of Westerns could plausibly be said to exist, we can allow it to modernize. Carolyn Williams in her work on Gilbert and Sullivan argues that parody is "a powerfully *modernizing*" (9) mode of representation, because it always updates its precursors; and so, aligning with the implications from Hutcheon, genre itself can be understood as perpetually modern, perhaps postmodern. (This claim about retrospection echoes that of Lee Clark Mitchell on the always-already-postness of the Western, which I quoted in the introduction to this book.) We can even dispense with the syllogism. Genre, like parody, is usually updating a precursor, so in that sense it is usually remaking itself as current or recurrent. Some genres have in their conventional plots the Western's historical theme of modernization and its nostalgia for the pre-telegraphic eras of pre-modernity (e.g., as in steampunk or various medievalisms), but the Western is almost certainly more popular and thereby especially apt as an explainer of genre in its relationship to parody (which relies on an audience's recognition of intertexts) and the "modernizing" effects of postmodernism.

In fact, Hutcheon's association between postmodernism and parody in *A Theory of Parody* (1985) seems entirely relatable to the Canadian Westerns published serially in the 1940s. Ironically, although Hutcheon cites Lyotard's view, in *The Postmodern Condition*, that postmodernism questions its culture's grand narratives, she focuses almost exclusively on high-cultural examples, such as Euripides, George Gordon Byron (i.e., Lord Byron), T. S. Eliot, Ezra Pound, René Magritte, and Umberto Eco, though she does mention relatively popular directors such as Brian De Palma and publications such as *Punch* and *Playboy*. The shortage of popular or low-cultural examples is a limitation of her early study, one that she corrects in *Re: Reading the Postmodern* with the inclusion of examples such as children's literature and graphic novels, but it otherwise offers much to this chapter. Hutcheon explains that postmodernism is "implicitly contesting . . . such concepts as aesthetic originality and textual closure" ("Politics" 180). Toronto's *Dynamic Western* clearly makes no attempt at "aesthetic originality"; on the contrary, it is unquestionably derivative of American models, and its pseudonyms suggest that few authors within its pages cared much for recognition as "originals" in the context of the pulps. *Dynamic Western*'s seriality undermines its potential for "textual closure" (as does the incompleteness of the archive), and its seriality—its repetitiveness—is a sign that it is parody, repetition with difference. A structural dimension such as seriality can be parodic because, for Hutcheon, parody needs a "codified form" (*Theory* 18) but need not be a mockery (5), as long as it is ironic (6, 104); it generally demonstrates "ironic inversion" (6), such as men playing women's roles and vice versa. Hutcheon seems to imply, then, that a mere cliché can be parody if it has a complexity that readers can distinguish in it, even if the author was not intending the complexity. Such an implication would seem logical to a postmodern reader, someone schooled on postmodern writing. While I doubt that Price and others in *Dynamic Western* were truly ahead of their time, or avant-garde, and while I find only a few gender-bending inversions in stories of Smokey Carmain, his roles are definitely "playing with multiple conventions," not always "with critical distance" (Hutcheon, *Theory* 7) but certainly with conventions of more than one genre, especially detective fiction. (Like a detective, he likes to explain mysteries, such as the one about his name.) A genre need not ridicule its provenance in other genres to be parodic. It simply needs enough variety in each iteration, and generic crossovers often present the variety on a silver platter—"intergenerational, intercultural, and intergeneric" (Sircar 11)—or at least a buffet table.

So we learn, then, that parody is both ironic and structural, in alignment with some theories of postmodernism. Furthermore, Smokey Carmain's self-parody (or at least his sardonic self-consciousness) and his ironic relationship to social mores gain a postmodern dimension that aligns with the "oppositional" and "contestatory" history of the nigh-outlawed Westerns of the '40s pulps. And in another meaningful sense, the prototypical postmodernism of Smokey Carmain invites us to change how we read: not chronologically but synchronically, reaching across iterations for patterns that reveal themselves only with every iteration at our fingertips at the same time.

A Gunstock Character: Smokey Carmain

Given enough time and money, a scholar's ideal method of studying genre—even the prolific genres—would be to read as much of it as possible and create a massively comparative project. Compromising in this chapter, I also have the convenience of the archive's very limited holdings: only nine readable issues (ten in total) of *Dynamic Western* and a few issues of related magazines (at the time of my visits, at least). I could read across authors in *Dynamic Western* to understand the genre; authorship, in theory, is not essential to the genre, but repetition is—and Luke Price's Smokey Carmain appears in nine of these ten issues. Partly because I am attempting to track icons of the genre, I chose Smokey as the outlaw to pair with the lawman of the previous chapter, the Muscular Christian Mountie.

Who is Smokey? He is, for starters, an American from the Southwest, in a series set throughout the Southwest and the Midwest in the United States, with only a rare mention of Canada. He is, in a sense, always new, because he never stays home at Hornspoon to deal with trouble there, mainly because he has already brought peace to the county. He is always "a stranger" ("Smokey Defies" 28), always a drifter reintroduced (eventually with his reputation preceding him). He has excuse after excuse to go to other counties outside of his jurisdiction and to step in where other sheriffs have faltered. His father was Irish, and his fatherly uncle a wanderer ("Smokey Signs Up" 15). These wanderings and reintroductions enable parody in Hutcheon's sense of it. Seemingly a man of the first decade of the 1900s, a turn-of-the-century man, as Price implies by setting the series just after "the nineties" ("Smokey Carmain" 56), Smokey is not as nationally branded as some Western figures set during and immediately after the Civil War. In terms of his identity, we see his physique and appearance more than anything—often literally in the illustrations accompanying the stories. In the illustrations, he is iconically the American cowboy: clean-shaven, handsome but wiry, dressed in denim and a cowboy hat—a classic Stetson ("Blight" 15). In "Smokey Defies an Army," he is "like a tall figure of bronze" (28). The blue, sometimes grey ("Blight" 5; "Smokey Stirs Up" 52), of his eyes is often mentioned. He has "firm lips" and "strong, white teeth" ("Smokey Stirs Up" 52), a "lean chin" ("Blight" 6) but "a capable pair of shoulders" ("Gunsmoke" 98) that are sometimes also called "powerful" ("Smokey Signs Up" 10). In one of the later stories, he is "a huge man" ("Blight" 24). Some of these details appear in a longer description in one of his early stories, when he is appraised by the bartender Baldy Stern:

> he saw a tall, withy-bodied fellow, evidently in his early twenties with a thatch of reddish-gold hair over steel-blue eyes, and a pair of capable shoulders. The glint of humor in those eyes was offset by a firm mouth and square, agressive [sic] jaw.... His slow drawl put the brand of the southwest on him. ("Smokey Carmain" 55)

That his "drawl" is "slow" is a sign that he is the action-oriented and laconic cowboy. He "never prided himself upon being the meek as Moses type" ("Blight" 8), and he prefers that his actions bely his meekness. "[A] man's got a right to keep his thoughts private" ("Gunsmoke" 100), says Smokey just after he punches out a man who had been trying to draw him into repartee and then a gunfight. Later, asked by the doctor how he was stabbed in the arm, he says, "It ain't important enough to wast [sic] palaver on" (105). He appears to be serious about the old joke: "It's hard to put a foot in a closed mouth" (Stone 12). When he does engage in conversation with men, his smugly confident sense of humour and his daring machismo suggest that he is like the Virginian in Owen Wister's novel of the same name, or like John Wayne in his developing roles through the late 1930s into the 1940s. Clint Eastwood, in all of his roles in Italian Westerns, and in later films such as *The Outlaw Josey Wales* (1976), follows these models closely, speaking not only rarely but also softly.

Metaphorically, Smokey is not entirely human. Many of Price's characters are metaphors of non-human animals, especially snakes that figure in for the villains. In "Hound Dog Justice," Smokey pours out some bad but expensive beer and tells a man, "Yuh can't make a hawse drink ef he don't want to, Mister" (47), alluding to himself as the horse—an extension of a long, medieval tradition of imagining knights as hybrid figures: half man, half horse (which I will explain in more detail at opportune moments in chapters 5 and 6). Later, he also implies that he's a dog or wolf because he "lopes" ("Hound Dog" 52). In more than one story, he is described as "a leashed dynamo" ("Valley of Vengeance" 63; "Smokey Signs Up for Trouble" 10), like either a dog or a horse. The horse-man metaphor is common in Westerns. In *Dynamic Western*, Smokey's horse Pancho is a big black stallion that he "wouldn't have taken a fortune for" ("Smokey Defies" 30). He loans Pancho to Helen in "Six-Gun Thunder" but gives his own body to no woman, controlling his urges and promising to settle down when he has savings and land of his own. When Pancho is stolen in "Smokey Defies an Army," he finds him and kills the man who stole the horse, asserting control over his horse as a parallel, I think, to the control over his own body epitomized in his expert marksmanship. Another parallel appears in "Smokey Signs Up for Trouble," when Smokey's *guns* are the dogs that he controls: "the Carmains' guns had *leaped* up, black *muzzles* exploding lead and smoke. The heavy *snarling* of sixguns beat the air" (17, emphasis added).

With these almost trickster-like transformations into the horse and dog, he is wily enough to be a smokescreen, and there is little detail of his background in any of the stories, other than what I have mentioned. Relatedly, in "Smokey Signs Up for Trouble," Smokey says, "I got no folks living" (11), attesting to his lack of family and his mysterious, unknown history. Pretending to be a rancher as a means of pursuing the villain in "Hound Dog Justice," Smokey chooses an X as his brand, "the unknown quantity" (50). In the same way that he is open to interpretation, he is "a man used to wide, open spaces" ("Six-Gun" 71). The "unknown" or uncertain aspect of his identity becomes a plot device in "Valley of Vengeance" when an impostor arrives. The real Smokey confronts the "phoney" and says, "I'm Carmain. . . . I don't like imitators" (65). But the fact that the impostor can be a bad guy and pretend to be a good guy suggests that Smokey does not have an essence that can be copied—an "aura," yes, but nothing more substantial beyond his body, including his horse. (Nevertheless, the remainder of this chapter does characterize him more specifically. It's just that the characterization is not apparent in any one issue of *Dynamic Western* and has to be condensed from many stories.)

As horse or dog, Smokey is sexualized; both animals have strongly sexual and gendered connotations in the metaphors and idioms that we use in comparing them to humans (e.g., being hung like a horse, or having sex doggy style). The sexuality of the cowboy or outlaw-lawman is not only animal, however. A generic trait of any cowboy is the masculinity often grossly symbolized by his gun—but Smokey, in spite of being named after a phallic discharge, has *not only* "no folks living" and no family, *but also* a mostly virginal experience in *Dynamic Western*. All the little deaths sublimate sexuality. In his very first story in *Dynamic Western*, "The Gunsmoke Sheriff," he (as a twenty-something) begins to develop a relationship with a girl "about nineteen or twenty, a golden blonde with deep blue eyes and strawberry lips," a "firm figure," and tanned "bare legs" (102) under her skirt. She is Betty Stryker, who has been orphaned and is trying to manage her family's ranch with the help of her younger brother, Bud. Smokey gives them a "silver dollar" to buy sweets and, he says to her, "a ribbon fur your purty hair" (104), flirting as well as he can. When Smokey defeats her enemy, his friend Ned Smart—later self-described, in "Hound Dog Justice," as "Smart by name and smart by nature. A smart guy, and a smart shooter" (49)—says to him, "Seems tuh me that accordin' tuh land law, with this hombre dead, the Triple X [the bad guy's ranch] passes into the hands o' the town. Don' see no reason why the town can't make yuh a weddin' present of it" (110). (This "land law," notably, ignores Indigenous claims to the land, as I describe below.) Smokey and Betty kiss, and as Ned leaves "he stopped at the desk and blew out the lamp Betty had used to create the ghostly effect but neither Smokey nor Betty knew or cared whether it was dark or light" (110). This experience is the only sex in the series.

Two stories later, Smokey and Ned are motivated by a posted reward, and Smokey wants his half to get a stake (land) that will make him equal partner in an eventual marriage to Betty, but she is otherwise ignored in this story and the previous one. Betty then seems to disappear. In "Valley of Vengeance," it is Nettie Raines who offers Smokey a partnership, if not a marriage, and Smokey declines: "too much prosperity makes Ned and me nervous" (76). He appears to be making excuses to avoid his own wedding; George Bowering has written in *Caprice* that "[r]omances had proposals of marriage at the end of them, and dime novels of the west had the threat of the hint of marriage at the end of them" (212). Later again, in "Six-Gun Justice," Helen Lenox and Jim Lawson decide to marry as soon as he's out of the hospital, but Smokey declines to be their best man while "patting his black horse's neck affectionately" (76). If the horse is gendered masculine because the outlaw-lawman can also hyphenate as horse-man, then it is as if his horse is a manly companion, a homosocial figure. He does promise, however, to "be here for the first christening" (76) of the Helen-Jim baby. He does the same for the christening of the Cherry-Stan baby in "Blight on Valhalla," but in this story he even chooses the name of the child, the same name as that of a murderous train robber who converts to the good side. He is not against family, and naming, but he wants to avoid the sexual occasions, whether or not he is waiting for Betty, whom he never marries in the extant archived magazines. He has an "indifference to romance, [but] was always interested in Beauty in distress" ("Smokey Signs Up" 11)—Beauty the ideal, not Betty the woman. In "Smokey Signs Up for Trouble," the "Beauty" is yet another woman, Grace Foster, fiancée of her father's foreman. Reference to this "damsel in distress" evokes the Freudian virgin/whore dichotomy that Westerns tend to assert along with the patriarchy, and with the Electra complex implied when a woman loves her father's protegé.

This characterization seems perfectly attuned to a likely audience of teenage boys, especially because Smokey is only in his early twenties. The same type of cowboy played by a not-so-young-anymore John Wayne or Clint Eastwood is less expected, maybe, but writers have dealt with this problem by killing off the family in the backstory or producing some other reason (e.g., shell shock after the Civil War, or, in some of the whisperings about the famous Shane, repressed homosexuality) for the cowboy's loneliness. Smokey's youth not only makes him a relatable character (even if he is quite flat) to boys, but it also confirms the logic of his missing backstory.

We do get a clue to where he came from—and his political alignment—in "Valley of Vengeance" when Smokey tells Nettie that he had worked in an oil company in Oklahoma (68). (See also this book's conclusion, on Westerns and the extractive industries.) We can infer that big business did not suit him, which is why he prefers to be an itinerant sheriff. Although we associate big business with conservatism today, Smokey's political alignment is clearly conservative in the sense that he believes in taking the law into his own hands even when he, as sheriff, is not the law, as when he is out of his jurisdiction; however, he does believe in government, in what he calls "statute-law" compared to "gun-law" ("Smokey Defies" 28). And he does seem to believe that the law is meant to protect the little guy from the unfairness produced by big numbers. In "Smokey Defies an Army," the conflict that he needs to resolve is between big-time ranchers, small-time cowmen, and "nesters" (i.e., family farmers).

More specifically, the conflict is between big business and entrepreneurs, and he sides with the latter against the ranchers and the "Army." Smokey says to himself, "Gun-law backed up by mortgages, notes, compound interest and political power can be mighty unhealthy for any community" ("Smokey Defies" 28); he had a similar view of the rich W. C. Hollow and his Hollow City in "Smokey Carmain Shoots It Out!" He says he "likes money" ("Smokey Signs Up" 10), but not that of the establishment. Big business in "Smokey Stirs Up Rebellion" is an octopus (56), its tentacles like the snakes that typically describe the outlaws in Smokey's stories. In the same story, rather than rely on the law, he foments "rebellion" that even becomes the creation of a union—the "Cortlett County Cattle Association" ("Smokey Stirs Up" 70)—to represent small ranches and their mutual interests. In "Smokey Defies an Army," he says to the nesters, "I'll help you if you can't manage alone" (32), a direct articulation of his modus operandi. This plot would later be echoed in Jack Schaefer's novel *Shane* (1946/1949), which became one of the most indelible of cinematic Westerns in 1953. Less elegant and decent than that novel's title character, Smokey nevertheless shares his basic sense of duty to smaller social units (individuals or families) over bigger ones (usually businesses but sometimes mayors and other representatives of government).

He also has a more selfish sense of honour and reputation than Shane. He *does* have some honour; in "Blight on Valhalla," Smokey "can't bear to let even a crook roast alive" (19). When he later shoots a corrupt deputy at his office, he apologizes to Cherry Hollister: "I don't like to kill even a crook in the presence of ladies" (25). ("Bosh!" she responds, claiming to have seen shooting and in fact to have killed a man who was trying to hurt her father.) About to be hanged by Brant Corning and his waddies in "The Gunsmoke Sheriff," Smokey reflects on himself:

> Dying didn't bother him. A man had to go sooner or later, and whether you were buzzard meat or worm fodder made little difference. It was what was going to be left behind. Betty Stryker and Bud without their seven precious steers. Ned Smart and Doc Hills and Walt Tailor thinking ill of him. (107)

Although "what was going to be left behind" here are people and their difficulties, his sympathy is divided, and he demonstrates a subtle self-pity on account of his reputation, the concern that someone might be "thinking ill of him." Of course, he rectifies the situation and saves his reputation; he is not hanged, and, as always, he gets the upper hand by drawing faster, shooting more accurately, and punching harder than any other man. By the fourth story in the series, his reputation was preceding him such that he becomes "the great Smokey" ("Valley" 63), "right prominent all through the West" ("Blight" 12), just as the story of his name was growing to mythical proportions—an anti-heroic dragon, not J. R. R. Tolkien's Smaug (from the 1937 novel *The Hobbit*) but Smokey.

His infamy or celebrity is likely a factor in how quickly he is accepted as a legitimate figure of the law, even when he is outside his own county and jurisdiction. In "Six-Gun Thunder," Smokey tells Flack Dolan, "I'm giving orders outa my own county" (55); in "Blight on Valhalla," Smokey disclaims, "I have no official position whatever" (9). It is a pattern in these stories. In most of them, when he encounters a new town and a new enemy to overcome, he is elected or acclaimed into the role of sheriff by people in the here and now, not by distant electors or politicians.

Smokey does not always, however, have this legitimacy, and—though he often reveals a surprisingly Mountie-like desire for order (a theme of the previous chapter)—he is almost always willing to step outside the law or to break codes of decent behaviour:

> If Rat Biggle had really carried out his threat and killed [Smokey's friend, the sheriff Jim] Lawson, Carmain was resolved to avenge his death, law or no law. ("Six-Gun" 56)

And:

> He wished that some magic carpet could suddenly transport him and the entire set-up to his own county where he, backed up by legal authority, could demand their surrender. Then, reminding himself that such wishing was a waste of time, he tensed, clapping his hands to his revolvers. (58)

Later in "Six-Gun Justice," outnumbered but with the advantage of cover, Smokey resorts to shooting men who can't shoot back: "He had shot men in the course of his duty. Had killed more than one who defied his authority. But he recoiled from this kind of affair" (59). But not always! He claims to prefer it "clean" but also appears to relish "dirty fighting" ("Smokey Stirs Up" 64). Offended by Jefferson Trump in "Smokey Defies an Army," Smokey "might have broken his own rule right then and there. His six-gun was half out of the leather before he reminded himself that shooting a man in the back would be a bad start-off for a sheriff" (28). His legitimate claim to representing the law is on occasion questionable, and he often teeters on the edge—though, in fairness, he often shoots other men in the gun (symbolism par excellence) to disarm them, or occasionally other parts of their bodies—for example, the hip ("Hound Dog") or more often the arm, almost always a metonym of the gun (a sidearm), or in proximity to the groin. As James Warner Bellah wrote of a different but related figure in another 1940s Western, though in the middlebrow *Saturday Evening Post*, Smokey "hewed so close to the line" ("Mission" 31).

The opening paragraph of "Smokey Carmain Shoots It Out!" includes this introduction:

> Smokey Carmain seemed born for trouble. It often came his way in bunches. But when it didn't, he went out to find it halfway. Whenever a place got too civilized, Smokey pulled out of it and headed for a further frontier which was as yet uninvaded by law and order. (52)

He is *almost* as much outlaw as lawman—an outlaw-lawman, that figure of symmetry again. Twice in "Smokey Signs Up for Trouble," characters observe the similarity between the name of Lightnin' "Cormon," one of the outlaws, and "Carmain" (11, 12). Smokey dismisses it as coincidence, but, later in a gunfight with Cormon, he "knew those vivid blue eyes. This was not Lightnin' Cormon, but his uncle—Jack Carmain—that man who had been his boyhood idol!" (14). Jack was, in fact, Smokey's father figure, because we learn in "Smokey Signs Up for Trouble" that the eponymous hero was an orphan raised by his uncle, another reason why marrying someone and starting a family is an unfamiliar concept to him. He is too close to the dark side.

Detective Smokey Carmain

Symmetry is about being half of one thing face to face with half of another, but it is not too much an extension to suggest that it applies less equally to Smokey's crossovers between genres too. The balance is tilted far to the side of the Western, but Price's contributions to *Dynamic Western* sometimes tilt toward noirish detective fiction, another of the crime fiction genres that were and are common to pulp fiction. The most recent crossovers of this type with which I am familiar are, first, Quentin Tarantino's most genre-bending Western, *The Hateful Eight* (2015), in which the Major, played by Samuel L. Jackson, is both a type of sheriff and a detective who assembles the suspects and tells the story of the crime as a conclusion to the film, à la Hercule Poirot by Agatha Christie (a character who predates Smokey by twenty years); second, on television, HBO's *Westworld* (2016–20), in which the futuristic creators of a Western-themed virtual reality are also busy trying to solve the mystery of how characters—which *they* have invented—are rewriting their scripts, their various genres (e.g., Western, detective, sci-fi). Most of Price's stories about Smokey have a crime to be solved, often a crime enveloped in mystery, and he engages in detection, subterfuge, disguise, and other gestures toward the other genre. They are often the tenor, so to speak, of metaphorical transformations of the vehicle, which is always the Western first and foremost.

So, for example, in "Blight on Valhalla," Smokey is asked to pretend to be a homesteader for the purposes of reconnaissance and ultimately of solving the mystery of why homesteaders are unwilling to "stick" (6) to the area. In "Smokey Carmain Shoots It Out!" he goes to a "town meetin'" (76) and certainly plays Christie's Poirot, about to explain the crimes after he puts a recovered gun down in front of Hollow as a key piece of evidence. Everyone implicated in the story—everyone who is still alive, that is— is present to hear Smokey's explanation. Squire Lainson, acting as chair of the meeting at Smokey's request, calls the meeting "a court of a sort" (77), increasing the symbolic suggestion that Smokey is now acting as a detective or lawyer—an explainer, a storyteller—rather than sheriff. This change from action hero to talker is one of the ironic inversions in Price's stories that provide evidence for Hutcheon's theory of parody. It's ironic simply because it's the opposite of the expected: words, not deeds. In this story, although gunfire erupts briefly after Smokey has made his case, he is not the one who has to shoot to resolve the conflict. His function has changed, though he reverts to action hero in later stories. The inversion in "Smokey Carmain Shoots It Out!" is also self-reflexive, as one might expect from postmodern fiction compared to popular fiction: there seems to be authorial awareness in the irony of the title, which is counterfactual to the resolution of the plot: he doesn't shoot it out; he talks it through.

Furthermore, in bending toward the figure of the detective or lawyer, and thus explainer and storyteller, these Westerns gain a dimension of self-reflexivity that amplifies the already obvious repetitions and homages that are a manifestation of self-reflection, if not self-reflexivity. They become stories about storytelling, much as we can infer from the "smoke signals" about Smokey's moniker that he is functioning as a teller of his own tale, a crafty crafter of his own persona, his own framing device.

Smokey and Indigeneity

My reference to "smoke signals" is no accident here, because many of the cowboys or outlaw-lawmen in Westerns have been hybrid figures, racial crossovers, both colonial and Indigenous. Consider John Wayne's Hondo, "part Indian," in the eponymous 1953 film, as a paragon or at least paradigm of this type of figure. Smokey, however, has almost no such connection to Indigeneity. His separation and his prejudices are evident and obvious. In "Smokey Carmain Shoots It Out!," his nemesis—the mayor, judge, businessman—named Hollow is described like so (and quite well too):

> Inches above six feet, broad-shouldered, craggy-faced, Hollow presented a series of flat contradictions in appearance, in taste, and in personality. His skin was bronzed, his black hair worn long in the fashion of the plainsmen of the old days. But his hands, small for one of his huge bulk, were smooth as a woman's, and manicured to a nicety. His face was shaved cleanly, and his well tailored brown coat and trousers were pressed neatly. A flaring red tie, done in a loose bow, Morocco boots, beaded belt and holster gave him an Indian aspect which his build and erect carriage seemed to bear out, and which was accentuated by an ornate necklace of alternated bear's claws and elk's teeth which hung in a double loop about his pillarlike neck. But the outstanding feature of the man were [sic] his eyes, and they were not the eyes of an Aborigine. Instead they were pale and of an indeterminate hue. (58)

Hollow, here, is the hybrid figure, and Smokey loses no time in offending him with a racial slur. Furthermore, instead of thinking that Hollow is partly like himself (white), he thinks that he is mostly different (non-white) because of Hollow's trappings of Indigeneity, which are not even all that convincing, partly because they also appear to be Orientalist (which makes sense if you consider the fundamental geographical error in using "Indian" to describe the Indigenous peoples of North America rather than certain South Asians). When Hollow asks him when he's leaving, which is the first thing he says to Smokey, Smokey ignores him and drinks to the health of Baldy while prefiguring anxieties about blood quanta: "Here's to you, old timer, and to any other white man on this range—if there is any" (58). In other words, he derisively dismisses Hollow as an "Indian," and he toasts the "white man" in general. He is a straightforward example of a white-supremacist ideologue, and yet he insists on purity in a series whose crossovers suggest a willing mongrelism.

Yes, this is curious: Why gladly hybridize genre and character but not race or racialization? These stories were appearing in the early 1940s, when the horrors of Nazi eugenics and genocide were probably not yet familiar to most readers outside Europe, but even in the 1950s Westerns were still prominently racist and even, at times, genocidal. John Wayne in a mid-fifties masterpiece such as *The Searchers* (if it can be qualified as such on the merits of aesthetics alone, its ethics being more complicated) still wants to eradicate miscegenation. But only a few years earlier, Wayne in *Hondo* (1953) provides a less canonical but more perfect comparison that deserves a brief digression—partly because I already considered *Hondo* in the context of Indigenous literature in chapter 2. Based on a story by Louis L'Amour, *Hondo* stars Wayne as Hondo Lane, a "part Indian" gunman who had lived with the Apache for five years but also worked riding dispatch for the cavalry—a man with few absolute allegiances except to principles of self-reliance and radically free will: "A long time ago I made me a rule. I let people do what they wanna do." He does, however, stop people from trying to kill him. Without hating either the Apache or the agents of colonialism who would kill and dispossess them, he ultimately sides with the cavalry in protecting the widowed Angie Lowe (Geraldine Page) and her boy, for whom he has become a symbolic husband and father. Like Smokey, Hondo has an only symbolic family, implying that the sort of mixing that must happen to make a family (e.g., socializing and sexual intercourse) is forbidden to him partly because of the risk of miscegenation.

The boy in *Hondo*, significantly, gets a symbolic brother but not a father among the Apache. When the Apache come to remind Angie that they told her to leave and she retorts that she was waiting for her husband, one of the chief's men clutches her. Her boy reacts by firing her pistol at him, missing. Brought to the Apache chief Vittorio (Michael Pate), he declares that he is not afraid of them. Vittorio says that Johnny is "brave like Apache boy," seizes his hand, and cuts their thumbs, intermingling their blood to make them family. He declares that she is now the mother of an Apache and may stay on their land to care for the boy. Later, Vittorio presents his men as prospective new husbands for Angie, but she is committed to the memory of her husband and her hope for a relationship with Hondo. The ideological rationale of these scenes is to show that the possibility of continuing the family line depends on refusing miscegenation and raising a family among the future winners of the Indian Wars. Chauvinistic and racist, the film associates racial purity with superiority and survival, and we get the impression that Hondo's Indigenous "part" is very small indeed—perhaps, in fact, a lie that he uses to delude himself so that he can accept his own sexual history with an Indigenous woman. Like Smokey, Hondo can be "part" something else, but only symbolically. The example of Hondo also informs a theory of why Smokey, contrary to form, doesn't kill Hollow: "part" of him recognizes his own cowboy-detective hybridity in Hollow's miscegenized racialization.

In Smokey's stories, this racist and colonial narrative sometimes triggers a commentary on the gun. Near the end of the series, in "Smokey Signs Up for Trouble," Grace Foster tells Smokey, "I often wish guns had never been invented." He responds with a big grin: "If they hadn't a-been, I guess this country would still belong to the Injuns, Miss Grace. But since there is guns, and bad men use 'em, we'll have to meet the devil with fire" (11). His enjoyment of the colonial narrative here implies that "good men" took the land from "the Injuns," and that "bad men" were now threatening the same land now owned by settlers. The irony is lost on him. In the final story in the archive, Smokey tells Laurie Wyndon, "Guns and blood have always been used in this country to win anything ("Smokey Stirs Up" 60). If "country" means "land," then he is wrong, because guns came with the armies and settlers. But he means the nation-state, or, perhaps more accurately, land dedicated by settlers to a particular business: ranching. He admits that he is "[a] stranger to this district, yes" (60) while asserting, "But still it's my country. The part of the country I was born and raised in. I love every foot of this cattle country, and I don't like seein' a bunch of stuffed Stetsons from back yonder in the East take over this range and run it with hired guns and threats and bribes" (60–1). Here, Smokey erroneously implies that he is native—"born and raised"—and that the land is properly his to protect from newcomers from the East. Again, the irony is lost on him. As a hero, Smokey falls short of today's ethics of representation in relation to race, especially racialization of the "Indian," but his view of guns remains popular on the right and at the centre of North American politics. (Some of the nostalgia for the present in the Western comes from its untrue reminder to gun owners that guns are a way of life, "always." When Smokey convinces twenty men to burn the ranch of the kingpin who had control of the law, "he reminded himself grimly" of "those times" ["Smokey Stirs Up" 66] when six-gun justice is seemingly necessary—*just like today*, we are meant to think.)

Price himself appears to be no better at understanding Hollow's Indigeneity, implying that he is "Indian," and in fact Price follows the Western tradition—in the genre and often writ large in the Western world—of imagining any Indigenous person as the Vanishing "Indian" (a trope that I considered more fully in chapter 2). Witness "Six-Gun Thunder":

> Three days after his arrival, Smokey visited Crazy Horse Hill. Evidently the name had come from an incident of pioneer days that had since been forgotten. He found the former mission building little more than a decayed heap of rubble and rotting timbers surrounded by ancient graves. The general desolation and unbroken silence got on his nerves. (63)

Smokey's irritation, or his unease, is uncanny: a return of the repressed, in this case the history of Native Americans such as Crazy Horse, whose name's English translation is another forgetting, another mistake; his Lakota name, Tȟašúŋke Witkó, translates better as "His Horses Have Spirit" (Diamond). Price invokes history here only insofar as it serves the stereotype of the Vanishing "Indian." Curiously, however, it is also a mistaken assumption of what could be called the Vanishing Christian, "the former mission building little more than a decayed heap," which could be a historical reality in a given instance but which does not align with the success of Christianity in the United States in the late nineteenth and early twentieth centuries ("success" in the sense of replacing Indigenous religions and forerunning other major religions). The Vanishing "Indian" absolves guilt, or turns guilt into the less specific unease, a minor complaint of the "nerves." Meanwhile, the Vanishing Christian gives the outlaw-lawman a licence to be less meek and forgiving, even if Smokey does feel pangs of guilt when shooting at men who can't shoot back, or at wanting to shoot them *in* the back. When Smokey is reunited with his fatherly uncle, Lightnin' Cormon, the uncle doesn't survive their gunfight against the outlaws that had been Cormon's allies: "It had been right and just that this Lightnin' should die, [Smokey] reminded himself. Yet his heart was heavy"; he then declares that his uncle "died fightin' sidewinders, and rates Christian iburial [*sic*]" ("Smokey Signs Up" 17). However dragon-like Smokey is, he believes himself to be against the snakes and on Jesus Christ's side.

Crazy Horse's "name," "forgotten," brings us full circle in this chapter, back to Smokey's self-fashioning as the smoke-loving dragon, a symbol in Christianity of the devil. This, too, might be an ironic inversion that confirms the parody in Price's stories. The parody is evident in his naming, obviously, but also in the twist on Christianity that bedevils a neutral reading of the stories. Unlike the Indigenous peoples stereotyped across the long history and even the recent history of the Western, a history that the Cree filmmaker Neil Diamond documents in *Reel Injun* (2009), Smokey has the privilege of naming himself as he sees fit. He calls himself, in effect, a smoke-maker. And in 1942, the great smoke-maker was the war machine, one with the genocidal potential of the Holocaust that could have unconsciously paralleled a death wish against Indigenous peoples whose unwillingness to vanish also sustained the wish, and Smokey's dawning awareness of his postmodern condition had not yet helped him effect a critique.

However regressively enjoyable the reading of Price's stories can be—a boyish thrill—I want to emphasize my dislike of the character as a figure that replicates the most problematic tropes of the Western. I cannot be certain that Price knew he was creating a devil, a monster, in Smokey Carmain. So much suggests the opposite. But Smokey is certainly typical of heroes in the Western; he "combines the town's morals with the outlaw's skills" (Altman, "Semantic" 11). Historically, eventually, "the town" turned against him again, and he began, not exactly to vanish, but to lose prominence to a host of cultural competitors. Ian Driscoll writes that "[t]he monthly thrills of a magazine like *Dynamic Western* or *Bill Wayne's Western Magazine* were no match for westerns at local cinemas or the 'Lone Ranger' series, which had just begun airing on television" ("Decline"). And the Lone Ranger and Smokey Carmain were both the type of character that revisionist Westerns would address when postmodern literature became a more obvious structural or formal experiment and, beginning in the 1970s in the United States and Canada, stood up in the West.

5

CanLit's Postmodern Westerns
Ghosts and the Cowgirl Riding Off into the Sunrise

Whereas the previous chapter illustrated, through the character of Smokey Carmain, a few premonitions of a historical period that Jean-François Lyotard describes as "the postmodern condition" in the 1979 book of that name, the books we turn to in this chapter tend to illustrate a more postmodern *intention* that we can infer from stylistic experimentation. In other words, I discern two facets of postmodernism: first, the almost unavoidable situation of living in a world where media and communications have dramatically changed how we think, what we know, and what we make; second, our creative responses to that situation, including literary simulations designed to call attention to and dramatize that same situation.[1] Luke Price's Smokey Carmain is a typical but early, and thus prototypical or emergent, anti-hero of the Canadian Western genre,[2] and his parodically self-referential self-naming gives me reason to suggest that he is on the train toward the derailment that is postmodernism. But he is not resistant to genre; he affirms it from within, rather than questioning it from within as postmodernists usually try to do (Hutcheon, *Poetics* 20;

---

1   I am not always strict about separating these facets, because they soon overlap, but we could identify writers as either "postmodern" or "postmodern*ist*" to imply the difference between condition and intention—when we are confident that we can tell the difference.

2   Beyond the Western, the anti-hero is not only a postmodern figure, of course. Ronald Sutherland in *The New Hero* (1977) finds several examples of anti-heroes in the literary fiction of his day, but this "loser" (4) is not new; the anti-hero goes through cycles of dormancy and awakening.

D'haen 184). The American Western seems more ready for postmodernism when the 1970s roll around—for example, after Ishmael Reed's novel *Yellow Back Radio Broke-Down* (1969) and with the films *Little Big Man* (Penn, 1970) and *Blazing Saddles* (Brooks, 1974).[3] Linda Hutcheon claims that the postmodernism of that era thrives on "the periphery or the margin ... [which is] also the frontier, the place of possibility" (*Canadian* 3); "the border is the postmodern space *par excellence*" (4)—hence the importance of Robert Kroetsch to Canadian literature of the West, if not the Western.[4] The postmodern intention in the Western is not only stylistic. Although readers since Fredric Jameson have found evidence of postmodern literature's complicity with late capitalism, other readers have discovered a resistance that at least attempts to question everything, including capitalism and its development of neoliberalism. It is coincidentally a resistance to the status quo of genre, an interrogation of the American hegemony of the genre, even and often *by* writers in America—including texts such as Clint Eastwood's arguably postmodern Westerns, perhaps especially his film *Pale Rider* (1985). Just as arguably, however, his *Unforgiven* (1992) backslides into the myth of regeneration through violence that I consider in more detail in the next chapter. For now, I will look at the following Canadian examples: briefly at Margaret Atwood's "Backdrop Addresses Cowboy" (1968) and bpNichol's *The True Eventual Story of Billy the Kid* (1970), somewhat more closely at Michael Ondaatje's *The Collected Works of Billy the Kid* (1970), and more thoroughly at Frank Davey's *The Louis Riel Organ and Piano Co.* (1985), George Bowering's *Caprice* (1987), and Paulette Jiles's *The Jesse James Poems* (1989), which I will read alongside Ondaatje's book.[5] They culminate in Thomas King's *Green Grass, Running Water* (1993), but that was the centrepiece of chapter 2. These examples reveal that Canadian writers chose postmodern, resistant positions from the beginning of America's own trend toward questioning that quintessential

---

3   Notable, especially in the context of Reed, are African-American Westerns such as Sydney Poitier's *Buck and the Preacher* (1972) and the Blaxploitation Western of Gordon Parks Jr.'s *Thomasine and Bushrod* (1974).
4   I would love the time and space to consider Kroetsch's *The Studhorse Man* (1969) as a Western, but even more obviously germane is *The Man from the Creeks* (1998), a gold rush Northern or Northwestern, which I examine in this book's conclusion.
5   Also because of time and space, I have left out Bowering's *Shoot!* (1994), but for a recent interpretation see Fehrle (251–70).

American genre and its assumptions about topics such as region, race, and gender. These moves countered not only American Westerns but also the complicit Canadian Westerns that had been published since the turn of the century.

Thinking through "the postmodern relationship to genre" (Hoberek 341), Andrew Hoberek argues that postmodernism "construes genre as a form of... formulaic mental labor that authors must work through rather than simply rejecting" (341). Although a postmodernist responds to a popular genre's seemingly simple and even "degraded mental labor" by doing different intellectual work, "postmodernism itself becomes institutionalized and takes on modernism's elitist values" (Hoberek 342; see also Toth 112). Partly for this reason, postmodernism is the paradox that Linda Hutcheon observes throughout her many studies on the topic. (Much of what I want to say about Hutcheon and postmodernism and the Canadian Western appeared in the previous chapter, because of the prototypical postmodernism that I detected in Luke Price's main character, Smokey Carmain.) It does not have easy answers, and it is full of contradictions and inconsistencies. By creating puzzles, inviting questions, and acting politically, postmodernism is a fundamentally intellectual genre or mode, and therefore it is a strange bedfellow with the Western, which is usually considered to be escapist entertainment (D'haen 185) and even anti-intellectual, in keeping with Richard Hofstadter's view of the demotic populism in Frederick Jackson Turner's frontier thesis (Bledstein 52). This paradox especially—of an intellectual, high-cultural genre or mode such as postmodernism, and an anti-intellectual, low-cultural genre such as the Western—is one of my own fascinations here.

Postmodernism tends to fit uneasily into the generic categories that it alludes to, and one of the entertaining results of postmodern literature and film is that the audience is drawn into a conversation about which genres are at work. Monika Fludernik believes that "[w]hat readers really do when they read a text largely depends to start with on the observable generic alignment of that text" (289).[6] Fludernik speculates that texts—such as

---

6   Fludernik is echoing a quotation from the introduction to this book: "an interpreter's preliminary generic conception of a text is constitutive of everything that he subsequently understands" (E. D. Hirsch qtd. in Scholes, "Towards" 103).

postmodern texts—that "defy categorization . . . force readers to decide" (286); "we read literary texts quite differently when [we recognize them as one genre rather than another]" (286). In the introduction to this book, I conveyed Rick Altman's observation that the adjectival modification or description of a genre—for example, Western scenics, Western melodramas, Western romances—can eventually become a genre of its own (*Film/Genre* 36, 52). After we have recognized postmodern lyric, postmodern science fiction, or postmodern Westerns, we can separate postmodernism from mode into a genre of its own. David Lodge in *Modes of Modern Writing* (1977) might still call it a mode; so might Frank Davey, who calls postmodernism a way of thinking, not a description of content ("Canadian" 10). But a way of thinking can soon rather easily be understood as the content of a text. Does it "have" this way of thinking? Does it also have cowboys? I am uncertain what is gained when we insist that form/style and content/substance are entirely separate or in what Fludernik calls "[a] one-to-one relationship" (280). If we insisted on their separation, the existence of a postmodern Western would be impossible because of the aforementioned difference in the intellectual demands of postmodernism and Westerns. And we simply have the fact of Westerns that readers and viewers can and do identify as post-Western and postmodern.

Audiences seem to be interpellated such that readers who are very different from each other suddenly find themselves reading the same books. Hoberek follows Leslie Fiedler's canonized essay "Cross the Border—Close the Gap" (1970) by explaining that postmodernism crosses the border between literary and popular cultures, high and low, and that its earliest writers chose the Western, sci-fi, and pornography as their genres. Commenting on his 1987 novel *Caprice*, George Bowering stated that "I noticed two things about the western: one, that they were all very male-centred, and, two, that it always has something to do with dry land. . . . And so I said O.K., I want to make a western which is female-centred. I would just turn everything around—that way it is not just a parody but an investigation of a western, putting it on trial, almost" (qtd. in Carrera 434). Bowering's intellectual work, here, is that of a detective, police officer, lawyer, judge, or jury. In that vein, his reference to writing "not just a parody" helps to explain the usually serious tone of a novel that can otherwise be quite comic. His reference to a "trial" furthermore implies that he is writing an anti-Western, something as oppositional as a case in a court of law. John Cawelti generalizes that "after [Sam] Peckinpah most successful Westerns have either been outright parodies of the genre... or attempts to produce anti-Westerns which have the same moral ambiguity as the urban adventure of the modern spy story" (qtd. in D'haen 190). Thus, *Caprice* and others among CanLit's postmodern Westerns are involved in the two major trends in Westerns after the 1970s, doing a sort of "upgraded" mental labour that involves "turn[ing] everything around," or if not "everything" then at least the norms of gender and sex, geography, plot, and time. (There seem to be exclusions, such as class; for context, see Hoberek 342.) The very ambition of this postmodern intention of dealing with "everything" suggests that any project constrained by time and space would necessarily fail to do it all. And this happens to be a strange subgenre of CanLit's postmodern Westerns: the text that projects beyond the project.

Ghostmodernism and the Canadian Western

I mean beyond what Cawelti calls the "anti-Western" and into what has more recently been called the "post-Western," because both align with postmodern, oppositional intentions. The post-Western is an area of inquiry staked out by the University of Nebraska Press, which has a series that includes recent books such as Neil Campbell's *Post-Westerns* (2013) and Lee Clark Mitchell's *Late Westerns* (2018). In the ever-expanding discourse of postness—postmodernism, post-colonialism, post-humanism, post-feminism, post-racism, et cetera—we are thinking of different kinds of afterlife. Wolfgang Funk explains that

> the concept of haunting in general, and [Jacques] Derrida's notion of "hauntology" as a form of spectral epistemology in particular, mirrors/speaks to a contemporary fatigue with postmodernity's perpetual, rationalised scepticism and constitutes an attempt to reintegrate the supernatural, in the shape of epistemological uncertainty, into cultural and academic discourse. (148)

The Westerns with which I begin in this chapter already contain "the supernatural" in their "discourse." In some of CanLit's postmodern Westerns—namely, those of Ondaatje, Jiles, and King—there are a surprising number of ghosts. This would not surprise Jane Tompkins in her book on American Westerns, *West of Everything* (1992), who gets her title from Louis L'Amour's "The Gift of Cochise" (1952), which was adapted into film as *Hondo* (1953), and echoes: "To go west, as far west as you can go, west of everything, is to die" (Tompkins 24).[7] Rather than dwell too much on a Derridian "hauntology," I am drawing on a concept that attempts to see ghosts in terms of genre or mode—the concept of ghostmodernism, a relatively new coinage from literary critic Sylvia Söderlind (2010).[8] Ghostmodernism simply means postmodernism with ghosts, or Gothic postmodernism, an oversimplification to which I will return. Ghostmodern Westerns are a sub-genre of the post-Western that is also a crossover with the horror genre, but not scary. In this section, my main question is why ghosts might make sense in the genre of the Western, and I offer two provisional answers that deepen our inquiry into the development of postmodernism as it relates to the Western.

My first answer is that hauntings involve the return of the dead or the return of the repressed, which is weirdly consistent with Richard Slotkin's theory of the myth of regeneration through violence in American Westerns: ghosts scarily regenerate our attachments to the past, and we often violently reject both the attachments and the ghosts. The ghosts in these texts tend to be our heroes, anti-heroes, or enemies; the postmodern intention seems to be to break us away from concepts such as heroism, or at least to destabilize the moral grounds on which we maintain concepts such as heroism. We do not quite reach this point in a film such as John Ford's *The Searchers* (1956), in which Ethan (John Wayne) regenerates his family by vindictively murdering the Comanche warriors (and their more innocent neighbours) who kidnapped his niece, though Ford

---

7   Aritha van Herk seems to comment on this line from L'Amour and Tompkins: "We live in a corner of the universe where the sun sets instead of rising, and yes, going west is a metaphor for death" (*Stampede* 92).

8   The term "ghostmodernism" also comes a little later from an entirely different context, an artists' collective called Art Codex, but I don't think that the coinages—those of Art Codex and Sylvia Söderlind—are strongly related.

is wise enough to include a former schoolteacher in the plot who predicts that we will eventually see Ethan (and perhaps Wayne) as retrograde and incompatible with the present. Ethan's heroism is pre-modern because it is epic (the parent genre of the Western), but many of the epic's journeys and quests are at least implicitly colonial. In an infamous scene, Ethan desecrates the grave of a Comanche warrior by shooting the eyes out of the body, and he justifies his actions by saying that "[if he] ain't got no eyes, he can't enter the spirit land, has to wander forever between the winds." In this case, regeneration through violence is making ghosts of his enemies. However, there are signs that he is making a ghost of himself too. Ethan survives the film, but wounded; he had been shot by a supposedly poisoned Comanche arrow some days earlier. He is rarely immune to harm, but he usually survives. Discussing the film with me, my wife observed that, when Ethan is shot by the arrow, Martin tells him, "Sure beats me, Ethan, how you could have stayed alive this long." Ethan interrupts to demand that Martin read his last will and testament. Usually, a will is not read aloud until after its writer's death. Symbolically, perhaps, Ethan *is* dead. He enters the afterlife but continues his search. When Martin says, "I hope you die," Ethan can scoff, "That'll be the day," because Martin doesn't realize he is already haunted.

King's *Green Grass, Running Water* inverts the pattern of Wayne's Westerns by plotting the invasion of one of Wayne's movies by the Indigenous "ghosts" who rewrite the ending so that Wayne loses. Crucially, for King the regeneration is through *metafictional* violence in a movie within a novel. Although there are frame stories within *The Searchers* too, it still promotes the myth of regeneration through *real* violence. The ghost generated in *The Searchers* is the ghost of the Comanche, the Vanishing "Indian," who represents the pre-modern world that the Western idealizes only when that world is controlled by colonial forces. In killing the "Indians," the Western regenerates an attachment to the pre-modern, social-Darwinist world in which "Indians" are doomed and only the colonist remains fit for the Hobbesian state of nature.

At the risk of detouring too much in this preamble, I want to indulge for a moment in another way of thinking about the state of nature, which is the ecology of the Western landscape. When Ethan in *The Searchers* blasts at the Comanche warrior in his grave, he is both literally blasting the land (an image that will return later with *Pale Rider*) and blasting a symbol of the land, the "Indian." I might be over-reading, because Atwood does not mention Indigenous people directly, but she seems to be identifying one problem of the Western as the reconstruction of the landscape into the movie set of her title, "Backdrop Addresses Cowboy." Acknowledged or not, this reconstruction or simulation is violence against Indigenous people who did not cede their land to colonists in a fair deal. In the poem, the speaker says that it (the speaker, who is the backdrop and "the horizon") "ought to be watching" the cowboy "in admiration / but I am elsewhere" (70). The "elsewhere" is haunted in the sense that the "I" or perhaps even the Comanche's "eyes" are all around: "Then what about the I / confronting you on that border . . . ?"; "I am also what surrounds you . . . the litter of your invasions" (70). Atwood concludes by describing the landscape as "the space you desecrate / as you pass through" (70). Making the I/eye connection to *The Searchers* might seem obvious, but less obvious is the implication that the cowboy too will "pass through" to the other side of a "border." For Atwood, it is the Canada-America border through which the "[s]tarspangled cowboy" will return. But it is also the life-death border (not necessarily in that order) implied by the poem's macabre invocations of "bullets" and "skulls" (70). Despite all its critique, the poem can be read as a lament for a pre-modern time—that state of nature again—before the reconstruction or simulation or terraforming of the Western landscape.

Thus, my second answer to the question of why ghosts make sense in the Western is that ghosts symbolize the past and thus align with the traditional anti-modernism of the Western (a term that I do not mean to imply is synonymous with postmodernism, which is an innovation rather than a tradition in the genre), including the nostalgia for a time when you could still run to the West (or the North) from modernity. To clarify: the Western is a genre in modernity that serves a desire for a pre-modern or nearly pre-modern time, and so it tends to critique modernity—its own time—in forms such as modern law, modern technology, modern social mores, and even modernism. Hence, its "natural law" of social Darwinism (Tranquilla 78), its preference for the horse over the train, and its obstinate patriarchal heroes. The anti-modernism is partly a feeling of dislike for the modern, and partly a feeling of longing for what "we" supposedly once had but then lost. Think of any ghost town as an invocation of this nostalgia.

(There's a 1987 episode of Disney's *DuckTales* about Scrooge McDuck prospecting in a ghost town, one that acknowledges the Gothic in Charles Dickens's 1843 tale *A Christmas Carol*.) With places such as ghost towns—dead but still liminally there—we have what Matt Foley calls the "purgatorial model of haunting" (1) in modernist texts. Very few Westerns are modernist, to my knowledge, but those by Atwood, Ondaatje, Jiles, King, and others are definitely on the spectrum toward postmodernism.

Why, then, can ghosts still make sense in the *post*-Western, which should be "over it"? The easy answer is that there is continuity between modernism and postmodernism, and that postmodernism will always be haunted by its forebears, in spite of its attempt to break more radically from the past than modernism could. In fact, it makes sense that the more radical the attempted break, the deeper the repression, the more powerful the ghost. In the context of what he calls "the aftergothic," Fred Botting explains that Gothic horror was "[o]nce the dark underside of modernity, [but] Gothic horror now outlines the darkness of the postmodern condition" (281). According to Josh Toth in *The Passing of Postmodernism* (2010), "postmodernism ... was *haunted* by a certain teleological aporia, a promise of the end represented by a type of humanism, a certain faith in historical progress, a sense of justice and/or meaning" (4, original emphasis). In other words, it was haunted by everything that its earlier incarnation of modernism was still trying to recuperate or regenerate.

Relative to Botting and Toth, Neil Campbell has an answer more specific to the Western. In his book *Post-Westerns*, Campbell explains that "post-Westerns are concerned with the afterlife of the classic Western and the regional mythos and with their consequences and reverberations in the contemporary world" (332). In his reading of Cormac McCarthy's 2005 novel *No Country for Old Men* and its 2007 film adaptation by the Coen brothers, Campbell hears Sheriff Bell refer to the assassin Chigurh as "a ghost," and he notices that the figures of the outlaw and the lawman are "uncanny ... as haunted and haunting presences of the West" (335). According to Campbell, the sheriff is "a critically posthumous being who lives the past in the present, [and] his perspective ... always *comes after* the event" (333, original emphasis). Bigger than the sheriff, the genre itself is "a ghostly figure" (335). If the genre once meant control over the frontier and the resulting destruction of the wilderness, then control is dead, and what comes back to life is only powerlessness and uncertainty (336), and not, in this version, even the wilderness. We can imagine the flood that breaks the dam in King's *Green Grass, Running Water* as a wilderness-as-revenant, and a symbol of the Indigenous Renaissance, but here it is bleak for everyone but mercurial anarchists. Linking to a diegetic story of an "Injun" but without commenting on Chigurh's or anyone else's racialization, Campbell nevertheless understands that the ghost is figurative, a stand-in and crucially a cypher for something else that has been made to "vanish." In terms of affect, the implication is that a creepy feeling—and possibly an anxiety and a guilt—has overcome nostalgia, which is otherwise the emotional core of the genre.

Campbell also interprets the genre in post-colonial terms of nation (as would Fredric Jameson or Svetlana Boym or Arjun Appadurai writing about nostalgia). Campbell describes the Western as "an uprising of the buried and repressed legacy of conquest endlessly visited on and challenging the present" (343). We're sensitive to this "legacy" in the context of Canadian literature too. In Canada, the term "ghostmodernism" comes from Söderlind's response to Davey's 1993 book *Post-National Arguments*, which Söderlind turns into an essay entitled "Ghost-National Arguments" (2006). She reprises the theme in a later essay on Leonard Cohen's 1966 novel *Beautiful Losers*. The nationalist versus transnationalist debate inspires bold thrusts from Söderlind and Davey, but I am side-stepping the debate because the transnational dimension of the following texts is so obvious in my case studies here of Ondaatje, Jiles, and King, all immigrants to Canada—King having satirized the debate most memorably in his brilliant short story "Borders" (1993, the same year as *Green Grass, Running Water*). (Jiles later moved back to the United States; Davey writes explicitly of cross-border movements in *The Louis Riel Organ and Piano Co*.) Partly because of the transnationality of the Western, I am including not only a brief reading of *The Searchers* (above) in this chapter, but also a reading of Clint Eastwood's *Pale Rider* (1985). At least one American example is needed to show a potential response to the ghost of Ethan and of *The Searchers* itself. The specific transnationality of *Pale Rider* is less obvious than that of the others in this chapter, but in my essay in *Film-Philosophy* on Eastwood's transition from Westerns to cop movies, I tracked him from the regional to the cosmopolitan (read: global), and that essay could well be repurposed to show a transnational movement or at least presence in Eastwood's films ("Do I Feel Lucky?").

But Söderlind argues that "Canadian ghosts tend to be personal or, at the most, regional" ("Ghost-National" 276), a claim that affirms the applicability of the concept to the regionalism of Westerns. Söderlind defines ghostmodernism very generally as "writing . . . produced in the transition between modernism and postmodernism" ("F" 270), which nevertheless makes sense to me because ghosts are transitional or liminal figures. When you turn away from modernism, you might become afraid of the ghost over your shoulder; ghostmodernism is also simply postmodernism haunted by modernism. More than that, however, Söderlind implies that ghostmodernism is synonymous with postmodernism's project of "ignor[ing] or at least abandon[ing] the futile [modernist] attempt to articulate that which cannot be articulated" ("F" 270). It responds also to the futile attempt to *visualize* that which cannot be *visualized*. This is where the ghosts come in. We struggle to visualize them—they are vaguely "between the winds"—and we struggle to renew the effort to express the political positions that serve to counter the remarkable aesthetic and ideological powers of the Western. Among those powers are the myths of open country and Vanishing "Indians," and the regeneration of these myths through new conquests and surrogate violence against Indigenous peoples and lands.

The Ghosts of Billy the Kid

Ondaatje's 1970 collection *The Collected Works of Billy the Kid* emerges from a postmodern context in which both Ondaatje and his friend and peer bpNichol were evidently having a lot of fun (though Ondaatje's work on Billy is far more serious—more brutal and ruminative and deeply felt—than Nichol's). Nichol's unpaginated pamphlet *The True Eventual Story of Billy the Kid* (also 1970) once led a student in one of my classes to exclaim, in epiphany, that she now understood postmodernism: as modernism by teenagers. Indeed, it is ribald:

> bill was born with a short dick but they did not call him richard.

> bill might've grown up in a town or a city. it does not matter.
> the true story is that bill grew & his dick didn't. sometimes
> he called it a penis or a prick but still it didn't grow. as he
> grew he called others the same thing & their pricks & penises were big & heavy as dictionaries but his dick remained—
> short for richard.
>
> billy was not fast with words so he became fast with a gun.
> they called him the kid so he became faster & meaner. (n.p.)

But *The True Eventual Story of Billy the Kid* is also signalling a ghost-modernism through this emasculation: "rumour has it that billy the kid never died. rumour is billy the kid. he never gets anywhere, being too short-lived" (n.p.). So, the culmination of Billy's relevance is that he himself becomes a short-dick joke, in Nichol's case because his "true eventual story" is only a pamphlet, a short stack, and in Ondaatje's because Billy ends up "hung from a horse," which when inverted implies that he is not at all "hung like a horse." I will return to this phallic amusement in the next chapter, in a post-humanist context, but even then I shall endeavour not to explain the comedy overmuch. Rather, it suffices, I think, to read Ondaatje's and Nichol's examinations of Billy as the first truly postmodern Canadian Westerns.[9] Compared to every other text that *could* be described as a postmodern Canadian Western, Ondaatje's and Nichol's works (and King's significantly later *Green Grass, Running Water*) are as unambiguously postmodern as such texts can be.

Before I interpret *The Collected Works of Billy the Kid*, it might be worth knowing that Ondaatje follows the same historical outline that Sam Peckinpah does in his slightly later film, *Pat Garrett and Billy the Kid* (1973). Billy, an outlaw on the run, is being pursued by his old friend, Pat Garrett, who has become a sheriff. In both texts, Garrett eventually tracks down his new nemesis at a cabin at night, and he kills Billy in a scene fraught with sexual tension and self-reflective symbolism. In spite of

---

9   Precedents of Canadian postmodernism that Ondaatje and Nichol would likely have known include Leonard Cohen's *Beautiful Losers* (1966) and Robert Kroetsch's *The Studhorse Man* (1969).

clever images of symmetry produced by a pond and a mirror, *Pat Garrett and Billy the Kid* might be described as formally and visually unremarkable in the context of other A-list Hollywood films and their high production values and aesthetics. Except for its initial prolepsis (a glimpse of Garrett's future, specifically his eventual murder), it has little of the postmodern experimentation with form seen in Ondaatje's book (as described below), though its postmodern condition versus its intention could be debated, perhaps especially in comparison with earlier and aesthetically edgier films by Peckinpah.[10] Regardless, it does raise questions about how legends are made—for example, by making ghosts of them first.

Most of my conclusions about *The Collected Works of Billy the Kid* from my first book, *The Metaphor of Celebrity* (2013), are still germane here, so I want to offer a précis, leading to its new contextualization as ghostmodernism. I argued in *The Metaphor of Celebrity* that

> Billy is dead, and some evidence [e.g., from Smaro Kamboureli and Dennis Cooley] suggests that at least part of his story is narrated when he is a ghost—[with] strange perspectives, *déjà vu*, and invisibility.... His *déjà vu* is to some extent both the return of the repressed and *his* return, as a ghost, to the narrative of his life and his celebrity. (140)

His "invisibility" should not be taken for granted, but it is implied in the "photograph" presented to us on the first page of the book—a frame with nothing in it. The interest in his "empty" image and his related celebrity is part of the postmodern turn away from high modernism toward popular culture and its supposed lack of substance. (The phrase "the postmodern turn" comes from Ihab Hassan and, later, Douglas Kellner and Steven Best.) For Hutcheon, *The Collected Works of Billy the Kid* is an example

---

10 According to Maximilian Le Cain, "[w]hereas the revisionist directors gleefully attacked the genre from outside with often glibly political ideas, Peckinpah used this film to deconstruct not the famous figures of the Western nor its landscape, but its narrative form. Peckinpah allows the oft-filmed characters of Pat and Billy to retain their mythological status unlike, say, [Robert] Altman's Buffalo Bill or [Arthur] Penn's Wild Bill Hickock" ("Drifting"). In spite of maintaining "status," "*Pat Garrett* deconstructs the Western in a number of ways" ("Drifting"). Le Cain gives several reasons why one could consider Peckinpah's film to be postmodern but not revisionist.

of the historiographic metafiction that she believes to be synonymous with postmodernism in Canadian literature; I noted in the opening pages of this book that a picture of Ondaatje himself appears in *The Collected Works of Billy the Kid* as a boy in the garb of a cowboy, standing in for the picture of Billy that seems to have been stolen from the frame (or could not be captured). Ondaatje's book is also a "genre paradox" (Hutcheon, *Canadian* 4–5) because it can appear to be biography, fiction, or poetry. I wrote, again in my first book, that

> Billy's legend is based on the historical fragments of his celebrity and the missing pieces of his biography. *The Collected Works of Billy the Kid* contains many kinds of texts, which all contribute to the impression of a collection of found documents that can only partially represent Billy's history despite the inclusion of supposedly autobiographical poems. Interviews with people who knew him and photographs of them, an excerpt and illustration from the "comic book legend" (as described in the book's credits) of *Billy the Kid and the Princess*, an "EXCLUSIVE JAIL INTERVIEW" promising that "THE KID TELLS ALL" (81)—these texts are more a part of the popular media than they are staid historical documents; indeed, as Dennis Cooley convincingly argues, even Billy's way of seeing is photographic... and cinematic. ... This incompleteness is conducive to legend—and a legend, like a ghost, is never fully there. (143)

Notably, this "incompleteness" means that the narrative line is broken. The pieces of his cinematic and fragmentary narrative line are easy to rearrange into non-linear, non-chronological forms, as Ondaatje does in things like deft poem-sized palindromes and intriguing retakes of the same scene. Ondaatje had once called his book the film that he couldn't afford to shoot. It is not merely cinematic; more than that, as Cooley (qtd. in Hutcheon, *Canadian* 46–7) and I understand it, Billy is effectively able to rewind, pause, and fast-forward through his own biopic.

This fragmentation of time is a hallmark of modernism that becomes, in postmodernism, the supposedly ahistorical moment. For Söderlind, ghostmodernism is preoccupied by temporal concepts such as firsts, precedents, antecedents, and belatedness ("Ghost-National" 674-5). In ghostmodernism, the ghost is the ahistorical figure—usually a figure of the past, yes, but one whose pastness has ceased to matter in one crucial way: the ghost lives on, superimposing temporal concepts with uncanny effects on what is familiar and what is strange.

Zerelda James and the Ghost of Her Son Jesse

Given the anachronism or atemporality of ghosts, there is little reason to proceed chronologically, so I will proceed comparatively and jump ahead from 1970 to 1988. In scope, form, and choice of main character, the most similar Western to Ondaatje's *The Collected Works of Billy the Kid* is Paulette Jiles's 1988 collection *The Jesse James Poems*. Jiles, like Ondaatje, moved to Canada in her twenties (but in her case from the United States) and established her career by publishing here, including *The Jesse James Poems*, with Polestar Press in British Columbia. She followed this book with the more conventional novel *Enemy Women* (2002), which focuses on a young woman's imprisonment during the Civil War and her aided escape back to the South. Although *The Jesse James Poems* is about Jesse and is narrated first by his father and then mainly by members of his gang, the book disrupts the patriarchy through a ghostmodernist critique.

Like *The Collected Works of Billy the Kid*, *The Jesse James Poems* features a series of set pieces that sometimes touch on events in the biography of the titular historical figure. The storyline involves Jesse's criminal history and his eventual murder, and it goes beyond the murder into Jesse's "afterlife" as a corpse on display and a photograph of that corpse. As with Peckinpah and Ondaatje (but not Nichol), Jiles treats her subject with great sympathy, in two particularly relevant ways: first, by reflecting on how American gun culture affects boys and men; second, by contextualizing Jesse's short life with the longer but still tough and complicated lives of his parents, particularly that of his mother. Arguably, *The Jesse James Poems* was the first book-length Canadian Western by a woman (Atwood's single poem "Backdrop Addresses Cowboy" coming around two decades earlier). Unlike Ondaatje's book, it appears to have been ignored in the scholarship, except in book reviews and interviews.

A more meaningful difference is that *The Jesse James Poems* has an introductory focus on the outlaw's mother, Zerelda James, and a more obvious critique of the myth of regeneration through violence that Slotkin has illustrated in such depth. Quite unlike the regeneration of the family and the patriarchy that we see in American films such as *The Searchers* (1956), *High Noon* (1952), and *Shane* (1953), for Zerelda, violence is mainly destructive. Notably, without the right to vote, she cannot "speak aloud of anything she knows to be true; / she is alive and yet without / a legal existence" (14). Because of the "yet" that follows the statement that she is "alive," she is a symbolic ghost—an implication, perhaps, that the Western is haunted partly by women who have been silenced. Indeed, Zerelda is presented sympathetically until we realize that "[i]n her mouth human speech becomes a skinning knife: / they're going to take our niggers away" (14). In spite of her racism and her Confederate reliance on the slave trade, her voice echoes throughout the book as her family breaks apart because of the robberies and murders perpetrated by her sons Jesse and Frank. When Jiles wrote the book in the late 1980s, incidents of urban gun violence in the United States were mediatized at rapid fire. Given a context in which so many young men in the United States were being killed in gang violence, Jiles's critique of urban gun violence is arguably a motherly critique. It has an added dimension too, in a set of anachronistic parallels between late nineteenth-century gun violence and the "critical mass" (25) of nuclear "warhead[s]" (80), a concern still present at the end of the Cold War in the 1980s when she was writing (and it haunts us still, as do guns).[11] This anachronism and other non-linear developments in *The Jesse James Poems* combine with uncanny representations of people's lives and deaths to produce a ghostmodern Western that is critical specifically of guns and idealized notions of independence related to gun ownership—that vaunted right that functions as a consolation for the increased federal powers that came with the Union.

The non-linearity of the book becomes noticeable as a pattern near the middle in the central poem (in both senses) of *The Jesse James Poems*,

---

11   Jiles's association of hauntings with technology also appears in her significantly later 2002 Western novel *Enemy Women*: "Always in the distance she could hear the sound of the St. Louis and Iron Mountain Railroad engines, their long wailing. Like the beginning note sounded by a choirmaster for a phantom choir that never sang" (166).

and it seems always related to matters of life and death. We have already seen Jesse die—"whereupon Robert Ford / shot him in the back of the head twice / at close range" (38)—and yet the "Wanted Poster" in the middle of the book (45) implies that he is still at large and can die again. The motherly critique gains a curious dimension at the scene of his death. It occurs in a poem entitled "Bandits' Wives" that focuses on Jesse's wife, Zee (notably the initial of his mother, Zerelda, and thus a sign of Oedipal conflict), and Frank's wife, Annie. The speaker says that "Zee never wanted to end up like . . . violent whores . . . diseased or dead" (36–7), and so she and Annie are much more traditionally domestic. Suffering from a bad cold, Zee asks Jessie to help with the dishes, and he does: "a desperate outlaw doing the dishes, wearing that / Navy Colt five-shot . . . singing 'I'm A Good Old Rebel' " (38). Immediately after finishing the dishes, Jesse raises his hands to level a picture frame, and Ford murders him, as if completing a task "outlaw[ed]" by his gender role had to be punished by death—another sympathetic illustration of the demands and consequences of patriarchally constructed roles. Later, the poster-poem describes his strictly delimited life and foretells his future death, which, in the sequence of the book, has already happened: "Jesse James was never confused about anything in his life, which will last exactly thirty-seven years, five months, three days, fourteen hours, and ten minutes" (45). We finally see "[t]he death picture" (76) itself in the poem "Assassination" many pages later. The impression is of experiencing history simultaneously or as synchronicity, implying the cyclical or perhaps continual nature of struggles against de facto laws of gender, and effectively subverting the sequence of cause and effect that defines history for most people.

Who could experience history in this way? For Jiles and the narrators of her book, it is a supernatural experience. In the section entitled "Guerrilla Warfare: Missouri 1856–1865," the narrators describe an eerie situation (here in first-person plural, probably Jesse's gang members):

> Our rifle barrels are hot as pokers
> we can't stop ourselves
> we are being run by something
> that lives in us as if we were an abandoned house. (25)

The "something" here that cannot quite be described in the "abandoned house" of ourselves is not obvious, which is perfectly appropriate for a ghost; our "house" is not only "abandoned" but also haunted. The narrators return to this image later in the book when they claim: "Nothing makes / Jesse so content as shooting people. We got other people living inside us" (56). The fantasy that our bodies are animated by souls or spirits (or demons) is another echo of *The Collected Works of Billy the Kid*: "the second narrative of [Billy's] death scene is narrated by a fused Billy-Garrett, whom we might also think of as Garrett possessed by the ghost of Billy, who has returned from the scene of his future murder to ensure that Garrett, alone, does not have the privilege of the last word" (Deshaye, *Metaphor* 149). These supernatural possessions are also a critique of the ideal of independence, which Jiles had already called into question by contextualizing the singular Jesse James as a son and brother whose reliance on family became eventually a reliance on his gang, which in turn is an extended family that includes his brother Frank. To complicate matters, Jesse's dependence on the ghost that haunts his body is uncomfortably related to his violence: "If I could have my body back again / I would release the thing that inhabited me / that went out at night, with a gun" (80). Although the "release" is ambiguous, because he claims to have enjoyed "a pistol, the old happy / aggression" (80), I think that the animation of Jesse's body toward gun violence is "something," a "thing" that he would be rid of so that he could sublimate his "aggression" and enjoy other activities such as listening to music and playing pool (80). These activities suggest that he wants to be accepted in the social world, not the anti-social world.

He also needs to hide from society, however, because he is an outlaw, a robber and murderer—and his uncanny ability to live in multiple moments of time also enables him to hide, invisible. Various descriptions of Jesse's position on the spectrum of visibility and invisibility, and various possible allusions to Ondaatje's Billy, appear throughout in the book. When Jesse is hiding from the law in Tennessee, we learn that "[h]e can think about [the people searching for him] and watch them from under his hat and choose not to appear to them" (63). We also learn that

> Jesse is hard to see
> he survives

> he is sixteen, he knows already to stay very
> quiet and
> aim for the middle
> he operates like an empty space, he shifts. (28)

The "empty space" seems to allude quite directly to the similarly empty frame of Billy's photograph on the first page of Ondaatje's *The Collected Works of Billy the Kid*. Contrary to these lines, however, Jiles's book has more actual photographs than does Ondaatje's book, some of which present the bodies of Jesse's gang—and Jesse himself—on display after they were shot and killed. Interspersed with descriptions of the actions of these men, the photographs create a dynamic of "shift[ing]" between dead and alive that accentuates the non-linearity that I have already explained. After showing the bodies of two "gang members" (58), the next poem describes the "unhappy outlaws" (59) "[s]itting around the Fire," and "[s]ome of them have no vital signs" (59). Like Zerelda in their unhappiness (1), they also seem like her in not having a "legal existence." They are outlaws whose actions drive them to the margins. And although at least some of them already seem to be ghosts fading out of history, through Jiles they express a desire to preserve their voices: "What's the point of being dead if you don't / have anything to say to posterity?" (59).

This self-reflective question is related to a crucial ideological self-reflection of the book that appears in the section entitled "The End of the War" when the narrators explain:

> This is what
> happens to
> winners. They begin to believe in winning.
> And now the federal government believes in guns.
> So do we.
> We believe in guns. (31–2)

The passage echoes a classic question: Do you "believe in" ghosts? The alliteration between "guns" and "ghosts" *almost* appears, but the *g* of the ghost is naturally not there. It is there only as the animating spirit behind the guns. On one hand, the guns are simply a tool, good or bad depending on the spirit of it. On the other, the guns are obviously implicated in conflict and dreams of "winning," of superiority between parts of the same society.

In sum, Jesse's "shift[ing]," his invisibility, and his own sense of being controlled by "other people" align with the cultural critique assumed to be postmodern—for example, if we take a basic definition from Brian Duignan in the *Encyclopedia Britannica*, in which postmodernism is characterized by "broad skepticism, subjectivism, or relativism; a general suspicion of reason; and an acute sensitivity to the role of ideology in asserting and maintaining political and economic power" ("Postmodernism"). The feminism of *The Jesse James Poems* displays that "acute sensitivity" toward an American gun culture and its associated arms races, and its ghostmodern non-linearity calls into question the extent of American progress.

I also like the definition above because of how well it describes Clint Eastwood. His trademark squint is to me a perfect expression of his "broad skepticism." To be "suspicio[us] of reason" is to be open to ghosts, as he is in *Pale Rider*. He plays a similar role in his earlier film *High Plains Drifter* (Eastwood, 1973) as what Peter Babiak calls a "specter" and "ghost" (65) of a murdered man. This chapter moves now to the later example of the 1985 film *Pale Rider* mainly because it is more fun to interpret than *High Plains Drifter*, and not for irrelevant reasons. It is arguably more likely to be diagnosed as a symptom of Lyotard's postmodern condition. *Pale Rider* is not as postmodern in style as it is in substance, certainly not in comparison with *The Jesse James Poems*; however, in substance, *Pale Rider* destabilizes some of the ideological premises of classic(al) Westerns. Babiak argues that "Unlike Classical Westerns, Eastwood's Westerns are generally concerned with the disruption of the dominant social order . . . consistently maintaining a critical stance in relation to patriarchal capitalism" (63). I am not entirely convinced that this "stance" is always critical, especially in his late films, in which "patriarchal" features are sometimes exaggerated by his age. Even as early as 1992's *Unforgiven* (which is not so much "postmodern" as it is in a reactionary mode such as operatic realism), Eastwood's outlaw comes out of retirement to save the women from the brothel and avenge his African-American friend, but these progressive goals are achieved in a bloodbath that regenerates the aging white man and the dominance of his gun (and the capitalism of the brothel; he himself becomes a prosperous shopkeeper, as the epilogue implies). He's more critical in *Pale Rider*, but even then the film predictably concludes with a gunfight and an assertion of the gun culture that Jiles would later disapprove of.

Anti-heroic Self-Parody in Eastwood's *Pale Rider*

Although ghosts are slightly outside the realm of Christian orthodoxy and can be found instead in the realm of paganism, they are allowed in as angels—spirits who live on in heaven or on earth as guardian angels—and Eastwood's *Pale Rider* is a good example. In the film, Eastwood's ghostliness is also associated with his religiosity as an angel summoned by prayer and as a preacher in a white collar (but black hat). Thus, almost by definition the preacher is a patriarchal figure, one who succumbs to the temptation to have sex with a middle-aged mother but not her young daughter. Briefly summarized, *Pale Rider* is a film about a guardian angel who is also an avenging angel who comes to protect a community of small-time miners while also taking revenge on the man who killed him, a corrupt marshal symbolized as hellish partly by his name, Stockburn. It need not be interpreted as a ghost story; it could be about a man who only happens to arrive to save the community and kill the man who injured him terribly, but the six bullet-wound scars in his upper torso suggest an attack that no one could survive—hence the ghost story.

Less well-known is the role of Megan, the fourteen-year-old girl whose earnestly questioning prayer calls forth the man known only as the Stranger (in the tradition of Eastwood films made famous by Sergio Leone in his trilogy) or the Preacher, or simply Preacher. (I wish I had space here to consider the horror-Western crossover in the American comic series *Preacher*, 1995–2000.) Megan's prayer involves Psalm 23, which is about walking through the valley of the shadow of death, and it continues to the book of Revelation in its foretold arrival of the Four Horsemen of the Apocalypse, the final of which is Death incarnate on a pale horse—the "pale rider" whose horse's colouring becomes his own identifier.[12] In an

---

12 The plot of a young woman's prayer being immediately answered by a hero emerging out of the wilderness of the West has a possible origin in Zane Grey's *Riders of the Purple Sage* (1912). In Canadian Westerns, the most obvious figuring of a cowboy as a Horseman of the Apocalypse might be in Paul St. Pierre's *Smith and Other Events* (1983): "Man and horse moved,

essay on Westerns in relation to Christianity, Biblical scholar Robert Paul Seesengood claims: "If [Megan's] recitation of the Psalm was imprecation, the reading of Revelation is incantation; Megan has summoned divine Justice, riding down from the surrounding hills (Ps. 121:1–2) to bring God's deliverance" (193). Unfortunately, the implications of this reading are not developed in Seesengood's essay, which focuses on the masculinity and Christianity of Western idealism in general. Megan's "summoning" is much more fascinating than it might appear, partly because of how she associates herself with the land being mined almost as if she were the Gaia or primordial mother of ancient Greek and pagan religions—an allegory that Söderlind would find "inherently ghostly" ("F" 273) as a structure of referring to what is not really there.

The association between Megan and the mined land helps to send the ecocritical message of the film: that the land is innocent, yet potentially fertile, and that big business threatens its sustainability. (I return to this message with various post-Westerns in the conclusion to this book.) This message is one of *Pale Rider*'s "reverberations in the contemporary world," to echo the previous quotation from Campbell's *Post-Westerns*. In their research on ecology and Westerns on film, Robin L. Murray and Joseph K. Heumann explain that mining narratives usually depict a conflict between big business and community-based business, along with the suggestion that sustainability is more likely to be achieved by the community than by distant corporate offices ("Mining Westerns" 57–8).[13] In *Pale Rider*, the ecocritical message is complicated by how the filmmakers imply that the mine is a gendered and spiritually meaningful site; the association between Megan and the mined land first appears when the boss of the corporate mining operation, Coy LaHood, mentions the criticism of how his operation is "raping the land." Murray and Heumann claim that this is "an obvious parallel" ("Eco-Terrorism" 128), and it is, but it also has an

---

batlike, in an erratic pattern through the trees and across moon-washed meadows, the wind shrieking, the horse grunting. Stettler's face was white, his teeth were bared. An apocalyptic horseman of no purpose, he fled from nothing, rode to nowhere, and the demons from deep hell came up to cheer them as man and horse went by" (31). St. Pierre's emphasis on negation here—"no," "nothing," "nowhere"—is a sign of ghostliness.

13   Although I do not comment much on Eastwood's role in *High Plains Drifter* (Eastwood, 1973), that film, too, has a mining company that is exploiting a community and protecting its interests by murdering people opposed to its corporate growth.

unexpected twist that I will return to in a moment. His son Josh, the site manager, literalizes this metaphor in two ways. First, when Megan visits the site, Josh describes the phallic imagery of huge hoses and built-up pressures that shoot fountains of liquid into the earth to expel the gold. She remarks, "It looks like Hell." Second, he then immediately attempts to rape Megan by dragging her from her horse and throwing her to the ground and attacking her in full view of his mainly cheering employees. When Preacher arrives to save her, he raises her onto his horse with him. Their riding together is a cypher. Remember that when Megan summoned him, she quoted the Bible's statement that "his name that sat on [the pale horse] was Death, and Hell followed with him." By riding behind him on the pale horse, she is effectively hell herself, and thus her description of the mine site as "hell" is a moment of anagnorisis or self-recognition. Her sudden change from virginal to hellishly sexual certainly insinuates that the Freudian virgin/whore or Madonna/whore dichotomy is at work in this Western (as it often is—for example, in *The Searchers*, where it tastelessly maps onto the prospective wives Laurie and Look), but it also implies a Christian denunciation of Gaia as a pagan belief—a denunciation that does not, however, stabilize Christianity as we might expect.

Instead, Megan as a Gaian figure diminishes Preacher. Megan's inspiration for summoning Preacher is the killing of her dog in the opening scene. Her feelings for her dog generate her questioning of the psalm: "[the still waters] restoreth my soul—but they killed my dog. . . . I *am* afraid." The killing of dogs in Westerns would be worth considering further, but for now my comments on dead dogs in chapter 2 will have to suffice. In *Pale Rider*, the dog is small and white, possibly a terrier. Immediately after she buries the dog, the shot dissolves to the sun behind the clouds, and a pan down to the mountain from which Preacher rides in a later dissolve. The choice of dissolve implies a fluid transition between the white dog and Preacher's pale horse—and obviously they are parallel four-legged animals, just different sizes. Given Preacher's metonymic association with his horse—as "pale rider"—I have to conclude that he is effectively her new lapdog. This interpretation gains credence when Megan calls to him at the end of the film, "Preacher! Preacher!," echoing the boy calling for Shane at the end of *that* preceding film—but Preacher doesn't come back either. He's a disobedient little dog, as when he passes his own "test" and refuses

Megan's temptation when she asks him to have sex with her and marry her. The true scandal of the scene of temptation is not the smoldering sexuality of a fourteen-year-old girl or the emasculation of the hero but the implication of bestiality—or, less scandalously, a post-humanist, ecocritical vision of interdependent species, thwarted ultimately by Preacher's departure. Otherwise, Preacher does what she summoned him to do, and then he leaves because, like other cowboy heroes, he does not belong in the social world.

Although Megan's Gaian powers have some sway over Preacher, his own supernatural powers—against other men—are still considerable. Murray and Heumann explain that "Preacher easily kills Stockburn's deputies one by one in ghost style, able to appear and disappear at will—demonstrating his seemingly supernatural status" ("Eco-Terrorism" 139). Similarly, Kathleen Murphy describes Eastwood's performances in a way that identifies a trait of his "ghost style": "His gait is that of a ghost or a predator, his poncho'd torso [or duster'd, in *Pale Rider*] remaining strangely still, propelled ahead by the long legs, as though swimming upright in slow motion" (16).[14] In fact, as she hints by mentioning "slow motion," what she describes is also the way a dolly moves, as Spike Lee has demonstrated in many winsomely absurd tracking shots in his films. As with Ondaatje's representation of Billy the Kid, Eastwood's performances of the Man with No Name suggests that he is like a camera on a dolly, the personification of a tracking shot—tracking with all its connotations of investigation and exploration. He is beholden to the landscape or location symbolized by Megan, but the major implication in *Pale Rider* is that Preacher is "behind the scenes" or behind *the seen*, possessing a power akin to that of the filmmaker. This is a subtle metafictional—or at least self-conscious—feature of the film that gives it some of its postmodern and ghostmodern substance: a display of auteurship all the more self-reflexive because Eastwood is both actor and director of *Pale Rider*, and yet all the more self-deprecating because the auteur is such a dog. He's not just the ghostmodern death of the author (as in Roland Barthes)

---

14   A likely influence on Eastwood's performance here is Errol Flynn at the gallows plaza in Michael Curtiz's *Dodge City* (1939).

but the dogging of the author. He's an unexpectedly postmodern figure of anti-heroic self-parody.

I choose to interpret Preacher as a post-industrial figure rather than an anti-modern figure whose terrorist attack on the mine is meant to revert mining to an earlier phase. True, the classic Western is repressing modernity, repressing a technologically enabled globalizing process that Westerners might not want to acknowledge. It is also repressing modern*ism* to maintain the conscious simplicity of the style of the genre, which we see in the plots with less talk, more action (instead of laconic modernism), the decisive shootouts, and the racialized and gendered binaries. *Pale Rider* generally maintains these, whereas *The Collected Works of Billy the Kid* and *The Jesse James Poems* are obviously more postmodern in style, with their non-linearity, their intermediality, and their polyphony. In its substance, however, *Pale Rider* has the subtle complexity of all the aforementioned destabilizations: of heroism, of authorship, of big business. Ondaatje and Jiles seem to work toward a more radical critique that reshapes even the way in which the story of the cowboy is told and retold. As ghostmodernism, these texts are revisionist but also palimpsestic, not quite able to erase the troubles of the past that they also find so hauntingly exciting. This, in fact, is an apt explanation of the Western in general.

Dav(e)y Crockett and Louis Riel

If Eastwood can be what I just described as an unexpectedly postmodern figure of anti-heroic self-parody, we might in contrast *expect* a postmodern writer such as Frank Davey to be curious about the same potential of anti-heroic self-parody, if he were to deconstruct the Western. Davey's 1985 collection of poems, *The Louis Riel Organ and Piano Co.*, questions the representations of the historical Métis leader and founding figure of Manitoba, Louis Riel, alongside heroes of the Western in popular culture. Thus far in this chapter, none of CanLit's postmodern Westerns has focused on an Indigenous figure, but Indigeneity is significant to my selections from both Davey and George Bowering (next in line), who were friends and colleagues at the *TISH* magazine in Vancouver in the 1960s—a history told by Davey himself in *When TISH Happens* (2011). Although *The Louis Riel Organ and Piano Co.* might be one of the texts that shows "a profound need on the part of non-Natives to connect to North America by associating with one of its most durable symbols, the Imaginary Indian" (Francis 223), it is also a remarkably self-reflective book about Davey's own imagining of this "Indian" and his own status in contrast with Riel and the much better-known American historical figure Davy Crockett, "King of the Wild Frontier."

Davey's 1985 reflection on the North-West Resistance of 1885 is the only interpretation besides *Gabriel Dumont's Wild West Show* (2017/2021) that I've found, so far, that puts Riel in the context of celebrity, the mass media, and the genre of the Western, a genre that has appropriated and usually distorted Indigeneity.[15] (Thus, this section would have also made sense in chapter 2, especially for its resonance with John Wayne in King's *Green Grass, Running Water*, but Davey is not an Indigenous writer offering an Indigenous perspective on the Western.) In fact, the developing late nineteenth-century genre of the Western was perhaps an inspiration to the news media when the historical Riel fled to the United States and was branded an outlaw with "a reward of $5,000 . . . offered for his arrest" (Stanley and Gaudry, "Louis Riel"). The reward implied to the public that Riel was responsible for murdering Thomas Scott, who was in fact executed by the provisional government of Manitoba, not by Riel personally. Although the mass media in Riel's lifetime were primarily newspapers, and some of them helped to create the infamy of Riel in Ontario (and to a lesser extent Quebec), Davey deconstructs Riel alongside Hollywood creations. Although his book is not an example of ghostmodernism as I understand it, *The Louis Riel Organ and Piano Co.* is a postmodern destabilization of our sense of being grounded in a historical reality, as ghost stories usually are. And it is "paranormal" as postmodern texts usually are, "para" meaning adjacent to or distinct from, and they expose how normality and historical reality are compromised by mass media and popular culture in the postmodern condition.[16]

In contrast with Hollywood creations, specifically the fictionalized Davy Crockett from television and film in the mid-1950s, Davey's persona

---

15   There are many other fictionalizations of Riel that focus on history or biography rather than genre, including more recent examples such as Chester Brown's *Louis Riel: A Comic-Strip Biography* (1999) and Gregory Scofield's *Louis: The Heretic Poems* (2011).

16   See also Ihab Hassan's *The Postmodern Turn* (1987) for two chapters that use the "para" prefix (for "paracritical" and "parabiography").

at first suggests that Riel is comparatively "real" because "[y]ou couldn't play / cowboys & Riels, you couldn't play / Riels & Indians" (49). The implications here are manifold: that "Indians" are fictional, not real; that "cowboys," too, are fictional; that Riel was neither cowboy nor "Indian." Although I discussed in chapter 2 Garry Gottfriedson's observation that some Indigenous people have adopted the identity of the cowboy, I cannot imagine how anyone could refuse to accept Riel as "Indian" if that term means "Indigenous." But, quite rightly, perhaps "Indian" is such a distortion that it is not a synonym; Indigenous people are real, and "Indians" are fictional. Davey implies that this problem is a result of the Western and its conventions of "cowboys and Indians," and it is compounded by Riel's notoriety in the mass media.

The Cree-Métis scholar and poet Emma LaRocque wonders whether we can "redefine Cowboys and Indians" (150) so that the terms are different from "the Wild West type" (150): less driven by mass media, less historically and generically dependent, less adversarial, less binary. Davey himself deconstructs the fact/fiction binary and soon thereafter raises the question of authenticity—a concept that postmodern theory defeathers into a very naked canard.[17] How it does so, briefly put, is through the Nietzschean idea that our selves are now so relative that we have no foundation or perspective from which to define an objective reality (Cangiano 342). We could be authentic if we could know who we are and what our principles are, and if we could rely on that selfhood in a changing world. Postmodern thinkers do not generally believe this to be the case. When Davey's speaker refers to "The Real Rebellion" (51), not the *Riel* Rebellion, as it is sometimes described, he remembers his mother saying that "[t]here was something fishy . . . / about Louis Real" (51). He was supposed to be historical, thus real (in mainstream logic), but he was "fishy" instead. Aligning with LaRocque's criticism (which Chelsea Vowel echoes) of the flawed appreciation of Indigenous "authenticity" (147-9) in other texts, Davey implies a similarity between historical reinterpretations of Riel and the inauthenticity of the Western. I think he is skeptical of the

---

17   For an attempted validation of authenticity in the context of postmodernism, see Alessandro Ferrara's *Reflective Authenticity: Rethinking the Project of Modernity* (1998). Highly conceptual, it comments on art in relation to intention, interpretation, and identity.

historical reinterpretations too, because they are a sign of what LaRocque calls a colonial "need for an authentic Indian" (149) that can even trigger an "identity crisis" (149) in some Indigenous people who worry that their contemporary Indigeneity is not authentic enough. To Davey's credit, he does not appear to be seeking "an authentic Indian." Rather, he is reflecting on where these ideas and images come from.

Although there are degrees, and we can think of Riel as "real" compared to the reel of the Western, Davey is still implying that "Louis Real" depends in some way on the alternating binary of "cowboys & Riels" and "Riels & Indians" that Canadians import from American popular culture. This hybrid status (not necessarily a racial hybridity but something more like that of genre) aligns with the American citizenship that the historical Riel gained while exiled in Montana before returning to Canada in 1884 as an ally to Dumont. Riel is thus transnational. Hybrids and transnationalism are of interest partly because Davey doesn't appear to believe in homogeneity, uniformity, unity, or anything so potentially simple; in his book *Post-National Arguments* (1993) he emphasizes contestations (15, 18, 24) and disputation (8, 24) between the diverse parts of the complex whole, and I think that he believes this to be the reality of the situation, "real" life.[18] Pragmatically, it means that Canadian cultures and Indigenous cultures have to deal with the power of American cultural exports.

For this reason, here I am aligning hybridity with not only transnationalism but also multiculturalism, even though it is common to think of hybridity on a much smaller scale than the other two.[19] Davey's Riel is a hybrid who symbolizes multiculturalism and its messy relationship with nationalism. As Kit Dobson writes in his book *Transnational Canadas* (2009), "Davey's well-known discomfort with both the national and the global side of the free trade debate signals a dawning awareness of the interpenetration of the two terms. Davey opts to support the nation in

---

18   Finding the discourse of conflict and contest in the work of Gerald Graff in the 1980s, Daniel Heath Justice suggests that Indigenous literary studies, too, offers "a self-critical (and always contested) understanding of literature as both artistic expression and political instrument and an assertion of literature within a larger matrix of relationships, influences, and effects" (335–6).

19   For a related commentary in the context of Indigenous literatures and cultures, see chapter 5 of Dee Horne's *Contemporary American Indian Writing* (1999), in which Horne explains Indigenous hybridity or multinationality as a defence against colonialism.

[*Post-National Arguments*], but one wonders if he would do so in the same terms today" (xvii). I would guess that his "support" would fluctuate, as mine does, depending on who the underdog is: the region versus the nation; the First Nations versus the nation-state; the nation-state versus the transnational corporation. I would disagree slightly with the suggestion that Davey is uncomfortable with the changing allegiances; Davey in fact once commented on the "anxiety" toward Canadian "incoherence" ("On Not Being Indigenous" 10) leading to the very first TransCanada conference, suggesting again his tolerance of contestations and disputations that are inevitable on the grand scale of multiculturalism and on the small scale of individual hybrids searching for identity.

Whether self-identifying Canadians are imagining a better future in multicultural folk traditions, or whether a hybrid is trying to find a home in the world, nostalgia is a problem. Davey suggests that he has acquired nostalgia from the United States in a cultural and economic exchange enabled by the mass media of film and television. Although Svetlana Boym traces nostalgia to seventeenth-century medicine, she adds that "[n]ostalgia as a historical emotion came of age at the time of Romanticism and is coeval with the birth of mass culture" (16). I would add *multi*-culture. To my fascination, the nostalgia for this hybridity is also what in 1989 Jameson called a "nostalgia for the present" (qtd. in Appadurai 30), because the decade of the 1980s was the first decade of official multiculturalism in Canada, and this multiculturalism resonated with postmodern writers who had committed themselves to categorical breakdown in the 1960s and '70s. The etymology of nostalgia defines the term as a longing for home, and the longing to make Canada home to more cultures was a temporary win-win situation that *seemed* to redress colonial problems *and* assuage colonial guilt. Boym explains that "[l]onging for home became a central trope of romantic nationalism" (12). Many of my teachers, colleagues, and friends have since argued that multiculturalism was not and is not enough, and that anti-racism is more direct and to the point, and I usually agree, and I suspect that the contestation implied in "anti-racism" would be appealing to Davey. I definitely agree with Jameson that "nostalgia for the present" is a sign of "false consciousness" (*Postmodernism* 282) about what is actually happening in the present. Hutcheon affirms this view by writing that "the ideal that is *not* being lived now is projected into the past" ("Irony"). Nostalgia can be "consciously denied but deeply felt" ("Irony"). In a phrase that crystallizes a problem and its critique, as Vowel also does (43), Michael Kammen calls it "history... without guilt" (qtd. in Boym xiv). In the present of the 1980s, when Davey was writing his *Louis Riel* and just before Jameson was writing his *Postmodernism* (1991), the nostalgia was vivid because the *theories* of multiculturalism and hybridity were current, and yet in Canada, *manifestations* as nationally powerful as Riel were perhaps only historical. In locating the ideal at a different historical moment, such as at Riel's time of potential self-government, the political comparisons become obvious. Furthermore, as Hutcheon claims, exposing the obviousness creates irony ("Irony"). Davey seems to have exchanged an imported and thus false nostalgia for a nostalgia that is more *authentic* because it is based on a present ideal of multiculturalism and hybridity—but yet *ironic* because it was embodied in the historical but unreal Riel.

Irony can stymie readers who are looking for political orientations. In *The False Traitor: Louis Riel in Canadian Culture* (2003), Albert Braz arrives at a different conclusion from mine. Braz writes: "unexpected in light of [Davey's] postmodernism is his apparent unreceptiveness to Riel's hybridity, the latter's proclivity to disregard boundaries" (66). Braz's claim about Davey's "unreceptiveness to Riel's hybridity" may well be true if the "Riel" section of Davey's book is read in isolation from the book's four other parts. Braz interprets so many representations of Riel that some nuance has to be sacrificed. The parts of Davey's book are entitled "Wacouster," "Dump," "Crockett," "Riel," and "The Thomas Organ and Piano Company," but time and space do not permit me, either, to explain how the ironies multiply with each.

The juxtaposition of the parts entitled "Crockett" and "Riel" is most significant as a commentary on the Western and related nationally relevant attitudes. Why not set Riel side by side with an Indigenous figure from the same time period in America, such as Sitting Bull, who, like Dumont, was once a performer in Buffalo Bill's Wild West Show? I do not have an entirely satisfying answer, but I speculate that Davey wanted a contrast between different degrees of celebrity and recognition in the mass media. And Davy Crockett was a historical figure who *was* in some ways parallel to Riel: a woodsy politician who stood up for Indigenous land claims, died because of a rebellion, and is now often remembered as a national hero of the frontier. Partly because Riel was originally associated with rebellion rather than Confederation, and partly because of the racialization that Davey calls attention to with the trope of the "Indian," Riel could never become as popular—even in the 1980s—as the fictionalized Crockett on TV and film. Davey seems to remark on the differences in popularity when he also compares himself to the fictionalized Crockett: "It was 1955 / Davey Davey Davey Davey / Crockett, they called me" (39). The repetition of "Davey" and "Davy" in this poem echoes the Crockett phenomenon partly inspired by Disney and the associated theme songs. Aware of his own nostalgia, Davey writes: "1950. We're all ten years old. The Alamo ricochets / onto the screen of the Abbotsford Odeon. / Of course it's myth," and, "[a]n army (we'll learn) / only Hollywood can dream" (40). In 1950, Davey himself *was* "ten years old," and so there is a "real" nostalgia of his memories of childhood superimposed on the false nostalgia of 1950s versions of Davy Crockett that recall the 1836 Texas Revolution. The Texas Revolution and the North-West Resistance are also in juxtaposition, implying different awarenesses of regional histories in American and Canadian cultures—a difference likely related to the fact that the North-West Resistance involved Indigenous peoples so centrally, people who were assumed to be vanishing in the national culture of the time.

Another implication of juxtaposing the Texas Revolution and the North-West Resistance is that war is conceptually parallel with hybridity or the trespassing of racial borders, and this raises questions about positive views of war or negative views of hybridity. Considering Davey's commitment to postmodern complexity, I do not think that he has such clear-cut views. Davey writes about Riel's actual border crossings: "Louis kept crossing the border. Down / to Minnesota up to Toronto," "[d]own to Minnesota / up to Assiniboia," "[d]own to Minnesota / up to Ottawa," "[d]own to Montana. Up to Duck Lake, Batoche" (56). These politically motivated exiles and negotiations can symbolize war, because "[t]he bullets / went back and forth" (56) too. The implication of violence associated with the United States in other books by Davey leads Aritha van Herk to offer the following commentary:

> Murders and murderers, [Davey] maintains, are read as partaking of an American sensibility rather than any ordinary Canadian experience.... Only Louis Riel and Marc Lépine, "Davey" says, proclaim the infamous brand of murderer.... The general opinion that murder is "un-Canadian" is one of our social myths. ("Frank Davey")

Here, Riel is one of the "un-Canadian" exceptions, aligned with American infamy. "Maybe he wears a six-gun" (54), Davey speculates. If we imagine Louis Riel as a cowboy in parallel with Davy Crockett, as suggested by the juxtaposition of their sections in Davey's book, we might wonder how American this Riel is, or is meant to be.

This view of Riel as a cowboy and thus an American is provocative, but we also have to think about the final section of *The Louis Riel Organ & Piano Company*, a section entitled "The *Thomas* Organ & Piano Company" (emphasis added). Davey probably intends the Riel-Crockett juxtaposition and its associated Canadian-American comparisons, but the book's title and the section's title differ only in the name of the brand of organ or piano—the brand being another sign of corporate identification and alignment with popular culture—and so Davey probably also intends a Riel-Thomas juxtaposition and comparison. In the centre of the book, Davey suggests that the idea for the comparison was in the memory of sheet music for the piano. He writes: "above each piece of music in my practice book / was a small picture of a black-bearded unsmiling man" (51) who reminded him of Timothy Eaton, Mackenzie King, and evidently Riel. How does "Thomas" stand in for "Riel"? What characteristics—what national signifiers—of the Thomas Company transfer metaphorically to the Riel Company and to the collective and individual meanings of "Riel"?

Local Heroes

Provenance is the main signifier. According to Davey, the Thomas organs were built in a factory in Woodstock, Ontario. Testifying to its globalization, however, some of its materials were imported. The rubber of the bellows, for example, came from "tarps that had covered fieldguns / on their way from Liverpool / to Fish Creek" (62), one of the sites of the North-West Resistance. So, yes, the signs of war and the signs of trade appear together, along with colonial signifiers. Although he doesn't specify, the rubber might have come from Liverpool too, but rubber is not produced from Canadian or English materials, as far as I know; it is usually associated with Asia and various countries in Africa. On the next page, Davey's concern with provenance is revealed to be a concern with buying locally; the speaker's mother would bring him on shopping trips from Abbotsford to Vancouver or across the border to Washington State, where anything they bought had to remain a secret from his girlfriend's father, who managed a local store (63). Showing his penchant for the comic, Davey then contrasts regional loyalties toward beer with the region-effacing cosmopolitanism of modernist writers:

> T. S. Eliot
> was from Missouri. "I'm from Missouri"—
> T. S. Eliot said that only once,
> much too late, & A. J. M. Smith
> was already world-famous across Canada
> for urging cosmopolitan standards. (66)

Borrowing Mordecai Richler's line, from *The Incomparable Atuk* (1963), about being "world-famous . . . all over Canada" (40), here Davey seems to resent "cosmopolitan standards" for effacing or erasing the small things in a big world. As Métis, like a Thomas organ, Riel is branded "Canadian" despite his component parts not fitting together comfortably under that brand: not all French Canadians identify as Canadian, just as many Inuit and First Nations do not identify as Canadian. As a big country in a much bigger world, Canada is made up of parts, the mosaic, and Davey seems to be urging us to remember the parts, the provenance, the Indigenous, when the globe beckons—even if the parts were put together as a result of war and colonization. They can serve different purposes now.

  The poem about cosmopolitanism that I just quoted has what Arjun Appadurai calls a "scalar dynamic" (32): a telescoping size from "small-town" (66) to state ("Missouri") to country ("Canada") to "world." This telescoping is a feature of Appadurai's conception of modernity "at large" in the world, which has serious implications. In contrast, Richler and Davey's joke is that Canada on the world stage *is* a joke. Davey's speaker muses,

> I always thought
> that if there were more bricks, poems
> & novels made in the small towns of Canada,
> somewhere in Canada
> there'd be a really good brick
> & poem, & novel. (72)

I suspect that the speaker's wish for something "really good" is partly a wish for a hero, a local hero, a figure of Eliot's status but Mazo de la Roche's popularity (72), and he comes up with Riel. He is not looking for a war hero, but an ironic hero, a multicultural hero. Although there is a moral to be affirmed in this view of Riel, it might still be what Emma LaRocque describes as a "White Man's heroic point of view" (143) that implicitly downgrades the moral claim of Indigenous people to their traditional lands and widens the surveying scope of imperialism by associating heroism with its modern derivative, celebrity, which is a mechanism of cultural colonization. The logic here is a logic of expansion, even if Davey suggests (with the irony of a doubling) that nothing better than "really good" could ever come of it.

It is an example of Davey's tendency, as editor and author, to publish what Smaro Kamboureli calls "writing that questions literariness" ("Frank Davey" 208) through its postmodern blending of literary and popular cultures, the mash-up of high and low. In a way, it asks why Crockett should be the televised hero of the 1950s for Canadians when Riel could have been that figure, in theory. In another way, and more controversially perhaps, the related question is why self-identifying Canadians could not entertain or be entertained by a hero coded as "Indian," at least until 1985; today, it is a little different, given that King and others are both canonized and entertaining, but LaRocque's concern about the pejorative connotations of "Indian" (as Savage or Noble Savage) still stands.

So, where does this leave us with *The Louis Riel Organ and Piano Co.?* First, Davey compares Riel's historicity to the inauthenticity of Hollywood's Western and seems to think that they are similarly created.

Second, Davey is playing with nostalgia by suggesting a paradox of real or authentic nostalgia for the present of the multicultural 1980s, while also providing evidence for Hutcheon's suggestion that we should understand this nostalgia as ironic. Third and final, another irony is that to accept Riel as a cowboy or "Indian" and thus as a convention of the Western, we have to ignore that Riel, as Métis, can be branded "Canadian" despite—or precisely *because of*—his component parts not integrating as Canadian. Davey explains that a literature or an identity is the sum of "the specific contentions and nexuses of the sites of its production" (*Post-National* 23). Ultimately, this is an irony of multiculturalism, especially when Canadians see multiculturalism as a cultural difference from American society.

A Western Heroine in Quebec

If the skeleton key of this project is the transnationalism of the Western and the resulting challenge to the nationalisms of the United States and Canada, then no one should be surprised that the key and our attention would eventually turn to Quebec. In fact, the two biggest and most lavish books on the Western in Canada come from Montreal: *Québec Western* (2013) from Éditions les Malins (printed in China) and *Once Upon a Time ... The Western* (2017) from the Montreal Museum of Fine Arts (printed in Italy). Neither book has anything to say about the Western in Canadian literature in English. Although there are French-language Westerns from France, such as Céline Minard's *Faillir Être Flingué* (2013), and from Quebec, such as Marie Hélène Poitras's *Griffintown* (2012), Dominique Scali's *In Search of New Babylon* (2015), and Olivier Dufault's *Benediction* (2019), here I am concentrating on George Bowering's *Caprice*, one of English Canada's postmodern Westerns—a category found mainly in the 1970s, '80s, and arguably the early '90s that includes those already considered in this chapter: Nichol's *The True Eventual Story of Billy the Kid*, Ondaatje's *The Collected Works of Billy the Kid*, Jiles's *The Jesse James Poems*, and Davey's *The Louis Riel Organ and Piano Co*. Davey's and Bowering's books are the only ones in which Indigenous characters are prominent; Bowering's is the only one with a woman as a main character (with the possible exception of Zerelda James as a central, framing figure in Jiles's book). It is also distinct from the others as the only one with an emphasis on the other "official" founding nation in Canada, the French of what is now Quebec.

Quebec's situation in Canada is itself distinct, of course. The independent spirit of Quebec has caused Canadian national crises of identity and unity in the twentieth century, and earlier French explorers such as Jacques Cartier shared with English and American nationalists an imperial drive to obtain lands and resources. French-Canadian traditions of trapping, fur trading, and exploration by canoe are motifs in a minority of early Westerns in print and film. Pierre Berton surveys some of them in *Hollywood's Canada* (1975), as does Dominique Brégent-Heald in *Borderland Films* (2015). Brégent-Heald focuses more narrowly on the 1910s but thereby offers insight into the historical period very close to the turn-of-the-century setting of George Bowering's *Caprice* (1987). *Caprice* takes place in the British Columbian interior, involving a villainous international border-crossing American and a heroic interprovincial border-crossing French Canadian. Regardless of their distance from actual borders, they interact in the imagined American-Canadian borderlands, "a wider and more inclusive zone of transnational and cultural interactions" (Brégent-Heald, *Borderland* 10). Farther east, Quebecers assert that they share a common ground with Americans and "their" genre of the Western: "Après tout, l'Amérique, c'est aussi nous, et l'Américain fait même bien souvent partie de la famille. . . . À cette familiarité s'ajoute nos racines communes: anglo-saxonne, nord-américaine, et notre âme de pionnier" ("After all, America, that's us too, and the American is often enough part of the family. . . . Added to this familiarity are the roots we share: Anglo-Saxon, North American, and our pioneer spirit"; Blondin et al. 13).[20] Evidently, the genre of the Western is an expression of culture that aligns with some points of view in Quebec, and seemingly for many Quebecers the Western has most of the same meanings that it has for self-described Canadians outside of Quebec. Simply, it means independence, authenticity, and nostalgia, perhaps also a highly problematic colonial fantasy. These meanings are precisely what Bowering is playing with in *Caprice*, which is about a young woman from Quebec in the 1890s who journeys to the interior of British Columbia to avenge her murdered

---

20   Unless otherwise noted, all translations from the French are my own.

brother. Bowering himself is from British Columbia, and, in his looking to the East, *Caprice* becomes a thought experiment. What would happen to the genre if the hero of the Western was not a man from the West but a woman from the relative East, specifically Quebec? Obviously, Quebec is still "West" relative to Europe, but it's "East" relative to the setting of *Caprice* in the interior of British Columbia, just as New England and the Eastern Seaboard are easternized in the genre of the American Western. My purpose here is to try to explain, first, how these relativities can be described as postmodern; and, second, how they relate to other seemingly postmodern dimensions of *Caprice*, such as its border crossings, its self-reflexivity, its gender-bending, and ultimately its *genre*-bending.

These relativities are a dimension of what Alexander MacLeod calls "postmodern-regionalism." MacLeod hyphenates the term because he believed that, when he was completing his research in 2003, postmodernism and regionalism were so opposed that they had to be "grafted" (10) together. MacLeod explains that "[b]ecause most scholars continue to interpret regionalist texts according to a resolutely empirical reading of geography, literary regionalism has fallen out of touch with the new kinds of 'unrealistic,' generic landscapes that now dominate North American culture in the postindustrial era" (ii). He is thinking partly of the surreal suburban malls and parking lots of American postmodernism. He does not include the Western as a sometimes postmodern example of an " 'unrealistic,' generic landscape," but I would add it. In terms of "unrealistic" and "generic," think of the false fronts of architecture in so many Westerns, and the constructed mesas and cacti implied in Margaret Atwood's "Backdrop Addresses Cowboy," which I considered briefly above. (Such elements are taken to new heights in John Landis's 1986 comic Western, *The Three Amigos*, perhaps especially in the nighttime campfire singalong scene.) MacLeod's research demonstrates that we cannot sufficiently understand Canadian postmodernism unless we understand it as a regional response to the suburban landscapes that most Canadians live in. Robert Kroetsch figures centrally in MacLeod's research, and both of them explain that writers from the West led the development of postmodernism, at least in the West if not throughout the country. MacLeod might prefer that we "read postmodernism regionally" (ii), and I agree that doing so is crucial; but now that he has done so, here I read regionalism postmodernistically.

The consequence of this thinking for a novel such as *Caprice* is that we cannot accept its borderland between the BC interior, Alberta, and the United States as a place that will be inevitably or essentially or fundamentally different from the heroine's origin in Quebec. As a result, my own interest in the regionalism of this novel has little connection to actual places (with one exception), and rather I find the regionalism in *characters* and in *metaphors* that interact with the postmodern dimensions that I have already listed: border crossings, self-reflexivity, gender-bending, and *genre*-bending.

Partly because we are thinking of region, and because the interpretation at work here is related to postmodernism, I want to acknowledge that an early version of this part of this chapter was presented at Congress 2018 in Regina, Saskatchewan, more historically at oskana kā-asastēki, or the place where the bones are piled up. The areas around Regina are the traditional lands of the Nêhiyawak (or Cree), the Anihšināpēk (or Saulteaux), the Dakota, Lakota, and Nakoda, and the Métis. Although it is not entirely compatible with Indigenous views to read a region postmodernistically, because of the risk of uprooting the knowledge that we find there, Bowering at least acknowledges Indigenous people and imagines how they might view the genre of the Western. As I have shown in my research on Thomas King's *Green Grass, Running Water* and Garry Gottfriedson's *Whiskey Bullets*, Indigenous views of the genre tend to be ambivalent but ultimately negative—which is understandable, given that the Western is usually a narrative that glorifies colonialism and the vanishing of the "Indian." But a postmodern reading of regionalism aligns with Indigeneity in at least one respect—namely, that the postmodern reading blurs borders, borders which colonists and settlers affirm very strictly, to the detriment of First Nations and Métis, who asserted and still assert a transnational fluidity to the land and their own movements.

Although the two Indigenous characters in *Caprice* are only observing the action from a frame story and are known to us only as "the first Indian" and "the second Indian," their sardonic remarks introduce the novel's questioning of the Western and its colonial and patriarchal implications. I will return to the post-colonial and anti-colonial themes, and I will begin with the imperfect feminist theme that the character Caprice and her novel imply, simply because the cover of the novel and the two Indigenous characters who get the first word all focus on her. The two Indigenous characters set up a central question about the nature and gender of the cowboy, here illustrated (literally, on the book's cover) by Caprice. Possibly the first heroine and female main character of a Canadian Western, Caprice also stands out as a francophone—and a poet—from Quebec. In a single sentence, the plot of *Caprice* involves her travelling alone (except for her horse) from Quebec to British Columbia (via Mexico) to avenge her brother, who was killed by an American near Kamloops. Her language and place of origin do not change what it means to go west. Her gender does—not because women stayed home while the men went west, but because she adopts the role of outlaw-lawman, someone out of her own jurisdiction taking the law into her own hands (mostly). Her age matters too, because the novel plays with differences between boys and men, and between girls and women. Age and gender are mapped onto regions to suggest that regions are symbolic constructs as much as real places. The other twist in the plot is that she eventually goes home, at least symbolically to a domestic space (which we don't see before the novel ends), invoking the nostalgia so characteristic of the Western and redoubling some of the ethical problems of the Western even as her eponymous novel tries to break out of them.

Gender-bending and genre-bending go hand in hand in *Caprice*, starting with the crossover genre implied on the cover of the novel. The cover displays Caprice and her horse in the semi-realistic, semi-pulp style of lurid illustrative painting recognizable especially on Harlequin romances and in middlebrow magazines of the 1940s such as *The Saturday Evening Post*. Bowering indirectly explains the painting as an alternative to "a picture of [Caprice] with [her] whip" (102) that a photographer in the novel proposes to her. In her critical study of the novel, Isabel Carrera observes that inside the book "Caprice's physical appearance is certainly suggestive of depictions of women in certain types of male fantasy literature [such as the Western, though she does not mention it here]. This figure, out of yet another sub-genre, male popular romance/comic magazine/pornography, is mostly silent" (435). Helene Staveley therefore calls Caprice an "enigma" and "a fetish for the male reader's gaze" (247, 248n). As "a French-Canadian Cinderella" (254), Caprice bends the Western toward the romantic novel, not so much for teenage girls and women as for teenage boys and men.

Extending Staveley's and Carrera's more sinister implications, we could also associate Caprice and her whip with a genre of S&M (sadism and masochism), but it could also be an allusion to a popular hero from earlier in the 1980s: Steven Spielberg's Indiana Jones, whose first film was *Raiders of the Lost Ark* in 1981. The Indiana Jones series became self-consciously a Western and an epic in *Indiana Jones and the Last Crusade* (1989, two years after *Caprice*), where, in the backstory, we see a landscape of mesas, a horse chase, and a fight atop a steam-powered locomotive. That it is in the backstory suggests that Indiana Jones was always a Western. (They also ride off into the sunset at the end of the film, but they are in the Middle East, near Petra.) Inasmuch as the cover of *Caprice* suggests that it, too, was always a Western, it signals other genres with an obviousness and insistence that imply it is self-consciously postmodern in the sense of strategically multi-categorical. Caprice's work as a poet, "a creator of wor(l)ds" (Carrera 435), helps to imply the authorial self-reflexivity. So does the novel's motif of eyes: " 'ordinary English eyes,' . . . American eyes, Indian eyes, male and female eyes" (Carrera 437). The motif of eyes draws the reader's attention to the fact that Caprice is a representation, not a reality, and her mythic quality is one excuse—however poor—for her objectification. Although she is described without her shirt in a brief love scene (75–6), it is no more explicit than "one high little breast followed by a second, sweet soft firm muscles, the freckles above them" (75). The Indiana Jones comparison is instructive: with his frequently half-unbuttoned shirts, he shows more skin than Caprice does on the cover of the novel, where her long-sleeved denim shirt is buttoned to the collar, her chest could almost be that of a strong male, and her blue jeans are thick and baggy. Even her hat is pulled low over her eyes. Her braids (more about them later) are the telltale sign of her femininity, and—though their girlishness becomes doubly problematic in light of the implications of pornography and S&M—they are part of a visual first impression that gender-bends away from Caprice as a woman toward both girlishness and mannishness.[21]

---

21   Caprice's masculinity is also potentially part of the tradition, in dime-novel Westerns, of women who pose as men and cowboys. Daniel Worden explains it (an explanation that Collin Campbell pointed out to me) as a sometimes critical response to "late nineteenth-century genteel norms and institutions, particularly through a proliferation of masculinities that are not essentially connected to a legibly male body" (*Masculine* 36).

Caprice also bends the genre by association with the regional and linguistic relativities of its heroine's home. Caprice is Québécoise; the novel thereby invites responses to Frank Davey's assertion that the sort of "transnational mapping" (*Post-National* 8) that I see in the Western tends to diminish the Canadianness of Quebec. I would argue that Bowering recognizes the westering nationalism of both solitudes. The strong similarity of the westering nationalisms in Quebec and the rest of Canada was attested to in 2013 by Jacques Blondin et al.'s *Québec Western: Ville Après Ville* and the Télé-Québec program of that name. Neither is an academic study, though a few books from academic presses can be found in its bibliography; *Québec Western* is a popular history and contemporary survey—a French catalogue of the country musicians, yodellers, fans, dancers, campers, truckers, writers, actors, filmmakers, fashionistas, and other Quebecers who adopt or have adopted a cowboy persona and the trappings of the genre to express their independence, their desire for self-governance, their authenticity, their love of the countryside, and the historical and commodified nostalgias also self-evident in places called Vieux Québec and Old Montreal. Throughout, the book asserts that this Eastern province is Western "ville après ville," wherever you go. It reads the Western into the folksy *chansonnier* genre, into false-front architecture, and into "rodeos" of motorcyclists. I do this sort of work too—thinking that the Western is a synecdoche for the Western world—so I can't complain. In the context of literary history, it admits that "[l]e Québec n'a évidemment pas pareille tradition littéraire [compared to the Western in the United States]—il faudra attendre les années 1960 pour voir plusieurs auteurs québécois s'intéresser à notre passé d'un point de vue nord-américain. Il a cependant lui aussi son digne pionnier" ("Quebec obviously does not have the same literary tradition; not until the 1960s would several Quebec authors become interested in their past from a North American point of view. Quebec, too, however, has its own pioneer"; Blondin et al. 174). Here *Québec Western* reveals some of its less apparent ideology. Tracing this dignity of the pioneer back to an exception to the rule, the authors find Quebecer Ernest Dufault, who wrote *Lone Cowboy: My Life Story* (1930) under the pseudonym Will James. Dufault/James remarks that French-Canadian trappers were "ceux qui sont arrivés les premiers partout" ("those who were the first to arrive everywhere"; qtd. in Blondin et al. 174), perpetuating the myth of *terra nullius*, nobody's land, the open range that is free for the taking. *Québec Western* does not speak back to Dufault/James; it does not significantly acknowledge Indigenous peoples in Quebec or elsewhere, nor does it appear to imply the so-called victim narrative or any related equation of the French minority in Canada with the Indigenous minority. There is recent scholarship in French on the figure of the "Indian" in the Western (e.g., Mathieu Lacoue-Labarthe's *Les Indiens dans le western américain* [2013]), but I chose *Québec Western* partly because it seeks a popular audience in a way similar to the Harlequin-like cover of *Caprice*. (Indeed, the covers of both books are similar in the pose of the cowboy on the landscape with an impression of movement from the horse on *Caprice* and the highway on *Québec Western*.) Furthermore, like so many popular Westerns even after the 1960s, it idealizes the Western as a search for Eden or utopia (Blondin et al. 174). Sue Sorensen juxtaposes West *as* Eden and West *of* Eden (6) in her edited collection, *West of Eden* (2008), which is about the West in general. "Being in Eden," she writes, quoting Dick Harrison, "also requires the writer or reader to think in terms of 'moral simplicity and optimism' " (4). I think this happens in *Québec Western* and many Westerns: it's easy to be optimistic if you omit ethical dilemmas caused by colonialism. This idealization has been a hallmark of regional literature in general, and Caprice herself wants no part in it.

Bowering's *Caprice* involves Quebec in the West and the Western quite differently, partly because the novel is framed by, and often interrupted by, the observations of two Indigenous men who remark ironically upon "the white people who have been thoughtful enough to come and pursue their living among us" (2), and partly because Caprice herself is not the typical cowboy. In fact, the two "Indians" begin the story by debating whether she may be called a "cowboy" when she is a girl or, more accurately, a woman (2–5). Bowering shows his self-consciousness about language in the same scene when the second "Indian" (the younger and the protégé) says, "I am not sure I can find the words" (2) to describe Caprice. Although we are probably reading an imagined translation from their Indigenous language, the second "Indian's" "words" imply not only that Caprice is difficult to describe but also that colonization—Caprice's "[c]oming from the east" (1)—has damaged his language. When the second "Indian" parodies Latin by calling the distant past the "etcet-era" later in the novel, the first "Indian" remonstrates: "No you dont [sic]. That is not an Indian pun" (128). Later still, an Indigenous boy in a residential school says of a pencil, "This thing. It does not understand my words" (175). Poignantly, his exclamation suggests that he has other "thing[s]" to say but that colonial technologies of writing have interrupted and supplanted his effective speech.

This damage, too, is implied by the context of the Western that Bowering introduces in his very first paragraph: "If you just had ordinary English eyes, you would have seen late-morning sunlight. . . . But if you had those famous Indian eyes you could . . . see something moving" (1). These "eyes" are "famous" because of the popularity of the Western, of course, and they reinforce stereotypes of the eagle-eyed—no, *hawk*-eyed—and stoic, laconic "Indian." The status of observer that the two Indigenous men share does not mean, however, that they cannot speak, because they are probably the most talkative characters in the book; their actual language is the question. According to Davey, the two observers "parody those discourses [of the Western] and speak themselves, rather, in the analytical language of anthropology, to which their role as spectators to another culture suits them" (*Post-National* 84). Whether this appropriation of language is assimilation or counter-appropriation is uncertain, but Bowering also refuses to insist that "English" is the only possible language of power: his character Everyday Luigi is an Italian working for a Chinese boss, Soo Woo, and he is perplexed by the Chinese language. I interpret Bowering's writing about the babel of language and his use of "Indian" framing devices, which evoke anthropological epistemology, as significantly post-colonial and postmodern.

By starting with "words" and their nationalities and related languages, Bowering's *Caprice* evokes the linguistic determinism of the Sapir-Whorf hypothesis—the idea that how we see the world depends on how our language sees it—but it also calls upon us to examine "our interpretive schemata" (Garrett-Petts 567), such as genre. Bowering imagines the space of the West as an "alphabet" (76), and its eponymous heroine as "living in a different [one]" (76). She might be "living" elsewhere, but she is a poet visiting the West, bringing with her a poet's perspective and a discomfort with the gun violence reputed to be endemic to the West. Caprice's different approach to the role of outlaw-lawman probably has more to do with her vocation as poet and her gender than with her French language or her provenance in Quebec, which at least according to *Québec Western* is a place of significant affirmation of the Western. Still, in *Caprice*, the heroine has gone west only to pursue two criminals, including the murderer of her brother; she will then return home. One of the criminals, Loop Groulx, is also French Canadian, suggesting that at least part of her search is for her old home in Quebec—a twist on the genre of the Western in which almost everyone wants a *new* home and not the one they left.

Regionalism in *Caprice* is therefore not only Western Canadian, and it is understood partly in relation to other cardinal directions, not only eastward but also northward. Eventually shot in the arm by Caprice in her quest to kill Frank Spencer, Loop Groulx tires of Spencer's lecture about the "freedom and opportunity" in the West; he "just wanted a white bed. He didnt [sic] care what direction it was in" (245). Loop's moniker, which appears to be a reference to the Loop Garoo Kid, the African-American cowboy in Ishmael Reed's parodic 1969 novel *Yellow Back Radio Broke-Down*, has geographical dimensions: "Loop" is a nickname, and his real name is Lionel Groulx (74, 105), which is also the name of an early twentieth-century figure, a Roman Catholic priest and religious nationalist in Quebec. The historical Groulx soon had a college and metro station named after him in Montreal; the Lionel Groulx station is a hub that has lines going in four directions—in other words, a cross, roughly the cardinal (not the priestly) directions. The fictional Loop Groulx/Lionel Groulx has a nickname that replaces the lion of "Lionel" and means "wolf" in French (but is pronounced "Lou," as in "the lady that's known as," as explained in this book's conclusion). Funnily, the nickname aligns the character with an animal known for its errant sense of direction, as in the phrase "as the wolf runs," meaning "not straight," or not "as the crow flies." The multiple ironies can be unpacked only briefly here, but for Montreal to name a metro station after Lionel Groulx is simultaneously to honour the recent past (Groulx having died in 1967) and to project Groulx's then dated religious nationalism into the future, the subway system being an infrastructural symbol of the modernization of Montreal and Quebec.

So, the cardinal directions are curiously related to time: past and future. In *Caprice*, Bowering's narrator reflects on regions in the late nineteenth century from an admittedly anachronistic post-*Shane* (1949 in print, 1953 on screen) perspective (110):

> By the 1890s the west had started to shrink. It had started noticeably to shrink by the time the first locomotives made the turnaround at Port Moody. Now or rather then it shrank with every word that was sent back from the dry country across the mountains and over the Atlantic Ocean. Some of the west spilled northward for a while and seemed to be expanding to its original size, but there too it would shrink, until the west became small enough to fit into eastern plans, to become a region in the eastern scheme of things. Out in the west the west was also, by the 1890s, becoming the past. The more one looked around in the west the more it seemed obvious that it was the past hanging on for a while. It became more clear all the time that the future was getting ready to move in, and the future of the west was going to be the east. (108)

The postmodern reversals and diversions in space-time here, the symbolic shrinking and expansion of West and North, help to provide evidence for the relativistic explanations of "the idea of West" in the introduction and first chapter of this book.[22] Here, Bowering's metaphor of the shrinking/expanding region is an explanation from physics: a fluid, something that "spilled," corresponding with images of gravity wells and, if you can imagine it as a container, a light cone. Later, the fluid metaphor wicks over to characters when Roy Smith, the schoolteacher and Caprice's lover, "remembered that Horace Greeley said the 'Indians' would have to disappear while the white people filled up the west" (176).

In fact, the two "Indians" have the cleverest view of how characterization and region align:

---

22   At the same time, however, Bowering lets a generality about Canadian/American difference stand, when Everyday Luigi is shot in one of the hold-ups perpetrated by Loop: "You did not often see shooting like that from the back of a quick-moving horse, at least not on this side of the medicine line" (123)—a practice that helped some Indigenous peoples to differentiate the empires.

"The white man in what he calls the west and we call the middle prizes action above all else. He thinks of himself as a man of action, and does not trust other men who are not. This includes most people from what he calls the east, and it includes people who read books, or engage in abstract conversation, or do not get dirty when they work."

"I do not like getting dirty when I work," said the second Indian.

"I have never had an opportunity to observe whether that is true," said the first Indian. . . . "The western man of action believes that his actions are saving his country, as he calls it, from the decay of its early promise that set in when life became easy enough back east for people to make their living without getting dirty. He therefore resents people in the west who survive on the practice of quiet. He thinks that his ideal might be undermined by lawyers, bankers, teachers, writers, and the like."

"Are bankers like writers?"

"Only in the sense that they do not get dirty—I am speaking literally—when they work." (191)

The comic timing and co-operation here are perfect, and the first man's attention to naming and his reference to "speaking literally" demonstrate Bowering's willingness to "authorize" the men and give them a say in what the regions mean. He is speaking literally but he is implying figuratively; his opinion is that bankers are untrustworthy and morally stained. The regions are not defined by actual geography, here, but by figurative and relative points of view held by characters with different beliefs. Similarly, a little later, Caprice is offered an American pistol to replace the German Luger that she had never fired, and she considers "the western man of action" already mentioned: "The trouble was thinking. The remedy was action. She was not sure that she believed it" (194). It was too simple, even if a thought followed by, or transformed into, an action is a sentient being's most basic temporal performance.

She is also unsure about other gendered characterizations that could link her to geography. On one occasion, she meets a homesteading wife and assumes that her interlocutor wants to hear about women's toughness in the West: " 'Women-folks,' she said in a language she was borrowing, 'have to be just as fierce as the weather around here' " (214). Of course, the "language" here is the English that supplants her French while she is on the trail of her brother's killer, but it can also be a language of signs pointing from gender ("women-folks") to place ("here"). The "here" is a place defined by "the weather," which is "fierce," though she is still learning how to shift from poet to avenger. In a previous chapter, I digressed by considering snow in the Western; here, *Caprice* shows that character, weather, and geography combine, and this might be as close to a real, material region as we come in my interpretation here: the acknowledgement that, in Canada, we are close enough to the North that weather and geography are often issues of life and death.

The metaphoricity of region therefore maps onto characterizations that symbolize regions. The reversal of time—that "the future of the west was going to be the east"—is involved in Caprice's venture in the West. If she symbolizes East, then she also embodies a feminist vision of the future, in which the future is multilingual, feminine, and more creative than violent. As a "cowboy" and thus theoretically a "girl" despite her obvious womanhood in the eyes of the Indigenous characters and anyone who has read the first few pages, Caprice blurs not only gender but also age in ways that here have regional significance. The narrator of the novel states:

> Children do not belong in myths. They are used in fairy stories, but myths are the domain of immortals. Children are reminders of change, or potential, of what is called in some places "becoming." Children make sense in a town that is looking forward to greatness in the twentieth century. But cowboys and lone riders and dangerous misunderstood gunfighters do not. (144)

So, insofar as Caprice is a "child," she "makes sense" in the future but is out of place in the Old West. In fact, her childishness relates to her regionality on the intertextual level too. Partly coded as regionally Eastern by her red braided hair's resemblance to that of Anne of Green Gables, and partly coded as "cosmopolitan" and "worldly" (Staveley 247) by her Spanish horse and French-Canadian heritage, Caprice is "from a different order of reality" (251). She crosses the regional/global divide, which is another sign of coming from the future, another of the temporal facilities that we see in Ondaatje's *The Collected Works of Billy the Kid*—its reruns and rewinds.

But in another sense, Caprice's coming from the future means that she is less a child than a ghost. In the future, we will all be dead; Carrera argues that Caprice is "murdered . . . by the ending of her story" (438), partly because she gives up on adventure. If Caprice is not only from elsewhere but also "from a different order of reality," I would add that she is also from "a different order" of genre, one in which "an instrument of death" (Staveley 252) need not kill her target at the end of the story. This "order" is romance, widely understood in Canada since Northrop Frye's *Anatomy of Criticism* (1957) as a narrative that circles back to the point of origin after death (187). Although Bowering writes that "[f]amily revenge belonged to Jacobean tragedies" (41), not romances, he also calls her journey from Quebec a "bitter quest" (60) on which "[s]he had spent more than a year meditating on death" (61). Furthermore, when Caprice is eventually photographed, the photographer thinks of the image that "[i]t was as if a ghost had stepped past without really being seen" (149). (Notably, she here aligns with my paranormal reading of Ondaatje's Billy the Kid and his blank photograph at the beginning of the book.) Death is central, as Frye explains:

> The complete form of the romance is clearly the successful quest, and such a complete form has three main stages: the stage of the perilous journey and the preliminary minor adventures; the crucial struggle, usually some kind of battle in which either the hero or his foe, or both, must die; and the exaltation of the hero. (*Anatomy* 187)

The deaths in *Caprice*, however, are symbolic. Both Frank Spencer and Caprice literally survive. Caprice's riding off into the sun*rise* is not merely a parodic reversal but also an inversion of the trope. In the Western, riding off into the sun*set* means both into death and into the frontier.²³ Caprice's parting words to her lover are, in French, "je vais voir l'ombre que tu devins" ("I will see the shadow that you became"; 266). As Staveley suggests, these words are "funereal" (256), but they also refer to "the shadow" in *his* imagination, not hers. C'est l'ombre qu'*il* devint—le passé simple de *devenir*. *He* was becoming a shadow. True, Caprice has a dark side too; she is a poet. In a poem in the novel that is not attributed to anyone but that is likely hers, the speaker seems to identify with "les êtres destinés / A partager les ombres désolées" ("the beings destined / To share the desolate shadows"; 83). But she does not identify strongly enough to stay.

Caprice does not dwell on how the English language affects her view of the West, but she does not dwell long *in* the West either. When her brother's murderers are safely behind bars, quite differently from the stereotypical Western, Caprice rides off into the sunrise. In *Caprice*, riding off into the sunrise is to return home, giving up on new frontiers—hardly a feminist message—and fulfilling a rebirth that has been called a "restorative nostalgia" (Boym xviii). Despite her success, and perhaps because of her anti-feminist return to the presumably domestic space (in that it is home), the novel concludes with a sense of defeat, a phantom feeling of the "nostalgic regret" (109). In *The Future of Nostalgia* (2001), Svetlana Boym describes two not altogether separable nostalgias, both of which can apply to *Caprice*:

> Restorative nostalgia stresses *nostos* [the return home] and attempts a transhistorical reconstruction of the lost home. Reflective nostalgia thrives in *algia*, the longing itself, and delays the homecoming—wistfully, ironically, desperately. Restorative nostalgia does not think of itself as nostalgia, but rather as truth and tradition. Reflective nostalgia dwells on the ambivalences of human longing and belonging and does not shy away from the contradictions of modernity. Restorative nostalgia protects the absolute truth, while

---

23   One exception is *Dodge City* (Curtiz, 1939), where the newlyweds (Errol Flynn and Olivia de Havilland) ride off into the sunset to start their new life together—*and* to continue their adventures in crime-fighting in the American West.

reflective nostalgia calls it into doubt. Restorative nostalgia is at the core of recent national and religious revivals; it knows two main plots—the return to origins and the conspiracy. Reflective nostalgia does not follow a single plot but explores ways of inhabiting many places at once and imagining different time zones; it loves details, not symbols. At best, reflective nostalgia can present an ethical and creative challenge, not merely a pretext for midnight melancholias. (xviii)

In the simplified language of the Western, restorative nostalgia wears the black hat, and reflective the white. In this sense, Caprice's restorative return home is problematic; however, the novel as a whole seems reflective in that it "dwells on the ambivalences of human longing and belonging and does not shy away from the contradictions of modernity." Bowering's remarks about the regions and their "time zones" of past and future are evidence of these "contradictions." Certainly, the "ethical and creative challenge" in *Caprice* is not only from its reflective nostalgia but also from its combination of the two nostalgias and its reversals of direction and regional directives. (The same could be said of Davey in *The Louis Riel Organ and Piano Co.*, where nostalgia is restorative because the past is usually another country and, thus, our nostalgia can be imported along with so many other components of our lives. It is also where nostalgia becomes self-deprecatingly *self*-reflective through Davey's recollection of his unheroic youth and its refrain: "Davey / Crockett.") The Western orders Caprice to kill Frank Spencer, but she spares him with help from the Mountie; it orders her to ride into the sun*set* and die at least symbolically, but she rides east and may well thrive, however problematically at home, domestically even, in Quebec. On the one hand, *Caprice* leans toward restorative nostalgia, despite the reflective aspects of its postmodernism, and it is not as subversive as it could be in its representations of women, even heroic women. In the same vein, Nichol's and Ondaatje's Billies subvert heroic masculinity but are still phallocentric—their ghostmodernism implying the death of only one kind of masculinity. On the other, remember the question that I asked in the beginning: What would happen to the genre if the hero of the Western was not a man from the West but a woman from the relative East, specifically Quebec? The hero does go home to the East, to Quebec, which is not quite as decolonial as going back to France, but it is in the right direction.

The gesture of returning home to Quebec has a conclusive theoretical implication too. I notice that Caprice leaves as easily as she came, without any story of the journey from place to place to place. Whether she returns to poetry is unknown, but these details affirm Hoberek's assertion that we should "read postmodernism dialectically, as the worldview not only of middle-class privilege but of the hollowness of this privilege: of the bitter discovery of one's lack of agency and inability to navigate the world" (341). Although Caprice presumably finds her way home, and showed agency in apprehending her brother's killer, she seems unsatisfied, even "bitter." The narrator states that she travelled and will travel again, but we do not see her "navigate the world," because she is simply there and then gone. She seems like a lost soul, and lostness is implicated in the refusal to show her travelling, her orienting herself on a trail through the landscape. Referring to Wayne Johnston's novel *Colony of Unrequited Dreams* (1998) and Guy Vanderhaeghe's *The Englishman's Boy* (1996), Alexander MacLeod argues that in other postmodern regionalist novels, "[b]ecause they cannot orient themselves in an ontologically unstable American cultural geography [such as the suburbs of American postmodernism], Johnston['s] and Vanderhaeghe's characters flee from the United States to re-establish themselves in a Canadian landscape that at least seems more stable and more metaphysically secure" (26). Caprice seems to be fleeing to a "more stable and more metaphysically secure" place too. Here and now, the Canadian West is like America—with the transience of its malls, parking lots, and knock-downs—and Quebec is like Canada (or Europe). Nothing could be a more ironically postmodern comparison.

Dick Harrison once predicted that, by the late 1970s, "you will probably get the impression that the two literatures [of Canada and the United States] are converging," because "writers on both sides of the border feel themselves cut off from a living past" ("Across" 54). Certainly this has not happened much between Quebec and the rest of Canada, except insofar as they share the genre of the Western. Harrison traces the interest in historical authenticity to this transnationally shared dilemma, but he also suggests that the problem for Canadians is less "discontinuity" than "lack of roots" (55). Caprice, unable to find roots (her brother being dead) or make roots (her lover being a bore), goes back from the West to Quebec, which is supposed to mean the "stable" and "secure" space of home, but it is never described. It is a mirage. Nostalgia as a drive to return home makes sense in a postmodern novel, because nostalgia is not necessarily rooted in a real place either; it is almost ahistorical. And perhaps what *Caprice* ultimately demonstrates is that Canadian postmodernism questions the idea of a "stable" and "secure" place but still dreams of it.

In the next chapter, we will see that this stability begins to break down even at the level of the gene.

6

Degeneration through Violence
Contemporary Historical Westerns and Post-human Horsemen

In 1787, several years before he became the third president of the United States, Thomas Jefferson expressed the view that "the tree of liberty must be refreshed from time to time with the blood of patriots and tyrants." This quotation has since been widely used as justification for the right to bear arms in the United States (Horowitz).[1] While Richard Slotkin does not appear to refer to it in *Regeneration through Violence: The Mythology of the American Frontier, 1600–1860* (1973), it seems a "founding" corroboration of Slotkin's theory.[2] For Slotkin, American society can be explained by history retold into myth: America was established through violence, such as rebellion against England and, later, the American Civil War; and so forever afterward, whenever society's rules become so densely woven and binding that they threaten freedom and individualism, violence can tear the social fabric and renew these fundamental American values.[3]

---

1 Josh Horowitz, an activist against gun violence, points out a reflection in Jefferson's letter that applies remarkably well in the current climate of opinion surrounding the political base of the former American president Donald Trump: "In the same letter, . . . Jefferson stated that the rebellion was 'founded in ignorance. . . . The people cannot be all, and always, well informed. The part which is wrong will be discontented in proportion to the importance of the facts they misconceive' " ("Thomas Jefferson").

2 The theme of renewal, but not necessarily *violent* renewal except through territorial expansion, also appears in the so-called frontier thesis that emerged from Frederick Jackson Turner's 1893 paper "The Significance of the Frontier in American History" (Conway 6–7).

3 In *The Frontier Club* (2013), Christine Bold implies that the myth of regeneration through violence was the "sleight of hand" of "a cultural elite violently protecting its privilege in the name of democracy" (1), democracy being presented by the elite as the fundamental American

297

Freedom and individualism are at stake in the myth because they were threatened, fundamentally, by "Indian war and captivity [and assimilation] narratives" that later inspired an American identity "defin[ed] by repudiation" (*Regeneration* 20, 22) of other identities—for example, Indigenous or British. Over time, the myth evolved, alongside the genres that circulated it:

> If the first American mythology portrayed the colonist as a captive or destroyer of Indians, the subsequent acculturated versions of the myth showed him growing closer to the Indian and the wild land. New versions of the hero emerged, characters whose role was that of mediating between civilization and savagery, white and red. (21)

As with Jefferson's metaphor of the "tree" of liberty, Slotkin's theory is signified by a metaphor of nature, of "*growing* closer to the Indian and the wild land." However, as I understand the "subsequent" version, it is a metaphor of Nature as a woman with whom the searcher or hunter symbolically and sexually merges, regenerating the American family and nation. This merger was not equal; it was about control, management—conservation in that sense. However, as Nature became Gaian, became Mother Nature or Mother Earth, the American transcendentalists were able to figure it as a restorative space—so it was, for Ralph Waldo Emerson, renewing, purifying, medicinal, and reproductive (11, 14, 27, 31), and similarly for other Americans it was nurturing, whole, true, beautiful, and bountiful (Kolodny 5).[4] Briefly put, one part of the value of nature in America was that it could foster cycles of regeneration, or a regression or return to innocence (Kolodny 6); however, nature was also a premise for violence and, in its forests, deserts, and valleys, dangers lurked.

---

value when, in fact, self-interest is obviously another one, which can both agree and disagree with democracy.

[4] For an inversion of the usual landscape-woman metaphor, see Irina Chirica's "Masculinity in the Western Genre" (2018). Chirica's view is that the landscape of the West is "a world where no woman can follow" (56). The landscape is masculine because it dominates the people of the Western, and it is associated with a freedom that was primarily masculine (57–8). I read this landscape as a construct whose potential masculinity, or its power of whatever gender, is projected by the genre onto its usually male heroes.

Vividly described by Clark Blaise in *Time Lord* (2000), these transformative ideas of nature in Jefferson were expanded by Charles Darwin and adopted throughout society. "The agents of degeneration, the dark legacy of Darwin's hopeful evolution, were everywhere," writes Blaise of the 1880s and the Victorian era in general. "Gypsies, shamans, medicine men, 'half-breeds' and 'octoroons,' Hindus, Catholics, Muslims, the miscegenist, the scholar who identified too strongly with his subject and 'went native,' becoming ... a monster, a Kurtz [the enigmatic nemesis in Joseph Conrad's 1902 novel *Heart of Darkness*], a madman" (118). These fears are precisely those that the myth of regeneration through violence was meant to allay. Nature was good only if it was "human nature," not the natures of plants and other animals. And "going native" or "going Indian" meant going too close to Nature, thereby acculturating and diminishing oneself.

For most of the nineteenth and twentieth centuries, the writers of the Western loved this simplification and its dynamics, which helped to produce the outlandish stereotypes of "cowboys and Indians" and the Freudian virgin/whore, characters that populated comic books, movies, and by extension teenage fantasies. Even when writers were mocking the genre's stereotypes with postmodern Westerns such as Ishmael Reed's *Yellow Back Radio Broke-Down* (1969) or Arthur Penn's *Little Big Man* (1970), or the Canadian examples from the previous chapter, they were re-inscribing them. And even when revisionist Westerns were opposing the genre's racism and sexism, they often readily accepted violence as a heroic act.[5]

The recourse was supposed to be to revisionist history: the historical novel, the historical Western. Jane Tompkins, though not writing about historical Westerns specifically, claims in passing that "facts are what the Western is always trying to face" (27); she is probably referring to facts of life and death rather than historical facts. But, as David H. Evans explains,

> there is an irony in identifying the mission of that novel [e.g., a revisionist or historical Western] as a simple overcoming

---

5   A fairly recent American example, an episode of *Justified* (Holcomb, 2010) called "The Collection," shows the marshal Raylan Givens (Timothy Olyphant) refusing to listen to racist, antisemitic slurs from Caryn Carnes (Katherine LaNasa), but he is perfectly willing to kill men without due process if he deems it "justified."

of traditional narratives, and a demystification of the myths they propagated, to the extent that this critical story is in effect another version of the classic western plot, of the winning of the West—not ... from wilderness and savagery but from the shady forces of illusion and fantasy. (407–8)

As I understand it, the revisionist Western was not (and is not) simply *historical* revisionism, but *mythic* revisionism, even mythic regeneration: recourse to "another version of the classic western plot."

As New Historicism began to influence readers and writers in the 1980s and '90s, two almost completely different Canadian Westerns signalled the change in the Canadian context. The first was Thomas King's *Green Grass, Running Water* (1993), which still seems familiar to me as the ultimate postmodern Canadian Western—or the first post-Western in Canada. One caveat for these terms, however, is Joanna Hearne's statement that the adjectives "post-Western" and "revisionist" do not perfectly describe millennial Indigenous responses to the Western, at least on film, "for rather than contemporary films 'ghosting' an old genre, Indigenous directors and performers participated and shaped this cinematic heritage from the beginning, working with and against the generic conventions of Hollywood" (8). Indeed, King's novel narrates early Indigenous participation through the character of Portland Looking Bear, an actor in early Westerns. To readers less familiar with intersections of Indigenous and colonial histories in media, *Green Grass, Running Water*—with its circular narrative and parodic inversions of canonical Western texts (e.g., the Bible)—will appear more postmodern (if not post-Western) than Guy Vanderhaeghe's *The Englishman's Boy* (1996), which is also "revisionist" and "post-Western," and it invokes postmodernism to teach historical lessons.[6] Because of the relative accessibility of its more linear or at least more conventionally framed stories (i.e., involving neatly separated time periods), *The Englishman's Boy* is probably the most influential novel in

---

6   Although there is good reason to be wary of using different types of postness (e.g., post-colonialism or postmodernism) to categorize contemporary Indigenous literature, as King explains in already-quoted passages in this book, Gerald Vizenor (Chippewa) is open to it in his edited collection *Narrative Chance: Postmodern Discourse on Native American Indian Literatures* (1989) (C. Smith 12–13).

renewing general and historical interest in the Western, leading to the boom in contemporary post-Westerns here.

My interest in Vanderhaeghe's trilogy of historical Westerns, which continued after *The Englishman's Boy* with *The Last Crossing* (2002) and *A Good Man* (2011), is mainly in how they reject the myth of regeneration through violence and propose a seemingly historical alternative that I call the myth of *de*generation through violence. It, too, is a myth, and a theory, but when these books first appeared, people who read them and talked with me about them told me that, finally, we could read Westerns that showed how the West really was. Although these novels were indeed more historically informed than was evident in the broad strokes of most classic Westerns, Vanderhaeghe himself has been perplexed that readers so often assume that his master's degree in history means that he is a historian.[7] Herb Wyile describes the history in this novel in terms of creative writing and other arts, such as dance, remembering the film *Dances with Wolves* (Costner, 1990): "[*The Englishman's Boy*] is an elaborate choreographing of historical material, a discursive orchestration that necessarily competes with other 'productions' of history" ("Dances" 23). We have to understand that history itself is sometimes defeated or taken over by "other 'productions' " in popular culture or cultural memory. And history, which demands time and effort, is not the remedy to myth that everyone prefers. We often prefer to answer one myth with another.

Following Wyile's reference to Kevin Costner's character, Dances with Wolves (a white soldier given the name as he acculturates himself into Sioux society), I would add that some of the "historical material" that we need to consider is the historical materiality of other animals, perhaps especially horses. Such animals are crucial to understanding the ambivalence of the degeneration through violence that seems to fascinate Vanderhaeghe in his Westerns. When Vanderhaeghe calls attention and cultural memory to colonial violence against Indigenous peoples, as demonstrated by the Cypress Hills Massacre in *The Englishman's Boy* and the imperial Christian mission in *The Last Crossing*, he also points out how non-human animals were implicated: the stolen horses in the former, and

---

7   Vanderhaeghe made this statement to me and other students in his creative writing class sometime in the late 1990s.

the sacrificed horse in the latter. They can motivate humans and thereby affect history, and indeed the companion species of horses and dogs (among others) have prominent roles in diverse historical developments involving religion, war, exploration, transportation, art, therapy, et cetera.

In parallel, companion species are also made to serve myth, first as anthropomorphic figures. J. J. Clark proposes that "[b]ecause the western genre emerged at the turn of the century alongside the already-popular genres of the plantation romance and minstrel show, ... a collaboration between these forms established the stereotype of the western horse through a re-tooling of the ubiquitous 'devoted slave' or 'Uncle Tom' stereotype" (158).[8] If Clark is correct, then a juxtaposition such as the horse Silver and the "Indian" Tonto in the Lone Ranger stories would imply a shared debasement from the position of sidekick: to slavery from supposed partnership or companionship, thereby serving a myth of fair dealing with the Other. But there is a second myth, that of learning from Nature (or living more naturally) and then treading more lightly on Mother Earth. In this myth, the natures of non-human animals are appropriated or honoured by zoomorphic figures such as Dances with Wolves or *The Last Crossing*'s Born of a Horse (a white missionary seemingly converting to Crow beliefs). In Westerns, zoomorphism can be degenerative, regenerative, or both, often depending on how a typically white author views non-human animals or Indigenous cultures or possibly Black cultures in that historical moment. Partly because such views are implicated in the acts of violence perpetrated against the Other in the Western, human or otherwise, the two morphisms are an index to attitudes toward violence that invites responses from cultural and animal studies.

Before re-approaching the horse, I will turn to a more common question about violence in the Western.

Violence and History in the Western

Most Westerns depict the Old West as a sensationally violent place and time—not a traditional war zone but not entirely different from a site of guerrilla warfare. My favourite historical counterpoint is from the

---

8   See Natalee Caple's *In Calamity's Wake* (2013) for a revisionist rebuttal of minstrelsy in the context of Westerns.

American scholar and teacher Helen Lewis, whom I have heard speak at conferences in New Orleans, San Diego, and Washington, DC. Lewis's research focuses on women's non-fictional accounts of settling the West. Drawing on sources such as Lillian Schlissel's *Women's Diaries of the Westward Journey* (1982) and the *Covered Wagon Women* series edited by Kenneth Holmes, Schlissel, and others (1995–2000), Lewis explains, for example, that in the Old West most gunshot wounds were accidental, and that—excepting the treatment of Indigenous peoples—settling there was far less violent than it was honest, hard work: toil and boredom in the shack or in the fields, mending clothes and hammering fence posts.[9] Similarly, referring to Annette Kolodny, Tompkins states that "[w]hen women wrote about the West [in the nineteenth century], the stories they told did not look anything like what we know as the Western" (41–2).[10] They looked more like real life.

Murders that did occur, according to Clare V. McKanna Jr., tended to be under the influence of alcohol and between friends or acquaintances (461), not outlaws and lawmen, though handguns were indeed the weapon of choice. McKanna contextualizes his study by alluding to the Western: "True to the numerous film, novel, and television portrayals of the American West, gunfights did occur. However, they certainly were not heroic" (472). McKanna rationalizes his comment about heroism partly by remarking that the people involved "were lousy marksmen" (472). Notwithstanding McKanna's small sample size (three counties), he presents some evidence that the West was more violent than the East in the United States (472); he also agrees with previous research that characterized the West as having "a regional culture of violence" (479–80), one that developed partly because of easy access to pistols and alcohol without the accountability of an established society on the frontier. Attempting to resolve the apparent contradiction between McKanna's socio-historical study and women's non-fictional accounts is beyond the scope of this

---

9   Helen Lewis, email message to the author, 25 April 2017. See also Polić, "Sisters" 132.
10 Norris Yates "partly" agrees with Tompkins, writing that some women did write formula Westerns, "but formula Westerns with a difference" (1), from classic Westerns and from the memoirs and historical fictions that are more often associated with women's writing. For a survey of recent women's scholarship of the American Western, see Sigrid Anderson Cordell and Carrie Johnston (2017).

chapter; there would be too many temporal and geographical microcosms to sort out, among other things. Suffice it to say that none of these historical studies approves of the myth of regeneration through violence and its associated notions of heroism.

To return to the historical Western while maintaining a connection to McKanna's observation about the role of alcohol in the violence of the West, I want to mention a precursor to Vanderhaeghe's novels, Michael Ondaatje's *The Collected Works of Billy the Kid* (1970), in which the historical figure Pat Garrett is depicted as an alcoholic whose drinking is calculated to numb him to the acts of violence he must commit. The book includes a parallel in the story that John Chisum tells of a madman named Livingstone who wanted to breed mad dogs by inbreeding and "giving them just alcohol to drink" (63). For Ondaatje, the violence of historical figures is obviously distilled into tall tales, and their madness involves various symptoms of degeneracy—even in Billy with the "blood planets in his head" (109). A related madness appears in Vanderhaeghe's *The Last Crossing*, which describes a brutal aspiring hero who is syphilitic—his disease a symbol of degeneration. The novel focuses partly on the syphilitic man, the mercurial Addington Gaunt, and his brother Simon, a comparatively meek English missionary on his way into the West. In conflict with Addington at times is Jerry Potts (a.k.a. Ky-yo-kosi or Bear Child), a historical figure of Kainai (Blood) and Scottish descent (Sealey), who participates in battles but arguably becomes the novel's true hero in a moment of refusing to be violent directly: by allowing the hallucinating Addington to be killed by the bear he was hunting in a bow-and-arrow mockery of Indigenous traditions.[11] Vanderhaeghe prefers the violence to be natural, environmental, a violence *accepted* and not *driven* by the individual person, in a gesture that mostly contravenes the dictates of the genre. Although *The Last Crossing* is not quite Gaian, he asks a *mythic* Nature to enact revenge; he does not ask his *historical* figure, Potts, to reverse the myth of regeneration.

---

11   Katherine Ann Roberts calls Jerry Potts "the forgotten or unacknowledged father of the Canadian nation" (58). Potts was an instrumental mediator between the Blackfoot and the North-West Mounted Police, leading to the signing of Treaty 7 (Sealey). He also figured prominently in Norma Sluman's historical Western *Blackfoot Crossing* (1959).

I also want to put Vanderhaeghe's novels and degeneration through violence in the context of two other Canadian writers who may be described as historical novelists, Fred Stenson and perhaps especially Gil Adamson. Adamson's *The Outlander* (2007) follows a woman who murdered her husband and is running from his vengeful brothers to the foot of Turtle Mountain in the old North-West Territories, where a massive avalanche on 29 April 1903 destroyed the mining town of Frank. More figuratively, Aritha van Herk describes "grand myths [that] are crumbling" (*Stampede* 96). Although I have quoted her in earlier chapters, I have not included van Herk here, partly because her texts "are not historical westerns but texts that ironize and mock that American myth" (Roberts 85).[12] I have been assuming that "historical westerns" speak more loudly against the myth—history versus myth—though I also believe that louder is not more substantive; what we get in supposedly historical Westerns is myth versus myth, or, as Johannes Fehrle puts it, myth and "countermyth" (112–13, 130–1). The Frank Slide in Adamson's *The Outlander* is in my view a revenge story, a Gaian response to the extractive industries that parallels the woman's murder of her husband.[13] The avalanche, as a *deus ex machina*, is certainly no machine; it is Adamson's mythology of Nature functioning to assert an eco-feminist view of a male-dominated field and its mistreatment of a feminized landscape. Stenson does something similar, though not as obviously feminist, with his recent novel *Who by Fire* (2014), which interrogates the practices of the oil and gas industry in Alberta since the 1970s. But *Who by Fire* is not a Western; arguably,

---

12   Van Herk's tone in *Stampede and the Westness of West* (2016) is not always easy to interpret, because sometimes she seems to defend (not "ironize and mock") the myths about the West that are often perpetuated by the Western: "Triumphalism: okay, beat the stuffing out of me, it's a triumphalist story, with winners and losers against the mural of a big sky" (80; see also 78). Indigenous peoples—stereotypically described as "losers" and who often assert their resilience and resistance to the stereotype—are mentioned only rarely in *Stampede*; she does acknowledge Tom Three Persons (48, 59) and Louis Riel (31). *Stampede* misses an opportunity to respond to the generic trope of the Vanishing "Indian" when she lists the many "vanishings" in the West: "The vanishing west, the vanishing world, vanishing horses, vanishing sky, vanishing vanishment . . . all vanished" (53). Van Herk's poem about a horse called "Pocahontas" (21) could also have reflected on the appropriation of the name of an Indigenous person for a horse that is represented negatively.

13   In *On Active Grounds: Agency and Time in the Environmental Humanities* (2019), Mario Trono and Robert Boschman muse that "[t]he sense that . . . an avenging Gaia has found a way of dealing with us hovers at the edge of consciousness" (2).

neither is his fur-trading epic *The Trade* (2000), which is so historical and "myth-shattering" (Dinka) that it has been used in history courses; but his novels *Lightning* (2003) and *The Great Karoo* (2008) can be read through the lens of the Western. *Lightning* is the tale of the Texan cowboy Doc, his cattle-driving into Canada in the 1860s, his love for Pearly, and his struggle against the murderer Overcross. "Another mark of the authentic western," writes Nicholas Dinka, is "some good old fashioned head-staving" ("Review").

Stenson's *Great Karoo* is more historical but is reminiscent of a cavalry Western in its relocation of a group of Albertan cowboys into Africa during the Second Boer War, and some of its representations of horses bring me around to the latter half of this chapter, which recontextualizes the theory of degeneration through violence alongside the human relationship with horses in the Western, a genre sometimes called "horse opera." The horse as a convention of the genre is as significant as the cowboy, "Indian," or gun, but "the characters who ride them don't pay them much attention, and as far as the critics are concerned they might as well not exist" (Tompkins 90). A single chapter by Tompkins appears to be the first sustained inquiry into horses in the genre. In Hollywood, horses came to prominence alongside a growing awareness of animal rights following the abuse of horses in the making of the first *Ben-Hur* film (Niblo, 1925) (Kristmanson 15–16); perhaps the first and slightly earlier Canadian Western that shows an awareness of animal rights is Luke Allan's 1921 novel *Blue Pete: Half Breed* (97–8). Individual horses eventually became characters in many Westerns, and in celluloid examples such as those of William S. Hart, Tom Mix, Gene Autry, and Roy Rogers, the horse often stole the show, appealing to a sympathetic audience that was nostalgic for the pre-modern, pre–Iron Horse as motor vehicles displaced the working animal from the lives of most Americans (Kristmanson 1–2; Tompkins 93). (In Canada, Emily Ursuliak's 2017 book of poetry and memoir, *Throwing the Diamond Hitch*, is framed by the horse-car relationship too, as I explain in the conclusion of this book.) The felt connection between humans and horses was so strong that it could be described as identification—a stage in which our feelings seem to confuse or conflate zoomorphism and anthropomorphism. Indeed, there is no better image of nostalgic identification with the horse at the dawn of the automobile than in the final words of Cormac McCarthy's *All the Pretty Horses* (1992), where horse and rider seem to fuse before "the bloodred sunset" (302): "horse and rider and horse passed on and their long shadows passed in tandem like the shadow of a single being. Passed and paled into the darkening land, the world to come" (302). This image of a "pass[ing]" implies not only the end of an era but also a death, and it thereby implicates the horse and horseman in the contemporary discourse of the post-human and of post-humanism.

Riding Off into the Sunset

It is as if the cowboy riding off into the sunset is closure not only for his one story but for all people of the West. The image appears again and again in American Westerns on film, with prominent examples in John Ford's *She Wore a Yellow Ribbon* (1949) and Sam Peckinpah's *Pat Garrett and Billy the Kid* (1973), among many others. In literature, it is perhaps less often only of men or for men; in George Bowering's *Caprice* (1987), which I considered in the previous chapter, "[i]n the early evening sun the prodigious black horse stepped to the summit of a grassy rise and stopped of his own accord, as if he wanted to take in the view. His shadow with the woman's shadow above it reached to the round edge and over into the general shadow" (211). Although Bowering genders the shadow as "the woman's," the gender or sex of the person would be indistinguishable from the shadow, just as the separation of the person and horse would not be perfectly clear. We see the same with Mary Boulton in Adamson's *The Outlander*: "Together, horse and rider melted into the long shadows" (376). The diction of "melt[ing]" illustrates the liminality, the transience, and the metaphorically post-human plasticity of the shadowy horseman (or horsewoman).[14] For Sean Johnston in *Listen All You Bullets* (2013), "the sun took forever to go down. The horse and the man seemed to walk forever toward its place on the horizon. As they moved the silhouette of the next town appeared, as if it was being drawn on a blank space ahead of them" (44); the horse-man silhouette has the staying power of "forever," here associated with the expansive colonial power taking over "a blank space."

---

14   The allusion to plastic in this metaphor reminds me of a comment in Donna Haraway's *The Companion Species Manifesto* (2003): "Metaplasm means a change in a word, for example by adding, omitting, inverting, or transposing.... The term is from the Greek *metaplasmos*, meaning remodeling or remolding" (20). Metaphor does with reality what metaplasm does with words.

And riding off into the sunset is not only for the white man either. The horse as a symbol or metaphor is written into modernity as the natural ancestor of the train (a.k.a. the Iron Horse). Both technologies—the train and the horse-as-vehicle—were tools of colonization. As Mark Jackson explains, "[c]ultures of modernity . . . became understood [during the cultural turn in scholarship] as enrolled within cultures of colonialism; where you find modernity, there too you will find colonialism in some form" ("Introduction" 2). From a colonial academic perspective, the horse was then appropriated by Native American and First Nations peoples to such an extent that they are closely and proudly identified with each other. From the Indigenous academic perspective of Yvette Running Horse Collin, who cites various origin stories, artifacts, and glyphs in her dissertation (108–15), horses were in the Americas before first contact with Europeans, and horses were then and are now spiritual creatures who are honoured by Indigenous peoples. Rather than vanish together into a sunset, they insist on the contemporary significance of redness. After the al Qaeda terrorist attacks on American soil on 11 September 2001, my friend Delvin Kanewiyakiho (Cree) sported a t-shirt on which a red-rimmed silhouette of an Indigenous warrior on horseback was captioned "Homeland Security Since 1492." Satirically recontextualizing colonization since Christopher Columbus alongside the American Department of Homeland Security and the classic cowboy—and our stereotypes in the West of terrorists as non-white—the image returns Indigenous people to the discourse even as it reminds us of how Indigenous philosophies tend not to separate humans and other animals and inanimate objects so strictly—for example, in the Okanagan animism of Harry Robinson's "You Think It's a Stump, But That's My Grandfather" (1992/2004).

For Jackson, the widening concept of the Other that emerged through the development of post-colonial theory was coincident with, if not a precursor to, the development of theories of the post-human and post-humanism ("For New" 20). These theories further expand the Other to include non-human animals and even inanimate objects such as the stump in Robinson's story. The prefix "post," rather than indicating that something is finished, implies various self-reflective and self-critical positions on "ongoing colonial oppression" (21). Realistically, we need the combination of post-colonial and post-human thinking and being that might address our ethical and environmental dilemmas, but if we were very strict about the current term "decolonization," we would demand that (we) cowboys ride off into the *sunrise*: to the *East*, backwards along the traditional paths of colonization and exploration in North America, as I suggested through Bowering's *Caprice* in the previous chapter. (We might also choose Cree as an official language, look to Indigenous peoples for our immigration policies, and resolve as many land claims as possible in the interests of Indigenous peoples, in an effort to set things right. Maria Campbell, speaking for the Indigenous Literary Studies Association conference in Vancouver in 2019, said that "reconciliation" is the wrong word, because it implies colonists once got along with the Indigenous peoples; "setting things right" is better—and even better in Michif or another Indigenous language.) The Western's sunset motif offers imagery easily exploited by postmodern and post-Western writers.

The Post-human and Post-humanism

I do not mean to imply that Westerns are typically concerned with the post-human or post-humanism, not with all their androcentrism, gold-rushing colonialism, and anti-intellectualism yoked to "common sense"—itself "the tyranny of doxa" (Braidotti 4). Rosi Braidotti admires "non-nostalgic post-human thinker[s]" (198), and these attributes are uncommon to makers of classic Westerns. But I do wonder about how the horseman or horsewoman, these crucial hybrids of the genre, encourage thought experiments about the coincidence of historical Westerns and emerging post-Westerns and post-humanism in the 1990s and 2000s. Braidotti imagines thinking as "a nomadic activity" defined partly by "[t]he politics of location, of situated knowledges" (199). The West as one such "location" may create "nomadic" knowledge thanks in part to the mobility of the horse—the first "technology" of rapid transportation for people. Even more than dogs, horses are part of what Donna Haraway calls "the body of technoscience" (5). The horse's speed was a major advantage in battle from its domestication until the First World War; it inspired Eadweard Muybridge's late nineteenth-century cinematic photography; it dramatized almost countless Westerns, as in the plot of "cutting off the train at the pass." Vanderhaeghe's *The Englishman's Boy* exposes the abuse of galloping horses in the making of Westerns for film and television (65), abuse that harmed the reputation of Hollywood studios which, in turn, humanized horses and promoted them as stars to prove their "humane" treatment (Kristmanson 3–4). Research into star horses in the Western offers another example, alongside those from Braidotti in *The Posthuman* (2013), of non-human animals whose lives become more valuable as commodities than the lives of many humans (8), such as Indigenous people. Capitalist adaptation is sometimes only the production of difference for the expansion of commodification (Braidotti 58)—a neoliberal precept of commodifying everything, with money the main value. Although the humanization of horses can be lauded as humane, it is also a sign of the post-human predicament in which capitalism depreciates some values and appreciates others (8) without concerning itself with an ethics beyond the self as defined in terms of self-interest. Certainly, in contrast with such an ethics, we might do well to try to think like a horse or another non-human.

Unfortunately, I am not certain that I am qualified to do so. Although my expertise is that of a critical reader of literature and other narratives who identifies partly as a writer, Braidotti seems skeptical that such expertise is enough; she believes that the "momentous" next step for critical theory is to develop "an understandable language" and "a new vocabulary" with "more conceptual creativity" (82) than we usually find in the humanities. I suspect that she would find much to consider in novels narrated by or focalized around non-human animals, such as Barbara Gowdy's *The White Bone* (1999) or André Alexis's *Fifteen Dogs* (2015), but she tends to draw on philosophy, history, geography, and other disciplines cognate with literary studies. Echoing Donna Haraway in *The Companion Species Manifesto* (2003), in which "dogs are not about oneself" (11), Braidotti implies repeatedly that she is not impressed by the tradition of personification and anthropomorphism in such novels,[15] and she does not appear to have gone looking for such novels that also include examples of constructed or invented languages to equip the non-human narrators. Nor have I, in the context of the Western,[16] wherein Braidotti's stated limitations on post-human thinking seem entirely valid. But I will attempt

---

15 Avoiding anthropocentrism is also one of the tactics of deep ecology (Murray and Heumann, *Gunfight* 14).

16 Beyond the Western, there are many examples for human and humanoid characters, as in J. R. R. Tolkien's writings in and around *The Lord of the Rings* (1954–5) and in Anthony

to bend my imagination to the possibility of post-human thinking after showing how *The Englishman's Boy* and other historical Westerns are expressing the genre alongside humanistic concerns such as history.

The Western's Horse in *The Englishman's Boy*

The Englishman's Boy is explicitly commenting on the Western. Set partly in Los Angeles in 1923, it spends time where Damon Ira Chance is setting up his film production. Hollywood and its environment are described as a land of "make-believe" (6), "a world half-wild, half-artificial" (12) that corresponds with Margaret Atwood's "Backdrop Addresses Cowboy" (1968) from the previous chapter, and indeed, if you compare a 1923 image of pastoral Hollywoodland with a 2001 NASA satellite photograph of Los Angeles, you will see how much the sprawling city limits of Los Angeles could have seemed like a frontier compared to its later, almost total envelopment of the surrounding area. Chance hires Harry Vincent, a Canadian in Hollywood, to write an epic Western that could rival the historic (if not accurately historical) *Birth of a Nation* (Griffith, 1915) as an American nationalist project. Vincent tells us: "Contrary to what you might expect, Hollywood was a ghost town after dark" (8). His screenwriting mentor Rachel Gold explains filmmakers by calling "[e]verybody an outlaw. Patent-breakers, fly-by-night independents, here today, gone tomorrow" (135). Harry also tells us that "[d]irectors of Westerns like flamboyance, it photographs well, which accounts for the way these boys [the actors playing cowboys] are duded up" (54). It explains historical details of how horses were handled and harmed in the making of Westerns (65). And in one character's cowboy drawl it reflects sardonically on the unenviable position of Vanishing "Indians" in the Western: "Those wild Indians the army used to jail for scampering off the reservation, directly they was locked up, they shrivelled and died. Wild Indian got to run free. I'd guess you lock a wild Indian up between the covers of a book, same thing is going to befall him. He's going to die" (145).[17] Not only does *The Englishman's*

Burgess's *A Clockwork Orange* (1962). I would also recommend China Miéville's 2011 novel *Embassytown*, a science fiction that includes the constructed language of the Ariekei.

17   Shorty McAdoo, the titular Englishman's boy who speaks these words, himself appears to be modelled visually on Clint Eastwood and similar outlaws. Although Shorty is short and Eastwood tall, each of them has what Vanderhaeghe memorably describes as "the gaunt,

Boy comment on the Western, but it also reflects on its own responsibility toward the depiction of Indigenous peoples in its own pages.

Vanderhaeghe's *Englishman's Boy* is historical fiction, not the historiographic fiction that Linda Hutcheon finds to be definitive of postmodern(ist) literature in Canada, but *The Englishman's Boy* seems to be self-consciously seeking a new (or old) footing for literature after postmodernism. Writing about Vanderhaeghe's influence, Vanja Polić explains:

> [T]he emergence of the new Western genre in Canadian writing is visible through the replacement of certain tropes and schematic plots from the traditional Western with more complex postmodern narrative techniques such as historiographic metafiction; dialogism and polyglossia; and a greater prominence of ex-centric characters such as women, peoples of the First Nations, and atypical cowboys. ("Reworkings" 206)

Vanderhaeghe hints at the revisionist poetic licence of historiographic metafiction when the villainous Damon Ira Chance envisions an epic Western made from "the poetry of fact" (20) to honour his "obsession with history" (16), while "[h]istory . . . disappeared from sight" (6). (Damon Ira Chance's initials, D. I. C., make me wonder if Vanderhaeghe is echoing bpNichol's microaggressive fun with short-dick jokes in *The True Eventual Story of Billy the Kid* [1970].) Although *The Englishman's Boy* is not strictly metafictional in the sense of being a book about the writing of the same book, it is a book about a writer, the main character Harry Vincent and his research. And the novel does describe Chance as a "Henry James character" (7) whose grandiloquence is "as if a Henry James character were launching an attack on James himself" (18). As a novel published so soon after King's *Green Grass, Running Water*, it appears to have learned some big lessons of postmodernism, such as the decentring of authorized, grand narratives akin to *Birth of a Nation*; the obsession with media, such as film, that acknowledges the mediated condition of any claim to truth, such

---

cadaverous look of the rural poor . . . [and] anthracite eyes [that] did the talking for him. They said: Expect no quarter. Give none. . . . He didn't string more than five words together at a time" (30).

as Chance's version of history; and the self-reflection and metacognition (if not quite self-reflexivity and metafiction) of authors on their acts of creation.

The self-reflection and metacognition are evident in the temporal structure of *The Englishman's Boy*, which ironically opposes the nostalgia of the Western. The novel provides us with both Harry's story of writing the film and the backstory of Shorty McAdoo, the old cowboy and later actor who consulted on the film and was once the relatively innocent "boy" of the novel's title. But its good old days are in fact a reimagining of the boy's witnessing of, and participation in, the historical Cypress Hills Massacre in 1873, hardly an occasion to be longed for. And its present (generally the 1920s) is a noirish tale of failed work and corporate greed and murder, not the triumph of industry; Vincent describes himself occasionally as a "detective" (37, 53), and his later hopelessness with a pistol demonstrates that he is definitely not a cowboy (161–4); John Motyka calls it a "California noir-meets-Wild-West" (23) story. All this is briefly framed by Harry's memories in the 1950s. He has occasions when, like Ondaatje's Billy the Kid, he sees himself as a camera would: "I become too aware of myself. I watch my hand slide along the banister. . . . Out of the corner of my eye I catch the ladder-backed chair isolated on the cold marble floor of the ballroom, the strangeness of its position" (25)—a scene that also alludes to a memorable set in the film *Sunset Boulevard* (Wilder, 1950) and its tale of another rich old "visionary" hiring a penniless new writer. Technically, all this is also framed again by an omniscient third-person narration, not Harry's close third-person narration, that focalizes around the Assiniboine men Fine Man and Broken Horn and their theft of the white men's horses that precipitated the Cypress Hills Massacre. This telescoping or nesting of stories is certainly a postmodern technique of redoubling perspectives and subjective distortions. Less obviously performative than the postmodernism of *Green Grass, Running Water* and its ebullient returns to the beginning of various stories, there is a circular structure in *The Englishman's Boy*; it ironically regenerates Shorty through the younger Harry Vincent, another dupe of men more evil, whose "bum leg" (33) is a sign of the degeneration resulting from acts of violence on people or their history.

His "bum leg" is on one hand simply a reason to redirect Vincent's efforts from his body to his mind, or at least to his eyes. But on the other it also invites us to think of the horse on the body-mind continuum. It is a phallic symbol related to what Tompkins calls "the inevitable Freudian query: horse as penis" (16). The horses in *The Englishman's Boy* are symbols of mobility associated with the train (a.k.a. the Iron Horse), but they are also complex symbols of this degeneration of legs (being that you usually have to shoot a lame horse), and a compensatory symbolic elevation. Edith Hamilton's *Mythology* contains the following paraphrase of the Greek myth of Poseidon: "He was the ruler of the sea, Zeus's brother and second only to him in eminence.... [H]e gave the first horse to man: Lord Poseidon, from you this pride is ours, / The strong horses, the young horses, and also / The rule of the deep" (28–9). A later religious source on horses in the Western-world tradition returns in Vanderhaeghe's short story "Man on Horseback," from his collection *Things As They Are?* (1992):

> In Christian art the horse is held to represent courage and generosity.... In the catacombs it was, with the fish and the cross, a common symbol. No one is absolutely certain what its meaning was, although it is assumed it represents the swift, fleeting, and transitory character of life. (51)

For Vanderhaeghe, horses are thereby existential figures that express ideas of life and death; in Adamson's *The Outlander*, the death of horses causes in the young girl an "existential gloom" (287). These are ideas common to other religious traditions too. In *The Studhorse Man* (1969), Robert Kroetsch writes that "[a]t one time in the China of T'ai Tsung there were 40,000 horses in the Imperial stables.... Even to the grave they sent a man with mortuary horses...; we pack a corpse off in copper and steel that it might for an extra year bewilder the dust" (155–6).[18] According to Tompkins, in the context of the Western, "[m]ore than any other single element in the genre, they symbolize the desire to recuperate some lost

---

18   In Kroetsch's much later novel, *The Man from the Creeks* (1998)—considered in this book's conclusion—he associates horses and death through the mass carnage of dead horses below the cliffs of mountain passes where prospectors found their ways to the Klondike.

connection to life" (94). Perhaps because of its implied ability to transport souls, the horse appears to symbolize freedom—as when in *The Outlander* "the chill of freedom had blown through them already" (286)—but in some cases also mastery and power (e.g., in terms of horsepower) (Tompkins 99), and the riches that power can bring: "On ne peut pas surestimer la fascination qu'exerce le cheval sur les gens de toutes les classes de la societé. Il symbolise la richesse, la puissance et la liberté" ("We cannot overestimate the fascination that the horse provokes in people from all classes of society. It symbolizes wealth, power, and freedom"; Blondin et al. 11). These meanings were also true for Indigenous people who depended on the horse in conflicts with colonists and with other Indigenous people. And, like the symbolism descending through Greek myth to Christianity, the horse for Indigenous people was sometimes linked to religious figures— for example, as a gift of the Great Spirit (for the Sioux) and as a creature blessed by Old Man Coyote (for the Crow).[19] Here, horses are inestimably, intangibly, and spiritually valuable.

Given these honorific and elevating uses of the horse, we might be surprised to see that they are also symbols of degeneration, but the degeneration can be explained when the horse is tethered to Western milestones of historical progress that involve departures from real horses to Iron Horses. When Chance describes McAdoo in *The Englishman's Boy*, he first identifies him as both "a tin god" and "the last bull buffalo of the old West" (20). He then adjusts the buffalo metaphor by explaining that McAdoo's story has to come from "the horse's mouth" (22).[20] In fact, people are described as a lot of animal species in the novel, but horses have a self-conscious significance. Ed Grace, the boy's one friend in the vengeful Tom Hardwick's gang of wolfers, asks the boy if he knows what a centaur is. The boy doesn't, so Grace explains: "A being, half man, half horse. . . . I've been

---

19 For related information, see the entries on "Horse," "Sioux," and "Crows" in David J. Wishart's *The Encyclopedia of the Great Plains* at the University of Nebraska (Lincoln): http://plainshumanities.unl.edu/encyclopedia/.

20 Speaking of horse's mouths, I should note that implications of horse-human hybridity have a long history in the Western, including the Canadian Western—for example, in "The Gunsmoke Sheriff" by Luke Price in the 1940s pulps that I considered in chapter 4. Smokey Carmain is introduced as being so close to his horse that the saddle "came as natural to the rider as the thatch of gold-tinted hair on his head" (98). Later, in "Hound Dog Justice," he tells a man, "Yuh can't make a hawse drink ef he don't want to, Mister" (47), alluding to himself as the horse, he of the horse's mouth again.

knocking around this country ten years—it changes a man. But I'm not all the way there yet. I'm not Tom Hardwick. I'm betwixt and between—half civilized, half uncivilized. A centaur" (191). Grace's evocation of the Greek myth of the "centaur" is not as odd as one might think,[21] because it has connections to the medieval epics and romances from which Westerns are derived; Susan Crane's essay on "Chivalry and the Pre/Postmodern" (2011) shows remarkable continuity between medieval ideas of a knight's relationship with his horse and ideas of the self today, and Anastasija Ropa's 2019 survey of medieval scholarship suggests that "[o]ne idea, which has gained much currency, is grounded in posthumanism, understanding the relation of the medieval rider and the horse through their blending in order to create a new, collective identity" (1). The notion of a "collective" diminishes the individuality of the subject. Similarly, Grace's statement illustrates one of Braidotti's very contemporary definitions of the post-human: as "becoming-animal" (67). According to Haraway, in the context of evolving alongside other animals, "it is a mistake to see the alterations of dogs' [or horses'] bodies and minds as biological and the changes in human bodies and lives ... as cultural, and so not about co-evolution" (31). Vanderhaeghe's Grace is not making that mistake because he appears to be open to "co-evolution." And according to Braidotti, "[p]ost-anthropocentrism [basically a synonym of post-humanism] displaces the notion of species hierarchy and of a single, common standard for 'Man' as the measure of all things. In the ontological gap thus opened, other species come galloping in" (67). Her own horse metaphor happens to align with Grace's statement, which also shows how meaningful the horse is to the Western: it enables not only the spatial liminalities of border crossing and a "connection" "between the human being and the earth" (Tompkins 93) but also the ontological liminalities of un/civilization, through which a person may experience "progress" or "regression," such as an atavistic and implicitly degenerative return to a more animalistic condition of being.

---

21   It also has a precedent in dime novels, specifically *Beadle's Popular Library*, vol. 1, no. 20, 1897, headlined by "Cowboy Chris, the Desert Centaur." According to Warren French, this "desert centaur" was different from other cowboys because he did not settle down at the end of the story (233–4). He was possibly the beginning of the cowboy understood to serve society without being a part of it, and his refusal to integrate might also reflect his hybridity with horses, which also invokes his mobility.

He might not be willing to say so because it would alert Hardwick to a potential sympathizer with the enemy, but Grace is also implying that the "uncivilized" condition is symbolically Indigenous, in line with the stereotypes of Indigenous people as primitives or, at best, "noble savages."

By invoking the mythical creature of the centaur, Grace also unwittingly re-inscribes the mythical nature of the Western genre in which he is participating as a character in a tale told later by the (colonial) Englishman's boy. Even more than this, he and later the boy re-inscribe Indigeneity as mythical too. The boy's recollection of this conversation with Grace is nested indirectly; we get it in the 1873 plot framed by Vincent's 1923 plot involving the making of Chance's epic film. But McAdoo also tells a similar tale to Vincent in the 1923 plot, one that is nested directly and explicitly: "McAdoo turns his face back to me [Vincent]. . . . 'I been to Canada,' he says. His voice changes, as if he is speaking out of a cavern. A cavern of regret, or sorrow. 'I went Indian up in Canada' " (151). The phrase "going Indian," which Kroetsch uses in the title of *Gone Indian* (1973), is sometimes meant disparagingly, but Kroetsch uses it to suggest that "the quest for an essentialist notion of identity will lead to a dead end" (Edwards) and to "pos[e] questions about historical attitudes that are based on the perceptions (or social constructions) of ethnic variations" (Edwards). Vanderhaeghe's project is similar. Both of McAdoo's stories, from his boyhood and from his adulthood fifty years later, are about "changes" (151, 191) to the presumed civility of the white man in "Indian country." He reflects what Daniel Coleman calls, in *White Civility* (2006), the English Canadian "obsession . . . with the problem of [white] civility" (5). The problem is, simply, how English culture normalized whiteness as the colour of privilege and has had to contend ever since with the ramifications of excluding others from such privilege. Quoting M. NourbeSe Philip, Coleman explains that there is an "ideological lineage to this belief system" (Coleman 7). Vanderhaeghe calls attention to this "lineage" by invoking it in the title *The Englishman's Boy*. So does McAdoo himself: "Lots of them Eastern boys riding at the studios *play* at cowboys and Indians. . . . Books don't make an Indian. It's country makes an Indian" (151, original emphasis). For McAdoo, there are performed identities (perhaps the only ones of which Kroetsch's postmodernism would approve) and an authentic identity (perhaps) rooted in the Canadian landscape and its original human inhabitants, the Indigenous peoples—but this binary of performed whiteness and authentic Indigeneity perpetuates the white privilege to *adapt* (i.e., perform) while Indigeneity is *rooted* and, however stable, thereby also immobilized, quite contrary to the mobility of the horse.

Ironically, McAdoo then casts doubt on his assertion of an authentic identity by going on to explain—with a comical alternative to the horse—how he had to pretend to be insane (or degenerate) to appear harmless to the Blackfoot men who surprised him once on the range. He pretended by imitating a pig "rooting through the slop . . . [and] wiggling my hams" (155), while he was in fact looking for his pistol in the vegetation. It was hardly post-human thinking or even method acting; it was totally faking it. He concludes his story by telling Vincent that "[t]hem old-timey, genuine Indians used to go off solitary in the wilderness so's to find their creature spirit. . . . That's where they learned it, in the wilderness" (157). He has to explain to Vincent: "Creature spirit. . . . Spirit they shared with some creature—grizzly spirit, elk spirit, coyote spirit, crow spirit. . . . What do you make of mine?" Vincent is caught off guard, and McAdoo remarks, "You ain't been listening, have you?" (157). McAdoo might well have enjoyed the fact that, just as he could not respond (as a boy at least) to Grace's question about the centaur, Vincent could not make sense of the anecdote about the pig. Instead of the horse, McAdoo sardonically adopts the pig as his "creature spirit." Although he does not and perhaps cannot articulate it, he acknowledges and seems to accept, self-deprecatingly, his colonial (Englishman's) heritage and its symbolism of the pig as dirty, greedy, and canny. If the horse is degenerate in the context of white human civilization, the pig is even farther gone, thereby returning a degree of nobility to the horse.

For Indigenous people, horses are among other animals that are relations of humans. *The Englishman's Boy* begins as Fine Man and Broken Horn are about to steal the horses, and one stands out: "a big blue roan . . . stained a faint blue [by the moon] . . . a Nez Percé horse from beyond the mountains which wore snow on their heads all the year round, a horse from behind the Backbone of the World" (2). The horse's association with the Nez Percé confirms that the horse is special as a result of being part of the oldest horse-human tradition; Vanderhaeghe seems to affirm an Indigenous origin story in which "a Blackfoot, Shaved Head by name, went west and obtained the first horses that were known to his people from the Nez Percé, who told him that they had taken them out of the water" (John Canfield Ewers qtd. in Collin 112)—possibly also the source of the memorable image of a horse emerging from beneath the liquid surface in Kroetsch's *The Studhorse Man*. Although an Indigenous interpretation would probably be different, to me it seems that the Nez Percé are at least midwives to the horse; there is a close relationship that is almost familial. About to take "the winter horse" (2) with him, Fine Man respectfully calls him "Little Cousin" (3) and vows to be good to him and the other horses, who relax when the winter horse does.[22] The novel returns to this opening scene in its final pages as Fine Man applies face paint while looking at himself in a hand mirror. The flecks of quicksilver in the mirror give him a vision of what to do next: "dab [the horse's] blue coat with white spots to make a picture of the night blizzard which four days ago had frozen the wolfers to the ground in sleep" (328). Painting frozen water onto the horse acknowledges its origin "out of the water," and the mirror's symbolism of self-reflection superimposed with an idea of the horse suggests that both Fine Man and Ed Grace imagine themselves to be related, as "Cousin" or "centaur," to horses. But for Fine Man, including horses among his relations is a sign of wider, inter-species social bonds than those implied by Grace, whose language of "civilization" implies a primitive opposition.[23]

---

22   The trope of the Indigenous relationship to horses is common in Westerns; it also appears memorably in Paul St. Pierre's *Smith and Other Events* (1983) when a character says, "A beautiful thing to see, how an Indian can talk to a horse. He never roughs him up. He never drives the irons into him. He just takes him out, after he gets a halter on him, and he talks to him. He has got just one turn of the halter rope around a snubbin post, like my finger there, and the Indian is on one side of the snubbin post and the horse is on the other side, and he just talks to him. Sometimes he spits in his face a little bit or he puffs his breath up into the horse's nostrils. Like this. Puh. Puh. That is the way he goes about it. A beautiful thing to see" (23). In contrast, the antiheroic titular character of Paulette Jiles's *The Jesse James Poems* (1988) is worried about talking to horses: "Because you have abandoned your daylight self with such urgency and such joy, because nobody knows your name, there is the danger of being absorbed by the language of animals" (64). One Indigenous perspective on horses is from Thomas King's 1993 novel *Green Grass, Running Water*, where the horse connects people to home: "Charlie put a pillow over his head and began counting horses, the kind of horses he and his cousins used to ride when he lived on the reserve" (210).

23   Ethan in *The Searchers* (1956) eventually, grudgingly, accepts that his family includes not only his part-Cherokee nephew Martin but also his acculturated Comanche niece Deborah; however, he refuses to go home to play his own part in this new family.

More important, Fine Man's "picture" of a "winter storm" (328) is *a moving picture*, a metaphor of film. (I will write more later about how the image of the centaur and the image of the blizzard reappear in Vanderhaeghe's following novel, *The Last Crossing*.) This metaphor becomes more certain as metaphor (in contrast to symbol, which is more open to interpretation) when Fine Man later visits "the holy man" (328) Strong Bull, who has recently begun to draw pictures in "a trader book" (331) to record the people in his life "so the grandchildren will recognize us" (331). Strong Bull was inspired to draw, after a time of uncertainty, when Thunderbird conjured a lightning storm and brightened away the darkness of his mind, giving him "knowledge of things to come" (330). Strong Man foretells that the One Above will transfer his "dreams of horses" (331) to Fine Man, the new keeper of their knowledge. In effect, Fine Man and Strong Bull have accepted the role of pictures and moving pictures in their shared history, which to King is a dangerous scenario (as I explained in the second chapter). The acceptance of film as a medium of history is surprisingly similar to Chance's view of writing history in the light(ning) of cinema (108): "if Griffith wrote history in lightning, the time has now come to *rewrite* history in lightning" (297). It is also similar to Vincent's view that an image "fill[s] the screen the way a dream fills the mind" (24). For Vanderhaeghe, history is a dream told and retold through the technologies of popular culture, and the horse symbolizes the historical movement of technologies of the picture. The horse powers film history.

It would be appropriate to pause and reflect on how other animals have powered history in general. Other quadrupeds such as donkeys have powered plows and carts full of produce; cows and many other animals have powered humans by literally "fuelling" them as food. But this is anthropocentric history that is not post-human. To think post-humanly, we might learn from Strong Bull, because he learns from Thunderbird, a mythic bird but still seemingly understood as a bird—or, at least, not as a human. Thunderbird's power ironically leads Strong Bull to anticipate film and history on film—profoundly anthropocentric developments—and this example shows how challenging it is to imagine a truly non-human point of view, such as that of a bird. Thunderbird in *The Englishman's Boy* might also be evidence of Vanderhaeghe's colonial imagination, because he reorients Strong Bull's vision toward a colonial technology. It is difficult enough to imagine someone else's point of view, notwithstanding a non-human point of view. (The Métis scholar and photographer Warren Cariou discussed Thunderbird's appearance in Indigenous literature about hydropower generation in his talk at the Indigenous Literary Studies Association conference in 2019, building on his earlier talks on bitumen.) And Vanderhaeghe also manages to admit to human and colonial "blindness" when thinking of non-human points of view—namely, in the unforgettable scenes with Hank's blind horse, notably a white horse that invokes and evokes various traditions and intertexts.[24] When the horse's blindness endangers Hardwick's quest to reclaim his stolen horses and enact revenge, Hardwick "matter-of-factly" (94) shoots and kills the blind white horse. This ill-fated horse was also attributed the ill-fated number 13, which gives Hardwick further pleasure in having eliminated it (96). The discussion of number 13 leads the Englishman's boy to think to himself "that nothing was different on the other side [of death], only darker and dimmer, and that the rider on the pale horse was again one of their party, the unlucky, the cursed thirteenth" (96). He thinks post-humanly to the extent that he imagines the afterlife of not only "the rider" but also "the pale horse."

And, of course, the pale horse and its rider have their own fatalistic numerology beyond number 13 in the Four Horsemen of the Apocalypse alluded to, as I explained in the previous chapter, in Clint Eastwood's *Pale Rider* (1985). If you recall, the girl hoping for a miracle in *Pale Rider* reads from Revelations 6:8, a Biblical verse in which a pale horse appears, ridden by Death and followed by Hell. In keeping with the Bible, the unnamed preacher played by Eastwood rides a pale horse, and the title of the film, *Pale Rider*, suggests that the close relationship between horse and rider is at least metonymic if not metaphoric. Eastwood takes on the role of avenging angel—and that of a ghost (having survived several shots to the chest that no human could have survived, as he proves when he kills the man who shot him in exactly the same way). By virtue of their shared characteristics, the horse, too, is a ghost, a spirit, perhaps also Death but not

---

24   There are also blind horses in Paulette Jiles's *The Jesse James Poems* (1988): "Sometime / in the night they will ride south on blind horses; the horses will have never seen / anything like this in their lives" (60). Potentially something more could be said about the subtle implication here that horses from the North are blind, which could be relevant to Jiles's dual citizenship.

Hell, because the preacher and horse ride together as one. And if in *Pale Rider* the pale horse and its metonymically associated rider are a magical reanimation of the murdered little white dog, its macabre dimension is another degeneration through violence akin to that of McAdoo's pig (above); he is a pale shadow of a beast less noble (to some) than a horse. As Death incarnate, his human body and its steed have another, and far more powerful, contesting identity. In one of my courses on the Western, Lana McCrae responded to these ideas by realizing that they also reveal the degeneration of the cowboy's connection to the mortal plane, a disconnection that bestows upon him the power to judge the soul of the next man he might kill. The apocalyptic judge in McCarthy's *Blood Meridian* (1985) is a fine example of this in literature—also arguably a paragon of regeneration through violence and thus a major counterpoint to some of my arguments in this chapter—and one that bleakly contradicts any model of the judge as a neutral, critical thinker or a humanistic force.[25]

Vanderhaeghe, too, rarely defers to nobility and its reassuring conclusions, though his opinion on the ultimate meaning of the horse throughout its transformations seems ambivalent. Sue Sorensen recognizes Vanderhaeghe's allusions to the Four Horsemen if not to *Pale Rider*:

> The pale horse in Revelation 6 carries Death, and the rider on the white horse in that chapter has been variously

---

25 I have thus far not quoted or considered at any length the various American novels in the background of this book, mainly because of my scope-limiting decision to compare (usually) American films and Canadian literature, as I explained in the introduction to this book. *Blood Meridian* would be the exception to this rule, were I to break it. Michael Herr blurbs the book (on the Vintage International edition of 1992) as "[a] classic American novel of regeneration through violence," though I am not certain that it is so simple. In the novel, the kid's experience with violence does change his identity. Shot but not fatally near the beginning, "the child [is] finally divested of all that he has been" (4). Later, the judge (seemingly the kid's eventual killer) tells his listeners that the course of "the degeneracy of mankind" (146) can be interrupted only by raising children to cope with violence; thereby, humans may "cull themselves" (146). The kid later has a chance to kill the judge, his pursuer, but he does not (298), possibly because he does in fact see the judge as a father figure (306). Instead, after a scene featuring a dancing bear, the judge dances in a parallelism to illustrate not a "degenerate" connection to other animals but that "[t]here is room on the stage for one beast and one alone. . . . Bears that dance, bears that dont [*sic*]" (331). Through an ambiguously impressionistic closing image of the naked judge as a skinned but still living bear whose embrace of the kid might in fact have killed him (333–4), McCarthy implies that the judge's regeneration is in the almost vampiric "culling" of his lessers—an example of social Darwinism unless, of course, we interpret the judge as the devilish nemesis that he often appears to be.

> interpreted, but can be associated with the Antichrist. . . .
> The white horse in Revelation 19, however, is definitely associated with the Messiah. Vanderhaeghe uses these contending symbols of good and evil interchangeably, although Hank's horse's blindness adds weight to the pathetic or ominous side of the equation. (35)

Reflecting a little later on the tension between Death and the Messiah here, Sorensen adds: "Commentary on religion in *The Englishman's Boy* is difficult because Vanderhaeghe's symbolism is not only ironic but overabundant, with possible identifications doubled or redoubled" (36). So, the likely allusion in *The Englishman's Boy* not only to the Bible but also to *Pale Rider* is partly an ironic foreshadowing, because Hardwick enacts revenge as he desired in chapters 27 and 29, massacring and raping and burning others alive, whereas in *Pale Rider* the preacher's sense of justice is far less offensive.[26] The Assiniboine girl in *The Englishman's Boy* is not saved as Megan is saved in *Pale Rider*. And the whiteness of the murdered blind white horse is ironic too, or at least very complex, because Fine Man's painting of the blue horse is meant to give it the whiteness and the movement of falling snow. Partly because painting the horse white produces a moving picture akin to film, a highly visual medium, there seems to be an irony in the reference to the blind white horse in the same novel. But more than that, the post-human thinking in the apocalyptic pale horse in *The Englishman's Boy* is a reorientation to a filmic point of view, not another animal's point of view, which for Vanderhaeghe has less future potential. Braidotti, coincidentally, refers to "the four horsemen of the posthuman apocalypse: nanotechnology, biotechnology, information technology and cognitive science" (59). Vanderhaeghe's horse-men, fused as they are not only across species but also with the technology of film, represent at least biotechnology and information technology. In transforming the horse into a moving picture, he skips its incarnation as the Iron Horse of nineteenth-century industry and lands in twentieth-century media (echoing Kroetsch's claim that Canadian literature skipped straight

---

26   Eastwood's vengeful character in *High Plains Drifter* (Eastwood, 1973) is far more ghastly, a protector but also a rapist.

to postmodernism). His novel depends on Biblical allusions, but it gets some of them from *Pale Rider*, showing its dependence on popular culture beyond the pop-cultural resonance that may be attributed to the Bible. In this sense, the novel is profoundly post-human: its vision of life and death does not reanimate anything except as technological simulation, a mark of hyperreality that is both post-human and postmodern. And if being a pale rider animated by a moving picture implies a prosthetic (as if film itself were the legs that give it movement), it is a condition that is both a degeneracy and a cyborg's improvement on the mere human.

Men Born of Horses

Until now, with this evolutionary theme in mind, I have concentrated on Vanderhaeghe's *Englishman's Boy* because of its canonical status as a historical Western that appears to have been the first Canadian Western after the postmodern trend began to dissipate in the late 1980s and early 1990s, and that appears as an early exemplar in a lengthening series of post-Westerns; however, its spiritual sequel, *The Last Crossing*, goes further in thinking through regeneration or degeneration through violence and the horse-man hybridity that exemplifies the post-human in these Westerns. Because it is a lesser-known novel compared to *The Englishman's Boy*, I relay a colourful synopsis from John Burns:

> The story is simple. Charles Gaunt and elder brother Addington travel into the lawless New World of 1871 searching for Charles's lost twin, Simon, last seen leaving England under the sway of a shady evangelist preaching the kind of religious claptrap so popular among the Victorians. The trip, whether rescue or inquest, is clearly doomed. Charles in England is a dreamer, a milk-fed artist in an eccentric but powerful family. Charles in America is a kipper out of water, butt of scorn and flinty humour from the posse he and Addington assemble.... But this is really all just a cunningly designed, immaculately stitched backdrop for the novel's central relationship between Charles and Addington Gaunt. It's a quest story transposed into the New World of the 1870s, the history and geography of the still-wild west

embodying the clash between gentle, modern Charles and Addington, ruthless servant to the Empire. Told back in England, in time-worn, implacable London, theirs would be another social novel of the Henry James variety. In the heaving West, a land redefining itself politically, socially, spiritually, it's a story with the potential to attain the level of myth. ("Review")

Partly because of this potential, and of the fact that this story is already "transposed" across countries, in this section I have a set of examples that show how the Western and Western-like texts in general—not only Canadian Westerns—are imagining the horse-man hybridity. *The Last Crossing* does so partly through the character of Custis Straw. Katherine Ann Roberts explains: "Sporting leg wounds suffered during the American Civil War . . . , haunted by his inability to a save a wounded comrade . . . , Straw is a man of introspection and humility" (59); he "is thus not only the 'man who knows Indians' within the classic American western iconography, [because] he is the man who knows horses and is . . . at home on the range" (59). By the end of the novel, "he manages to scale down violence, rein in [a] drive for vengeance, and resolve conflict by 'talking quiet.' His turning away represents a significant evolution away from the generic western's triumphalism and regeneration through violence" (63). But for me, the better example in *The Last Crossing* is Simon, the English missionary whose "regeneration" is a transnational acculturation into Indigenous ways of knowing, all starting with a more "knowing" or intimate (actually, familial more than sexual) relationship with a horse.

Indeed, its opening scene of hybridity is a node in an intertextual and transnational network of Westerns and Western-like texts from both Canada and the United States. Degeneration through violence is perhaps nowhere more obvious than when, near the beginning of *The Last Crossing*, the lost missionary on the wintry plains is about to die of exposure to cold. To survive, he kills and repurposes his horse: cutting open the warm body, he creates a shelter and crawls inside to the guts, "burrow[ing] into the balmy pocket. . . . Safe in the slick, rich animal heat, out of the cruel wind. . . . An embryo, curled in the belly of the dead horse" (8–9). In addition to various transnational echoes that I hear below, there is an echo of what

Annette Kolodny calls America's "single dominating metaphor: regression from the cares of adult life and a return to the primal warmth of womb or breast in a feminine landscape" (6)—here a positive "regression" to childhood and mothering. As this metaphor plays out in Westerns and related texts, it is not always so innocent.[27] Simon is later renamed Born of a Horse (344–5) by the Two-Spirited person who observes his birth and then becomes his lover and spiritual re-educator outside the Christian tradition.[28] In the context of the missionary, the rebirth is ironic, because it leads to Simon's non-heteronormative relationship with a Two Spirit, a *bote*. It thereby also leads to his adoption and acculturation into a Crow community, which to his English family is likely another captivity narrative and another degeneration—one in contrast with his imperial brother Addington, whose degeneracy through violence is represented symbolically by the syphilis that eventually drives him to attempt to hunt a bear without benefit of his modern weaponry.

Addington becomes animalistic in *The Last Crossing*, but he lacks the animalistic nobility and Indigenous spirituality that his brother gains through the horse and Indigenous respect for horses. According to Roberts, "Addington symbolizes . . . the hypocrisy and decay beneath the veneer of Victorian moral and sexual propriety. As Wyile . . . points out, Vanderhaeghe, through his portrait of the Gaunt brothers, 'figures imperialism as a migration of the ills of Victorian society outward to the margins of empire, subverting the trope of the genteel Victorian being confronted with the lawless, depraved Wild West' " (50). Roberts explains in detail:

---

27 No one asks, for example, what the horse would think of being used. J. J. Clark observes that "there is a stark difference between the actual behaviour of horses and the behavior of the stereotypical western horse of literature, film, and television. These fictional horses are presented as celibate males who . . . are readily obedient and submissive to the cowboy" (157). I, too, learned from experience that the stereotype is not true. In filming a short promotion for this book with my colleague Jamie Skidmore, I was recorded talking at the camera with a microphone on my lapel and a live horse over my shoulder. The horse ate the mic. The horse's owner (or protector) seemingly pushed her whole arm down the throat of the horse to get the mic. I'm sure the scene was funnier to me than the horse.

28 A similar plot can be found in *A Man Called Horse* (Silverstein, 1970) when an English slave of the Sioux refuses to be treated like a horse, a refusal that the "Indians" mock by renaming him "Horse" thereafter (Tompkins 105). A line in Gil Adamson's *Ridgerunner* (2020) about who could "resurrect a horse" (77) suggests that this sort of rebirth is also a sort of reincarnation.

> Addington exposes the "rot" not only at the heart of Victorian imperialism but also at the heart of Theodore Roosevelt's turn-of-the-century frontier myth. . . . Roosevelt's peculiar racist historiography and its veneration for the hunter/aristocrat/military figure is completely turned on its head in *The Last Crossing* through the portrait of Addington. Burdened by an ignominious past—he commanded his regiment to shoot Irish civilians at Dunvargan to quell their revolt—the captain searches fleetingly in the West for a path to rebirth (regeneration through violence) but is instead slowly overtaken by an untreated case of syphilis and reduced to a crazed monster, slathering himself in mercury [that futuristic liquid metal that *Terminator 2* (Cameron, 1991) would use so memorably in another narrative about anti-imperial technological appropriation]. Vanderhaeghe's novel contains phrases that seem to be taken almost verbatim from Roosevelt's theory on the need for physical activity. Given what the reader knows of Addington's character and the moral degradation this "exercise" is supposed to remedy (he suffers from venereal disease), these passages have a poignant irony: "This is what he was born to do. Live like a Mongol khan." (50–1)

One irony is that Addington has no idea what it is to live "like a Mongol khan," and another is that his vision of being "born" again in the West is nothing like his brother's rebirth and Indigenous acculturation as Born of a Horse. The key difference: Simon's rebirth has few of the imperial overtones of Addington's much more degenerative experience of the West. Simon's rebirth suggests that becoming horse-like, and befriending Indigenous people, is progress.

But here we should look beyond the Canadian Western, because this scene of taking shelter in an animal that has just died is probably more familiar to many of us from a *Star Wars* movie, *The Empire Strikes Back*

(Kershner, 1980),[29] when Luke Skywalker (Mark Hamill) has succumbed to the elements in a blizzard on a remote planet.[30] The science-fictional context is crucial, because it implies a diegesis in which civilization has progressed (complicated, of course, by all the dystopian narratives in sci-fi). To save Luke, his friend Han Solo (Harrison Ford, costumed in most scenes to evoke a space cowboy) cuts open an alien beast of burden, into which he pushes Luke to preserve his remaining warmth. "I thought they smelled bad on the outside," Han says, but we see little of the animal's insides; instead of an animalistic rebirth, we soon see Luke suspended with tubes and wires and recovering in a huge glassed-in tank of presumably warm water or some other healthful fluid. This example of "the posthuman as becoming-machine" (Braidotti 89) is at home in science fiction but is also, as we will see below, an emerging interest of the Western; here it implies that "becoming-machine" is a survival tactic in the face of an imperial threat, as Wyile and Roberts see it—but in the context of "becoming-animal"—in *The Last Crossing*. In *The Empire Strikes Back*, Luke is born not from a horse or other non-human animal but from a futuristic technology, one aligned more closely with his father, Darth Vader (David Prowse), than with his dead mother. The key difference between this scene and related scenes in Westerns is that the horse-like animal is a temporary saviour, while his transformation is future-friendly rather than anti-modern—as when Luke later equips himself with a bionic hand to replace the one that his father Darth Vader cut from him.[31] Still, Luke's becoming like Vader is clearly a degeneracy.

In *The Revenant* (Iñárritu, 2016), the scene from *The Empire Strikes Back* reappears but in an American context that refuses *The Last Crossing*'s

---

29   For readers of the Northwestern, it might also be familiar from Jack London's "To Build a Fire" (1908), in which a man freezing to death in the Yukon contemplates killing his dog in order to use the body to stay warm.

30   The earliest example that I know of in print is Bram Stoker's "The Squaw" (1893), where a character confidently states: "nothin's too terrible to the explorin' mind. Spent a night inside a dead horse while a prairie fire swept over me in Montana Territory—an' another time slept inside a dead buffler when the Comanches was on the war path an' I didn't keer to leave my kyard on them" (260). He then goes thrill-seeking in an iron maiden, with predictable results. I thank Andrew Loman for calling my attention to this one.

31   An early future-friendly example, though one of dramatic irony, is in *Dodge City* (Curtiz, 1939) when Colonel Dodge, ensconced in a comfortable compartment with other elites on the train, describes progress as "Iron Men and Iron Horses—you can't beat 'em."

partial integration of colonial and First Nations people. In *The Revenant*, the main character, Hugh Glass (a historical figure played by Leonardo DiCaprio), dies three times: first, when he is nearly killed by a bear;[32] second, when he is left for dead by his companions who partly bury him alive; and, third, when he rides his horse off a cliff (chased by "Indians") and, stranded in a gully with an oncoming snow storm, guts the horse, strips naked, and climbs inside. (I do not recall that this scene appears in one of the movie's source texts, Michael Punke's 2002 novel, *The Revenant*.) His deaths echo the various haunted Westerns that I considered in the previous chapter. When Glass re-emerges, however, no Indigenous people are there to witness the scene and allow him to join them. He had already had a relationship with a Pawnee woman, and they had a child together, but she was killed by whites and, after he raised his interracial child alone, the same man who wanted to leave him for dead after the bear attack also killed his son. The American movie (though directed by Alejandro Iñárritu, who is Mexican) assumes that white-Indigenous families will not survive, whereas *The Last Crossing* assumes that they will—simply not as traditional nuclear families led by heterosexual couples, and therefore not likely to create a lineage except by further adoptions. Symbolically, the horse in *The Revenant* has less power to give life—to regenerate—than in *The Last Crossing*, attesting perhaps to the former's stronger sense of conflict with the natural world.

For *The Last Crossing*, *The Empire Strikes Back* might well have been the inspiration for the birthing scene, but it likely has Indigenous origins, possibly in traditional storytelling, to which I have no access. However, in *Whiskey Bullets: Cowboy and Indian Heritage Poems* (2006), Garry Gottfriedson (whose work I looked at in the chapter devoted to Indigenous perspectives) introduces a figure known as Horsechild in a series of poems. He explained in an interview that "[Horsechild is part of] the imagery [that] comes from the Secwepemc land in Kamloops and around that area. . . . So it's really about my love for the land, I'm Horsechild and it's the land that's calling me back to it" (Gottfriedson qtd. in Ripplinger 5). He

---

32   He is later seen draped in a huge bearskin poncho, suggesting that his transformation into a horse was preceded by a transformation into a bear, the latter possibly alluding to James Fenimore Cooper's *The Last of the Mohicans* (1826), when two different characters don a bearskin in similar fashion.

identifies explicitly as Horsechild here, but it is possibly an identity that can be shared with other Indigenous people—for example, when he attributes the identity of Horsechild to the Kwakiutl painter George Littlechild ("Ode to Horsechild," 120). It is also possible that Horsechild in *Whiskey Bullets* is an allusion to the historical figure Horse Child, also known as Joe Pimi, son of the Cree chief Big Bear. Horse Child was adopted into a Métis family when Big Bear surrendered after the 1885 Resistance, and he later gave Big Bear's medicine bundle to the American Museum of Natural History in 1934 (Lusty 20). He lived at Poundmaker's Reserve near North Battleford, Saskatchewan, until his death in 1952 (20). To me, Gottfriedson seems to respect and identify with Horsechild and/or the historical Horse Child, the former because of a connection to the beckoning land, the latter (if I am not over-reading or misrepresenting the history) because of his survival and adaptation on colonized land in the context of the anti-colonial resistance of Horse Child's father, Big Bear. For Gottfriedson, being Horsechild enables or involves a beneficial return to the land, not at all a degeneracy.

Whether Vanderhaeghe found inspiration for Born of a Horse in Indigenous sources or *The Empire Strikes Back* or somewhere else, my own favourite source of the idea is Ondaatje's *The Collected Works of Billy the Kid*, which I looked at in the previous chapter. In an outrageous and darkly comic set piece, Ondaatje implies that the relationship of horse to man is less a utility than a kinship or even symbiosis. The sheriff Pat Garrett has captured Billy and other outlaws, and is leading them to jail the long way, through the desert and without hats, as a cruel punishment that echoes Tuco's (Eli Wallach) torture of Blondie (Clint Eastwood) in Sergio Leone's *The Good, the Bad, and the Ugly* (1966). Whereas Blondie is on foot and Tuco on horseback, Billy and his captors are riding, and Billy's shackles are chained around the horse's stomach to prevent his escape. Without protection from the blazing sun, Billy succumbs to heat stroke and begins hallucinating that the sun has reached down through his head to his penis, literally turning him inside out. Finally, Billy collapses—but merely slides down the side of the horse and remains chained there, hanging underneath: "And I rolled off the horse's back like a soft shell-less egg . . . but the chain held my legs to the horse and I was dragged picking up dust . . . as I travelled in between his four trotting legs at last thank the fucking christ, in the shade of his stomach" (81). The metaphor of Billy as an egg hanging beneath the horse's stomach suggests that he has regressed, or degenerated, to an embryonic phase, as in some of the texts above; he now has a new mother: the horse, who herself has degenerated into a pre-mammalian, egg-laying animal. Notably, in every case so far, the transformation has been driven by necessity, and they all share a more resistant attitude to imperial power than to horsepower.

The painfully hilarious hung-from-a-horse scene in *The Collected Works of Billy the Kid* is replayed less as regression and more as progression in the more recent movie *Gunless* (Phillips, 2010), a much more deliberately Canadian perspective on the Western genre. In the opening scene, the Montana Kid (Paul Gross) rides into town backwards, dragging a broken branch from the noose around his neck. Back(ward) in the saddle, he is a sign of looking back to the United States—but not with much nostalgia, given that he narrowly escaped a hanging by the outlaws who still pursue him.[33] Arriving wounded and semi-conscious at a general store in small-town Alberta, he tips forward and sideways, sliding down until he is hanging upside down under the horse, as Billy does. His hanging in the opening scene is already his second hanging, so it calls attention to the differences between how he was treated in the United States compared to Canada. In a reversal of the plot of Mark Twain's *A Connecticut Yankee in King Arthur's Court* (1889), he goes forward in time, at least time measured by stereotypically Canadian ideals of social progress, and *he* becomes the anachronism: freed from bondage by a second-generation Chinese-Canadian citizen (the Korean-Canadian Melody Choi), whom he mistakes for someone more foreign than him, and welcomed into an emerging pluralistic society whose government he (again) fails to recognize through the portrait of Queen Victoria on the wall in the store. He is out of sync with the economy, government, and culture. Inside the store, after buying bullets on credit, the Montana Kid loses patience with the salesmen and shoots both a teacup—symbol of civility, though it contains prohibited whisky—and the portrait of the queen, symbol of empire.

---

33 For earlier examples of this plot in American films, see Richard G. Baker (115–19). For medieval sources of the backwards ride, see Esther Cohen: "The backwards ride upon an ass . . . was . . . a common form of *charivari* [or ritual public derision]" (175).

The shooting identifies him as a savage but an independent, though he is now reborn. Through a process of disorientation and reorientation begun under the horse, he eventually becomes voluntarily interdependent as the suicidal urges of his internalized gunslinger change from actual to symbolic. He chooses a life without guns and becomes an honorary modern liberal Canadian, forward-thinking and reoriented toward community, however idealized this view of Canada is.

If *Gunless* is the most recent iteration of the rebirth scene, the earliest I know of in Canada is from comics in the 1940s, and it warrants inclusion even though I've otherwise excluded comics from this book. In the Canadian publication *Triumph Comics* (number 9, from 1941), a comic-book story called "The Capture of 'Red' " in the *Tang* series by René Kulbach involves Buddy, himself barely older than the "kid" he was when the series began, shooting and cutting open a buffalo to survive a wildfire. When Buddy truly *was* a kid in the first few issues of *Triumph Comics*, he was kidnapped by a Sioux chief who adopted him and taught him Sioux ways. Killing the buffalo and taking shelter inside is credited to the chief: "Spotted Eagle knew a lot of tricks—hope this is the right one!" (Kulbach 42). For Buddy, surviving inside a buffalo suggests that his acculturated Indigeneity (which is appropriated by Kulbach) is not a degeneration but an evolution into a fitter person. And although Buddy tries to make peace with some of the "Indians" in the *Tang* series, he also kills many of them, and Kulbach usually presents them as "savages," perpetuating the racist notion that "a good Indian" is a white man.

That the transformation of the Kids is both protective and empowering is less obvious in "The Capture of 'Red,' " *The Collected Works of Billy the Kid*, and *Gunless* than it is in the classic film *High Noon* (Zinnemann, 1952), when the sheriff becomes the outlaw-lawman by accepting and harnessing the power of the horse. As with Billy, the sheriff (Gary Cooper) is eventually captured, in the sense of being trapped in a barn full of horses and prevented from leaving by the danger of nearby shooters. And, as with Billy in the sun, the sheriff in *High Noon* is endangered by the heat. The scene becomes a firefight in two senses when the gang sets fire to the hay in the barn. Desperate, the sheriff gathers the horses and stampedes them out of the fiery barn, hanging off the side of his mount to avoid being shot in a scene reminiscent of the escape from the forest fire in Zane Grey's *Wildfire*

(1916). Although we can discern him in the stampede, his more horizontal position and his partial indistinguishability in the eyes of his attackers are signs that he, too, is a horse-man hybrid—but not only a horseman: also a phoenix. He is reborn in the flames. Embracing an elemental power, his wild side, he is still no match for Frank Miller (Ian MacDonald) and his gang. The significance of his transformation becomes clearer when his new wife, Amy (Grace Kelly), still in the white of her wedding dress, *also* contravenes her own Quaker ethic of non-violence in a moral decision to shoot an outlaw and save her husband. Although only one of them becomes a horseman, both experience the related degeneration of ethics (their principles break down) and the regeneration of morality (they "do the right thing" for the situation at hand). Rebirth as a horseman in this American context shows the perhaps enviable adaptability of American society and morals to new situations, but, whereas *Gunless* encourages America to adapt to a (falsely) gunless life, *High Noon* suggests that the adaptation must be of non-violence to violence.

Of course, not all Canadians are pacifists, and not all Canadian Westerns are either. Nor are all horses in the Western horse-men, and some of them seem to want anything but a metaphorical fusion with people. This is because most humans cannot relate well to other animals, as one of Stenson's characters suggests: "If you can't imagine what it feels like to be a horse, try being human" (*Lightning* 181). In Stenson's 2008 novel *The Great Karoo*, however, the horse that wants no connection with people is linked to them anyway—though in Stenson's other Western, *Lightning*, "[h]orses were Lippy's closest friends" (10); "[a] horse was not a dog, not a pet" (108).[34] In the North-West Mounted Police's horsemanship training early in *The Great Karoo*, the recruits are put to the test by the historical figure Lieutenant Colonel Sam Steele, who wants every man to be toughened by being thrown from a horse. (Later, they go to South Africa to fight the Boers for the farmland that the British wanted, and they get first-hand experience with both the open country and the infamous prisoner-of-war camps managed by the British.) Stenson introduces the wildest horse as

---

34   To shift the focus from horses to canines as companion species in Canadian Westerns, see the classic *The Call of the Wild* (1903) by Jack London, and compare with the quick succession of Natalee Caple's *In Calamity's Wake* in 2013 and Nadia Bozak's *El Niño* in 2014.

"a monkey-coloured outlaw" (35), using not only "outlaw" but also "monkey" to imply that the horse is a kind of "missing link" in the evolution of non-human animals toward human civilization. Given their cavalry's mission in Africa and the attitudes of characters such as Steele, calling the horse "monkey-coloured" is a potentially racist reference to Africans that belies any notion of Canada's own better evolution from England. Calling the horse an "outlaw" simply suggests that notions of the law are relative to one's own country. But, as usual, the real and symbolic borders are both called into question in this Western. When hapless Albert begins riding the bucking outlaw, "both stirrups were lost. At times, Albert's only connection to the horse was a death grip on the saddle horn" (37). A moment later something changes: "Into his next combination the horse poured so much wild energy that he shot a rear hoof into and through one of the empty stirrups. Now, he was bucking on three legs, and still it was more than Albert could handle" (37). The horse, now three-legged instead of four, is taking steps—or great leaps—toward bipedalism.[35] No wonder that "it dawned on Albert that he was serving no useful purpose" and "let go" (37). The horse is supplanting him. He jokes, "Well, boys, . . . you know me, I can ride most anything with hair. But, when a horse puts his hoof in the stirrup and tries to get on behind, I reckon it's time to let him go" (37). The image of a horse trying to ride himself is similar to the image of Ouroboros, the snake that eats its own tail. It is a natural symbol of cycles of life, death, and life: regeneration. Suiting the comedy of the scene, Albert's evasion of being ridden also implies that he has avoided being screwed by the horse that "tries to get on behind," avoiding miscegenation and leaving the horse in an incestuous or at least masturbatory relationship with himself. If only Canadian war-making and peacekeeping could always be only that offensive.

In sum, through these transnational fantasies about horse-human hybridity, we discern mainly an anti-imperialist attitude, one that can be generalized (even in the case of *High Noon*) as a resistance to threatening powers that are perceived to be immoral. Although any position on the political spectra could play host to this attitude, the protective

---

35 The mention of "combination" in this scene also seems to allude to recombination, a technique in genetic manipulation.

nature (or Nature) of horse-human hybridity suggests that an idea of (co)evolution is at work, and it is liberal in its attitude to borders, or at least human-inhuman borders. The levity of many of these scenes—Stenson's and Ondaatje's sexual comedies, Phillips's goofy nationalism, even Han Solo's bad joke—suggests that we have learned to dissipate some of the tension involved in imagining human evolution as devolution. In other words, we are beginning to accept (or are accepting again) that humans will not always be human. The question is, how much bigger—and better or worse—could we become?

Becoming Earth in the Western

The Ouroboros implied by the "monkey-coloured outlaw" horse in Stenson's *The Great Karoo* is related to another ancient myth, that of Gaia. In *The Outlander*, by Gil Adamson, the story focuses occasionally on horses, but the narrative arc of the novel becomes far more geological than biological at the climax, and only in the dénouement does biology—specifically that of humans—reassert itself. In the novel, the widow who murdered her husband escapes two twin assassins and disappears into the woods, eventually meeting the Ridgerunner, who becomes her lover, and joining a camp of men to work with them adjacent to a mountain mine. (The Ridgerunner also becomes the titular character in the sequel in 2020, and mining towns are again a prominent setting.) The final dramas of the story involve what might happen to her baby if she is convicted of her husband's murder. The return to the biological imperative of sex and child-rearing is a humanistic end to a story that could have been post-human and post-humanistic, especially given the mark of science fiction on its otherwise historical fiction. But it definitely bears the marks of the Western: first, it is billed by its publisher, Anansi, as "[p]art historical novel, part Gothic tale, and part literary Western" (on its website showcasing its A List series); second, I heard in an interview with Adamson that her title for *The Outlander* is drawn in part from a Sean Connery space Western, *Outland* (Hyams, 1981; confirmed by Adamson in an email interview); third, it is set on the frontier in the late nineteenth-century West (technically, the early twentieth century of 1903); and finally, it focuses on an outlaw—the widow who murdered her husband—and her pursuit by two brothers whose twinning motif is very common among the symmetries (e.g., outlaw-lawman) of the Western. *The Outlander* interests me partly because of how it plays with genre but also because of how its environmental themes re-inscribe the relationality of genre: like everything on earth, any genre is interdependent with other genres and the system of circulation that supports them all. In a different context, Braidotti theorizes "the open-ended, inter-relational, multi-sexed and trans-species flows of becoming through interaction with multiple others. A posthuman subject thus constituted exceeds the boundaries of both anthropocentrism and of compensatory humanism, to acquire a planetary dimension" (89). Adamson's *Outlander* has a Gaian dimension that may be described as planetary, but it also has what Braidotti describes as "a way of humanizing the environment, that is to say, as a well-meaning form of residual anthropomorphic normativity, applied to non-human planetary agents" (86), which she calls "compensatory humanism," a sort of compromise between radical post-humanism and its forebears.

Possibly for this reason, in Adamson's *The Outlander*, as with so many other Westerns, horses are not understood on their own terms (to the extent that we could imagine them post-humanly and post-humanistically); neither are the horses hybrids of humans, not quite, but they are clearly metaphors of humans and their contrastingly gendered dispositions, the gendering adding a new dimension to the representations of horses in the Canadian Western. The widow, whose name is later revealed to be Mary Boulton, has an identity strongly associated with that of her husband—hence her definition, as "the widow," in terms of marriage. Adamson writes that

> Until she was married, [the widow had] never ridden anything but a "girl's horse"—gentle animals, usually old and slothful by temperament. Once married, she was introduced to a wholly different species: massive, powerful monsters with hairy forelegs and broad backs, stupid beasts with ferocious tempers. (287)

Obviously, a horse cannot be differentiated from another horse as "a wholly different species," so Adamson is doing something else here. She is in fact comparing the "different" horses to men in contrast with women, specifically Boulton's husband and his physical characteristics such as "hairy forelegs," hairy legs being gendered masculine. And the personality traits that contributed to her decision to kill him, his traits of being "stupid" and "ferocious," are projected onto the horses of her marriage too. They are clearly implicated in the domesticity and gendering of Boulton's household. In contrast, in a previous comparison but from a later time in her life, Boulton looked upon the horses of the town of Frank and noticed that people's horses "followed them around like lapdogs" (262)—more shades of Eastwood's paranormal terrier-horse transformation in *Pale Rider*. (In fact, when some of the miners are telling ghost stories about the sights and sounds in the darkness of the mine shafts, one of them says, "Ghosts don't exist. It's gas and white dogs" [234].) One horse even follows an owner into his own house: "Everyone heard the soft clop of unshod hooves and the warning cracks of the floorboards. The boy . . . impelled it backwards out the door, knocking its head on the lintel" (263). The horse then goes around the house to look through the window "like a governess peering into a playhouse" (263). Tompkins explains that horses are gendered feminine, despite the Freudian connotation of the phallus (17), and that "[i]t is here, in the society of man and horse, that the problems women and language pose for the Western hero come closest to being solved" (96): horses satisfy the lack of women in the West. Similarly, Adamson's references to "a governess" and "a playhouse" obviously gender horses in relation to domestic roles traditionally assigned to women. The references imply that, after her murder of her husband, Boulton has found in the town of Frank a safer and more peaceable relationship to other men, who have accepted her as they have not accepted other femininities.[36]

Notwithstanding this peace at the micro level of individuals, the men of Frank are involved in a macro project that cannot be simply described as peaceful: the mining of the nearby Turtle Mountain. Bronwyn Drainie's review of *The Outlander* claims that "a novel that had the hallucinatory quality of Ondaatje or Peter Oliva's brilliant *Drowning in Darkness* [1993] turns into straightforward historical fiction" ("Review") when the Frank

---

36 In a way, the safety of Frank implies that the codes of masculinity inscribed into the Western have done their work of producing a temporarily peaceful time and place. Edward Buscombe asserts the rationale of the genre: "A society without violence, a society fit for women, can only be established *through* violence" (59, original emphasis).

Slide happens, but it is also profoundly allegorical. The Gaian element of the novel serves as a conversation-starter for Braidotti's notion of "the posthuman as becoming-earth" (81). As in *Pale Rider*, the mining can be understood as the figurative rape of the land and hence a symbolic attack on Gaia, Mother Earth. In the American context generally, the classic study of the Gaian theme is Kolodny's *The Lay of the Land* (1984). Kolodny speculates on "what is probably America's oldest and most cherished fantasy: a daily reality of harmony between man and nature based on an experience of the land as essentially feminine" (4). Kolodny then explains that "those who had initially responded to the promise inherent in a feminine landscape were now faced with the consequences of that response: either they recoiled in horror from the meaning of their manipulation of a naturally generous world . . . or they succumbed to a life of easeful regression" (7). In *The Outlander*, it is the former: the miners notice that their mining is having an effect on the mountain to which they also assign a gender: "We got ground tremors now. She shakes all on her own. We don't even have to set charges much any more. She shifts a little every day, and down comes rock" (233). They also notice ominous sparks in the shafts, described by the narrator as a "bowel" (232), that one of them interprets as fairies (233). Eventually the landslide occurs with brightened imagery of light: "For a full minute, the mountain seemed to billow, then slowly collapse, floating downward, lit palely from within. It luminesced from pure friction" (294), but its inner light is also a symbol of the Gaian spirit of the mountain. Inasmuch as the landslide is the mountain's injury and death, it is also its phoenix-like rebirth (hence the "luminescent" aura) and reformation of the landscape.

Notably, Adamson is self-conscious about this symbolism, implying that it accords with colonial stereotypes about Indigenous beliefs: "Indians didn't spend too much time in Frank. The common wisdom was that they were superstitious about the mountain and believed it was alive—a view that was much ridiculed in Frank. In Frank, there was ridicule of pretty much everything" (290). She seems to be acknowledging a limit to her point of view, or at least to the masculinity "[i]n Frank" of reasonably scoffing at people who are being "superstitious," and perhaps this accounts for the way in which she describes the aftermath of the landslide:

> The widow moved amid the trimmings of a nightmare forest. Blown debris was piled up everywhere. Branches and stones. Trees leaned drunkenly, many broken halfway up their tall shafts, heavy heads tilted crazily. On everything was a pale dust, giving the dark green vegetation a leprous air. Small, colourful bodies were strewn on the ground like Easter eggs, bright fallen birds, killed by the first blast of hot wind. . . . Farther on, a young lynx lay bloodied. . . . A hat was dangling from a high branch. (299–300)

The anthropomorphic language of "a nightmare" and "drunke[n]" trees and birds that appear decorated "like Easter eggs" is possibly why Braidotti tends to avoid literature in *The Posthuman*. But to me—at a time of climate crisis resulting from the same sorts of extractive industries interrogated in *The Outlander*—such descriptions are better than the irresponsible disregard of nature. They elicit sympathy and possibly, through identification, empathy (however anthropomorphic the identification is). When in *The Outlander* "[a] maddened horse dashed insanely up and down the new shoreline" (303) and over the debris of the landslide, we also feel what Tompkins discerns as a guilt and a nostalgia for a time before when we "broke" horses (103) and, I would add, degenerated them. And yet I respect Braidotti's concern about our not being able to respect nature until we can imagine its points of view without the interference of our own. In the settler tradition, contemporary poets such as Tim Lilburn, Sue Goyette, Don McKay, Mary Dalton, and many others have done remarkable work for this imagination, but the Western is about how landscapes have human value as resource and homestead; it is part of the same epic and romance tradition of family plots in which knights save damsels in distress.

Near the end of the novel, the widow is pregnant with a child fathered by a man known mainly as the Ridgerunner, a man whose identity as such is defined in terms of his interaction with the landscape of ridges in the mountains, in contrast with the widow's identity, defined as it is in terms of her marriage. (His real name is William Moreland, a name that still defines him in terms of land, but with a more colonial emphasis on "more," rather than the relational activity of "running" in his nickname.) But the pregnancy is one of the signs of the widow's Gaian relationship as a mother who will give birth to a child of the mountain's ridges. And it resonates with incidents in the novel when the widow is penetrated by nature (rather than by Moreland), such as the arrow (143–4) and, during the landslide, a twig (297). We could even read the pregnancy in *The Outlander* as an almost-immaculate conception, a depersonalized incubation.

The birth is relevant for the surrounding landscape because the mountain has been damaged by the mining and the subsequent landslide. In a Gaian reaction against Anthropocenic terraforming, "[w]hat used to be a river was now a shallow lake, swelling upward along the fissures and runnels that wandered up the mountainside" (302). Later, the Ridgerunner discovers this "new lake" (368) near "the original riverbed that stood low and empty now, wide and slick and strewn with debris, and down its middle ran a scrawny stream, lifeless and foul-smelling" (369). The regeneration of the landscape is not complete; Gaian terraforming may not entirely clean up the pollution from the mine. For the Ridgerunner, however, the destruction is close enough: "It struck him suddenly, ridiculously, that this place would not acknowledge him, even in reflection. The human world erased in one brutal swipe" (369). The apocalyptic language of erasure and extinction here is human. It also suggests masculine or male privilege. Tompkins claims that "the Western is secular, materialist, and antifeminist" (28) (though in chapter 2 the Muscular Christianity of early Canadian Westerns calls "secular" into question, as does the transcendentalism at the start of this chapter); here in *The Outlander* Adamson is reorienting the genre toward religious, intangible, and feminist values for Nature, "swip[ing]" at a *man's* "world" more than any other. Thus, the feminism of the novel might in fact work against its post-humanism, because its ideology serves people as much as Nature. Furthermore, the implication that a symbolic Mother Earth (the widow's and the Ridgerunner's child) will outlive humans is only *symbolically* post-human, because Adamson lets the widow escape her death sentence and leaves open the possibility (in the sequel, *Ridgerunner*) that the Ridgerunner will find her and create a bigger family with her in the future.

In *The Outlander*, there is no planet B, because there is no need for one. The Frank Slide destroys Frank—and symbolically Frank's style of masculinity, indicated perhaps by "the pointless industry of the living" (313)—but the post-human message is ultimately overcome by the humanistic family plot. I mentioned above that part of the inspiration for the title *The Outlander* was a Sean Connery space Western, *Outland*, which adapts the plot of *High Noon* (Arnold, "Unlikely"). In *Outland*, the action takes place at a mining colony on one of Jupiter's moons, Io, but Earth itself remains a livable planet. Rather than learn our lessons about stripping bare our own planet, we have continued on other astral bodies.

"Becoming-Machine"

The sci-fi connection that *The Outlander* presents in its title, and its potential to develop Braidotti's conception of "the posthuman as becoming-machine" (89), is not, as far as I know, developed in Canadian literature. So I will be brief in concluding this chapter. In American film and television, however, there is the example of Michael Crichton's *Westworld* (1973) and its adaptation into (among others) the recent HBO television series by the same name (2016–20). As futuristic as it seems to be, *Westworld* is a near-perfect representation of the regressive aspects proposed in Slotkin's theory. Until *Westworld*, the most memorable example for me was Eastwood's *Unforgiven* (1992), in which the cowboy who tries to retire from his tough-on-crime life of vigilante justice is inexorably drawn back to it—and thereby away from his newly liberal life (with his best friend, an African-American man, and his Indigenous wife). In *Westworld*, the androids created to simulate humans in an immersive Wild West theme park eventually avenge their abuse at the hands of humans by attempting to massacre them. Braidotti argues that "the posthuman as becoming-machine" is now "beyond metaphorization" (89) because technology has caught up to our imaginations, but this claim is far from being true. We might all now be androids to some extent, but "metaphorization" persists. In *Westworld*, the androids stand in for Indigenous people, who have almost entirely vanished in the *Westworld* narrative, including its main characters (at least in the first season), and their rebellion against humans briefly holds the promise of a new land beyond the oppressive big business and R&D of the Westworld parks. Nothing here is degenerative; in fact, in their quest for freedom and sovereignty, the androids supposedly gain the potential to upgrade themselves, in addition to repairing their bodies and their beauty. But how progressive can this vision be?

In contrast with *Westworld*, the recent X-Men film *Logan* (Mangold, 2017) goes much further in questioning the myth of regeneration through violence. Although it is not strictly a Canadian film, it has various Canadian elements, including the titular character, Logan (a.k.a. Wolverine, played by Hugh Jackman), whose origin story tracks him from northern Alberta to the United States and around the world. And although it is not strictly a Western either, *Logan* is explicitly presented as a crossover between superhero and Western genres in a scene where Charles Xavier (a.k.a. Professor X, played by Patrick Stewart) views the classic film *Shane* (Stevens, 1953). Watching with him is the young girl Laura (Dafne Keen), who memorizes Shane's final words to the boy who looks up to him: "Joey, there's no living with, with a killing. There's no going back from it. Right or wrong, it's a brand, a brand that sticks. . . . Now you run on home to your mother and tell her . . . there aren't any more guns in the valley." Shane's promise of peace resonates with Laura because *Logan*'s plot unfolds in a dystopian near-future involving a governmental crackdown on mutants like her—humans born with special powers for which they have been ostracized. Set at first near Mexico, the narrative moves toward "Eden" in North Dakota before the persecuted mutants escape into Canada. Logan's particular mutation is an ability to regenerate rapidly, which grants him near-invulnerability in battle and, until recently, a perpetual youth. The theme of regeneration is juxtaposed with the theme of aging; Hugh Jackman is now aging perceptibly as an actor, and so the film rationalizes Jackman's body by explaining that his mutation is failing him, aligning him more and more with his elderly and demented mentor, Professor X. In yet another related juxtaposition, Logan learns that Laura is his daughter, whose regenerative ability is in its prime. In a metafictional twist that rationalizes heroism as celebrity, Logan complains that Laura and her nurse are following directions to "Eden" from an X-Men comic book that, though based on a true story (*his* true story), is now almost completely fantastic and false. The Christian allusions to "Eden," and the potential problem of the film's imagining Canada as not only a haven but also a promised land or another Manifest Destiny, become more obviously colonial when, at the scene of an accident on the highway and much like Fine Man in *The Englishman's Boy*, Professor X uses his telepathic ability to act as a "horse whisperer" and calm the horses who survived. (It is one of the few examples that isn't an unfortunate weaponization of mutant abilities in the franchise, armed conflict being its narrative drive.) This connection helps to demonstrate that the X-Men franchise, as yet another example of generic overlap with the Western, displaces Indigenous people through symbols (the mutants) who replace them. At the end of *Logan*—and the end of Logan's life, his regenerative power finally having failed him—the mutant children regenerate the territorial expansion of the Western by retreating into the forest as in *Dances with Wolves*, going into the North. The film's fascinating commentary on the Western becomes less a rejection and more a transformation of the myth of regeneration through violence. The saving grace is perhaps the implication that Logan's regeneration was compromised by the degenerative sci-fi experiment that turned his primarily defensive power into an offensive one: the torturously, surgically installed adamantine bone reinforcements and retractable claws that make him more obviously post-human, a mad military scientist's idea of a wolverine-human hybrid.

The nearest example to a representation of science alongside an interrogation of the myth of regeneration through violence in Canadian literature is *The Sisters Brothers* (2011) by Patrick deWitt, which was remade into an American-French co-production (Audiard, 2018). (The only other sci-fi Western that I know from Canada is the independent film *Six Reasons Why* by the Campagna brothers in 2008, which follows enigmatic stock characters through a post-apocalyptic West where the oil has run dry and the world's remaining batteries are highly sought after.) *The Sisters Brothers* qualifies as Canadian because deWitt was born on Vancouver Island, lived for a while in Canada, and published it with Anansi in Toronto, where it won various Canadian awards. As usual in the Western, in *The Sisters Brothers* we see a contrast of pre-modernity, such as the old woman's curse, and modernity, such as the emerging technologies of toothpaste and dental analgesia. Indeed, chemistry rather than mechanical engineering is the science of *The Sisters Brothers*; the enigmatic prospector Hermann Kermit Warm is attempting to perfect the formula of a liquid chemical that can be poured into a stream to make hidden gold glow—in effect, a divining potion. The potential to find gold is why the Sisters brothers, Charlie and Eli Sisters, are hired to steal the formula, but they end up helping Warm and his accomplice Morris to test the formula, which works beautifully. Alas, they use too much of the chemical, which begins to irritate their skin and rapidly worsens to burn them horribly. Nature, in their hands, loses its restorative powers and, polluted, enacts a revenge akin to that of *The Outlander*. Warm and Morris die, and Charlie eventually loses his hand, a personal injury that parallels, first, the briefly mentioned maimed dog (142) and, second, the environmental degradation (or degeneration) that the formula causes in the stream. When the "Indians" happen upon them and steal their gold, the Sisters brothers return in retirement to their single mother (Charlie having killed his father years prior). Charlie's disfigurement is poetic justice for a man whose trigger finger had snuffed out so many lives in their career of assassination: degeneration through violence par excellence, and post-human too, if he has also become a mama's boy foreshadowed by the maimed dog.

The Sisters Brothers also circles us around—in a final example here (though I will return to *The Sisters Brothers* in the conclusion)—to the Western's concern with the horse. As the infamous murderer Eli Sisters, Eli has slowly developed a conscience, especially as he has observed his horse, Tub, degenerate physically with age. Eli identifies with Tub early in the novel, because he thinks of himself as fat, and Tub is not in good shape. Eli's fatness is not degenerative, but he resolves to lose it so that he can more easily enter the social world of consensual sexual relationships—for example, with the hotel woman (66). It is a sign of his growing realization of his heavy conscience. Notably, he does not lose Tub; he decides to sell an impressive black horse and keep Tub instead (77–8, 85–6). By the end of the novel, he recognizes the cost of subordinating other animals: "What a life it is for man's animals, what a trial of pain and endurance and senselessness" (241). When he behaves violently, he asks himself, "Why do I relish this reversal to animal?" (246). He claims to suffer "shame" and "degradation" (246) that indicate the theme of degeneration through violence more explicitly.[37] *The Sisters Brothers* as a novel if not a film may be

---

37 In Ron Charles's review of the novel, he remarks that, "[f]or no reason that I can understand, Canadian novels are a notoriously hard sell in the United States," but he thinks that *The Sisters Brothers* "deserves a chance" ("Patrick deWitt"), and indeed it was made into a film, albeit not an entirely American film—something hardly possible any more anyway. Quite possibly the degeneration theme is simply too much a reversal from the classic Western to be appealing to American audiences; notably, the film version ends with the brothers going home rich, a triumphalist homecoming very different from that of the novel.

a sign that twenty-first-century Westerns and post-Westerns are following the revisionist trend of changing the myth, if not the history.

In this chapter, we have zoomed out to an interplanetary perspective from the comparatively small world of human beings and their relationships with other animals such as horses. But the implications of these relationships are extraordinary. The horse in the Western chronicles the notions of progress that accord not only with ethical and existential questions of human, inhuman, and post-human developments—but also with an obsession with what Coleman calls white civility (as in my examination of *The Englishman's Boy* above) that seems to underwrite ideas of the post-human in the Western and in related texts. Relationships with horses are thus germane to the ethics of our relationships with other people, perhaps especially the colonial-settler relationship with Indigenous peoples, whose connection to the land and respectful appropriation of the horse are inconsistently remodelled by the Western. It is a genre nostalgic for such a connection but, especially on film, willing to inflict pain and death on both horses and Indigenous people to show dominance and produce entertainment. Horses also seem to stand in for Indigenous peoples, at least occasionally, effecting another "vanishing" that calls into question the progressive credentials of post-Westerns, revisionist Westerns, and historical Westerns. Even in historical Westerns in Canada, Indigenous people tend to be significantly displaced, and narratives of violence continue to be dramatized to epic proportions that belie the sometimes much more banal history of the West—notwithstanding how reprehensibly colonial empires have treated Indigenous peoples on the lands that they have taken. In general, as the fascination with horses above suggests, historical Westerns simply show how myth has supplanted history even in the popular imagination of "history," as I argued in chapter 2, "Tom King's John Wayne."

But now—as this book concludes—we turn to various twenty-first-century Westerns and post-Westerns that demonstrate how the popular imagination has been recently drawn to Westerns again, effecting a new revival of the genre. Why now? What historical and especially political contexts have remade the Western into a tool for expressing our transnational, international, and national concerns? And given the crossover fever that has persisted throughout postmodernism, where will the Western go next—*what* now?

Conclusion
Mining the Western in the Twenty-First Century

In the small market of Canadian literature, the genre of the Western and its post-Western spinoffs have recently been booming. The resurgence since the year 2000—and I would stretch this date back at least as far as Robert Kroetsch's 1998 novel *The Man from the Creeks*—includes Guy Vanderhaeghe's *The Last Crossing* (2002) and *A Good Man* (2011); Fred Stenson's trilogy *The Trade* (2000), *Lightning* (2003), and *The Great Karoo* (2008); Brad Smith's *All Hat* (2004, adapted to film by Leonard Farlinger in 2007) and *The Return of Kid Cooper* (2018); Gil Adamson's *The Outlander* (2007) and *Ridgerunner* (2020); Lee Henderson's *The Man Game* (2008); Patrick deWitt's *The Sisters Brothers* (2011, adapted to film by Jacques Audiard in 2018); Sean Johnston's poetry in *Listen All You Bullets* (2013); Natalee Caple's *In Calamity's Wake* (2013); Nadia Bozak's *El Niño* (2014); Dayle Furlong's *Saltwater Cowboys* (2015); Alix Hawley's *All True Not a Lie in It* (2015) and *My Name Is a Knife* (2018); Clifford Jackman's *The Winter Family* (2015); Bill Gallaher's *High Rider* (2015); Jordan Abel's poems in *Un/Inhabited* (2014) and *Injun* (2016); Emily Ursuliak's poems in *Throwing the Diamond Hitch* (2017); Tyler Enfield's *Like Rum-Drunk Angels* (2020); Gary Barwin's *Nothing the Same, Everything Haunted: The Ballad of Motl the Cowboy* (2021); and Bob Armstrong's *Prodigies* (2021). In Canadian film and theatre, we also have *Six Reasons Why* (Campagna and Campagna, 2008), *Gunless* (Phillips, 2010), *Forsaken* (Cassar, 2015),

Maliglutit (Kunuk and Ungalaaq, 2016), and *Gabriel Dumont's Wild West Show* (Dalpé et al., 2017).[1]

Having briefly illustrated the post-humanist and ecocritical movements in Adamson's *The Outlander* and deWitt's *The Sisters Brothers* at the end of the previous chapter, on "Degeneration through Violence," I want now to return to these books for another glance from a slightly different perspective, alongside Kroetsch's *The Man from the Creeks*, Furlong's *Saltwater Cowboys* (which also coincidentally brings me "home" to the East, where I live and where this book started), and Ursuliak's *Throwing the Diamond Hitch* (which brings me home to the West, where I was raised). Coming full circle is a sign of Planet Earth that is not a mere cliché; it is meaningful but also urgent, because if people in cultural studies such as literature and film want to contribute to slowing the devastating increase in global temperature, we have a moral imperative to (1) think critically about texts that might positively or negatively influence our imagination of our environments, and (2) think creatively about how to shift away from fossil fuels, plastics, and other petroleum products (e.g., in a circular economy). I am in part answering Robin L. Murray and Joseph K. Heumann, in *Gunfight at the Eco-Corral* (2012), who call for "historicized views of environmental degradation or sustainable development" (6, 10) in Westerns and related scholarship. I am leaving many other issues of twenty-first-century Westerns in Canada for future research in order to "mine the Western" here, to interpret these texts mainly from the ecocritical perspective that I have been working on.

Some of the new Canadian Westerns above return to familiar scenes of boom towns and gold rushes to comment on today's extractive industries and their political contexts.[2] Not coincidentally, the Canadian boom comes at a time when the Western is popular again in the United States (Worden, "Neo-Liberalism" 225) and the extractive industries are again (or on again, off again) the "engine" of the Canadian economy. Oil came relatively late, however, to the economy of the Canadian West, with nine-

---

1 In Canadian television, the single-season CBC series *Strange Empire* (2014–15) imagined a nineteenth-century Canadian-American borderland in which most of the men had been killed and women survived in the roles typically assigned to men.

2 The most recent American example is C. Pam Zhang's 2020 novel *How Much of These Hills Is Gold*.

teenth-century mining towns built around coal,[3] as suggested by the title of Ralph Connor's *Black Rock*, the 1898 novel that might in fact be the first Canadian Western. Part of my own twenty-first-century interest in early industrial Westerns comes from Paul Thomas Anderson's film *There Will Be Blood* (2007)—with its brilliantly imaginative linking of blood, oil, and milkshakes—and this interest more generally arises in Canadian culture from the dramatic expansion of the oil sands in Alberta in the years of the Harper government (2006–15). Murray and Heumann describe such an expansion as a "rush for oil" (*Gunfight*, ch. 4) in relation to *There Will Be Blood*, describing the historical realities of conflict and competition that arise from "advancing" the industrial frontier. During the years of the Harper government, some Canadian writers implied a comparison between Alberta's oil sands and much earlier developments in capitalizing on the West and its natural environment as a natural resource—"natural resources" being a reframing of nature and Nature according to a neoliberal language of inescapably economic values, rationalized inequality, and uneven development. This span of years, 2006 to 2015, includes some of the novels that are my focus here: *The Outlander*, from 2007; *The Sisters Brothers*, from 2011; and *Saltwater Cowboys*, from 2015. Of these, only *Saltwater Cowboys* is set in contemporary times, specifically the 1980s, a decade coincident with Reaganomics and Thatcherism, which were economic and cultural phenomena that developed toward the Harper government in Canada just as they were later echoed by the Trump administration in the United States.

Unquestionably, Donald Trump posed and still poses problems for many otherwise cogent analyses of American culture, perhaps especially in relation to the Western. Personally and politically, Trump's indecency and valorization of extreme wealth are at odds with classic Western courtesy and frugality; however, his isolationism and contempt for non-Americans and supposedly un-American activity seems consistent with a mindset of the closing of the American frontier—the notion that there is nowhere else to go, hence the retrenchment, hoarding, and identity policing. Thus, the

---

3   As an example of turning from coal to oil, in the pulp fictional short story "Valley of Vengeance" (1941) in the Smokey Carmain series in *Dynamic Western* magazine, natural gas is exploited as a poison by villains to intimidate and kill small-time ranchers.

Cowboys for Trump organization promotes border protections, and more germane to this conclusion, they claim to "want to stand up and support rural America thru [sic] greater access to public lands, natural resources, and rural industries. We advocate against the attacks of environmental and radical endangered species acts. The backbone of America is found in the logging, ranching, mining, farming and oil and gas industries" ("Cowboys for Trump"). Such a claim is possibly a distortion of the values of the Western—a conflation of the values of the Western with some of the values of the West (even though, admittedly, I often suggested earlier in this book that the Western scales up from genre to region to nation and "Western world"). Murray and Heumann show that Westerns often prefer one type of business over another, usually local business over big business, but I have seen and read few Westerns that truly support these industries on any scale. Most Westerns rue natural degradation by industry even if they also seem to posit that it is an inevitability of modernity that can only be heroically resisted. One risk of the continued influence of Trump and his brand of Reaganomics on world markets is further deregulation and a resulting environmental cost. However much the authors of Canadian Westerns in this conclusion would support or oppose extractive economics, their novels all address the problem of industrial damage to Nature and to humans who are inextricable—unextractable—from Nature.

Reflecting the potted history of political contexts of the Western from the introduction to this book, *The Man from the Creeks, Saltwater Cowboys, The Outlander,* and *The Sisters Brothers* are revisionist Westerns or post-Westerns that are themselves "mining the Western" to comment on neoliberalism, concentrating on plots that feature coal and gold mining. Similar to Westerns such as HBO's *Deadwood* series (2004–6) in interrogating "how neo-liberal reasoning produces social effects" (Worden, "Neo-Liberalism" 231), each of these novels rejects the myth of the West as what Richard White calls "the He-Man Land" (qtd. in Quam-Wickham 135) of capable masculinity. They also impugn the related myth, which Northrop Frye conceptualized, of the "no-man's-land" (Frye, "Conclusion" 220) of the Canadian landscape. Frye's theory applies to the West in general because, if there are no men working that land, then it is open to the "He-Man," the man who can come and "dominate a feminine nature" (White, qtd. in Quam-Wickham 135), as we saw in the previous chapter with the Gaian mountain that eventually destroyed the historical and yet aptly named town of Frank. The plots of these novels culminate in disaster, disfigurement, and shame associated with men's failure to become rich through mining. Nancy Quam-Wickham writes that "[t]he West was a profoundly gendered region: a place where men conquered Mother Nature" (135), and she explains that "it was men who exploited these [natural] resources, men who laboured in the forests and mines, men who built a distinctive regional economy," men who were "masculine heroes" (136). When the heroine of Adamson's *The Outlander* arrives at the coal mine, she asks her "Indian guide," Henry, where all the people are. "People?" he answers. "The *men* are underground. In the mine" (147, original emphasis). Her assumption that there would be women in the West is crucial, partly because obviously there *are* and *were* women such as herself and Henry's wife, Helen, and partly because the myth of the West is that it was empty except for the white men who went there to make their fortunes. The phrase "make your fortune" suggests that riches are built and worked at. These gender roles involve managing "the distribution of power under capitalism" (Quam-Wickham 139) and coping with the risks of extraordinarily dangerous industrial work (140), but the "heroes" are not to be found in these novels. Their reversal of the rags-to-riches narrative (with the partial exception of *The Man from the Creeks*) is clearly skeptical of neoliberalism; less clear is how these novels align with the politically complex ecocriticism identified in the mining plots of American Westerns by Robin L. Murray and Joseph K. Heumann ("Mining" 58–9), who attended to Clint Eastwood's *Pale Rider* (1985), as seen in my chapter on postmodern Westerns. How much of the conservationism of early conservatism remains in today's neoliberalism?

This question fascinates me, because I find an earlier American Republicanism equally problematic and appealing—the Republicanism that Canadians got through popular culture once upon a time, that of Spencer Tracy, Jimmy Stewart, and even Clint Eastwood. Eastwood's *Pale Rider* is one of the films that compares different economic models without calling into question all of the Western and American (and Canadian) ideals of the landscape. This comparison is itself a questioning of neoliberalism—a capitalism that accepts no alternative—even if the family-run, community-oriented mining operation protected by Eastwood's Preacher is different from the boss-and-son's operation mainly by virtue of that very community orientation (and its scale, of course). Each of the novels in this conclusion presents a slightly different economy of scale, from the singular inventor and his secret experiments in *The Sisters Brothers* to the mass popularity of rushing and mining for resources in *The Man from the Creeks*, *The Outlander*, and *Saltwater Cowboys*. With the possible exception of the Ridgerunner's views of Nature in *The Outlander*, none of these novels comments directly on a conservationism related to early conservatism. Each of them proposes, however, that capitalism has costs—human costs and costs to Nature—that might be borne with the usual Western stoicism but that could be avoided by minimizing greed.

Allow me to sketch a now familiar picture: the open country of the Western, the untouched landscape, the promised land, a proving ground for the mobile and self-reliant masculinity embodied in the heroes of the genre. Now imagine graffiti on the idyllic picture I have just drawn to mind. By graffiti I mean the mark of the revisionist Western whose purpose is to uncover the often hidden grit of the clean-shaven heroes of movies such as *High Noon* (Zinnemann, 1952), *Shane* (Stevens, 1953), and of course *True Grit* (Hathaway, 1969; Coen and Coen, 2010). Usually the revisionist Western tries to correct the classic Western for historical reasons, often to call attention to historical atrocities perpetrated by colonists and soldiers in the West—or, quite the opposite, to enlarge the stature and status of the Western hero by suggesting that, historically, the West was much rougher, tougher, and more violent than the classic Western had ever shown. Although I am not a historian, I think that the revisionist Western has over-corrected toward atrocity, much like the mass media over-correct by revealing true crime to such an extent that we believe it's much more common than it is. For example, Eric Hobsbawm claims that "the total number of deaths caused by gun wounds in the major cattle towns in the 15-year period between 1870 and 1885 amounted only to 45" (qtd. in Polić, "Sisters" 132). Kevin Grant states that violence in Westerns "cried 'authenticity' at the same time as being blatantly absurd" (34–5). Life in the Old West would probably have been boredom and plenty of hard work. Much of this hard work would have been in the early industries of the West, such as mining. The novels I am studying here suggest that the risk to men in the Western, which we usually assume to be other men, is actually industrial.

"Pitched on His Head, and Pumped Full of Lead"

On the surface, Kroetsch's *The Man from the Creeks* could easily be read as a restoratively nostalgic novel about mining gold in the Klondike if it were not for the fact that all of its heroes, except the narrator, die by gunshot at the end. *The Man from the Creeks* borrows its title and conclusion from Robert Service's epic poem "The Shooting of Dan McGrew," from *Songs of a Sourdough* (1907), also published as *The Spell of the Yukon* in the United States in the same year. The poem is arguably one of the Northerns or Northwesterns that first turned attention to the North as a new frontier. My own father has entirely memorized the poem, with consequences for my own recollection:

> A bunch of the boys were whooping it up in the Malamute
>   Saloon;
> The kid that handles the music-box was hitting a jag-time
>   tune;
> Back of the bar, in a solo game, sat Dangerous Dan McGrew;
> And watching his luck was his light o' love, the lady that's
>   known as Lou. (45)

The poem implies a love triangle between Lou, McGrew, and the stranger who later appears at the bar one fateful night, but it also implies that money is at stake—not only here in the "solo game" but also in the pinching of pokes (from the poem's final line) that Kroetsch transforms into his narrator's obsession with money throughout *The Man from the Creeks*. Kroetsch refers to and quotes the poem most often in the final section, entitled "1899" (a centennial date that gives me licence to think of Kroetsch as writing a turn-of-the-millennium Western here), when the plot of the novel coincides with that of the poem:

> When out of the night, which was fifty below, and into the
>   din and the glare,
> There stumbled a miner fresh from the creeks, dog-dirty
>   and loaded for bear. (qtd. in Kroetsch 277)

The poem is mum on the identity of this stranger "from the creeks," but the responding novel is not. Kroetsch creates the character of Ben Redd, a cooper by trade, who falls in love with Lou on their journey with the other stampeders to the Klondike. Rather than stock up on the necessary goods that will equip him for the journey, Ben fills several barrels with whisky and labels them "salt herring" as, well, a red herring. He then trades the whisky as needed along the way, paying for things with whisky that others would pay for with gold. The whisky's function as currency (a fool's gold) and its placement in barrels lead me to think of it as symbolic oil, oil being a product that is often measured in barrels.[4] *The Man from the Creeks* might appear to romanticize the extractive industries of the West by expanding on Service's poem with the novel's own affections, and I was surprised by this possibility given Kroetsch's career of writing subversively postmodern novels such as *The Studhorse Man* (1969) and *Badlands* (1975); however, it can also be read as a parable about our culture's addiction to oil rather than alcohol, one that culminates in violent death.

Probably my interpretation of *The Man from the Creeks* as an ecocritical novel about the deadly consequences of oil will be questionable to some readers, especially in the West, where oil is almost sacred, and especially because the novel lacks most of the trappings of postmodernism that we might expect from Kroetsch, such as temporal play (e.g., in 1977's fragmented *Seed Catalogue*),[5] farcical mythopoeia (e.g., the uproarious sex in a tornado in *Badlands*),[6] and satirically neoclassical allusions (e.g., the allegorical Demeter in *The Studhorse Man*).[7] But Kroetsch's transformation of the poem's mysterious minor character—"the lady that's known as Lou"—into the novel's most important character also has potential as a

---

4   Granted, oil was a probably a commodity that was less brought into the West than extracted there.
5   The millennial coincidence of the late 1890s and the late 1990s, and the narrator's unlikely age of 114 (305), are possible exceptions.
6   Kroetsch might be referring to one of his own most famous scenes when Peek says of his lover Gussie Meadows that "[t]rying not to look at her was like trying not to look at a tornado" (156). Curiously, her status as his "true love" is implied by her lack of gold, despite the wealth she earned at her hardware store: "The one thing she wasn't wearing was gold" (125).
7   *The Man from the Creeks* is arguably historiographic metafiction, however, which becomes more obvious when Peek disputes Service: "the poet wasn't there. He, not the miner, was the stranger of whom he goes on to speak. Why are poets such bluffers and prevaricators, such dotards in the face of the bald truth? Why do poets fail, ever, to look at the facts themselves?" (278).

revision that is critical of gold rush capitalism and its afterlife as petroculture. Aritha van Herk explains that Lou

> refuses to take up Dangerous Dan McGrew's offer of a share in the Malamute, turning down a partnership because she knows that [he] does not treat his investors well. . . . [S]he challenges the economy of the gold rush story so that it climaxes in neither wealth nor romance, but in the peripheral happiness of an anonymous woman who uses the occasion to evade her own category and name herself into existence. ("Turning" 136)

I am not certain that Lou would have been happy to die in the arms of her lover, which is what happens at the climax, but she does indeed become known as Lou because she tells men to call her that (5), and she "challenges the economy" and the capitalist imperative of upward mobility by choosing wages over property. And the novel imitates this production of alternatives for interpretation too. The sort of bait and switch implied by the red herring of the "salt herring" is also implied elsewhere. The novel's epigraph from "The Shooting of Dan McGrew" is one such place, and it frames the entire book:

> Then I ducked my head, and the lights went out, and two guns blazed in the dark,
> And a woman screamed, and the lights went up, and two men lay stiff and stark.
> Pitched on his head, and pumped full of lead, was Dangerous Dan McGrew,
> While the man from the creeks lay clutched to the breast of the lady that's known as Lou. (Service 49)

If the teller of the tall tale admits to having "ducked [his] head" as the story played out "in the dark," then we can assume that the readers face a similar difficulty. Perhaps even Service was unconsciously thinking of oil when he chose the words "pitched" and "pumped" (pitch being a distillate of tar, and pumping being a method of extracting oil), though oil was much later to replace gold and coal as the primary commodity of the Canadian West. Kroetsch himself certainly allows for barrels to be full of curiosities: he invents a subplot in which Ben meets Dangerous Dan McGrew (before the latter became known as "Dangerous") when McGrew hides for his life in one of Ben's barrels. Peek naively remarks that "Lou had a way of believing that people harboured secrets" (133), and in fact they obviously do. Lou becomes a heuristic that exposes problems of the economy and its violent enablers. Such interpretations extend the ecocritical and feminist work in the previous chapter and chapters 3 and 4, which criticized the Muscular Christianity and devilish masculinity of early Westerns. God, devil, or firewater, men are part of the problem.

But these replacement operations—McGrew standing in for whisky or oil in the barrel—are evident in other similes, metaphors, and metonyms of *The Man from the Creeks*. After all, money as a currency is a replacement for commodities, especially gold, and commodities are partly interchangeable; we saw in the introduction to this book that a milkshake replaces oil in the famous scene from *There Will Be Blood*. Early in *The Man from the Creeks*, the narrator—Peek, Lou's son, a teenager of 14 going on 15 who is not in the original poem and tells the story retrospectively from the age of 114 (305)—compares "silver dollars" to "snowflakes" in "a dream of money" (54). In fact, Peek is obsessed with money, mainly because he is anxious about the inflating cost of goods on the way to the Klondike—inflation eventually meaning that their barrelled whisky was "worth its weight in gold" (173). While the stampeders have a penchant for literality, as when they give the name of Dead Horse Pass to the way past a gulch full of dead horses (68–9), they also choose metaphors that transform ordinary things into their own "dream[s]," such as the climb through the mountains that becomes "The Golden Stairs" (90). Relatedly, Peek imagines that Lou and Ben have "turned their small space on the floor in their room in The Nugget [the Ole Nugget Saloon] into a cozy den of sorts" (70)—gold becoming a metaphor of home. Gold is later associated with whisky quite directly: "They could taste the faraway promise of gold, along with the whiskey" (157). The metonym here can easily be extended to oil, partly because Kroetsch sometimes figures gold as a liquid, as if oil were liquid gold: "I guess she'd expected a golden colour, given that the Klondike was fed by more gold creeks that [sic] anyone had bothered to count" (182). So Ben's barrels of whisky in the 1890s are easy enough to interpret as oil for Kroetsch in the 1990s.

All the more fascinating, then, that Kroetsch has Peek involve himself in the final scene by shooting the last barrel of whisky when Ben appears "out of the night" and unexpectedly co-opts the piano for his haunting, threatening solo performance. Ben's otherworldly command of the ivories renders the patrons and staff at the saloon "squirmy and riveted and sweating and cold at the same time" (289). Taking one of McGrew's classic Western six-guns—a Colt .45 Peacemaker (293)—from a drawer behind the bar, Peek aims and then takes the shot: "I hit the keg that was sitting on the grand piano" (296). He claims to have wanted to "keep the peace" (296), but the shot catalyzes the violence: Ben shoots and kills McGrew, McGrew shoots and kills Ben. And yet Peek's purpose in the story is to correct Service's version: "What the poet and his poem do not tell you is that Ben and Lou had in fact been struck by one and the same bullet" (300). How ironic, this "2 for 1" (a standard capitalist promotion but with a double death that symbolizes worse-than-expected externalities). The fateful "bullet" is fired by the man whom Ben once found in a barrel, the man who embodies some of the addictive substances of the West: whisky, gold, and oil. Peek's shooting of the barrel can be interpreted as the boldest action that a shy young man could take; had he been bolder or meaner, perhaps he would have thought to shoot McGrew himself, rather than McGrew's representation in the barrel. (Nevertheless, his draining of the barrel again evokes *There Will Be Blood* and Daniel Day-Lewis's braggadocio about "drain[ing]" the oil out of his neighbour's land.) Peek also could have had in mind, as a teenager barely out of his boyhood, that the barrel was a sort of pinata—on the one hand, a festive container to surprise everyone with a treat and thereby please the thirsty crowd; on the other, a game to relieve the unbearable uncanniness of Ben's song. Surely relief from tension was part of his plan. The shooting of the symbolic Dangerous Dan McGrew was probably not intended as a macho performance of gender, a waste in the colloquial sense of "wasting somebody," but it might have been unconsciously meant in the sense of wasting a valuable commodity. In the latter sense, Peek was enacting the same challenge to the economy that van Herk identifies in his mother Lou's refusal to be a partner with McGrew in the ownership of the Malamute Saloon. If he was following a role model in a performance of gender, it was his mother. His intuition was to achieve "peace" by reorienting the crowd away from their evening commerce of gambling and drinking—in other words, away from activities that might degenerate into the degenerative violence that I considered in chapter 6, and away from the extractive industry of gold mining that supported those activities. Whether gold, whisky, symbolic oil, or all of them, the commodities of *The Man from the Creeks* lead to violence even against the best intentions of the storyteller.

Gold over Guns

Kroetsch's concern about men's greed in *The Man from the Creeks* reappears in deWitt's *The Sisters Brothers*, with similar ramifications for gender—and, again, violence between men seems to stand in for industrial-occupational hazards. In *The Sisters Brothers*, where we might expect a showdown and a killing, the climax of the plot involves a toxic spill, a failed get-rich-quick scheme, and a maiming. In brief, what happens in *The Sisters Brothers* is that two notorious assassins, Charlie and Eli Sisters—"the fabled Sisters brothers" (236)—are hired to kill a man and take a scientific formula from him in California during the 1851 gold rush. (I offered a similar plot summary in the previous chapter, with a different emphasis.) Instead, they cross their own employer to join the scientist and participate in his experiment. The scientist is really a hybrid of pre-modern alchemist and modern technician; his formula is "a *diviner*" (191), and he plans "to dam a river" (223) and then flood the resulting pond with the formula to make the gold glow, thereby enabling rapid and effective panning for gold. Unfortunately, the chemical is toxic and quickly burns the men wading in the river. The scientist's name is Hermann Kermit Warm, and his warmth becomes an ironic, symbolic fire (perhaps also a symbolic whisky or firewater again) as he and his assistant are "immolated" (286) by the toxic spill. Eli and Charlie were not fully submerged and were exposed only once, so they survive—but Charlie loses his hand and his ability to work as usual: as a gun for hire alongside his brother Eli.

That the hand is a phallic symbol linked metonymically with the handgun was manifested to me in *The Good, the Bad, and the Ugly* (Leone, 1966), when the close-up of the hand of Angel Eyes by his holster and groin reveals that one of his fingers is missing a fingernail—implying a vulnerability that proves true when Blondie kills him. In that film, Blondie gets the gold. In *The Sisters Brothers*, some Indigenous passersby steal the gold from the chemically injured white men (299–300).[8] The brothers cut their losses, choosing not to risk their lives by chasing the Indigenous people to recover the gold. In a related essay on the meaning of gold in HBO's *Deadwood*, Kyle Wiggins and David Holmberg argue that,

> [i]n the Western, autonomy is commonly signified by a proficiency with firearms, which in turn gets morphed into the phallic worship that [Jane] Tompkins and [David] Lusted identify. Death and reproduction conflate, and the key instrument in the Western's crude symbolic order is something wielded by individual agents. However, this ideology is supremely dehistoricized, even within the genre's own timeless logic, and effaces the economic or material circumstances that dictate who can access power in the frontier. (293)

Instead, Wiggins and Holmberg claim, access to gold, not guns, is the more historically accurate opportunity to act. Although *The Sisters Brothers* is self-conscious about myths of the West, through its themes of pseudo-science, superstition, and cinematic mythopoeia (e.g., in the novel's "intermission"), it is not historical fiction; it is not that kind of revisionism. But it does adjust focus from guns to gold, and to the economic subtext of trading with "Indians" and taking "Indian" land. The implication is that the Western's idea of masculinity is premised on taking the land in order to gain agency through mineral rights. Similarly, *Deadwood* "reconfigures phallic power, one of the dominant signifiers in the traditional Western, as a guarantor of financial independence rather than its axiomatic meaning of sexual longevity or destructive authority" (Wiggins and Holmberg 284). In *The Sisters Brothers*, "phallic power" fails sexually *and* financially,

---

8 For a transnational historicization of colonial resource extraction as a form of theft, and the re-appropriations that might ensue, see Fenn Elan Stewart's "Hiawatha / Hereafter: Re-appropriating Longfellow's Epic in Northern Ontario" (2013).

though Eli does succeed in murdering his boss,[9] what might be called an ironic gesture of "authority and independence from the boss" (Quam-Wickham 142). Then he and his emasculated brother Charlie give up their careers and go live with their mother in a matriarchal, fatherless home that codifies their symbolic relationship as sisters rather than brothers.[10]

The refusal to run down the "Indians" in *The Sisters Brothers* has a remarkable echo in Dayle Furlong's *Saltwater Cowboys*. The latter novel's plot has many of the Western's conventions with the exception of a nemesis and a singular act of violence at the climax. The initial tension arises from the familiar tale of westward expansion for settlement and resource extraction, but instead of a nineteenth-century setting we have a late twentieth-century family from Newfoundland—as far to the East as you can go in North America—who move west to Alberta to work in the gold mining industry when the mines in Newfoundland lay off workers. So, when Jack McCarthy and his family move west with their best friends, another family in mining, he is soon involved in stealing gold from their mine alongside other men described only as "cowboys." When they are eventually arrested, the novel implies that the police fail to recover all the stolen property, which Jack's wife, Angela, gives to its one Indigenous character (246-7), Olive St. James. Furlong gives her an individual identity, unlike deWitt's anonymous band of "Indians," but her identity does not appear to be an entirely original creation. Olive St. James is a Cree musician seemingly styled after the Cree musician Buffy Sainte-Marie's early costumes and performances, with a "feather at the back of her head, tucked into a buckskin headpiece, [that] was covered in red beads" (154)—a gesture to tradition but also potentially a stereotype of the "Indian" unable to modernize, a stereotype countered by Indigenous writers such as Jordan Abel and Thomas King, as seen in the second chapter of this book.

---

9   Notably, in Jacques Audiard's film adaptation of *The Sisters Brothers*, Eli does not have to kill his boss, who is already dead when they arrive to kill him. In the novel, Eli drowns the Commodore in his bathtub, echoing a theme of ironic cleanliness and purity from other Westerns (Gaines and Herzog 180). In the film, they find the Commodore in his open casket at the wake, and Eli punches the body, whether to be sure that he is dead or in anger at having missed his chance.

10   In contrast, in the Kiefer and Donald Sutherland vehicle *Forsaken* (Cassar, 2015), the gunslinger—John Henry Clayton (Kiefer Sutherland) returns to the home of his father, his mother having died years ago. In this case, however, it is the beginning of the story.

Here the plot implies the post-colonial guilt of wanting to give back, or surrender, to Indigenous people what was stolen by the whites, or it implies that the ultimate emasculation is to lose to the "Indians." In *The Sisters Brothers*, Eli and Charlie effectively give their gold to the Indigenous interlopers by deciding not to pursue them. Rearmed, they could have tracked and killed them, who had only one rifle and numbered "a half-dozen" (299): odds that the brothers had easily defeated in the past thanks to their expertise as hired killers. If indeed it's a gift, then, in *Saltwater Cowboys*, Angela's gift to Olive is a similar, dramatically insufficient restitution: an afterthought and a gift unlikely to remain in Indigenous hands. Because the gift is golden in these novels, it is a symbolic attempt to pay penance and maybe even to recover phallic power. In *Saltwater Cowboys*, Angela has to wait many years to recover this power in the form of her husband, whose jail term makes him a shadow of the man he was. His release and their reunion hardly make for an optimistic ending. Like Charlie, he has been symbolically castrated, and, like the Sisters, the whole family has been emasculated. If the family represents some sort of union, as do the gold bands of marriage, then by synecdochal extension these families might represent a reconfiguration of national, federal power. I should say that *Saltwater Cowboys* was published in 2015, the same year in which the Truth and Reconciliation Commission of Canada published its final report (and in which Justin Trudeau and the Liberals gained power at the expense of Stephen Harper's Conservatives). Widely discussed, the Truth and Reconciliation Commission was and is Canada's biggest anti-colonial project, one focused on addressing the harms caused by a policy of moving Indigenous children from their homes to residential schools to be forcibly assimilated into colonial culture. I wonder whether the novel was intended as a subtle commentary on the very late and questionably effective restitution offered by the Canadian government for its colonial project in the West. Regardless of the intention, *Saltwater Cowboys* implies a new Western mentality, one that *The Sisters Brothers* imagines as a sort of mature *Bildungsroman* about the development of sensitivity and conscience—the transformation, as Vanja Polić writes, of "a villain with a heart" ("Sisters" 139).

Giving the gold back to the Indigenous people happens more symbolically in Adamson's *The Outlander*, when the historic landslide at Frank,

Alberta, in 1903 effectively buries the "black gold," the coal, and keeps it in the earth to which Indigenous people have such an elemental connection in the Western. (The avalanche in *The Man from the Creeks* has less significance but conveys the dangers of the North and West just as well.) Prior to the landslide in her novel, Adamson describes an arrival at the mine as a movement "from wilderness to wasteland" (148). When the avalanche happens, Adamson describes it like so, in a quotation worth repeating from chapter 6: "This was no mere avalanche; the entire cap of the mountain was coming down toward the town of Frank.... For a full minute, the mountain seemed to billow, then slowly collapse, floating downward, lit palely from within. It luminesced from pure friction" (294). The coincidence of the historical town's masculine name, Frank, with the landslide's symbolic destruction of industrial masculinity must have seemed just right to Adamson. Murray and Heumann remind me that, in the Humphrey Bogart vehicle *The Treasure of the Sierra Madre* (Huston, 1947), one of the gold miners wants to decommission the mine because "[i]t's the least we can do to show all our gratitude for all the wealth she's given us." In response, the miner played by Bogart says, "You talk about that mountain as if she were a real woman" (qtd. in Murray and Heumann, "Mining" 62). In *The Outlander*, after the dust settles there is a "terrible new landscape" (294), "terrible" partly because it reminds us of awe, of the awful, of the sublime nature that industry exploits and attempts to control. This nature is feminized in *The Outlander* as it is in *The Treasure of the Sierra Madre*. As I concluded previously, the Frank Slide is, in effect, Mother Nature's revenge against industry and the feminized landscapes of so many other Westerns, including *The Treasure of the Sierra Madre* and *Pale Rider*.

Furthermore, the consequences of nation making are not as expected; the nation making is supposed to be engendered by the self-made manhood that ensures that the nation's citizens are both self-reliant and co-operative. In *The Sisters Brothers*, when Eli tells his brother, "This is the last job for me, Charlie" (216), he intends to live off his profits while ending his partnership with Charlie—which doesn't happen, because Charlie's emasculating injury reconfigures their brotherhood toward non-profit. In other words, their brotherhood is no longer in business; similarly, in *The Man from the Creeks*, Peek's family business—that of prospecting and mining for gold—is abruptly terminated in the saloon by the murder of his mother, Lou, and his symbolic father, Ben, by Dangerous Dan McGrew, leaving him at work as a tour guide who sells an oversimplified version of his own story to uncritical fans.[11] In *Saltwater Cowboys*, Jack and Peter could have remained friends if Peter had not insisted on continuing to steal more and more gold from their mine. In *The Outlander*, the collapse of the mountain above the town of Frank precedes the widow's fight with the twin brothers, which results in her being jailed for killing her husband. When she escapes, the twins are disheartened and cannot agree to pursue her again, because they associate her with "[t]he trackless eternity of trees" (379). Her integration into the "trees" is a symbolic power of connecting with nature that the men could not muster. Although we have seen this disappearance into the trees before, as a problematic mark of the Vanishing "Indian" in films such as *Dances with Wolves* (Costner, 1990), in these twenty-first-century Canadian Westerns, traditional masculinity is more likely to go the way of the dinosaurs. Such masculinity is the fossil fuel of culture: a force that has been powerful until now but must be minimized in favour of new masculinities oriented to the future.[12]

These themes of a futuristic masculinity associated with fuel appear with a twist in the 2008 film *Six Reasons Why*, directed by (and starring) Matthew and Jeff Campagna. *Six Reasons Why* is set in a near future in which oil wells have run dry and one of the most sought-after fuels is the battery. Thus, electric power has become the "gold." The men in the story (there are virtually no women) are variously driven by revenge, greed, and a desire to escape the desert, either back to their homes or across to the presumably still verdant (but never pictured) paradise in the West. In a revealing scene that establishes the environmental context, some of the men—who have monikers such as the Criminal, the Sherpa, the Nomad, and the Entrepreneur, no personal names—are thirsty from wandering in the Badlands. They are about to drink from a shallow river, which runs

---

11   This outcome in *The Man from the Creeks* is echoed in Gil Adamson's *Ridgerunner*, which ends in Banff National Park. According to Bob Armstrong, "[p]arks are, after all, rife with our frontier fantasies.... They are where we seek an authentic experience in an area that has been artificially delineated as a wild place—supposedly stripped of human influence, except for that of commerce. They even provide tourism entrepreneurs with dreams of gold—yet another chapter in the ongoing quest for El Dorado" ("Writing").

12   An example of such new masculinities is *Brokeback Mountain* (2005), Ang Lee's adaptation of the Annie Proulx short story.

below a bluff where an abandoned oil well stands, but their guide warns them, "That ain't no water. At least, not any more." The implication is that the river was poisoned by the oil well. Later, they are sitting around a campfire at night. Until this point, the setting might almost have been confused for the late nineteenth or early twentieth centuries, but they had already exchanged a battery instead of gold. One of them opens the newly re-energized "tune box" and plays a country song—"drinking music, not talking music"—while they all drink too much sarsaparilla (itself possibly a symbolic gold, in light of *The Man from the Creeks*). The silliness and defamiliarization of the scene reframe the film as a parody of the Western, even if the remainder of the film is often serious and indeed portentous.

Like Oil and Water: Horses, Trains, Car Culture

But the portentousness of *Six Reasons Why* is rationalized by the ecocritical theme of the end of oil and the transition to greener electric power. A subplot of the film involves the extension of an existing monorail out of the remaining communities, across the desolate Badlands and westward into an almost mythic utopian land. To me, the ambition of the plan can be discouraged as another colonial venture that will help the post-apocalyptic dystopia "travel" into the utopia by virtue of the train, whatever its power supply. The monorail seemingly wants to point—rather literally— to an Edenic gardenscape, but it also reproduces the imagery of colonial expansion that the train conventionally delivers in the Western, thereby calling into question the necessary alignment of ecocritical and anti-colonial ideals. In other words, *Six Reasons Why* is surprisingly complex and pragmatic: progressive ideals are not always compatible with each other.

Although there is no train in the 2010 Paul Gross vehicle *Gunless*, there is a North-West Mounted Police barracks that implies that the train has already reached the film's setting in late nineteenth-century Alberta. Instead of the train, the only sign of industry akin to a mining operation is Jane's (Sienna Guillory) windmill-powered well, which she is trying to complete to bring more water (not oil) to her farm. Having left her abusive husband in a backstory that echoes that of *The Outlander*, Jane is developing her self-reliance on the range, and the introduction of the Montana Kid shows him to be comparatively emasculated at every turn: hanging like a flaccid penis beneath his horse, handling a broken pistol, forced to wear Chinese clothing that he seems to think of as feminine or at least too decorative for his manliness, ultimately begging for a showdown so that he can die in a secretly assisted suicide. But his agreement to help Jane finish the well is one step toward his integration into Jane's society, including that of her neighbours and the local NWMP. The well is a subtle suggestion that water (or wind), not gold or oil or electric power, will be the treasured resource of the future. (Hydro power plays out somewhat differently in Eastwood's *Pale Rider*, where the miners pressurize water to blast through the landscape in their search for gold, and where Preacher uses dynamite to destroy the hydro-power operation. *Pale Rider* continues to associate heroism with explosive power.) For the Montana Kid—later rather funnily unmasked as "Sean"—masculinity has to be adjusted away from the power of gunpowder and other earlier industrial technologies and fuels. More natural sources of energy are required, and *Gunless* proposes that they will be less dangerous and less deadly than the fiery fuels on which we still rely. To grow up from the Kid to Sean, he has to avoid certain kinds of power.

The traditional masculinity that Sean learns to moderate and complicate is specifically the industrial and nation-making masculinity that underlies so much of the anxiety about modernity in the Western more generally. In today's context, when a climate crisis is happening and Canadian and American federal leaders show little concern—or at least commit distantly to so few practical transformations of our power systems—these texts are a political critique. To me, the critique questions a style of conservatism that produces illusions of empowerment while subordinating individual men and their brotherhoods to corporate and national interests that do serious harm—to their individuality, their bodily coherence, their relationships, and their environment. Envisioning an ecocritical interrelationship between humans and the landscape, and all other animals with whom we should begin a rapprochement—is the way forward.

Emily Ursuliak's narrative poem and surrogate memoir, *Throwing the Diamond Hitch* (2017), puts a hitch in this plan, if only to tie it up differently later. Whereas the extractive industries in the previously considered texts are often linked with men's violence, vehicles powered by fossil fuels in *Throwing the Diamond Hitch* initially seem to be an attractive symbol of empowerment—this time for women. (Indeed, it raises the question of how oil is gendered, if landscapes are usually gendered feminine and extraction masculine.) Ursuliak's book draws on her grandmother's diary of a 1951 road trip from Victoria, British Columbia, to Red Deer, Alberta, in a "beloved 1927 MG Roadster that Phyllis [her grandmother] and Anne saved up for and bought together for $150" (1). They name the car Jason and learn how not only to push "his" buttons but also how to "dissect / his iffy engine" (11). Their ability to "dissect" implies that they are scientists of the roadster, and, billed as a Western, the book suddenly reminds me of the scientist Doc Brown (Christopher Lloyd) in the *Back to the Future* trilogy (Zemeckis, 1985, 1989, 1990), which features the iconic gull-winged DMC DeLorean coupe that the Doc has modified into a time machine and which culminates in a Western. In some ways, Cormac McCarthy's *All the Pretty Horses* (1992) is a better American comparison, because of its often rose-coloured look back to the same era of a regrettably emerging car culture when the halcyon days of necessary horses were still with us. In Canada, Brad Smith's *The Return of Kid Cooper* (2018) is similar. Set in 1911, Smith's novel memorably describes the advent of the automobile as "hard on the ears" (69): as a "loud cacophony of bleating and barking, as if a mutant strain of sheep had invaded the range" (17).[13] But Ursuliak's manipulation of symbols of time is a little more like that of *Back to the Future*. At the end of *Back to the Future II* (1989), Doc is in the now flying DeLorean when it is struck by lightning—a power surge that sends him back in time to the Old West in 1885. In the third and final film, Doc is unable to time travel from the Old West because a 1980s sports car cannot be repaired with the existing nineteenth-century technologies. There is no gasoline, for example, to enable the car to reach the requisite eighty-eight miles per hour and catalyze the "flux capacitor" of the time machine. Doc and his sidekick Marty (Michael J. Fox) try to use a team of horses to pull the DeLorean, but they fall short of eighty-eight miles per hour. (Doc then decides to push it with a dynamite-powered train, obviously.) The horse-car dynamic in *Back to the Future III* strongly relates to *Throwing the Diamond Hitch*, because Phyl (as she is known) and Anne have planned

---

13   A subplot of *The Return of Kid Cooper* involves a crooked senator's role in an "interstate highway project" (97): roads are dirty.

not to drive the MG back to Victoria. Rather, they will go by horse, looking for alternatives to the car as in *Back to the Future III*.[14]

It is not explicit, but the MG and the horses in *Throwing the Diamond Hitch* enable a symbolic time travel: forward from a place marked by nineteenth-century empire (that of Queen Victoria) to a place marked as a future frontier—a once "open country" in the West. Red Deer also figures as a *past* frontier, because to Ursuliak and her readers Red Deer is a city with the heritage of ranchland and oil country all around it. Their travel also offers a freedom from men: weeks of independence and companionship on the road together. Whereas many formula Westerns, even by some women, "invoked values associated with the rural past, including a lost frontier, and looked backward in time to the female image that had pervaded the domestic novel for an earlier readership" (Yates 3), Ursuliak is recovering a more progressive "female image." Although her image of "the rural past" seems fairly conventional, the sense of a "lost frontier" is less troublesome, partly because her travelling women do a circuit from Victoria to Red Deer to Victoria, leaving nothing behind—unlike the abandoned train from Don McKay's *Deactivated West 100* (2005) that I mentioned in chapter 1, and unlike the destroyed train that Doc Brown leaves in the gully in *Back to the Future III*. They don't stay. Vancouver Island and Victoria were and are colonized, but symbolically Phyl and Anne decolonize the landscape by leaving; they arrange to have their car driven home as they ride, refusing a modern technology while also not treating it as obsolete garbage in the process of experimenting with an alternative. In this symbolic decolonization, they reflect Caprice's movement back home (but to the East—namely, Quebec) in George Bowering's 1987 novel with her name as title, as explained in chapter 5, which also presents the most detailed account of Svetlana Boym's typology of nostalgia in this book. By looping not only through space but also through time in her book, Ursuliak indulges in the restorative nostalgia of trying to piece together her grandmother's road trip, but she also uses nostalgia

---

14   The Western written by Sam Shepard in collaboration with director Wim Wenders, *Don't Come Knocking* (2005), is another example: partly a road movie (through Utah, Nevada, and Montana), but one in which the movement is prominently on horseback. The main character, an actor in Westerns, unhappily leaves the set of a film and goes by horse instead of car.

as an occasion for reflection on, and critique of, women in the car (and truck) culture of the West.

The most obvious reflection on gender and fuel appears early in *Throwing the Diamond Hitch*. In spite of their affection for Jason, the MG, Ursuliak's speaker admits that

> Jason's legacy [is]
> twenty years
> of breath
> by combustion. (9)

By naming "Jason" here, Ursuliak implies that "combustion" is men's "legacy" or responsibility, as with the historical Frank and the associated coal mine in Adamson's *The Outlander*—the mining and burning a cause of lung disease. Such an assignation would not be especially critical except that it is in the context of "breath." People and other animals need fresh air to breathe safely, and the West was once vaunted for its fresh air and other benefits of unpolluted nature.[15] In the context of combustion, of burning things, Ursuliak also calls a map "a route / scorched / against the land's will" (29).

Although there is not time or space to consider the implications of the potentially Gaian "will" here, Ursuliak elsewhere makes clear that we can respect the best interests of other animals and the land even if they cannot express these interests in human language. Ursuliak's speaker also admits that Jason and his ilk are at odds with their other favoured mode of transportation: the horse, an animal whose breath is true breath and far safer than that of a sports car. *Throwing the Diamond Hitch* has three notable horses: Monty, Peaches, and Pedro, the latter becoming one of the main characters. After seeing exactly the respect alluded to above, Anne says to Phyl,

> in the West
> a man

---

15 The West in North America in recent years has been beset by long droughts (especially in the American Southwest) and uncontrollable wildfires whose severity and frequency are associated with climate crisis, one result being air pollution.

gives a bigger house
to his horses
than himself. (19)

Later, when Anne and Phyl discover that Bun Bolton doesn't know how to tie the near-mythical diamond hitch, Bun gives them "dubious" (28) directions to another source, saving his better help for the horses:

His last act of kindness:
some added padding
to Pedro's cinch,
his best sock
cut up for the job. (28)

The alluring combination of sparingly resourceful pragmatism and simple generosity here seems to be an unheralded response to a statement from earlier in the book, in a poem about the celebrity sighting of one of the actors who played Clarence E. Mulford's turn-of-the-century cowboy, Hopalong Cassidy. Phyl claims that "Hopalong's too soft" (13). Rather, "a cowboy" is defined as being "lean...hard...well-weathered...preferably scarred. That's cowboy" (13). Only later does Bun's "act of kindness" toward Pedro demonstrate an arguably nobler cowboyishness, one strongly associated with the cowboy's sense of affection and care for the horse.

Thus, several scenes in *Throwing the Diamond Hitch* demonstrate a clash between cowboy culture and car culture (68, 86, 88, 99). In the poem "Barbed Wire," a speeding car almost hits Anne and Phyl on their horses: "The horses jolt" and as the dust settles we see that "[t]he car has cut / a black scar / through the grass" (68), almost hitting a barbed wire fence. The blackness of the "scar" evokes burning rubber, even though the surface is grass and not something harder; the point is that the environmental damage to the "grass" is linked so closely to the barbed wire, which is another form of "scar" on the prairie topography. (It is not that different from the symbolic "black scar" of the river in *Six Reasons Why* that is polluted or blackened by the oil well above.) In much of the West (and elsewhere), fences demarcate roads and thereby indicate directions, and Ursuliak comically reflects on this fact in "Getting Directions." With the horses causing a traffic jam of "[b]unched cars," the narrative perspective zooms in to the centre, where we find the horse Pedro staring at "the road sign / he reads / for directions" (86). As we saw in the previous chapter, Westerns often personalize horses, and so we later sympathize with the already lame Pedro when a blue Ford attempts to pass him and "his hindquarters / grind / against the bumper" (88). Luckily, the incident leaves only a "residue" (89) upon Pedro, and the car swerves into the ditch. (In *Back to the Future III*, the DeLorean is irreparably destroyed by a train: an Iron Horse—a related poetic justice for the automobile.) In one of the final poems, "The Home Stretch," Ursuliak writes that "[t]he horses endure / trolley buses / and traffic lights" (99), but I like to think that they at least "endure" and could perhaps thrive again.

For Ursuliak, the horse is obviously more integral to the fabric of the Western than the car, but both resonate for the West today. I have already mentioned that Phyl and Anne's route to Alberta is reversed by the return trip on horseback. Their circular route is almost metafictional, because Ursuliak frames the book with self-conscious metaphors of narrative— that is, the "strand[s] of story" (3)—hence the "fabric" metaphor. She states in the end: "Every hitch thrown / makes a fleeting story / from a line of rope" (102). The rope here is crucial, and so is the adjective "fleeting." The title of *Throwing the Diamond Hitch* refers to "the packer's knot" (25) used to secure a load to a moving horse. The Platonic form of the knot is one that will not come undone until the moment when it needs to be untied. In its resemblance to the symbol of infinity (the figure eight on its side, or even an hourglass), the diamond hitch is also a symbol of time, and time is tied to rare wisdom:

> The search for this knowledge
> resulted in a string of names,
>
> . . .
>
> and so far none of them
> able to demonstrate the knot. (25)

Eventually, Phyl and Anne find a teacher and learn the knot, and the knot and its lesson are a microcosm of the larger story. Having learned the knot, and thereby having completed the journey home on horseback, the speaker of *Throwing the Diamond Hitch* and the author of the book assert the centrality of horses in the genre. They have completed a circle, a return to a life less dependent on fossil-fuelled vehicles—a life of sustained, sustainable animal companionship.

When Phyl and Anne sell their horses in the epilogue, we learn that their shared experience was a "last hurrah" (103) before their respective marriages. As with the nineteenth-century Westerns by women that Norris Yates studies in *Gender and Genre* (1995), *Throwing the Diamond Hitch* "mute[s] the messages about competence and self-reliance conveyed through active heroines . . . by propelling these heroines into domesticity at closure" (5). One difference is that Ursuliak's book is partly her grandmother's memoir, so it simply conveys a truth about a time and place where women had fewer options: the 1950s were remarkably like the late 1800s. Another difference is that it does not quite have a happy ending for Phyl and Anne. Symbolically, their husbands replace their horses when they tie the knot of marriage, and the sense of loss (compounded when we read of Phyl's funeral and Anne's eulogy many years later) is of the close relationship between women and animals who are not men, despite masculine names such as Pedro. The sense of loss is that the women of the West lost something as we allowed car culture to overcome Western traditions of ranching, riding, and even storytelling. In response, the "search" is a Proustian and deliberate search for (a) lost time, a trip through time to one's youth—but not our own youth. It is someone else's youth, and it is filtered through "a fleeting story" "in a string" that could well describe the nostalgic transference or vicariousness of the horse opera itself.

The Lasso

We will probably not see this way back from car culture and its associated freedom of mobility in the West or elsewhere. As I circle a rope around this book—more a performative gesture than a real attempt to tie something up—I reflect on Svetlana Boym's sense of critical thinking about the emotional appeal of the genre of the Western. It remains a nostalgic genre that typically hopes to restore or regenerate unprogressive notions of human relationships based on gender, nation, and other constructs, while maintaining emotional distance from almost every other animal except the horse. When we pair Boym's work with Richard Slotkin's career-long theorization of regeneration through violence, we readers of Westerns can see that the genre's emotional appeal is not only that of longing but also that of cathartic violence and, as an ironic result (because of the longing), closure. We want the story to end but not end. We crave the moral clarity of an ending, but we also yearn to keep a simpler life alive. The ambivalence can be especially bitter if we realize that we will not get what we want, because the past is not easy to retrieve in reality, and a neat resolution to our current problems is unlikely.

Progress is difficult because there is no consensus about what it would look like or how we would achieve it. But one of the insights of this study, and one of the areas of potential ethical growth in the Western, is in the fusion of horse and human in the centaur-like figures of the horsemen and horsewomen that appeared in the previous chapter, chapter 6, especially through the works of Guy Vanderhaeghe and Gil Adamson. I wanted the horseman/woman to call into question ideas of progress and regression related to the role of violence in human society, primarily to dispute (unfortunately not refute) the view that violence is still a necessary and evolutionary step. Slotkin's explanation of regeneration through violence exposes a myth that revisionist Westerns in the United States and Canada have questioned too, partly by imagining the social, economic, and environmental externalities or unacknowledged costs of this violence. For Canadian Westerns at least, the myth of regeneration through violence is revised through figures of degeneration rather than regeneration: violence unmakes men and their power, rather than remaking them and their society. Patrick deWitt's brothers, the aptly named Sisters, lose or give up their power (a little of both) and an associated style of violent masculinity. Their return home to their mother might well be a sign of a better society to come, but we do not see it in deWitt's book. In partial contrast, Emily Ursuliak's Anne and Phyl return to car culture and the heteronormative nuclear family, after their good life together on the road, and the ending is a calculated disappointment. For both writers, the real story is not in how it ends but what led to the end; however, deWitt shows us what we need to leave behind (a greedy world in which the lives of humans and horses are undervalued and prevented from going on together), while Ursuliak shows us what we needed to keep (a friendlier world in which the lives of humans and horses can come together without judgment). As this book has demonstrated, the revisionism of the Western is informed partly by post-humanism and concepts of the post-human, which can also be found outside the Western in science fiction and other genres, concepts that shift the focus from humans to other animals and that question very seriously whether the reason and openness of humanism have much hope in the future. And as the Campagna brothers imply, we must also wonder whether environmentalism will be effective against the short-sighted visions of growth and commercial or colonial expansion that are sometimes believed to be unlimited.

Strongly associated with these post-human ideas is the ghostmodern trend in most of the postmodern Canadian Westerns that I considered in chapter 5, such as those by bpNichol, Michael Ondaatje, and Paulette Jiles. The ghostmodernism of these books situates the postmodernism of postmodern Westerns or post-Westerns as a way of thinking that is not merely an intellectual revision of an anti-intellectual genre; it is also an emotionally intelligent literalization of the feeling of being haunted by the past, a feeling similar to the reflective nostalgia that Boym explains. It is not as hopeful as bringing something back to life. Instead, it evokes fear and the uncanny. If you recall the signs of a Western ghost town in St. John's, Newfoundland, that I described in the opening paragraphs of this book, you might also be interested in a crooked headstone in the Belvedere Roman Catholic Cemetery in St. John's, where you can find the final resting place of William J. Carroll, sheriff of Newfoundland (1861–1940), and his wife, Mary Ryan Carroll (1867–1950). The epitaph reads "*Gloria in excelsis Deo.*" Although Newfoundland still has an Office of the High Sheriff for administrative purposes in the court system—and not because of any influence of a genre from the United States—I cannot help but see the headstone obliquely, through the lens of the Western, resulting in the displacement of the Western to the East and to the very years around the island's entrance into Confederation in 1949. Similarly, in Canadian literature, the weirdness of ghostmodernism helps us to reflect on the temporal distortion of the Western, its own haunting by the past and, just maybe, the prospects of certain futures—personal, familial, or socio-economic—as imagined more recently by Ursuliak in *Throwing the Diamond Hitch.* And in the same way that it helps to reverse timelines, it helps in George

Bowering's *Caprice* to reverse narratives of westering, back to the East, creating the thought experiment of what decolonization might theoretically or symbolically entail—say, honest valedictions, actual leave-takings from colonized lands and back to other homelands elsewhere.

But, in practice, postmodern Westerns in Canada have been more transnational than decolonial, as suggested by the complex positions of border-crossing authors such as Ondaatje and Jiles (and of course Kroetsch, and later examples such as Thomas King and Patrick deWitt). The transnational dimension of Canadian postmodernism aligns with one of the central tenets of this book, that the Western has had well over a century of being not only American. It is also not tantalizingly, totalizingly Canadian. (This book has not dwelled on the regional differences of Canadian Westerns, notwithstanding the significant space in chapter 1 that was devoted to regionalism in theory.) Bowering and Jiles in British Columbia, and Dayle Furlong from Newfoundland—and many in between—have written Westerns and post-Westerns with different regional preoccupations and movements toward or away from colonial centres. The scalar dimension of modernity (*pace* Arjun Appadurai) spatializes the Western by telescoping it from nation to region and back again, ultimately gaining the momentum to swing a pendulum across oceans. Sometimes it grows a region into a global mould; sometimes the mould breaks as the region grows too big. We are basically seeing an interplay—and a proposed, provocative interchangeability—of globe/nation/region, one that illustrates contemporary anxieties about identity, belonging, race, and tribe.

In another example of resisting conventional wisdom in this book, the theoretical discovery of chapter 4, on the 1940s pulps, was that postmodern Canadian literature might have originated earlier than we thought, partly because we define its period so often in terms of canonical literature that represents the so-called high culture. But it makes sense to have it begin with the archival rediscovery of the pulp fiction of Luke Price in *Dynamic Western*, with the antinomy of popular and literary cultures, as a transition from what in retrospect seem to be the pretentiously didactic novels of Ralph Connor and H. A. Cody. Connor and Cody, as novelists of the early Canadian Westerns (or, relatedly, Northerns or Northwesterns), were working through the regionalism of the Western and expanding it into national visions of white civility on a Western model. They were aspirationally literary, but they are barely canonical even by today's more open standards. In chapter 3, I suggested that their status is in part a negotiation between genres (i.e., as crossover genres) that connote different values depending on whether adults or children are the primary readership. But in fact all genre has a crossover dimension, with the Venn diagram being a better model than the hierarchy. Crossover itself also enables us to conceptualize the border-crossing, transnational movements of the Western that are so central to this book. Nevertheless, hierarchy and categorical separation had ramifications on early Canadian Westerns; I read Connor's and Cody's novels for their Muscular Christianity but also for the devious pressures of the formulaic distillation of the Western genre—a deviousness perfectly embodied by Price's later hero, Smokey Carmain—on the upstanding moralism of their adventure stories.

But for my own attempt at ethical criticism, I began reading the literature of this book, in chapter 2, with Indigenous perspectives on the Western genre. Many studies of Indigeneity by and for Indigenous peoples exist, but there are very few on Indigenous views of the Western, and it makes sense that Indigenous writers and allies would echo and mock popular culture as a contested site of resistance to cultural imperialism and the colonial doctrine of the Western. In looking for an Indigenous alternative to the Western's John Wayne, I considered Thomas King himself as an author with some of the requisite star power; I also looked back to Gabriel Dumont as a "Canadian" alternative to Wayne as a hero and performer; but, ultimately, I turned to Zacharias Kunuk and Natar Ungalaaq's approximate remake and revision of John Ford's *The Searchers* (1956), *Maliglutit* (2016), where a woman finally saves the man who was trying to save the women, and where land is not obviously divided along racial, cultural, or national lines.

Coincidentally, I see genre itself as a site of non-obvious demarcations, of relationality more than category. I would never insist that the relationship between Northwesterns and Westerns means that they are identical, but I do insist that they be read for continuity. Hybridity and crossover are the terms for the relationality of genre that I tried to explain throughout this book, especially in chapters 1 and 3. If categories can be neat and tidy, hybridity and crossover can mess them up. The continuity between classic Westerns and revisionist Westerns is in their shared settings and other icons or conventions, but it is also in the gradual change of how much generic and moral messiness readers and viewers could tolerate. I have suggested throughout this book that the Western has tended to become less conservative and more liberal over time, especially in the genre's development in Canada, and such a change is epistemological. The makers of Westerns and their audiences have learned to tolerate and even enjoy uncertainty (of who the bad guy is, or what genre this really is). The postmodern condition has required us to accept uncertainties and multiplicities (and, yes, it tempts us or frustrates us with fusions and illusions of sameness). As a result, we cannot "think in silos" anymore, as the saying goes in academia. Interdisciplinarity, connection—the fragments of modernity are later reframed as pieces of a puzzle.

The conclusion of this book, with its emphasis on the relationality of living things (and even inanimate things) on Planet Earth, is a lesson from settler-colonial writers such as deWitt and Adamson—especially those with an affinity for companion species such as the horse, and especially those with a critical eye on late capitalism or perhaps more accurately late industrialism. This lesson precedes them in Indigenous traditions that are continued today by writers and directors such as King, Kunuk, and Garry Gottfriedson—and even from substantially post-humanistic writers such as Jordan Abel, who sees through the nostalgic guises of the Western to a deconstructed future in which decolonial dreams are conjured from a post-Western world. When I think of where we as a species are going, I think that people like me have much to learn from Indigenous traditions of knowing while not subjugating the land—or other species, given that it is increasingly practical for humans to survive in the Western world without killing them for food. Related non-Indigenous epistemologies with similar ethics are equally crucial. In spite of the isolationist, anti-globalist, adversarial dynamics that are emerging around the world, we must realize that many of our problems are global in nature and cannot be solved without extensive co-operation between countries and the existing blocs.

Why have there recently been so many new Westerns and Western-like books in Canada, as in the list at the beginning of this conclusion? To ignore this question is to risk marginalizing creative interventions by Indigenous writers in the "cowboys and Indians" narrative. It risks decontextualizing the historical popularity of genres that can reveal ideological trends: the myths that we want to believe and reify. It might also perpetuate a false, often elitist, dichotomy between popular and literary cultures. The early twenty-first-century resurgence of the Western in Canada has major political implications, partly because the Western is so strongly associated with the United States, and partly because the Canadian appropriation of the genre entails a symbolic realignment of the geographic axis of western expansion in North America. One of the more interesting theories, as I explained in chapters 1 and 3, is that Canadian writers turn the idea of West northward so that Canada becomes the new frontier (or at least Western and Northern Canada do, sometimes for inhabitants of both Canada and the United States). Understanding this realignment will help us to understand colonization in general, whether territorial or cultural, from 1492 to the present; colonization is a process driven in part by an idea of the frontier that the Western illustrates more than any other genre besides science fiction, which derives its idea of a "final frontier" (i.e., outer space as described in examples from *Star Trek*) from the Western. And we must understand that regional concerns, which can echo Indigenous concerns, are becoming increasingly relevant as resistance to the homogenizing effects of globalization. Realignments of cardinal directions are, on the one hand, a destabilization resulting from globalization; on the other, they can be reassertions of regionalism and its potential to expand into larger conceptions of nation and world, a manifestation of the telescoping effects of modernity—and the Western—that can help as a cypher for where we are today.

WORKS REPRODUCED IN PART

Every effort has been made to seek permission to reproduce portions of copyrighted text. These include:

From "Considering the Death of John Wayne" from *The Journal of Popular Culture,* vol. 7, no. 3, 1979, p. 265, by Louis Phillips. Copyright (c) 1979 by Louis Phillips. Used by permission of Louis Phillips.

From *Deactivated West 100* by Don McKay. Copyright (c) 2005 by Don McKay. Used by permission of Gaspereau Press.

From "Dear John Wayne" from *Original Fire* by Louise Erdrich. Copyright (c) 2003 by Louise Erdrich. Used by permission of HarperCollins Publishers.

From *The Louis Riel Organ and Piano Company* by Frank Davey. Copyright (c) 1985 by Frank Davey. Used by permission of Turnstone Press.

From *Throwing the Diamond Hitch* by Emily Ursuliak. Copyright (c) 2017 by Emily Ursuliak. Used by permission of University of Calgary Press.

From *The True Eventual Story of Billy the Kid* by bpNichol. Copyright (c) 1970 by bpNichol. Used by permission of Eleanor Nichol for the estate of bpNichol.

From *Whiskey Bullets: Cowboy and Indian Heritage Poems* by Garry Gottfriedson. Copyright (c) 2006 by Garry Gottfriedson. Used by permission of Ronsdale Press.

WORKS CONSULTED

Abel, Jordan. *Injun*. Talonbooks, 2016.

———. "Jordan Abel and Renée Saklikar in Conversation: Accumulation as a Political Act." Interview with Daniel Zomparelli. *Lemon Hound*, 7 Mar. 2014, https://lemonhound.com/2014/03/07/accumulation-as-a-political-act-in-conversation-with-jordan-abel-and-renee-saklikar/.

———. "Seven Questions for Jordan Abel." Interview with rob mclennan. *Touch the Donkey*, Blogspot, 24 Sept. 2015, http://touchthedonkey.blogspot.ca/2015/09/ttd-supplement-36-seven-questions-for.html.

———. *Un/inhabited*. Project Space/Talonbooks, 2014.

Acree, William G. Jr. "A Mythical Gaucho and the Making of Modern Popular Culture." Introduction to *The Gaucho Juan Moreira: True Crime in Nineteenth-Century Argentina*, by Eduardo Guttiérrez, Hackett, 2014, pp. ix–xxxiv.

Adamson, Gil. *The Outlander*. Anansi, 2007.

———. "Re: [the title of *The Outlander*.]" Email interview. Conducted by Joel Deshaye, 17 Aug. 2020.

———. *Ridgerunner*. Anansi, 2020.

Alexie, Sherman. *The Lone Ranger and Tonto Fistfight in Heaven*. Grove Atlantic Press, 2013.

Allan, Luke. *Blue Pete, Half Breed: A Story of the Cowboy West*. McClelland and Stewart, 1921.

Allen, Chadwick. *Trans-Indigenous: Methodologies for Global Native Literary Studies*. U of Minnesota P, 2012.

Altman, Rick. *Film/Genre*. British Film Institute, 1999.

———. "A Semantic/Syntactic Approach to Film Genre." *Cinema Journal*, vol. 23, no. 3, 1984, pp. 6–18.

Altman, Robert. *McCabe & Mrs. Miller*. Perf. Warren Beatty and Julie Christie. Warner Bros., 1971.

Anderson, Benedict. *Imagined Communities: Reflections on the Origin and Spread of Nationalism*. Verso, 1983.

Anderson, Paul Thomas. *There Will Be Blood*. Perf. Daniel Day-Lewis. Paramount, 2007.

Andrews, Jennifer, and Priscilla L. Walton. "Rethinking Canadian and American Nationality: Indigeneity and the 49th Parallel in Thomas King." *American Literary History*, vol. 18, no. 3, 2006, pp. 600–17.

Appadurai, Arjun. *Modernity at Large: Cultural Dimensions of Globalization*. Oxford UP, 1997.

Armstrong, Bob. "Writing into the Sunset: In the Saddle with Canadian Novelists." *Literary Review of Canada*, June 2021, https://reviewcanada.ca/magazine/2021/06/writing-into-the-sunset/.

Arnold, Gary. "Unlikely 'Outland.'" *The Washington Post*, 23 May 1981, https://www.washingtonpost.com/archive/lifestyle/1981/05/23/unlikely-outland/c8996007-0975-47c2-b61e-80f63a7a502c/.

Atwood, Margaret. "Backdrop Addresses Cowboy." 1968. *Selected Poems: 1965–1975*. Houghton, 1976.

———. *Survival: A Thematic Guide to Canadian Literature*. Anansi, 1972.

Audiard, Jacques. *The Sisters Brothers*. Annapurna Pictures, 2018.

Babiak, Peter. "Icons and Subversion in the Westerns of Clint Eastwood." *CineAction*, vol. 59, 2002, pp. 62–8.

Baker, Richard G. " 'Nothing But Hill and Hollow': The Canadian Border as American Frontier in the Hollywood Northern." *Comparative American Studies*, vol. 13, nos. 1–2, 2015, pp. 107–21.

"Barack Obama and Joe Biden Pass Democratic Baton to Hillary Clinton and Tim Kaine." *CBC News*, 27 July 2016, http://www.cbc.ca/news/world/democratic-convention-day-3-1.3696782.

Barnett, LeRoy. "Ghastly Harvest: Montana's Trade in Buffalo Bones." *Montana: The Magazine of Western History*, vol. 25, no. 3, 1975, pp. 2–3.

Barnholden, Michael. "Introduction." *Gabriel Dumont Speaks*, translated by Michael Barnholden. Talonbooks, 2009, pp. 11–36.

Barrera, Jorge. "Author Joseph Boyden's Shape-Shifting Indigenous Identity." *APTN National News*, 23 Dec. 2016, http://aptnnews.ca/2016/12/23/author-joseph-boydens-shape-shifting-indigenous-identity/.

Bartlett, Brian. *Ringing Here & There: A Nature Calendar*. Fitzhenry and Whiteside, 2014.

Barwin, Gary. *Nothing the Same, Everything Haunted: The Ballad of Motl the Cowboy*. Penguin, 2021.

Bazin, André. "The Western, or the American Film *Par Excellence*" and "The Evolution of the Western." 1956. *What Is Cinema?*, translated and edited by Hugh Gray. U of California P, 1971, pp. 140–57.

Beaty, Bart. "High Treason: Canadian Nationalism and the Regulation of American Crime Comic Books." *Essays on Canadian Writing*, no. 62, 1997, pp. 85–107.

Bechtel, Greg. "The Word for World Is Story: Syncretic Fantasy as Healing Ritual in Thomas King's *Green Grass, Running Water*." *Journal of the Fantastic in the Arts*, vol. 19, no. 2, 2008, pp. 204–22.

Beebee, Thomas O. *The Ideology of Genre: A Comparative Study of Generic Instability*. Pennsylvania State UP, 1994.

Bélanger, Damien-Claude. "L'antiaméricanisme et l'antimodernisme dans le discours de la droite intellectuelle du Canada, 1891–1945." *Revue d'histoire de l'Amérique française*, vol. 61, nos. 3–4, 2008, pp. 501–30.

Bellah, James Warner. "Mission with No Record." *The Saturday Evening Post*, 27 Sept. 1947, pp. 31–1, 138–44.

Bentley, D. M. R. "The Mower and the Boneless Acrobat: Notes on the Stances of Baseland and Hinterland in Canadian Poetry." *Studies in Canadian Literature*, vol. 8, no. 1, 1983, pp. 5–48.

———. "Rummagings, 5: Northrop Frye's 'Garrison Mentality.'" *Canadian Poetry*, no. 58, 2006, pp. 5–9.

Berlin, Isaiah. "Two Concepts of Liberty." 1958. *Four Essays on Liberty*. Oxford UP, 1969, p. 118–72.

Berton, Pierre. *Hollywood's Canada: The Americanization of Our National Image*. McClelland and Stewart, 1975.

———. *The Last Spike: The Great Railway, 1881–1885*. McClelland and Stewart, 1971.

Betz, Virginia Marie. "On the History of the Mexican Charro: A Review Essay." *Journal of the Southwest*, vol. 37, no. 3, 1995, pp. 510–17.

Black, Conrad. *Rise to Greatness: The History of Canada from the Vikings to the Present*. McClelland and Stewart, 2014.

Blaise, Clark. *Time Lord: Sir Sandford Fleming and the Creation of Standard Time*. Vintage, 2000.

Bledstein, Burton J. "Frederick Jackson Turner: A Note on the Intellectual and the Professional." *The Wisconsin Magazine of History*, vol. 54, no. 1, 1970, pp. 50–5.

Blondin, Jacques, Melissa Maya Falkenberg, and Marie Hélène Lebeau-Tascherea. *Québec Western: Ville après Ville*. Éditions les Malins, 2013.

Bloom, Clive. *Cult Fiction: Popular Fiction and Pulp Theory*. St. Martin's, 1996.

Boddy, William. "'Sixty Million Viewers Can't Be Wrong': The Rise and Fall of the Television Western." *Back in the Saddle Again: New Essays on the Western*, edited by Edward Buscombe and Roberta E. Pearson, BFI, 1998, pp. 119–40.

Bold, Christine. "Did Indians Read Dime Novels? Re-Indigenising the Western at the Turn of the Twentieth Century." *New Directions in Popular Fiction: Genre, Distribution, Reproduction*, edited by Ken Gelder, Palgrave, 2016, pp. 135–56.

———. *The Frontier Club: Popular Westerns and Cultural Power, 1880–1924*. Oxford UP, 2013.

———. "The Voice of the Fiction Factory in Dime and Pulp Westerns." *Journal of American Studies*, vol. 17, no. 1, 1983, pp. 29–46.

Bowering, George. *Caprice*. Viking, 1987.

Boyd, Shelley. *Garden Plots: Canadian Women Writers and Their Literary Gardens*. McGill-Queen's UP, 2013.

Boym, Svetlana. *The Future of Nostalgia*. Basic Books, 2001.

Bozak, Nadia. *El Niño*. Anansi, 2014.

Braidotti, Rosi. *The Posthuman*. Polity, 2013.

Braz, Albert. *The False Traitor: Louis Riel in Canadian Culture*. U of Toronto P, 2017.

Brégent-Heald, Dominique. *Borderland Films: American Cinema, Mexico and Canada during the Progressive Era*. U of Nebraska P, 2015.

———. "James Oliver Curwood: Advertising Canada across the Border." *Journal of Canadian Studies*, vol. 52, no. 3, 2018, pp. 691–717.

Breitbach, Julia. "Rewriting Genre Fiction: The *DreadfulWater* Mysteries." *Thomas King: Works and Impact*, edited by Eva Gruber, Camden House, 2012, pp. 84–97.

Brim, Connie. Review of *Whiskey Bullets: Cowboy and Indian Heritage Poems*, by Garry Gottfriedson. *BC Studies*, no. 154, 2007, https://bcstudies.arts.ubc.ca/book_film_review/whiskey-bullets-cowboy-and-indian-heritage-poems/#content.

Broad, Graham. *A Small Price to Pay: Consumer Culture on the Canadian Home Front, 1939–1945*. U of British Columbia P, 2013.

Brode, Douglas. *Dream West: Politics and Religion in Cowboy Movies*. Texas UP, 2013.

Brown, Kirby. "Citizenship, Land, and Law: Constitutional Criticism and John Milton Oskison's *Black Jack Davy*." *Studies in American Indian Literatures*, vol. 23, no. 4, 2011, pp. 77–115.

Brown, Wendy. "American Nightmare: Neoliberalism, Neoconservatism, and De-democratization." *Political Theory*, vol. 34, no. 6, 2006, pp. 690–714.

"Buffalo Bones Being Loaded onto a CPR Freight Train in Moose Jaw, Saskatchewan, c. 1885." NA-4967-10. Glenbow Museum, Calgary, 5 Oct. 2014.

Burns, John. Review of *The Last Crossing*, by Guy Vanderhaeghe. *Quill & Quire*, n.d., https://quillandquire.com/review/the-last-crossing/. Accessed 13 Oct. 2021.

Buscombe, Edward. *Stagecoach*. BFI, 1992.

Butler, Judith. *Gender Trouble*. Routledge, 1990.

Butts, Edward. "North-West Mounted Police." *The Canadian Encyclopedia*, 6 Dec. 2016, https://www.thecanadianencyclopedia.ca/en/article/north-west-mounted-police.

Calder, Alison. "The Importance of Place: Or, Why We're Not Post-Prairie." *Place and Replace: Essays on Western Canada*, edited by Esyllt W. Jones, Adele Perry, and Leah Morton, U of Manitoba P, 2013, pp. 169–78.

———. "Reassessing Prairie Realism." *A Sense of Place: Re-evaluating Regionalism in Canadian and American Writing*, edited by Christian Riegel and Herb Wyile, U of Alberta P, 1998, pp. 51–60.

———. "Unsettling the West: Nation and Genre in Guy Vanderhaeghe's *The Englishman's Boy*." *Studies in Canadian Literature*, vol. 25, no. 2, 2000, pp. 96–107.

———. "Why Shoot the Gopher? Reading the Politics of a Prairie Icon." *West of Eden: Essays on Canadian Prairie Literature*, edited by Sue Sorensen, CMU, 2008, pp. 243–59.

Calder, Alison, and Robert Wardhaugh. *History, Literature, and the Writing of the Canadian Prairies*. U of Manitoba P, 2005.

Campagna, Jeff, and Matthew Campagna. *Six Reasons Why*. Perf. Daniel Wooster, Christopher Harrison, and Mads Koudal. THINKFilm, 2008.

Campbell, Collin. "Ugly Boys in the Canadian Western: Landscapes of Desire and Indigeneity in William Lacey Amy's *Blue Pete, Half-Breed*." ACCUTE Conference, 29 May 2018, U of Regina.

Campbell, Maria and Nicola Campbell. "Responding to Truth and Reconciliation through Indigenous Literatures: A Conversation between Maria Campbell and Nicola Campbell." Indigenous Literary Studies Association conference, 4 June 2019, University of British Columbia, Vancouver.

Campbell, Neil. *Post-Westerns: Cinema, Region, West.* U of Nebraska P, 2013.

Cangiano, Mimmo. "Against Postmodernism: Paolo Sorrentino and the Search for Authenticity." *Journal of Italian Cinema and Media Studies*, vol. 7, no. 3, 2019, p. 339–49.

Caple, Natalee. *In Calamity's Wake.* HarperCollins, 2013.

Carrera, Isabel. "*Caprice* and *No Fixed Address*: Playing with Gender and Genre." *Kunapipi: Journal of Postcolonial Writing and Culture*, vol. 16, no. 1, 1994, pp. 432–9.

Cassar, Jon. *Forsaken.* Entertainment One, 2015.

Cawelti, John G. "*Chinatown* and Generic Transformation in Recent American Films." 1978. *Film Genre Reader III*, edited by Barry Keith Grant, U of Texas P, 2003, pp. 498–511.

———. *The Six-Gun Mystique Sequel.* Bowling Green State U Popular P, 1999.

CBS News. [John Wayne Visits Harvard University.] CBS, 15 Jan. 1974.

Certeau, Michel de. *The Practice of Everyday Life.* U of California P, 1984.

Charles, Ron. "Patrick deWitt's 'The Sisters Brothers' Wins Governor General's Award in Canada." *The Washington Post*, 16 Nov. 2011, https://www.washingtonpost.com/blogs/arts-post/post/patrick-dewitts-the-sisters-brothers-wins-governor-generals-award-in-canada/2011/11/15/gIQArjMARN_blog.html.

Chester, Blanca. "Western Fictions in Welch's *Fools Crow*: Languages of Landscape and Culture." *Telling the Stories: Essays on American Indian Literatures & Cultures*, edited by Elizabeth Hoffman Nelson and Malcolm A. Nelson, Peter Lang, 2001, 93–108.

Chirica, Irina. "Masculinity in the Western Genre." *Romanian Journal of Artistic Creativity*, vol. 6, no. 4, 2018, pp. 55–64.

Chisholm, A. M. *The Land of Strong Men.* H. K. Fly Company, 1919.

Christie, Stuart. "Thomas King Meets Indigenous Convergent Media." *Thomas King: Works and Impact*, edited by Eva Gruber, Camden House, 2012, pp. 67–83.

Clark, J. J. "The Slave Whisperer Rides the Frontier: Horseface Minstrelsy in the Western." *Animals and Agency: An Interdisciplinary Exploration*, edited by Sarah McFarland and Ryan Hediger, Brill, 2009, pp. 157–80.

Clarke, Michael Tavel, and David Wittenberg. "Introduction." *Scale in Literature and Culture*, edited by Michael Tavel Clarke and David Wittenberg, Palgrave Macmillan, 2017, pp. 1–32.

Cody, H. A. *The Frontiersman: A Tale of the Yukon.* William Briggs, 1910.

———. *The Long Patrol: A Tale of the Mounted Police.* William Briggs, 1912.

———. *Rod of the Lone Patrol.* McClelland and Stewart, 1916.

Cohen, Esther. *The Crossroads of Justice: Law and Culture in Late Medieval France.* Brill, 1993.

Cohen, Margaret. "Narratology in the Archive of Literature." *Representations*, no. 108, 2009, pp. 51–75.

Coleman, Daniel. *White Civility: The Literary Project of English Canada.* U of Toronto P, 2006.

Collin, Yvette Running Horse. *The Relationship between Indigenous Peoples of the Americas and the Horse: Deconstructing a Eurocentric Myth*. PhD dissertation, U Alaska Fairbanks, 2017.

Conway, Christopher. *Heroes of the Borderlands: Mexican Westerns in Film, Comics, and Music*. U of New Mexico P, 2019.

Cook, Pam. *Screening the Past: Memory and Nostalgia in Cinema*. Routledge, 2005.

Cooley, Dennis. " 'I Am Here on the Edge': Modern Hero/Postmodern Poetics in *The Collected Works of Billy the Kid*." *Spider Blues: Essays on Michael Ondaatje*, edited by Sam Solecki, Véhicule, 1985, pp. 211–39.

Connor, Ralph. *Black Rock: A Tale of the Selkirks*. Mershon, 1901.

———. *Corporal Cameron of the North West Mounted Police: A Tale of the Macleod Trail*. Westminster, 1912.

———. *Postscript to Adventure: The Autobiography of Ralph Connor (Charles W. Gordon)*. Hodder and Stoughton, 1938.

Cooper, Catherine. *The Western Home: Stories for Home on the Range*. Pedlar, 2014.

Cooper, Courtney Ryley. *Go North, Young Man!* Little, Brown and Co., 1929.

Cordell, Sigrid Anderson, and Carrie Johnston. "Gender and the Cultural Preoccupations of the American West." *Studies in the Novel*, vol. 49, no. 3, 2017, pp. 299–303.

Corkin, Stanley. "Cowboys and Free Markets: Post-WWII Westerns and U.S. Hegemony." *Cinema Journal*, vol. 39, no. 3, 2000, pp. 66–91.

———. *Realism and the Birth of the Modern United States: Cinema, Literature, and Culture*. U of Georgia P, 1996.

"Cowboys for Trump," 20 Aug. 2020, https://www.cowboysfortrump.org (no longer available to access at time of writing).

Cox, James H. " 'All This Water Imagery Must Mean Something': Thomas King's Revisions of Narratives of Domination and Conquest in *Green Grass, Running Water*." *American Indian Quarterly*, vol. 24, no. 2, 2000, pp. 219–46.

Craig, Terrence. "Ralph Connor (Charles William Gordon)." *The Canadian Encyclopedia*, 2 Apr. 2008, https://www.thecanadianencyclopedia.ca/en/article/charles-william-gordon/.

Crane, Susan. "Chivalry and the Pre/Postmodern." *Postmedieval: A Journal of Medieval Studies*, vol. 2, no. 1, 2011, pp. 69–87.

Cruise, Cian. "*Maliglutit* Remakes the Western in Its Own Image." *TIFF.net*, 13 Jan. 2017, https://www.tiff.net/the-review/maliglutit-remakes-the-western-in-its-own-image/.

Curwood, James Oliver. *The Flaming Forest: A Novel of the Canadian North-West*. Copp Clark, 1923.

Dalpé, Jean Marc, David Granger, Laura Lussier, Alexis Martin, Andrea Ménard, Yvette Nolan, Giles Poulin-Denis, Paula Jean Prudat, Mansel Robinson, and Kenneth T. Williams. *Gabriel Dumont's Wild West Show*. Dir. Mani Soleymanlou. Typescript described as "Final ENGLISH DRAFT—January 2018." 2017.

Daniells, Roy. "Glengarry Revisited." 1967. *Writers of the Prairies*, edited by Donald G. Stephens, U of British Columbia P, 1973, pp. 17–25.

Daniels, Bruce C. " 'We Are Not Tenants and They Are Not Landlords': Canadian Popular and Political Perceptions of the United States." *Journal of Popular Culture*, vol. 22, no. 3, 1988, pp. 85–100.

Daniels, Rudolph. *Trains Across the Continent*. 2nd ed. Indiana UP, 2000.

Darias-Beautell, Eva. "Rescaling CanLit: Global Readings." *Canadian Literature*, vol. 238, 2019, pp. 6–11.

Davey, Frank. "Canadian Postmodernisms: Misreadings and Non-readings." *Re: Reading the Postmodern: Canadian Literature and Criticism after Modernism*, edited by Robert David Stacey, U of Ottawa P, 2010, pp. 9–38.

———. *The Louis Riel Organ and Piano Company*. Turnstone, 1985.

———. "On Not Being Indigenous." *Canadaria*, no. 4, 2008, pp. 7–14.

———. *Post-national Arguments: The Politics of the Anglophone-Canadian Novel since 1967*. U of Toronto P, 1993.

———. "Surviving the Paraphrase." *Canadian Literature*, no. 70, 1976, pp. 5–13.

———. "Toward the Ends of Regionalism." *A Sense of Place: Re-evaluating Regionalism in Canadian and American Writing*, edited by Christian Riegel, Herb Wyile, Karen Overbye, and Don Perkins, U of Alberta P, 1998, pp. 1–17.

———. *When TISH Happens: The Unlikely Story of "Canada's Most Influential Literary Magazine."* ECW Press, 2011.

Davidson, Arnold E., Priscilla L. Walton, and Jennifer Andrews. *Border Crossings: Thomas King's Cultural Inversions*. U of Toronto P, 2003.

Dawson, Michael. *The Mountie from Dime Novel to Disney*. Between the Lines, 1998.

"Dead Dog Café Comedy Hour." *Rewind with Michael Enright*. CBC Radio, 28 Mar. 2013.

Deranger, Susana. "Our Home on Native Land: The Celebration of Colonization in Canada." *Briarpatch*, no. 40, 2011, p. 40.

Derrida, Jacques. "The Law of Genre," translated by Avital Ronell. *Critical Inquiry*, vol. 7, no. 1, 1980, pp. 55–81.

Deshaye, Joel. " 'Do I Feel Lucky?': Moral Luck, Bluffing, and the Ethics of Eastwood's Outlaw-Lawman in *Coogan's Bluff* and the Dirty Harry Films." *Film-Philosophy*, vol. 21, no. 1, 2017, pp. 20–36.

———. "Irving Layton's Televised 'Public Poetry' and *The Pierre Berton Show*." *Canadian Poetry: Studies, Documents, Reviews*, no. 73, 2013, pp. 32–53.

———. *The Metaphor of Celebrity: Canadian Poetry and the Public, 1955–1980*. U Toronto P, 2013.

Desmarais, Mary-Dailey, and Thomas Brent Smith, editors. *Once upon a Time . . . The Western: A New Frontier in Art and Film*. 5 Continents, 2017.

deWitt, Patrick. *The Sisters Brothers*. Anansi, 2011.

D'haen, Theo. "The Western." *International Postmodernism: Theory and Literary Practice*, edited by Hans Bertens and Douwe Fokkema, John Benjamins Publishing, 1997, pp. 183–93.

Diamond, Neil. *Reel Injun*. Resolution Pictures and National Film Board of Canada, 2009.

Dinka, Nicholas. Review of *Lightning*, by Fred Stenson. *Quill & Quire*, n.d., https://quillandquire.com/review/lightning. Accessed 13 Oct. 2021.

Dippie, Brian W. "One West, One Myth: Transborder Continuity in Western Art." *American Review of Canadian Studies*, vol. 33, no. 4, 2003, pp. 509–41.

Dobson, Kit. *Transnational Canadas: Anglo-Canadian Literature and Globalization*. Wilfrid Laurier UP, 2009.

Drainie, Bronwyn. Review of *The Outlander*, by Gil Adamson. *Quill & Quire*, n.d., https://quillandquire.com/review/the-outlander. Accessed 13 Oct. 2021.

Driscoll, Ian. "Corrupting Morals." Library and Archives Canada, 2005, https://www.collectionscanada.gc.ca/pulp/ (no longer available to access at time of writing).

———. "Decline of the Pulps." Library and Archives Canada, 2005, https://www.collectionscanada.gc.ca/pulp/ (no longer available to access at time of writing).

———. "Tales from the Vault!: Canadian Pulp Fiction 1940–1952." Library and Archives Canada, 2005, https://www.collectionscanada.gc.ca/pulp/ (no longer available to access at time of writing).

Druick, Zoë. "TV News Parody as a Critique of Genre." *Television and New Media*, vol. 10, no. 3, 2009, pp. 294–308.

Duignan, Brian. "Postmodernism." *Encyclopedia Britannica*, 4 Sep. 2020, https://www.britannica.com/topic/postmodernism-philosophy.

Dummitt, Christopher. "The 'Taint of Self': Reflections on Ralph Connor, His Fans, and the Problem of Morality in Recent Canadian Historiography." *Histoire sociale/Social History*, vol. 46, no. 91, 2013, pp. 63–90.

Dumont, Gabriel. *Gabriel Dumont Speaks*. Translated by Michael Barnholden. Talonbooks, 2009.

Durante, Jaymes. "*Maliglutit*." *4:3*, 13 June 2017, https://fourthreefilm.com/2017/06/maliglutit.

Ďurovičová, Nataša. "Preface." *World Cinemas, Transnational Perspectives*, edited by Nataša Ďurovičová and Kathleen E. Newman, Routledge, 2010, ix–xv.

Dwyer, Carlota Cárdenas de. "Westering and the Chicano Literary Tradition." *The Westering Experience in American Literature*, edited by Merrill Lewis and L. L. Lee, Bureau for Faculty Research, Western Washington U, 1977, pp. 206–12.

Dwyer, Tessa. "Mad Max, Accented English, and Same-Language Dubbing." *Locating the Voice in Film: Critical Approaches and Global Practices*, edited by Tom Whittaker and Sarah Wright, Oxford UP, 2016, pp. 137–56.

Eastwood, Clint. *Pale Rider*. Perf. Clint Eastwood, Michael Moriarty, and Carrie Snodgress. Warner Brothers, 1985.

Edwards, Justin D. "Going Native in Robert Kroetsch's *Gone Indian*." *Studies in Canadian Literature*, vol. 26, no. 1, 2001, pp. 84–97. *ProQuest*, https://www.proquest.com/docview/214495837?pq-origsite=primo&accountid=12378.

Eggleston, Wilfrid. *The Frontier and Canadian Letters*. Ryerson P, 1957.

Ellingson, Chloë. "Riding the Tshiuetin." *The Walrus*, vol. 14, no. 9, pp. 54–61.

Elliott, Alicia. "CanLit Is a Raging Dumpster Fire." *Open Book*, 7 Sept. 2017, http://open-book.ca/Columnists/CanLit-is-a-Raging-Dumpster-Fire.

Emerson, Ralph Waldo. *Emerson's* Nature—*Origin, Growth, Meaning*, edited by Merton M. Sealts Jr. and Alfred R. Ferguson. Dodd, Mead, and Co., 1969.

Eneas, Brian. "Sask. First Nation Announces Discovery of 751 Unmarked Graves Near Former Residential School." *CBC News*, 24 June 2021, https://www.cbc.ca/news/canada/saskatchewan/cowessess-marieval-indian-residential-school-news-1.6078375.

Erdrich, Louise. "Dear John Wayne." 1984. *Original Fire: Selected and New Poems*. Harper Perennial, 2003.

Evans, David H. "True West and Lying Marks: *The Englishman's Boy, Blood Meridian*, and the Paradox of the Revisionist Western." *Texas Studies in Literature and Language*, vol. 55, no. 4, 2013, pp. 406–33.

Eyre, Chris. *Smoke Signals*. Perf. Adam Beach, Evan Adams, Gary Farmer, Irene Bedard. Miramax, 1998.

Fagan, Kristina, and Sam McKegney. "Circling the Question of Nationalism in Native Canadian Literature and its Study." *Review: Literature and Arts of the Americas*, vol. 41, no. 1, 2008, pp. 31–42.

Falconer, Rachel. "Crossover Literature." *International Companion Encyclopedia of Children's Literature*, edited by Peter Hunt, Routledge, 2004, pp. 556–75.

Farrow, John. *Hondo*. Perf. John Wayne. Paramount, 1953.

Fee, Margery. *Literary Land Claims: The "Indian Land Question" from Pontiac's War to Attawapiskat*. Wilfrid Laurier UP, 2015.

———. "Romantic Nationalism and the Image of Native People in Contemporary English-Canadian Literature." *The Native in Literature*, edited by Thomas King, Cheryl Calver, and Helen Roy, ECW, 1987, pp. 15–33.

Fehrle, Johannes. *Revisionist Westerns in Canadian and U.S. American Literature*. PhD dissertation, University of Freiberg, 2012.

Ferrara, Alessandro. *Reflective Authenticity: Rethinking the Project of Modernity*. Routledge, 1998.

Fisher, Jaimey. "In the Horror Mode? Weimar Flashbacks and Generic Hybridity in 1950s West German Cinema." *New German Critique*, no. 126, 2015, pp. 91–114.

FitzMaurice, Kevin. "Transgressing the Boundaries of Native Studies: Traces of 'White Paper' Policy in Academic Patterns of Indigenization." *Canadian Journal of Native Studies*, vol. 31, no. 2, 2011, pp. 63–76.

Flaherty, Kathleen. "Tom King and the *Dead Dog Café*." *Thomas King: Works and Impact*, edited by Eva Gruber, Camden House, 2012, pp. 312–13.

Fludernik, Monika. "Genres, Text Types, or Discourse Modes? Narrative Modalities and Generic Categorization." *Style*, vol. 34, no. 2, 2000, pp. 274–92.

Foucault, Michel. "Of Other Spaces," translated by Jay Miskowiec. *Diacritics*, vol. 16, no. 1, 1986, pp. 22–7.

Francis, Daniel. *The Imaginary Indian: The Image of the Indian in Canadian Culture*. Arsenal Pulp Press, 1992.

Frankiewicz, Shane Joseph Willis. *Revisionism and the Subversive Cowboy in the Classic Western: Challenging the Definitions and Boundaries of the American Western*

Literary Genre of the 19th and Early 20th Century. PhD dissertation, University of Freiburg, 2017.

Frayling, Christopher. "Europeans." *The BFI Companion to the Western*, edited by Edward Buscombe, Atheneum, 1988, pp. 118–20.

French, Warren. "The Cowboy in the Dime Novel." *The University of Texas Studies in English*, no. 30, 1951, pp. 219–34.

Frow, John. *Genre: The New Critical Idiom*. Routledge, 2006.

Frye, Northrop. *Anatomy of Criticism: Four Essays*. Princeton UP, 1957.

———. "Conclusion to a *Literary History of Canada*." *The Bush Garden: Essays on the Canadian Imagination*. Anansi, 1971, pp. 213–51.

Furlong, Dayle. *Saltwater Cowboys*. Dundurn Press, 2015.

Gaberscek, Carlo. "Zapata Westerns: The Short Life of a Subgenre (1966–1972)." *Bilingual Review/La Revista Bilingüe*, vol. 29, nos. 2–3, 2008, pp. 45–58.

Gaines, Jane Marie, and Charlotte Cornelia Herzog. "The Fantasy of Authenticity in Western Costume." *Back in the Saddle Again: New Essays on the Western*, edited by Edward Buscombe and Roberta E. Pearson, BFI, 1998, pp. 172–81.

Garneau, David. "Cross Addressing [in fact, *Cross (Ad)dressing*]." *Geist*, vol. 27, no. 99, 2015, p. 35.

Garrett-Petts, W. F. "Novelist as Radical Pedagogue: George Bowering and Postmodern Reading Strategies." *College English*, vol. 54, no. 5, 1992, pp. 554–72.

Garvie, Maureen. "Not Just for Children Anymore: Literature for the Young Is Reaching a Growing Audience of Adult Readers Special Report on Children's & Educational Publishing [Includes List of Crossover Books]." *Quill & Quire*, vol. 64, no. 10, 1998, pp. 1,16. *ProQuest*, https://www.proquest.com/docview/235736510?pq-origsite=primo&accountid=12378

"Gaucho Literature." *Encyclopaedia Britannica*. Encyclopaedia Britannica, 2015.

Gaudry, Adam. "Gabriel Dumont." *The Canadian Encyclopedia*, 3 Apr. 2015, https://www.thecanadianencyclopedia.ca/en/article/dumont-gabriel.

Gittings, Christopher. "Imaging Canada: The Singing Mountie and Other Commodifications of Nation." *Canadian Journal of Communication*, vol. 23, no. 4, 1998, pp. 507–22. *ProQuest*, https://www.proquest.com/docview/219528523/C6BAA44DE8624EE8PQ/1?accountid=12378.

Goldie, Terry. "Fanciful Indigeneity." *Cross/Cultures*, no. 149, 2012, pp. 119–28.

Gordon, Charles. "Ralph Connor and the New Generation." *Mosaic*, vol. 3, no. 3, 1970, pp. 11–18.

Gordon, J. King. "Introduction." *Postscript to Adventure: The Autobiography of Ralph Connor (Charles W. Gordon)*. Hodder and Stoughton, 1938, pp. 9–16.

Gottfriedson, Garry. "Ode to Horsechild." *In Honour of Our Grandmothers*, edited by Reisa Schneider and Garry Gottfriedson, Theytus, 1994, p. 120.

———. *Whiskey Bullets: Cowboy and Indian Heritage Poems*. Ronsdale, 2006.

Gould, Glenn. "Idea of North." CBC Radio, 1967.

Grace, Sherrill E. *Canada and the Idea of North*. McGill-Queen's UP, 2001.

Grant, Kevin. *Any Gun Can Play: The Essential Guide to Euro-Westerns*. Fab Press, 2011.

Grant, Shelagh D. "The Importance to Arctic Sovereignty: How the Find [of the HMS *Erebus*] Affects Canada's Case." *Canadian Geographic*, Dec. 2014, pp. 60–1.

Guillén, Claudio. *The Challenge of Comparative Literature*. Harvard UP, 1993.

Hackworth, Jason. "Compassionate Neoliberalism? Evangelical Christianity, the Welfare State, and the Politics of the Right." *Studies in Political Economy*, vol. 86, no. 1, 2010, pp. 83–108.

Hamilton, Edith. *Mythology: Timeless Tales of Gods and Heroes*. 1942. Signet, 1969.

Hammill, Faye. *Canadian Literature*. Edinburgh UP, 2007.

Haraway, Donna. *The Companion Species Manifesto: Dogs, People, and Significant Otherness*. Prickly Paradigm Press, 2003.

Harrison, Dick. " 'Across the Medicine Line': Problems in Comparing Canadian and American Western Fiction." *The Westering Experience in American Literature*, edited by Merrill Lewis and L.L. Lee, Bureau for Faculty Research, Western Washington University, 1977, pp. 48–56.

———. *Unnamed Country: The Struggle for Canadian Prairie Fiction*. U of Alberta P, 1977.

Hassan, Ihab. *The Postmodern Turn: Essays in Postmodern Theory and Culture*. Ohio State UP, 1987.

Healey, Michael. *Proud*. Dir. Ruth Lawrence. Perf. Patrick Foran, Marie Jones, and Steve O'Connell. Resource Centre for the Arts, LSPU Hall, St. John's, 14 Nov. 2015.

Hearne, Joanna. *Native Recognition: Indigenous Cinema and the Western*. State U of New York P, 2012.

Hendryx, James B. *Blood on the Yukon Trail: A Novel of Corporal Downey of the Mounted*. Doubleday, Doran and Co., 1930.

———. *Connie Morgan with the Mounted*. G. P. Putnam's Sons, 1918.

Hill, Colin. *Modern Realism in English-Canadian Fiction*. U of Toronto P, 2012.

Hillhouse, Emily. "*White Sun of the Desert.*" *Directory of World Cinema: Russia*, edited by Birgit Beumers, Intellect, 2011, pp. 221–3.

Hitt, Sarah. "The Oil Roughneck: 'Cowboy' of the New West?" Popular Culture Association-American Culture Association (PCA-ACA) Conference, New Orleans, 4 Apr. 2015.

Hoberek, Andrew. "Postmodernism and Modernization." *Twentieth Century Literature*, vol. 57, nos. 3–4, 2011, pp. 341–53.

Hochbruck, Wolfgang. " 'Native American Literature': Developments, Contexts and Problems." *Antigonish Review*, nos. 93–4, 1993, pp. 265–76.

Holcomb, Rod. "The Collection." *Justified*, 20 Apr. 2010.

Hopson, Travis. "Filmfest DC Review: 'Searchers' Is a Thrilling, Inuit Remake of John Ford's Classic." *Punch Drunk Critics.com*, 22 Apr. 2017, http://www.punchdrunkcritics.com/2017/04/filmfest-dc-review-searchers-is.html.

Horne, Dee. *Contemporary American Indian Writing: Unsettling Literature*. Peter Lang, 2004.

———. "To Know the Difference: Mimicry, Satire, and Thomas King's *Green Grass, Running Water*." *Essays on Canadian Writing*, no. 56, 1995, pp. 255–73.

ProQuest, https://www.proquest.com/docview/197240969?accountid=12378&pq-origsite=primo&forcedol=true#.

Horowitz, Josh. "Thomas Jefferson and 'The Blood of Tyrants.' " *Huffpost.com*, 17 Oct. 2009, https://www.huffingtonpost.com/josh-horwitz/thomas-jefferson-and-the_b_273800.html.

Howell, Charlotte E. "Legitimating Genre: The Discursive Turn to Quality in Early 1990s Science Fiction Television." *Critical Studies in Television*, vol. 12, no. 1, 2017, pp. 35–50.

Hulan, Renée. " 'Everybody Likes the Inuit': Inuit Revision and Representations of the North." *Introduction to Indigenous Literary Criticism in Canada*, edited by Heather Macfarlane and Armand Garnet Ruffo, Broadview, 2015, pp. 202–20.

Huston, John. *The Treasure of the Sierra Madre*. Perf. Humphrey Bogart, Walter Huston, and Tim Holt. Warner Bros., 1948.

Hutcheon, Linda. *The Canadian Postmodern: A Study of Contemporary English-Canadian Fiction*. Oxford UP, 1988.

———. "The Glories of Hindsight: What We Know Now." *Re: Reading the Postmodern*, edited by Robert David Stacey, U of Ottawa P, 2010, pp. 39–53.

———. "Irony, Nostalgia, and the Postmodern." *University of Toronto English Library*, 1998, www.library.utoronto.ca/utel/criticism/hutchinp.html.

———. *Irony's Edge: The Theory and the Politics of Irony*. Routledge, 1994.

———. *A Poetics of Postmodernism: History, Theory, Fiction*. Routledge, 1988.

———. "The Politics of Postmodernism: Parody and History." *Cultural Critique*, no. 5, 1985/1986, pp. 179–207.

———. *A Theory of Parody: The Teachings of Twentieth-Century Art Forms*. U of Illinois P, 1985.

Hutchison, Don. *Scarlet Riders: Pulp Fiction Tales of the Mounties*. Mosaic, 1998.

Iñárritu, Alejandro. *The Revenant*. Perf. Leonardo DiCaprio, Tom Hardy, and Domhnall Gleeson. 20th Century Fox, 2016.

Indick, William. *The Psychology of the Western: How the American Psyche Plays Out on the Screen*. McFarland, 2008.

Ingold, Tim. "Landscape or Weather-World?" *Being Alive: Essays on Movement, Knowledge and Description*. Routledge, 2011.

Interlandi, Jeneen. "Why Doesn't the United States Have Universal Health Care?" *The New York Times*, 14 Aug. 2019.

Jackson, Mark. "For New Ecologies of Thought: Towards Decolonising Critique." *Coloniality, Ontology, and the Question of the Posthuman*, edited by Mark Jackson, Routledge, 2018, pp. 19–62.

———. "Introduction." *Coloniality, Ontology, and the Question of the Posthuman*, edited by Mark Jackson, Routledge, 2018, pp. 1–17.

Jameson, Fredric. "Cognitive Mapping." *Marxism and the Interpretation of Culture*, edited by Cary Nelson and Lawrence Grossberg, U of Illinois P, 1988, pp. 347–60.

———. *The Political Unconscious*. Cornell UP, 1981.

——. *Postmodernism, or the Cultural Logic of Late Capitalism*. Verso, 1991.

Jarmusch, Jim. *Dead Man*. Perf. Johnny Depp, Gary Farmer, and Lance Henriksen. Miramax Films, 1995.

Jennings, John. *The Cowboy Legend: Owen Wister's Virginian and the Canadian-American Frontier*. U of Calgary P, 2015.

Jiles, Paulette. *Enemy Women*. HarperCollins, 2002.

——. *The Jesse James Poems*. Polestar, 1988.

Johnson, Brian. "Plastic Shaman in the Global Village: Understanding Media in Thomas King's *Green Grass, Running Water*." *Studies in Canadian Literature*, vol. 25, no. 2, 2000, pp. 24–49.

Johnston, Sean. *Listen All You Bullets*. Gaspereau, 2013.

Johnston, Wayne. *The Colony of Unrequited Dreams*. Vintage, 1999.

Jones, Ted. *All the Days of His Life: A Biography of Archdeacon H. A. Cody*. New Brunswick Museum, 1981.

Joudrey, Susan L. "What a Man: Portrayals of Masculinity and Race in Calgary Stampede Ephemera." *Cultural Studies <=> Critical Methodologies*, vol. 16, no. 1, 2016, pp. 28–39.

Justice, Daniel Heath. "Currents of Trans/national Criticism in Indigenous Literary Studies." *American Indian Quarterly*, vol. 35, no. 3, 2011, pp. 334–52.

Kamboureli, Smaro. " 'Frank Davey' and the Method of Cool." *Studies in Canadian Literature*, vol. 32, no. 2, 2007, pp. 201–26.

——. "Outlawed Narrative: Michael Ondaatje's *The Collected Works of Billy the Kid*." *Sagetrieb: A Journal Devoted to Poets in the Imagist / Objectivist Tradition*, vol. 7, no. 1, 1988, pp. 115–29.

Kane, Thomas H. "The Deaths of the Authors: Literary Celebrity and Automortography in Acker, Barthelme, Bukowski, and Carver's Last Acts." *Lit: Literature Interpretation Theory*, vol. 15, no. 4, 2004, pp. 409–43.

Katerberg, William H. "A Northern Vision: Frontiers and the West in the Canadian and American Imagination." *American Review of Canadian Studies*, vol. 33, no. 4, 2003, pp. 543–63.

Keahey, Deborah. *Making It Home: Place in Canadian Prairie Literature*. U of Manitoba P, 1998.

Keene, Adrienne. "Valentino Didn't Learn Anything." *Native Appropriations*, 23 Mar. 2017, http://nativeappropriations.com/2017/03/valentino-didnt-learn-anything.html.

Kellner, Douglas. "Film, Politics, and Ideology: Reflections on Hollywood Film in the Age of Reagan." *The Velvet Light Trap*, Spring 1991, pp. 9–24.

Kelly, Robert A. "The Gospel of Success in Canada: Charles W. Gordon (Ralph Connor) as Exemplar." *Historical Papers 1998*. Canadian Society of Church History, Annual Conference, U of Ottawa, 29–30 May, 1998, pp. 5–15.

Kershner, Irvin. *The Empire Strikes Back*. Perf. Mark Hamill, Harrison Ford, and Carrie Fisher. 20th Century Fox, 1980.

Khan, Shahrukh. "A New Kind of Colonialism: Intellectual Property Rights." *Harvard International Review*, vol. 35, no. 3, 2014, pp. 37–9.

Killingsworth, Colleen. "Animal-Welfare Activists vs. the Calgary Stampede: 'That's Entertainment?' " *Public Relations Journal*, vol. 6, no. 1, 2012, pp. 1–27.

King, Thomas. "Godzilla vs. Post-Colonial." *Journal of Postcolonial Writing*, vol. 30, no. 2, 1990, pp. 10–16.

———. *Green Grass, Running Water*. HarperCollins, 1993.

———. *The Inconvenient Indian: A Curious Account of Native People in North America*. Penguin, 2012.

———. "An Interview with Thomas King (August 1999)." Interview with Margery Fee and Sneja Gunew. *Canadian Literature*, 1 Aug. 1999, https://canlit.ca/an-interview-with-thomas-king-august-1999/.

———. *The Truth about Stories*. Anansi, 2003.

———. *Truth & Bright Water*. Harper, 1999.

Knight, Chris. "If The Searchers Was a Western, Inuit Film Maliglutit Is a Northern." *National Post*, 12 Jan. 2017, http://nationalpost.com/entertainment/movies/if-the-searchers-was-a-western-inuit-film-maliglutit-is-a-northern.

Kollin, Susan. "Wister and the 'New West.' " *Reading the Virginian in the New West*, edited by Melody Graulich and Thomas Tatum, U of Nebraska P, 2003, pp. 233–54.

Kolodny, Annette. *The Lay of the Land: Metaphor as Experience and History in American Life and Letters*. U of North Carolina P, 1984.

Kopecky, Arno. "Title Fight: The Tsilhqot'in Nation Got Its Land Back. Canada Will Never Be the Same." *The Walrus*, vol. 12, no. 6, 2015, pp. 30–9.

Kreisel, Henry. "The Prairie: A State of Mind." *Trace: Prairie Writers on Writing*, edited by Birk Sproxton, Turnstone, 1986, pp. 3–17.

Kristmanson, Lynn. "Trigger Happy: The Celebrity Horse in Western Cinema." Master's thesis, Memorial University, 2018.

Kroetsch, Robert. *The Man from the Creeks*. Random House, 1998.

———. *The Studhorse Man*. 1969. Random House, 1995.

Krotz, Sarah Wylie. *Mapping with Words: Anglo-Canadian Literary Cartographies, 1789–1916*. U of Toronto P, 2018.

Krueger, Misty. "Teaching Jane Austen's Northanger Abbey as a 'Crossover' Text." *Persuasions: The Jane Austen Journal On-Line*, vol. 34, no. 2, 2014. ProQuest, https://www.proquest.com/docview/2309792329?pq-origsite=primo&accountid=12378.

Kulbach, René L. "The Capture of 'Red.' " *Tang, Triumph Comics*, no. 9, 1941.

Kunuk, Zacharias, and Natar Ungalaaq. *Maliglutit*. Perf. Benjamin Kunuk, Karen Ivalu, and Jonah Qunaq. Kinguliit Productions, 2016.

Lakoff, George, and Mark Johnson. *Metaphors We Live By*. U of Chicago P, 1980.

L'Amour, Louis. *Heller with a Gun*. Bantam, 2011.

LaRocque, Emma. "When the 'Wild West' Is Me: Re-Viewing Cowboys and Indians." *Challenging Frontiers: The Canadian West*, edited by Lorry Felske and Beverly J. Rasporich, U of Calgary P, 2005, pp. 136–53.

Le Cain, Maximilian. "Drifting Out of the Territory: Sam Peckinpah's Pat Garrett and Billy the Kid." *Senses of Cinema*, no. 13, 2001, http://www.sensesofcinema.com/2001/70s-us-cinema/garrett/.

Lecker, Robert. *Keepers of the Code: English-Canadian Literary Anthologies and the Representation of Nation*. U of Toronto P, 2013.

Leone, Sergio. *The Good, the Bad, and the Ugly*. Perf. Clint Eastwood, Lee Van Cleef, and Eli Wallach. United Artists, 1966.

Lincoln, Kenneth. *Native American Renaissance*. U of California P, 1983.

London, Jack. *The Call of the Wild*. 1903. Penguin, 1994.

———. *Son of the Wolf*. 1902. Edited by Charles N. Watson Jr. Oxford UP, 1996.

———. "To Build a Fire." 1908. *Lost Face*, U Pennsylvania P, 2005, pp. 61–98.

"Lost Franklin Expedition Ship Found in the Arctic." *CBC News*, 9 Sept. 2014, https://www.cbc.ca/news/politics/lost-franklin-expedition-ship-found-in-the-arctic-1.2760311.

Lu, Jie. "Reconsiderations on the Crises of Comparative Literature Study." *CLCWeb: Comparative Literature and Culture*, vol. 19, no. 5, 2017, pp. 2–9.

Lusty, Terry. "Big Bear's Bundle: New Answers Raise Additional Questions." *Windspeaker*, vol. 4, no. 24, 1987, p. 20, *AMMSA*.com, https://ammsa.com/publications/windspeaker/big-bears-bundle-new-answers-raise-additional-questions.

MacGillivray, Royce. "Refusing to Go Away: The Case of Ralph Connor." *Past and Present*, Oct. 1984, pp. 8–9.

MacKenzie, David Bruce Hollis. "The Culture Cube: A Three-Dimensional Model of Political Thought." Master's thesis, Regent U, 2015.

Mackie, John. *Sinners Twain: A Romance of the Great Lone Land*. T. F. Unwin, 1895.

MacLaren, Eli. "The Magnification of Ralph Connor: *Black Rock* and the North American Copyright Divide." *Papers of the Bibliographical Society of America*, vol. 101. no. 4, 2007, pp. 507–31.

MacLeod, Alexander. *Between a Rock and a Soft Place: Postmodern-Regionalism in Canadian and American Fiction*. PhD dissertation, McGill U, 2003.

MacLeod, David I. "Act Your Age: Boyhood, Adolescence, and the Rise of the Boy Scouts of America." *Journal of Social History*, vol. 16, no. 2, 1982, pp. 3–20.

MacSkimming, Roy. *The Perilous Trade: Book Publishing in Canada, 1946–2006*. 2nd ed. McClelland and Stewart, 2007.

Mandel, Eli. "Images of Prairie Man." *A Region of the Mind*, edited by R. Allan, Canadian Plains Research Centre, 1973, pp. 201–9.

Mangold, James. *Logan*. 20th Century Fox, 2017.

Mannell, Julie. "Featured Review: *Injun* by Jordan Abel." *Vallum: Contemporary Poetry*, Wordpress, 14 Dec. 2016, https://vallum.wordpress.com/2016/12/14/featured-review-injun-by-jordan-abel-a-review-by-julie-mannell/.

Marovitz, Sanford E. "Myth and Realism in Recent Criticism of the American Literary West." *Journal of American Studies*, vol. 15, no. 1, 1981, pp. 95–114.

Marubbio, M. Elise. "Decolonizing the Western: A Revisionist Analysis of *Avatar* with a Twist." *The Post-2000 Film Western: Contexts, Transnationality, Hybridity*, edited by Marek Paryz and John R. Leo, Palgrave, 2015, pp. 167–90.

Marx, Leo. *The Machine in the Garden: Technology and the Pastoral Ideal in America*. Oxford UP, 1964.

McCarthy, Cormac. *All the Pretty Horses*. Vintage, 1992.

———. *Blood Meridian: Or, the Evening Redness in the West*. 1985. Vintage, 1992.

———. *No Country for Old Men*. Vintage, 2005.

McCourt, Edward. *The Canadian West in Fiction*. 1949. Ryerson P, 1970.

McGee, Patrick. *From Shane to Kill Bill: Rethinking the Western*. Blackwell, 2007.

McGimpsey, David. "Catnip for Canadians." *Geist*, no. 98, 2015, p. 29.

McKanna, Clare V. Jr. "Alcohol, Handguns, and Homicide in the American West: A Tale of Three Counties, 1880–1920." *Western Historical Quarterly*, vol. 26, no. 4, 1995, pp. 455–82.

McKay, Don. *Deactivated West 100*. Gaspereau, 2005.

McKay, Ian, and Jamie Swift. *Warrior Nation: Rebranding Canada in an Age of Anxiety*. Between the Lines, 2012.

McMahon, Ryan. "The New Wild West: An Interview with Ryan McMahon of *Indian & Cowboy*." Interview with Liza Yeager. *Native Appropriations*, 30 Dec. 2016.

McNaron, David L. "From Dollars to Iron: The Currency of Clint Eastwood's Westerns." *The Philosophy of the Western*, edited by Jennifer L. McMahon and B. Steve Csaki, UP of Kentucky, 2010, pp. 149–70.

Meeuf, Russell. *John Wayne's World: Transnational Masculinity in the Fifties*. U of Texas P, 2013.

Mexal, Stephen J. *Reading for Liberalism: The* Overland Monthly *and the Writing of the Modern American West*. U Nebraska P, 2013.

Miller, J.R. *Shingwauk's Vision: A History of Native Residential Schools*. U of Toronto P, 1996.

Mitchell, Lee C. *Late Westerns: The Persistence of a Genre*. U of Nebraska P, 2018.

———. "'Who *Are* These Guys?': The Advent of the Beleaguered Western Hero." *Once upon a Time . . . The Western: A New Frontier in Art and Film*, edited by Mary-Dailey Desmarais and Thomas Brent Smith, 5 Continents, 2017, pp. 260–4.

———. "Whose West Is It Anyway? or, What's Myth Got to Do with It? The Role of 'America' in the Myth of the West." *American Review of Canadian Studies*, vol. 33, no. 4, 2003, pp. 497–508.

Monkman, Leslie. *A Native Heritage: Images of the Indian in English-Canadian Literature*. U of Toronto P, 1981.

Monticone, Paul. "The *Noir* Western: Genre Theory and the Problem of the Anomalous Hybrid." *Quarterly Review of Film and Video*, no. 31, 2014, pp. 336–49.

Mora, Carlos. *Mexican Cinema*. U of California P, 1982.

Moran, Rodger J. "Hiram Alfred (H. A.) Cody." *The Canadian Encyclopedia*, 15 Dec. 2013, https://www.thecanadianencyclopedia.ca/en/article/hiram-alfred-ha-cody.

Moretti, Franco. *Distant Reading*. Verso, 2013.

Moss, Laura. *Is Canada Postcolonial? Unsettling Canadian Literature*. Wilfrid Laurier UP, 2003.

Motyka, John. Review of *The Englishman's Boy* by Guy Vanderhaeghe. *New York Times Book Review*, 5 Oct. 1997, p. 23.

Mowat, Farley. *Canada North Now: The Great Betrayal*. McClelland and Stewart, 1976.

Murphy, Kathleen. "The Good, the Bad & the Ugly: Clint Eastwood as Romantic Hero." *Film Comment*, vol. 32, no. 3, May/June 1996, pp. 16–24.

Murray, Robin L., and Joseph K. Heumann. "Eco-Terrorism in Film: *Pale Rider* and the Revenge Cycle." *Ecology and Popular Film: Cinema on the Edge*. State U of New York P, 2009, pp. 127–42.

———. *Gunfight at the Eco-Corral: Western Cinema and the Environment*. U of Oklahoma P, 2012.

———. "Mining Westerns: Seeking Sustainable Development in McCabe and Mrs. Miller." *Journal of Ecocriticism*, vol. 2, no. 2, 2010, pp. 57–72.

Nance, Susan. "Outlaw Horses and the True Spirit of Calgary in the Automobile Age." *Calgary: City of Animals*, edited by Jim Ellis. U of Calgary P, 2017, pp. 10–21.

Naughton, Yulia Pushkarevskaya and Gerald David Naughton. "'Westward Went I in Search of Romance': The Transnational Reception of Thomas Mayne Reid's Western Novels." *CEA Critic*, vol. 75, no. 2, 2013, pp. 142-57.

"NDP Guelph: Tom King Introduces Himself." YouTube.com, uploaded by NDByElectionHQ, 12 Aug 2008. https://www.youtube.com/watch?v=cevaHCg3-vs&ab_channel=NDPByElectionHQ.

Neale, Steve. *Genre and Hollywood*. Routledge, 2000.

———. "Vanishing Americans: Racial and Ethnic Issues in the Interpretation and Context of Post-war 'Pro-Indian' Westerns." *Back in the Saddle Again: New Essays on the Western*, edited by Edward Buscombe and Roberta E. Pearson, BFI, 1998, pp. 8–28.

Nestruck, J. Kelly. "Welcome to the Future of Canadian History Theatre [on *Gabriel Dumont's Wild West Show*]." *The Globe and Mail*, 12 Nov. 2017, https://www.theglobeandmail.com/arts/theatre-and-performance/the-future-of-history-theatre-avoiding-conflict-by-including-everyonesvoice/article36677967/.

New, W. H. *A History of Canadian Literature* McGill-Queen's UP, 1989.

Newman, Judie. Review of *John Wayne: The Politics of Celebrity*, by Garry Wills. *Journal of American Studies*, vol. 32, no. 1, 1998, pp. 157-8.

Ngai, Sianne. "Our Aesthetic Categories." *PMLA*, vol. 125, no. 4, 2010, pp. 948–58.

Nichol, bp. *The True Eventual Story of Billy the Kid*. 1970. above/ground, 2005.

Nir, Oded. "World Literature as a Problem of Scale." *Scale in Literature and Culture*, edited by Michael Tavel Clarke and David Wittenberg, Palgrave Macmillan, 2017, pp. 225–51.

Nischik, Reingard M. "The English-Canadian Short Story since 1967: Between (Post) Modernism and (Neo) Realism." *History of Literature in Canada: English-Canadian and French-Canadian*, edited by Reingard M. Nischik, Camden House, 2008, pp. 330–51.

"Old-West Sheriff Costumes Donned by Protesting Police Force in Châteauguay, Que." *CBC News*, 14 Nov. 2014. https://www.cbc.ca/news/canada/montreal/old-west-sheriff-costumes-donned-by-protesting-police-force-in-ch%C3%A2teauguay-que-1.2835682.

Ondaatje, Michael. *The Collected Works of Billy the Kid*. Anansi, 1970.

Owram, Doug. *Promise of Eden: The Canadian Expansionist Movement and the Idea of the West, 1856–1900*. U Toronto P, 1980.

Pacey, Desmond. "Fiction 1920–1940." *Literary History of Canada: Canadian Literature in English*, edited by Alfred G. Bailey, Claude Bissell, Roy Daniells, Northrop Frye, and Desmond Pacey, U of Toronto P, 1965, pp. 558–693.

Pearson, Sarina. "Cowboy Contradictions: Westerns in the Postcolonial Pacific." *Studies in Australasian Cinema*, vol. 7, nos. 2–3, pp. 153–64.

Peckinpah, Sam. *Pat Garrett and Billy the Kid*. Metro-Goldwyn-Mayer, 1973.

Percy, Owen. "Imagining Vancouvers: *Burning Water*, *Ana Historic*, and the Literary (Un)settling of the Pacific Coast." *National Plots: Historical Fiction and Changing Ideas of Canada*, edited by Andrea Cabajsky and Brett Josef Grubisic, Wilfrid Laurier UP, 2010, pp. 208–22.

Phillips, Louis. "Considering the Death of John Wayne." *Journal of Popular Film and Television*, vol. 7, no. 3, 1979, p. 265.

Phillips, William. *Gunless*. Alliance Films, 2010.

Pippin, Robert B. "What Is a Western? Politics and Self-Knowledge in John Ford's *The Searchers*." *Critical Inquiry*, no. 35, 2009, pp. 223–46.

Pitts, Gordon. *Stampede! The Rise of the West and Canada's New Power Elite*. Key Porter, 2010.

Poitier, Sydney. *Buck and the Preacher*. E & R Productions; Belafonte Enterprises, 1972.

Polack, Fiona, and Danine Farquharson. "Offshore Rig." *Fueling Culture: 100 Words for Energy and Environment*, edited by Imre Szeman, Jennifer Wenzel, and Patricia Yaeger, Fordham UP, 2017, pp. 252–4.

Polić, Vanja. "The Reworkings of the Western from the Northern Side of the Medicine Line: Caple's *In Calamity's Wake*, Vanderhaeghe's *The Englishman's Boy*, and Stenson's *Lightning*." *British Journal of Canadian Studies*, vol. 28, no. 2, 2015, pp. 205–21.

———. "The Sisters Brothers Pack Heat: or How the Sisters Fared in the West." *Facing the Crises: Anglophone Literature in the Postmodern World*, edited by Ljubica Matek and Jasna Poljak Rehlicki, Cambridge Scholars, 2014, pp. 128–46.

Porter, Edwin S. *The Great Train Robbery*. Edison, 1903.

Post, Robert C. "A Theory of Genre: Romance, Realism, and Moral Reality." *American Quarterly*, vol. 33, no. 4, 1981, pp. 367–90.

Prats, Armando José. *Invisible Natives: Myth and Identity in the American Western*. Cornell UP, 2002.

Price, Luke. "Blight on Valhalla." *Dynamic Western*, June 1942, pp. 4–26, 49.

———. "The Gunsmoke Sheriff." *Dynamic Western*, Aug. 1941, pp. 98–110.

———. "Hound Dog Justice." *Dynamic Western*, Oct. 1941, pp. 42–54.

———. "Six-Gun Thunder." *Dynamic Western*, Feb. 1942, pp. 52–76.
———. "Smokey Carmain Shoots It Out!" *Dynamic Western*, Sept. 1941, pp. 52–78.
———. "Smokey Defies an Army." *Dynamic Western*, May 1942, pp. 27–47.
———. "Smokey Signs Up for Trouble" *Dynamic Western*, July 1942, pp. 9–17.
———. "Smokey Stirs Up Rebellion." *Dynamic Western*, Oct. 1942, pp. 51–71.
———. "Valley of Vengeance." *Dynamic Western*, Dec. 1941, pp. 63–76.
Purdy, Al. *The New Romans: Candid Canadian Opinions of the US.* M. G. Hurtig, 1968.
Quam-Wickham, Nancy. "Rereading Man's Conquest of Nature: Skill, Myths, and the Historical Construction of Masculinity in Western Extractive Industries." *Men and Masculinities,* vol. 2, no. 2, 1999, pp. 135–51.
Redekop, Magdalene. "Ernest Thompson Seton." *The Canadian Encyclopedia*, 4 Mar. 2015, https://www.thecanadianencyclopedia.ca/en/article/ernest-thompson-seton.
Richler, Mordecai. *The Incomparable Atuk*. McClelland and Stewart, 1963.
Ricou, Laurie. *Vertical Man / Horizontal World: Man and Landscape in Canadian Prairie Fiction*. U of British Columbia P, 1973.
Rieder, John. "On Defining SF, or Not: Genre Theory, SF, and History." *Science Fiction Studies*, vol. 37, no. 2, 2010, pp. 191–209.
Rifkind, Candida. "When Mounties Were Modern Kitsch: The Serial Seductions of Renfrew of the Mounted." *ESC: English Studies in Canada*, vol. 37, nos. 3–4, 2011, pp. 123–46.
Ripplinger, Sarah. "Gottfriedson's Poetry Shoots *Whiskey Bullets*." *The Ubyssey*, 17 Nov. 2006, p. 5.
Ritter, Kathleen. "Ctrl-F: Reterritorializing the Canon." *Un/inhabited*, by Jordan Abel. Project Space/Talonbooks, 2014, pp. ix–xix.
Roberts, Katherine Ann. *West/Border/Road: Nation and Genre in Contemporary Canadian Narrative*. McGill-Queen's UP, 2018.
Robinson, Harry. "You Think It's a Stump, But That's My Grandfather." 1992. *Nature Power: In the Spirit of an Okanagan Storyteller*, 2nd ed., edited by Wendy Wickwire, Talonbooks, 2004, pp. 35–42.
Rodness, Roshaya. "Thomas King's National Literary Celebrity and the Cultural Ambassadorship of a Native Canadian Writer." *Canadian Literature*, no. 220, 2014, pp. 55–72, 204. *ProQuest*, https://www.proquest.com/docview/1638915546?accountid=12378&pq-origsite=primo&forcedol=true#.
Ropa, Anastasija. *Practical Horsemanship in Medieval Arthurian Romance*. Trivent, 2019.
Rushdie, Salman. " 'Commonwealth Literature' Does Not Exist." 1983. *Imaginary Homelands: Essays and Criticism, 1981–1991*. Granta, 1991, pp. 61–70.
———. "Imaginary Homelands." 1982. *Imaginary Homelands: Essays and Criticism, 1981–1991*. Granta, 1991, pp. 9–21.
Samutina, Natalia. "Fan Fiction as World-Building: Transformative Reception in Crossover Writing." *Continuum: Journal of Media and Cultural Studies*, 11 Feb. 2016.
Schneider, Reisa, and Garry Gottfriedson. *In Honour of Our Grandmothers*. Theytus, 1994.

Scholes, Robert. "On Realism and Genre." *NOVEL: A Forum on Fiction*, vol. 2, no. 3, 1969, pp. 269–71.

———. "Towards a Poetics of Fiction: An Approach through Genre." *NOVEL: A Forum on Fiction*, vol. 2, no. 2, 1969, pp. 101–11.

Schroeder, Jonathan David Shelly. "The Painting of Modern Light: Local Color before Regionalism." *American Literature*, vol. 86, no. 3, 2014, pp. 551–81.

Schwantes, Carlos A., and James P. Ronda. *The West the Railroads Made*. U of Washington P, 2008.

Scott, Jamie S. "Colonial, Neo-Colonial, Post-Colonial: Images of Christian Missions in Hiram A. Cody's *The Frontiersman*, Rudy Wiebe's *First and Vital Candle* and Basil Johnston's *Indian School Days*." *Journal of Canadian Studies*, vol. 32, no. 3, 1997, pp. 140–61.

Sealey, D. Bruce. "Jerry Potts." *The Canadian Encyclopedia*, 4 Feb. 2008, https://www.thecanadianencyclopedia.ca/en/article/jerry-potts.

Seesengood, Robert Paul. "Western Text(s): The Bible and the Movies of the Wild, Wild West." The Bible in Motion: A Handbook of the Bible and Its Reception in Film. Vol. 2, edited by Rhonda Burnette-Bletsch, De Gruyter, 2016, pp. 193–207.

Service, Robert. "Clancy of the Mounted." *Ballads of a Cheechako*. William Briggs, 1911, pp. 119–28.

———. "The Shooting of Dan McGrew." *The Spell of the Yukon and Other Verses*. Barse and Hopkins, 1907, pp. 45–9.

Shively, JoEllen. "Cowboys and Indians: Perceptions of Western Films among American Indians and Anglos." *American Sociological Review*, vol. 57, no. 6, 1992, pp. 725–34.

Sircar, Sanjay. "Australian Popular Culture, Genre-Parody, and Cross-over Writing." *Bookbird*, vol. 36, no. 4, 1998, pp. 11–17.

Slotkin, Richard. *Fatal Environment: The Myth of the Frontier in the Age of Industrialization, 1800–1890*. 1985. HarperPerennial, 1994.

———. *Gunfighter Nation: The Myth of the Frontier in Twentieth-Century America*. Atheneum, 1992.

———. *Regeneration through Violence: The Mythology of the American Frontier, 1600–1860*. Wesleyan UP, 1973.

Slotkin, Richard, with Mary-Dailey Desmarais. "Cumulative Genre Effect." *Once upon a Time . . . The Western: A New Frontier in Art and Film*. 5 Continents, 2017, pp. 147–50.

Smart, Robert. "Landscape as Moral Destiny: Mythic Reinvention from Rowdy Yates to the Stranger." *New Essays on Clint Eastwood*, edited by Leonard Engel and Drucilla Cornell, U of Utah P, 2012, pp. 18–35.

Smith, Brad. *All Hat*. Henry Holt, 2003.

———. *The Return of Kid Cooper*. Arcade, 2018.

Smith, Carlton. *Coyote Kills John Wayne: Postmodernism and Contemporary Fictions of the Transcultural Frontier*. UP of New England, 2000.

Smith, Michelle Denise. "Soup Cans and Love Slaves: National Politics and Cultural Authority in the Editing and Authorship of Canadian Pulp Magazines." *Book History*, vol. 9, no. 1, 2006, pp. 261–89.

Söderlind, Sylvia. "F the Ineffable! The Allegorical Intention in Ghostmodernism." *Re: Reading the Postmodern: Canadian Literature and Criticism after Modernism*, edited by Robert David Stacey, U of Ottawa P, 2010, pp. 269–92.

———. "Ghost-National Arguments." *University of Toronto Quarterly*, vol. 75, no. 2, 2006, pp. 673–92.

Sontag, Susan. "On Style." 1965. *Susan Sontag: Essays of the 1960s & 70s*, edited by David Rieff, Library of America, 2013, pp. 21–41.

Sorensen, Sue. "West of Eden." *West of Eden: Essays on Canadian Prairie Literature*, edited by Sue Sorensen, CMU, 2008, pp. 1–25.

Spivak, Gayatri Chakravorty. *A Critique of Postcolonial Reason: Towards a History of the Vanishing Present*. Harvard UP, 1999.

———. *Death of a Discipline*. Columbia UP, 2003.

Stacey, Robert David. "Introduction: Post-, Marked Canada." *Re: Reading the Postmodern*, edited by Robert David Stacey, U of Ottawa P, 2010, pp. xi–xxxviii.

Stanley, George F. G., and Adam Gaudry. "Louis Riel." *The Canadian Encyclopedia*. 22 Apr. 2013, https://www.thecanadianencyclopedia.ca/en/article/louis-riel.

Staveley, Helene. *Playful Citizens: Utopian Intersections of Play, Sex and Citizenship in Contemporary Canadian Fiction*. Dissertation, Memorial University, 2008.

Stefanucci, Tracy. "Afterword." *Un/inhabited*, by Jordan Abel. Project Space/Talonbooks, 2015, pp. iii–v.

Stenson, Fred. *The Great Karoo*. Doubleday, 2008.

———. *Lightning*. Douglas and McIntyre, 2003.

———. *The Trade*. Douglas and McIntyre, 2000.

Stephens, Donald G. "Introduction." *Writers of the Prairies*, edited by Donald G. Stephens, U of British Columbia P, 1973, pp. 1–6.

Stewart, Fenn Elan. "Hiawatha/Hereafter: Re-Appropriating Longfellow's Epic in Northern Ontario." *Ariel: A Review of International English Literature*, vol. 44, no. 4, 2013, pp .159–80.

Stewart, Susan. *On Longing: Narratives of the Miniature, the Gigantic, the Souvenir, the Collection*. Duke UP, 1993.

Stoker, Bram. "The Squaw." 1893. *Horror Stories: Classic Tales from Hoffmann to Hodgson*, edited by Darryl Jones, Oxford World's Classics, 2014, pp. 252–63.

Stone, Ted. *Cowboy Logic: The Wit & Wisdom of the West*. Lone Pine, 1997.

St. Pierre, Paul. *Smith and Other Events: Tales of the Chilcotin*. Doubleday, 1983.

Strange, Carolyn, and Tina Loo. "From Hewers of Wood to Producers of Pulp: True Crime in Canadian Pulp Magazines of the 1940s." *Journal of Canadian Studies*, vol. 37, no. 2, 2002 pp. 11–32.

———. "Maple Leaf Pulps." *The Beaver*, vol. 84, no. 2, 2004, pp. 14–17. EBSCO Host, https://web-s-ebscohost-com.qe2a-proxy.mun.ca/ehost/detail/

detail?vid=1&sid=b4345c09-79bb-4639-a91a-71e30c3b1e3e%40redis&bdata=JkF1d GhUeXBlPWlwLHVybCx1aWQmc2l0ZT1laG9zdC1saXZlJnNjb3BlPXNpdGU%3d #AN=13025105&db=a9h.

Sugars, Cynthia, and Gerry Turcotte, editors. *Unsettled Remains: Canadian Literature and the Postcolonial Gothic*. Wilfrid Laurier UP, 2009.

Sutherland, Ronald. *The New Hero: Essays in Comparative Quebec/Canadian Literature*. Macmillan, 1977.

Sweet, Matthew. "The First Native American Director. Or Was He?" *The Guardian*, 23 Sept. 2010, https://www.theguardian.com/film/2010/sep/23/first-native-american-director.

Szklarski, Cassandra. "Debate over Cultural Appropriation a Centuries-Old Battle for Indigenous Groups." CTV News, 9 May 2017, https://www.ctvnews.ca/entertainment/debate-over-cultural-appropriation-a-centuries-old-battle-for-indigenous-groups-1.3402073.

Tan, Kathy-Ann. *Reconfiguring Citizenship and National Identity in the North American Literary Imagination*. Wayne State UP, 2015.

Taylor, Drew Hayden. "It May Be Harmless Appropriation to You. But It's Our Preservation." *Globe and Mail*, 17 May 2017, https://www.theglobeandmail.com/opinion/it-may-be-appropriation-to-you-but-its-our-preservation/article34981797/.

———. "Not 'Native Enough'?" *Quill & Quire*, vol. 161, no. 12, Dec. 1995, p. 11.

Taylor, Kate. "Maliglutit: All-Inuit Drama a Compelling Tale about Family Love." *The Globe and Mail*, 13 Apr. 2017, https://www.theglobeandmail.com/arts/film/film-reviews/maliglutit-all-inuit-drama-a-compelling-tale-built-around-family-love/article33673211.

Taylor, M. Scott. "Buffalo Hunt: International Trade and the Virtual Extinction of the North American Bison." *American Economics Review*, vol. 101, no. 7, 2011, pp. 3162–95.

Teh, Ian. "China's New Deserts." *The Walrus*, vol. 16, no. 9, 2019, pp. 52–61.

Teo, Stephen. *Eastern Westerns: Film and Genre Outside and Inside Hollywood*. Routledge, 2018.

Thacker, Robert. "Canada's Mounted: The Evolution of a Legend." *Journal of Popular Culture*, vol. 14, no. 2, 1980, pp. 298–312.

———. *The Great Prairie Fact and Literary Imagination*. U of New Mexico P, 1989.

———. "Mountie versus Outlaw: Inventing the Western Hero." *Journal of Canadian Studies*, vol. 20, no. 1, 1985, pp. 161–9.

———. "Reading North through the One-Way Mirror: Canadian Literature, the Canadian Literary Institution, and Alice Munro." *American Review of Canadian Studies*, vol. 41, no. 4, 2011, pp. 406–14.

Tompkins, Jane. *West of Everything: The Inner Life of Westerns*. Oxford UP, 1992.

Toth, Josh. *The Passing of Postmodernism: A Spectroanalysis of the Contemporary*. State U of New York P, 2010.

Tranquilla, Ronald. "Ranger and Mountie: Myths of National Identity in Zane Grey's *The Lone* Star Ranger and Ralph Connor's *Corporal Cameron*." *Journal of Popular Culture*, vol. 24, no. 3, 1990, pp. 69–80.

Trono, Mario, and Robert Boschman. "Ecocritical Agency in Time." *On Active Grounds: Agency and Time in the Environmental Humanities*, edited by Robert Boschman and Mario Trono, Wilfrid Laurier UP, 2019, pp. 1–30.

"Trump Receives Wayne Family Endorsement." *The New York Times*, 19 Jan. 2020, https://www.nytimes.com/video/us/politics/100000004154174/trump-receives-wayne-family-endorsement.html.

Turner, Frederick Jackson. *The Frontier in American History*. Henry Holt, 1920.

"Uniforms and Equipment." *Royal Canadian Mounted Police*, 17 Dec. 2014, https://www.rcmp-grc.gc.ca/en/uniforms-and-equipment.

Ursuliak, Emily. *Throwing the Diamond Hitch*. U of Calgary P, 2017.

Vanderhaeghe, Guy. *The Englishman's Boy*. McClelland and Stewart, 1996.

———. *A Good Man*. McClelland and Stewart, 2011.

———. *The Last Crossing*. McClelland and Stewart, 2002.

———. "Man on Horseback." *Things As They Are?* McClelland and Stewart, 1992.

van Herk, Aritha. "Frank Davey and the Firing Squad." *Studies in Canadian Literature*, vol. 32, no. 2. https://journals.lib.unb.ca/index.php/SCL/article/view/10576.

———. *Stampede and the Westness of West*. Frontenac House, 2016.

———. "Turning the Tables." *National Plots: Historical Fiction and Changing Ideas of Canada*, edited by Andrea Cabajsky and Brett Josef Grubisic, Wilfrid Laurier UP, 2010, pp. 131–47.

———. "Washtub Westerns." *Unsettled Pasts: Reconceiving the West Through Women's History*, edited by Sarah Carter, Lesley Erickson, Patricia Roome, and Char Smith, U of Calgary P, 2005, pp. 251–66.

Vowel, Chelsea. *Indigenous Writes: A Guide to First Nations, Métis and Inuit Issues in Canada*. Highwater Press, 2016.

Wachhorst, Wyn. " 'Come Back, Shane!' The National Nostalgia." *Southwest Review*, vol. 98, no. 1, 2013, pp. 12–25.

Walden, Keith. *Visions of Order: The Canadian Mountie in Symbol and Myth*. Butterworths, 1982.

Warner, Michael. *Publics and Counterpublics*. Zone, 2002.

Warrior, Robert. "Native American Scholarship and the Transnational Turn." *Cultural Studies Review*, vol. 15, no. 2, 2009, pp. 119–30.

Watt, F. W. "Western Myth: The World of Ralph Connor." 1959. *Writers of the Prairies*, edited by Donald G. Stephens, U of British Columbia P, 1973, pp. 7–16.

Webb, Peter. " 'A Righteous Cause': War Propaganda and Canadian Fiction, 1915–1921." *British Journal of Canadian Studies*, vol. 24, no. 1, 2011, pp. 31–48.

Weber, Bob. "Canada's Sudden North Pole Claim Surprised Government Officials, Internal Emails Suggest." *National Post*, 10 Nov. 2014, https://nationalpost.com/

news/canada/canadas-sudden-north-pole-claim-surprised-government-officials-internal-emails-suggest.

Whetter, K. S. *Understanding Genre and Medieval Romance*. Routledge, 2017.

Wiggins, Kyle and David Holmberg. " 'Gold Is Every Man's Opportunity': Castration Anxiety and the Economic Venture in *Deadwood*." *Great Plains Quarterly*, vol. 27, no. 4, 2007, pp. 283–95.

Williams, Carolyn. *Gilbert and Sullivan: Gender, Genre, and Parody*. Columbia UP, 2011.

Williams, Linda. "Melodrama Revised." *Refiguring American Film Genres*, edited by Nick Browne, U of California P, 1998, pp. 42–88.

Wills, Garry. *John Wayne: The Politics of Celebrity*. Faber, 1997.

Wilson, Keith. *Charles William Gordon*. Peguis, 1981.

Wister, Owen. *The Virginian*. 1902. Penguin, 1988.

Wolff, Mark. "Western Novels as Children's Literature in Nineteenth-Century France." *Mosaic: A Journal for the Interdisciplinary Study of Literature*, vol. 34, no. 2, 2001, pp. 87–102. *ProQuest*, https://www.proquest.com/docview/205341917?pq-origsite=primo&accountid=12378.

Wood, Susan [Joan]. *The Land in Canadian Prose, 1840–1945*. Carleton UP, 1988.

Worden, Daniel. *Masculine Style: The American West and Literary Modernism*. Palgrave, 2011.

———. "Neo-Liberalism and the Western: HBO's *Deadwood* as National Allegory." *Canadian Review of American Studies*, vol. 39, no. 2, 2009, pp. 221–46.

Wright, Will. *Six Guns and Society: A Structural Study of the Western*. U of California P, 1975.

Wyile, Herb. *Anne of Tim Hortons: Globalization and the Reshaping of Atlantic-Canadian Literature*. Wilfrid Laurier UP, 2011.

———. "Dances With Wolfers: Choreographing History in *The Englishman's Boy*." *Essays on Canadian Writing*, no. 67, 1999, pp. 23–52.

———. " 'Trust Tonto': Thomas King's Subversive Fictions and the Politics of Cultural Literacy." *Canadian Literature*, nos. 161–2, 1999, pp. 105–24.

Yates, Norris Wilson. *Gender and Genre: An Introduction to Women Writers of Formula Westerns, 1900–1950*. U of New Mexico P, 1995.

Young, Neil. "Journey through the Past." *Time Fades Away*. Reprise, 1973.

"Zacharias Kunuk Reimagines the Classic Western in His New Film *Searchers*." *Q with Tom Power*. CBC Radio, 20 Jan. 2017.

Zemeckis, Robert. *Back to the Future III*. Perf. Michael J. Fox, Christopher Lloyd, and Mary Steenburgen. Universal Pictures, 1990.

Zinnemann, Fred. *High Noon*. Perf. Gary Cooper and Grace Kelly. United Artists, 1952.

INDEX

A

Abel, Jordan, 27, 31, 38, 54, 111, 121, 142-149, 154, 206, 347, 360, 376
Acree, William G. Jr., 50
Adamson, Gil, 9, 32-33, 42, 173, 305, 307, 314-315, 326n, 335-341, 344, 347-349, 352, 361-363, 368, 372, 376
agriculture, 77-79, 103, 111, 169, 187-189, 350, 364
Alaska, 38-39, 100-101, 169, 174
Alberta, 2, 14, 26, 45, 65, 73, 75, 90, 107, 164-165, 282, 305, 331, 342, 349, 360, 362, 364, 366, 370
alcohol, 42, 104, 184-185, 187, 203, 303-304, 331, 354, 356-358, 364
Alexie, Sherman, 112, 120
Allan, Luke (William Lacey Amy), 139n, 160
Allen, Chadwick, 54n
Altman, Rick, 31n, 55-62, 84n, 86, 159, 191, 194, 243, 248
Altman, Robert, 36n, 106, 257n
Anderson, Benedict, 14, 74, 170n
Anderson, Paul Thomas, 36, 349
Andrews, Jennifer, 51, 128-131, 134, 136
anti-Americanism, 45, 134-135, 214-219
Appadurai, Arjun, 4-5, 28n, 44, 55, 78, 105n, 117, 177-179, 254, 273, 277, 374
archetypes, 21, 23 35, 57, 86, 186
archives, 29, 207-208, 213, 227-228, 232, 240, 374
Armstrong, Bob, 27, 347, 363n
Arnold, Gary, 341
Atwood, Margaret, 11, 26, 32, 135, 221, 225, 246, 252-253, 259, 281, 311

Audiard, Jacques, 343, 347
Australia, 19, 21, 66, 123

B

Babiak, Peter, 264
Baden-Powell, Robert, 14, 199, 200n
Baker, Richard G., 157, 183n, 331
Barnett, LeRoy, 95
Barnholden, Michael, 138
Barrera, Jorge, 143
Bartlett, Brian, 94n
Barwin, Gary, 27, 347
Bazin, André, 2
Beaty, Bart, 210, 215-216
Bechtel, Greg, 124
Beebee, Thomas O., 57, 60-61, 196
Bélanger, Damien-Claude, 225n
Bellah, James Warner, 235
Bentley, D. M. R., 63n, 71
Berlin, Isaiah, 9
Berton, Pierre, 58, 66, 102, 159-161, 170-171, 280
Betz, Virginia Marie, 50
Billy the Kid, 3, 11, 19, 25, 30, 32, 38, 41, 59, 61, 65, 71, 120, 136-137, 173, 225-226, 246, 255-259, 262-263, 268-269, 279, 292, 304, 307, 312, 313, 330-332
Black, Conrad, 130n
Blackness, 48, 49n, 59, 80, 106, 246, 264, 302, 334, 341; Black cowboys 3, 51, 288
Blaise, Clark, 98, 99-100, 108, 168, 299
Bledstein, Burton J., 247
Bloom, Clive, 207, 213, 217

403

Boddy, William, 217-218
Bold, Christine, 48-49, 52-53, 74, 111, 113, 170, 186n, 211-212, 297n
Boone, Daniel, 37
borders, 7, 16, 29, 41, 52-55, 59-62, 73, 78, 113, 129, 160, 178-179, 181, 211, 218, 246, 248, 252, 282; Canada-US border, 3n, 12, 15, 24, 52, 59, 63-65, 73, 99, 101, 111, 129, 134, 159-160, 179-183, 190, 252, 254, 275, 277, 280-282, 289, 295, 334, 348, 374-375; US-Mexico border, 3n, 15n, 26, 29, 50, 350
Boschman, Robert, 305n
Bowering, George, 26, 32, 41, 59, 74, 170, 191, 225, 232, 246, 248-249, 269, 279-296, 307, 309, 367, 374
Boy Scouts, 14, 158, 191-193, 196-197, 199-201, 203
Boyd, Shelley, 66n
Boym, Svetlana, 4-5, 45, 47, 52n, 99, 254, 273-274, 293, 373
Bozak, Nadia, 25-27, 33, 333, 347
Braidotti, Rosi, 309-310, 316, 323, 328, 336, 338-339, 341
Braudy, Leo, 56
Braz, Albert, 274
Brégent-Heald, Dominique, 76, 156-157, 160, 166, 168, 280
Breitbach, Julia, 119n
Brim, Connie, 126
British Columbia, 73, 133, 184, 214-215, 259, 280-281, 283, 366, 374
British. *see* United Kingdom
Broad, Graham, 209
Brode, Douglas, 8
Brown, Kirby, 148
Brown, Wendy, 13
buffalo, 4, 77, 94-96, 99-100, 102, 108, 125, 140, 315, 332
Burns, John, 324-325
Buscombe, Edward, 122, 337n
Bush, George W., 13
Butler, Judith, 32n, 220
Butts, Edward, 174

C

Calamity Jane, 65, 137
Calder, Alison, 31, 69, 75-77, 79, 111
Calgary Stampede, 19n, 20, 31, 45, 78-80
Campagna brothers (Jeff and Matthew), 93, 107, 343, 346, 363, 373
Campbell, Collin, 139, 284n
Campbell, Maria, 309
Campbell, Neil, 22, 253-254
canoes, 6, 280
capitalism, 13, 32n, 33n, 34, 36n, 48, 54-55, 57, 72, 123, 168-169, 178-179, 186n, 189, 224n, 246, 264, 310, 351-352, 355, 357, 376
Caple, Natalee, 27n, 33, 302n, 333n, 347n
car culture, 34, 78, 99, 116, 306, 364-372
Carrera, Isabel, 248, 283-284, 292
Cassar, Jon, 347, 360
cattle, 16, 23, 125, 133, 178, 233, 240, 306
Cawelti, John G., 49, 226, 249
celebrity, 35, 38, 80, 115, 120-121, 129-130, 137, 140, 165, 171, 234, 257-258, 270, 274, 278, 342, 369
Certeau, Michel de, 5, 102
Charles, Ron, 344n
Chester, Blanca, 148
China, 46, 314; Chinese people, 46, 89, 287, 331
Chirica, Irina, 298n
Chisholm, A. M., 10-11
Chrétien, Jean, 13
Christianity, 27n, 39, 68, 119, 130-131, 153, 155-158, 162-165, 171, 175-177, 184, 190, 201-203, 205, 241-242, 265-267, 301, 314, 326, 342; missionaries, 38, 68, 104, 162, 164, 166, 175-176, 183-184, 192, 301-302, 304, 325-326; Muscular Christianity, 27n, 32, 39, 87, 154, 158, 161, 175, 196, 206, 228, 340, 356, 375; preachers, 106, 265, 321-322, 115, 288
Christie, Stuart, 118
Clark, J. J., 302, 326n
Clarke, Michael Tavel, 6n, 43-44
climate change, 8, 34-35, 103, 108, 339, 350, 365, 368n

Cody, Buffalo Bill, 4-5, 20, 61, 80, 85n, 112, 138-142, 159, 168, 257n, 274
Cody, H. A., 3n, 14, 17, 26, 39-40, 58, 60-61, 66-68, 74, 80, 104-105, 107-108, 156-158, 161-165, 167, 169-177, 188n, 190-203, 205-206, 217, 374-375
Cohen, Esther, 331n,
Cohen, Margaret, 55
Cold War, 11, 260
Coleman, Daniel, 39, 102, 154, 158, 175, 203, 317, 345
Collin, Yvette Running Horse, 308, 319
colonialism, 7-9, 30-31, 33, 37-39, 78-79, 89-90, 92, 94-96, 104-105, 113, 116n, 125-126, 133, 135-136, 139, 141-142, 145-148, 151-156, 167, 169, 175-179, 239-240, 251-252, 272-273, 277-278, 286-287, 300-301, 307-309, 320-321, 345, 352, 359n, 361, 364-367, 373-377
comics, 10, 29-30, 55, 134n, 159, 170, 208, 210-211, 213-218, 258, 265, 270n, 283, 299, 332, 342
Connor, Ralph (Charles W. Gordon), 3n, 7n, 10, 14, 16, 26, 37, 39-40, 58, 61, 65-70, 87, 90, 92n, 104, 108, 156-158, 161-172, 175-177, 179-190, 200n, 201-203, 205-206, 349, 374-375
conservatism, 9-14, 20, 33, 35, 49, 68, 75, 76, 79, 90, 114, 123, 127, 131, 157, 175, 192, 214-215, 233, 351-352, 365, 376
Conway, Christopher, 21, 25n, 29, 50, 86, 297n
Cook, Pam, 120
Cooley, Dennis, 61, 226, 257-258
Cooper, Catherine, 4, 8, 21, 138
Cooper, Courtney Ryley, 90-91, 93, 100-101
Cooper, James Fenimore, 37, 50, 80, 186, 192, 329n
Cordell, Sigrid Anderson, 303
Corkin, Stanley, 11, 82
cowboys, 1-2, 4, 6, 22-23, 32, 41, 50, 61, 77, 82n, 85-86, 98, 125-127, 133, 135, 137, 150, 160, 173, 183n, 217, 229, 240, 252, 269, 271, 285-286, 297, 307-309, 316, 322, 341, 369

Cowboys for Trump, 15, 57, 350
Cox, James H., 133
Craig, Terrence, 164
Crane, Susan, 316
Cruise, Cian, 149-151
Curwood, James Oliver, 156-157, 159, 163, 166-168, 203
Custer, George, 38, 63, 121-122

D

D'haen, Theo, 245-247, 249
Daniells, Roy, 165
Daniels, Bruce C., 12, 134-136
Daniels, Rudolph, 101
Darias-Beautell, Eva, 6
Davey, Frank, 32n, 41, 56n, 81n, 82n, 103, 112n, 138n, 144, 221-223, 225, 246, 248, 254, 269-279, 285, 287, 294
Davidson, Arnold E., 128-131, 134, 136
Dawson, Michael, 48n, 161, 163, 166, 169-171, 175, 203, 209, 212
Day-Lewis, Daniel, 36-37, 357
de Certeau, Michel, 5, 102
decolonization, 22, 30-31, 33, 53-54, 59, 125-126, 153, 193, 215, 249, 254, 282, 287, 295, 300, 308-309, 330, 361, 367, 374, 376
democracy, 16, 31, 47, 85n, 128, 167, 169, 297n-298n
Deranger, Susana, 31
Derrida, Jacques, 59, 103, 250
Desmarais, Mary-Dailey, 20n, 28n, 38, 85n, 134n
deWitt, Patrick, 19, 27, 42, 160n, 173, 343-344, 347-348, 358, 360, 372, 374, 376
Diamond, Neil, 241-242
Dinka, Nicholas, 306
Dippie, Brian W., 63, 78
disease, 41, 304, 326-327, 368
Dobson, Kit, 6, 22n, 32n, 272
dogs, 127-128, 230-231, 267-268, 328, 333, 344
Drainie, Bronwyn, 337
Driscoll, Ian, 166, 215, 243
Druick, Zoë, 210

Duignan, Brian, 264
Dummitt, Christopher, 164, 172, 175, 187
Dumont, Gabriel, 80, 112n, 137-142, 149, 154, 206, 270, 272, 274, 348, 375
Durante, Jaymes, 153
Ďurovičová, Nataša, 177-178
Dwyer, Carlota Cárdenas de, 49
Dwyer, Tessa, 34n

E

East, 2, 21, 39, 45-49, 73-76, 80, 95, 98, 101, 155, 157, 161, 175, 184, 192, 197, 206-207, 240-241, 281, 285-286, 289-295, 309, 348, 360, 367, 373-374
Eastwood, Clint, 22n, 23, 29, 33, 35, 36n, 46, 58-59, 61, 87, 106-107, 112, 138, 155, 173, 193n, 205, 230, 232, 246, 254-255, 264-269, 311n, 321, 323n, 330, 337, 341, 351, 365
ecocriticism, 42, 46, 266, 268, 348, 351, 354-356, 364-365
Eden. *see* garden myths
Edwards, Justin D., 317
Eggleston, Wilfrid, 6n
Ellingson, Chloë, 97
Elliott, Alicia, 216n
Emerson, Ralph Waldo, 127, 298
Eneas, Brian, 151
environment, 7-8, 34-35, 43, 70, 96-97, 117, 137, 304-305, 309, 336, 344, 348, 350, 363, 369, 372-373,
Erdrich, Louise, 112, 116-118, 120n
Evans, David H., 119, 121, 299-300
Eyre, Chris, 120n

F

Fagan, Kristina, 135
Falconer, Rachel, 193, 196
Farquharson, Danine, 2
Farrow, John, 122
Fee, Margery, 7, 89, 133n, 135
Fehrle, Johannes, 17n, 25n, 73, 131n, 246n, 305
Ferrara, Alessandro, 271n

film, 10, 27n, 28-30, 35, 61-62, 107-108, 115-116, 122-123, 134, 136, 213-214, 273, 300, 307, 311, 320, 323-324
Findlay, Len, 52n
Fisher, Jaimey, 84
FitzMaurice, Kevin, 11n
Flaherty, Kathleen, 129
Fludernik, Monika, 247-248
Ford, John, 10, 39, 48, 87, 89, 119, 122, 149-154, 173, 206, 250, 307, 375
Foucault, Michel, 5, 93, 212
Fowler, Alastair, 84
Francis, Daniel, 50, 52n, 63, 111, 270
Frankiewicz, Shane Joseph Willis, 49n, 59
Franklin, John, 90, 94, 101
Frayling, Christopher, 16, 19, 47-48
freedom, 9, 17, 44, 47, 51n, 93, 96, 103, 133, 146-147, 185, 189, 239, 286, 288, 297-298, 311, 315, 341, 367, 371; free trade, 9, 135, 207, 272
French, Warren, 316n
French Canadians, 142, 166, 170, 183, 277, 279-288, 291-293
Freud, Sigmund, 36, 232, 267, 299, 314, 337
frontiers, 6, 8-9, 11n, 14-18, 23n, 49, 63-75, 88-103, 168-169, 246-247, 297n, 327, 349, 367, 377
Frow, John, 22n, 85, 220-221
Frye, Northrop, 21, 49, 57-58, 63, 69-72, 76, 84, 135, 138n, 292, 350
fur trade, 23n, 87, 95, 98, 178-179, 192, 280, 285, 306
Furlong, Dayle, 2n, 25-26, 27, 33, 42, 347-348, 360, 374

G

Gaberscek, Carlo, 47
Gaines, Jane Marie, 1, 360n
Galan, F. W., 56
garden myths, 7, 66-68, 75, 87, 198, 286, 342, 364
Garneau, David, 137-138
Garrett, Pat, 71, 173, 256-257, 262, 304
Garrett-Petts, W. F., 287
garrison mentality, 49, 63, 69-71, 76

Garvie, Maureen, 196-199
Gassett, Ortega y, 61
Gaudry, Adam, 80, 270
gender, 32, 40, 85, 107, 139, 175, 193, 220, 227, 231, 247, 249, 261, 266, 281-284, 288, 291, 338, 351, 358, 366, 371; feminism, 32, 264, 282, 291-293, 305, 340; masculinity, 153, 203, 232, 284, 294, 298, 337-340, 350-352, 356-359, 362-363, 365, 368, 372; women, 32-33, 48, 86, 107, 142, 150-153, 170, 190-191, 209, 260, 283-284, 291, 294, 303, 312, 337, 348, 351, 363, 366-368, 371, 375
genre, 3, 21-24, 29, 34-35, 55-63, 72-73, 81-87, 119, 160, 175, 193n, 194-197, 203, 219-221, 226-228, 239, 246-253, 287, 336, 375; adaptation, 36, 62, 77n, 83n, 88, 107, 120n, 161, 167, 250, 253, 318, 341, 347, 360n, 363n, American Westerns, 4, 19, 24-25, 28, 31, 37, 41, 65, 108, 112, 137, 183, 246, 303; anti-Westerns, 16, 51, 70, 72, 214, 249; Australian Westerns, 19; Canadian Westerns, 6-7, 10n, 18-19, 24-30, 56-59, 68, 73, 87-88, 179, 225, 245-247, 300, 349; cavalry Westerns, 14, 23, 306; Christian Westerns, 27; cop movies, 22, 58, 254; detective fiction, 86, 119, 160, 211, 227-228, 236-240; Eastern Westerns, 245-246; epic, 22, 31, 36, 57-58, 82-83, 89, 122, 195, 251, 284, 306, 311-312, 316, 339, 359; fantasy, 85, 120-121, 132-133, 203; Gothic, 250, 253, 335; Harlequin romance, 27, 85, 283, 286; historical Westerns, 60, 87, 178, 299-301, 304-305, 309-311, 324, 345; historiographic metafiction, 59-60, 258, 312, 354; homage, 18-19, 35, 237; Indo Westerns, 19, 46; Italian Westerns, 44, 46-47, 58, 123 193, 230; literary Westerns, 3, 21, 30, 60-64, 72, 118-119, 206, 245, 335, 375; magic realism, 38, 121, 131; melodrama, 58, 84-85, 164, 191-192, 248; Mexican Westerns, 3n, 25n, 29-30, 50; mode, 27n, 82-84, 119n, 191n, 197, 220-221, 226, 247-248, 250; myth, 16-17, 55-57, 60, 69-72, 297-305, 345; noir, 2n, 84, 194, 236, 313; Northerns or Northwesterns, 18, 39, 59, 65 156, 159-171, 190, 246, 328; parody, 13, 16, 18-19, 24, 32, 84, 129, 220-229, 237, 242, 248, 265, 269, 287, 364; post-Westerns, 2n, 17n, 22-27, 41, 61, 86, 36n, 112, 119, 248-250, 253, 266, 300-301, 309, 324, 345, 343, 350, 373-374, 376; Prairie fiction, 7n, 64, 69, 76-79, 81-83, 87, 108, 111; pulp, 10, 29-30, 35, 40, 61, 63, 74, 159-160, 164, 166, 191, 201-228, 315, 349, 374; realism, 23-25, 46, 56, 81-87, 108, 131, 200, 264; revisionist Westerns, 24-25, 49n, 60, 62, 83, 91, 119, 121, 243, 257, 269, 299-300, 345, 350, 352, 372, 375; romance, 22, 27, 57-58, 85, 183, 195, 248, 292, 302, 316, 339; science fiction, 85, 223, 248, 311, 328, 335, 373, 377; space Westerns, 84, 194, 335, 341; Soviet Westerns, 46, 47, 123
ghosts, 106, 249-270, 292, 321, 337; ghost towns 1, 2n, 252-253, 311, 373
Gittings, Christopher, 162
globalization, 5, 8, 14, 28n, 43, 47-48 52-55, 75, 77, 135, 160, 176-179, 190, 269, 276, 377; *see also* transnationalism
gold, 35, 37, 78, 88, 145n, 169, 246n, 267, 309, 343-344, 348, 350, 353-365
Goldie, Terry, 144
Gordon, J. King, 158, 165
Gottfriedson, Garry, 111, 125-126, 149, 154, 206, 329-330, 376
Gould, Glenn, 75, 88-89
Grace, Sherrill E., 2n, 18, 64, 74, 89-90
Grant, Kevin, 47-48, 352
Grant, Shelagh D., 91n
Greeley, Horace, 90, 289
Grey, Zane, 10, 22, 146, 186, 191n
Gross, Paul, 19, 35, 331, 364
Gruber, Frank, 23n
Guillén, Claudio, 21, 28, 46
guns, 4, 69, 86, 120, 151-153, 170, 180-186, 210, 231, 233, 235, 237, 240-241, 259-264, 287, 297, 332, 342

H

Hackworth, Jason, 13n
Hamilton, Edith, 314
Hammill, Faye, 130-131
Haraway, Donna, 307n, 309-310, 316
Harper, Stephen, 13-16, 90-91, 101, 349, 361
Harrison, Dick, 19n, 64-74, 82, 169, 186-187, 286, 295-296
Hassan, Ihab, 221n, 257, 270n
hats, 2, 6, 13, 18, 24, 77-78, 84, 124, 133n, 137, 173, 196, 205, 217, 220, 229, 265, 284, 294
Hawley, Alix, 27, 33, 37, 137n, 347
Healey, Michael, 91
Hearne, Joanna, 113-114, 300
Hendryx, James B., 157n, 160
heroes, 2, 14, 18, 40, 57, 68, 70, 83, 87, 126, 137, 142, 149, 158-159, 171-172, 205, 237, 250-251, 276-279, 281, 292, 298, 337, 351-352, 357; anti-heroes, 11, 39-40, 50, 161, 234, 245, 250, 265-269
Herzog, Charlotte Cornelia, 1, 360n
Heumann, Joseph K., 266, 268, 310n, 348-351, 362
high/low culture, 3n, 29-30, 61, 216-217, 219, 227, 235, 247-248, 278, 283, 374
Higley, Brewster, 4, 6
Hill, Colin, 56n, 81
Hillhouse, Emily, 46
Hirsch, E. D., 23, 247n
Hitt, Sarah, 2
Hoberek, Andrew, 247-249, 295
Hochbruck, Wolfgang, 51, 143n
Holcomb, Rod, 299n
Hollywood. *see* film
Holmberg, David, 359
home, 4-5, 8-9, 31, 48, 99, 176, 273, 288, 293, 344n, 348, 356, 367, 372
"Home on the Range," 4, 8, 138, 325
Hopkins, Pauline, 59
Hopson, Travis, 153
Horne, Dee, 31, 126, 272n
Horowitz, Josh, 297

horses, 50, 106-107, 116, 230-232, 302, 305-311, 314-335, 336, 344-345, 368-370; contrasted with motorized vehicles, 115-116, 188, 252, 286, 306, 308, 309, 323, 367-368, 370; horse opera, 42, 306, 271; horse-human hybrids, 230, 315-320, 323-326, 333-334, 372; Horsemen of the Apocalypse, 265-266, 321-323
Howell, Charlotte E., 26
Hulan, Renée, 114
Hutcheon, Linda, 59-61, 146, 220-227, 229, 237, 245-247, 257-258, 273-274, 279, 312
Hutchison, Don, 166-167, 169, 171

I

ideology, 10, 36-39, 57-61, 70-72, 89, 136, 175, 183-184, 264
immigrants, 16, 31n, 48-49, 52-53, 71, 89, 160, 168, 170, 254
imperialism. *see* colonization
Iñárritu, Alejandro, 106, 121, 328-329
Indick, William, 35
Indigenous peoples, 7, 38-39, 51-54, 97, 111-154, 170, 174-175, 177, 238-255, 269-279, 282-283, 286-287, 300, 308-309, 317-318, 345, 361, 375-376
individualism, 70-71, 160-161, 167, 211, 297-298
Ingold, Tim, 103, 105
Interlandi, Jeneen, 51n
Internet, 61, 134, 144, 190, 209
Inuit, 88-89, 108, 111, 149-154, 158, 277
isolation, 18, 21, 23n, 49, 66, 71, 80, 88, 149, 195, 211
isolationism, 8, 19, 21, 47, 349, 376

J

Jackson, Mark, 77n, 308
James, Jesse, 65, 136-137, 171, 259-264
Jameson, Fredric, 4, 33n-34n, 36n 44, 57, 61, 221-223, 226, 246, 254, 273-274
Japan, 45-46, 123
Jarmusch, Jim, 91n, 93, 95n
Jennings, John, 3, 77, 95, 162n,

Jiles, Paulette, 26, 29, 32, 33, 38, 41, 59, 136, 160n, 225, 246, 250, 253-254, 259-265, 269, 279, 319n, 321n, 373-374
Johnson, Brian, 122, 126, 134
Johnston, Carrie, 303n
Johnston, Sean, 27, 307, 347
Johnston, Wayne, 94n, 295
Jones, Ted, 162-163, 176
Joudrey, Susan L., 78
Justice, Daniel Heath, 112-113, 272n

K

Kamboureli, Smaro, 6n, 257, 278
Kane, Thomas H., 121
Katerberg, William H., 14-15, 18, 63-65, 68, 73, 160, 185,
Keahey, Deborah, 8n
Keefer, Janice Kulyk, 75
Keene, Adrienne, 143n
Kellner, Douglas, 56, 257
Kelly, Robert A., 169
Kershner, Irvin, 327-328
Khan, Shahrukh, 146
Killingsworth, Colleen, 79n
King, Thomas, 10, 22, 27, 37-38, 51-43, 59, 80, 94-96, 105, 108, 111, 113-116, 118-137, 143, 146, 149, 154, 160n, 175, 205-206, 225, 246, 250-251, 253, 254, 256, 270, 278, 282, 300, 312, 319n, 320, 360, 374-376
Knight, Chris, 89
Kollin, Susan, 91
Kolodny, Annette, 66n, 298, 303, 326, 338
Kopecky, Arno, 133n
Kreisel, Henry, 69
Kristmanson, Lynn, 306, 310
Kroetsch, Robert, 40, 42, 69, 76-78, 185n, 210, 221-222, 246, 256n, 281, 314, 317, 319, 323, 347, 348, 353-357, 374
Krotz, Sarah Wylie, 33-34, 92
Krueger, Misty, 194, 197
Kulbach, René L., 332
Kunuk, Zacharias, 88-89, 108, 111, 124, 149-150, 154, 206, 348, 375-376

L

L'Amour, Louis, 173, 239, 250
Lakoff, George, 35-36
landscape, 2, 5, 17, 47, 66-67, 69-71, 76, 79, 92, 101, 103-109, 137-138, 143, 149, 177-178, 183, 252, 268, 281, 286, 298n, 305, 338-340, 352, 362, 365-366
LaRocque, Emma, 120n, 124-125, 271-272, 278
Le Cain, Maximilian, 257n
Lecker, Robert, 81
left (political). *see* liberalism
Leone, Sergio, 44, 48-49, 59, 87, 93, 173, 265, 358
liberalism, 8-14, 33, 90, 114, 123, 157, 332, 335, 341, 361, 376
Lincoln, Kenneth, 51
London, Jack, 39, 157, 159, 163, 165-166, 328n, 333n,
Lone Ranger, 1-2, 118, 120, 128, 131-132, 170, 217, 243, 302
Loo, Tina, 209, 211, 213, 215-216
Lu, Jie, 24
Lusty, Terry, 330

M

MacGillivray, Royce, 164-165
MacKenzie, David Bruce Hollis, 9n, 36n
Mackie, John, 39, 157
MacLaren, Eli, 38n, 162-163, 165-166, 179, 182-184
MacLeod, Alexander, 281, 295
MacLeod, David I., 199, 200n
MacSkimming, Roy, 208, 209, 217
magazines, 10, 29-30, 40, 146, 162, 164, 166, 191, 201-202, 207-243, 269, 283, 349n, 374
Mandel, Eli, 5n
Mangold, James, 25, 342
Manifest Destiny, 39, 52, 68, 73n, 100, 105, 135, 147, 169, 174-175, 183, 190, 342
Manitoba, 88, 90, 138-139, 165, 269-270
Mannell, Julie, 146

mapping as metaphor, 5, 17, 24n, 33-34, 78, 81-82, 90, 92, 102, 156, 267, 285, 291, 368
Marovitz, Sanford E., 20n, 82n, 83n, 85n
Marubbio, M. Elise, 38n
Marx, Leo, 66n
mass media, 16, 20, 52, 118, 122, 129-130, 134, 142, 161, 166, 209, 214-215, 217, 258, 270-274, 352
May, Karl, 46-47
McCarthy, Cormac, 4n, 26, 196-197, 206, 253, 307, 322, 366
McCourt, Edward, 6n, 69, 73
McGee, Patrick, 10n, 49n, 83, 172n
McGimpsey, David, 107n
McKanna, Clare V. Jr., 303-304
McKay, Don, 1-2, 94, 96-98, 108, 339, 367
McKay, Ian, 13-14
McKegney, Sam, 135
mclennan, rob, 148
McMahon, Ryan, 144
McNaron, David L., 205
Medicine Line. *see* borders: Canada-US
Meeuf, Russell, 123
Métis, 137-141, 154, 174, 269, 277, 279
Mexal, Stephen J., 82
Mexico, 3n, 17, 47, 49-50, 59, 72, 78, 155, 283, 342
Miles, D. O., 9n
Miller, J.R., 124, 150
mining, 42, 83, 97, 169, 184-185, 265-269, 305, 335-341, 349-354, 358, 360-365, 368
Mitchell, Lee Clark, 3, 16-17, 19, 22-23, 26-27, 36n, 65, 226
modernism, 12, 40, 81-82, 222, 247, 252-258, 269, 277; anti-modernism, 36, 48, 50, 76-77, 93, 192, 210, 226, 252, 269, 328
modernity, 5, 49, 55, 79, 108-109, 115-116, 176-177, 252-253, 277, 293-294, 308, 343, 350, 365, 374, 376-377; modernization, 34, 49, 80, 100, 161, 226-227, 360
Monkman, Leslie, 111

Monticone, Paul, 84, 194
Mora, Carlos, 50
Moran, Rodger J., 162-163
Moretti, Franco, 19, 43-44, 62, 86
Morton, W. L., 165
Moss, Laura, 31
Motyka, John, 313
mountains, 91, 102, 106, 133, 184, 202, 305, 314, 338-340, 351, 356, 362-363
Mounties. *see* policing: Royal Canadian Mounted Police
Mowat, Farley, 91
multiculturalism, 11, 15, 80, 139, 272-274, 278-279
Murphy, Kathleen, 268
Murray, Robin L., 266, 268, 310n, 348-351, 362
music, 4, 8, 128, 171, 194, 217, 275-276, 353, 357, 360, 364

N

Nance, Susan, 78-79
nationalism, 7, 11, 31, 37, 52-53, 56, 59, 73, 77, 81-82, 135-136, 142, 165, 175, 183, 190, 206, 210, 272-273, 311
Neale, Steve, 10-11, 86, 194
neoconservatism, 12-13, 16
neoliberalism, 13, 16, 52, 54, 246, 310, 349-351
Nestruck, J. Kelly, 141
New, W. H., 100n
New Brunswick, 162, 192, 197
Newfoundland, 1-2, 5, 26, 34, 75, 88, 94n, 360, 373-374
Newman, Judie, 123
newspapers, 61, 162, 270
Ngai, Sianne, 145n
Nichol, bp, 3n, 11, 25n, 30, 32, 38, 136, 225, 246, 255-256, 259, 279, 294, 312, 373
Nir, Oded, 19, 34n, 44n
Nischik, Reingard M., 40
North, 2, 17-18, 39, 65-66, 72, 74-75, 87-91, 96-97, 100-103, 108, 149-150, 153, 157-158, 166-168, 203, 289, 353

North-West Mounted Police. *see* policing: North-West Mounted Police
North-West Resistance, 38, 65, 80, 128, 174, 270, 275-276
North-West Territories, 66, 73, 101, 305
nostalgia, 2, 4-5, 15, 30, 44-49, 56, 75, 78, 119-121, 197, 226, 241, 252-254, 273-275, 279, 293-296, 367

O

oil, 2, 33-37, 42, 305, 343, 348-350, 354-358, 363-366
Ondaatje, Michael, 3, 5, 11, 19, 30, 38, 41, 59, 61, 70-71, 136, 160, 173, 225-226, 246, 250, 253-259, 262-263, 268-269, 279, 292, 294, 304, 313, 330, 335, 337, 373-374
Ontario, 65, 67, 101, 164-165, 168, 187, 200n, 270, 276, 359n
outlaw/lawman figures, 22n, 26, 39, 58, 138, 155, 169-174, 184, 190, 198, 203, 205-208, 213, 220, 231-232, 236, 238, 242, 253, 283, 288, 303, 332, 336
Owram, Doug, 68, 73, 87, 100

P

Pacey, Desmond, 10, 164n
past, 5, 48-49, 75-81, 93-94, 99, 120, 124, 222-226, 252-253, 259, 294-295, 367, 373
Pearlman, Judith, 88-89
Pearson, Sarina, 19n
Peckinpah, Sam, 249, 256-257, 259, 307
Percy, Owen, 31
Phillips, Louis, 114-116, 123
Phillips, William, 19, 107, 331, 347
Pippin, Robert B., 127
Pitts, Gordon, 13, 75
Poitier, Sydney, 51, 106, 246
Polack, Fiona, 2
Polić, Vanja, 303n, 312, 352, 361
policing, 18, 86, 100n, 151, 166, 170, 173, 190, 207, 210, 214-215, 219-220, 233-237, 253, 330, 373; North-West Mounted Police, 38, 66, 155, 161, 171, 179, 184-188, 304, 333, 364; Royal Canadian Mounted Police, 18, 23n, 56, 65, 69-72, 155-163, 165-171, 176, 179-181, 184-186, 203, 205, 209-210, 235, 294
pornography, 30, 209, 215, 248, 283-284
Porter, Edwin S., 62n, 93
Post, Robert C., 22n, 83
post-colonialism. *see* decolonization
post-humanism, 249, 307-310, 316, 323, 328, 336-341, 373
postmodernism, 22, 40-41, 59, 79-80, 219-228, 245-296, 300, 312-313, 373-376
Prats, Armando José, 111
Price, Luke, 10n, 74, 160n, 203, 212, 219, 223, 227, 229, 241-242, 315n, 374
Purdy, Al, 210, 214

Q

Quam-Wickham, Nancy, 350-351, 360
Quebec, 18n, 19n, 97, 270, 279-296, 367

R

race, 88, 106, 124, 128, 131, 149, 151, 154, 176, 183, 194, 238-241, 247, 254, 269, 272, 275, 374, 375
railways, 39, 64, 73, 80, 88-89, 92-101, 108-109, 115, 155-156, 159, 168, 177, 184, 187-190, 202, 245, 252, 260, 308, 314, 364, 367
range. *see* landscape
Reagan, Ronald, 12-13, 160, 224, 349-350
realism. *see* genre and mode
Redekop, Magdalene, 201n
regionalism, 5n, 8n, 15, 18, 46, 73-88, 103, 253-255, 285, 292, 374, 377
Richler, Mordecai, 277
Ricou, Laurie, 69, 156n
Rieder, John, 22n
Riel, Louis, 80, 112n, 128, 137-142, 269-279, 305n
Rifkind, Candida, 39, 154, 158, 163, 165-166, 196, 203
right (political). *see* conservatism
Ripplinger, Sarah, 329

Index *411*

Ritter, Kathleen, 145-148
Roberts, Katherine Ann, 3, 7, 32-33, 73, 304n-305, 325-326, 328
Robinson, Harry, 308
rodeo, 19, 32, 79-80, 125-126, 285
Rodness, Roshayaid, 129
Ronda, James P., 98-99
Roosevelt, Theodore, 49, 162, 165, 168, 170, 179-182
Ropa, Anastasija, 316
rural-urban relationships, 22, 50, 75-77, 79, 98, 160-161
Rushdie, Salman, 3n, 5n, 20n
Russia, 6, 8, 38, 46-47, 100, 123, 174

S

saloons, 85-86, 115n, 173, 184-185, 187, 353, 356-357, 362
Samutina, Natalia, 193n
Saskatchewan, 58, 65, 90, 107, 138, 167, 174, 207, 282, 330
scale, 5-6, 43-45, 82, 177-178, 190, 196
Schneider, Reisa, 125
Scholes, Robert, 23-24, 33, 84-85, 247n
Schroeder, Jonathan David Shelly, 81n
Schwantes, Carlos A., 98-99
Scott, Jamie S., 162-163, 176
Sealey, D. Bruce, 304
Seesengood, Robert Paul, 266
Service, Robert, 160, 163, 353-355, 357
settlement, 7, 31, 33-34, 39, 47, 52, 64-66, 77, 83n, 91n, 89, 92, 100, 149, 154-156, 166, 169, 188, 282, 360
sex work, 36n, 261, 264; virgin/whore dichotomy, 232, 267, 299
sexuality, 40, 231, 232, 265, 268, 335, 354
sheriffs. *see* policing
Shively, JoEllen, 80, 124, 133
sidekicks, 2, 131, 187, 206, 302, 366
signposts, 1, 33-34, 37
Sircar, Sanjay, 228
Sitting Bull, 140, 274

Slotkin, Richard, 20, 23, 28-29, 36n, 38, 41, 45, 52, 70, 85n, 119, 122, 168-169, 250, 260, 297-298, 341, 372
Smart, Robert, 46
Smith, Brad, 27, 347, 366
Smith, Carlton, 2n, 52n, 116n, 118, 120, 221n, 300n
Smith, Michelle Denise, 208, 210, 212-213
Smith, Thomas Brent, 134n
snow, 102-108, 291, 318, 329
social order, 9, 23, 36n, 50, 64-67, 82, 99, 160, 186-187, 211, 217, 219, 235-236, 264
socialism, 9, 12, 47n, 72, 123, 131
Söderlind, Sylvia, 250, 254-255, 258-259, 266
Sontag, Susan, 22n
Sorensen, Sue, 76, 286, 322-323
South, 39, 50, 51, 89, 102, 107, 158, 162, 166, 259
South Africa, 14, 306, 333-334
Southwest, 1, 16, 74, 102, 149, 210, 220, 228-229, 368
Soviet Union. *see* Russia
space, 6, 8-9, 84, 102, 194, 328, 335, 341, 377
Spivak, Gayatri Chakravorty, 8n, 30-31, 33, 38, 144
Stacey, Robert David, 221-222
Stanley, George F. G., 270
Staveley, Helene, 283-284, 291-293
Steele, Harwood, 10n
Stefanucci, Tracy, 54
Stenson, Fred, 14, 19, 32, 179, 305-306, 333, 335, 347
Stephens, Donald G., 76, 90, 165
Stetsons. *see* hats
Stevens, George, 40, 68, 342, 352
Stewart, Fenn Elan, 359n
Stewart, Susan, 5n, 34, 78n
Stoker, Bram, 328
Stone, Ted, 229
Strange, Carolyn, 209, 211, 213, 215-216
Sugars, Cynthia, 31n

sunsets, 1, 117, 196, 250n, 284, 293-294, 307-309
Sutherland, Ronald, 72-73, 161n, 245n
Sweet, Matthew, 113n
Swift, Jamie, 13-14
Szklarski, Cassandra, 142

T

Tan, Kathy-Ann, 7-8, 146
Taylor, Drew Hayden, 134n, 143, 147
Taylor, Kate, 150
Taylor, M. Scott, 95
Teh, Ian, 46
television, 28, 88, 131, 142, 167, 213-218, 273, 303, 309
Teo, Stephen, 17n, 45-46
Thacker, Robert, 18-19, 69, 72, 82, 156, 163, 167, 169
theatre, 27, 91, 112, 129, 134n, 138-142, 168, 209, 302, 347
Tompkins, Jane, 86, 250, 299, 303, 306, 314-316, 326, 337, 339-340, 359
Tonto, 2, 128, 131, 302
Toth, Josh, 41n, 83n, 247, 253
trains. *see* railways
Tranquilla, Ronald, 16, 69-70, 167, 252,
transnationalism, 5-6, 8, 19, 22n, 24, 32n, 39, 50-56, 72, 109, 155, 177-183, 190, 254-255, 272-273, 285, 325, 345, 374-375; *see also* globalization
Trono, Mario, 305n
trucks. *see* car culture
Trump, Donald, 15-16, 47, 54, 57, 141, 207, 224, 297n, 349-350
Turcotte, Gerry, 31n
Turner, Frederick Jackson, 17, 63-64, 75, 116, 161, 168, 247, 297n

U

Ungalaaq, Natar, 39, 88-89, 108, 111, 149, 206, 348, 375
United Kingdom, 7, 49, 64-66, 68, 71, 73, 82, 91, 100, 102, 116, 122, 160, 165, 169-170, 174, 179, 182, 185-187, 225, 298, 333

Ursuliak, Emily, 27, 306, 347-348, 365-373

V

van Herk, Aritha, 1n, 18-20, 32-33, 45, 74, 78, 250, 275-276, 305, 355, 357
Vanderhaeghe, Guy, 10, 27, 32, 41, 60, 76, 92-93, 101, 107, 112, 119, 178, 197, 206, 295, 300-301, 304-305, 309, 311-323, 326-327, 330, 372
violence, 9, 32, 36n, 37, 41, 69-70, 99, 131, 151, 153, 154, 171, 183, 190, 197, 200, 210, 215, 218, 220, 246, 250-255, 260-262, 275, 287, 297-313, 322, 324-327, 337, 342-344, 352, 357-360, 372
Vowel, Chelsea, 139, 147, 271, 274

W

Wachhorst, Wyn, 45, 191, 195
Walden, Keith, 56, 66, 159-161, 209
Walton, Priscilla L., 51, 128-131, 134, 136
war, 32, 130n, 156, 192, 197, 200, 203, 217, 275-278, 302, 334; Afghanistan, 13; American Civil War, 23n, 38, 51, 87, 153, 159, 229, 232, 259, 297, 325; Boer Wars, 13-14, 306, 333; Indian Wars, 23, 63, 138, 187, 240, 298; Iraq, 44; Vietnam, 44, 123; War of 1812, 122; World War I, 115, 164-165, 168, 179, 181-182, 197-198, 214, 309; World War II, 11, 45, 205-219, 242
Wardhaugh, Robert, 69, 75-76
Ware, John, 3
Warner, Michael, 214
Warrior, Robert, 17n, 53
Warwick, Jack, 17-18
Watt, F. W., 164, 168
Wayne, John, 8, 15n, 16, 26, 38, 54, 87, 106, 111-154, 173, 224, 230, 232, 239, 250-251, 270, 375
Webb, Peter, 164-165
Weber, Bob, 101
West, Elliott, 21
West, 2, 21, 44, 54, 68-69, 74-76, 94, 98, 101, 137, 146, 148, 250, 252-253, 283, 289, 291, 298n, 305n, 309, 350-352,

West (*continued*)
371; American West, 14-17, 19, 63-66, 91, 159, 170, 303; Canadian West, 14, 18, 34, 38, 63-67, 73-76, 87, 90-91, 169, 180-181, 222, 295; Midwest, 13n, 15-16, 67, 228; Old West, 18n, 91, 119, 191, 291, 302-303, 315, 352, 366; Western world, 12, 14, 21, 30, 39, 146, 178, 241, 285, 308, 314, 350, 376; Wild West, 20n, 54, 58, 63, 98, 119, 144, 180, 271, 324, 326, 341

Westfell, William, 18
Whetter, K. S., 84
Wiggins, Kyle, 359
Wild West shows, 61, 80, 140-142, 159, 168, 274
Williams, Carolyn, 226
Williams, Linda, 84-85, 191n
Wills, Garry, 112, 123
Wilson, Keith, 164-165, 179, 182, 201
Wister, Owen, 3, 22, 35, 49, 61, 65, 67-68, 146, 162, 167, 172n, 186, 191n, 230
Wittenberg, David, 6n, 43-44
Wittgenstein, Ludwig, 22
Wolff, Mark, 192, 199
Wood, Susan [Joan], 18, 156
Worden, Daniel, 13, 284n, 348, 350
Wright, Will, 24n, 57
Wyile, Herb, 20, 74-75, 80, 131, 133-134, 301, 326, 328

Y

Yates, Norris Wilson, 23n, 190, 191n, 303n, 367, 371
Young, Neil, 5n
Yukon, 39, 73, 88, 169, 171, 176, 328n

Z

Zemeckis, Robert, 99, 119, 223, 366
Zinnemann, Fred, 48, 85n, 93, 205, 332, 352